TCP/IP Explained

TCP/IP Explained

PHILIP MILLER

DIGITAL PRESS

Boston Oxford Johannesburg Melbourne New Delhi Singapore

Library of Congress Cataloging-in-Publication Data
Miller, Philip, 1956-
    TCP/IP explained : Philip Miller.
       p.   cm.
    Includes bibliographical references and index.
    ISBN 1-55558-166-8 (pbk. : alk. paper)
    1. TCP/IP (Computer network protocol)   I. Title.
TK5105.585.M564   1997
004.6'2—dc20   96-41116
                                             CIP

British Library Cataloguing-in-Publication Data
A catalogue record for this book is available from the British Library.

The publisher offers special discounts on bulk orders of this book.
For information, please contact:
Manager of Special Sales
Butterworth–Heinemann
313 Washington Street
Newton, MA 02158–1626
Tel: 617-928-2500
Fax: 617-928-2620

For information on all Digital Press publications available, contact our World Wide Web home page at: http://www.bh.com/dp

Order number: EY-V417E-DP

10 9 8 7 6 5 4

Printed in the United States of America

To my children Stuart and Nicole, and my wife Karen.
Without their patience and love, my world would be incomplete.

Table of Contents

Chapter 20 – The Simple Network Management Protocol (SNMP)..361

Chapter 21 – Miscellaneous Protocols 381

Chapter 22 – Communications Over Wide Area Links......397

Preface

Computer systems are in use in every walk of life. In the early days these were large machines that required armies of people to manage them. In addition, few were allowed anywhere near them due to their price and complexity. Today, the story is very different. Cheap components, open technologies and accessible, easy to use software means that almost anyone can harness the power of the silicon chip. Who would have imagined just those few years ago, that the power locked away in the back room would explode onto peoples desks and into peoples lives. A PC on each employees' desk, and one in the home was a mere pipe dream then, but today it is already history. Now we can browse through global libraries and find almost any information that we could possibly need.

With this accessibility comes the thirst for knowledge. Today, the home PC makes the megalithic giants of the dark ages of the sixties pale into insignificance. Our PC today with it's Pentium™ power, its gigabyte disks and its point-and-click graphical interface makes the mainframes of the past look like the dinosaurs that they are. One thing that these minature giants lack though is a real in-built method of communications. And by this we mean the ability to share information.

One thing we must thank our forebears for is communications because the old mainframes did know a trick or two. Even the earliest systems were able to communicate and to share information. True this was proprietary and *emulation* was the watchword for those vendors who wanted to compete in multi-vendor environments. But as the markets opened, so did the systems. The age of standards was upon us and manufacturers moved from large centralized machines into a distributed environment. Networking was born.

It is this latter area that this book is designed to address. It is not really designed to be unique in this since there are countless books on the subject already. Equally, there are many different protocols that can, and are, used to allow machines to communicate. This book looks at just one suite of protocols, the Internet Protocol Suite.

For those that have read books on the subject before, you will be aware that so many spend a great deal of time theorizing and explaining why things work the way that they do. The approach of this book however is to discuss how they work as opposed to why. No real pre-requisite is required and it can be read directly one chapter after another gradually building knowledge from the cable through to the application. For more experienced readers and those that have understood the basics of the protocols, each chapter should stand as a reference. Indeed, by examining the practical traces included within the text, the principles behind communications with TCP/IP are clearly demonstrated.

Two difficulties with communications are that firstly people have differing views and secondly ideas change so fast. This book is based upon the standards, the only definitive documents. Thus references are made throughout, pointing the reader where to look for additional information. Where changes have been made to enhance the suite, these have been incorporated making the text itself as up-to-date as possible.

This book could be broadly split into four sections. Chapters 1 to 8 and 14 deal with the basics of the TCP/IP suite and how data is transported between two systems. Chapters 9 to 14 deal with routing principles and protocols. Chapters 15 to 21 deal with applications. Finally, Chapters 22 to 24 deal with miscellaneous areas. For example, many books exclude the so called Link-Layer when discussing the ways in which computer communications operate. In Chapter 22 we discuss the common protocols used across wide area links, and how we can dial into host networks. In Chapter 23, we discuss practical methods of securing networks against malicious attack, and in Chapter 24 we delve into the future of IP to see how it will continue to provide us with a communications infrastructure.

Many people have assisted in the production of this book. Amongst those that require special mention are my employers at Whittaker Xyplex and countless individuals within the organization which include (but are not limited to) Greg Shortell, Simon McCormack, and especially Derin Mellor for his contribution to Chapter 23. In addition, Mike Cummins, Brian Hill, Tony Mulchrone and Mike Shepherd deserve special mention for reading the text at various stages of production and debating many of the points that it makes. Finally, I would like to thank Tony Kenyon and Bob Brace of Grid Technologies for their inspiration and encouragement, and allowing me to use their packet trace decoding utility (μSCOPE) throughout the text.

Introduction

In today's information rich society, we sometimes take for granted the technologies that provide us with that information. Equally, it is sometimes difficult to appreciate the infrastructure that must be in place when we send an electronic mail message around the world. Truly we live in an information age that few people comprehend and, even fewer understand in its entirety.

Today our world is one where we need not touch the telephone nor use the postal system. Instead, if we wish to converse with aunt Mary in Australia we need only send her a message by some form of electronic mail. True this is less personal than sending a letter, but the service is quicker than any postal service could ever hope to be (measured in minutes rather than days). No exotic stamps are used, leaving Uncle Bill sad that he will never get his first day cover – but this is the price that we must pay for technological advancement.

Certainly for the *man-on-the-street* this rates as just another *impersonalization* of an already faceless society. But who is the man-on-the-street? Today, computers invade every facet of life and everybody can name at least one time when they have encountered or used them. This then leaves us with business. That small thing driving our world from day to day. We have had 24-hr services for some time, but today 24-hr banking, shopping, and insurance are commonplace. Although we may disagree with the inhuman aspect of it, we surely have to marvel at the technology that made this possible.

To an extent though, all of this is immaterial since here we are going to discuss the *how* as opposed to the *why*. We all appreciate that these facilities are available, but do we understand how they are delivered? How is it possible to send an eMail?, and what do our computers actually do with the data that they receive? It is these questions (and more) that this book is hoped to address.

1.1   What is TCP/IP?

TCP/IP (or more correctly) the *Internet Protocol Suite* is a suite of protocols aimed at providing meaningful computer communications. With TCP, the *Transmission Control Protocol* and IP, the *Internet Protocol* being two of the major protocols used within the suite, it is thus given its colloquial name of TCP/IP.

Originally developed for the United States Department of Defense Advanced Research Projects Agency *DARPA* network, the protocols are now used to link many commercial, university and military establishments world-wide. Additionally, these protocols have now become the commercial choice of many other *smaller* businesses throughout the world since they provide a flexible method of computer communications.

TCP/IP is not the only protocol suite in use today and it has never achieved anything like International Standard status. It has however become the *de-facto* standard for networking and is therefore bound to be around for a good many years to come. TCP/IP is not some new protocol suite. Far from it, it pre-dates many protocols that would claim a wider following, and users are still continuing the migration to TCP/IP while waiting for these other suites to be completed.

In addition, TCP/IP breaks many of the rules that we normally associate with protocol architectures. It uses four not seven layers. It is however interesting to note that while the best known architecture (that developed for OSI) claimed seven layers was required at its conception, it is now adding a layer for use in Local Area Networks (LANs). The architecture of TCP/IP however, pre-dates this and has remained constant throughout its life.

1.1.1 A Brief History of TCP/IP

It was during the 1970s that work commenced and much research was started. Essentially, the developers were experimenting with new protocols that would provide reliable, yet simple, communications between various major sites. In the early days, the Network Control Program (NCP) was used, but by 1983 the conversion to the new TCP/IP protocols was complete.

To speed the transition and to speed development, DARPA funded two major organizations to produce a low cost implementation of the protocol suite. These organizations were the Bolt, Beranek and Newman company and the University of California based in Berkeley. At this time most of the universities ran the Unix operating system and this was distributed by the University of California (the so called *Berkeley distribution*). Now, TCP/IP was incorporated into Unix and it received the widest possible audience, in the shortest possible timescale and at the smallest possible cost. Academics and other researchers were, without even knowing it, now testing the protocols and assisting those involved in computer research to develop the utilities that we now use every day.

Originally, few applications could use this new protocol suite. A File Transfer and a Virtual Terminal package were really the mainstay. Graphical User Interfaces (GUIs) had not been invented and the idea of a computer, or even a terminal, on everyone's desk was pure fantasy. Sustained bursts of high traffic levels were not required and the original computers used in the experiment were large machines linked by serial Wide Area links. These links were slow by today's standard but this mattered little, inter-operability between vendors through a common operating system had begun and with it our protocol suite was born.

Since this time, the suite of protocols and the functionality offered has increased dramatically. New papers and articles postulate on what is possible and vendors co-operate in a way that is unprecedented knowing that to survive today, inter-operability is key. At one time many people felt that TCP/IP would become a stepping stone for users that would then migrate to the newer OSI protocols. This is especially true of government departments that insisted vendors should be able to provide OSI connectivity, or at least commit to it for the future. To this end we see elements of OSI within some of the later protocols particularly those involved with management. The transition however has never been fully exploited and the more cynical might say that it never will.

The original pioneers can never have foreseen the extent to which their work would be used. The visionaries who saw a need for low cost computing, networking and *information for all* have achieved this in less than a decade. How many man hours has it taken? We shall never know. One thing is clear though, and that is in our shrinking world just about anything is possible today.

1.1.2 The Internet Protocol Suite

The Internet Protocol Suite comprises many different protocols and it is these that are the subject of this book. Figure 1-1 shows many of them (although this is by no means exhaustive) and their relationships to each other. Appendix B lists the major protocols and their current status. Obviously things are changing constantly and the reader is urged to consult the latest *Internet Official Protocol Standards* document for the very latest information.

The protocols themselves can (and normally are) grouped by function such as Applications, Services etc. The suite itself however does not try to re-define established standards. Where these exist, the Internet Protocol Suite uses them. After all, there is no point in redesigning something that is perfectly adequate for the task that you wish to put it to.

- **Underlying Network Technologies**
  The Internet Protocol Suite generally does not define any new network technologies. Instead, it is independent of the underlying network and relies on those already standardized by other bodies such as IEEE, ANSI and others.

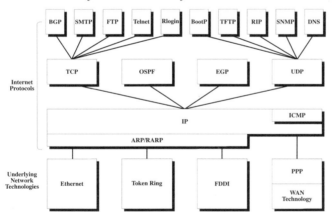

Figure 1-1: The Internet Protocol Suite

Some work was required and two new protocols ARP and RARP were introduced in order to map the addressing scheme used by IP to that used by the underlying network technology itself. Arguably these are not actual Internet protocols but instead are more general purpose in nature. However since they do not comfortably fit elsewhere they are included here.

In addition, the suite also introduces the Point-to-Point Protocol (PPP) in order to control Wide Area links. Again this can be considered general purpose since it can be used for protocols other than the Internet Protocol Suite.

- **The Internet Protocol (IP)**
  This is the very cornerstone of the Internet Protocol Suite and provides the mechanism that all other protocols use. Connectionless in nature, IP attracts only a small overhead in terms of additional control information, yet it is rich in features.

  IP itself has no error reporting mechanism and generally relies on the upper layer protocols to provide reliability. Some low level reporting is required however and this is outside the scope of the protocol. To provide this functionality IP uses the Internet Control Message Protocol (ICMP), which is considered integral to IP itself.

- **Transport Protocols**
  The Internet Protocol Suite has two transport protocols. The first, the Transmission Control Protocol (TCP) is key to the suite as a whole since it is this that provides the guaranteed, connection oriented transport system used by the key user applications.

  The second, the User Datagram Protocol (UDP) is connectionless and relies on the application itself to provide reliability where required. In essence, UDP provides no additional reliability over that of IP. It does however provide a compact transport system for use where reliability is either not an issue or where this can be provided through the application.

- **Routing Protocols**
  To make networks adaptive, it is important to use protocols that can detect changes in network topology and react accordingly. Two major groups of routing protocol exist, namely the Interior Gateway Protocols (IGPs) and the Exterior Gateway Protocols (EGPs).

  IGPs are used within what are known as Autonomous Systems and define the policies in use by that administration. These protocols include the Routing Information Protocol (RIP) and the Open Shortest Path First protocol (OSPF).

  EGPs are used to join Autonomous Systems and therefore define the policies that we wish to apply between these administrations or domains. This protocol group includes the Exterior Gateway Protocol (EGP) and the Border Gateway Protocol (BGP).

- **End User Applications**
  The Internet Protocol Suite provides a number of user applications. Arguably the most well known and popular of these are the File Transfer Protocol (FTP), and Telnet. In addition, there is a Telnet-like application available in many implementations of UNIX known as Rlogin that relies on *trusted hosts*. Possibly one of the lesser known, although not less important protocols, is the Simple Mail Transfer Protocol (SMTP), for it is through this that end user eMail services are provided

New applications are being added all the time and today, if asked about applications used, many people would cite one of the many Web browsers available. These applications, such as Netscape and Mosaic, attempt to bring together all the more traditional applications under one common graphical interface. The face of networking is therefore changing as these applications develop.

- **Supporting Services**

  To use many of the applications, we rely heavily on a standardized host naming convention known as the Domain Name System (DNS). In much the same way that ARP allows the mapping of IP addresses to MAC addresses, this protocol allows the mapping of names to IP addresses. This then makes it easier for human operators to use network resources.

  Supporting users is not the only task that we have to consider. On the periphery of the suite, other support protocols are used by devices so that they can learn about their environment without the need for operator intervention.

  The Bootstrap Protocol (BootP) is one such protocol used heavily by IP devices that load image files across the network. Since this protocol provides good general purpose qualities though, it has now also been adopted and indeed extended by other systems such Windows NT for the discovery of host configuration information. So, what was started by the Internet Protocol Suite is now providing solutions to today's problems. An example of the flexibility provided by the protocols.

  Finally, we must not forget the equally important Trivial File Transfer Protocol (TFTP). This extremely uncomplicated and small protocol is much loved by hardware designers since it allows them to load files across networks with the absolute minimum of coding. This then makes it ideal for programmers to code directly into Read Only Memory (ROM).

- **Management**

  The Simple Network Management Protocol (SNMP) was originally designed to be replaced by the newer OSI management protocols when they became available. Now so widely used, it seems unlikely that this replacement will ever actually take place although much of it is OSI ready.

1.2 The Internet

Today the Internet is part of our lives. Advertisements carry addresses that can be used for further on-line information, and as we have already said global communication is literally *at our fingertips.*

It is the Internet, to which we owe the maturing of TCP/IP since it was with this network in mind that TCP/IP was developed. True, the success of the Internet could never have been imagined. When those first machines, used what at the time must have unstable software, who could have imagined where it would all lead. TCP/IP itself was born out of necessity. It provided a solution to a problem quickly and easily. Not satisfied with this, the developers then went further and opened new doors. Originally only file transfer and virtual terminal packages were available but today we have electronic mail, and the ability to browse through on-line libraries almost anywhere in the world.

People now talk less of the Internet preferring to call it the *World Wide Web*, the largest network of computers ever known. In reality the World Wide Web is just a sub-set of the Internet since this only refers to those systems that allow Web access. It has however attracted attention of late and it is this portion of the Internet about which a whole industry has developed.

1.2.1 The Growth of the Internet

In truth, the Internet has become a victim of its own success and now we can see the cracks appearing in some of the older protocols. We are suffering from a gross shortage of address space and still new devices are being attached. User demands are fuelled by imagination and although we may think that we have wonderful systems today, our children will look at them and think them primitive by comparison with what they have. Thankfully technology opens new doors all the time and we are able to increase the bandwidth of our links to keep pace with the demands placed on them. New protocols are being developed to make our networks more adaptive and faster, and therefore at least keep pace with our needs. Finally new applications are bringing the services to the desktop in a far more user friendly form. In truth though are we just treading water unable to make significant strides ahead? And does the Internet really have a future if it continues expansion at this rate?

In the simple terms of raw data transmission, traffic levels have increased exponentially and are likely to continue to do so. Applications place larger demands on our network infrastructures and processing speed is a watch word to the computer industry as a whole. When the first PC was launched, it was hailed as a wonderful invention that then went on to outsell the manufacturers wildest dreams. How many people today though would swap their high powered device for one of the earlier models. In short, we have become a race that needs information, we need it fast, and our thirst for knowledge cannot be quenched. This is of course obvious but it is somehow sobering when walking around a museum you can remember using some of the exhibits. In a similar way, those early pioneers of the Internet must look back in wonder at what they have created.

In the early days of development of TCP/IP, the Internet was small. For example in August 1981 there were only 213 hosts. By October 1985 however, there were nearly 2,000. Since then the growth has been explosive as Figure 1-2 shows with the number of connected hosts in January 1996 being 9.5 million. Of course these latter figures are only estimates. Certainly while the Internet was small it was easy to administer and therefore to gather accurate statistics. Each machine connected had to have a hard coded *hosts* file that identified all other systems. Adding another host to the network then required the hosts file of each machine to be updated, an arduous task but one that was at least manageable. As anything grows however it becomes harder to control, especially when we have something that has grown quite rapidly like this. As a result, estimates of numbers of hosts are just that, estimates.

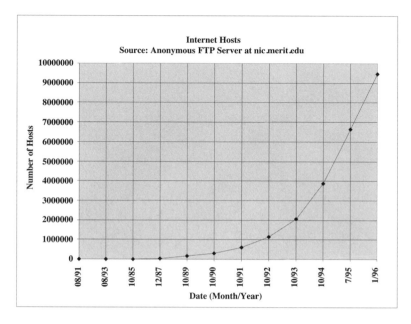

Internet Hosts
Source: Anonymous FTP Server at nic.merit.edu

Figure 1-2: Internet Growth 1981-1996

Estimating the number of Internet users is an even more difficult task. As a rule it is accepted that to estimate user numbers, one should take the number of host computers and then multiply this number by 10. In October 1993 then, we can say that approximately 20 million users had access to the Internet compared to only 2,000 in 1981. By 1996 however, this number had risen to a staggering 94.5 million if we are to use this formula!

In a similar fashion, the number of registered domains has also increased. Domains are issued to organizations and form part of the unique naming system used within the Internet. For example, the source of these statistics is NIC.MERIT.EDU, in this case NIC is the host system that resides in the domain MERIT.EDU. A full discussion of the Domain Name System however, appears in Chapter 15.

In 1988 only 900 domains had been issued. By 1996 though some 240,000 were in existence. Figure 1-3 shows this growth in graphical form.

Figure 1-4 shows the distribution of hosts over the top 10 domains by percentage. Of course, without knowing the overall figures to which these percentages relate, the data is effectively meaningless. So, to put this into context, it is useful to bear the figures shown in Table 1-1 in mind:

Table 1-1: Top Ten Domains by Percentage

Domain	com	edu	net	gov	org	mil	de	uk	ca	au
Hosts	2430954	1793491	758597	312330	265327	258791	452997	451750	372891	309562

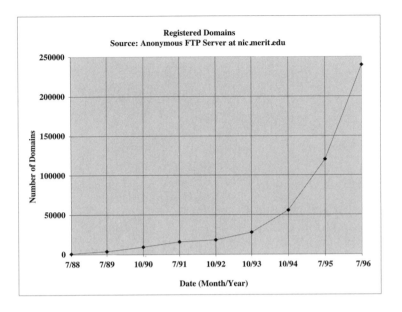

Figure 1-3: Registered Domains 1988 to 1996

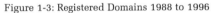

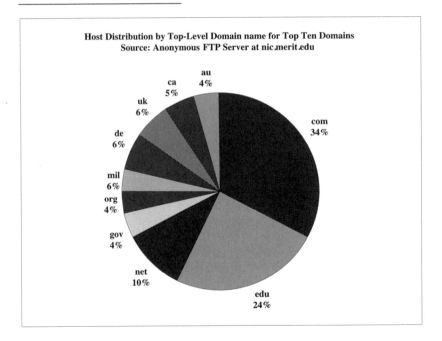

Figure 1-4: Host Distribution by Top Level Domain Name – Top Ten Hosts

Introduction

1.3 Summary

When talking about the Internet it is easy to lose sight of the fact that it is really a vast collection of networks all working together to form a global communications infrastructure. In the early days, each of the networks were named individually but today it is easier to consider them as one large communications infrastructure.

Without the Internet, there would be no TCP/IP. The Internet Protocol Suite was developed with the communications between the original machines that formed what we now call the Internet in mind. Obviously much development has been necessary since then and the original, relatively few, applications that existed have changed dramatically. In the early days, there were Telnet and FTP type applications and very little else. Certainly there were some rudimentary routing protocols but in reality these bear little resemblance to what we have today. Now we have a rich suite of protocols that provide functionality few could have dreamed of in those early days and we have much to thank those early visionaries for.

We could say that the Internet is out of control, and to an extent this would be true. Certainly, the growth of the Internet has surpassed all expectations. Problems also exist since nothing is perfect. In truth we are looking at something that is now a victim of it's own success and much work that is done today merely papers over the cracks that have appeared. That is not to say that the protocols are any less robust. In fact the stability of these is now far greater than any of those earlier attempts. Now we must introduce a better infrastructure that will take us forward for the next 20 years.

Standardization

As we saw in the previous chapter, the creation of "*The Internet*" was the driving force behind the development of the protocol suite that we now refer to colloqui-ally as TCP/IP. It is important to note that no one person or company owns The Internet, rather it is an alliance of small networks that have agreed to allow inter-communication using a *standardized* set of protocols. With the explosive growth of this internetwork and internetworking in general, clearly a central administra-tive authority had to take control of the protocols in use and steer the improve-ments and enhancements that naturally occur. Within the Internet community, this administrative authority is called the *Internet Architecture Board* and it is through this body that all work on protocols passes.

In this section we shall examine the work of the Internet Architecture Board and its subsidiary groups. We shall also examine the route that protocols take to becoming *standards*, the associated documentation, and finally the architecture of the protocol suite itself.

2.1 The Internet Architecture Board

The Internet Architecture Board (IAB) was originally founded in 1983 (then called the *Internet Activities Board*) to guide the evolution of the Internet Protocol suite in an advisory capacity. In June 1992, the IAB was placed under the control of the 'Internet Society'[1] and given the following charter that is documented fully in RFC-1358[2] and from which the following extract is taken:

The IAB shall provide:

- Expert and experienced oversight of the architecture of the world-wide Internet.

- The editorial management and publication of the Request for Comments (RFC) document series, which constitutes the archival publication series for Internet Standards and related contributions by the Internet research and engineering community.

---

1. The Internet Society is a non-profit making organization operated solely for academic, educational, and charitable purposes.
2. The term *RFC* refers to Request For Comments documents, the vehicle used for documenting all Internet activities. RFCs are discussed later in this section.

- The development, review, and approval of Internet Standards, according to a well-defined and documented set of "Procedures for Internet Standardization". Internet Standards shall be published in the form of specifications as part of the RFC series.

- The provision of advice and guidance to the Board of Trustees and Officers of the Internet Society concerning technical, architectural, procedural, and (where appropriate) policy matters pertaining to the Internet and its enabling technologies.

- Representation of the interests of the Internet Society in liaison relationships with other organizations.

Under this charter, the IAB may consist of up to 15 members '. . . *serving in the capacity of individuals and not as representatives of any company, agency, or other organization . . .'* In this way, the IAB remains impartial and has only the best interests of its users at heart.

The IAB, in its charter, is also empowered to create task forces, committees, and other working groups as it sees fit. Initially, in 1992, two such task forces existed; the *Internet Engineering Task Force* (IETF) and the *Internet Research Task Force* (IRTF). Today these task forces play a vital role in the development and maintenance of the protocols that we currently use, and which we will use tomorrow.

2.1.1 The Internet Engineering Task Force

The Internet Engineering Task Force (IETF) is responsible for protocol engineering, development and standardization, and indeed no protocol may use the word **standard** unless it is ratified by the IETF. The IETF was initiated in 1986 as a forum for the technical co-ordination of the contract companies involved in the development of the ARPANET, the U.S. Defense Data Network, and the Internet Core Gateway System. Since that time however, it has evolved into a large open international community of network designers, operators, vendors, and researchers concerned with the evolution of the Internet protocols and the smooth operation of the Internet.

Managed by the *Internet Engineering Steering Group* (IESG), the IETF has the responsibility for generally making the Internet work, and for the resolution of all short to mid-term protocol and architectural issues. The charter of the IETF (taken from RFC-1160) includes:

- The responsibility for specifying the short and mid-term Internet protocols and architecture, and recommending standards for IAB approval.

- The provision of a forum for the exchange of information within the Internet community.

- The identification of pressing and relevant short to mid-range operational and technical problem areas and the convening of working groups to explore solutions.

The IETF is organized around eight technical areas, each of which is managed by a technical area director. The management group, the IESG, is then formed from a chairperson and each of these eight area directors. The area directors are chosen for both their managerial and technical skills but most importantly, their judgement, for it is these area directors who decide where resources are best placed through a number of *working groups*. Working Groups are assigned specific tasks, thus their focus tends to be very narrow, aimed only at their particular assignment. Additionally, by their very nature, these working groups are transient and exist only for the life of the individual project although of course there are certain exceptions to this.

The IETF meets quarterly and extensive minutes and reports from the various working groups are then published. It is important that such meetings take place since the IETF is a major source of proposed protocol standards awaiting final approval by the IAB. As we have already seen, it is only through the IAB that protocols may be formalized, and indeed these protocols rely heavily on the work carried out by the IETF.

2.1.2 The Internet Research Task Force

The Internet Research Task Force (IRTF) is a body of individuals primarily responsible for research into networking and the development of new technology. The people that comprise this group therefore have an interest in the more long-term strategies of the Internet and the protocols in use. Since there exists only a fine line between engineering and research, there is considerable overlap between the activities of the IETF and the IRTF. Cross-fertilization and the transfer of technical ideas are vital in the world of Internetworking. Consequently, this healthy extension is a necessity to the general well being of The Internet.

The IRTF is governed by its own steering group called the *Internet Research Steering Group* (IRSG). The IRTF is then organized into a number of Research Groups each concerned with a broad area of research on specific topics dictated by the IAB. The operational stability of the Internet is of prime concern to its users. The tools used to gather data and assist in the isolation of faults and to analyze performance are critical and are therefore high on the agenda of the IRTF.

2.2 Internet Protocol Standards

In this section we shall deal with the processes and phases involved in a protocol eventually becoming a standard. Generally, Internet Standards are specifications for protocols that are stable, with several implementations, and also provide a useful purpose to at least some small part of the Internet.

The *Internet Protocol Suite*, commonly known as TCP/IP, is the principal set of Internet Standards. As the Internet evolves, new protocols and services, particularly those evolving around *Open Systems Interconnection* (OSI), have been, and will be deployed in traditional TCP/IP environments. This will then lead to an Internet that supports multiple protocol suites. Remember though, that the vast majority of protocol development within the Internet community takes place within the various working groups of the Internet Engineering Task Force.

2.2.1 Protocol States

The development of a *Standard* protocol does not occur overnight. Instead much work must be completed and typically this is overseen by one (or more) of the IETF's working groups. Protocols that eventually become Standards normally proceed through a series of states namely *Proposed Standard*, *Draft Standard*, and finally, *Standard*. This process, which at first may seem somewhat painful, reflects the operation of the Internet's governing body. Remember that the IAB comprises the IRTF and the IETF, with the latter consisting of a number of working groups made up of individuals with only the best interests of the Internet at heart.

Table 2-1: Protocol States

State	Description
Standard Protocol	This has become an established protocol and has been assigned a Standard (STD) number. These protocols form two groups, namely the IP protocol and above (those that apply to the whole Internet), and network specific protocols (since IP should be implemented over particular network types).
Draft Standard Protocol	This protocol is being considered for promotion to a Standard Protocol, by the IESG. At this stage, the IESG requires the protocol to be extensively tested and requires as much feedback as possible.
Proposed Standard Protocol	Protocols that may be considered for future standardization are given this title. Much work is still to be carried out on protocols in this state and it is unlikely that they will emerge as Draft Standards without even minor modification.
Experimental Protocol	These protocols are generally developed as part of an on-going research project. Only those systems participating in the experiment implement the protocol and then only after proper co-ordination with the development group responsible. Many protocols in this state are themselves mature and reliable and indeed this state is sometimes applied to protocols that are not intended for operational use.
Informational Protocol	Certain protocols, developed by other Standards organizations or independent vendors and that have no direct applications in the Internet may be published as RFCs with this state. These are for general convenience only.
Historic Protocol	These protocols are unlikely to become Standards since they have been either superseded or else interest has merely died.

In order for the Internet community to consider and subsequently respond to any standardization proposal, it is normal that a minimum delay of six months be imposed in the transition from *Proposed Standard* to *Draft Standard*. Equally, the transition from *Draft Standard* to *Standard* normally takes at least four months. These delays allow time for all members of the various assigned working groups to consider and fully research the protocol before it is advanced. It is general practice that before a Proposed Standard may be promoted to a Draft Standard, the IESG must first agree, and at least two independent implementations should be operational. This assures operational experience, and that inter-operability of the protocol has been demonstrated. Where there is any doubt, the IESG may delay the advancement of the protocol while more experimentation is undertaken.

When a protocol receives the title Proposed Standard, an important milestone is reached, since this means that the protocol is designated as an eventual candidate for formal standardization. Such a protocol is then said to enter the *Standards Track*. Its promotion to Draft Standard is a warning to the Internet community that, unless major objections are received within the four month minimum period, this will become a Standard. Figure 2-1 shows the Standards Track.

The figure shows the route that a simple idea must take before being granted *Standard* status. As you will note from the figure, a protocol may go from Draft to Proposed or even from Standard to Draft many times. Additionally, when the protocol has reached the end of its useful life, the eventual fate of all protocols is that of *Historic*.

So, when a protocol enters the Standards Track, does this mean that it will become a standard? The answer is of course No! Many things can, and do, go wrong. There are countless examples of protocols that have become Proposed or Draft Standards only to falter at the final hurdle. Maybe the very idea of this particular protocol sparks the imagination of somebody else, and a better solution is proposed. Maybe the protocol was proposed as a short-term solution for a problem that has been resolved by other methods – who can tell? In any event, the hope is that the work performed will not have been in vain and at least something will have been achieved.

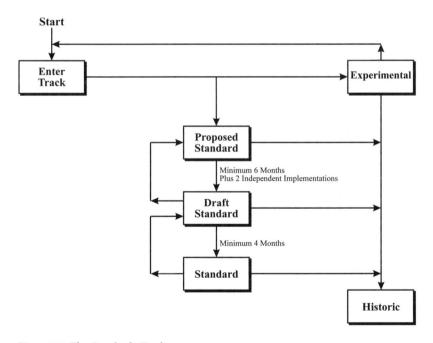

Figure 2-1: The Standards Track

Of course we have discussed the normal process taken en-route to standardization. A few vendor specific protocols have received both widespread acclaim and acceptance within the Internet without either the sanction of the IESG or any part the process described above. This however is rare and the IAB recommends that to preserve maximum inter-operability the standards process is maintained.

2.2.2 Protocol Status

In addition to its State, each protocol is also assigned a *Requirement Level* or *Status*. Table 2-2 describes these statuses:

Table 2-2: Protocol Statuses

Status	Description
Required	A Required protocol is one that a system MUST implement.
Recommended	All systems should implement Recommended protocols.
Elective	A system may, or may not, implement these protocols. The idea being, if you are going to implement a protocol to perform this function, then it should be implemented in this way.
Limited Use	These protocols are for use in limited circumstances only. They may either have an Experimental State, be of a specialized nature, have limited functionality or be Historic.
Not Recommended	These protocols are not recommended, due to their limited, experimental or specialized nature.

An important distinction must now be made between different devices that exist on the Internet or indeed any inter-network. For example, it would be wholly inappropriate to suggest that every *Required* and *Recommended* protocol MUST be supported on every device connected to the Internet. Devices may typically be divided into two major groups namely *Hosts* and *Gateways*, each of which perform a specific function and naturally have different protocol requirements. It would therefore be wrong to assume that all *Recommended* protocols will be present on all machines that are connected to the Internet. For example; The Transmission Control Protocol[3] (TCP) described in RFC 793, has a status of Recommended but not all systems need to implement it. Take the case of a Hub that is SNMP[4] manageable – must this really incorporate the overhead of TCP when it will not be used by the management system? Equally, the Exterior Gateway Protocol[5] (EGP) is also Recommended. What of local routers that have no need to implement the protocol?

2.2.3 The Request For Comments (RFC)

At the very heart of the standardization process is a set of documents called *Request For Comments* or RFCs. This naming of important documents again

---

3. The Transmission Control Protocol (TCP) is described in detail in Chapter 7.
4. The Simple Network Management Protocol (SNMP) is discussed in Chapter 20.
5. The Exterior Gateway Protocol is used to advertise routes to networks in different autonomous systems. This concept is described in Chapter 9, and the protocol itself is discussed in Chapter 12.

reflects the very open nature of the Internet community. The rules are very simple. Anyone may submit a document for publication via eMail to the RFC Editor. Once published, the RFC is reviewed by members of the appropriate task force and individual technical experts as appropriate, and *Comments* are returned. An RFC could be on any topic of interest to the Internet community in general, from the minutes of a meeting to a full and detailed specification of a complex protocol. Note: *All standards are published as RFCs however, not all RFCs specify Standards.*

Unlike other standards organizations, where a Standard is assigned a number or other designation and then different revisions are published, once an RFC has been published, it will never be re-issued with the same number. This has the advantage that, if you have an RFC, you must always have the latest revision of it. The disadvantage of such a system is that, as protocols change and improvements are made, it will be re-documented using the RFC as its vehicle. By re-issuing the document of course, a new number is assigned, potentially leading to confusion as to whether you have the latest document in the series.

To overcome this problem of which document describes the current Standard, approximately every quarter, an RFC is published that lists the Internet Official Protocol Standards. Of course since this is an RFC, its number will also change each time it is issued so a close track must be kept on all RFC numbers by those that are interested. Appendix B lists the current Standard Protocols (based on RFC 1800 – the current reference at the time of writing).

Finally, the members of the Internet community are anything but dull, many RFCs have a distinctly humorous flavor, and the titles of others are anything but clear. For example:

- *"All Victims Together"* (RFC-967) discusses how networking code is integrated with various operating systems.

- *"Twas the Night Before Start-up"* (RFC-968) discusses problems that may arise and associated debugging techniques used when bringing a new network into operation.

- *"A Standard for the Transmission of IP Datagrams on Avian Carriers"* (RFC-1149) discusses the possibility of transporting IP Datagrams by carrier pigeon. However, since this RFC is dated 1 April, it should not be taken seriously.

Dr. Stephen Crocker (the father of the RFC and definitely one of the luminaries of the Internet) writes a history of the RFC, and cross-references the first 999 documents in RFC-1000. This RFC, although now somewhat dated, does provide an interesting insight into the start-up of the Internet and is certainly recommended reading.

2.3 Internet Protocol Architecture

Whenever we wish to transfer data between two systems, problems (which are not necessarily immediately apparent) may occur. Many machines are mutiprocessing hosts with only limited communications capability, giving rise to problems such as:

- How can we cope with more than one transmission at a time?

- If there is more than one link between machines, on what basis do we select the link to be used?

- What would happen if one machine used one code set to represent characters while the other used a completely alien code set?

- Must the two applications at each end of our link be identical? And what will happen if this is not the case?

Traditionally, vendors solved such issues with proprietary protocols and methodologies, but now we are working with multi-vendor, *Open*, solutions and this is plainly no longer possible. One major hurdle still exists however, that of choosing the best solution for the task at hand.

Whenever any problem requires resolution, man has always broken the problem down into smaller, more manageable, pieces. In this way we are able to solve the riddle in stages. Such modular techniques are generally referred to as the *Software Architecture* or *Software Model*. In this section we shall examine the *Layered* Architecture used in the TCP/IP protocol suite.

2.3.1   The Open Systems Interconnection (OSI) Model

Possibly the best example of a layered architecture is that of the OSI Basic Reference Model. Introduced in 1984, this model was the result of some six years collaboration of the *International Organization for Standardization* and the *CCITT* [6]. Figure 2-2 shows this model and briefly describes the function(s) of each layer.

Within this framework, each layer only exists to provide services to the layer above. By isolating the functionality of each layer in this way, the model allows changes to be made to a particular function without affecting the overall operation of the model. This assumes, of course, that the interface between layers remains consistent at all times.

- **The Physical Layer**
  The physical layer provides a direct connection to the physical medium. This layer is therefore responsible for the transmission and reception of the raw bit stream across the medium itself. In general, it defines the electrical, mechanical, and signal characteristics of the interface to the transmission medium. In this way it provides us with a transparent communications path between the two Data-Link layer entities at each end of the connection.

---

6. CCITT stands for the Consultative Committee on International Telephony and Telegraphy, a Standards Making Body from France.

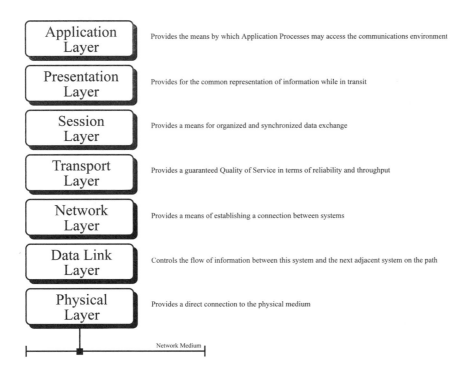

Application Layer — Provides the means by which Application Processes may access the communications environment

Presentation Layer — Provides for the common representation of information while in transit

Session Layer — Provides a means for organized and synchronized data exchange

Transport Layer — Provides a guaranteed Quality of Service in terms of reliability and throughput

Network Layer — Provides a means of establishing a connection between systems

Data Link Layer — Controls the flow of information between this system and the next adjacent system on the path

Physical Layer — Provides a direct connection to the physical medium

Network Medium

Figure 2-2: The OSI Seven Layer Model

- **The Data Link Layer**

  The Data Link Layer is responsible for controlling the flow of data between this system and the next adjacent system on the path to the destination or *target* system. Since we require to pass data between stations, it is imperative that each is uniquely addressed. Each station is assigned a unique address either during the manufacture of the station itself or during the manufacture of the network interface card that will be installed. In the case of Ethernet, Token Ring, or FDDI interfaces, this address is six octets in length and is recorded in a field that forms part of the header applied to data at this layer. This *Physical* or *MAC* addressing, as it is known, is described in Chapter 3.

  Additionally, through the provision of simple error detection mechanisms, this layer attempts to eliminate data loss and corruption. It is also responsible for the packaging of data into acceptable size *Frames* ready for transmission by the Physical layer.

- **The Network Layer**

  The Network Layer provides a means through which a connection may be established between systems. It enables such connections to exist even where the co-operating end systems reside on different networks and where these networks are of different types.

- **The Transport Layer**
  The Transport layer provides the upper layers with a guaranteed quality of service in terms of both throughput and reliability. This Quality of Service, which is requested by the Session Layer, is achieved through the multiplexing of multiple connections to enhance throughput, and through the use of error correction schemes to enhance reliability.

- **The Session Layer**
  The Session layer is responsible for the establishment of a framework for dialogue between systems. This framework then provides an organized and synchronized exchange of data between systems. For example, should the data be sent in one direction only (simplex), in alternate directions (half duplex), or in both directions simultaneously (full duplex).

- **The Presentation Layer**
  The Presentation layer provides for the common representation of information whilst in transit. For example, since two communicating systems may use different character sets to represent different symbols, the presentation layers on each system must negotiate a common representation scheme. Having agreed on the scheme, the presentation layer on the transmitting host will translate the data received from the Application layer into that common form. The presentation layer on the receiving host will then translate the data back before passing it to its own Application layer.

- **The Application Layer**
  The Application layer provides the user processes with access to the communications environment and therefore provides the communication services to the host machines' end users. Such services may be File Transfer services, Virtual Terminal services, Electronic Mail, Network Management or any one of hundreds of other applications that the user desires. In essence, all of the subordinate layers exist only to make possible the activities that take place at this layer.

2.3.2   The OSI Model and LANs

Sadly, the OSI architecture was designed long before LANs became commonplace. As a result, changes have had to be made to the model to accommodate the vast array of LAN technologies. For example, 802 networks (as distinct from Ethernet) split the Data Link layer into two separate sub-layers, the Logical Link Control layer (LLC), and the Media Access Control layer (MAC) as Figure 2-3 shows.

- **The Media Access Control Layer**
  The MAC layer is the lower sub-layer of the OSI Data Link Layer, and is responsible for the generation and reception of frames, the validation of data integrity through Frame Check Sequences, addressing, and other functions that control access to the network medium itself. As such, the MAC sub-layer will differ depending upon the access technique employed by the LAN technology.

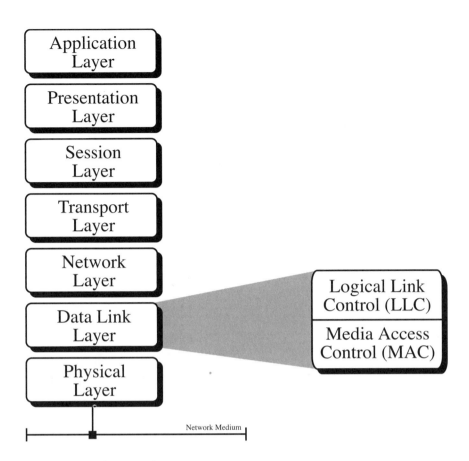

Figure 2-3: Data Link Layer Sub-Layers

- **The Logical Link Control Layer**

  Two major types of LLC exist namely, *an unacknowledged connectionless ser-vice*, and an *acknowledged connection oriented service.* In the first instance, a system is able to exchange information with its peer without the need for large overheads. Where reliability is required in this scenario, it then must of course be provided by the upper layers. In the second situation, a system establishes a link-level connection with its peer prior to the transfer of any information and is able to provide additional error recovery and sequencing.

  A third type of LLC does exist although it is rarely implemented. This service, a hybrid of those previously described, is the *acknowledged connectionless ser-vice* allowing all of the inherent reliability of an acknowledgement system without the overhead of connection management.

  Some architectures take this sub-division further by splitting the functionality of both the Data Link and Physical layers. One such architecture is that of the Fibre

Distributed Data Interface (ANSI X3T9.5)[7] and is shown in Figure 2-4:
The functions of each of these sub-layers are described below:

- **The Physical Medium Dependent Layer (PMD)**
  This layer is responsible for the definition of the wavelength of the optical transmission, the fibre optic connections, the characteristics of the transmitter/receiver circuitry and, where used, optical bypass switches. It is therefore also responsible for the overall configuration limits of the system.

  Since its original conception, the specification of this layer has been extended such that today three separate specifications exist. One for Multi-Mode Fibre (Multi-Mode PMD or MMF-PMD), one for Single Mode Fibre (SMF-PMD), and one for Twisted Pair Copper Cable (TP-PMD).

- **The Physical Layer (PHY)**
  The PHY Layer is the upper sub layer of the Physical Layer and is responsible for the clocking and framing of data, and the encoding scheme used (NRZI 4B5B).

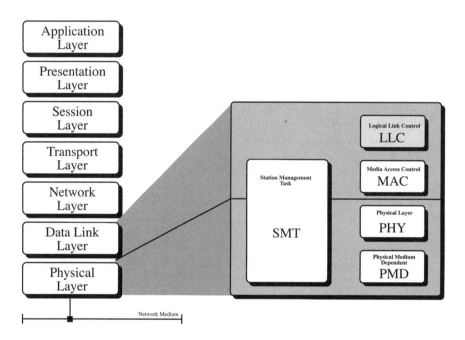

Figure 2-4: FDDI in Relation to the OSI Model

7. The basic operation of FDDI will be described in Chapter 3. For a complete description, you should consult either the ANSI X3T9.5 standard or other literature.

Standardization

- **The Media Access Control Layer (MAC)**
  This layer is the lower sub layer of the Data Link Layer, and in much the same fashion as 802 type networks is responsible for addressing, the verification of data integrity, and the generation and reception of frames.

- **The Logical Link Control Layer (LLC)**
  The LLC layer does not form part of the FDDI Standard however, its functionality is as previously described since the same LLC layer is used both in FDDI, and 802 type networks.

- **The Station Management Task (SMT)**
  The SMT is responsible for ring station and general ring configuration, and provides the controls necessary for proper ring operation. Such tasks are station and ring initialization, the isolation of, and the recovery from, faults and the collection of ring statistics.

2.3.3   The Internet Protocol Suite Model

Just as the OSI Model uses a layered architecture, the Internet Protocol Suite is also based around a layered model. In contrast to the seven layer model described in the previous section however, the Internet Protocol Suite is based upon just four layers. It is interesting that a layered approach was employed, especially when you consider that the Internet Protocol Suite predates the OSI protocols by some ten years. It is hardly surprising though, that the number of layers differ in such a marked fashion.

Before looking at the layers that comprise the Internet Protocol Suite in detail, let us first consider why there is such a difference between the two models. Firstly the OSI model was created by a committee of some of the best minds in networking and took some six years to come to fruition. Even today, many of the protocols that will eventually occupy the layers are not completed and, with the widespread adoption of LAN standards, many now argue that the Data Link Layer should be permanently split in two. This will then make an eight layer model rather than our familiar seven layer version. The Internet Protocol Suite, on the other hand, was born of necessity and, especially when its age is considered, represents a major milestone in networking history. That being said, Dr. Stephen Crocker writes in RFC-1000:

'If we had only consulted the ancient mystics, we would have seen immediately that seven layers were required.'

Figure 2-5 shows the four layer model used by the Internet Protocol Suite model.

- **The Network Access or Physical Layer**
  The *Network Access* or *Physical* Layer is not defined by any Internet standards.[8] Instead, the upper three layers build upon network access methods defined by other standards making bodies. Examples of such access protocols are listed in Table 2-3:

---

8. A full description of this layer is beyond the scope of this text since, to gain an understanding of even those access protocols listed in the table would require a great deal of discussion. Instead, Chapter 3 briefly describes standard access methods and protocols commonly associated with them.

Table 2-3: Network Access Protocols

Standard	ISO Std	Description
IEEE 802.3	8802-3	Carrier Sense, Multiple Access with Collision Detection (CSMA/CD)[9]
IEEE 802.4	8802-4	Token Passing Bus
IEEE 802.5	8802-5	Token Passing Ring (Token Ring)
ANSI X3T9.5		Fibre Distributed Data Interface (FDDI)

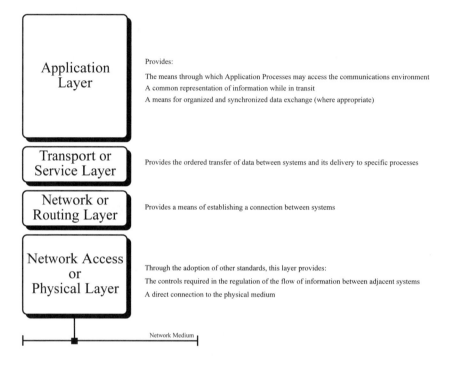

Figure 2-5: The Internet Protocol Suite Model

This layer is equivalent to the OSI Physical and Data Link Layers combined.

- **The Network or Routing Layer**
  This layer is responsible for the routing and delivery of data between networks. Such operations may become quite complex where differences exist between the *low level naming* or addressing schemes used. As such, this layer must make the appropriate translations where required. The Internet Protocol (IP) together with the Internet Control Message Protocol (ICMP) is used at this layer and, since it must function with all network types, is independent of underlying net-

9. Ethernet, while using the CSMA/CD Access Method, is more commonly used than 802.3. There are however minor differences between these two access protocols and while they may co-exist on the same network, they should not be confused.

Standardization

work architectures. IP therefore brings its own addressing scheme that is discussed in Chapter 4.

Since IP must work with any network access protocol, IP also includes a means by which data from one network may be *fragmented* before continuing its journey over another network. This is an important feature since different network access protocols allow the transportation of different amounts of data in a Link Layer frame.

This layer is equivalent to the Network Layer in the OSI Model.

- **The Transport or Service Layer**

  This layer is broadly equivalent to the Transport Layer in the OSI Model however we shall see in later sections that some Session Layer functionality is inherent here also. In general, it provides a delivery service to a specified Application layer *port*.

  Two protocols may be used here depending upon the application requirements namely the *Transmission Control Protocol (TCP)* or the *User Datagram Protocol (UDP)*. In the first case, TCP provides the application process with an error checked, flow controlled, sequenced, data stream through the provision of a virtual circuit between users. The connection oriented environment requires the establishment, maintenance, and eventual orderly closure of such circuits, and is commonly used where reliability is required.

  UDP provides a connectionless environment, requiring that the application process deals with error checking, sequencing and flow control, and is used where low network traffic overhead is of prime concern. Typically UDP would be used for network control and management.

- **The Application Layer**

  The Application Layer, as in the OSI Model, provides the application process with access to the communications environment. This is broadly equivalent to the Presentation and Application Layers of the OSI Model, although certain application protocols do provide synchronization and error detection. It is thus difficult to show clear demarcation between the layers of the two model types.

  Examples of Application Layer protocols are:

Table 2-4: Application Layer Protocols

Protocol	Description	See Chapter
TELNET	The Network Virtual Terminal Emulation Protocol	16
FTP	The File Transfer Protocol	17
TFTP	The Trivial File Transfer Protocol	19
BOOTP	The Bootstrap Protocol	19
SNMP	The Simple Network Management Protocol	20

2.4 A Comparison of Major Architectures

Before leaving the subject of architectures and standardization, it is interesting to compare and contrast several major architectures that are found in networking. Figure 2-6 shows four such architectures and compares these to the OSI Model.

OSI	Internet	DECnet	SNA
Application	Application	User	User
Presentation		Network Application	Transaction Services
			Presentation Services
Session		Session Control	Data Flow Control
Transport	Transport or Service	End Communications	Transmission Control
Network	Network or Routing	Routing	Path Control
Data Link	Network Access or Physical	Data Link	Data Link
Physical		Physical	Physical Control

Figure 2-6: A Comparison of Common Architectures

The one thing that all of these architectures have in common is that they are all based upon a layered system. Equally, each use either the same or similar naming for the layers that have a common functionality. This is both unusual and refreshing, especially when two architectures are proprietary (DECnet, and SNA), and the Internet architecture is a de-facto, rather than Internationally agreed Standard.

2.5 Summary

We have seen that the Internet Protocol Suite is certainly not the only suite of protocols available for networking today. While this suite is significant by the numbers of networks that employ it, it certainly cannot be considered either the best nor the most up to date. What it does have though, is the fact that it was there when people needed it rather than being an empty unfulfilled promise.

IP has evolved although not without natural selection. The IAB provides a vital role in steering the Internet community and, through the time given freely by its members, sets the standards by which protocols and systems are developed. Part of this standardization process, and the main vehicle, is the Request for Comments document (the RFC). Through this, comments from all interested parties are requested, and new ideas are communicated. True it is the various committees that eventually decide upon the overall direction, but it remains that anyone may comment.

Some of the best industry brains are involved with the IAB and have only the best interests of the Internet at heart. Protocols must go through stages of acceptance and can be in one of many states. Equally, before acceptance, at least two independent implementations must be produced to ensure compatibility can be acheived, and that the work carried out is viable. Sometimes this may seem that the work is pitifully slow, but it is better to have the small delays imposed by this regime than both late delivered promises or incomplete research.

An Overview of Network Technologies and Relay Systems

C H A P T E R   3

Before we can usefully discuss the operation of the Internet protocols, we must first have a basic understanding of how Local and Wide Area Networks operate. In addition, there are a number of different devices that are used to interconnect our networks and an idea of their operation, advantages and shortcomings is equally important. This chapter is not designed to be a definitive discussion of LAN and WAN technologies. Instead, as its title suggests, this is an overview. There are many books on this subject and where further information is required, the reader is urged to either consult such a book or refer directly to the relevant standards.

For LAN technologies, most commonly today we find Ethernet, Token Ring, and the Fibre Distributed Data Interface (FDDI) used. As for WAN technologies, many standards exist including RS-232C, RS-442/9, X.21, X.25, V.35, and ISDN. In this chapter we shall look at these LAN/WAN technologies and how the various inter-networking devices and the Internet protocols are used with them. In Chapter 22, we also look at the transmission of the Internet protocols over serial WAN links and see how TCP/IP can be used in wide area networks.

3.1 Ethernet and IEEE 802.3

Possibly the most prevalent of all LAN access methods is Ethernet. Be warned though, many people that use 802.3 LANs will also refer to them, albeit wrongly, as being Ethernet. When used in this context, the terms Ethernet and 802.3 are generally used to refer to the types of cabling, the topology of the network, and the access method employed. In reality though, these terms hold far more information than just that.

3.1.1 802.3 Specifications

It was during the early 1970s that work originally began to develop an experimental network that has since evolved into both Ethernet II and 802.3. Xerox began work in 1972 and by 1976 had a demonstrable prototype system. They were then joined by Intel and Digital (forming what has since become known as DIX), and in 1980 introduced Ethernet version 1.0.

At this time, the American Institute of Electrical and Electronic Engineers (IEEE) was looking for a starting point for their Carrier Sense, Multiple Access with Collision Detection (CSMA/CD) LAN access method. They chose to use the work

27

begun by DIX and, based upon the draft documents of the IEEE, in 1982 DIX then released Version 2.0 of their Ethernet LAN access method. Sadly this was an opportunity missed since the IEEE then went on to further refine their work and, in 1983, they introduced the 802.3 standard that differs from Ethernet in one key area. Since then, much further work has been undertaken and now a whole suite of standards exist.

- **10Base5**

  The original IEEE specification (802.3) based upon a 10Mbps system utilizing *Baseband* signalling techniques over 50 ohm coaxial cable with a maximum of 500m cable segments that must be terminated in 50 ohms at each end. The topology here is a *bus*, with all stations (maximum 100 per cable segment and, at least, a theoretical maximum limit of 1024 stations in total) connected to a common cable. This is often referred to as *Thick Ethernet*.

  Station connection for 10Base5 is by a *Transceiver* and *Attachment Unit Interface* (AUI) cable. The transceiver is a simple device that is responsible for the transmission and reception of data, and the detection of collisions amongst other things. Two types of transceiver exist. A so-called *Vampire* (or *Beesting*) and an *N Type*. In the first case, the transceiver attaches to the cable by piercing the insulation and can be attached while the network is live. The N Type transceiver, on the other hand, employs two N Type sockets and requires that the cable be broken during installation.

- **10Base2**

  Standardized by IEEE 802.3b and introduced in 1988, this defines a similar (bus topology) coaxial system to 10Base5. Here however the cable type is RG58 (which is thinner and therefore cheaper than traditional 10Base5 cabling) but with a maximum segment length of 185m. Again, cable segments must be terminated at each end with a 50 ohm terminator, and each segment supports a maximum of 30 stations. This system is often referred to as *Thin Ethernet*.

  Connection here is also by way of a transceiver although many interface cards actually have these built on-board. Connection of the transceiver to the cable is achieved via a *Bayonet Neill Concelmann* (BNC) 'T' piece and, although this connection method is slightly different, 10Base2 is still actually a Bus.

- **10BaseT**

  Introduced in 1990 and specified by IEEE 802.3i, this system is a 10Mbps Baseband system, but uses Twisted Pair cabling (often simply referred to as *UTP*). Typical cable lengths are up to 100m, however this is dependent upon the type of cable used. The topology here is *point-to-point* with stations connected to a special device known as a Hub.

  The standardized connector here is the *RJ45* plug (and socket) and uses pins 1, 2, 3, and 6 as two pairs (one for transmit and the other for receive). Care must be exercised, since 8 core (4 pair) cable is generally used and the cables used for pins 3 and 6 *must* form a pair. This is because a mode of transmission known as *Balanced Differential* is employed that uses both a positive and negative element for each of the transmit and receive pairs.

  In order to simplify connection, vendors reverse the transmit and receive pairs at the station so that simple straight through cables can be used to connect them to the hub. Where two Hubs are to be interconnected using 10BaseT however, a cross-over cable must be used to maintain the correct connections.

As with 10Base2, 10BaseT also uses a transceiver to connect the station to the medium (cable). Again though, most station interface cards actually have this circuitry incorporated, presenting the user with only a RJ45 socket. Hubs have their station ports presented simply as RJ45 sockets, or as a set of 50 pin *Telco* connectors that can be connected directly into a Structured Cabling System. Where Telco connections are used, each connector can then support up to 12 stations maximum.

- **10BaseF**

IEEE 802.3j defines this specification for a 10Mbps Baseband system over Fibre cable. Introduced in 1992, three individual specifications are included each describing a point-to-point topology:

- **10BaseFP**

A Passive Star system incorporating passive hubs to interconnect devices

- **10BaseFB**

A Backbone system to connect repeaters using synchronous repeater links

- **10BaseFL**

Also referred to as the Fibre Optic Inter-Repeater Link (FOIRL), this allows stations and/or repeaters to be connected in a point-to-point fashion.

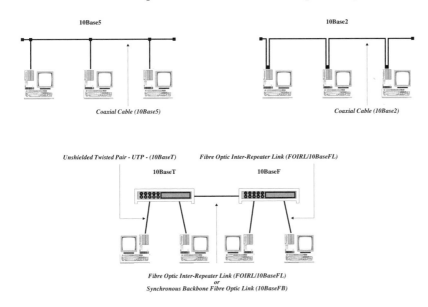

Figure 3-1: Ethernet/802.3 Topologies

Typically the cable used is known as 62.5/125 Multi-Mode, Graded Index. The figures mean that the inner core of fibre is 62.5 microns in diameter, and that the overall diameter is 125 microns. Multi-Mode refers to the type of fibre itself (Multi-Mode as opposed to Single Mode) and Graded Index, that the refractive index of the core changes as the light signal travels away from the center of it. Some installations will use Single Mode fibre since this allows far greater distances between devices. The cost for such installations however is considerably greater.

Figure 3-1 shows the topologies for these different specifications.

3.1.2 Ethernet/802.3 Frame Structure

The Ethernet II and IEEE 802.3 frame structures are very similar but the one small difference between them does preclude Ethernet and 802.3 stations from communicating. The frame itself is shown in Figure 3-2 which also indicates where these technologies differ. As you will see, it is the interpretation of the field immediately following the *Source Address* where the difference lies with Ethernet using this as an indication of the type of data, and 802.3 using it to determine the length.

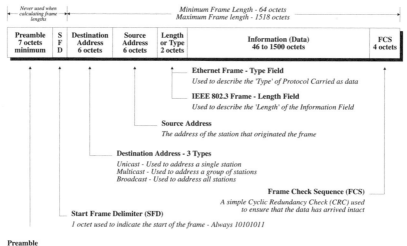

Figure 3-2: Ethernet/802.3 Frame Structure

Although the interpretation of this field prohibits Ethernet and 802.3 stations from communicating, it does not stop them from co-existing on the same physical medium. DIX and the IEEE were very careful when designing their systems, and as a result the values of these fields do not conflict. For example, the largest amount of information that can be carried is 1500 octets (in decimal) which translates to 05DC in hexadecimal. The smallest value of this field in Ethernet environments though is 0600 (hex) thus, the two systems can co-exist without mis-interpretation. Ethernet systems merely discard 802.3 frames as carrying invalid protocol information, while 802.3 systems consider Ethernet frames as

An Overview of Network Technologies and Relay Systems

being too long and likewise discard them. Examples of some valid Ethernet Type Codes are shown in Table 3-1.

Table 3-1: Ethernet Type Codes

Ethernet Type	Protocol	Ethernet Type	Protocol
0600	Xerox XNS	8035	RARP
0800	IP	8137	Novell IPX
0806	ARP	8138	Novell IPX

An indication of the type of information being carried is essential since it is through this field that multi-protocol devices decide how frames should be handled. In Ethernet we have the *Type* field however where 802.3 is used, further information such as *Logical Link Control* (IEEE 802.2) and/or the *Sub Network Access Protocol* (SNAP) is included that indicates this. A further discussion of these other protocols however is beyond the scope of this text.

The *Preamble* and *Start Frame Delimiters* are used to synchronize the stations and to indicate the actual start of the frame respectively. These fields though are generally not included when discussing the contents of the frame.

All devices on a network must be uniquely addressable, and this is achieved through a 6 octet[1] address normally expressed in hexadecimal. The address itself comprises a 3 octet Vendor ID that can be used to identify the manufacturer of the device. The remaining 3 octets are then used to uniquely identify this device amongst all those manufactured by the vendor. For example, an address of 08-00-87-12-34-5D identifies the device as having been manufactured by Xyplex Inc. Since 08-00-87 is their Vendor ID. 12-34-5D then identifies this particular device from all the others that they have made.

The *Destination* and *Source Address* fields naturally contain the address of the target station and that of the station that originated the frame. If we turn our attention to the Destination Address field specifically though, we find that three types of address exist. Firstly, where we wish to communicate only with a single device (known as a *Unicast*), this field will contain the address of that device. Normally, the address of a device is either printed on it, or the vendor supplies a utility that allows it to be obtained. In any event without this vital piece of information, communication will not be possible.

On occasion, we may wish to simultaneously communicate with a group of devices (but not all) on the network. This is known as *Multicasting*. This type of transmission is not a problem since Ethernet/802.3 is a broadcast technology, meaning that all stations receive the transmissions of all others and simply ignore those that are not addressed to them. In this case, we set the lowest order bit of the highest order octet (referred to as the Individual/Group Address bit) to indicate that we wish to multicast. Examples of multicast addresses are 01-80-C2-00-00-00, and 09-00-87-12-34-5D. Stations that participate in these multicast groups will then respond to their own (unicast) address and also the group address(es) of the group(s) to which they belong.

1. The actual IEEE 802.3 standard also allows for two octet addressing. This scheme is rarely used in todays networks however.

Finally, a station may need to simultaneously communicate with all stations on a network (known as *Broadcasting*). Here, the Destination Address field is set to all ones (FF-FF-FF-FF-FF-FF) and it is a requirement that all stations must be able to receive (and act on) these frames.

The *Information* field carries the actual data being transferred which must be between 46 and 1500 octets in length. The reasoning behind the maximum value, is that this technology is a *contention based* system and therefore we must be able to provide fair access to the medium itself. Allowing frames that are too large would not be conducive with this, thus a maximum has been defined. The reasons for a minimum size however are more involved and are based upon the fact that, being contention based, two or more stations may attempt to transmit at the same time. When this takes place, *collisions* occur corrupting the data from each of the stations involved. Obviously where we have collisions we must be able to detect them and take appropriate action. This facility is discussed in some detail in the next section.

The Frame Check Sequence (FCS) is a simple Cyclic Redundancy Check (CRC) sequence that is used to ensure that data arriving at a destination is intact. Simply put, the station transmitting the frame calculates a special value based upon the values of all octets from the start of the Destination Address field through to the end of the FCS.[2] This 4 octet value is then appended to the frame. On reception, stations recalculate this and then compare the calculated value to the value contained in the FCS field to determine whether errors have occurred. Where they match, the frame is deemed to be good and is then processed accordingly. However, where the values are different (indicating an error) the frame is discarded.

3.1.3 Ethernet/802.3 Operation

As we said in the previous section, Ethernet/802.3 is contention based meaning that all stations must contend to use the medium. This is why this type of technology is referred to as being *Carrier Sense, Multiple Access with Collision Detection* (CSMA/CD). It is *Carrier Sense* because all stations must listen to the medium at all times. In other words they must be able to sense that another station is using the medium by detecting its *carrier*. *Multiple Access* means that each station has equal right to use the medium provided that it is not currently in use by another station. Finally since there is no scheduling and any station may use the medium, it is possible that two (or more) stations may detect that the medium is idle at the same time, and therefore chose to transmit together. In this case the data is said to collide causing it to become corrupted and obviously requiring it to be re-transmitted. Hence we must be able to detect collisions (*Collision Detection*). Figure 3-3 shows an example of Ethernet/802.3 in operation.

In the first part of the figure, the medium is idle and has been so for some time. Only Station A has data to transmit so it begins its transmission. Since data takes a finite amount of time to travel along the cable, when the data has reached point 1, Stations P, Q and Z will still consider the medium to be idle.

Next we will assume that Station Z now has data to transmit as shown in the second part. It thinks that the medium is idle so it commences its transmission. The

---

2. For the purposes of calculating the FCS, the value of this field is generally considered to be all zeroes.

result is that the data collides at point 2 and the resulting collision signal is propagated along the entire length of the cable as shown in the final part of the figure.

Since the collision itself propagates along the cable, all of the stations will be able to detect that a collision has occurred. Stations P and Q will effectively ignore it since they were not involved. Stations A and Z however will know that it was their data that has been corrupted, since they will still be transmitting when the collision reaches them. This then is the reason for the minimum size frame. The only way that a station is able to detect that *it* has experienced a collision, is to still be transmitting when the collision signal reaches it. The frame then *must* be long enough to enable this to happen!

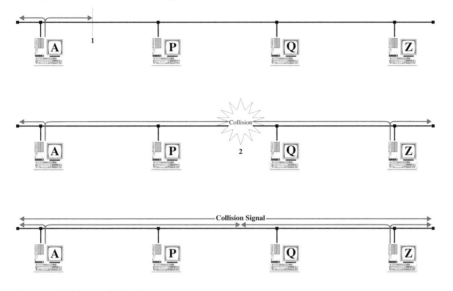

Figure 3-3: Ethernet/802.3 Operation

When a station is involved in a collision, it is said to back off. In other words, it firstly transmits a small (32 bit) signal of 10101 . . . known as a Jam signal, and then stops transmitting for a random amount of time. It then listens to the medium as before, and re-transmits the data when the medium is free again.

In this way, Ethernet/802.3 provides fair access to the medium although it is not without cost. The higher the traffic levels, the worse the access time will become. Worst of all though, the point at which saturation occurs is difficult if not impossible to predict. CSMA/CD type LANs do however provide a reasonable overall response with careful design, and are certainly popular particularly where they can be kept small.

3.2 Token Ring

Certainly the main driving force behind the Token Ring Access method has been IBM. In 1981, IBM announced that it would be developing Token Ring products and, through an agreement with Texas Instruments, commenced the joint development of the chipset required. The IEEE was also instrumental, with the standardization of the access method in their 802.5 standard in 1985. Since then, the standard has received much publicity and a great deal of further development has taken place. The 802.5 standard itself was re-published in 1989 and IBM have also added a number of extensions particularly in the area of management. Vendors who wish to enter this potentially lucrative market must therefore be compliant with both the latest versions of the 802.5 standard and equipment from IBM.

Token Ring was originally based upon *Shielded Twisted Pair Cable* (STP). Today however, a number of different cable types can be used. Just as Ethernet/802.3 allows the use and integration of coaxial, twisted pair and fibre cable, Token Ring allows the use of twisted pair and fibre. No standards currently exist for the use of coaxial cable, although many vendors are looking into this possibility to allow their customers to migrate from Ethernet to Token Ring at some later date.

A major difference between Ethernet and Token Ring cabling though is that Token Ring can (and does) use many different types of twisted pair. For example in Token Ring environments, users can use both Shielded and Unshielded cabling systems. Also where shielded cabling is used, different types can be employed. The only operational difference between these is then the number of stations that can be connected, and the distances that can be employed.

Finally, Token Ring/802.5 networks can be connected in such a way as to overcome a break in the cable thereby making it more resilient than Ethernet or 802.3 networks. Token Ring actually uses a single ring of cable to pass data but can detect when a cable break occurs, and then *heal* the ends. When this happens, depending on the way that the network is wired, we either end up with two independent rings, or alternatively we can use an alternate (backup path) to maintain network connectivity.

3.2.1 802.5 Specifications

Several different specifications exist for Token Ring. In 1985 when the original specification was published, it included 1Mbps and 4Mbps systems. When re-published in 1989 the standard no longer mentioned the 1Mbps specification, however a 16Mbps system was introduced. The major specifications for Token Ring/802.5 are:

- **802.5F**
  This defines Token Ring/802.5 at 16Mbps. The original specification (1985) defined both 1Mbps and 4Mbps systems. The 1989 specification withdrew support for 1Mbps and introduced 16Mbps although 16Mbps was not fully defined. 802.5F attempts to remedy this by fully defining Token Ring at 16Mbps.

- **802.5I**
  Token Ring/802.5 Systems can be used in a mode known as Early Token Release (ETR) that allows more of the available bandwidth to be used. Typically though it is only 16Mbps systems that employ this method of medium access and IEEE 802.5I provides the definition of this system. The operation of Token Ring networks (with and without Early Token Release) is discussed in section 3.2.3.

- **802.5J**

  In today's networks many users are turning to fibre optics for station attachment. Defined by 802.5J, this allows stations to be connected by fibre optic cable thereby increasing the distance between the station and its attachment unit, and increasing security due to egress radiation.

- **802.5K**

  Since Token Ring/802.5 networks can employ so many different cable types, the IEEE has now standardized both the types of cable that can be used and the numbers of stations that can be attached. As we have already said, Token Ring/802.5 networks can use both Shielded and Unshielded Twisted Pair cable. However since lower quality cables increase both the attenuation and Jitter introduced to the signal, the number(s) of stations that can be attached is naturally affected.

  Regardless of the work the IEEE has completed, IBM has also defined several cable types and it is these that users normally refer to. The following cable types are defined by IBM:

- **IBM Type 1A**

  Used as the *standard* Token Ring cable plant, this is shielded twisted pair cable comprising two pairs of 22AWG (American Wire Gauge) conductors. The cable will work at both 4Mbps and 16Mbps and has been tested to 350Mhz.

  Three variants of this cable are used namely *Indoor, Outdoor* and *Plenum* cable with the latter being used within air conditioning ducts. The cores here are solid and the cable is enclosed in a braided cable shield. The connector type is either the *Medium Interface Connector* (MIC) or the 9 pin *'D' Type* (DB9)

- **IBM Type 2A**

  Similar in performance to Type 1A cable, this has an additional 4 pairs of 22AWG shielded cable between the braid and the outer jacket. Two versions of this are available namely Indoor and Plenum however due to local regulations this cable type is not widely used outside the USA.

- **IBM Type 3**

  Otherwise known as Voice Grade cable, this is similar to that used by Ethernet/802.3 installations and comprises four pairs of 24AWG unshielded cable. Tested to 4Mbps, this cable is technically good enough to run 16Mbps systems and uses the *RJ45* connector as standard.

- **IBM Type 5**

  This cable type is Fibre Optic generally for use between repeaters. The cable is of 100/140 micron construction although several vendors now use 62.5/125 cable with ST connectors in its place. This then brings it in line with both Ethernet/802.3 and FDDI networks.

- **IBM Type 6A**

  This cable is normally used for patch or drop cables since it is of a stranded (as opposed to solid) construction. The cable itself comprises two shielded pairs of 26AWG cable and is capable of carrying data at 16Mbps. Like Type 1 cable, the connectors used here are the MIC connector and DB9.

- **IBM Type 8**
  This is known as under-carpet cable and is constructed of two twisted pairs of 22AWG solid cable laid flat. The cable itself is tested to 16Mbps and has a foil shield.

- **IBM Type 9A**
  This cable is similar to Type 1 and is often used as an alternative to it due to its price and flexibility. Again, as with Type 1 cable, the connectors are the MIC and the DB9 connectors. It operates comfortably at 16Mbps but allows fewer stations to be connected because it uses 26AWG (thinner) cable.

- **802.5M**
  The method used to bridge Token Ring/802.5 frames differs dramatically from that used to bridge Ethernet/802.3. In Ethernet/802.3 networks the bridging method is known as *Transparent* bridging while that used in Token Ring is known as Source Route bridging. 802.5M describes the Source Route Bridging method and is discussed in section 3.4.2.

3.2.2 802.5 Frame Structure

The main frame format used in Token Ring/802.5 is shown in Figure 3-4 however, a special frame known as the Token is also used in this type of environment. Taking the data frame first, we see that there are three main sections – the Start of Frame Sequence, the main body of the frame, and the End of Frame Sequence. Notice that there are no Type fields to identify the protocol carried. To this extent 802.5 is similar to 802.3 (as opposed to Ethernet) and needs to carry LLC[3] (802.2) information to provide a protocol identifier.

The *Start of Frame Sequence* comprises two fields known as the *Start Delimiter* and *Access Control*. The Start Delimiter is simply a special sequence of bits that identifies the start of the frame. The Access Control field however is slightly more complex since it is this that defines whether this is a frame or a token, and also provides a method for ring prioritization.[4]

The *Frame Control* field is used to identify which of the two possible types of frame this is. So called *MAC* frames are used to control the ring, while *LLC* frames are used to carry user data.

The *Destination* and *Source Address* fields have the same meanings as they do within Ethernet/802.3 environments and are of the same format. An exception to this is in an IBM environment where addresses are generally *locally administered* and set by the user. In either case, both fields are 6 octets long and, in the case of the Destination Address, can be used to address single stations, groups of stations or all

---

3. You will recall from Chapter 2 that the Data Link Layer is split into two for use with LAN technologies. LLC Frames then relate to the upper portion of Layer 2.

4. Token Ring frames can be one of eight priorities. Few protocols take advantage of this however IP does (at least in theory) have this capability through the Type of Service (precedence) field. This type of service capability is discussed in Chapter 5.

stations on the ring. The Source Address field in Token Ring environments differs slightly however since it is legal for this to indicate a group address – normally considered illogical. Where the Source Address field has the Individual/Group Address bit set, this is taken to mean that the Routing Information field is present and that the frame is a Source Routing frame. This should not be confused with routing though, since *source routing* is the name applied to the method of bridging that Token Ring uses. Source routing is discussed in section 3.4.2.

The *Information* field contains the actual data being transported. Unlike Ethernet/802.3, Token Ring does not have a defined maximum and minimum amount of data. Instead no data need be carried at the lower end of the scale, while the maximum amount of data is controlled by a timer at the transmitting station. When we look at the operation of Token Ring in the next section though, this will become clearer.

The *Frame Check Sequence* (FCS) is used to ensure that the data arrived at its destination error free. As with Ethernet/802.3 this is a simple CRC and operates in an identical manner.

The *End Delimiter*, like the Start Delimiter is a special sequence of bits, only this time it identifies the end of the frame, and also has an *Error* bit that may be set by any station. The Error bit can then be used to indicate (amongst other things) that the FCS was incorrect for example.

From the figure though it is clear that the End Delimiter is actually not at the end of the frame and is followed by a further field, the *Frame Status*. This last field contains bits to indicate whether the address was recognized and/or whether the frame was copied. The frame is structured in this way so that a station can indicate whether all data (i.e. the entire frame) was actually received.

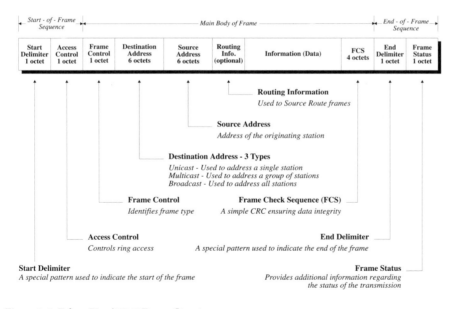

Figure 3-4: Token Ring/802.5 Frame Structure

At the start of this section we said that there was also a another type of frame called a Token. Token Ring/802.5 networks rely on a token to circulate constantly to act as an invitation to transmit. Without this, no stations can send data, and the network is therefore effectively dead. The token is simply constructed as three fields and comprises a Start Delimiter, an Access Control field, and an End Delimiter. No data is ever carried in the token and there can only ever be one token on the ring at any time.

3.2.3   802.5 Operation

The topology of Token Ring is, as its name suggests, a ring. Stations are connected to Multi-station Access Units (MAUs) which are then in turn connected together to form the ring itself. In truth this may appear as a ring of stars, however, through the internal circuitry of the MAU, each station is actually connected to its neighbor in a ring configuration as Figure 3-5 shows.

The Token Ring protocol itself is far more complicated than that of Ethernet/802.3 and is best described by the example shown in the lower half of Figure 3-5. In this example, we shall firstly assume that none of the stations have any data to transmit. A Token is therefore circulating, being passed from A to B, to C, to D and then back to A etc. All stations recognize the Token since, as we have said, it is identified by the Access Control field of the frame.

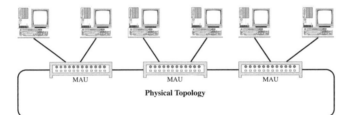

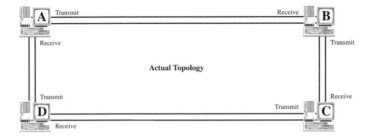

Figure 3-5: Token Ring/802.5 Topologies

Next we shall assume that Station A wishes to transmit data to station C so it waits until the token is received (being the invitation to transmit) and then transmits its data. In effect the token is removed from the ring, however in practical terms the token is modified by the insertion of extra fields and modifying the Access Control field to change it from a token to a frame. Station A is now said to be *Holding the Token* and it starts a timer known as the *Token Holding Timer*. The station may now transmit a frame the maximum size of which is determined by the Token Holding Timer and the speed of tranmission (4Mbps or 16Mbps).

The data frame(s) transmitted are now passed around the ring. Station B receives the frame(s) and will simultaneously both copy and re-transmit it/them onwards to station C. Station B knows that these are frames (as opposed to a token) by the Access Control field and therefore although it too may have data to transmit, it will not attempt to do so.

A station determines whether the frame is addressed to it through the *Destination Address* field. Where the destination address matches that of the station, the station will, in addition to processing the frame to check for errors, process the data. Thus, when the frame arrives at Station C it is transmitted towards D, copied, and processed. The station also modifies certain bits in the *Frame Status* field to indicate that this has occurred.

Although a station has now recognized the frame as being destined for it, it must still re-transmit the frame since it is possible that the frame is either addressed to a group of stations or is being broadcast. In addition, Token Ring can be said to provide a measure of guaranteed delivery through the Frame Status field. Thus, it is important that Station A receives the frame back. Eventually Station A does receive its own frame(s) back which it then *strips* from the ring and then releases a new token thereby allowing other stations to transmit.

What has been described so far is the traditional method of Token Ring operation. Today however, most implementations (especially 16Mbps systems) use what is known as *Early Token Release* (ETR). With ETR, a station need not wait for its frames to be returned to it before releasing a token. Instead, when the last frame has been transmitted a token is released. This does not upset the basic principles of ring operation since a station that transmits data frames will still receive them back so that it can determine if the data was delivered. Also, even with this system no more than one token will ever be on the network at any time therefore an ordered sequence of data transmission still prevails. Finally, ETR is fully compatible with the older (traditional) implementation of ring protocol but has the advantage of being able to use more of the available bandwidth.

3.3   Fibre Distributed Data Interface (FDDI)

Like Token Ring/802.5, FDDI is based upon a Token passing access method. In fact, the operation of Token Ring and FDDI is very similar with data being passed from neighbor to neighbor until it arrives back at the originating station. Also as with Token Ring networks, stations for whom the data is destined also copy it to their buffers for processing.

Work was started on FDDI in 1982 by the American National Standards Institution (ANSI) under the sub-committee X3T9.5. At the same time, the IEEE was working on its own 802.x standards and had already completed much of the work for its 4Mbps 802.5 specification. Indeed the IEEE 802.5 specification then became the basis for FDDI, although this was to work at the much higher speed of 100Mbps.

FDDI networks operate with a dual counter-rotating ring in much the same way that Token Ring networks can be wired. This provides resilience should a cable break by allowing the data to be routed through the backup ring. Also, FDDI introduces several new terms that describe the different types of device that can be used, and how they are connected. Topologically, FDDI can be described as a Ring of Trees with large trees of devices being created which are then interconnected via a ring. Figure 3-6 shows these various device types which are also described below:

- **Dual Attached Stations (DAS)**
  These are devices that are integral to the operation of the ring and are connected directly to the main trunk cables (that is Dual Attached). If these devices fail or are powered off, the ring is momentarily disrupted and data is routed via the backup path. Thus, only essential devices and those that have a high perceived up-time are ever connected in this way. A single cable break (or device failure) in the main trunk is tolerable but two (or more) breaks or failures can result in the ring becoming split into many parts.

- **Dual Attached Concentrators (DAC)**
  These devices are attached to the main trunk and allow the connection of Single Attached devices (either Single Attached Stations or Single Attached Concentrators). A DAC device, since it is connected to the main trunk, must be capable of high up-time in much the same way that DAS devices are. A break in a single attach cable merely isolates that part of the tree but a break in the main trunk potentially isolates whole parts of the ring. DAC devices can therefore be considered as being the root of the tree system that they form.

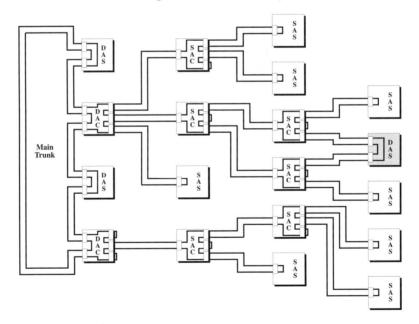

Figure 3-6: FDDI Topology

- **Single Attached Concentrators (SAC)**

  Like DAC devices, these are used to attach either stations or further concentrators. These devices cannot be placed on the main trunk since they have only a single ring connection. In practice, these can be considered as the branches of the tree formed with a DAC at its root.

- **Single Attach Stations (SAS)**

  These are typically end user devices that, if powered off, will cause no disruption to the network. SAS devices are always connected to concentrators and, like SACs, can never be connected to the main ring. If FDDI is to be thought of as a *ring of trees* topology, then these devices are the leaves.

Besides the devices mentioned above, FDDI also provides a connection method know as Dual Homing that allows a Dual Attached Station (DAS) or concentrator (DAC) to be connected to two Concentrators. This provides resilience against cable breakage, concentrator failure, and allows the Dual Attached device to be removed without causing disruption to the main ring itself. The DAS device shown shaded in Figure 3-6 is connected in this way.

As we said previously, FDDI is able to overcome a single break in the main trunk cable. This is achieved by the ports either side of the break entering a state known as *wrapped* where the inputs and outputs are automatically joined. Indeed, it is not only main trunk ports that do this. Any port will wrap where a cable break occurs and in Figure 3-6 we see the unused ports on the concentrators shown in this state.

If we were to trace the signal around the network, we would see that the topology is indeed a ring, and that only one of the two trunk cables was in use. Now if we were to assume that the cable between one of the DAC and DAS devices was broken, the ports either side of the break would wrap. Following our signal now would show that both main trunk cables are used where this situation arises, and how only a single main trunk breakage can in fact be tolerated.

3.3.1 FDDI Specifications

As its name suggests, FDDI was originally designed to work exclusively with fibre optic cable. In this case 62.5/125 multi-mode cable was chosen although several *Physical Medium Dependant* layer types (as they are called) now exist. Thus, the connection of Multi Mode fibre, Single Mode fibre and twisted pair copper cable is possible and these can be mixed as required.

As a general rule, FDDI supports 1000 connections (or 500 stations) connected to the dual ring. The total ring length can then be up to 100km and the maximum distance between stations cannot exceed 2km where Multi-Mode fibre is used.

- **MMF-PMD**

  The original specification for FDDI using 62.5/125 Multi-Mode fibres. The maximum distance of 2km between stations is derived from this specification although to be absolutely correct, we should really talk more in terms of the amount of light loss that is acceptable. In the case of MMF-PMD, this value is 11dB.

- **SMF-PMD**

  Since some users wish to place their stations at distances in excess of 2km, the Single Mode Fibre (SMF) specification was introduced. In this case, the maximum separation between stations is limited by the amount of light loss (or *Loss Budget* as it is known). For SMF-PMD, this value is either 10 or 32 dB depending upon the type of cable used and the wavelength of the light source.

- **TP-PMD**

  Twisted Pair (TP) is the most recent addition to the list of FDDI specifications. TP-PMD is often referred to as CDDI.

  TP-PMD defines the use of FDDI over shielded or unshielded twisted pair cable. This is not recommended for use within the main trunk where fibre should be used, but is instead designed to be used where FDDI to the desktop is required. Obviously twisted pair cabling is both cheaper and easier to install, and except where security is of the utmost concern is by far the best way to achieve high data rates to the desktop over currently standardized networks.

3.3.2 FDDI Frame Structure

FDDI frames are very similar to their Token Ring/802.5 counterparts. This is not remarkable since FDDI has its roots firmly in Token Ring technology. Like the Token Ring frame, FDDI has no immediate method for protocol identification. Instead, it too relies on the LLC protocol. The actual data frame format is shown in Figure 3-7.

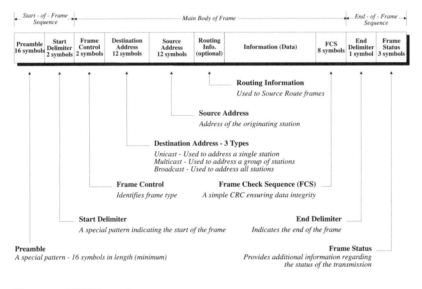

Figure 3-7: FDDI Frame Structure

The frame itself is broadly self explanatory with the possible exception of the term *symbol*. This term comes from the encoding techniques used, and is described in section 3.3.3. For most normal purposes however, we can consider a symbol to be half of one octet.

An Overview of Network Technologies and Relay Systems

3.3.3 FDDI Operation

In operation, FDDI is similar to Token Ring/802.5 as we described in section 3.2. One exception is that FDDI works exclusively with Early Token Release however, so stations release a token immediately after they have finished transmitting their data. Another difference that is interesting, is that the data rate and the actual rate of transmission are different. In FDDI environments, the actual speed of the ring is really 125Mbps although the data rate is only 100Mbps. This difference is because *Non-Return to Zero, Inverted* (NRZI) is used as the signalling method. While this is perfectly acceptable, where large strings of zeros are to be transmitted there will be no signal transitions and the stations will drift out of synchronization. This obviously cannot be tolerated, so each four bit pattern is actually encoded as five bits. This means that for the 16 possible four bit patterns, 32 are available. All those 5 bit patterns that have more than two consecutive zeroes, and those that start with more than 1 zero, are then unused. This then avoids any synchronization problems.

The only problem now is that to recover data at 100Mbps, we must transmit it 25% faster (at 125Mbps), and that we can no longer talk about octets since these are now 10 bits long. As a result, when talking about FDDI we generally refer to each 4 (or more correctly 5) bit nibble as a symbol.

3.4 Relay Systems

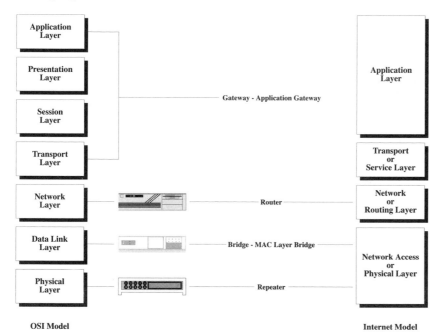

Figure 3-8: Internetworking Devices

In talking about the underlying network technologies, our discussion has so far centered on the communication of participating *End Systems.* However, what happens when data needs to be transferred between networks of either the same or dissimilar types? In these cases, a relay system called a *Router* or *Gateway* must normally be used.

A Router (generally referred to as a *Gateway* in the Internet world) is responsible for the routing of traffic between networks. Notice that the phrase applied here is not *LANs* even though many such networks today are in fact single LANs of one technology or another. Gateways in the OSI world are normally considered *application gateways* that provide a conversion from one application protocol to another. At the risk of creating confusion, we shall call those devices that route traffic between networks *Routers* even though much Internet documentation would disagree with this naming.

So, are Routers the only internetworking devices that relay information? Simply, the answer is no. True, routers are key devices especially when we consider protocols such as IP, and indeed much of this text is devoted to routing. However, we shall now briefly consider other types of internetworking devices before proceeding, in the hope that some myths may be dispelled. The devices that are generally used are shown in Figure 3-8 and are then discussed separately.

3.4.1 Repeaters

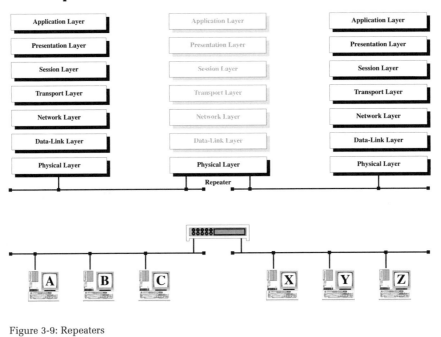

Figure 3-9: Repeaters

Repeaters are non-intelligent devices designed to connect LANs of similar type. Their purpose, as their name suggests, is to *repeat* the electrical signal from one interface to all the others. In so doing, repeaters naturally re-time and amplify the signal thus reducing the effects of attenuation and jitter introduced by stations connected to the physical LAN.

Repeaters operate with no regard for addressing and are therefore transparent to end stations on the LAN. Equally, Repeaters make no assumption whether the traffic repeated in this way is destined for the target LAN, nor indeed whether that data is good. Repeaters therefore provide no *segmentation* or checking of network traffic for errors.

These devices are said to operate at the Physical Layer of the OSI model (Network Access or Physical Layer in the Internet Model). Their operation with regard to the OSI model and in practice, in an Ethernet environment, is then shown in Figure 3-9.

The logical representation of the repeater shown at the top of this figure shows that it really only needs to implement the Physical Layer. In practice however repeaters today generally implement all layers applicable to their architecture since by doing this they can provide a management capability. Hence the other layers are shown, yet they need not actually be used to simply repeat data.

In the lower part of the figure, a practical implementation is shown where two Ethernet LANs are linked by a repeater. Since repeaters do not make any decisions whether a frame should be forwarded, any data generated by the stations on the left hand LAN will automatically appear on the right hand LAN. Stations X, Y, and Z will therefore receive any traffic generated by exchanges between say, stations A, and C.

One further point must be made clear about repeaters and that is we cannot form resilient networks with them. Two (or more) repeaters must never be placed in parallel between two LANs since this would create a loop and result in packets circulating endlessly. Resilience is therefore not an option where repeaters are used unless proprietary redundancy methods are employed.

3.4.2 Bridges

Bridges operate at the OSI Model Data Link Layer (Network Access or Physical Layer in the Internet Model). They are sometimes referred to as *Store and Forward* devices because in operation, they store an incoming frame and then decide whether to forward it or not based upon addressing information. Since a bridge operates at the Data Link Layer though, it is ignorant of the upper layer protocols carried within the physical network frame making it a protocol independent device.

Depending upon the LAN technology in use, the bridge may operate as either a *Transparent, Source Routing,* or *Translational* bridge. Typically Ethernet bridges operate as Transparent bridges while Token Ring and FDDI bridges operate as Source Routing devices. Where it is desirable to bridge between different LAN technologies a Translational or a newer type of bridge known as a *Source Routing, Transparent* (SRT) bridge may be used. In this latter case, the bridge is able to detect the type of frame arriving on a port and then behave accordingly.

- **Transparent Bridges**
  These bridges operate by storing the frame as it arrives from one LAN, and then interrogating it for the Physical Address of the destination station. A decision

whether to *Forward or Filter* (discard) the frame is then made, thus allowing a degree of traffic isolation to be achieved.

Where the bridge decides to forward the frame, the device will forward the frame in the manner dictated by the LAN access method. Where the frame is to be filtered, it is merely discarded since the bridge has determined that both source and destination station stations reside on the same physical LAN, or through some other filter criteria. This therefore avoids wasting network bandwidth by transmitting the frame onto other attached LAN(s) where it is not required.

As the name suggests, this type of bridge is transparent to the end stations connected to the attached LANs, and all of the forwarding decisions are made by the bridge itself. These bridges *learn* the whereabouts of stations by interrogating *all* frames received for the physical address of the source station. In doing this, they will then know on which port the station resides. This process is simple since these devices are used on broadcast LANs and thus will receive all traffic transmitted. End station intelligence therefore only needs to be low to allow bridging to be performed in this type of environment.

A potential problem exists when Transparent bridges are used. What happens when a resilient network is to be constructed and duplicate paths exist? Loops are not allowed when constructing networks since frames may circulate endlessly. Clearly a solution must be found to this dilemma allowing designers to introduce backup paths that can then be automatically deployed in the event of a link or component failure.

One solution is to employ a *Spanning Tree Algorithm* (such as that standardized by IEEE 802.1d) that examines the network to determine where loops exist and block selected, worst cost, paths. This system then leaves a single path open to each LAN segment. However should one of the operative bridges fail, one that is blocking traffic (and therefore eliminating the current loops) will start to forward data. Resilience is therefore a feature of these devices.

Figure 3-10 shows MAC layer bridges in use. In this figure, of the four bridges shown, only two are actually carrying user data (those on the left). The bridges on the right are then in a blocking state (as shown by the broken lower interfaces) to eliminate the three major loops (shown dotted). Should one of the bridges on the left fail however, the corresponding bridge on the right will take over the task of forwarding data.

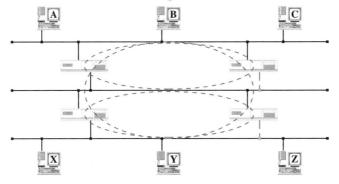

Figure 3-10: Transparent Bridges and Spanning Tree

An Overview of Network Technologies and Relay Systems

As with repeaters these devices do not need to implement all protocol layers. Where management is required (as is normally the case) however, they must be implemented. Bridges actually need only implement the lower two layers (Physical and Data Link) since the decision process is carried out on information contained in the frame header. The example that follows serves to demonstrate this point.

Let us assume that station A is sending data to station C, and that station C is responding by sending data back. In short, the two stations are communicating. Each frame that station A transmits will be heard by all stations on the LAN (stations B and C, and both of the bridges at the top). The bridge on the top right will ignore the frame since it is blocking user traffic. The bridge on the left however, will take the frame and buffer it so that it can make a decision as to whether the frame should be forwarded or not.

By interrogating the Destination Address field of the frame, the bridge will know the ultimate destination. The bridge next consults a table of addresses and the ports on which they have been heard that it has constructed from the source address fields of frames on the LAN. On seeing that the frame is meant for station C, the bridge will now discard the frame since it knows that station C resides on the LAN over which the frame was received.

This argument holds true only where the bridge knows the location of station C. If station C has never transmitted a frame before however, the bridge cannot have learnt this information. As such, the bridge will need to be safe and forward the frame to the middle LAN even though this is not required. When station C sends its first frame however, the bridge will know where station C resides because it will see the source address of the frame, and it will know the port on which it was heard.

In this way a level of isolation is achieved between our LANs and, with the exception of a small number of frames where we have no information about the destination, only data destined for any LAN segment will ever be sent there.

- **Source Routing Bridges**
  Unlike their *Transparent* counterparts, these bridges require that end stations participate in the decision process of how the frame is passed from source to destination. Source Routing Bridges (typically used in *Ring* type environments) first send exploratory frames and then decide the optimum route for all successive frames. These frames then dictate the route that should be used to route future frames between devices.

  Again these devices operate in the *Store and Forward* mode. However, with Source Routing, the device examines a special field (the *Routing Information Field*) rather than the ultimate destination address of the frame. Since end stations need to be able to create this field within the frame, it follows that interaction is required by these devices and that a corresponding increase in end station intelligence is needed.

  Contrasting these bridges with the Transparent bridge, it is clear that since the end stations decide the ultimate route that frames should follow, a Spanning Tree is not strictly required. Of course where broadcast traffic is to be used or where multiple possible routes exist, a Spanning Tree can however be employed. Figure 3-11 shows such bridges in operation with the bridge that links rings 1 and 3 (Bridge 2) blocking user data through Spanning Tree and thereby eliminating a potential loop. It must be stressed however that Spanning Tree is not necessarily used by all Source Routing Bridges.

In the figure, if we assume that station A wishes to communicate with station C we have a problem since it is logical to assume that station A will not know where station C resides. In this case, station A sends a special *Explorer* frame that is passed from ring to ring until it eventually arrives at station C. As it travels between rings, the bridges stamp the ring and bridge numbers into the Routing Information field gradually expanding it at each hop. On reception, station C then returns the frame to station A by using the routing information, but in reverse. Thus the frame returns to station A traversing bridges in the reverse order but maintaining the Routing Information field intact. The route between the two stations can now be determined by station A by merely interrogating the Routing Information field in the frame.

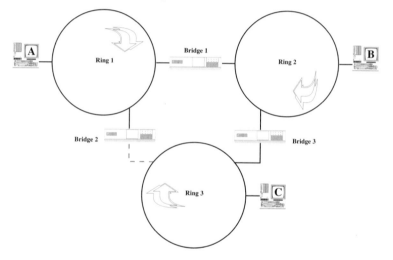

Figure 3-11: Source Routing Bridges

- **Translational Bridges**

  A Translational Bridge is able to connect LANs of different types (typically Ethernet and FDDI). This is because when a packet is received, the *Layer 2* header is removed and replaced by a Layer 2 header of the type required by the LAN to which the frame is forwarded. The frame is therefore *Translated* from one LAN technology to another.

  This type of bridging is relatively simple since it follows the normal methods described by Transparent bridges. In this case although the frame format is translated, the layer 2 addresses remain unchanged. So the source and destination addresses of the FDDI frame are identical to those that the source Ethernet station used. The bridge then learns the location of stations attached to its local Ethernet by listening to all local traffic. It then need only copy frames from the FDDI (and

An Overview of Network Technologies and Relay Systems

of course translate them to Ethernet) that are directed to stations known to be located on its attached LAN. One exception though, is that Broadcast and Multicast frames will be copied regardless of course.

Translational bridges then seem the answer to many of the problems faced by designers working with mixed technologies today – but do they really provide us with the panacea to cure these particular ills? Simply the answer is no. Consider what would happen if a frame containing say 4500 bytes of data were sent from a FDDI station, destined for a station connected to the Ethernet. An Ethernet LAN can handle only 1500 bytes of data maximum in a frame, so how can we handle it? The simple answer would be to *fragment* the data and pass it to the destination station in multiple frames each containing no more than the destination LAN was able to handle. Unfortunately though fragmentation relies on upper layer protocols and not all such devices implement this. In this latter case, our only alternative would be to discard the frame.

- **Encapsulation Bridges**

  Many early Ethernet to FDDI bridges operated as Encapsulation bridges. These bridges take an Ethernet frame at the source, and then encapsulate it in its entirety as the data field of the FDDI frame. The problem here is that the FDDI bridges must now send the frames to each other since the original Layer 2 information is embedded deep in the frame. As a result these bridges need a proprietary protocol that passes local addressing information amongst themselves.

  An advantage of such a system is that there are no associated frame size problems. However, since these bridges encapsulated frames this meant that Ethernet stations could not talk to directly connected FDDI devices or vice versa.

- **Source Routing Transparent Bridges**

  These bridges incorporate the features of both Transparent and Source Routing Bridges and are very common in mixed Ethernet/Token Ring environments. When a frame is received at a bridge port, it is examined to determine whether a Routing Information Field exists and, if it does, then the bridge will forward the frame as dictated by this field. If there is no Routing Information Field, then the frame is bridged transparently.

  As we saw earlier, should this bridge be part of a larger meshed network, it is possible that some of the bridge ports will be blocked and therefore not passing user data. Where the bridge has one or more ports in this state though, a Source Routed frame will be forwarded (even through blocked ports) if the Routing Information field instructs it to do so.

  Of course one problem that can arise when bridging between Ethernet and Token Ring is what should the maximum length of frame be? When processing Source Routing exploratory frames, bridges en-route to the destination station can set a *Length* indicator in the Routing Information Field that indicates the maximum amount of data that may be handled by the attached LAN. When the exploratory frame is eventually returned to the source station, this indicator can then be examined to determine how much data may be sent in any frame. This then overcomes the problems of connecting LANs of different technologies with different data lengths (or Maximum Transmission Units – MTUs as they are called).

- **Routers**

  A Router performs a similar function to a bridge in that decisions as to whether to *Forward* a packet are made, based upon addressing information. With Routers (generally termed *Gateways* in the Internet world) however, this decision is based upon information contained in the *Information* field of the frame. The relevant information is held in the header of the layer three protocol, and is then used to determine the *Network,* rather than *physical*, address of the target device. There are many such protocols that may operate at this layer of our model. IP, the Internet Protocol, is the one that concerns us and is one of the main topics of this text.

  A Router is never transparent to end stations since these devices will only forward packets when explicitly requested to do so. As such, participation by end stations is key to the operation of a routed environment. Routing itself is discussed in detail in Chapter 9, and the various protocols on which it relies are then discussed further in Chapters 10 to 13.

3.5 WAN Links

Today, Wide Area Networks (WANs) are integral to the proper operation of our businesses, linking the various offices of our organizations. No discussion of underlying technologies can therefore be complete without at least mentioning them. WAN links pre-date LANs by many years and, during this time many standards have evolved. True they all deal with the same basic idea of allowing the serial transmission of data, however with the introduction of digital lines, speeds have increased dramatically. Many standards exist for serial data communications, some of which are briefly described below:

- **RS-232C/V.24**

  Equivalent to the CCITT V.24 specification, the RS-232C standard was developed by the EIA. Possibly the most widely known and used standard for this type of communications, it has served the computer industry well despite its shortcomings. For example, distances between devices must be kept to a minimum and speeds rarely exceed 9600 bps.

- **RS-422/V.11**

  The need to increase the distances between devices and the need for higher transmission speeds led to the development of the RS-422/V.11 standard. Unlike RS-232C/V.24, this specification calls for a *balanced differential* system where the transmit and receive signals each have two elements, and it is the difference between them that is interpreted as data. In contrast, RS-232C/V.24 systems have all signals that are referenced to a common ground.

- **RS-449**

  Two specifications actually exist for RS-449 depending upon whether balanced or unbalanced signalling is used. In real terms, this standard provides enhancements over the previous standards listed since this provides for even greater distances between devices.

- **V.35**

  V.35 interfaces are used where higher speeds (typically in the range 48-168kbps) are required. Since the specification calls for a mixture of balanced and unbalanced lines, no greater device separation is normally achieved. Some applications however call for only the transmit and receive lines (with their associated clocks) which are always balanced. In these cases, longer cables can therefore be used.

- **X.21**

  This specification is normally used when a device is to be connected to a public data network (PDN) or where higher speeds are required. Two versions exist, namely X.21, and X.21 bits with the latter being the more popular of the two.

So which devices use WAN links? Clearly since Repeaters must repeat all data at the same rate that it arrives they cannot use links of this type. Currently no 10Mbps services exist, and in any case it would be undesirable to repeat all data that appears on one LAN to another. Bridges and routers however are a different story. These devices do not need to transmit every frame that they receive on a LAN and indeed if they did, they would be providing no added functionality over that of a repeater. Thus, since they need to forward less, the WAN links can run at speeds considerably less than those of the LAN. Indeed for many smaller networks, the speed of the WAN link need not exceed say 64kbps.

Having joined our LANs with either bridges or routers, we must now concern ourselves with the data that is to pass over these Wide Area links. Going back only a small amount of time, we find that there was scant choice. Few standards existed for the transmission of data in this way and most vendors provided only proprietary solutions. Each end of the link then had to have equipment from the same vendor, making the construction of large multi-vendor Wide Area Networks an impossibility.

From a purely Internet Protocol perspective, Serial Line IP (or SLIP as it is known) was the starting point of the Wide Area revolution and although the RFC that defines it is entitled "*A non-standard for transmission of IP datagrams over serial lines*" it is extremely important. Now the Internet Protocol (IP) could be carried in a *standardized* form over WANs. The one problem is that, as its name suggests, SLIP can carry only IP and ignores the needs of all other protocols. Other wide area protocols existed such as X.25, Frame Relay etc. and they are still in wide usage today. However since these are not specific to IP, they are not covered by this volume.

Next came the Point-to-Point Protocol (PPP) which allows a multitude of protocols to be carried, and at the same time. This protocol has now become the standard for use over point-to-point WAN links and it is true to say that most vendors now support it at least at its most rudimentary level. Both SLIP and PPP are more than a little significant to networking then and are discussed in detail in Chapter 22.

3.6 Summary

In this chapter we have looked at some of the underlying network technologies over which the internet Protocol Suite commonly runs. The descriptions included are not designed to be exhaustive but are instead designed to give the reader a feel for both some of the problems facing network designers and also the advantages and disadvantages that different technologies offer.

Probably the most common technology today is Ethernet. True this offers only relatively slow speeds compared to others such as Token Ring and FDDI but based upon cost per port, Ethernet probably offers best value for money. As networks evolve, other technologies will become available and indeed high speed networks such as ATM are available today albeit at a prohibitive cost to many. For the future, who can tell. Certainly we can be sure that two factors will drive development, namely speed and cost. Today, organizations require higher and higher speeds but at lower cost. Thus, we can be sure that we will look to higher speed networks in the future.

Where security is an issue, fibre optic cabling is generally employed and will almost certainly continue to be so since there is both no radiation and it is difficult to tap. Such technology comes at a price though so more traditional copper cable is generally considered the norm for most designers in todays markets.

Internet Addressing

In this chapter we shall examine the addressing scheme used by the Internet Protocol Suite, why it is required, the format of addresses used, and the problems that such a scheme potentially introduces. Internet users are under extreme pressures to conserve a rapidly diminishing address space – but why? Surely the designers could have foreseen the requirements of todays computer reliant generation? Do we need an addressing scheme anyway? If we do, why aren't existing schemes capable of providing us with a scheme that is flexible enough?

This chapter attempts to provide answers to these questions and more, and in so doing defines a framework without which the Internet Protocol Suite cannot exist.

4.1   The Need for an Addressing Scheme

It is a requirement that each station on a network must have a unique address. The postal service cannot deliver letters to you unless they are clearly marked with a unique address. In just the same way, stations on networks cannot receive data unless they too possess a unique address.

We have already seen that each station has a unique address in the form of its Layer 2 (Data Link) or *MAC* address. So why the need to complicate matters further by the introduction of another scheme? Is the scheme used by Ethernet, or that used by Token Ring or FDDI, inadequate for our needs? Or is it just that the architects failed to see the usefulness of existing schemes?

Simply, the answer to all of the questions posed thus far is a resounding No! The Internet address is not some kind of cruel joke, nor was it designed to supplement an ill-conceived or inadequate addressing scheme introduced at Layer 2. Instead, it was designed so that all underlying LAN technologies could be used without the need for any changes to be made. Plainly put, if the Internet Protocol Suite were to rely on say, the addressing scheme implemented by the designers of Ethernet, then the protocol would work happily on LANs using this access method or addressing scheme. It is unlikely however, that it would work over other LAN technologies that used either two or eight octet addresses for example. The designers then created an addressing scheme that, in their eyes, was as future proof as could conceivably be at the time. One goal has certainly been achieved – that of making the scheme future proof in terms of underlying network technology. Sadly, this is anything but the case when the total address space available is considered in line with the growth of the Internet itself.

4.2 Internet Addressing

As we have just stated, one of the prime goals in designing an addressing scheme was to make the address independent of the underlying LAN (or indeed WAN) technology in use. However certain other criteria had to be met:

- The address must lend itself to the easy *Routing* of traffic between networks.[1] This concept is briefly described in section 4.3 and discussed in detail in Chapter 9.

- RFC 791 tells us that the addressing scheme implemented had to "*. . . provide for flexibility in assigning addresses to networks and to allow for the large number of small to intermediate sized networks. . . .*"

- Again from RFC 791, we learn that "*. . . The local address*[2] *. . . must allow for a single physical host to act as several distinct physical hosts.*" This concept, known as Multihoming, is also discussed later.

The architects of the Internet decided to use a 32 bit (four octet) address, which was totally independent of any addressing scheme used at Layer 2. Thus one goal was accomplished. Now 2^{32} (or 4,294,967,295) possible stations could be interconnected, each with a unique address! But this was not enough. An addressing scheme of this nature, on its own, would require a central authority to oversee the allocation of addresses on a *per station* basis – A Herculean task by any standard.

To make the available address space as flexible as possible, it was decided that the 32 bits should be divided into a universally administered *Network ID* (Network Address) and a locally administered *Host ID* (Host Address). This served two purposes. Firstly, it meant that only networks (and not hosts) had to be registered, resulting in less administrative overhead. Secondly, by careful encoding of the address bits, it allowed for the following network types to be accommodated:

- A small number of networks with a large number of hosts attached.

- A moderate number of networks with a moderate number of hosts attached.

- A large number of networks with a small number of hosts attached.

The flexibility sought would now be achieved – but how could this be encoded? The original RFC documenting the Internet Protocol (RFC 791) details that the address space should be divided into three distinct *Classes* of address to serve the ideals required above. Figure 4-1 shows these three major classes (Class A, B, and C) and how the 32 bits available are encoded. The figure also shows how the addressing scheme has been enhanced to provide a mechanism for *Multicasting* that is described in some detail in Chapter 14.

---

1. Routing refers to the process by which a packet is passed from network to network until it is eventually delivered. A *Network*, in this context refers to a collection of LANs and/or WANs over which these data packets travel.

2. That assigned by the local Network Administrator.

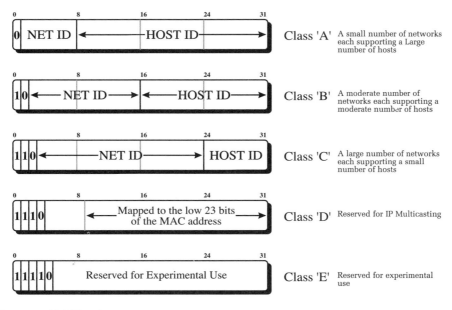

Figure 4-1: IP Addressing

The "most significant" bits in the address are the key to the division of the available 32 bits into distinct Network and Host IDs. Where the most significant bit is a 0, a Class A address is represented. This indicates that the remaining seven bits of the highest order octet are used to identify the Network, and the remaining 24 bits (three octets) are used to represent the Host. Where the most significant bit pattern is '10', a Class B address is implied. This results in 14 bits of the address being used for the Network ID, and the remaining 16 bits for the Host ID. Class C addresses are indicated by the most significant bits of the address being set to '110'. This then allows 21 bits to be used to identify the Network and 8 bits to identify the Host. In all cases, the Host ID is locally administered.

Class D addresses are a special case since all addresses in this range are reserved for Multicasting[3] and Class E addresses are reserved for experimental use. Only stations participating in the experiment would ever implement addresses in the range assigned to Class E.

4.2.1 Dotted Decimal Notation

As humans, we generally find remembering long strings of numbers extremely difficult. No more so than when those numbers comprise only a zero and a one. Imagine if you wished to connect to a host system whose IP Address was 10101100000100000000101000000010? The chance of remembering the address is

---

3. Multicasting is the means by which a single station may communicate with a group of (but not necessarily all) other stations. This is described in Chapter 14.

in the first instance is low, and the possibility of entering the address incorrectly is extremely high. A better way of expressing this address had to be found. Thus, manufacturers found a friendlier method by expressing the 32 bit pattern in either hexadecimal or decimal form. In both cases, the 32 bit value of the address is divided into four octets, and then each of these octets is expressed as follows:

- In hexadecimal, each octet may assume a value of between 00 and FF. Where 00 represents each of the eight bits that comprise the octet being all zeroes, and FF represents each of the bits being 1s, that is 00000000 to 11111111.

- In decimal, each octet is represented by the decimal value of its constituent bits. This means that a value of 0 would represent all eight bits being 0, and 255 would represent each of the eight bits being 1s. The decimal weightings of the eight bit positions are calculated from right to left where the rightmost (least significant) bit has a decimal value of 1, and the leftmost (most significant) bit has a value of 128. A binary progression then exists between these bits, 1, 2, 4, 8, 16, 32, 64, and 128.

In the case of decimal representation, by far the most popular, each of the decimal values that represent the individual octets are then separated by decimal points (or dots) so that no confusion arises. Our address 10101100000100000000101000000010 may then be represented as 172.16.10.2, far easier to remember. This convention is referred to as *Dotted Decimal Notation*.

4.2.2 Identifying IP Addresses and Rules

From our preceding discussion, you will see that, when an address is written down, the *Class* of address (and therefore how large the Host ID address space actually is) is immediately shown. For example:

- With Class A addresses, the first octet will be a number between 0 and 127. In actual fact, a value of zero as the Network ID means *this network* and a complete address of 0.0.0.0 has the meaning, *this host on this network*[4]. Thus, you will never see this address, nor a network address of 0 actually on the network. In addition, the network address 127 is reserved for *loopback testing*, used where the network hardware or software is to be tested. Typically 127.0.0.1 is used for this purpose and should also never be seen on a network. Class A addresses then always have a leading octet in the range 1 to 126, and have 24 bits assigned to the Host ID. In addition, no Host ID of all ones is allowed since this has special significance which will be discussed later. Class A stations therefore, will always have addresses in the following range:

  1.0.0.1 to 126.255.255.254

- With Class B Addresses, the first octet will always be in the range 128 to 191, and the last two octets (16 bits) form the Host ID. Our address shown above is therefore a Class B address meaning host 10.2 on network 172.16.0.0. As before, a Class B station will therefore have an address in the range:

  128.0.0.1 to 191.255.255.254

4. We shall see later that this is not always the case since many *older* implementations also use what is referred to as an *all zeroes broadcast*.

- With Class C Addresses, the first octet will always be in the range 192 to 223, with the last 8 bits reserved as the Host ID. This then leads to Class C stations having addresses in the range:

  ```
  192.0.0.1 to 223.255.255.254
  ```

- Class D, or Multicast Addresses are special types of address and are explained in detail in Chapter 14. They will however, always have their first octet set to between 224 and 239.
  With Multicasts, the lower 24 bits have a special significance and do not specify an individual host. Instead, these bits identify groups of devices that respond to both their own IP Address, and that of the *Multicast Group* to which they belong.

- Class E Addresses will have their first octet set to between 240 and 255. However, since these are reserved for experimentation, they are of little importance to general Internet users. Unless you are involved in experimentation, and have registered the address(es) that you wish to use, this class of address may be ignored. These groups of addresses may thus be considered transitory and are therefore not discussed here.

Certain patterns of bits within the Host ID portion of the address must be also be avoided since they too have special meaning. For example:

- You may not assign a Host ID of all zeroes, since this is used to describe either the network itself, or a broadcast[5] to all hosts on that network. For example, 10.0.0.0 could identify the Class A network 10, or it could mean broadcast to all devices on network 10. Similarly, 192.168.22.0 could be used to identify the Class C network 192.168.22, or alternatively, could mean broadcast to all hosts on network 192.168.22. Typically it is older hosts that consider Host IDs of all zeroes to indicate a broadcast and the convention of using zeroes to mean *this network* is now used as a convenience when viewing tables of addresses.

- A Host ID of all 1's is the more normal representation of a *Broadcast* to all stations on a network. For example, 172.16.255.255 means broadcast to all stations on network 172.16.0.0. For this reason Host Ids such as x.255.255.255 (where x identifies a Class A network) must be avoided.

4.2.3 Choosing the Right Addressing Scheme

The classes and rules discussed in the preceding sections show that certain constraints have been placed on the available address space. For instance, there are only 126 possible Class A addresses available (1 to 126). Similarly, when using Class C addresses, each network can support only 254 hosts (since host 0 and 255 cannot be used). So how do I choose an addressing scheme that is right for me? Do I use a Class A, Class B, or a Class C address, and do I need to register an address once I have chosen the scheme I wish to use?

---

5. Broadcasting is discussed in Chapter 14.

The Internet Protocols themselves impose only one rule when choosing an addressing scheme, namely that each host system must be uniquely identifiable. The following three points describe all possible scenarios:

- If you are setting up a private network that requires no communication with outside systems, then you are free to choose any network address(es) that you wish, and assign unique IP Addresses to each device. Should you choose to use more than one Network ID however, you will have to use a *Router* [6] to pass traffic between the networks.

- If you wish to use a "service provider" to gain access to The Internet, you will be assigned at least the Network ID portion of the address that must be used. It is entirely possible that your provider may also assign a block of Host Ids. Whichever is the case, how you distribute the Host Ids is entirely up to you. Remember though that each host must have a unique ID.

- Where you are setting up a private network that requires no communication with external systems today, but may at some time in the future, it is probably best to apply for a registered address. Addresses can be issued, on request, from the Network Information Center (NIC) or from your Internet Service Provider (ISP).

Be warned, nobody issues addresses without justification – Addresses are now fast becoming a scarce commodity. With just 126 available Class A addresses, only the largest organizations, typically government or military, are granted addresses in this class. Class B addresses, with only some 16,000 combinations in total, are now limited, and an extremely good justification is required before these are issued. Class C addresses, with over 2 million possible combinations, are still reasonably plentiful. Indeed, network addresses in this class are now being issued in blocks to those organizations with more than 254 hosts to connect, rather than a single Class B address.

4.2.4 Free Addresses

The Internet community realize that there are many organizations that have networks that will either never be connected to the Internet, or at the very least are unlikely to be. As such, a group of addresses are reserved for *private internets*. RFC 1597 defines three such groups as follows:

- 10.0.0.0 – A single Class A network address.

- 172.16.0.0 – A single Class B network address.

- 192.168.0.0 – 254 individual Class C network addresses.

Of course, if there is never any desire to attach a private internet to the Internet, any addresses can be chosen. What is significant about these addresses in particular though is that all Internet Service Providers (ISPs) must block any traffic to/from

---

6. Routing and Router operation is discussed in Chapters 9, 10, 11, 12 and 13.

Internet Addressing

them. Thus, organizations that wish to expand their individual networks beyond those *legally* obtained, can use these network addresses with absolute impunity.

4.3 Routing Fundamentals

The motivation behind any addressing scheme is to allow successful communication between co-operating hosts. We have seen that each host will have a unique address in much the same way as our homes do. Now we shall examine how two hosts communicate by using this address and how other devices assist us in the delivery of our data. Routing is discussed in detail in Chapter 9, however in order to understand the motivation for grouping our machines into *Networks*, we must at least touch on the subject here.

Devices may only directly communicate with each other if they reside on the same network, a process called *Direct Routing*. In this case, the device itself is responsible for data delivery to the other system, in a similar manner to you placing a memo on a colleagues' desk if you work in the same department. Where devices reside on different networks, they must rely on the services of another device known as a Router in much the same way that if you wished to communicate with somebody on the other side of the world, you would rely on the postal service. Figure 4-2 shows these two scenarios.

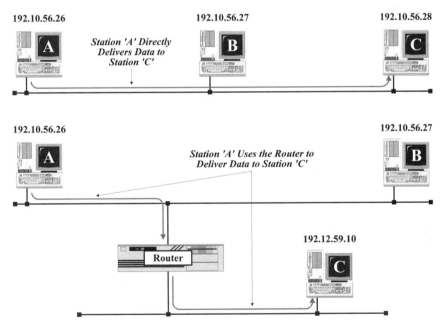

Figure 4-2: Basic Routing

Before one host can communicate with another, it must first know two things; its own IP Address, and the IP Address of the other system. It is logical to assume that all devices will know their own IP Address since this must form part of the device configuration. It is equally logical to assume that if it does not know the address of the station that it wishes to talk to, it probably has no need to pass data to it in the first place. For this latter address (that of the destination), we can assume that either the application has this address, or the operator provides it when a connection is to be made.

Since our device is now in possession of these two key pieces of information, by examining the high order bits of the two addresses it can determine their class and therefore how many bits are assigned to the *Network ID*. A simple comparison of these Network Ids will now tell us if the two devices reside on the same network or not, and therefore whether we are able to perform direct routing.

Routers have more than one interface and therefore have connections to multiple networks. Where we need to use a router to reach distant hosts, the station sends its data to the router and then uses it to deliver the data on its behalf. Again, if we were to consider our example of sending a letter to somebody on the other side of the world, we would post it in a post box. Stations then, need to be pre-configured not only with their own IP Address, but also with the IP Address of a router that can take responsibility for delivering data where we cannot deliver it ourselves. This router is normally known as a *Default Gateway*.[7]

4.4 The Resolution of MAC Addresses

We have now seen that a station will have a unique IP Address and will therefore be able to communicate with other stations. In this section, we shall look into the mechanics of this, since the actual process of data transmission is not really quite that simple.

The Internet Address relies on a 32 bit addressing scheme that is completely independent of all underlying physical addressing schemes. We therefore need to translate (*map*) the Internet Address to the Physical (MAC) Address in some way. This however is not necessarily straightforward and is indeed complicated by three main issues:

- Incompatible Address Lengths
  The underlying network technology is unlikely to use a 32 bit addressing scheme. Indeed, if we examine the common technologies Ethernet/IEEE 802.3, Token Ring, and FDDI we will see that these each utilize 48 bit addresses. Clearly there can be no direct correlation between such physical addresses and the Internet Address assigned.

- Incompatible Representations of Addresses
  Ethernet and IEEE 802.3 addresses are always represented and transmitted in what is known as *canonical form*. In these cases, each byte that comprises the address will be both shown and transmitted least significant bit first. In the case of both Token Ring and FDDI networks however, the address is represented and transmitted in *non-canonical form,* where each byte is depicted, and most importantly transmitted, most significant bit first.

7. You will recall from Chapter 3 that in the Internet world a router is referred to as a *gateway*. Therefore, be careful not to confuse router and gateway functionality here.

- The susceptibility to change

  Generally, network interfaces are assigned their MAC Address at the time of manufacture, making it impossible to encode a 32 bit Internet Address onto the card. Equally, if the network hardware were ever to require replacement, the physical address would also change, leading to more configuration problems.

4.4.1 The Address Resolution Protocol (ARP)

The designers of the Internet Addressing scheme found a generic solution to the problem by developing a general purpose protocol known as the Address Resolution Protocol (ARP). This protocol, described in RFC 826, allows the dynamic mapping of IP to MAC addresses over any *broadcast* network, such as Ethernet, Token Ring etc. The ARP protocol then, allows any station on the network to determine the MAC address of a target host when knowing only the target's IP Address.

ARP is a low level protocol that uses the services of the MAC (Data Link) Layer and, as with all protocols, ARP is then encapsulated in a physical network frame. In this case, the Source Address field of the physical frame will indicate the station that is requesting the address resolution, while the Destination Address field will contain the broadcast address. Where a Type field is present, this will contain a code to indicate the ARP protocol, so that receiving stations will be able to correctly process the frame. For example, in the case of Ethernet, the Type field will contain 0806_{16}.

Consider the example of an Ethernet network shown in Figure 4-3.

Station C wishes to communicate with Station F. Station C will first need to determine that the two machines are on the same network, and will then broadcast the ARP frame. Since Ethernet is a broadcast network, all stations will receive the frame and examine the Destination Address field. Since the Destination Address indicates a broadcast, each station must now pass the information to the protocol module indicated by the Type field (ARP in this case) and will process the Information field of the frame. The Information field will carry the ARP protocol that, in turn, will convey three important pieces of information namely the MAC and IP addresses of the sending station and the IP address of the target station.[8]

Only the target station (Station F) will recognize its own IP address, and all other stations will discard the frame as irrelevant. Station F will now record the address information about station C, and return the frame to the originating station. The returned frame will be a unicast with the information previously contained, plus its own MAC address. Since each station now knows the MAC address of the other, normal communication between the stations may now commence.

Of course, broadcasts to all attached network devices are anything but desirable since these will consume large numbers of processing cycles, particularly on machines to which the ARP request is not directed. Thus, instead of broadcasting ARP frames each time that communication is to be established, machines implement a special cache called the *ARP Cache.* This cache then allows resolved IP to MAC address pairings to be stored and reused as required. Obviously, such caches

8. The complete protocol format is described in section 4.4.2.

are finite in size. Most caches therefore are implemented with an *age timer* that allows entries that have not been referenced within the timer period to be discarded. This provides two important functions. Firstly, the ARP cache will be kept to a relatively small size and secondly, if the age timer is reasonably short, old information (such as where a station's MAC address has changed) will not be used.

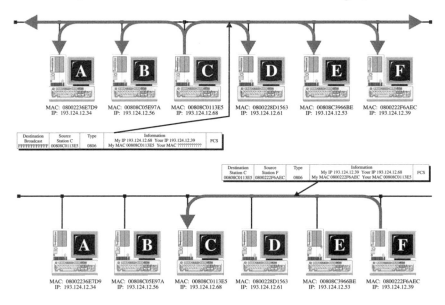

Figure 4-3: ARP Basic Operation

Where it is desirable to have a longer age timer, some implementations operate aging in two stages. When the expired time is short, the entry is assumed to still be valid and will therefore be used directly when communication with a target is required. Where the expired time is nearing the age timer value, the station will send an ARP packet to the target to check that it is still alive, but will use a unicast physical frame instead of a broadcast.

One other enhancement to ARP is where a device can promiscuously listen to ARP traffic on the local network. In this case, it is entirely possible that since station F or station C may have sent ARPs to other stations before, each could already be in possession of the the the others MAC address.

4.4.2 The ARP Protocol Format

Most protocols employ a fixed format header where each field is a pre-defined length. The Address Resolution Protocol however was designed to be general purpose, and to work with any network technology and with any upper layer protocol. For this reason, many fields are of variable length relying on other fields as pointers.

Figure 4-4 shows the ARP format where the upper layer protocol employs a four octet address and the network technology uses six octets as would be found in IP over Ethernet for example.

This packet format allows the buffer to be reused where a reply is generated, since replies are the same length as requests, and several fields are the same. The value of the two octet *Hardware Type* field is obviously the same for both requests and replies and is taken from Table 4-1 of major hardware types.

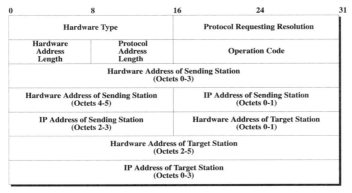

Figure 4-4: The ARP Protocol Format

Table 4-1: Hardware Type Codes for ARP

Code Hex.	Code Dec.	Description
0001	1	Ethernet 10Mbps
0003	3	Amateur Radio AX.25
0004	4	Proteon ProNET Token Ring
0005	5	Chaos
0006	6	IEEE 802.x type networks
0007	7	ARCNET
000B	11	LocalTalk
000C	12	LocalNet (IBM PCNet or SYTEK LocalNET)
000D	13	Ultra link
000E	14	SMDS
000F	15	Frame Relay
0010	16	Asynchronous Transfer Mode (ATM)

ARP is a generic protocol, thus it is important that the protocol that is requesting the resolution be identified. This is achieved through the second 16 bit (two octet) field that, in the case of an Ethernet frame, will use the standard Ethernet type codes (0800_{16} for IP).

The next two fields, the *Hardware* and *Protocol Address Lengths* are redundant for most practical purposes since a station should be able to determine the lengths of addresses based upon the Hardware Type and the Protocol in use. In practice, these two fields are included merely for consistency checking.

The *Operation Code* is essential since this will determine whether the packet is either a *Request* or a *Reply*. A value of 1 indicates an ARP Request while a value of 2 indicates an ARP Response. There are two other possible values, 3 and 4, which are used to indicate *Reverse Address Resolution Protocol* Requests and Replies respectively. This latter protocol will be discussed in detail in section 4.5.

The fields *Hardware Address of Sending Station* and *IP Address of Sending Station* are absolutely necessary. It is through these fields that the need for the target station to ARP the source station is eliminated. Instead, the addresses indicated in these locations may be directly used by the target machine and entered into its translation table. Furthermore, these addresses are then used to form the ARP Response.

The *IP Address of the Target Station* is also essential, since it is through this field that a machine may determine whether it should reply to a received request. The *Hardware Address of the Target Station* has no meaning in a Request since the whole purpose of the request was to determine the value of this field. In practice, this field may contain either nulls or may be the buffer contents following the previous request. In either case the receiving station will ignore this field in a request and replace it with the requesting station's hardware address in a reply.

The overall frame formats for our example in Figure 4-3 are now shown below. Remember that Station C wishes to communicate with Station F, therefore Station C will generate an ARP Request and Station F, an ARP Response. For the purpose of clarity, we have ignored the layer 2 (MAC) details.

- Station C creates an ARP request with the following information:

Hardware Type	0001	Ethernet
Protocol Requesting Resolution	0800	IP
Hardware Address Length	06	48 bit MAC Address
Protocol Address Length	04	32 bit IP Address
Operation Code	0001	ARP Request
Hardware Address of Sending Station	00808C0113E5	MAC Address of Station C
IP Address of Sending Station	C17C0C44	IP Address of C (193.124.12.68)
Hardware Address of Target Station	000000000000	Null string – purpose of request
IP Address of Target Station	C17C0C27	IP Address of F (193.124.12.39)

- Station F will respond as follows:

Hardware Type	0001	Ethernet
Protocol Requesting Resolution	0800	IP
Hardware Address Length	06	48 bit MAC Address
Protocol Address Length	04	32 bit IP Address
Operation Code	0002	ARP Response
Hardware Address of Sending Station	0800222F6AEC	MAC Address of Station F
IP Address of Sending Station	C17C0C27	IP Address of F (193.124.12.39)
Hardware Address of Target Station	00808C0113E5	MAC Address of Station C
IP Address of Target Station	C17C0C44	IP Address of C (193.124.12.68)

Figure 4-5 shows a trace of an actual ARP exchange:

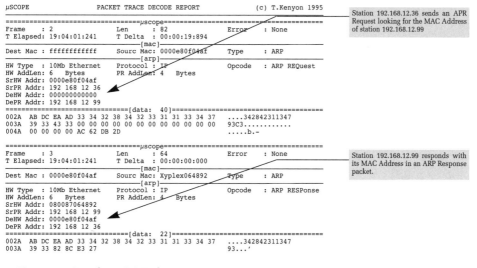

```
============================μscope============================
Frame   : 2              Len    : 82            Error    : None
T Elapsed: 19:04:01:241  T Delta : 00:00:19:894
------------------------------[mac]-
Dest Mac : ffffffffffff   Sourc Mac: 0000e80f04af   Type    : ARP
------------------------------[arp]-
HW Type  : 10Mb Ethernet  Protocol : IP            Opcode  : ARP REQuest
HW AddLen: 6    Bytes     PR AddLen: 4    Bytes
SrHW Addr: 0000e80f04af
SrPR Addr: 192 168 12 36
DeHW Addr: 000000000000
DePR Addr: 192 168 12 99
============================[data:  40]============================
002A  AB DC EA AD 33 34 32 38 34 32 33 31 31 33 34 37   ....342842311347
003A  39 33 43 33 00 00 00 00 00 00 00 00 00 00 00 00   93C3............
004A  00 00 00 00 AC 62 DB 2D                            .....b.-


============================μscope============================
Frame   : 3              Len    : 64            Error    : None
T Elapsed: 19:04:01:241  T Delta : 00:00:00:000
------------------------------[mac]-
Dest Mac : 0000e80f04af   Sourc Mac: Xyplex064892   Type    : ARP
------------------------------[arp]-
HW Type  : 10Mb Ethernet  Protocol : IP            Opcode  : ARP RESPonse
HW AddLen: 6    Bytes     PR AddLen: 4    Bytes
SrHW Addr: 080087064892
SrPR Addr: 192 168 12 99
DeHW Addr: 0000e80f04af
DePR Addr: 192 168 12 36
============================[data:  22]============================
002A  AB DC EA AD 33 34 32 38 34 32 33 31 31 33 34 37   ....342842311347
003A  39 33 82 8C E3 27                                 93...'
```

Station 192.168.12.36 sends an APR Request looking for the MAC Address of station 192.168.12.99

Station 192.168.12.99 responds with its MAC Address in an ARP Response packet.

Figure 4-5: Complete ARP Exchange

4.4.3   Problems with Address Resolution

We saw earlier that one of the reasons why a dynamic address resolution protocol was attractive was because of the potential incompatibility of address representation. Recall however that Token Ring and FDDI networks express their addresses in a *non-canonical* form (i.e. Most Significant Bit First), but what may not be immediately apparent is that data is carried in *canonical* form (Least Significant Bit First). This means that Source and Destination addresses in the Layer 2 (MAC) frame header will be specified in non-canonical form, while the data area of the frame, and hence the ARP packet, will be in canonical form. Thus potential confusion over addresses may occur.

So can the Address Resolution Protocol help us in this? Sadly the answer is no, and such solutions that do exist are generally implementation or vendor specific.

4.4.4   Address Resolution for Non-Broadcast Networks

Where address mappings are required over a non-broadcast network such as X.25, these must be established through static entries in a host maintained table. Obviously it would be undesirable to attempt to contact all attached stations over such network types however, since the X.25 address is unlikely to change regardless of changes made to hardware components, a static entry is potentially the best solution.

4.5   The Reverse Address Resolution Protocol (RARP)

We have seen that through the Address Resolution Protocol, it is possible for a machine to map IP Addresses to physical or MAC addresses. So, where is the IP address stored in the first place? Normally a machine's IP address will be stored as part of its configuration files (maybe either on disk or in some form of non-volatile Ram) that will be read when the machine boots. So the question of IP configuration in the absence of such files must be raised.

Many of even today's simplest devices require an *image* file (a copy of their operating system) to provide the rich functionality demanded by users. These images must be downloaded from network hosts using a file transfer protocol such as TFTP.[9] Equally these devices need to be managed by network management protocols such as SNMP[10] but in order to perform either of these functions they must be assigned an IP address. Should the device have no non-volatile Ram, or backing storage such as disk, it must then obtain this information from some other source.

Such devices have, when first powered on, one vital piece of information that uniquely identifies them from any other device on the network, namely their individual physical or MAC address. It is this address that is then used, via the RARP protocol, to query a server located on the network and hence find the IP address that should be used for this particular MAC Address. A RARP server may be any device on the network, the configuration of which is implementation specific. For example a UNIX host on an Ethernet network, configured to operate as a RARP server, will probably have two configuration files. The first */etc/ethers,* maps Ethernet addresses to unique *device identifiers.* The second */etc/hosts,* maps the IP address of the device to the unique identifier specified in the *ethers* file. Other systems, including Windows™ based network management products, implement a single, separate, table of mappings. Figure 4-6 shows a UNIX based RARP server in operation.

RARP, which is described in RFC 903, operates in a very similar fashion to ARP; indeed it uses exactly the same format. In this case, the station requesting the resolution of its MAC address to its IP address will broadcast an ARP packet with a Type Identifier of 8035_{16} and an operation code of 0003_{16}. In this case however, the device's own MAC address will be specified in both the Sending and Target Stations Hardware Address fields and the Operation Code will identify it as RARP. Obviously IP addresses will not be specified since these will not be known.

From the discussion above, you will note that where diskless or other such devices are used, it is imperative that at least one RARP server is available. We can also see that, unlike ARP, RARP makes a clear distinction between clients and servers but, makes no distinction as to which server should supply its information. So what will happen if multiple RARP servers are available to the device? Consider a device that broadcasts a RARP request onto the network. Should multiple servers be available, multiple responses will be received. This is not a problem since the device will take the first response and use that information. It would however be of concern if each server contained different information, since this would result in inconsistent configuration of the device in question. Thus, where multiple servers are to be used, each must contain identical information – the administrative price paid for resilience.

9. The Trivial File Transfer Protocol is discussed in Chapter 19.
10. The Simple Network Management Protocol is described in Chapter 20.

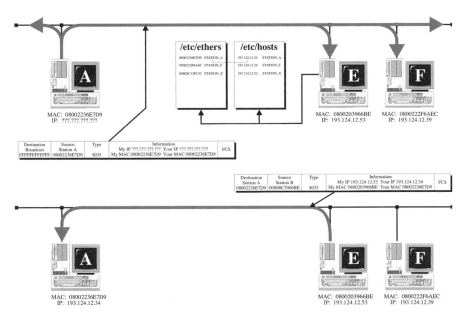

Figure 4-6: RARP Operation

Station A wishes to determine its IP address and Station E is configured as a RARP server. The complete exchange will now be as shown below:

- Station A will create an RARP packet with the following information:

Hardware Type	0001	Ethernet
Protocol Requesting Resolution	0800	IP
Hardware Address Length	06	48 bit MAC Address
Protocol Address Length	04	32 bit IP Address
Operation Code	0003	RARP Request
Hardware Address of Sending Station	08002236E7D9	MAC Address of Station A
IP Address of Sending Station	00000000	IP Address of A (unknown)
Hardware Address of Target Station	08002236E7D9	MAC Address of Station A
IP Address of Target Station	00000000	IP Address of Target (unknown)

- The RARP Server (Station E) will respond with:

Hardware Type	0001	Ethernet
Protocol Requesting Resolution	0800	IP
Hardware Address Length	06	48 bit MAC Address
Protocol Address Length	04	32 bit IP Address
Operation Code	0004	RARP Response
Hardware Address of Sending Station	0800203966BE	MAC Address of Station B

IP Address of Sending Station	C17C0C35	IP Address of B (193.124.12.53)
Hardware Address of Target Station	08002236E7D9	MAC Address of Station A
IP Address of Target Station	C17C0C22	IP Address of A (193.124.12.34)

4.6   Subnetting

Organizations with very large numbers of hosts will probably have an extremely complex network that comprises many LANs and WANs, and employs a single Class A or Class B address. Similarly some smaller organizations may wish to assign logical groupings to their hosts, thus making the task of management easier. There are many reasons why this grouping is desirable:

- The organization may employ different LAN technologies. That is, it may have some equipment on an Ethernet LAN and some connected to a Token Ring or FDDI LAN.

- Limits of the technologies in use. All LAN technologies impose limits, based on electrical or optical parameters, on the number of hosts that may be connected, and on the total length of the cable. Where the connection of many hosts is required, it is easy to exceed these limits.

- Areas of high network utilization. With today's applications, it is likely that a small subset of hosts on a LAN may generate large amounts of network traffic. Commonly, organizations concentrate these hosts on separate cables, thus ensuring that they do not affect other network users.

- Point-to-Point links, i.e. The organization may wish to interconnect LANs using Point-to-Point links that have only one station (typically a router) at each end.

It would be nice to assign a different Network ID to each of these logical groupings, but that would make very inefficient use of an addressing scheme that is already under pressure. So how can we group hosts in this way?

The address that we have discussed so far in this chapter defines two levels of hierarchy, namely a Network ID and a Host ID. What we require is the ability to define a further level of hierarchy, a *Subnet,* allowing *Hosts* to reside on *Subnets* which in turn may be grouped together to form *Networks.* RFC 950 describes a method whereby the Host ID portion of the address may be *partitioned* allowing the assignment of Subnet Numbers to each LAN.

What we achieve when we Subnet, is the assignment of more bits that will be considered as part of the Network ID. We see the groups that we have created as Subnets, while the devices that are affected see them as further networks. But how can we achieve this when the class of the address (and therefore the number of bits assigned to the Network ID) is fixed, and is identified solely by leading bits of the address itself? Does 158.152.30.248 mean host 30.248 on network 158.152.0.0, or does it mean host 248 on Subnet 30 of network 158.152.0.0? We clearly need a mechanism that will tell us exactly how many bits the Network ID really occupies.

Devices that support Subnetting have a programmable *Subnet Mask*, a 32 bit mask that identifies which bits in the address should be considered as Network ID bits, and correspondingly, which should be considered as Host ID bits. In the case of a SUN™ Workstation for example, entering the command *ifconfig le0*, (where le0 is the interface name) would display the following:

```
le0: flags=63<UP,BROADCAST,NOTRAILERS,RUNNING>
     inet 158.152.30.248 netmask ffffff00 broadcast 158.152.30.0
     ether 8:0:20:3b:59:5c
```

In order to determine our actual address, consider the example of Figure 4-7:

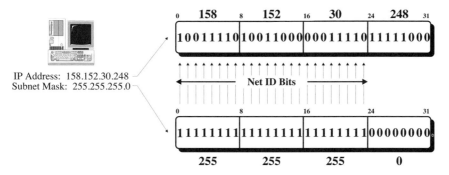

Figure 4-7: Example of a Subnet Mask in Action

Here, as humans, we view the address as being host 248 on Subnetwork 30 of network 158.152.0.0. The station views itself as being station 248, residing on network 158.152.30.0. This difference is of no importance since data delivery is based upon whether the source and target stations reside on the same network. Therefore a station that perceives itself as being on network 158.152.30.0 will know that it must use a router to contact another station on say network 158.152.40.0.

4.6.1 Natural Subnet Masks

Before leaving the subject of how Subnet masks are applied, we should also consider the term *Natural Subnet Mask* since this term describes the mask that would be used if a Subnet were not to be required. What we have described so far assumes that if we employ Subnets, all stations must be configured with a Subnet Mask. We shall see in Chapters 6 and 18 (ICMP and BootP) that this configuration may be derived from other network hosts, and we shall examine a variation of the ARP protocol (Proxy ARP) in Chapter 9 where Subnet Masks may not be required, even in subnetted environments. However, in this section, we shall examine the mask that is used when no Subnets are required on our internet.

We have said that the Subnet Mask defines which bits of the address should be considered as Network ID bits, and therefore which should be employed to define the Host ID. If we have no Subnets in use, then the *Subnet Masks* (or *Natural Subnet Masks* as they are known) for each of the address classes are as follows:

- **Class 'A' Addresses**

  Since the first eight bits of the 32 bit address are assigned as Network ID bits, the Natural Subnet Mask will be 255.0.0.0; i.e. The first eight bits of the mask are all on (1's) indicating that the first eight bits of the address are Network ID bits. The last 24 bits of the mask are off (0's) indicating that the last 24 bits of the address are Host ID bits.

  A host with the address 10.0.0.54 will have the Subnet mask 255.0.0.0.

- **Class 'B' Addresses**

  In this address class the first 16 bits of the address are assigned as Network ID bits therefore the Natural Subnet Mask will be 255.255.0.0; i.e. The first 16 bits of the address are all on (1's) indicating that the corresponding bits in the address are Network ID bits, and that the remainder are used to define the Host ID.

  A host with the address 129.53.8.12 will have a natural Subnet mask of 255.255.0.0.

- **Class 'C' Addresses**

  With Class C addresses, the first 24 bits are reserved as the Network ID, leaving the last 8 bits to define the Host. In this case, the Natural Subnet Mask would be 255.255.255.0 indicating that the first 24 bits are to be considered as Network ID bits, and the last 8 bits as the Host ID.

  A host with the address 194.23.74.241 would be configured with the Subnet mask 255.255.255.0.

4.6.2 Obtaining Subnet Masks

So, is it desirable to implement Subnets, and if so, how are they obtained? The answer is simple – All Subnet masks are merely extensions to the original addressing scheme described at the start of this chapter, and as such, they are always locally administered!

4.6.3 Guidelines for Implementing Subnet Masks

The only real rule in assigning Subnet Masks is that a mask of either all 1's or all 0's must not be assigned. Apart from this, there are no *hard and fast* rules as to how Subnet bits (and therefore masks) should be implemented. The decision to Subnet and the scheme employed is entirely up to the local site. From our previous discussions, you may have seen that *any* of the 32 bits could be used to define the Subnet. In practice, it is always best to assign Subnet masks on either 4 or 8 bit boundaries – consider this example:

```
A host is assigned the address: 129.101.194.130   (10000001 01100101 11000010 10000010)
Subnet mask:                     255.255.192.192   (11111111 11111111 11000000 11000000)
```

While this scheme may seem to provide an extremely flexible method of Subnetting and, possibly make best use of the address space available, imagine the confusion that could be introduced should documentation be weak! Remember the basic algorithm introduced in section 4.3 above and consider that we must now change our basic premise upon which routing decisions are made. Remember we said previously that devices can only communicate if they are on the same network. Now, with the introduction of Subnetworks, they may only communicate if they are on the same Subnet!

The example above provides us with 2^{14} possible hosts on each of 2^4-2 (14) Subnets (you should not allocate a mask of either all 1's or all 0's). But on which of our 14 possible Subnets does this host reside? Since the last two octets of the address are 194.130, we can determine that the two highest order bits of the first octet of the Host ID are 1's, as is the highest order bit of the second. This then means that the host is 2.2 on Subnet 14 of network 129.101.0.0, but it has certainly not been made as apparent as it could have been! Calculating which Subnetwork a station is on is easy for intelligent devices but, given our example, it would be extremely difficult for a human operator to quickly calculate the Subnet and Network numbers of the station. Great care should therefore be taken when applying such Masks since the results may not be immediately apparent to a human operator.

4.7 Multi-Homing

As we have already seen, an IP address is used to identify a particular network host. But what of hosts that have multiple network interfaces such as routers or other systems? Router ports should each connect to a different network. It is also possible to connect multiple physical interfaces of conventional computing equipment to different networks. In this case they may act as routers, or alternatively, these ports could be connected to the same network in which case the host is said to be *Multi-Homed*. So what now of our IP address?

RFC 791 states "*. . . a single physical host must be able to act as if it were several distinct hosts to the extent of using several distinct internet addresses.*" We should therefore not say that an IP address identifies a host, but instead that the IP address identifies the physical connection.

4.8 Assigning Multiple IP Addresses to a Single Physical Connection

In addition to the assignment of addresses to multiple interfaces, it is sometimes desirable to assign multiple IP addresses to a single physical connection. For example, consider Figure 4-8.

Here we have three distinct logical networks that exist on our two physical cables. In this case hosts on logical network 192.10.6.0 may all intercommunicate without the need to use the router. Similarly those hosts on network 192.10.7.0 may also send data to each other directly. Transmission of data between any of these three logical networks though, requires the router to deliver data on behalf of the communicating stations.

Notice that in this figure, our router has been configured with a single IP Address on one of its interfaces (192.10.5.100), and two IP Addresses (192.10.6.100, and 192.10.7.100) on the other. While it must be appreciated that not all routers can be configured in this way, for the purposes of our example we shall assume that our router supports this type of configuration. These addresses then reflect the three logical networks that the router interconnects.

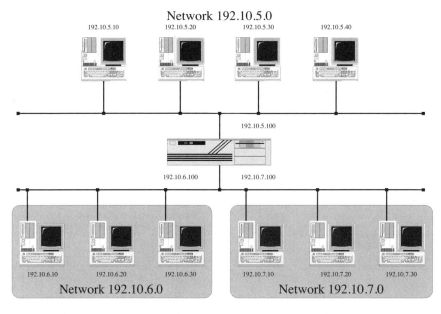

Figure 4-8: Assigning multiple IP addresses to a single physical interface

Setting up a network in this way has certain advantages, for example:

- We may be in the process of migrating from one locally assigned IP address group to another, universally assigned group.

  In this way, we may migrate over a period of time while still maintaining full connectivity between all network hosts.

- We may wish to stop communication between logical networks 192.10.6.0 and 192.10.7.0 but, due to the physical locations of the hosts, it may be undesirable or even impossible to place these on physical networks of their own.

  In this case, if our router supported a means of providing *filtering*, we could prohibit communication between networks 192.10.6.0 and 192.10.7.0 yet allow communication between either of these networks and network 192.10.5.0.

4.9   The Future of The Internet Addressing Scheme

One thing is clear, IP addresses are now in extremely short supply. In many respects, the Internet protocols are a victim of their own success and now we are faced with a dwindling supply of IP addresses and an ever increasing number of subscribers to the Internet. Who could have foreseen when the addressing scheme was first devised, the proliferation of computing systems in use today and the need for interconnection? It must be remembered that, when the addressing scheme was first developed, Personal Computers had not been thought of, the need for everyone to have a computer terminal was never imagined, and the idea of sharing data on the scale that we have today would have been laughable. So where do we go from here? Listed below are some suggestions together with their relative merits:

- Increasing the length of the address from 32 bits to maybe 48 bits or even more.

  While this would overcome many of our current problems and would certainly solve the short term crisis, it would require a major change to every IP module currently in use. The so called IP next generation or IP version 6 proposes just this by increasing the address to 128 bits. The problems are apparent and the transition is likely to be anything but smooth. However, this step, no matter how painful, must be taken. IPv6, because it represents such a radical change, is discussed seperatly in Chapter 24.

- Do nothing. IP is supposed to be replaced by OSI protocols already implementing 48 bit addressing.

  If we are to believe all that has been written about OSI protocols in recent years, nobody would be implementing IP and all development in this area would have stopped. In actual fact, more people than ever are now implementing IP, and the trend is set to rise still further.

- Force Subnet masking in order to reuse address space, or to use the terms currently under consideration, to use *Classless Internet Domain Routing* (CIDR), or *Supernetting*.

  In this way, we would be able to reuse the entire Class C address range as pseudo Class B addresses. Of course though, with this scheme, there are no classes. For example, if we were to present the address 192.168.0.0 with the mask 255.255.0.0 this would allow the re-allocation of each of the 254 networks in the range 192.168.1.0 to 192.168.254.0. If we now multiply this by the number of Class C networks originally available, this gives us more than enough extra address space until the more permanent solution of version 6 can be implemented.

4.10 Summary

At it's simplest level, the addressing scheme used by IP provides us with a flexible method to uniquely identify hosts, and networks. For routing, this two level *heirarchy* is all that is required, however, such a scheme does not nessecarily make best use of the available address space. As such, subnetting is available to us whereby we can further divide our address space such that we now have the concept of hosts that reside on subnets that can then be grouped into networks.

In part, the Internet Protocol Suite has become a victim of it's own success with the Internet community now extremely short of addresses. Much is being done to relieve the pressure with work being carried out to test the viability of a much larger address. The problems though are potentially enormous. For example, if we were to implement an addressing scheme that used 128 bit addressing, while this would solve our problems regarding address space, other problems would need to be overcome. Hosts that need to talk to those running older implementations would need to either implement both versions of IP address, or alternatively gateways would need to be implemented that could convert between the two. Equally, from an pure implementation point of view, the costs are potentially enormous with the new hardware and software needed.

The 32 bit IP address has served us well to date and will be with us for many years to come. True it is not ideal but few things in any area of life are perfect. One thing that we must not lose sight of is that the Internet Protocol and with it the addressing that it uses pre dates many other suites. As such we must accept its limitations and work within the boundaries that it sets.

The Internet Protocol (IP)

The Internet Protocol (IP) may best be described as a connectionless *datagram* delivery system. It is connectionless since each unit (a datagram) is delivered in isolation, even with reference to other related packets. With IP there are no connections nor logical circuits. Many say that the service provided is *unreliable* since no guarantees are made that the datagram will ever arrive at its destination. IP provides no acknowledgements; datagrams may be lost, duplicated, or arrive out of sequence at the destination host. IP has no way in which to inform the transmitting station. Equally, IP has been described as being a *best efforts* delivery system. This is because datagrams may legitimately be discarded due to insufficient resources, again without informing the source host. While true, these statements paint a bleak and unfair picture of what has become an extremely robust and versatile protocol.

IP, as outlined by RFC 791, defines that IP performs two basic functions, namely addressing and fragmentation. In the previous chapter we saw the basic addressing scheme employed and how this is split into two sections, specifically the Network ID and the Host ID. Also in the previous chapter we saw how routers or *Gateways* are used to connect different networks. In Chapter 9, we shall see how this routing works in detail, by being able to determine paths to route datagrams towards their eventual destinations. In this chapter we shall see that, through the use of specific fields in the IP header, it is possible to fragment datagrams for transmission over small packet networks, and many of the other features that it provides. These features are briefly outlined below:

- Type of Service
  This may be used to specify a particular *Quality of Service* required. This feature, although always intended to be implemented on routers, is only now starting to be used. In general, it allows users to request certain services provided by networks between the source and destination hosts. Considering that IP is some 14 years old, it is sad to think that it is only with the latest routing protocols, that Type of Service may actually be used. Indeed today, many routers will still ignore this field completely.

- Time-to-Live
  Within a routed environment, there is always the possibility that a loop may exist, or that a datagram may not be deliverable. The Time-to-Live therefore provides a self-destruct timer, after which the datagram will be removed from the network. All datagrams must therefore be delivered within their own Time-to Live timer.

- Options

  IP provides a number of options that, although unnecessary in most communications, may be used to provide useful control functions.

- Header Checksum

  In order to ensure that the control information has arrived either at the destination or some intermediate station intact, IP checks the information contained in the header.

- Error Reporting

  Although we have said that IP has no inherent error reporting mechanism, a further protocol, the *Internet Control Message Protocol* (ICMP), conveys messages about errors and other conditions. ICMP is considered an integral part of IP however, since it is a protocol in its own right, we shall consider it separately in the next chapter.

5.1 The IP Datagram

IP datagrams travel encapsulated within physical or MAC frames. Because of this encapsulation, the actual size of each datagram fragment may not exceed the length of the data area of the frame. This limit is referred to as the *Maximum Transmission Unit* (or MTU) of the network.

Since each network technology may place a different limit on the amount of data that may be carried, a problem exists when trying to determine the maximum amount of data that an IP datagram should carry. Obviously we would wish to make the best use of any network technology in use. This includes always making the best use of available bandwidth. But how can this be achieved when each technology places its own upper bound? We could limit the size of IP datagrams to the smallest MTU, but while this would make best use of one particular network technology, it would make very poor use of technologies whose MTUs may be larger. IP overcomes this problem and allows it to remain independent of network technology by means of fragmentation, (this will be described later). Figure 5-1 shows the format of the IP datagram.

The four bit *Version* field identifies the version of the IP protocol and therefore the format of the IP header. IP will not negotiate over versions. Thus, reception of a datagram with an unrecognized version will result in the datagram being rejected immediately. Currently the version of IP is 4.

The four bit *Internet Header Length* field is used to specify the length of the IP header in 32 bit words, and therefore indicates where the IP data begins. The IP header may be considered to be of variable length up to a maximum of 60 octets where options are incorporated. However in the absence of options, as is normally the case, the header length will be 20 octets long, yielding the minimum value of 5 for this field.

The *Type of Service* allows hosts to define the Quality of Service that is desired. In general terms, the bits are used to select the actual parameters that should be used when a datagram is transmitted through a network. RFC 791 defines that the eight bits that comprise this field, shown in Figure 5-2 to the right, shall have the following meanings.

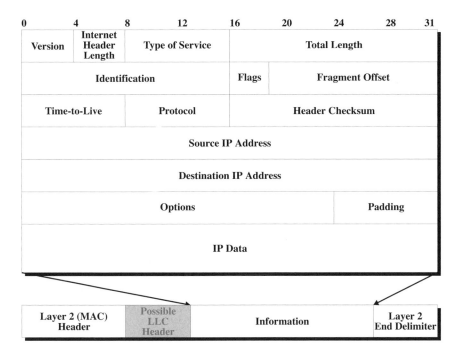

0	4	8	12	16	20	24	28	31
Version	Internet Header Length	Type of Service		Total Length				
Identification				Flags	Fragment Offset			
Time-to-Live		Protocol		Header Checksum				
Source IP Address								
Destination IP Address								
Options						Padding		
IP Data								

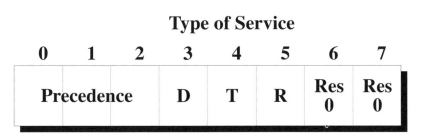

Layer 2 (MAC) Header	Possible LLC Header	Information	Layer 2 End Delimiter

Figure 5-1: IP Datagram Format

The three *precedence* bits allow hosts to specify the importance of this datagram, and may therefore give priority to network control traffic over normal user data. The precedence levels range from 0 for *routine* datagram delivery through to 7 for *Network Control*. Many network technologies allow the setting of service precedence. In these cases, only traffic above a certain priority will be transmitted, say, at times of high load. Token Ring networks have such a facility by varying the priority of the token and therefore restricting the data that stations may transmit. Sadly this is rarely implemented in today's networks, but does provide us with a potential framework for future technologies.

Type of Service

0	1	2	3	4	5	6	7
Precedence			D	T	R	Res 0	Res 0

Figure 5-2: The Type of Service Field

Table 5-1: Type of Service Bits

D	T	R	Meaning
0			Treat with Normal Delay
1			Treat with Low Delay
	0		Provide Normal Throughput Path
	1		Provide High Throughput Path
		0	Provide Normal Reliability Path
		1	Provide High Reliability Path

The D, T, and R bits are used to specify the delay, throughput and reliability requested respectively. Where multiple routes exist to a given network, and the routing protocol in use supports Type of Service routing, these bits would be used in determining the best path in an attempt to provide better overall performance. Obviously, no guarantees can be given as to whether the network is able to support such requests. Therefore, where such support is not implemented, the routing algorithm in use chooses the route taken and these bits are ignored. These bits then are used to define routes, however in order to determine how good the route actually is, some sense of cost must also be applied. Type of Service routing is not found in all routing protocols, but is found in OSPF[1] and certain proprietary protocols. Table 5-1 above defines the exact meaning of the bits.

Bit six is redefined by RFC 1349 *Type of Service in the Internet* to have the meaning, "*Minimize Monetary Cost*". This RFC is defined by RFC 1800 the *Internet Official Protocol Standards* document as a Proposed Standard with a status of *Elective*. It is therefore introduced here for completeness although it is unknown when RFC 1349 will reach full Standard status. Bit seven remains reserved and is always set to zero.

RFC 1122 *Requirements for Internet Hosts — Communication Layers* (a current standard) states that the TOS field comprises a three bit precedence and five bit TOS. RFC 1349, when approved, will therefore probably be treated as an update to this information.

RFC 1700 (Internet Assigned Numbers) specifies that, where implemented, specific Types of Service should be used. Generally, where any interaction with a human operator is involved, the Type of Service selected should reflect minimal delays. Obviously, where any bulk data transfer is involved, the Type of Service should be set to provide maximum throughput. RFC 1700 further states that any application may (at the request of the user) substitute 0001 (minimize monetary cost) for any value listed. The *Assigned Numbers* document then further states that when all bits are set (1111), this should be taken to mean route the datagram using maximum security. No recommendations as to which protocols should implement this TOS are specified however.

Table 5-2 outlines these TOS preferred values.

---

1. The Open Shortest Path First (OSPF) protocol is discussed in detail in Chapter 11.

Table 5-2: TOS Preferred Values

Protocol	Notes	D	T	R	M[2]	Description
		TOS Value				
TELNET	And other interactive protocols	1	0	0	0	Minimize Delay
FTP Control		1	0	0	0	Minimize Delay
FTP Data	And other bulk transfer protocols	0	1	0	0	Maximize Throughput
TFTP		1	0	0	0	Minimize Delay
SMTP Command	Where implementations do not	1	0	0	0	Minimize Delay
SMTP Data	Support changing TOS, use 0000	0	1	0	0	Maximize Throughput
DNS	UDP Query	1	0	0	0	Minimize Delay
DNS	TCP Query	0	0	0	0	No TOS selected
DNS	Zone Transfer	0	1	0	0	Maximize Throughput
NNTP		0	0	0	1	Minimize Cost
ICMP Errors		0	0	0	0	No TOS
ICMP Requests		0	0	0	0	No TOS
ICMP Responses	Always use same TOS as Request					Variable
IGPs	Any Interior Gateway Protocol	0	0	1	0	Maximize Reliability
EGP		0	0	0	0	No TOS
SNMP		0	0	1	0	Maximize Reliability
BOOTP		0	0	0	0	No TOS

Finally, although RFC 1349 is not currently an Internet standard, it is interesting that the Assigned Numbers document includes the Minimize Monetary Cost bit. While many implementations will not support the setting of this bit, we can see that efforts are being made to force generally high volume, low priority, traffic such as the *Network News Transfer Protocol* (NNTP), to travel over the least *monetary* cost route.

The 16 bit *Total Length* field is used to describe the total length of the datagram (both header and data), measured in octets. Since this field is 16 bits long, the maximum datagram size allowed is 2^{16} or 64kb. Obviously, this is impractical for many hosts and no network technology is capable of supporting a payload of this size. While this upper bound is therefore never used, it is accepted that all hosts must be able to accept datagrams of up to 576 octets, whether they arrive as a whole or in a number of fragments. Equally, hosts must only send datagrams that exceed 576 octets if they are sure that the target host is capable of receiving the larger datagram size.

The reasoning behind a minimum upper limit figure is to ensure that a reasonable sized data block may be transmitted in addition to the mandatory IP header. For example: The maximum size that is allowed for an IP header (including options) is 60 octets. If we assume that a reasonable size of data would be 512 octets, then we shall carry only 572 octets in total. Furthermore, since the standard IP header is only 20 octets, by allowing 576 octets in total, we shall be able to carry 512 octets of data plus have a margin for headers of upper layer protocols.

The *Identification* field contains a unique 16 bit integer that identifies this datagram, and therefore each of its fragments should fragmentation become necessary. This value is assigned by the transmitting host and may not be changed by any intermediate station. In order to avoid errors, it is imperative that this field is long enough to ensure that no duplicate numbered datagrams exist on the network at

2. M, in this instance, should be taken to mean Minimize Monetary Cost.

any time. A 16 bit field provides us with 2^{16} or 65,536 possible combinations, surely sufficient for this purpose.

The *Flags* field provides three flags, of which two are implemented. These flags, used in the processing of datagram fragments, are as shown in Figure 5-3. The first bit is reserved, as shown, and will always be zero. The second bit, the *Do Not Fragment* flag, indicates that under no circumstances must this datagram be fragmented. Datagrams arriving at a router with this flag set, will be discarded if their size exceeds the MTU of the next network to be traversed. In this event, an ICMP[3] message will be returned to the transmitting host to inform it that data has been lost. The final bit, the *More Fragments Follow* bit, is used in multi-fragment datagrams in conjunction with the *Identification* and *Fragment Offset* fields. This flag will not be set where a datagram has not been fragmented, nor in the final fragment of a multi-fragment datagram.

Flags

0	1	2
Reserved Must be 0	Do Not Fragment	More Fragments Follow

Figure 5-3: The Flags Field

The 13 bit *Fragment Offset* field informs receiving hosts of the relative position of this fragment within the overall datagram structure. Since this field is only 13 bits in length but a relative position anywhere within a 64kb block needs to be specified, the offset is always measured in 64 bit (8 octet) units referred to as *Fragment Blocks*. Each fragment (except for the last) therefore must contain a multiple of 8 octets and must be at least 8 octets long.

The 8 bit *Time-to-Live* field is used to indicate the maximum amount of time that this datagram is allowed to exist within the internet. The value, measured in seconds, is decreased by at least one each time that the datagram passes through a router. Where the value of the field has been decremented to zero, the datagram is discarded and an ICMP message is sent to the source host. Since the router must decrement this value by whole amounts (even where the datagram has been processed in less than one second) this value should be considered as the maximum amount of time that the datagram may exist. Indeed, most routers today tend to ignore the real meaning applied to this field and, instead of decrementing the field accurately, merely decrement it by one as the datagram is processed. In this way, the Time-to-Live could, and normally is, considered a *Hop Count* or the number of router hops that the datagram is allowed to take.

The 8 bit *Protocol* field indicates the next higher level protocol being carried in the data area of the datagram. In this way, the datagram becomes self-identifying, with this field identifying the format and contents of the data area. Table 5-3 lists some of the more common protocol numbers, however for a full list consult the *Internet Assigned Numbers* document RFC 1700.

3. ICMP is discussed in Chapter 6.

The Internet Protocol (IP)

The 16 bit *Header Checksum* field provides an integrity check on the IP datagram header. The actual value contained in this field is computed by first breaking the header down into a series of 16 bit words. These words are then summed using one's compliment arithmetic, any carry is then added in, and finally the one's compliment of the result is taken. This resulting value is then placed in the Checksum field. Naturally, the checksum is re-computed at each receiving host to verify that there has been no corruption. However, since the *Time-to-Live* field is modified each time the datagram is processed by a router, the *Header Checksum* must also be re-computed by each router en-route to the destination.

Table 5-3: IP Protocol Type Codes

Decimal	Hex	Keyword	Description
1	01	ICMP	The Internet Control Message Protocol
2	02	IGMP	The Internet Group Management Protocol
3	03	GGP	The Gateway-to-Gateway Protocol
4	04	IP	IP in IP encapsulation
6	06	TCP	The Transmission Control Protocol
8	08	EGP	The Exterior Gateway Protocol
9	09	IGP	Any private (proprietary) Interior Gateway Protocol
17	11	UDP	The User Datagram Protocol
29	1D	ISO-TP4	The ISO Transport Protocol Class 4
88	58	IGRP	Cisco's proprietary Interior Gateway Routing Protocol
89	59	OSPFIGP	The Open Shortest Path First (OSPF) Protocol

The 32 bit *Source* and *Destination Address* fields specify the transmitting host, and ultimate destination or target machine(s), respectively.

The variable length *Options* field allows multiple options to be specified in the IP datagram header. These options are discussed in detail in the next section.

The *Padding* field may be between 1 and 3 octets in length and is used to ensure that the datagram header ends on a 32 bit (4 octet) boundary. You will recall that the *Internet Header Length* field specifies the length of the header in 32 bit words. Since the options are of variable length, it may therefore be necessary to pad the header to ensure this alignment.

5.2   IP Datagram Options

The presence of options in the IP header is specific to the implementation of IP on the transmitting host. The ability to process options present in a received datagram however, must be implemented in all IP modules.

Each IP datagram may contain zero or more options, each of variable lengths, as shown in Figure 5-4. Although not directly shown, there are two basic option formats. In the first case, the option comprises a single octet of only option type. In the second case, we have a variable length option as shown in the diagram.

The *Option Type* octet consists of three distinct fields. Firstly, the *Copy Flag* identifies whether this option should be copied to all fragments of the datagram in the event that fragmentation occurs. When on (binary 1), the option will be copied. The *Option Class* field defines whether this option is classified as a control or debugging option. Only two classes have been defined to date, namely zero for control options, and 2 for debugging. Any other value in this field is considered illegal and will be ignored. Finally, the *Option Number* field uniquely identifies this option as shown in Table 5-4 below. The *Option Length* octet then contains the length of the entire option including the *Option Type*, *Length* and *Data* fields.

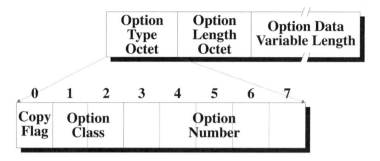

Figure 5-4: IP Datagram Options

Table 5-4: IP Options

Option Class	Option Number	Option Length	Option Name and Description
0	0	–	End of Option List. This option occupies only 1 octet and has no Length field.
0	1	–	No Operation. This option occupies only 1 octet and has no Length field.
0	2	11	Security. Used to carry security restrictions compatible with DoD requirements.
0	3	Variable	Loose Source Routing.[4] Used to route IP datagrams through an internet based on host supplied information.
2	4	Variable	Internet Timestamp. The only Debugging option currently specified. Used to calculate round trip delay times.
0	7	Variable	Record Route. Used to trace the route an IP datagram takes between source and destination.
0	8	4	Stream ID. Used to carry the SATNET stream identifier – This is now obsolete.
0	9	Variable	Strict Source Routing. Used to route IP datagrams through an internet based on host supplied information.

5.2.1 End of Option List

Because options occur in lists that are otherwise un-delimited, it is important that we have a marker to show the end of the option list. This option is used to indicate the end of the option list where the list would not normally coincide with the end of the IP header. It will occur only once, but since options need not be

---

4. The terms Source Routing (either Loose, or Strict) have no relationship with Source Routing as applied to IBM Token Ring Environments. In the IBM world, Source Routing is a term used in bridging. In the Internet world, Source Routing relates to routing methodologies.

The Internet Protocol (IP)

duplicated when fragmentation is required, it may be copied, introduced, or deleted when fragmentation occurs.

5.2.2   No Operation

This option is typically used between options to align the start of a subsequent option on a 32 bit boundary. As with the *End of Option List* option, this option may be copied, introduced, or deleted where fragmentation occurs.

5.2.3   Security

The Internet Protocol was originally developed for the U.S. Department of Defense and as such incorporates security options that allow hosts to send security, compartmentation, handling restrictions and closed user group parameters. Typically, this option is not used apart from within secure environments and is therefore not discussed here. Where used, the option must only appear once and must be copied in the event of fragmentation occurring.

5.2.4   Loose and Strict Source Routing

More correctly, these options should be defined as *Loose Source and Record Route* (LSRR) and *Strict Source and Record Route* (SSRR) since these options provide mechanisms for hosts to define (and record) a route that datagrams should take to their destination. This option appears at most once, is always copied, and is of variable length. As such, the length octet is used. The *Option Data* comprises a single octet pointer and a variable number of 4 octet fields, each of which contain the IP address of a host on route to the final destination.

The sending station will create the IP header that contains the Source Routing option (either LSRR or SSRR). On reception by a host system, the *Length* and *Pointer* fields are examined. Where the Pointer is greater than the Length, the list of IP addresses contained as data has been exhausted, and all further routing is based solely upon the Destination Address field of the IP datagram header. Where the Pointer is less than the Length, the Destination Address field of the IP header is replaced by the IP address in the option, as indicated by the Pointer value. The IP address that the Pointer is indicating is then replaced by the address of the interface on which the datagram is about to leave, and the Pointer is incremented by four.

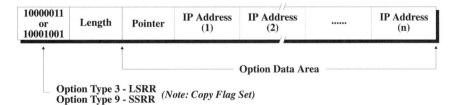

Figure 5-5: Source Routing Options

In the case of Loose Source Routing, a router may choose to use a route that has any number of intermediate routers to reach the next address stored in the Source Route option itself. In the case of Strict Source Routing, a router must send the datagram directly to the next address contained in the option through a directly connected network. No intermediate router *hops* are allowed, to the extent that if the datagram cannot be sent over a directly connected network, it will be discarded.

5.2.5 Record Route

This option (Type 7) allows the route taken by a datagram to be recorded. The option only ever appears once in an IP datagram header and the copy flag is never set. In this way, the route taken by the first fragment will be recorded but potential routes taken by other fragments will never be noted.

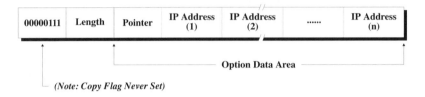

Figure 5-6: Record Route Option

In this case, the sending station creates an IP datagram with the Record Route option. The option will contain a data area that will be used to record the 4 octet IP addresses of routers that process the datagram en-route to the destination. Initially this data area will be all zeroes and the pointer will indicate the first 4 octet entry in the data area. The size of the data area should be large enough to accommodate all of the addresses expected, and should be a multiple of 4 octets (plus one octet for the pointer). No expansion of the area is allowed once created.

On reception of a datagram by a host, if the Record Route option is present, the host will examine the Length and Pointer fields and insert its own IP address at the location specified by the Pointer. If the Pointer is greater than the Length, the datagram will be forwarded as it is. If there are less than 4 octets left, the data area is considered corrupt and the datagram is discarded. Note that in either of these cases, the receiving host may send an ICMP[5] Parameter Problem message back to the source host.

5.2.6 Internet Timestamp

The Internet Timestamp option allows a host to determine delay times between itself and intermediate hosts. There are three ways in which the information may be recorded, but the option only ever appears once in an IP datagram header, and the copy flag is never set. Figure 5-7 shows this option.

_____

5. ICMP is discussed in Chapter 6.

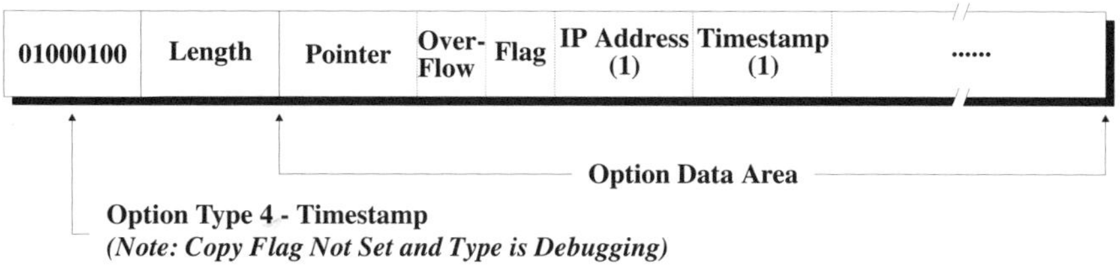

01000100	Length	Pointer	Over-Flow	Flag	IP Address (1)	Timestamp (1)	......

Option Type 4 - Timestamp
(Note: Copy Flag Not Set and Type is Debugging)

Option Data Area

Figure 5-7: Internet Timestamp

As with all options that are used to record information, this option is of variable length and uses both length and pointer fields. However in this case, the pointer points not to 4 octet fields, but 8 octet pairs. The Pointer value is then counted from the beginning of this option, and points to the space that starts the next timestamp.

Sending hosts should always create the data area of this option large enough to accommodate all timestamp information expected. The 4 bit Overflow field is a count of how many hosts were not able to record their information in the timestamp data area. This is caused when the area is full (where the pointer value is greater than the length). If there is insufficient room to contain a complete timestamp entry (8 octets), or if the Overflow field itself overflows, the datagram is considered to be in error and will be discarded. As with the Record Route option, either of these cases may cause an ICMP *Parameter Problem* message to be sent to the source host.

The 4 bit Flag field is used to determine the type of information recorded as shown in table. The timestamp data area should carry all zeroes, IP address/Timestamp pairs, or Timestamp/zero pairs depending upon the flag selected.

Table 5-5: Timestamp Option

Flag Value	Meaning
0	Timestamps only recorded. These are recorded in consecutive 32 bit words.
1	Each timestamp is preceded by the IP address of the host that registered the timestamp
3	The IP addresses are specified by the source host. Only those hosts identified by their IP addresses in the list should enter a timestamp.

On receiving an IP datagram with this option, the host will, depending on the value of the flag field, place the current time (measured in milliseconds since midnight GMT) in the 32 bit right justified timestamp field. If the host is unable to specify the time in this way, it may place any time into the field, provided that it identifies that it is non-standard by turning on (setting to 1) the highest order bit of the field.

5.3 Datagram Fragmentation

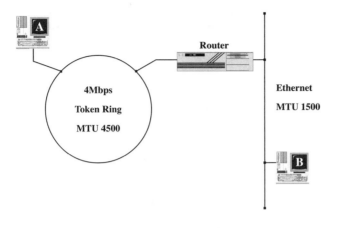

Figure 5-8: Datagram Fragmentation

Where a datagram must travel across a network whose MTU is smaller than the datagram length, it is necessary to fragment the datagram. Figure 5-8 shows where such fragmentation would be required:

In this case, Host A wishes to send data to Host B. It is possible that any datagram that Host A transmits would contain more than 1500 octets of data. Thus, fragmentation at the router would be required. Remember, fragmentation may only take place where the *Do Not Fragment* flag has not been set by the originating station. Where this flag has been set (for example in downloading an image file), the datagram would be discarded by the router, and an ICMP message sent to Host A. Where fragmentation occurs, reassembly will take place only at the destination host. No intermediate router will attempt to reassemble the datagram. Instead, each intermediate router will treat each fragment as a datagram in its own right, and even *re-fragment* it if required.

Receiving stations will know that a fragment has arrived by examining the *Flags* and *Fragment Offset* fields in the datagram header. Each fragment of the datagram will contain the same *Identification*, *Protocol*, and *Source* and *Destination Address* fields, therefore all fragments that comprised the original datagram will be easily identifiable. Two problems do however exist for the receiving host:

- Datagram fragments may arrive out of order. This is overcome by the *Fragment Offset* field which identifies the fragments actual position within the whole datagram.

- The receiving host will have no way of knowing the overall size of the datagram. The *Total Length* field will identify the length of the fragment only, so how will the receiving host know how much buffer space to allocate? The only real advice that RFC 791 gives us on this matter, such as it is, is that all hosts must be able to handle datagrams of up to 576 octets whether they arrive whole

The Internet Protocol (IP)

or in fragments. The allocation of buffer space is therefore totally specific to any particular implementation.

On reception of the first fragment of a multi-fragment datagram, the destination host will allocate buffer space and start a timer (the reassembly timer). All fragments then have to be received before this timer expires. In the event that this timer expires before all fragments have been received, all fragments received so far will be discarded, and an ICMP message sent to the source host.

Where fragmentation occurs, the following fields in the IP datagram header may be affected:

- The *Options* field.

  Since not all options are copied to every fragment, the options field may be changed. Typically the first fragment would contain all options specified in the original datagram. Subsequent fragments however, will only contain those options with the *Copy Flag* set.

- The *More Fragments* flag.

  The More Fragments flag will be set in all fragments with the exception of the last. By examination of the More Fragments flag and the Fragment Offset field, the receiving host is able to detect the first, last, and intermediate fragments.

- The *Fragment Offset* field.

  This field will be all zeroes in the first fragment, and will contain the relative position (in modulo 8) of all other fragments. In this way each fragment may be placed in the correct position within the actual datagram.

- The *Internet Header Length* field.

  Where options exist but have not been copied, the header will be shorter as indicated by the Internet Header Length field. Remember that this field specifies the length of the header in 4 octet words.

- The *Total Length* field.

  This field will identify the total length of *this* fragment. Therefore, since it is unlikely that all fragments will be of an equal length, this field will naturally be different in at least one of the fragments.

- The *Header Checksum* field.

  Since several of the header fields will change when fragmentation occurs, it naturally follows that the checksum must also change. This field will also change for every router hop, whether fragmentation occurs or not, since the Time-to-Live field will be decremented by each router and the checksum will be re-calculated.

As an example, let us consider Figure 5-9 where Host A wishes to transmit a datagram containing 2000 octets of data to Host B. For the sake of simplicity, we shall assume that there are no options present, and that each fragment will carry an equal amount of data.

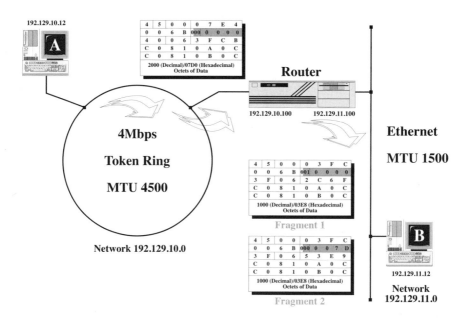

Figure 5-9: Fragmentation Example

During fragmentation the router copies the original header to each fragment as it is created (less any options without the Copy Flag set). The Internet Header Length and Total Length fields are then adjusted accordingly, and the Time-to-Live decremented. Finally, the More Fragments flag, and Fragment Offset field are set, and the Header Checksum is re-computed.

In our example, our original 2000 octet datagram is split into two 1000 octet fragments. While it would be unusual for two equal fragments to be created in this way, we will make this assumption here for simplicity. Both fragments contain the original Version (4), Internet Header Length (5), and Type of Service (00). The Total Length ($03FC_{16}$) translates to 1020_{10} octets, being 1000 octets of data and 20 octets for the header. The original Identification field (006B) is copied unchanged. Since the original datagram allowed fragmentation (the Do Not Fragment flag set to 0), this flag is copied unchanged. However in the first fragment only, the More Fragments flag is set indicating that this is the first or intermediate fragment. The Fragment Offset field in the first fragment (0000) shows the relative position of this fragment as being the start of the datagram. In the second fragment, the offset field (007D) shows that the start position of this fragment is $007D_{16}$ * 8, which equates to 125_{10} * 8, or 1000 octets. Finally, our two fragments show the Time-to-Live decremented by 1 (40_{16}-1=3F) and the checksum re-computed.[6] Obviously, the Source and Destination IP Addresses are copied from our original datagram unchanged, since this information is necessary for successful routing.

6. The Checksums shown in this example are not accurate, but are instead examples of how the checksum may change.

The Internet Protocol (IP)

5.4 Summary

The Internet Protocol (IP) is at the very heart of the Internet Protocol Suite. It is responsible for specifying a Time-to-Live that will eliminate packets caught in routing loops, a Type of Service that enables the packet to be treated with the correct precedence, and the ability to fragment packets for transmission over all network technologies.

IP itself provides only a connectionless, unreliable, best efforts delivery system and relies upon other protocols within the suite to handle reliability and error reporting. IP does provide us with a number of options although sadly these are rarely used. Indeed, many features of IP have been overlooked by the Internet community generally. That said, IP is a robust protocol and it is probably the widest used of all. Being the foundation upon which many applications are built, IP with its flexible addressing structure and numerous support protocols will be with us for many years to come.

The Internet Control Message Protocol (ICMP)

The Internet Protocol (IP) has no way in which to report errors or to send control messages to transmitting hosts. So what happens when a datagram cannot be delivered for some reason or when a problem is detected within a datagram? And how can hosts be informed of better routes when they become available? The *Internet Control Message Protocol* (ICMP) is the mechanism through which all of these functions are performed. ICMP is an integral part of IP, and must be implemented in all IP modules. However, since it utilizes IP for delivery, it is discussed here as a totally separate protocol.

Because ICMP relies upon IP, ICMP does not make IP more reliable. Where extra reliability is desired, an upper layer protocol must implement these mechanisms. ICMP messages are typically sent to report errors that have occurred in the processing of datagrams. They may also be sent where a datagram cannot be delivered to its destination, where the router has insufficient resource to buffer an incoming datagram, and where it would be desirable to send datagrams via a shorter route. Since ICMP is used to report errors, it is possible that a datagram carrying an ICMP error message may also be in error. The one exception to the operation described above, is that where an ICMP error message itself causes an error, no error message will be generated. This avoids the situation of recurrent error messages being generated. Equally, where an error is detected on a multi-fragment datagram, only errors associated with the first fragment are reported. All other fragments are discarded without warning.

ICMP messages were originally defined in RFC 792, however extensions have now been added. In this chapter we shall concentrate on those messages defined by RFC 792, and also some extensions to this.

Figure 6-1 shows the basic ICMP message format, and its relationship with both IP and the physical frame in which it must travel. ICMP messages are always carried in the data area of an IP datagram as shown, and always have a fixed format header. The first octet of the ICMP header is a *Type* field that is used to specify the format of the ICMP message. Different message types will have different data areas depending upon the type of message to be conveyed. The *Code* field is used to further specify the type of message. The 16 bit *Checksum* field provides an integrity check on the entire ICMP message (both header and data areas). The actual value contained in this field is computed by first breaking the message down into a series of 16 bit words. These words are then summed in one's compliment arithmetic, any *carry* is then added in, and then the one's compliment is taken of the result. It is this final value that is placed in the *Checksum* field. The IP Header is not used in the computation of the ICMP checksum. The variable length *ICMP Data* area is used to convey the actual message itself. Certain messages, those that are reporting errors in particular, will require that this area holds the IP header of the datagram that is being reported, together with the first 64 bits of IP Data. The reasoning behind this is so that the station to whom the report is directed will know which datagram was in error, together with the protocol and application.

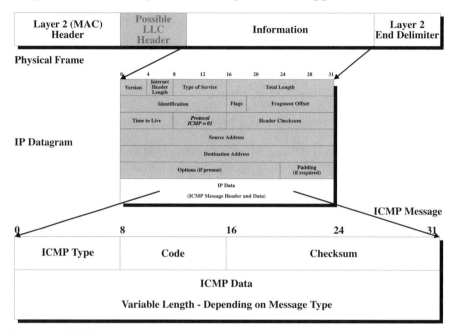

Figure 6-1: ICMP Message Encapsulation

6.1 ICMP Message Types

The complete list of ICMP type codes are listed in Table 6-1. As we have already said, most of these types were introduced with RFC792. However, with the introduction of *Subnetting*, it became necessary to introduce two further types, namely 17 and 18 in order that hosts could determine the Subnet masks that they should use. RFC 950, the *Internet Standard Subnetting Procedure* then introduced these Types.

ICMP messages are split into two distinct classes. Firstly there are the ICMP error messages: Destination Unreachable, Redirect, Source Quench, Time Exceeded, and Parameter Problem. Secondly, there are the query messages: Echo (Request and Reply), Information (Request and Reply), Timestamp, and Address Mask (Request and Reply). Regardless of class however, all ICMP messages should be transmitted with a Type-of-Service equal to *Normal* or 0. If an ICMP message is received where the type is unknown, it is discarded without itself generating an ICMP message. Remember that ICMP messages must not be generated about ICMP messages.

92   The Internet Control Message Protocol (ICMP)

Table 6-1: ICMP Message Types

Type Code Decimal	Type Code Hex	Message Type Description
0	00	Echo Reply
3	03	Destination Unreachable
4	04	Source Quench
5	05	Redirect
8	08	Echo Request
11	0B	Time Exceeded for Datagram
12	0C	Parameter Problem on Datagram
13	0D	Timestamp Request
14	0E	Timestamp Reply
15	0F	Information Request (Obsolete)
16	10	Information Reply (Obsolete)
17	11	Address Mask Request
18	12	Address Mask Reply

6.1.1 Destination Unreachable

Both routers and hosts will send ICMP Destination Unreachable messages to source hosts under certain circumstances. Routers will send these messages where they are either unable to route or deliver a datagram. For example, a datagram may be received that specifies a destination address that relates to a network that is either unknown or unreachable. Equally, a datagram may be received by a router that has a direct connection to the target network, but this router determines that the target host is unavailable. Finally, a router may need to fragment a datagram to onward route it, but the Do Not Fragment flag is set, or a Source Routing option may fail. In any of these cases, Destination Unreachable messages will be sent to the source host. Hosts send Destination Unreachable messages where the protocol specified in the IP header is not available, or where the upper layer protocol has specified an unavailable Port.[1] Ports are the mechanism that ensure the correct application processes are selected, and are always specified in the first few octets of the layer 4 header. This is one of the reasons why this type of message is always sent with the IP header, and the first 64 bits of IP data as part of the message.

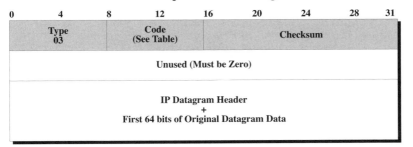

Figure 6-2: ICMP Destination Unreachable

1. The concept of ports will be discussed in detail in Chapter 7, TCP, and Chapter 8, UDP.

The Code field further specifies the type of message and provides us with a method of determining exactly what has failed. The table below lists these codes.

Table 6-2: Destination Unreachable Codes

Code Decimal	Code Hex	Code Description
0	00	Network Unreachable
1	01	Host Unreachable
2	02	Protocol Unreachable
3	03	Port Unreachable
4	04	Fragmentation Required, but the Do Not Fragment flag is set
5	05	Source Route Failed (LSRR or SSRR)
6	06	Destination Network Unknown
7	07	Destination Host Unknown
8	08	Source Host Isolated
9	09	Communication with Destination Network is Administratively Prohibited
10	0A	Communication with Destination Host is Administratively Prohibited
11	0B	Network Unreachable for the Specified Type of Service
12	0C	Host Unreachable for the Specified Type of Service

Do not confuse codes 11 and 12 with 0 and 1. Codes 11 and 12 are used when the network or host would have been reachable if a different TOS was selected, 0 and 1 will be used in all other cases of network and host un-reachability. The 32 bit Unused field is not used in this particular message type and is therefore always zero. Finally, the message contains a copy of the IP datagram header that caused the problem, together with the first 64 bits of data. This is of particular importance to Host generated messages, since the data will inform us which protocol or application has failed.

The Destination Unreachable message is not infallible when applied to routers since many network technologies, such as Ethernet, do not provide acknowledgements. What will happen if a router starts to transmit datagrams to a target host, and then after the transfer has commenced the host is switched off? IP and ICMP have no way of knowing that the host is now unavailable, and no Destination Unreachable message will be generated. The trace of Figure 6-3 shows a Destination Unreachable packet.

```
µSCOPE                  PACKET TRACE DECODE REPORT          (c) T.Kenyon 1995
===============================µscope==========================================
Frame     : 9          Len      : 74              Error   : None
T Elapsed: 19:38:41:721  T Delta  : 00:00:00:007
-------------------------------[mac]-------------------------------------------
Dest Mac : Sun   1bc95a  Sourc Mac: 0000e80f04af   Type     : IP
-------------------------------[ip]-------------------------------------------
IP Ver   : 4           IP HLen  : 20 Bytes
TOS      : 0x00        Pkt Len  : 56
Flags    : FRAG:Ā.LAST  Frag Ptr : 0     (8 Octet)  Seg ID  : 0x0003
PID      : ICMP (  1)   Checksum : 0xa3   (Good)     TTL     : 32
Dst IP <C: 192.168.12.171  Src IP <C: 192.168.12.36
-------------------------------[icmp]-----------------------------------------
ICMP Type: Destination Unreach        ICMP Code: Port Unavailable
Checksum : 0xe8a6                      ICMP Para: 0x00000000
===============================[data:  32]====================================
002A  45 00 00 2F E6 6D 00 00 3B 11 FF 30 C0 A8 0C AB   E../.m..;..0....
003A  C0 A8 0C 24 0F 7E 04 BD 00 1B 00 00 71 5C 67 BC   ...$.~......q\g.
```

Station 192.168.12.36 sends an ICMP Destination Unreachable message to station 192.168.12.171.

IP Datagram Header + first 64 bits of IP Data. In this case, the Datagram is carrying UDP (Protocol 11_{16}), Source Port $0F7E_{16}$, Destination Port $04BD_{16}$, Length $001B_{16}$, and no Checksum 000_{16}. The final 4 octets are the Ethernet FCS.

Figure 6-3: A Destination Unreachable Packet

6.1.2 Time Exceeded

As datagrams pass from one router to the next en-route to their destination, the Time-to-Live field contained in the IP header is decremented. Any router that finds this field decremented to zero must discard the datagram and inform the source host that this has occurred via the Time Exceeded message. Similarly, when a target host receives the first fragment of a multi-fragment datagram, it will start a timer. All fragments of the datagram must now be received before this timer expires. In the event that the timer expires before all fragments are received, the fragments received so far will be discarded and a Time Exceeded message sent to the source host. No reassembly ever takes place at intermediate routers, therefore this type of Time Exceeded message will always be sent from the target host. Remember also that errors are not reported for all fragments of a multi-fragment datagram, only one error is reported and that is for the first fragment. So what happens when the first fragment has not been received? In this case, no Time Exceeded message need be sent at all, thus reliance is placed on the upper layer protocol detection mechanisms to detect this case.

Figure 6-4 shows the Time Exceeded packet format which always uses a Type field of $0B_{16}$. As with the Destination Unreachable message, the Code field then further specifies the type of message. In this case, the code field specifies which timer has expired:

Table 6-3: Time Exceeded Codes

Code Decimal	Code Hex	Code Description
0	00	Time-to-Live Exceeded – Always sent from a router
1	01	Fragment Reassembly Timer Expired – Always sent from a host

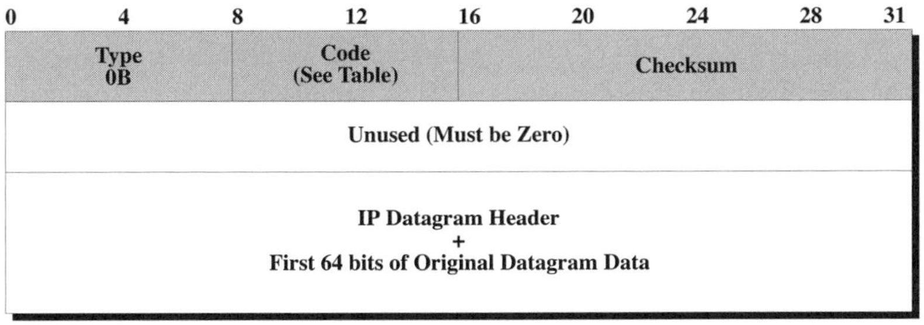

0	4	8	12	16	20	24	28	31

Type 0B	Code (See Table)	Checksum
Unused (Must be Zero)		
IP Datagram Header + First 64 bits of Original Datagram Data		

Figure 6-4: ICMP Time Exceeded Message

6.1.3 Parameter Problem

Any router or host may send an ICMP Parameter Problem message where it finds a problem in the header parameters of an IP datagram. Where a problem is encountered, the datagram must be discarded and the Parameter Problem message must be sent to the source host.

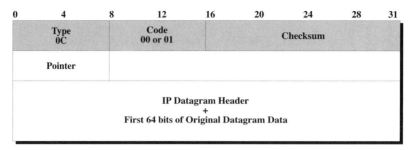

Figure 6-5: ICMP Parameter Problem Message

The Pointer field is used to identify the octet of the original IP datagram header where the error was detected. For example, a Pointer value of 1 would indicate that there was a problem with the Type of Service field, and a value of 20_{10} (14_{16}) or more, that there was a problem with one of the options. The Code field is generally unused and set to zero, indicating that the value in the Pointer field identifies where the problem is. However, in military applications, the Code field can be set to 01_{16}; indicating that a required option is missing and the Pointer field is not used.

6.1.4 Source Quench

The Source Quench message is an elementary form of flow control within an internet. Where datagrams arrive at a host or router faster than they can be processed, they will be buffered. Such buffers are necessarily finite and therefore datagrams will be discarded when these are exhausted. When discards due to buffer exhaustion occur, ICMP Source Quench messages are sent to the source host informing it that the datagram must be re-sent. Upon reception of a Source Quench message, the source host will also slow the rate at which it is sending datagrams until it no longer receives Source Quench messages thus providing flow control. Since there is no message with an opposite meaning to Source Quench, hosts will then begin to increase the rate at which they are sending. They will do this until they again receive Source Quench messages and then again slow down. In this way an equilibrium is achieved between the rate at which the host can send, and the rate at which the router or destination host can process what it has buffered.

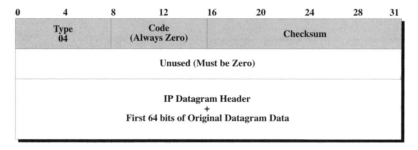

Figure 6-6: ICMP Source Quench Message

In some implementations, a router or host may send Source Quench messages when the buffer capacity is approached, rather than waiting for exhaustion. In this case, the datagram that caused the Source Quench message will be delivered and could result in duplicate datagrams arriving at the destination host. This should not cause a problem since IP has the ability to discard such duplicates as they arrive.

6.1.5 Redirect

Only routers ever send Redirect messages to source hosts informing them that a better route exists to a target network. Routers that implement a *Routing Protocol*[2] will generally have better routing information than hosts. For example, a host will probably be configured with a *Default Gateway* address, (the router to send datagrams to in the event that no other information is held). However, this information is normally static so when topology changes occur, the source host will be ignorant of them.

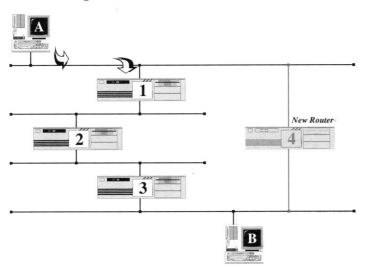

Figure 6-7: An ICMP Redirect Example

If host A wishes to send datagrams to host B, it needs to use the services of a router. In this case, we shall assume that Router 4 is not installed and that host A has been pre-configured with the address of Router 1 as its default gateway. Host A will therefore send datagrams destined for Host B to Router 1, so that they may be onward routed to their final destination via Routers 2 and 3.

On receipt of these datagrams, Router 1 will consult its routing table and see that it must now pass the datagrams to Router 2 for eventual delivery. Normal routing is therefore accomplished.

---

2. Routing Protocols are used between routers to allow the detection of topology changes in the internet.

Now let us consider the effects of installing Router 4. Assuming that we have implemented a routing protocol, Router 4 will start to advertise the networks to which it has a direct connection. Thus Routers 1 and 3 will now know that a better route exists between the top and bottom networks. Unfortunately, since most small systems are unable to listen to these router advertisements, Host A will remain unaware of the existence of Router 4. Now when Host A sends datagrams to Router 1 for delivery to Host B, Router 1 will again check its routing table, but this time will identify the best route as being via Router 4. Router 1 will onward route the datagram via Router 4 (the best route). Since Router 4 shares the same network as the source host, Router 1 will also send an ICMP Redirect message back to Host A. This informs station A that Router 4 has a better route to the destination network.

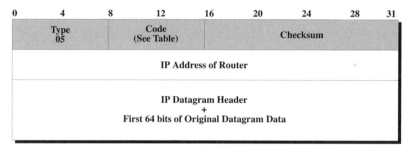

Figure 6-8: ICMP Redirect Message

The Code field is used to specify the type of Redirection required. Currently there are four valid Codes although today hosts do not need to implement the last two of these.

Table 6-4: Redirect Codes

Code Decimal	Code Hex	Code Description
0	00	Redirect datagrams for the Network
1	01	Redirect datagrams for the Host
2	02	Redirect datagrams for this Type of Service and Network
3	03	Redirect datagrams for this Type of Service and Host

Where routers implement all four codes, they should generate a Code 3 Redirect when it applies to IP packets requesting a particular TOS. Routers generate Code 1 Redirects when the optimal next hop on the path to the destination would be the same for any TOS. The Routers IP address in the Redirect message is the address of the router to which traffic for the network specified in the destination address field of the original IP datagram header should be sent. In our previous example, Router 1 would therefore have sent this message specifying Router 4's IP address.

6.1.6 Echo Request/Reply

It is sometimes useful to determine the reachability of a remote network or host by sending a small test packet. The ICMP Echo Request/Reply message pair perform this simple function effectively and with little network overhead. Indeed this has now become one of the most useful debugging tools in IP networking. The format of this message type is shown in Figure 6-9.

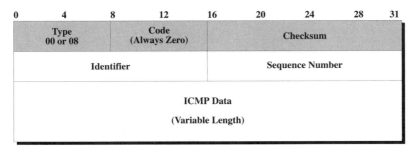

Figure 6-9: ICMP Echo Request/Reply Message

The basic method of operation is a host or router sends an ICMP Echo Request (Type 08) to the distant router or host. On receipt of such a message, the destination must return all information contained in the message intact to the source machine via an ICMP Echo Reply (Type 00). On receipt of the Echo Request message, the target host will change the ICMP Type field to a reply (Type 00) and recalculate the Checksum. The optional (and variable length) data must be left intact, as must the Identifier and Sequence Number fields. Remember that the Checksum calculation is based upon the ones compliment of sixteen bit words. Should the data be an odd number of octets in length therefore, it is padded with a single octet of zeroes for the purposes of calculating the checksum. How does the recipient know where to send the reply? Simple, ICMP is an integral part of IP. Therefore, since the IP header will contain the original Source and Destination addresses, these merely need to be switched!

We have already said that this message type is one of the most useful tools in networking today. Many vendors have implemented a *Ping* (Packet InterNetwork Groper) command that invokes an ICMP Echo Request to check for Internet Reachability. Some of these implementations are basic, simply providing a single shot Request and only reporting whether the target host has responded before a pre-defined timeout period. Others are far more sophisticated, and make full use of the message format shown above. For example, RFC 792 states that the Identifier and Sequence Number fields "*. . . may be used by the echo sender to aid in matching the replies with the echo requests.*" It also suggests that the Identifier field might be used to identify a particular session, and that the Sequence Number could be incremented for each Echo Request transmitted. As such, many implementations allow the user to set up the amount of data to be transmitted and the number of iterations to use. The program then reports round trip delays for each iteration, based upon a timer that is started when the *Request* is sent, and stopped when the corresponding *Reply* is received.

The trace in Figure 6-10 shows a typical ICMP Echo Request/Reply (Ping) exchange. Here, the first two frames show the ARP Request and Response enabling the source station 192.168.12.36 to determine the MAC Address of the destination station. The next two frames then show the actual Echo Request and Reply packets.

```
=========================================μscope==========================================
Frame    : 1                     Len     : 82              Error    : None
T Elapsed: 19:32:28:489          T Delta : 00:00:00:669
---------------------------------------[mac]---------------------------------------------
Dest Mac : ffffffffffff          Sourc Mac: 0000e80f04af   Type     : ARP
---------------------------------------[arp]---------------------------------------------
HW Type  : 10Mb Ethernet         Protocol : IP             Opcode   : ARP REQuest
HW AddLen: 6   Bytes             PR AddLen: 4   Bytes

SrHW Addr: 0000e80f04af
SrPR Addr: 192 168 12 36

DeHW Addr: 000000000000
DePR Addr: 192 168 12 171
=====================================[data:  40]=========================================
002A  AB DC EA AD 33 34 32 38 34 32 33 31 31 33 34 37   ....342842311347
003A  39 33 43 33 00 00 00 00 00 00 00 00 00 00 00 00   93C3...........
004A  00 00 00 00 0D 52 FD 05                           .....R..
```

ARP Request from station 192.168.12.36 sent to determine the MAC Address of station 192.168.12.171.

```
=========================================μscope==========================================
Frame    : 2                     Len     : 82              Error    : None
T Elapsed: 19:32:28:489          T Delta : 00:00:00:000
---------------------------------------[mac]---------------------------------------------
Dest Mac : 0000e80f04af          Sourc Mac: Sun  1bc95a    Type     : ARP
---------------------------------------[arp]---------------------------------------------
HW Type  : 10Mb Ethernet         Protocol : IP             Opcode   : ARP RESPonse
HW AddLen: 6   Bytes             PR AddLen: 4   Bytes

SrHW Addr: 0800201bc95a
SrPR Addr: 192 168 12 171

DeHW Addr: 0000e80f04af
DePR Addr: 192 168 12 36
=====================================[data:  40]=========================================
002A  AB DC EA AD 33 34 32 38 34 32 33 31 31 33 34 37   ....342842311347
003A  39 33 43 33 00 00 00 00 00 00 00 00 00 00 00 00   93C3...........
004A  00 00 00 00 80 24 8E A1                           .....$..
```

ARP Response from station 192.168.12.171

```
=========================================μscope==========================================
Frame    : 3                     Len     : 110             Error    : None
T Elapsed: 19:32:28:489          T Delta : 00:00:00:000
---------------------------------------[mac]---------------------------------------------
Dest Mac : Sun  1bc95a           Sourc Mac: 0000e80f04af   Type     : IP
---------------------------------------[ip]----------------------------------------------
IP Ver   : 4                     IP HLen  : 20 Bytes
TOS      : 0x00                  Pkt Len  : 92              Seg ID   : 0x0001
Flags    : FRAG:*.LAST           Frag Ptr : 0    (8 Octet) TTL      : 32
PID      : ICMP ( 1)             Checksum : 0x81   (Good)
Dst IP <C: 192.168.12.171        Src IP <C: 192.168.12.36
--------------------------------------[icmp]---------------------------------------------
ICMP Type: Echo Request          ICMP Code: 0
Checksum : 0x4790                 ICMP Para: 0xdead0000
=====================================[data:  68]=========================================
002A  29 23 BE 84 E1 6C D6 AE 52 90 49 F1 F1 BB E9 EB   )#...l..R.I....
003A  B3 A6 DB 3C 87 0C 3E 99 24 5E 0D 1C 06 B7 47 DE   ...<..>.$^....G.
004A  B3 12 4D C8 43 BB 8B A6 1F 03 5A 7D 09 38 25 1F   ..M.C.....Z}.8%.
005A  5D D4 CB FC 96 F5 45 3B 13 0D 89 0A 1C DB AE 32   ].....E;.......2
006A  A6 D3 04 E9                                        ....
```

ICMP Echo Request sent from source station 192.168.12.36 to destination station 192.168.12.171. The Identifier used is DEAD$_{16}$, and the Sequence Number is 000$_{16}$. The overall length (including IP Header) of the Datagram is 92 octets. Thus with 20 octets used by the Datagram Header, and 8 octets used by the ICMP Header, this leaves 64 octets of Data. The frame shown indicates 68 data octets however the last 4 of these are the Ethernet FCS.

```
=========================================μscope==========================================
Frame    : 4                     Len     : 110             Error    : None
T Elapsed: 19:32:28:489          T Delta : 00:00:00:000
---------------------------------------[mac]---------------------------------------------
Dest Mac : 0000e80f04af          Sourc Mac: Sun  1bc95a    Type     : IP
---------------------------------------[ip]----------------------------------------------
IP Ver   : 4                     IP HLen  : 20 Bytes
TOS      : 0x00                  Pkt Len  : 92              Seg ID   : 0xe5ca
Flags    : FRAG:*.LAST           Frag Ptr : 0    (8 Octet) TTL      : 255
PID      : ICMP ( 1)             Checksum : 0x3bb6 (Good)
Dst IP <C: 192.168.12.36         Src IP <C: 192.168.12.171
--------------------------------------[icmp]---------------------------------------------
ICMP Type: Echo Reply            ICMP Code: 0
Checksum : 0x4f90                 ICMP Para: 0xdead0000
=====================================[data:  68]=========================================
002A  29 23 BE 84 E1 6C D6 AE 52 90 49 F1 F1 BB E9 EB   )#...l..R.I....
003A  B3 A6 DB 3C 87 0C 3E 99 24 5E 0D 1C 06 B7 47 DE   ...<..>.$^....G.
004A  B3 12 4D C8 43 BB 8B A6 1F 03 5A 7D 09 38 25 1F   ..M.C.....Z}.8%.
005A  5D D4 CB FC 96 F5 45 3B 13 0D 89 0A 1C DB AE 32   ].....E;.......2
006A  BD 23 E0 D6                                        .#..
```

ICMP Echo Reply message returned to 192.168.12.36 showing data returned intact.

Figure 6-10: ICMP Echo Request/Reply Exchange

6.1.7 Timestamp Request/Reply

In order to effectively calculate round trip delays and congestion in host systems, ICMP provides us with a Timestamp Request/Reply message pair. In this case, the source host sends a Request message with the format shown in Figure 6-11 and specifies a Type of $0D_{16}$.

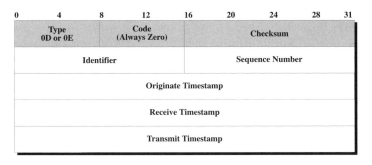

Figure 6-11: ICMP Timestamp Message

The originating host places the time that it sent the Request (specified in milliseconds since midnight GMT) in the 32 bit Originate Timestamp field. The 32 bit Receive and Transmit Timestamp fields will contain zeroes since these will be entered by the destination host.

On reception of a Timestamp Request, the target host enters the time that the message was received in the 32 bit Receive Timestamp field, and then prepares the message for return to the source host. This includes changing the Type from $0D_{16}$ to $0E_{16}$, but leaving the Identifier and Sequence Number fields unchanged. Immediately prior to the transmission of the Reply message, the target host enters the time in the 32 bit Transmit Timestamp field and then recalculates the Checksum. Again, all times are in milliseconds since midnight GMT. Should a host be unable to enter the time in milliseconds or be unable to enter times with respect to midnight GMT, it may enter any time. In order to indicate that a non-standard time has been entered, the host then sets the highest order bit of the field.

As with the Echo Request/Reply pair, the Identifier and Sequence number fields are used by the source host to match requests with responses.

6.1.8 Information Request/Reply

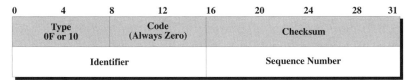

Figure 6-12: ICMP Information Request Message

Now replaced by RARP and BootP, this request/reply pair was once used by source hosts to determine their network addresses at start-up. In this form, the source host sent an ICMP message with the format shown in Figure 6-12. The network addresses in the IP header Source and Destination Address fields were set to zero (indicating *This Network*) in the Request, and would be fully specified in the

Reply. Thus the source host could now obtain its network address. As with other ICMP messages of this type, the Identifier and Sequence Number fields were to allow the source host to match Requests with Replies.

6.1.9 Address Mask Request/Reply

The ICMP Address Mask Request/Reply message formats were introduced by RFC 950 the *Internet Standard Subnetting Procedure*. Specifically, the Request format allows a host to broadcast a request to an authoritative host (typically a router) to determine its *Subnet Mask*. As we have already seen, it is important that hosts know which bits of their address are Network (or Subnet) bits, and which are locally assigned or host bits. This will then allow hosts to participate fully in a subnetted environment.[3]

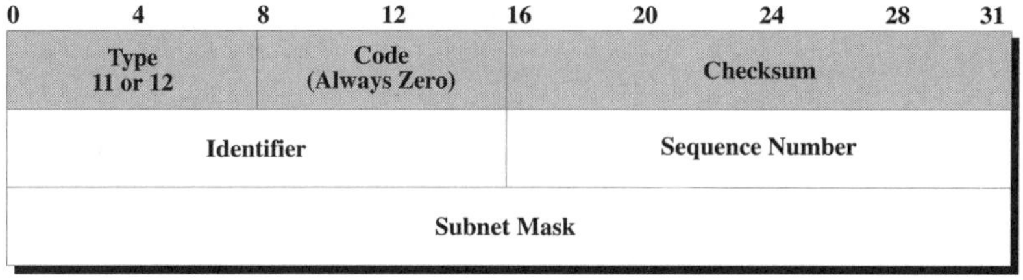

0	4	8	12	16	20	24	28	31
Type 11 or 12		Code (Always Zero)		Checksum				
Identifier				Sequence Number				
Subnet Mask								

Figure 6-13: ICMP Address Mask Request/Reply Message

The source host broadcasts the ICMP Address Mask Request message (Type 11_{16}) with the 32 bit Subnet Mask field set to zeroes. Upon receipt, a host authorized to provide this information (an authoritative host) enters the Subnet Mask for the network on which the Request was received into the Subnet Mask field. It then changes the Type from a Request to Reply (Type 12_{16}), and returns the message as a local unicast. In the event that the original IP datagram header contained zeroes in the Source IP address field (that is, the source host was not in possession of its IP address) replies are then broadcast. This in itself is not a problem since any network can only ever be assigned one Subnet Mask. Considering the fundamental concept of a single Subnet Mask for any given network, why do we need the Identifier and Sequence Number fields? In essence of course, we do not. There is no real need to match Requests and Responses for this format of message, and many implementations actually leave these fields blank.

6.2 ICMP Extensions

ICMP is a realtively old protocol originally designed to enhance the operation of IP. Naturally as the Internet Protocol suite has been updated and new protocols have been added, it has become necessary to update and enhance other areas – ICMP is no exception. In particular, routing protocols have improved significantly since IP was first conceived, and the deficiencies inherent in hosts with regard to routing have been addressed through two simple ICMP messages.

3. Where hosts are unaware of their Subnet Mask, correctly configured routers are able to assist through Proxy Arp which is discussed fully in Chapter 9.

6.2.1 Router Discovery

As we saw in section 4.3, a station must know the address of at least one router to which it can pass data for onward delivery to other networks. Typically this is achieved by pre-configuring the host through a configuration file. This however makes the routing process non-adaptive and, when network topology changes occur, we must rely on the router to re-direct traffic and to send ICMP Redirect messages (section 6.1.5). Thus to transmit a single packet via a router, three packets may actually be required – the original packet, the re-directed packet, and the ICMP Redirect message.

Some, more powerful, hosts are able to listen to routers exchanging their update messages and therefore determine to which router a packet should be sent. This however relies upon the fact that the host can recognize the routing protocol and is generally not implemented for the most advanced protocols such as OSPF.[4]

RFC 1256 defines a *Router Advertisement*, and a *Router Solicitation* message. These ICMP messages are not a routing protocol but simply a method by which hosts can discover routers on their network. In operation, routers implementing the Router Discovery Protocol (RDP) periodically multicast[5] unsolicited *Advertisements* over each of their interfaces. Hosts then discover the router by listening to these advertisements. In addition hosts, at startup, may multicast a *Solicitation* message that requests routers running RDP to respond with an immediate *Advertisement*.

Advertisements are generally sent to the *All-Systems Multicast* IP Address (224.0.0.1) although it is legal to broadcast these advertisements using the *Limited-Broadcast* IP Address (255.255.255.255). Equally, Solicitations are normally sent to the *All-Routers Multicast* IP Address (224.0.0.2) although again the use of limited broadcasts is allowed. Chapter 14 contains a complete discussion of Broadcasting and Multicasting in an IP environment and should be consulted for further information on these particular addresses.

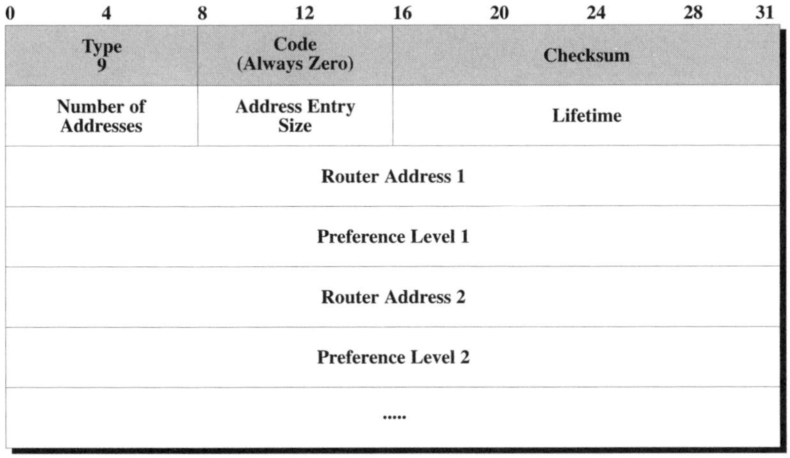

0   4   8   12   16   20   24   28   31
Type 9	Code (Always Zero)	Checksum
Number of Addresses	Address Entry Size	Lifetime
Router Address 1
Preference Level 1
Router Address 2
Preference Level 2
.....

Figure 6-14: Router Discovery Advertisement

---

4. OSPF is discussed in Chapter 11.
5. IP Multicasting is described in Chapter 14.

The 8 bit *Number of Addresses* field is used to convey how many router addresses are being advertised in this message, and the 8 bit *Address Entry Size* field indicates how many 32 bit (4 octet) words are used to describe each entry. Currently, the value of this field is always 2.

The 16 bit *Lifetime* field is used to define the maximum number of seconds that the router addresses contained in this message can be considered current. The 32 bit *Router Address* fields (Router Address 1, 2, etc.) indicate the IP Address(es) associated with the interface over which this message was transmitted. The associated 32 bit *Preference Levels* then indicate the preferability of each address as the default router address, relative to other routers on the same network. This latter field is presented as a signed twos compliment value, where the higher the value means that the route is more preferable.

Figure 6-15 (below) shows the format of the Router Solicitation message. In this message format the *Type* field is set to 10 and, as before, the *Code* field is unused and set to zero. No other fields are used in this message type.

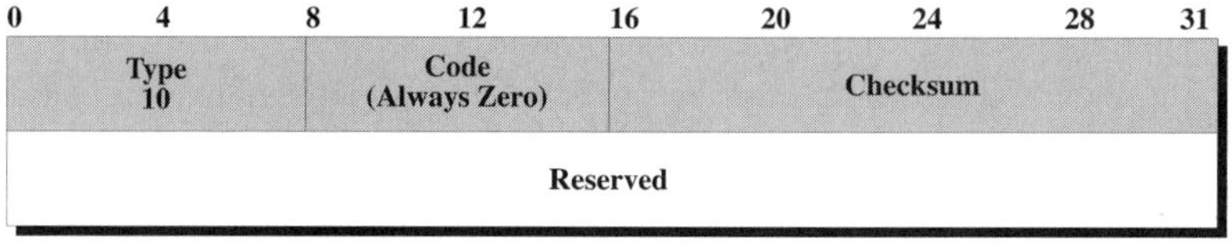

Figure 6-15: Router Solicitation Message

The trace Figure 6-16 shows a typical Router Advertisement message.

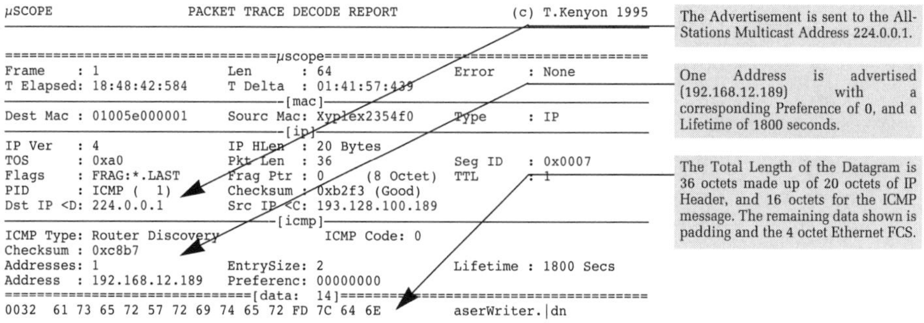

Figure 6-16: Router Advertisement Trace

6.3 Summary

The Internet Protocol does not have any inherent error reporting mechanism or management. As such, IP relies heavily upon ICMP to perform these tasks for it. ICMP is regarded as an integral part of IP and indeed the *Requirements for Internet Hosts* RFC states that implementation of ICMP is mandatory. In reality of course,

ICMP is also a user of IP thus making it impossible to report errors about itself – a slight drawback but not one that has unduly affected it overall.

ICMP along with other protocols has also undergone changes throughout it's life. The introduction of the Router Discovery Protocol (RDP) is just one example. Equally, many things in ICMP have not changed since its introduction and are now taken for granted. For example, almost everyone has heard of Ping, the application that allows us to test for network reachability. This is now one of the mainstays of network management, yet it relies totally upon the ICMP Echo Request/Reply packets discussed in this chapter.

Work still continues on ICMP and new ideas are being put into practice all of the time. With the introduction of IP version 6, new elements will need to be added to ICMP. Indeed today, it is almost impossible to decide where IP stops and ICMP begins and in the future, this delimitation can only become more confused.

The Transmission Control Protocol (TCP)

CHAPTER 7

The Transmission Control Protocol (TCP) is a Connection Oriented, End-to-End Reliable protocol. It is not designed to interface with underlying network technologies since it does not provide any means to address other, distant, hosts. Similarly, it provides no methods for fragmentation or reassembly, nor for the transport through intermediate routers, or for specifying precedence. The Internet Protocol, as we have already seen, performs these tasks on behalf of the upper layers, in this case TCP. The protocol makes few assumptions as to the reliability of underlying

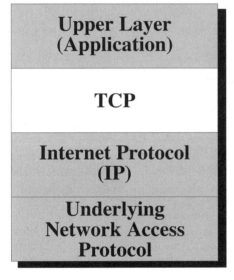

Figure 7-1: The Four Layer Model

protocols, making it general purpose in nature.[1] Upper layers, such as application processes, need not implement further mechanisms aimed at increasing reliability, since TCP dictates that all data sent be acknowledged within specified timeout periods. Where such acknowledgements fail to arrive, TCP will re-send data, thus overcoming the potentially unreliable nature of lower level protocols such as IP.

TCP is designed to support multiple network applications. We shall see in this chapter that the protocol, as described by RFC 793, provides a method of reliably interfacing with multiple application processes (such as Telnet, FTP, etc.) through the use of *Sockets*.[2] This makes TCP a reliable, process-to-process service, and is therefore in use as an interface between our application process and IP itself. An application will pass data to the TCP module for eventual transmission onto the local network, and ultimate delivery to a destination host. The TCP module will, in turn, call on the

---

1. Although generally used in conjunction with IP, theoretically TCP could be used with any other layer 3 protocol.

2. Sockets were briefly introduced in Chapter 6 (ICMP). We shall discuss the concepts of sockets in more detail in this chapter.

underlying protocol (probably IP) that packages the unit of TCP data into a datagram. Finally the datagram is passed to the network access protocol for encapsulation in a physical frame and transmission onto the network media.

As we saw in Chapter 5, intermediate routers may need to perform fragmentation or even further encapsulation in order to accomplish the delivery process. Intermediate routers will therefore strip the physical frame header from the local packet and examine the resulting datagram. Where fragmentation is required for onward routing, this will be performed except in circumstances where the *Do Not Fragment* flag is set. Finally, the resulting datagram(s) are encapsulated in the layer two header relevant to the local network onto which the datagram(s) are to be dispatched, and transmitted onto the network media.

7.1 TCP Operation

As we have already said, TCP was designed specifically to provide a reliable *logical circuit* or connection between application processes on different machines. We have also said that IP, the protocol upon which TCP normally sits, is generally considered to be *unreliable*. In order to therefore provide a reliable communications system, the following facilities are required.

7.1.1 Basic Data Transfer

TCP is able to both transmit and receive data streams simultaneously. At first sight this may seem opposite to the basic concept of data transmission in most underlying network technologies. In Ethernet, Token Ring and FDDI environments, only one station may transmit at any time. However we must accept that at the TCP layer, we potentially have *perceived* Full Duplex transactions. This is not to say that all communication at the TCP layer is full duplex in nature. We shall see later that during the life of a connection we have half duplex, full duplex, and simplex phases of operation.

The data unit transmitted from our TCP layer is referred to as a *Segment*. The size of these segments and the timing at which they are sent is generally left to the TCP module, thus ensuring that TCP users make the best use of available network bandwidth. So what happens when a user needs to transmit a small amount of data (that is short of the optimum segment size) in a timely manner? In this case, TCP users may request that the data is *Pushed*, instructing the TCP module to deliver all data up to that point to the remote TCP module.

7.1.2 Reliability

The reliability of TCP stems from the fact that each Segment must be acknowledged. Acknowledgements are carried in TCP segments together with data flowing from the remote host, and thus provides us with both the reliability that we require, and the ability to conserve network bandwidth. Let us consider the following examples:

The Transmission Control Protocol (TCP)

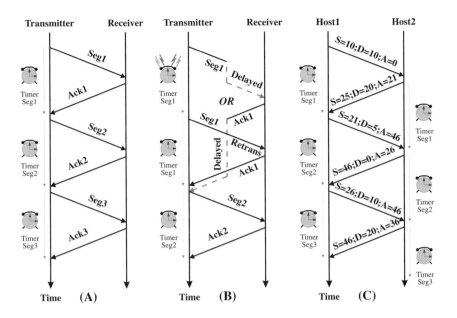

Figure 7-2: Reliable Data Transfer with Positive Acknowledgements

TCP provides reliable communications through a *Positive Acknowledgement* system. This system (diagram A), requires that each segment sent be acknowledged. A timer is started when the segment leaves the transmitting host and an acknowledgement must be received before the timer expires.

The system must also be able to recover from data that is lost, damaged, duplicated, or delivered out of sequence. In order to overcome these conditions, TCP assigns a sequence number to each octet transmitted and requires the receiving host to acknowledge each octet received. Where acknowledgements are not received within a specified timeout period, retransmission of the *presumably lost* octets takes place. So what happens if a segment is received correctly, albeit late, or the resulting acknowledgement is delayed in the network? In this case, the receiving host will potentially receive a duplicate segment. This must be examined and, based upon the sequence number used, be discarded. Equally, the transmitting host could receive a duplicate acknowledgement. In this case, since each octet is acknowledged, the duplicate should also be discarded based upon the acknowledgement number (diagram B). Naturally, a segment or an acknowledgement may be lost completely. In the case that a segment does not arrive at the receiving host, no acknowledgement will ever be received. The transmitting host will therefore retransmit the segment. In the case of a lost acknowledgement, the transmitting host will assume that the segment never arrived, and again re-transmit the segment. This results in the receiving host again receiving a duplicate segment (which must be discarded) and transmitting a duplicate acknowledgement.

Of course it would be extremely wasteful of network bandwidth to send an acknowledgement packet for each octet individually, particularly true when you appreciate the overhead of sending a complete TCP segment. Instead, before transmission, TCP increments the Sequence number by the number of octets contained in the last segment. The Acknowledgement returned is incremented by the number of octets received, thus informing the transmitting host that data has been received without error (diagram C). You will notice from diagram C that we have renamed our hosts as Host 1 and Host 2 since this example shows our perceived Full Duplex operation. In the first exchange, Host 1 sends 10 octets of data (D=10) with a sequence number of 10 (S=10) and no acknowledgement (A=0). The response from the receiver, Host 2, is to send 20 octets of data (D=20) with a sequence number of 25 (S=25), and an acknowledgement of 21 (A=21). Note that the acknowledgement sent is always the number of the *next* octet of data that we expect to receive. Host 1 now sends a segment containing 5 octets of data, and an acknowledgement of Host 2s' data and the transfers continue.

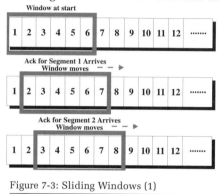

Figure 7-3: Sliding Windows (1)

What we have described so far, is a system that provides the reliability that we desire. But does it make best use of the available network bandwidth and resources of machines' en-route? Plainly the answer is no if we are to wait for one segment to be acknowledged before we may send the next, particularly when you consider the possible, considerable, delays involved over wide area links. So, instead of acknowledging each segment and waiting for that acknowledgement to arrive, TCP employs a system whereby multiple segments may be transmitted before an acknowledgement is required. This system, known as *Sliding Windows*, allows a transmitting station to transmit multiple segments, and therefore have multiple segments unacknowledged at any time.

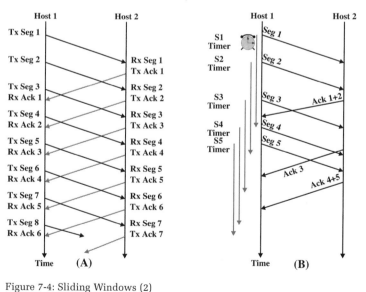

Figure 7-4: Sliding Windows (2)

The Transmission Control Protocol (TCP)

In theory, the sliding windows' principle works as follows: A window is placed over the data such that any data to the left of the window has been transmitted and acknowledged, data under the window has been transmitted but an acknowledgement is yet to be received, and data to the right of the window is, as yet, untransmitted. When an acknowledgement for the lowest numbered, unacknowledged, segment is received, the window is then slid to the right, thus allowing the transmission of further segment(s). In Figure 7-3 we have chosen a window size of six, thus allowing for six segments to be unacknowledged at any time. In Figure 7-4, diagram A shows a possible exchange using a window size of three.

We have already seen that TCP is built upon the principle that we should make the best use of available network resources. Allowing multiple unacknowledged segments to be on the network at any time is one way of achieving this. Allowing data and acknowledgements to be *piggybacked* in the same segment is another. But what happens when one side has no data to transmit or is maybe running slower than the other? Must it still send an acknowledgement for each segment received? Diagram B of Figure 7-4 shows that multiple segments may be acknowledged at the same time. You will now see that vast savings of network bandwidth can be made where this facility of acknowledging multiple segments is combined with the transmission of data in the same segment.

7.1.3 Flow Control

TCP provides a flow controlled environment, allowing the receiver to govern the amount of data that transmitting hosts may send. In order to achieve this, each acknowledgement sent by the receiving host contains a *window* that indicates the number of octets that the receiver is prepared to accept. In this way, a transmitting host will know how much data to send, and receiving hosts, by adjusting the window, can communicate the state of their buffers.

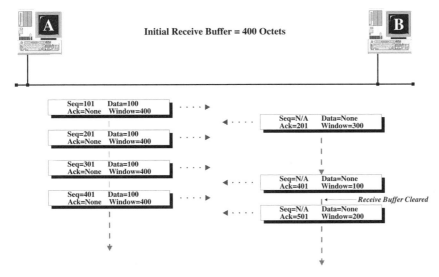

Figure 7-5: The Receive Window

One important consideration when discussing buffer usage is that data held in the transmit buffer cannot be removed until it is acknowledged, since the transmitter may need to re-send it. Equally, received data may not be removed immediately after it arrives due to delays imposed by other processes running on the receiving host. Figure 7-5 shows two hosts involved in a TCP data transfer. Both hosts have an initial receive buffer of 400 octets and, to simplify the diagram, we shall assume that only Host A has data to send. Host B will therefore merely acknowledge all correctly received data and advertise how much more data it is prepared to accept.

Another consideration, and one that has led to a great deal of research, is the algorithm used when advertising available buffer space through the window facility. Where a receiver advertises a small buffer space whenever it becomes available, the transmitter is at liberty to use it. Now, if the transmitter uses that incremental space to transmit data (no matter how small), the result will be a pattern of small data segments being transmitted, making inefficient use of network resources. This is known as the *Silly Window Syndrome*. RFC 1122, *Requirements for Internet Hosts,* recommends that the following formula be used to overcome this:

`RCV.BUFF — RCV.USER — RCV.WND >= min (Fr * RCV.BUFF, Eff.snd.MSS)`

Where:

`RCV.BUFF` Is the total buffer space.

`RCV.USER` Is the amount of data received from the remote TCP layer and Acknowledged. At any time a variable amount of received data may occupy the receive buffer.

`RCV.WND` Is the amount of buffer space advertised through the TCP window facility.

`Fr` Is a fraction (recommended value 0.5).

`Eff.snd.MSS` Is the effective maximum segment size negotiated at the establishment of the TCP connection.

The result is that the receiver "lies" when advertising the amount of available buffer space, and will allow the window to shrink to zero until such time that a reasonable size window is available.

So what about the transmitting host? We have already said that generally, segments are sent when the TCP module can make either best use of the available bandwidth, or when data is *Pushed*. Many applications, particularly virtual terminal applications, require that single characters are sent over a TCP connection. So if the receiver is lying about the amount of buffer space available, surely we should still send small segments?

The Nagle algorithm proposes a method of limiting the number of small segments where there is unacknowledged data. Nagle recommends that if there is unacknowledged data, then the TCP module should buffer all user data (even if pushed) until the outstanding data has been acknowledged. RFC 1122 also states that the Nagle algorithm must be implemented. Of course we still have a problem with *real-time* applications, and those that truly require small data transfers. RFC 1122 therefore recommends that application processes must be able to disable the Nagle algorithm in these cases.

7.1.4 Multiplexing

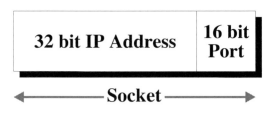

Figure 7-6: The TCP Socket

TCP provides a connection oriented environment for many processes within a single host, simultaneously. TCP provides a set of *Ports* (application addresses) which, when concatenated with the IP address of the host, provides a *Socket* that uniquely identifies this application process anywhere within the internet. The assignment of port numbers, and their binding on individual machines, is undefined and is therefore implementation-specific with the learning of these normally involving some dynamic process.

A list of universal or *Well Known*[3] ports that identify common applications, is published in the Internet Assigned Numbers document. All hosts must adhere to this document, and may therefore only use those ports listed, for the applications specified.

7.1.5 Connections

The reliability that we have described so far relies on each end of our connection being in possession of certain sequence number information. TCP therefore must establish, maintain and, wherever possible, *gracefully* close connections. When we talk of opening connections between hosts, we should be more specific since RFC 793 defines two types of *Open*.

- A *Passive* Open is where a process wishes to accept incoming service requests, rather than to actively pursue a connection. A Telnet or FTP Server process will initiate such an open, and then accept a connection request from other calling hosts.

- An *Active* Open is where a process wishes to actively initiate a connection with another host. Telnet and FTP client processes will operate in this way, and open a connection with a previously opened server process.

From this discussion, it is apparent that two host processes will never be able to establish a connection if they each issue *Passive* Opens. A connection can only ever be established where each end knows the port identifier of the remote process, and as we have already said, apart from our *Well Known* ports, these are dynamically assigned. Processes issuing Passive opens normally assign a Destination Port of all zeroes, or some other unspecified identifier. Although this means that it is only

---

3. A table of common Well Known Ports is provided in section 7.2.

possible to establish a connection when an Active Open is received, it also leaves
the server process free to establish a connection with any remote host.

7.2 TCP Segment Header

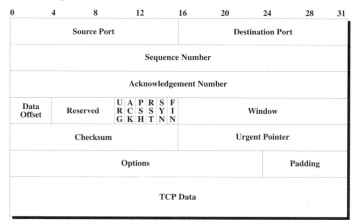

Figure 7-7: The TCP Segment Header

As with IP datagrams, the TCP segment comprises a header, and a variable length
data area that ultimately carries application data. The TCP segment, as it is called,
is carried as IP datagram data, and therefore immediately follows the datagram
header. Figure 7-7 shows the basic segment header format.

As we have seen, the two sixteen bit *Port* fields (Source Port and Destination
Port) identify application processes on the source and destination hosts respectively. More generally however, we should say that the ports are used to name the
ends of logical connections that carry our conversations. Since servers must provide services to extensive *unknown* hosts, a service contact point is defined by a set
of reserved ports known as *Well Known Ports*. RFC 1700 (Internet Assigned
Numbers) specifies these reserved port numbers, and Table 7-1 lists the four most
common protocols with their associated ports when used with TCP. As we have
already said, the allocation of *Source Port* numbers in client processes is usually
dynamic in nature, and implementation-specific. This is therefore not covered here.

Table 7-1: TCP Well Known Listener Ports

Port No. Decimal	Port No. Hex	Keyword	Description
20	0014	ftp-data	File Transfer Protocol (Default Data Connection)
21	0015	ftp	File Transfer Protocol (Default Control Connection)
23	0017	telnet	Telnet Server Listener Port
25	0019	smtp	Simple Mail Transfer Protocol Listener Port

Clearly we must have a method of identifying processes on a host, and indeed
we have already seen this in action. Figure 7-8 however may serve to demonstrate
this more clearly.

The Transmission Control Protocol (TCP)

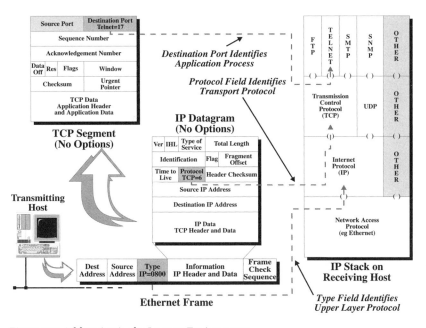

Figure 7-8: Addressing in the Internet Environment

The 32 bit *Sequence Number* field represents the sequence number of the first octet of data carried in this segment, except where the *SYN* flag is set. Where the SYN flag is set, the source host is attempting to establish a connection, and to therefore assign an *Initial Sequence Number* (ISN) from which all other sequence numbers will be derived. In this case, the first octet of data transmitted will be the value of the initial sequence number plus 1. TCP uses very large sequence and acknowledgement numbers (2^{32}), resulting in a possible 42,949,672,96 octets of data per connection being allowed in transit, and therefore unacknowledged, at any one time. A number that should, under any circumstances, be impossible to achieve and indeed, someone once calculated that it would take 9½ hours for a host, transmitting at a constant 2Mbps, to *wrap* these fields.

The determination of an ISN is not fixed, and will generally not be zero. Instead, the ISN will normally be derived from an internal clock in an attempt to ensure that duplicate numbers do not exist on the network. Imagine the problems that might arise should one end of an established connection crash and be restarted. The host, on restart, would dynamically assign port numbers that may have been in use before the crash. Equally, if the initial sequence number always started from a known base, it is possible that a new segment could be transmitted with the same number as a segment that is still in transit. A receiving host, unaware of the problems experienced at the far end could then receive two unrelated segments with the same sequence number!

The 32 bit *Acknowledgement Number* is valid only when the *ACK* flag is set. Where this is the case, the Acknowledgement Number field will contain the sequence number of the first octet in the next segment that the receiver is expecting to receive. In other words, since TCP is able to acknowledge every octet sent, an acknowledgement of X indicates that all octets up to, but not including X, have been received.

The 4 bit *Data Offset* field is used to indicate the length of the TCP segment header. In the same way that the *Internet Header Length* field in the IP datagram measures the length of the header in multiples of 32 bit (4 octet) words, so does this field. This means that all segment headers, whether they contain options or not, must end on a 32 bit boundary and therefore may require padding. The 6 *Reserved* bits are undefined, and must be set to zero in all segment headers. The 6 Control flags, *URG*, *ACK*, *PSH*, *RST*, *SYN*, and *FIN* have the following meanings when set to a binary 1:

URG   The Urgent Flag indicates that the Urgent Pointer field is valid and should be used. This facility allows the presence of urgent data, embedded in the data stream, to be communicated to the receiving host.

ACK   The Acknowledgement flag is used to indicate to the receiving host that the *Acknowledgement* field is valid, and therefore the segment is conveying an acknowledgement. Whether the segment is also carrying data is irrelevant to the state of this flag, since this would be signalled by the Sequence field. Where the ACK flag is set, the acknowledgement number field will identify the next data octet expected at some point in the future.

PSH   In order to allow small amounts of data to be transferred in a segment, the *Data Stream Push* function is requested by the application process. Where a transmitting host wishes to use this function, it sets the Push flag indicating that all data up to and including that assembled so far should be transmitted immediately. On reception of a segment with the Push flag set, the receiving TCP module should pass the data to the application process indicated by the Destination Port field, when it is ready to receive it.

RST   The Reset flag indicates that the connection should be reset, and must be sent if a segment is received which is apparently not for the current connection. On receipt of a segment with the RST bit set, the receiving station will immediately abort the connection. Where a connection is aborted, all data in transit is considered lost, and all buffers allocated to the connection are released.

SYN   The Synchronize flag is set only during connection establishment. The SYN flag is used to indicate to the receiving host that the number contained in the *Sequence Number* field is valid and should be treated as an *Initial Sequence Number* (ISN). Where the receiving host wishes to proceed with the establishment of the connection, it will then acknowledge the sequence number supplied. Connection establishment is discussed in detail later in this chapter.

FIN   The FIN or Final flag is used to indicate that the transmitting host has no more data, and that it wishes to close the connection. This *graceful* close does not indicate that the connection should be terminated immediately but simply that this host will send no more data. The host that sent the FIN will continue to accept data from the remote end, thus effectively turning the connection into a *Simplex* link.

The *Window* field is used to communicate the amount of data (in octets) that the receiving host is prepared to accept, starting with the octet identified by the Acknowledgement field. We saw previously how this mechanism functions, and it is through this field that flow control is achieved.

The *Checksum* field provides a mechanism to ensure that data has been received error free. Unlike the IP datagram header that checks only the header fields, the TCP segment checksum operates over both the TCP header and data. In addition, a 96 bit pseudo header, as shown in Figure 7-9, is conceptually prefixed to the segment.

0	4	8	12	16	20	24	28	31
Source Address							
Destination Address							
Zero		Protocol		TCP Length (Includes both TCP Header and Data but not pseudo header)			

Figure 7-9: TCP Pseudo Header

The checksum is calculated in a similar fashion to that used in the IP datagram header checksum, as the 16 bit one's compliment of the one's compliment sum of all 16 bit words including any bits carried. In this case though, both the header and data areas are checked. For the purposes of calculating the checksum, the checksum field itself is assumed to be zeroes. Where the segment is carrying an odd number of 16 bit words, it is padded with a single octet of zero for the purposes of calculating the checksum. Neither the pseudo header, nor this pseudo data pad, is ever transmitted.

The *Urgent Pointer* field is only valid where the URG flag is set. Where valid, this field is used to convey to a receiving host where within a data stream urgent data is located. In essence, the value contained in this field is the offset (in octets) from the sequence number indicated by the Sequence Number field. Urgent data may include an Xoff (Ctrl S) signal from a terminal that must be handled before any data preceding it (within the segment) is processed. Exactly how this is achieved is unspecified, thus making the mechanism implementation-specific.

7.3   TCP Options

Although the TCP header supports a variable number of options, in reality only three have been defined and of these only one, the Maximum Segment Size option, has any real relevance.

The *End of Options List* option was originally designed to indicate the end of the options field, and would only ever appear once. It was required since options, in theory at least, could be of variable length, and the end of the list might not coincide with the end of the segment header. In this case, Padding would be required. It would not be used where the options list ended at the end of the header. So, since the only really applicable option (the Maximum Segment Size option) is 4 octets in length, this is actually never used. The *No-Operation* option was designed to be used between options as a delimiter. However, since the only valid option is the Maximum Segment Size option, (and that may appear only once) this too is never used. The *Maximum Segment Size* option is always 32 bits in length and, where used, conveys the maximum receive segment size that the transmitting TCP module is prepared to accept. This option may only ever appear once in a segment, and may only ever be present during the connection establishment phase (that is where the SYN bit is set). Where the option is not used, any segment size is valid.

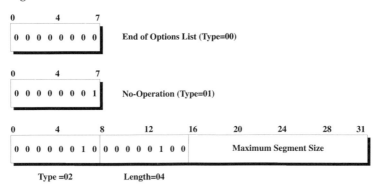

Figure 7-10: TCP Segment Header Options

7.4 Connection Management

We have already seen the reliability and flow control mechanisms applied to TCP data transfer. However, such connections must be initialised and synchronised so that we can maintain certain status information. The combination of sockets, sequence numbers, and window sizes is referred to as a TCP connection, uniquely identified by the socket numbers on each side. A connection therefore has three distinct phases in its lifetime namely: *Connection Establishment*, *Connection Maintenance*, and *Connection Closure*.

7.4.1 Connection Establishment

The Connection Establishment phase is where the two TCP modules exchange synchronization information in order to establish the connection. This procedure is normally initiated by one TCP module and responded to by another. However, the procedure, known as a *Three Way Handshake*, works equally well if two TCP modules simultaneously initiate the procedure.

Where two TCPs initiate a Three Way Handshake, each will receive a segment with the SYN flag set with no segment carrying an acknowledgement following. Figure 7-11 shows two examples of TCP connection establishment. The first shows a simple *Three Way Handshake,* and the second shows where both sides attempt to initiate the connection at the same time. In both cases superfluous information, *Windows*, *Ports*, and *Lengths,* etc. have been ignored to clarify the exchanges.

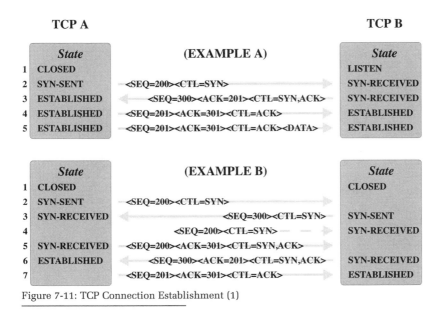

TCP A		TCP B

Figure 7-11: TCP Connection Establishment (1)

In example A, we see that TCP module A transmits a segment with the SYN bit set, and indicating that it will use a sequence number of 200 (Line 2). TCP module B responds (line 3) by acknowledging the segment sent from A, and indicating that it will use sequence number 300. Notice that this segment has both SYN and ACK flags set indicating that both fields are valid, and that TCP module B now expects to receive sequence number 201. TCP A now transmits an empty segment with the ACK flag set and indicating that it is expecting sequence number 301 from TCP B (line 4). Finally, TCP A commences data transmission (line 5) by sending a segment that contains data. Notice that this segment has the ACK flag set (indicating that the Acknowledgement field is valid) and that the sequence number used is the same as in line 4. This latter point is important since it demonstrates the basic principle that the Acknowledgement itself does not occupy any sequence number space. If this were not the case, we would be encumbered with acknowledging acknowledgements as they arrive.

Example B shows us the exchanges that take place where both ends attempt to establish a connection simultaneously. In this example, both ends start with their respective TCP modules in the *Closed* state. Lines 2 and 3 show that both TCP modules send synchronization segments at the same time. Line 4 is a representation of the fact that TCP A still believes that its SYN segment is in transit and therefore unacknowledged. In line 5 we see that TCP A recognizes the fact that it has received a SYN segment from TCP B, and therefore acknowledges Bs SYN and sends its own SYN (sequence 200). The next transfer, line 6 shows TCP B responding to the SYN segment from A and reasserting its own sequence number to ensure that no confusion exists. Finally in line 7, TCP A responds with what is normally the last phase of the handshake, and the connection is established.

We have seen what happens in the case of a normal connection establishment, and also where both sides try to initiate a connection simultaneously. But what happens where a duplicate segment with the SYN flag set is received part way through the establishment phase? Figure 7-12 shows one use of the RST flag by demonstrating this scenario. In this case, the receiving TCP module aborts the connection part way through, and then re-establishes the connection from the start.

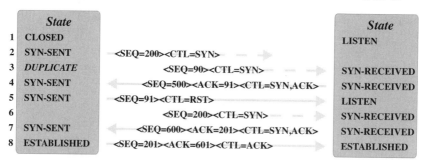

Figure 7-12: TCP Connection Establishment (2)

In this figure, we can see the effects of a duplicate SYN segment being received. TCP A sends a SYN segment with an initial sequence number of 200. This segment is however delayed in transit. In line 3, TCP B receives a delayed SYN segment (from TCP A) that indicates a sequence number of 90. Since this is the first SYN received, TCP B transmits an acknowledgement and indicates that it will use an initial sequence number of 500 (line 4). TCP A will have assumed that the SYN segment that caused this acknowledgement had failed to reach its destination, hence the reason that the segment in line 2 was sent in the first place. It will therefore sense that the acknowledgement field sent from B is incorrect, and will reject the segment by sending a reset (an empty segment with the RST flag set) as demonstrated by line 5. Notice that TCP A uses a sequence number of 91 in this reset segment in order to make the segment believable. TCP B has never received an initial sequence number of 200 from A so a value of 200 or 201 could not be used. Reception of a segment with the reset flag set will cause TCP B to re-enter the LISTEN state as shown. Assume now that the SYN segment that was delayed in line 2 finally arrives at TCP B (line 6). TCP B responds by acknowledging it in the normal fashion with its own *new* sequence number. TCP A acknowledges that initial sequence number (line 8) and the connection is established.

Finally, when discussing *Connection Establishment*, we must look at what happens where two processes are communicating normally and one side crashes. In this case, we assume that when the crashed host is up again, it will use some kind of error recovery mechanism. One possible scenario is that it will attempt to send on the connection that was previously open. This will fail, since the TCP module will have been restarted and will therefore have no knowledge of the connection. Alternatively, after the crashed host is up, it may attempt to re-open the connection using the same source port number as before. In this case, since the other host still believes the previous connection to be open, a reset is forced, resulting in a complete re-establishment of the connection.

Figure 7-13 demonstrates this point.

The Transmission Control Protocol (TCP)

Figure 7-13: TCP Crash Recovery

TCP module B considers itself to be in a synchronized state. Thus, when it receives the SYN segment in line 3, it checks the sequence number and finds that it is outside the sliding window. TCP B responds to this by transmitting an acknowledgement indicating that it expects sequence number 150 (Line 4). TCP A sees that the received segment does not acknowledge anything that it believes it has sent. Therefore, being in an unsynchronized state, it issues a reset causing TCP B to abort (Line 5). TCP A can now attempt to establish a connection with a simple *Three Way Handshake* as started in line 7.

Two other possible scenarios exist when discussing Connection Establishment. Firstly, after one side has crashed, the other (*Active*) side can cause a reset to occur. In Figure 7-14, TCP A has crashed. TCP B, unaware of the events at TCP A, sends a segment containing data. On receipt of this segment, TCP A transmits a reset, since it is unaware that such a connection exists. Since the reset is a perfectly valid response, TCP B will abort the connection.

Figure 7-14: TCP Connection Reset After a Crash

Secondly, there is a possibility that both TCP modules may be open with *Passive* connections, that is both listening for a SYN segment. An old duplicate SYN segment arriving at one of the TCP modules will then cause it to enter the connection establishment phase. In Figure 7-15, TCP B receives this *rogue* segment in line 2. This causes TCP B to transmit its own SYN segment, and acknowledge the other host's sequence number (a SYN/ACK). On receipt of this segment, TCP A will determine that the acknowledgement is unacceptable, and will therefore issue a reset. TCP B must accept the reset segment (since these are non-negotiable) and return to its passive open state of listening.

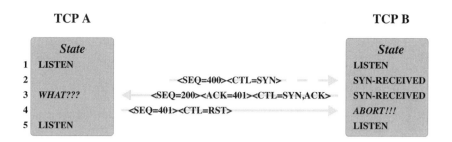

TCP A

TCP B

	State		*State*
1	LISTEN		LISTEN
2		<SEQ=400><CTL=SYN> ⟶	SYN-RECEIVED
3	*WHAT???*	⟵ <SEQ=200><ACK=401><CTL=SYN,ACK>	SYN-RECEIVED
4		<SEQ=401><CTL=RST> ⟶	*ABORT!!!*
5	LISTEN		LISTEN

Figure 7-15: TCP Reset on Passive Sockets

The trace of Figure 7-16 shows how a simple connection is established between a station (at IP Address 192.168.12.36) and the management port of a router (at IP Address 192.168.12.99).

```
µSCOPE              PACKET TRACE DECODE REPORT            (c) T.Kenyon 1995


=============================µscope=============================
Frame    : 1              Len    : 82          Error   : None
T Elapsed: 19:03:41:347   T Delta : 00:01:01:556
----------------------------[mac]------------------------------
Dest Mac : ffffffffffff   Sourc Mac: 0000e80f04af   Type    : ARP
----------------------------[arp]------------------------------
HW Type  : 10Mb Ethernet  Protocol : IP          Opcode  : ARP REQuest
HW AddLen: 6   Bytes      PR AddLen: 4   Bytes

SrHW Addr: 0000e80f04af
SrPR Addr: 192 168 12 36

DeHW Addr: 000000000000
DePR Addr: 192 168 12 36
==========================[data:  40]==========================
002A  AB DC EA AD 33 34 32 38 34 32 33 31 31 33 34 37  ....342842311347
003A  39 33 43 33 00 00 00 00 00 00 00 00 00 00 00 00  93C3...........
004A  00 00 00 00 C6 7F 69 4A                          ......iJ


=============================µscope=============================
Frame    : 2              Len    : 82          Error   : None
T Elapsed: 19:04:01:241   T Delta : 00:00:19:894
----------------------------[mac]------------------------------
Dest Mac : ffffffffffff   Sourc Mac: 0000e80f04af   Type    : ARP
----------------------------[arp]------------------------------
HW Type  : 10Mb Ethernet  Protocol : IP          Opcode  : ARP REQuest
HW AddLen: 6   Bytes      PR AddLen: 4   Bytes

SrHW Addr: 0000e80f04af
SrPR Addr: 192 168 12 36

DeHW Addr: 000000000000
DePR Addr: 192 168 12 99
==========================[data:  40]==========================
002A  AB DC EA AD 33 34 32 38 34 32 33 31 31 33 34 37  ....342842311347
003A  39 33 43 33 00 00 00 00 00 00 00 00 00 00 00 00  93C3...........
004A  00 00 00 00 AC 62 DB 2D                          .....b.-


=============================µscope=============================
Frame    : 3              Len    : 64          Error   : None
T Elapsed: 19:04:01:241   T Delta : 00:00:00:000
----------------------------[mac]------------------------------
Dest Mac : 0000e80f04af   Sourc Mac: Xyplex064892   Type    : ARP
----------------------------[arp]------------------------------
HW Type  : 10Mb Ethernet  Protocol : IP          Opcode  : ARP RESPonse
HW AddLen: 6   Bytes      PR AddLen: 4   Bytes

SrHW Addr: 080087064892
SrPR Addr: 192 168 12 99

DeHW Addr: 0000e80f04af
DePR Addr: 192 168 12 36
==========================[data:  22]==========================
002A  AB DC EA AD 33 34 32 38 34 32 33 31 31 33 34 37  ....342842311347
003A  39 33 82 8C E3 27                                93...'
```

In this implementation, the station always sends an ARP packet to its own address as it starts to ensure that no other station is using it. This practice is implementation specific.

Station 192.168.12.36 sends an ARP Request looking for the MAC Address of the router, 192.168.12.99. Although not strictly part of TCP Session Establishment, it is included here for completeness.

Router 192.168.12.99 responds with its MAC Address in an ARP Response packet. Normal IP operation (and therefore TCP operation) may now commence.

The Transmission Control Protocol (TCP)

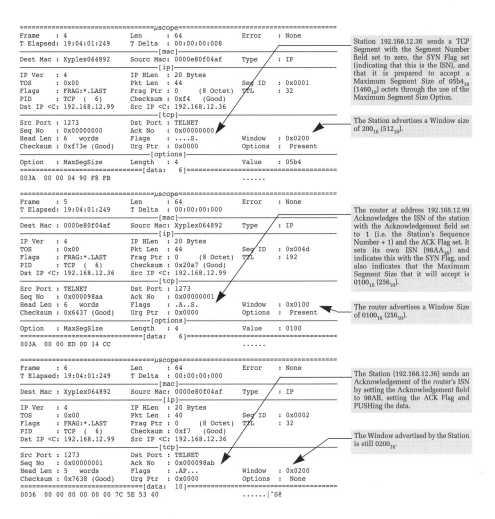

```
===========================µscope=========================
Frame    : 4                Len    : 64            Error   : None
T Elapsed: 19:04:01:249     T Delta : 00:00:00:008
-------------------------[mac]-----------------------------
Dest Mac : Xyplex064892     Sourc Mac: 0000e80f04af  Type  / : IP
-------------------------[ip]------------------------------
IP Ver   : 4                IP HLen  : 20 Bytes
TOS      : 0x00             Pkt Len  : 44            Seg ID  : 0x0001
Flags    : FRAG:*.LAST      Frag Ptr : 0    (8 Octet) TTL    : 32
PID      : TCP ( 6)         Checksum : 0xf4   (Good)
Dst IP <C: 192.168.12.99    Src IP <C: 192.168.12.36
-------------------------[tcp]-----------------------------
Src Port : 1273             Dst Port : TELNET
Seq No   : 0x00000000       Ack No   : 0x00000000
Head Len : 6   words        Flags    : ....S.         Window  : 0x0200
Checksum : 0xf73e (Good)    Urg Ptr  : 0x0000         Options : Present
-------------------------[options]-------------------------
Option   : MaxSegSize       Length   : 4              Value   : 05b4
===========================[data:   6]====================
003A  00 00 04 90 F8 FB                       ......
```

Station 192.168.12.36 sends a TCP Segment with the Segment Number field set to zero, the SYN Flag set (indicating that this is the ISN), and that it is prepared to accept a Maximum Segment Size of $05b4_{16}$ (1460_{10}) octets through the use of the Maximum Segment Size Option.

The Station advertises a Window size of 200_{16} (512_{10}).

```
===========================µscope=========================
Frame    : 5                Len    : 64            Error   : None
T Elapsed: 19:04:01:249     T Delta : 00:00:00:000
-------------------------[mac]-----------------------------
Dest Mac : 0000e80f04af     Sourc Mac: Xyplex064892  Type  / : IP
-------------------------[ip]------------------------------
IP Ver   : 4                IP HLen  : 20 Bytes
TOS      : 0x00             Pkt Len  : 44            Seg ID  : 0x004d
Flags    : FRAG:*.LAST      Frag Ptr : 0    (8 Octet) TTL    : 192
PID      : TCP ( 6)         Checksum : 0x20a7 (Good)
Dst IP <C: 192.168.12.36    Src IP <C: 192.168.12.99
-------------------------[tcp]-----------------------------
Src Port : TELNET           Dst Port : 1273
Seq No   : 0x000098aa       Ack No   : 0x00000001
Head Len : 6   words        Flags    : .A..S.         Window  : 0x0100
Checksum : 0x6437 (Good)    Urg Ptr  : 0x0000         Options : Present
-------------------------[options]-------------------------
Option   : MaxSegSize       Length   : 4              Value   : 0100
===========================[data:   6]====================
003A  00 00 ED 0D 14 CC                       ......
```

The router at address 192.168.12.99 Acknowledges the ISN of the station with the Acknowledgement field set to 1 (i.e. the Station's Sequence Number + 1) and the ACK Flag set. It sets its own ISN ($98AA_{16}$) and indicates this with the SYN Flag, and also indicates that the Maximum Segment Size that it will accept is 0100_{16} (256_{10}).

The router advertises a Window Size of 0100_{16} (256_{10}).

```
===========================µscope=========================
Frame    : 6                Len    : 64            Error   : None
T Elapsed: 19:04:01:249     T Delta : 00:00:00:000
-------------------------[mac]-----------------------------
Dest Mac : Xyplex064892     Sourc Mac: 0000e80f04af  Type  / : IP
-------------------------[ip]------------------------------
IP Ver   : 4                IP HLen  : 20 Bytes
TOS      : 0x00             Pkt Len  : 40            Seg ID  : 0x0002
Flags    : FRAG:*.LAST      Frag Ptr : 0    (8 Octet) TTL    : 32
PID      : TCP ( 6)         Checksum : 0xf7   (Good)
Dst IP <C: 192.168.12.99    Src IP <C: 192.168.12.36
-------------------------[tcp]-----------------------------
Src Port : 1273             Dst Port : TELNET
Seq No   : 0x00000001       Ack No   : 0x000098ab
Head Len : 5   words        Flags    : .AP...         Window  : 0x0200
Checksum : 0x7638 (Good)    Urg Ptr  : 0x0000         Options : None
===========================[data:  10]====================
0036  00 00 00 00 00 00 7C 5E 53 40             ......|^S@
```

The Station (192.168.12.36) sends an Acknowledgement of the router's ISN by setting the Acknowledgement field to 98AB, setting the ACK Flag and PUSHing the data.

The Window advertised by the Station is still 0200_{16}.

Figure 7-16: Establishing a Simple TCP Connection

7.4.2 Connection Maintenance

We have seen that connections are maintained throughout their lifetime by the acknowledgement of each octet of data transmitted. Where a segment is lost due to network failure or congestion, or where a segment is received corrupted, retransmission takes place after the timeout period. Duplicate segments may result due to these re-transmissions. However, the TCP module is responsible for checking sequence and acknowledgement numbers and discarding these.

Sending hosts must keep track of the next sequence number to use, and the receiver tracks which sequence number to expect. Equally, the sending host tracks the oldest unacknowledged sequence number sent. Naturally, where the connection has been idle, these three variables will all be equal.

7.4.3 Connection Termination

Normally connections are terminated gracefully, that is both sides transmit all data that they have to send before the connection is finally closed. In a TCP connection, we assume that one side will finish transmission and will indicate to the other side that it wishes to close the connection (denoted by the FIN flag being set). This segment may, or may not, contain data, however in either case this segment requires acknowledgement. The remote end will respond by acknowledging the first hosts desire to close, but if it still has data to send, neither end will attempt to fully close the connection. In this state, the first machine will continue to accept as much data as is sent from the remote machine, acknowledging each segment as normal. This host, having indicated its desire to close the connection, will not however attempt to send any further data. We can therefore say that the connection is no longer *Full Duplex*, but instead has entered a *Simplex* phase.

Eventually, the remote end should finish sending data, and send a segment indicating that it too wishes to terminate the connection, again denoted by the presence of the FIN flag. This segment must then be acknowledged by the first host, at which time the connection is deemed closed. Buffers are released, and information stored about the connection is deleted at this time. Essentially, there are three cases:

- A user application initiates the close by telling the TCP module to close the connection.

  Here, a FIN segment is constructed, and transmitted after the last queued data segment. No further data segments will be transmitted, with the exception of re-transmissions that occur where an acknowledgement has not been received within the timeout period. The same is also true for the FIN segment itself. Should an acknowledgement not be received, it too will be re-transmitted. All data received from the remote end will be acknowledged by the host that initiated the close, as normal. Indeed, in this state, the initiating host will continue to accept data until it receives a FIN segment from the remote machine. Note, the remote host will only send its own FIN segment when its application process has requested that the connection be closed.

- The remote TCP module initiates the close sequence (at the request of its application process) by transmitting a segment with the FIN flag set. This is the same as the previous example, except that it is viewed from the perspective of the remote, rather than local, TCP module.

  Where we receive an unsolicited FIN segment, the TCP module acknowledges the segment, and will inform the application process that the connection is closing. The application process will respond with a close request of its own, resulting in the construction of a FIN segment which will be queued and transmitted after all outstanding data segments have been sent. The connection will not be deemed closed until such time as all outstanding segments (including the FIN segment) have been correctly acknowledged. Should the FIN segment not be acknowledged (as would be the case where the remote host is disconnected from the network prematurely), the connection will be aborted and the application process informed.

- Both ends of the connection attempt to initiate the close simultaneously.

Here simultaneous close requests are initiated by both application processes, causing each end of the connection to transmit a FIN segment. In this case, neither end will acknowledge the FIN segment until all data segments have been processed and acknowledged in the normal way. Once completed, both hosts will acknowledge the FIN segments, and once the remote acknowledgement has been received, will declare the connection closed.

Figure 7-17 demonstrates these scenarios.

In this figure, example A shows a TCP module A transmitting a segment with the FIN flag set, indicating its desire to close the connection (Line 2). TCP B then responds by acknowledging this segment (Line 3). From this point forwards, TCP A will send no further data segments (except those requiring retransmission), but will acknowledge any data segments received. Effectively, between lines 3 and 4, many data segments could be transmitted from TCP B, and an equal number of acknowledgements from TCP A. However, for clarity, we have assumed that TCP B has no further data to send across this connection. In Line 4, we see that TCP B wishes to close the connection by the transmission of its segment with the FIN flag set. TCP A acknowledges this segment in line 5, and the connection is destroyed with both TCP modules accepting that the connection is now closed.

Figure 7-17: TCP Connection Closure

In example B, we see the effects of both TCP modules attempting to simultaneously close the connection. In this case, each transmits a segment with the FIN flag set, as indicated by the first two segments in line 2. The third segment of the second line indicates that the segment from TCP module A is still valid, and has now reached TCP B. In line 3, both TCP modules transmit acknowledgements to the FIN segments received and the connection is declared closed.

The trace of Figure 7-18 shows an example of a connection termination.

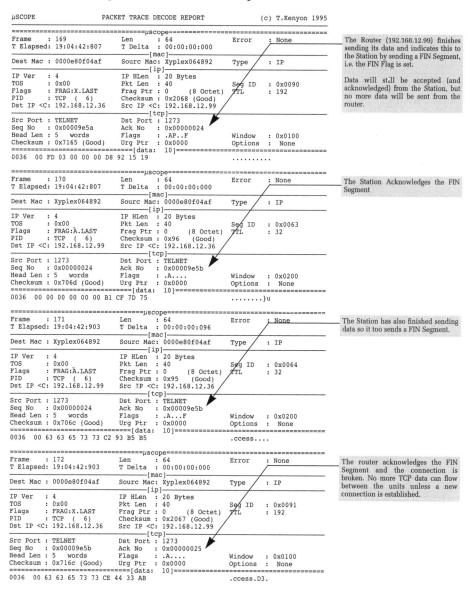

```
µSCOPE                PACKET TRACE DECODE REPORT            (c) T.Kenyon 1995

==============================µscope=====================================
Frame    : 169         Len    : 64          Error    : None
T Elapsed: 19:04:42:807    T Delta  : 00:00:00:000
                           [mac]
Dest Mac : 0000e80f04af    Sourc Mac: Xyplex064892    Type    : IP
                           [ip]
IP Ver   : 4           IP HLen  : 20 Bytes
TOS      : 0x00        Pkt Len  : 40           Seg ID   : 0x0090
Flags    : FRAG:X.LAST    Frag Ptr : 0     (8 Octet)    TTL      : 192
PID      : TCP ( 6)    Checksum : 0x2068 (Good)
Dst IP <C: 192.168.12.36    Src IP <C: 192.168.12.99
                           [tcp]
Src Port : TELNET      Dst Port : 1273
Seq No   : 0x00009e5a    Ack No   : 0x00000024
Head Len : 5   words    Flags    : .AP..F        Window   : 0x0100
Checksum : 0x7165 (Good)    Urg Ptr  : 0x0000           Options  : None
==============================[data:   10]==============================
0036   00 FD 03 00 00 00 D8 92 15 19           .........

==============================µscope=====================================
Frame    : 170         Len    : 64          Error    : None
T Elapsed: 19:04:42:807    T Delta  : 00:00:00:000
                           [mac]
Dest Mac : Xyplex064892    Sourc Mac: 0000e80f04af    Type    : IP
                           [ip]
IP Ver   : 4           IP HLen  : 20 Bytes
TOS      : 0x00        Pkt Len  : 40           Seg ID   : 0x0063
Flags    : FRAG:Ā.LAST    Frag Ptr : 0     (8 Octet)    TTL      : 32
PID      : TCP ( 6)    Checksum : 0x96    (Good)
Dst IP <C: 192.168.12.99    Src IP <C: 192.168.12.36
                           [tcp]
Src Port : 1273        Dst Port : TELNET
Seq No   : 0x00000024    Ack No   : 0x00009e5b
Head Len : 5   words    Flags    : .A....        Window   : 0x0200
Checksum : 0x706d (Good)    Urg Ptr  : 0x0000           Options  : None
==============================[data:   10]==============================
0036   00 00 00 00 00 00 B1 CF 7D 75           ........}u

==============================µscope=====================================
Frame    : 171         Len    : 64          Error    : None
T Elapsed: 19:04:42:903    T Delta  : 00:00:00:096
                           [mac]
Dest Mac : Xyplex064892    Sourc Mac: 0000e80f04af    Type    : IP
                           [ip]
IP Ver   : 4           IP HLen  : 20 Bytes
TOS      : 0x00        Pkt Len  : 40           Seg ID   : 0x0064
Flags    : FRAG:Ā.LAST    Frag Ptr : 0     (8 Octet)    TTL      : 32
PID      : TCP ( 6)    Checksum : 0x95    (Good)
Dst IP <C: 192.168.12.99    Src IP <C: 192.168.12.36
                           [tcp]
Src Port : 1273        Dst Port : TELNET
Seq No   : 0x00000024    Ack No   : 0x00009e5b
Head Len : 5   words    Flags    : .A...F        Window   : 0x0200
Checksum : 0x706c (Good)    Urg Ptr  : 0x0000           Options  : None
==============================[data:   10]==============================
0036   00 63 63 65 73 73 C2 93 B5 B5           .ccess....

==============================µscope=====================================
Frame    : 172         Len    : 64          Error    : None
T Elapsed: 19:04:42:903    T Delta  : 00:00:00:000
                           [mac]
Dest Mac : 0000e80f04af    Sourc Mac: Xyplex064892    Type    : IP
                           [ip]
IP Ver   : 4           IP HLen  : 20 Bytes
TOS      : 0x00        Pkt Len  : 40           Seg ID   : 0x0091
Flags    : FRAG:X.LAST    Frag Ptr : 0     (8 Octet)    TTL      : 192
PID      : TCP ( 6)    Checksum : 0x2067 (Good)
Dst IP <C: 192.168.12.36    Src IP <C: 192.168.12.99
                           [tcp]
Src Port : TELNET      Dst Port : 1273
Seq No   : 0x00009e5b    Ack No   : 0x00000025
Head Len : 5   words    Flags    : .A....        Window   : 0x0100
Checksum : 0x716c (Good)    Urg Ptr  : 0x0000           Options  : None
==============================[data:   10]==============================
0036   00 63 63 65 73 73 CE 44 33 AB           .ccess.D3.
```

The Router (192.168.12.99) finishes sending its data and indicates this to the Station by sending a FIN Segment, i.e. the FIN Flag is set.

Data will still be accepted (and acknowledged) from the Station, but no more data will be sent from the router.

The Station Acknowledges the FIN Segment

The Station has also finished sending data so it too sends a FIN Segment.

The router acknowledges the FIN Segment and the connection is broken. No more TCP data can flow between the units unless a new connection is established.

Figure 7-18: Sample TCP Connection Termination

7.4.4 The TCP Finite State Machine

As we have seen throughout the previous examples, connections progress through a series of states during their lifetime. The states, *LISTEN*, *SYN-SENT*, *SYN-*

The Transmission Control Protocol (TCP)

RECEIVED, ESTABLISHED, FIN-WAIT-1. FIN-WAIT-2, CLOSE-WAIT, CLOSING, LAST-ACK, TIME-WAIT, and *CLOSED* are briefly described in the following text:

- **LISTEN**

  This state represents a TCP module waiting for a connection request from any remote host. This is equivalent to the state entered after a *Passive Open*.

- **SYN-SENT**

  This is the state where a TCP module is waiting for an acknowledgement and matching connection request, having sent a connection request (SYN segment) of its own.

- **SYN-RECEIVED**

  Represents a TCP module that is waiting for a connection acknowledgement after both receiving a synchronization (SYN) segment and sending a corresponding synchronization (SYN/ACK) segment. ,

- **ESTABLISHED**

  This state represents an open connection and is the normal state for the data transfer phase of the connection. In this state, all data received can now be passed to the application process.

- **FIN-WAIT-1**

  This represents the state where the TCP module is waiting for either a connection termination request from the remote host, or an acknowledgement of the termination request that it has already sent.

- **FIN-WAIT-2**

  This state is entered when the TCP module is waiting for a connection termination request from the remote host.

- **CLOSE-WAIT**

  Represents the state of a TCP module that is waiting for a connection termination request from the application process.

- **CLOSING**

  The state that represents a TCP module waiting for a connection termination request acknowledgement from the remote host.

- **LAST-ACK**

  This state represents a TCP module that is waiting for an acknowledgement of a connection termination request that has previously been sent to the remote host.

- **TIME-WAIT**

  This represents the TCP module waiting for enough time to pass to be sure that the remote host received the acknowledgement of its connection termination request.

- **CLOSED**

  This represents the state where no connection exists, and the establishment phase has not been entered.

Figure 7-19 shows how a TCP module may progress through these states in response to events passed from the application process, incoming segments, and time-outs. The events from the application process, or *user calls*, are OPEN, SEND, RECEIVE, CLOSE, ABORT, and STATUS. Incoming segments that have the SYN, ACK, RST, and FIN flag(s) set also trigger events. The figure shows only state changes, the events that caused them, and the resulting actions.

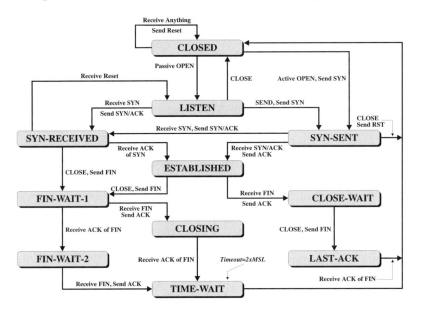

Figure 7-19: TCP Finite State Machine

All connections start from the *CLOSED* state at the top of the diagram. From here, a *Passive OPEN* takes us to the *LISTEN* state and an *Active OPEN*, to the *SYN-SENT* state. In order to progress to the *ESTABLISHED* state, we must progress through the entire Three Way Handshake operation, in which we wish to establish the connection from *LISTEN*. In the case of our *Active OPEN*, we expect to receive a SYN/ACK segment in response to our SYN segment, and we must then acknowledge the SYN/ACK from the remote host.

When closing a connection, we transition from the *ESTABLISHED* state to either the *FIN-WAIT-1*, or *CLOSE-WAIT* state. In the first case, the *CLOSE* is issued from the local host and requires receipt of an ACK, to move to the *FIN-WAIT-2* state. From this state, if we receive a FIN segment from the remote host, we acknowledge the FIN segment and enter the *CLOSING* state awaiting acknowledgement of our FIN. Where the request to close the connection is generated by the remote host, we receive a FIN segment from the network. We will then send an acknowledgement and enter the *CLOSE-WAIT* state. Eventually, when our own application has finished sending data, it issues a CLOSE to the local TCP module. Upon receipt of this *CLOSE*, we will send a FIN segment of our own, and enter the *LAST-ACK* state, where we await an acknowledgement.

The Transmission Control Protocol (TCP)

The *TIME-WAIT* state is important since it is in this state that we wait for assurance that our acknowledgement of the final FIN segment has reached the remote host. TCP modules keep track of the maximum life of a segment (*MSL*), the amount of time that any segment should live on an internet. Typically we wait in the *TIME-WAIT* state for twice this maximum segment life before we will transition to the *CLOSED* state.

The following trace (Figure 7-20) shows a simple TCP exchange illustrating TCP Connection Establishment, Maximum Segment Size Negotiation, data transfer and Window Advertisements, and finally Connection Closure.

```
µSCOPE                    PACKET TRACE DECODE REPORT          (c) T.Kenyon 1995     Ethernet Header

                                                                                    IP Header
=======================µscope===========================
Frame    : 4              Len      : 64          Error    : None
T Elapsed: 19:04:01:249   T Delta  : 00:00:00:008                                   TCP Header. Notice that the Data
=======================[data:    64]====================                            Offset and Flags fields (6002) indicate
0000  08 00 87 06 48 92 00 00 E8 0F 04 AF 08 00 45 00   ....H.........E.             that there are 6 words in the Header
0010  00 2C 00 01 00 00 20 06 00 F4 C0 A8 0C 24 C0 A8   .,.... .......$..             (Max Segment Size option present)
0020  0C 63 04 F9 00 17 00 00 00 00 00 00 00 60 02      .c...........`..              and that the SYN Flag is set.
0030  02 00 F7 3E 00 00 02 04 05 B4 00 00 04 90 F8 FB   ...>............

                                                                                    Ethernet FCS
=======================µscope===========================
Frame    : 5              Len      : 64          Error    : None                    Padding
T Elapsed: 19:04:01:249   T Delta  : 00:00:00:000
=======================[data:    64]====================                            TCP Header. The Data Offset and
0000  08 00 E8 0F 04 AF 00 00 87 06 48 92 08 00 45 00   ..........H...E.             Flags fields (6012) indicate that there
0010  00 2C 00 4D 40 00 C0 06 20 A7 C0 A8 0C 63 C0 A8   .,.M@... ....c..              are 6 words in the Header (Max
0020  0C 24 00 17 04 F9 00 00 98 AA 00 00 01 60 12      .$...........`..              Segment Size option present) and that
0030  01 00 64 37 00 00 02 04 01 00 00 00 ED 0D 14 CC   ..d7............              both the SYN and ACK Flags are set.

=======================µscope===========================
Frame    : 6              Len      : 64          Error    : None                    TCP Header with the Data Offset and
T Elapsed: 19:04:01:249   T Delta  : 00:00:00:000                                   Flags fields (5018) indicating that
=======================[data:    64]====================                            there are 5 words in the Header (no
0000  08 00 87 06 48 92 00 00 E8 0F 04 AF 08 00 45 00   ....H.........E.             options present) and that both the
0010  00 28 00 02 00 00 20 06 00 F7 C0 A8 0C 24 C0 A8   .(.... .......$..             ACK and PSH Flags are set.
0020  0C 63 04 F9 00 17 00 00 00 01 00 00 98 AB 50 18   .c............P.
0030  02 00 76 38 00 00 00 00 00 00 00 00 7C 5E 53 40   ..v8........|^S@

=======================µscope===========================
Frame    : 7              Len      : 67          Error    : None                    TCP Data (Telnet Data) containing
T Elapsed: 19:04:01:249   T Delta  : 00:00:00:000                                   Telnet Option Negotiation (See
=======================[data:    67]====================                            Chapter 16).
0000  00 00 E8 0F 04 AF 08 00 87 06 48 92 08 00 45 00   ..........H...E.
0010  00 31 00 4E 40 00 C0 06 20 A1 C0 A8 0C 63 C0 A8   .1.N@... ....c..
0020  0C 24 00 17 04 F9 00 00 98 AB 00 00 00 01 50 18   .$............P.
0030  01 00 75 34 00 00 FF FB 01 FF FD 03 FF FB 03 C5   ..u4............
0040  CC 52 85                                          .R.
```

Frames 7 to 17 are TELNET Negotiation.
Frames 8 to 16 removed from trace.

```
=======================µscope===========================
Frame    : 17             Len      : 64          Error    : None
T Elapsed: 19:04:05:600   T Delta  : 00:00:00:000
=======================[data:    64]====================
0000  00 00 E8 0F 04 AF 08 00 87 06 48 92 08 00 45 00   ..........H...E.
0010  00 28 00 52 40 00 C0 06 20 A6 C0 A8 0C 63 C0 A8   .(.R@... ....c..
0020  0C 24 00 17 04 F9 00 00 98 B4 00 00 00 0B 50 10   .$............P.
0030  00 FF 77 2E 00 00 0D 00 00 00 00 00 39 59 7C 9C   ..w.........9Y|.

=======================µscope===========================
Frame    : 18             Len      : 64          Error    : None
T Elapsed: 19:04:05:695   T Delta  : 00:00:00:095
=======================[data:    64]====================
0000  00 00 E8 0F 04 AF 08 00 87 06 48 92 08 00 45 00   ..........H...E.            5 octets of TCP (Telnet) Data sent
0010  00 2D 00 53 40 00 C0 06 20 A0 C0 A8 0C 63 C0 A8   .-.S@... ....c..             from 192.168.12,99 (C0A80C63):
0020  0C 24 00 17 04 F9 00 00 98 B4 00 00 00 0B 50 18   .$............P.             0D000A0723$_{16}$
0030  01 00 3D 19 00 00 0D 00 0A 07 23 00 E7 2F 9F F4   ..=.......#../..             (<CR><Null><LF><Bell>#)

=======================µscope===========================
Frame    : 19             Len      : 64          Error    : None
T Elapsed: 19:04:05:695   T Delta  : 00:00:00:000
=======================[data:    64]====================
0000  08 00 87 06 48 92 00 00 E8 0F 04 AF 08 00 45 00   ....H.........E.            TCP Segment from 192.168.12.36
0010  00 28 00 09 00 00 20 06 00 F0 C0 A8 0C 24 C0 A8   .(.... .......$..             (C0A80C24) with ACK and PSH Flags
0020  0C 63 04 F9 00 17 00 00 0B 00 00 98 B9 50 18      .c...........P.              set - No Data but Window size
0030  01 FB 76 25 00 00 00 00 00 00 00 00 3D BA 29 9C   ..v%........=.).             reduced to 01FB$_{16}$.

=======================µscope===========================
Frame    : 20             Len      : 64          Error    : None
T Elapsed: 19:04:05:695   T Delta  : 00:00:00:000
=======================[data:    64]====================
0000  08 00 87 06 48 92 00 00 E8 0F 04 AF 08 00 45 00   ....H.........E.            TCP Segment from 192.168.12.36
0010  00 28 00 0A 00 00 20 06 00 EF C0 A8 0C 24 C0 A8   .(.... .......$..             (C0A80C24) with ACK and PSH Flags
0020  0C 63 04 F9 00 17 00 00 0B 00 00 98 B9 50 18      .c...........P.              set - No Data but Window size
0030  02 00 76 20 00 00 00 00 00 00 00 00 FD F2 7D 6E   ..v ........}n               restored to 0200$_{16}$.
```

```
=============================µscope=============================
Frame    : 21              Len    : 64           Error   : None
T Elapsed: 19:04:06:733    T Delta : 00:00:01:038
=============================[data:   64]=============================
0000  08 00 87 06 48 92 00 00 E8 0F 04 AF 08 00 45 00   ....H.........E.
0010  00 29 00 0B 00 00 20 06 00 ED C0 A8 0C 24 C0 A8   .)........ .....$..
0020  0C 63 04 F9 00 17 00 00 00 0B 00 00 98 B9 50 18   .c............P.
0030  02 00 15 1F 00 00 61 00 00 00 00 00 F9 D1 C4 8D   ......a.........
```
TCP Segment from 192.168.12.36 (C0A80C24) with ACK and PSH Flags set – 1 octet of Data 61_{16} (a).

```
=============================µscope=============================
Frame    : 22              Len    : 64           Error   : None
T Elapsed: 19:04:06:741    T Delta : 00:00:00:008
=============================[data:   64]=============================
0000  00 00 E8 0F 04 AF 08 00 87 06 48 92 08 00 45 00   ..........H...E.
0010  00 28 00 54 40 00 C0 06 20 A4 C0 A8 0C 63 C0 A8   .(.T@... ....c..
0020  0C 24 00 17 04 F9 00 00 98 B9 00 00 00 0C 50 10   .$............P.
0030  00 FF 77 28 00 00 61 00 00 00 00 00 63 30 D5 65   ..w(..a.....c0.e
```
TCP Segment from 192.168.12.99 (C0A80C63) with ACK Flag set – No Data but Window size reduced by 1 octet to $00FF_{16}$.

Frames 22 to 168 are TELNET Data and Acknowledgements.
Frames 23 to 166 removed from trace.

```
=============================µscope=============================
Frame    : 167             Len    : 139          Error   : None
T Elapsed: 19:04:42:799    T Delta : 00:00:00:080
=============================[data:  139]=============================
0000  00 00 E8 0F 04 AF 08 00 87 06 48 92 08 00 45 00   ..........H...E.
0010  00 79 00 8F 40 00 C0 06 20 18 C0 A8 0C 63 C0 A8   .y..@... ....c..
0020  0C 24 00 17 04 F9 00 00 9E 09 00 00 00 24 50 18   .$...........$P.
0030  01 00 FF CD 00 00 0D 00 0A 0D 00 0A 58 79 70 6C   ............Xypl
0040  65 78 20 2D 30 32 30 2D 20 4C 6F 67 67 65 64 20   ex -020- Logged
0050  6F 75 74 20 70 6F 72 74 20 30 20 6F 6E 20 73 65   out port 0 on se
0060  72 76 65 72 20 58 30 36 34 38 39 32 20 61 74 20   rver X064892 at
0070  31 36 20 4A 61 6E 20 31 39 39 36 20 20 31 38 3A   16 Jan 1996  18:
0080  35 39 3A 30 33 0D 00 48 5F 6D 5F                  59:03..H_m_
```
TCP Segment from 192.168.12.36 (C0A80C24) with ACK and PSH Flags set – 80_{10} octets of Data.

```
=============================µscope=============================
Frame    : 168             Len    : 64           Error   : None
T Elapsed: 19:04:42:807    T Delta : 00:00:00:008
=============================[data:   64]=============================
0000  08 00 87 06 48 92 00 00 E8 0F 04 AF 08 00 45 00   ....H.........E.
0010  00 28 00 62 00 00 20 06 00 97 C0 A8 0C 24 C0 A8   .(.b.. ......$..
0020  0C 63 04 F9 00 17 00 00 00 24 00 00 9E 5A 50 18   .c.......$...ZP.
0030  01 AF 70 B7 00 00 00 FD 03 00 00 00 86 2C 2F 87   ..p..........,/.
```
TCP Segment from 192.168.12.36 (C0A80C24) with ACK and PSH Flags set – No Data but Window size reduced to $01AF_{16}$.

```
=============================µscope=============================
Frame    : 169             Len    : 64           Error   : None
T Elapsed: 19:04:42:807    T Delta : 00:00:00:000
=============================[data:   64]=============================
0000  00 00 E8 0F 04 AF 08 00 87 06 48 92 08 00 45 00   ..........H...E.
0010  00 28 00 90 40 00 C0 06 20 68 C0 A8 0C 63 C0 A8   .(..@... h...c..
0020  0C 24 00 17 04 F9 00 00 9E 5A 00 00 00 24 50 19   .$.......Z...$P.
0030  01 00 71 65 00 00 00 FD 03 00 00 00 D8 92 15 19   ..qe............
```
TCP Segment from 192.168.12.99 (C0A80C63) with ACK, FIN and PSH Flags set – No Data.

```
=============================µscope=============================
Frame    : 170             Len    : 64           Error   : None
T Elapsed: 19:04:42:807    T Delta : 00:00:00:000
=============================[data:   64]=============================
0000  08 00 87 06 48 92 00 00 E8 0F 04 AF 08 00 45 00   ....H.........E.
0010  00 28 00 63 00 00 20 06 00 96 C0 A8 0C 24 C0 A8   .(.c.. ......$..
0020  0C 63 04 F9 00 17 00 00 00 24 00 00 9E 5B 50 10   .c.......$...[P.
0030  02 00 70 6D 00 00 00 00 00 00 00 00 B1 CF 7D 75   ..pm..........}u
```
TCP Segment from 192.168.12.36 (C0A80C24) with ACK Flag set – No Data but Window size restored to 0200_{16}.

```
=============================µscope=============================
Frame    : 171             Len    : 64           Error   : None
T Elapsed: 19:04:42:903    T Delta : 00:00:00:096
=============================[data:   64]=============================
0000  08 00 87 06 48 92 00 00 E8 0F 04 AF 08 00 45 00   ....H.........E.
0010  00 28 00 64 00 00 20 06 00 95 C0 A8 0C 24 C0 A8   .(.d.. ......$..
0020  0C 63 04 F9 00 17 00 00 00 24 00 00 9E 5B 50 11   .c.......$...[P.
0030  02 00 70 6C 00 00 00 63 63 65 73 73 C2 93 B5 B5   ..pl...ccess....
```
TCP Segment from 192.168.12.36 (C0A80C24) with ACK and FIN Flags set – No Data.

```
=============================µscope=============================
Frame    : 172             Len    : 64           Error   : None
T Elapsed: 19:04:42:903    T Delta : 00:00:00:000
=============================[data:   64]=============================
0000  00 00 E8 0F 04 AF 08 00 87 06 48 92 08 00 45 00   ..........H...E.
0010  00 28 00 91 40 00 C0 06 20 67 C0 A8 0C 63 C0 A8   .(..@... g...c..
0020  0C 24 00 17 04 F9 00 00 9E 5B 00 00 00 25 50 10   .$.......[...%P.
0030  01 00 71 6C 00 00 00 63 63 65 73 73 CE 44 33 AB   ..ql...ccess.D3.
```
TCP Segment from 192.168.12.99 (C0A80C63) with ACK Flag set. All communications has now ceased.

Figure 7-20: Complete TCP Session

7.5 Summary

TCP is, to an extent, the workhorse of the Internet Protocol Suite. It takes the typically *unreliable* nature of IP and provides a connection oriented environment that

The Transmission Control Protocol (TCP)

incorporates a positive acknowledgement system. In addition, through the use of Ports and Sockets, TCP allows applications to be addressed. Flow Control is also inherent with TCP with the Window system used to ensure that neither side of the connection is swamped with data. In effect TCP *throttles* stations to ensure even data flow.

Many common applications use TCP namely Telnet, FTP, and SMTP. Even the latest routing protocol, BGP, uses it to provide the reliable communications needed. But using TCP is not without cost. TCP provides an overhead of some 20 octets on each packet sent. So those applications where overhead has to be kept to a minimum would normally use the simpler User Datagram Protocol (UDP). Certainly where we wish to manage devices with say the Simple Network Management Protocol (SNMP), TCP would provide an unacceptable overhead and would be counter productive. Where absolute reliability is required however in the transfer of files say, then there is no argument—TCP has to be the choice.

The User Datagram Protocol (UDP)

The User Datagram Protocol (UDP) is designed to provide application processes with the ability to transfer data to other application processes on remote machines, with a minimal overhead. In the previous chapter, we saw that the Transmission Control Protocol (TCP) provided a mechanism to interface with multiple applications through Sockets. UDP achieves the addressing of processes on a host in a similar way.

UDP, as described by RFC 768, assumes that the Internet Protocol (IP) is in use as the underlying protocol and uses the protocol address 11_{16}, 17 (in decimal). As with TCP, UDP is unable to interface directly with the access protocols of underlying network technologies, however unlike TCP, UDP provides no added reliability. No acknowledgements are sent, the data is not ordered on receipt, and except for those provided by ICMP, there are no flow control mechanisms. Instead, UDP is a *connectionless*, *best efforts* protocol, described as being *transaction* oriented and relying on the application process to provide any reliability over that supplied by IP. As such, when using UDP, delivery cannot be guaranteed, duplication of datagrams can occur, or they may even be discarded if they arrive faster than the destination host can process them. Nevertheless, UDP is a fundamental protocol upon which many functions of an internet are built.

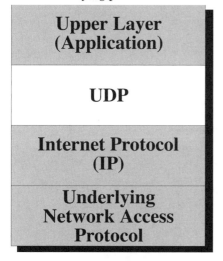

Figure 8-1: UDP and the Four Layer Model

Many diskless devices such as say, *Terminal Servers*, or even *Routers*, are unable to perform their functions unless first loaded with an *image* file (a file that holds their operating system). Where they cannot load it locally, they must look to servers located somewhere on the network. These devices have little intelligence without this file, so designers and developers need protocols with little overhead that can be programmed into ROMs or Flash memory. Applications such as the Bootstrap Protocol (BootP) and the Trivial File Transfer Protocol (TFTP) rely on

UDP, as does the Simple Network Management Protocol (SNMP), the Domain Name System (DNS), and some of the major routing protocols. Since UDP is connectionless in operation, the overhead and intelligence required is greatly reduced, making it an ideal choice for these applications.

8.1 UDP Multiplexing

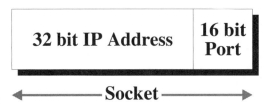

Figure 8-2: UDP Multiplexing

UDP multiplexes to multiple applications in the same way as TCP. Ports are used, which when combined with the IP address of the host, form a 48 bit socket. In this way, as with TCP, we are able to identify any process, on any host, anywhere within our internet.

8.2 UDP Datagram Header

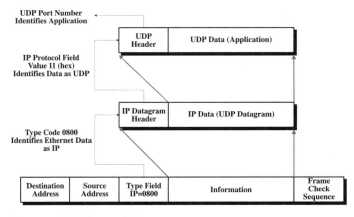

Figure 8-3: UDP Encapsulation

As is common with most protocols, UDP utilizes a fixed length header and variable length data area. The UDP *datagram*, as it is called, travels within an IP datagram that, as with TCP, is then encapsulated in the relevant physical frame. Figure 8-3 shows UDP/IP encapsulated in an Ethernet frame.

The segment header itself is small in comparison with other protocols, just 64 bits in length. As Figure 8-4 shows, the header provides only rudimentary information for the upper layer protocol. Being compact however, makes it ideal for certain applications as we have already discussed.

The two sixteen bit *Port* fields (Source Port and Destination Port) identify application processes on the source and destination hosts respectively. The *Source Port* field is, effectively, optional. Where used, it is the port to which all replies should be sent. However, as we saw with TCP, server applications may choose not to use this field, or alternatively could use a port number of zero. Table 8-1 shows some of the Reserved UDP Port Numbers:

0	4	8	12	16	20	24	28	31

Source Port	Destination Port
Length	Checksum
UDP Data	

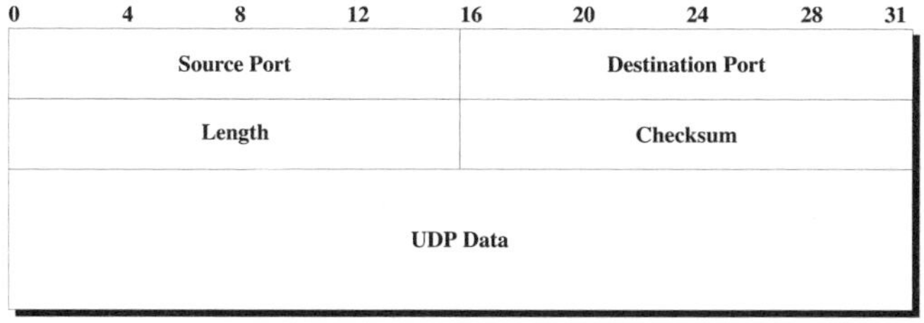

Figure 8-4: UDP Header Format

Table 8-1: Reserved UDP Port Numbers

Port No. Decimal	Port No. Hex	Keyword	Description
7	0007	echo	Echo Protocol
9	0009	discard	Discard Protocol
11	000B	systat	Active Users Protocol
13	000C	daytime	Daytime Protocol
17	0011	qotd	Quote of the Day Protocol
19	0013	chargen	Character Generator Protocol
37	0025	time	Network Time Protocol
42	002A	nameserver	Host Name Server Protocol
43	002B	nicname	Who Is Protocol
53	0035	domain	Domain Name Server
67	0043	bootps	Bootstrap Protocol (Server Process)
68	0044	bootpc	Bootstrap Protocol (Client Process)
69	0045	tftp	Trivial File Transfer Protocol
161	00A1	snmp	Simple Network Management Protocol
162	00A2	snmptrap	Simple Network Management Protocol Trap

You will notice that Table 8-1 lists some client processes, for example the BootP Client. In these cases however, the server process uses the defined port as the destination for data requested by the client. In a way the client is acting as a server process, for the purpose of receiving this specific data.

The *Length* field provides the length (in octets) of this *User Datagram,* including both the header and data areas. The minimum length of a UDP datagram is therefore 8 octets. The *Checksum* is calculated in a similar fashion to that of TCP, being the 16 bit one's compliment of the sum (including any carry) of the 16 bit one's compliments of a pseudo header, the UDP header and the data. This checking of the data area affords protection against corruption. Since this calculation assumes that the total UDP datagram will be treated as 16 bit words, where there is an odd number of octets the data field is padded with a single octet of zero. As with other protocols, this padding is never transmitted, and for the purposes of calculating the checksum, the field is assumed to contain all zeroes. The pseudo header conceptually prefixed to the real header of the UDP datagram is shown in Figure 8-5. As with TCP, we see that the pseudo header contains both Source and Destination addresses, Protocol and Length fields and again, as with TCP, is never transmitted.

0	4	8	12	16	20	24	28	31
Source Address								
Destination Address								
Zero		Protocol		UDP Length				

Figure 8-5: UDP Pseudo Header

It is possible that the calculation of the checksum could result in a value of all zeroes. If this happens, the Checksum field will be transmitted as all ones. This is because hosts receiving UDP datagrams with an all zeroes checksum assume that the transmitter did not generate one (use of the checksum field is actually optional). This however, is normally only used for debugging purposes, or where the application protocol does not care.

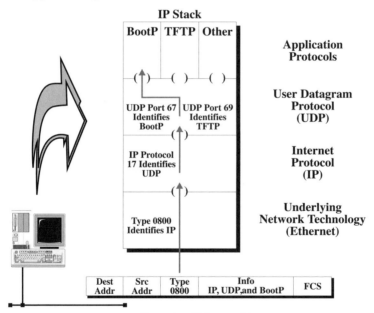

Figure 8-6: UDP Port Usage

Figure 8-6 shows how UDP might be used to deliver a datagram to an application process such as BootP.

The trace, shown in Figure 8-7 then shows an SNMP exchange between a management station and host. It also shows a SNMP Trap being delivered to the management station, thus demonstrating the use of UDP and, in particular, the use of Destination Ports.

```
µSCOPE              PACKET TRACE DECODE REPORT        (c) T.Kenyon 1995

==========================µscope=============================
Frame   : 1              Len     : 86           Error    : None
T Elapsed: 18:32:52:487  T Delta  : 00:15:59:611
------------------------------[mac]-------------------------
Dest Mac : Xyplex056866  Sourc Mac: Sun    1bc95a    Type    : IP
------------------------------[ip]--------------------------
IP Ver  : 4             IP HLen  : 20 Bytes
TOS     : 0x00          Pkt Len  : 68
Flags   : FRAG:*.LAST   Frag Ptr : 0      (8 Octet)   Seg ID  : 0xef28
PID     : UDP ( 17)     Checksum : 0x42da (Good)      TTL     : 60
Dst IP <C: 192.168.12.250  Src IP <C: 192.168.12.171
------------------------------[udp]-------------------------
Dest Port: 161           Src Port : 2000
Length   : 48            Checksum : 0x0000 (NoCheck)
------------------------------[snmp]------------------------
Version  : 1
Community: "public"
Command  : GetRequest
RequestID: 00
ErrStatus: 00
ErrIndex : 00
Object ID: Iso.IE-Org.DoD.Inet.Mgt.Mib.sys.sysUpTime.
     1.3.6.1.2.1.1.3.0
String   :
==========================[data:   0]=======================

==========================µscope=============================
Frame   : 2              Len     : 89           Error    : None
T Elapsed: 18:32:52:494  T Delta  : 00:00:00:007
------------------------------[mac]-------------------------
Dest Mac : Sun   1bc95a  Sourc Mac: Xyplex056866   Type    : IP
------------------------------[ip]--------------------------
IP Ver  : 4             IP HLen  : 20 Bytes
TOS     : 0x00          Pkt Len  : 71
Flags   : FRAG:*.LAST   Frag Ptr : 0      (8 Octet)   Seg ID  : 0x0041
PID     : UDP ( 17)     Checksum : 0x2dbf (Good)      TTL     : 64
Dst IP <C: 193.168.12.171  Src IP <C: 192.168.12.250
------------------------------[udp]-------------------------
Dest Port: 2000          Src Port : 161
Length   : 51            Checksum : 0x0000 (NoCheck)
------------------------------[snmp]------------------------
Version  : 1
Community: "public"
Command  : GetResponse
RequestID: 00
ErrStatus: 00
ErrIndex : 00
Object ID: Iso.IE-Org.DoD.Inet.Mgt.Mib.sys.sysUpTime.
     1.3.6.1.2.1.1.3.0
Object   : 238D32
==========================[data:   0]=======================

==========================µscope=============================
Frame   : 3              Len     : 88           Error    : None
T Elapsed: 18:37:54:328  T Delta  : 00:05:01:834
------------------------------[mac]-------------------------
Dest Mac : Sun   1bc95a  Sourc Mac: Xyplex056866   Type    : IP
------------------------------[ip]--------------------------
IP Ver  : 4             IP HLen  : 20 Bytes
TOS     : 0x00          Pkt Len  : 70
Flags   : FRAG:*.LAST   Frag Ptr : 0      (8 Octet)   Seg ID  : 0x0042
PID     : UDP ( 17)     Checksum : 0x2dbf (Good)      TTL     : 64
Dst IP <C: 192.168.12.171  Src IP <C: 192.168.12.250
------------------------------[udp]-------------------------
Dest Port: SNMP_TRAP [ 162]   Src Port : 161
Length   : 50                 Checksum : 0x0000 (NoCheck)
------------------------------[snmp]------------------------
Version  : 1
Community: "public"
Command  : Trap
Trap Type: Auth Failure
==========================[data:   0]=======================
```

The IP Protocol Field indicates Protocol 17_{10} (11_{16}) – UDP.

Destination Port is 161_{10} – SNMP.

Source Port 2000_{10} – Implementation Specific.

No Checksum in use (value 0000).

SNMP decode of Management Station (192.168.12.171) interrogating a Network Device (192.168.12.250) – See Chapter 20.

Response packet from the Network Device to the Management Station.

Destination Port 2000_{10} – As selected by the Management Station. Source Port 161_{10} – SNMP.

SNMP Response packet decode – See Chapter 20.

SNMP Trap (unsolicited information – See Chapter 20). Source Port 162_{10} – SNMP Trap. Destination Port 161_{10} – SNMP.

SNMP Trap Decode – See Chapter 20.

```
===============================μscope============================================
Frame    : 4              Len     : 86              Error    : None
T Elapsed: 18:38:04:068   T Delta : 00:00:09:740
------------------------------------[mac]----------------------------------------
Dest Mac : Xyplex056866   Sourc Mac: Sun   1bc95a   Type     : IP
------------------------------------[ip]-----------------------------------------
IP Ver   : 4              IP HLen  : 20 Bytes
TOS      : 0x00           Pkt Len  : 68             Seg ID   : 0xef32
Flags    : FRAG:*.LAST    Frag Ptr : 0     (8 Octet) TTL     : 60
PID      : UDP  ( 17)     Checksum : 0x42d0 (Good)
Dst IP <C: 192.168.12.250  Src IP <C: 192.168.12.171
------------------------------------[udp]----------------------------------------
Dest Port: 161                   Src Port : 2006
Length   : 48                    Checksum : 0x0000 (NoCheck)
-----------------------------------[snmp]----------------------------------------
Version  : 1
Community: "xyplex"
Command  : GetRequest
RequestID: 05
ErrStatus: 00
ErrIndex : 00
Object ID: Iso.IE-Org.DoD.Inet.Mgt.Mib.sys.sysDescr.
    1.3.6.1.2.1.1.1.0
String   :
============================[data:   0]==========================================
```

Further SNMP Request sent from the Management Station at Address 192.168.12.171 to the Network Device at 192.168.12.250. In this example a new session has been started thus the Source Port chosen by the Management Station is now 2006_{10}.

Figure 8-7: A Sample UDP (SNMP) Exchange

8.2.1 UDP and ICMP

Recall from our discussions of ICMP, that when a parameter problem is detected in an IP datagram, ICMP sends a *Parameter Problem* message. This message, apart from containing the ICMP header and the IP header of the offending datagram, also contains the first 64 bits of the IP data (TCP, or UDP header). This is to ensure that there can be no confusion as to exactly what caused the problem and hence why the ICMP message has been sent. As we have seen, the specification of the application is by Port number. Therefore by including the first 64 bits of IP data, we shall be able to determine the source and destination applications of this datagram.

8.3 Summary

This chapter discusses the User Datagram Protocol. UDP is a simple protocol used in place of TCP that provides only a small overhead for mainly management applications. UDP itself uses just a simple 8 octet header to identify the applications through the Source and Destination Ports, the length of the data, and a Checksum field whose usage is actually optional. In essence, UDP provides no additional reliability over IP, and is used merely to identify processes on the hosts.

Routing Principles

We said in Chapter 4 that one of the main aims of the IP Address was to provide for the easy routing of traffic between networks, and briefly introduced how this is achieved. In this chapter we shall study the actual mechanics of routing, the maintenance of routing tables, and define the operation of routers generally.

All stations are responsible for the delivery of data, either directly to another station, or to a router for eventual delivery to a distant host. Routers are concerned with the reachability of networks and maintain tables (*Routing Tables*) that list those networks that are reachable. These tables also include a measure of the quality (the *metric*) of the route used, and the address of the next relay system (*hop*) used to onward route the data. Routers also use a series of specialized protocols in order to *learn* about routes to new networks as they become available, and to delete routes that become unusable due to failures. In this way, meshed networks can be created that require an absolute minimum of operator maintenance.

In Chapter 5 we saw how IP incorporates the concept of *Type of Service*. This allows applications to request that particular routes are chosen over those that may not otherwise offer the best *cost* in terms of Throughput, Reliability, or Delay. Through the routing protocol, routers are able to make routing decisions based upon the best and most up to date information available, thereby ensuring that the optimum route is always used. Finally, routers do not forward broadcast[1] frames thus, broadcasts generated at layer two, are never passed.

9.1 Direct and Indirect Routing

Consider the delivery of a simple frame of data to another machine within an organization. The procedure followed by the computer is described below, and shown pictorially in Figure 9-1. Note that although this example ignores the existence of Subnets, it does serve to simply introduce the mechanics of routing.

- Once the data is ready for transmission, it is passed, together with the IP address of the target machine, to the IP module on the source machine.

- The IP module then identifies whether the target machine resides on the same network as itself. It does this by comparing the *Network ID* portion of the target

---

1. Broadcasting with IP is discussed in Chapter 14.

machines IP address with the *Network ID* portion of its own address. Recall that the highest order bit(s) will indicate the length of the *Network ID*.

If the result of the comparison indicates that both machines reside on the same network, the machine will attempt to directly deliver the data. This process is called *Direct* or *Local* Routing.

- Where the result of the comparison indicates that the machines reside on different networks, the source machine will send the data to a *Router*. The router will now be responsible for the onward routing and eventual delivery to the target host. This is called *Indirect Routing*.

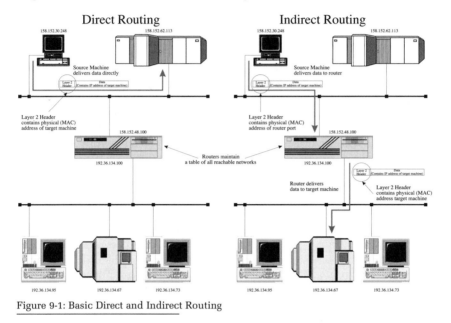

Figure 9-1: Basic Direct and Indirect Routing

Routers perform similar calculations on data as it arrives. Each router maintains a table of Network IDs and how these may be reached. Essentially, a router will determine whether it must pass the data to another router, or whether it can deliver the data directly to the target host. Figure 9-2 shows this concept, and demonstrates that data is passed from router to router until it eventually arrives at a router that is able to *directly* deliver it.

9.1.1 Routing Protocols

As we have already said, routers use special protocols to learn of changes to routes. These protocols, known as Gateway Protocols, fall into two broad categories namely *Interior Gateway Protocols*, and *Exterior Gateway Protocols*. Interior Gateway Protocols, or IGPs, are used within internets that fall under one administrative body, or an *Autonomous System* (AS) as it is more commonly called. Examples of these protocols are the *Routing Information Protocol* (RIP), the *Open Shortest Path First* protocol (OSPF), and Cisco's proprietary *Interior Gateway*

Routing Protocol (IGRP). Exterior Gateway Protocols, or EGPs, then link autonomous systems together. Examples of EGPs are the *Exterior Gateway Protocol* (EGP), and the *Border Gateway Protocol* (BGP). These protocols are discussed in detail in the next chapters.

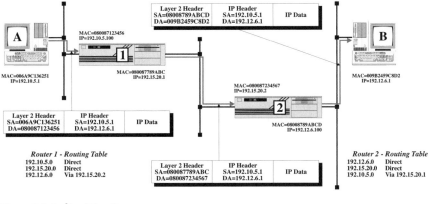

Figure 9-2: Indirect Routing

When a router is first powered on, it will know little about the environment in which it is operating. It will have been programmed with IP Addresses for each of its ports, and possibly have some pre-programmed *static* routes as well. Typically however, routers dynamically learn about reachable networks by exchanging information with their neighbors. A router tells its neighbor(s) about the networks to which it has a direct connection and therefore to which networks *it* can directly route. Its neighbor(s) update their routing tables, and in turn provide information about reachable networks that they know about. These neighbors also tell their neighbors of the new route(s) advertised by our new router, and in this way information is propagated through our internet.

9.1.2 Static and Default Routes

A Static route is one that has been programmed into the device such that it will know the route to a distant, destination network. Although the use of this type of route makes routing less *adaptive*, their use is common where we wish to limit routing update traffic over say a packet switched network such as X.25, or over ISDN.

A Default route is normally programmed into a router where it would be impractical to hold reachability information about every possible network. For example, if we wish to attach to the Internet via a service provider, it would be wholly impractical to assume that our router would hold reachability information about every available network. Instead, we would program our router with a default route that points at our Internet provider, and packets to all destinations for which we do not have an explicit route, would be routed this way.

9.2   Routing and Subnet Masks

Where Subnets are employed, the routing algorithm changes slightly, since we no longer rely upon the Class of address to determine whether we are able to directly route. Recall from our discussion of Subnets in Chapter 4, that where a bit in the Subnet Mask is On (i.e. it is a 1), the corresponding bit in the IP Address should be considered as forming part of the Network ID. Equally, where a bit in the Subnet Mask is Off (i.e. it is a 0), the corresponding bit in the IP Address should be considered as forming part of the Host ID.

In order to determine whether we need to use a router to deliver our data, the station performs a *bitwise AND* of its IP Address and its Subnet Mask, the result of which is to mask off the Host ID bits. In this way, the station may determine both its own *Subnetwork,* and also that of any host to which it wishes to communicate. Our model of operation, described in the previous section, is now changed as shown by Figure 9-3 depicting a Class B network that has been divided into 254 Subnets. The text that follows then describes this operation.

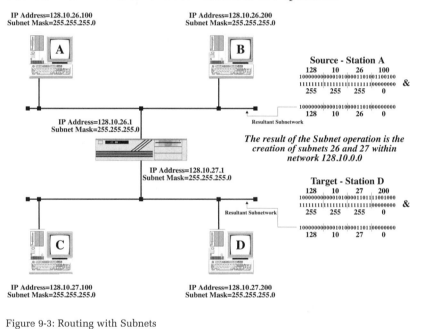

Figure 9-3: Routing with Subnets

- Once the data is ready for transmission, it is passed, together with the IP address of the target machine, to the IP module on the source machine as before.

- The IP module determines whether the target machine resides on the same Subnetwork as itself by ANDing both its own IP Address and that of the target machine with its own Subnet Mask. This results in the Host ID bits of its own address (and the *perceived* Host ID bits of the target machine) being set to zero. It may now compare the results of the two operations to see whether the machines are co-resident on the same Subnetwork. In this case, no attention is paid to the highest order bit(s) of the IP Address.

- Where the result of the above comparison is *False*, this indicates that the machines reside on different Subnets. The source machine will now send the data to a *Router* for onward delivery.

9.2.1 Variable Length Subnet Masks

So far we have considered examples where a single Subnet mask would be applied throughout our entire internet. However, how could we divide our address space if we have many networks each with a small number of attached hosts, and a single network that must accommodate a large number of hosts? Obviously in this instance, a single Subnet mask will not suffice.

Consider the case where you have been assigned a Class B network address and you have a requirement to configure one Subnet with at least 1000 hosts, many Subnetworks with between 100 and 254 hosts, and two point-to-point links (with only two hosts on each). Figure 9-4 below shows this as it would be configured on a multi-port router.

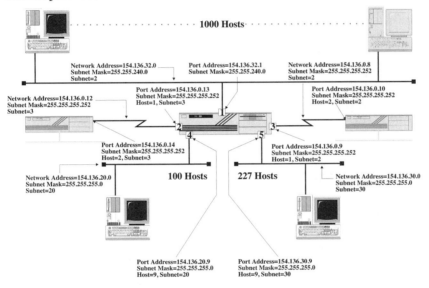

Figure 9-4: Routing with Variable Length Subnet Masks

Assume that the Class B network address is 154.136.0.0 as shown above. The requirements for the point-to-point links are for only two host connections, (the routers at each end of the link) therefore two bits must be assigned to the Host ID for these networks (remember that a Host ID must not be all zeroes or all ones, thus two bits are required). The Subnet field, in this instance, could therefore occupy 14 bits placing the left WAN link on Subnet 12, and the right WAN link on Subnet 8. The network requiring 1000 hosts would need to be assigned at least 10 Host ID bits ($2^{10} = 1024$). In our example above, we have chosen to assign 12, leaving 4 bits for the Subnet field, making this Subnet 2. Our networks that are to accommodate 100 to 254 hosts will need at least 8 Host ID bits ($2^8 = 256$) thus we have chosen to assign 8. This leaves 8 bits for the Subnet field resulting in the creation of Subnets 20, and 30 respectively. This would now seem to make optimum use of the available address space. It must however be noted, that the notion of Subnets now has little relevance when we have masks of different lengths applied to each router port.

Where we wish to deliver data to a host that resides on a different Subnet of our internet, a router must be employed. Routers make decisions as to whether they can directly route traffic or need to onward route it to another router in the path, based upon their own interface address and configured Subnet Mask. In addition, all stations on a Subnetwork (including the router port itself) must use the same Subnet mask. Without this latter requirement, the router would consider itself on a different Subnetwork to that of the hosts connected to the same physical network. Direct routing would then never be possible between the router and its local hosts.

Clearly any host may be assigned any Subnet mask, thus it follows that any router port may also be assigned a different Subnet mask to other ports on the same router. Does this now solve our problem? Sadly the answer is only maybe, since it will depend on the *Routing Protocol* in use. The RIP[2] protocol for example, does not advertise Subnet masks. Thus, given the example Class A network of Figure 9-5, Routers B, C, and D would all be seen by Router A to be advertising routes to network 25.170.0.0. However, since OSPF[3] does advertise Subnet Masks with the Network Ids of reachable networks, this would not prove to be a problem.

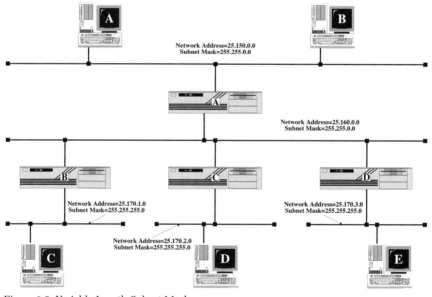
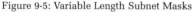

Figure 9-5: Variable Length Subnet Masks

---

2. The Routing Information Protocol (RIP) is discussed in detail in Chapter 10. In addition, a newer version of RIP (RIP II) does allow the advertisement of Subnet Masks.
3. Open Shortest Path First (OSPF) is discussed in detail in Chapter 11.

With OSPF Routing, the Subnet Mask is advertised along with the Network ID. In this case, since the routing tables held by the routers may contain what appears to be multiple routes to the same network, an algorithm is required to determine which Subnet is required. The flowchart shown in Figure 9-6 shows this algorithm based upon a simplified routing table.

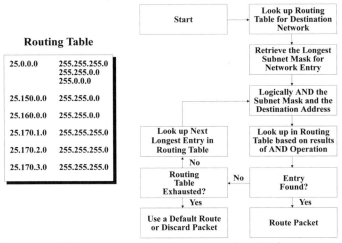

Figure 9-6: OSPF Routing with Variable Length Subnet Masks

9.3   ARP and Subnetted Environments

As we have seen, a router must be used in order for two stations residing on different Subnets to communicate. We have examined the actual mechanics of routing and seen that where Subnets are involved, a fundamental change to the routing algorithm is required. So are all IP devices able to operate in the presence of Subnets, or is there some other method by which this could operate?

9.3.1   Proxy ARP

Proxy ARP, as described by RFC 917, provides a method whereby routers can answer ARP requests on behalf of other stations (by proxy). Since ARP relies on absolute honesty by the responding station, any station that responds will be believed. Proxy ARP is therefore sometimes known as promiscuous ARP.

From Figure 9-7, you will note that only the router has been configured with a Subnet mask, however two distinct Subnets are in use, namely 150 and 200. Should Station A wish to communicate with Station X then, using the algorithm previously outlined, it would assume that both devices shared a common network (where no Subnet mask is specified, stations assume the Natural Subnet Mask should be used). The left side of the diagram shows that Station A would send an ARP packet as a broadcast since it would assume that both Station X and itself were on the same Subnet. Routers do not forward broadcast packets, thus Station X would never receive the ARP Request.

On the right hand side of the diagram, we see that the router responds to the ARP Request even though the target IP address in the ARP packet is that of Station X. From this point on, Station A believes that it has contacted Station X and will now send data to the router in the belief that it is performing direct routing. The router will, on reception of the packets, forward the data to Station X in the normal way. Thus Indirect Routing is taking place without the need to configure either a Subnet Mask or a Default Gateway.[4]

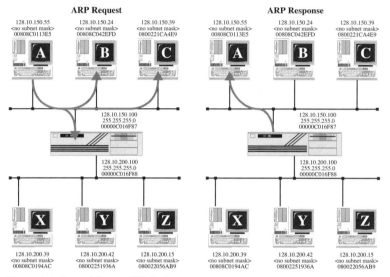

Figure 9-7: Typical Proxy ARP Exchange

The complete exchange may now look as follows:

- Station A wishes to communicate with Station X. Station A will create an ARP packet with the following information:

Hardware Type	0001	Ethernet
Protocol Requesting Resolution	0800	IP
Hardware Address Length	06	48 bit MAC Address
Protocol Address Length	04	32 bit IP Address
Operation Code	0001	ARP Request
Hardware Address of Sending Station	00808C0113E5	MAC Address of Station A
IP Address of Sending Station	800A9637	IP Address of A (128.10.150.55)
Hardware Address of Target Station	000000000000	Null string – purpose of request
IP Address of Target Station	800AC827	IP Address of X (128.10.200.39)

- The Router will respond with:

Hardware Type	0001	Ethernet
Protocol Requesting Resolution	0800	IP
Hardware Address Length	06	48 bit MAC Address
Protocol Address Length	04	32 bit IP Address
Operation Code	0002	ARP Response

4. The concept of *Default Gateways* are discussed in Chapter 4.

Hardware Address of Sending Station	00000C016F87	MAC Address of Router Port
IP Address of Sending Station	800AC827	IP Address of X (128.10.200.39)
Hardware Address of Target Station	00808C0113E5	MAC Address of Station A
IP Address of Target Station	800A9637	IP Address of A (128.10.150.55)

9.4 Summary

So far we have considered the mechanics of routing. Routers can be configured with a series of *Static routes* (sometimes known as *fixed routing*) where, in these cases, the routers are programmed with all of the information required to deliver packets to the desired destination. While this is sufficient for small static networks, no account can be made for changes that may occur, a link failing, a new route becoming available etc. without operator intervention. *Adaptive routing* through the use of routing protocols is therefore more common in most networks. In addition, we have seen that where we wish to join a large backbone network, it would be impracticle to hold information about every network. Thus, in these cases a *default route* is used to direct packets to a specific router where we have no other, or better, information.

In the next chapters we shall examine the way that routers exchange network reachability information through various routing protocols. Specifically, we will look at the Routing Information Protocol (RIP), the Open Shortest Path First (OSPF) protocol, the Exterior Gateway Protocol (EGP), and the Border Gateway Protocol (BGP). With these protocols our internets become adaptive and less reliant upon operators and network administrators. In truth, all but the smallest of newtorks use routing protocols and this then allows our routers to make better decisions as to how data should be routed.

The Routing Information Protocol (RIP)

RFC 1058, upon which the Routing Information Protocol (RIP) is based, tells us that "*Routing is the task of finding a path from a sender to a desired destination.*" In fact, we should say that routing is the task of finding the *best* path from a sender to a destination, since multiple paths could and often do exist. The Routing Information Protocol then, provides us with one of a series of standardized protocols designed to make the task of routing adaptive. That is one where routers will respond to changes in network topology when they occur. When routing is adaptive in this way, a change in network topology detected by one router will be advertised to all other routers in the internet. In this way, operator intervention is reduced, and overall network uptime is increased.

RIP is designed to be used as what is called an *Interior Gateway Protocol* (IGP), a routing protocol that is used within an autonomous system (an internetwork controlled by a single administrative or technical authority). While the size of autonomous systems that use RIP must be modest (no more than 15 intervening networks between the source and the destination), RIP provides a robust protocol that has now become a de-facto standard for the exchange of routing information among routers and hosts. Where we wish to link these autonomous systems together, as in a nation-wide (or even global) network, these are then linked via Exterior Gateway Protocols (EGPs), such as the *Exterior Gateway Protocol*, or the *Border Gateway Protocol* (BGP).

The Routing Information Protocol is based upon the *routed* program that was originally distributed with the 4.3 Berkeley Software Distribution making it a widely accepted and implemented protocol for use within IP internets. Most Router vendors support RIP however, some vendors have taken RIP as a basis and then added their own proprietary enhancements making inter-operability impossible. Equally, although originally intended for use with IP, RIP is a general purpose protocol and has now been adopted to work with a number of other protocols such as Novell's IPX.

10.1 Gauging Route Quality

Since the purpose of RIP is to find the best route between a source and destination, we must have some means of gauging just how good a particular route is. RIP is based upon the *Bellman-Ford*, *distance-vector* algorithm that simply counts the number of *network hops* (the number of networks that must be traversed) between the source and destination. This hop count is also referred to as the *metric*. RIP therefore should not be used when real-time parameters such as measured delay, load, or reliability are to be considered in determining best routes.

Where multiple routes exist to the destination, the one that has the fewest hops (the smallest metric) is the one that is chosen. From the previous discussion, selection of routes based purely upon the number of networks traversed does not necessarily provide us with the optimum route as Figure 10-1 shows. In this figure, we see that two distinct routes exist between the source and destination networks. The route on the right traverses a single, slow, serial link while that on the left, two fast serial links and a fast LAN. With RIP, faced with a routing decision such as this, the route to the right would be chosen although patently this is not the best route.

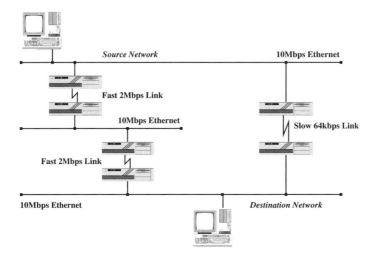

Figure 10-1: Routing Metrics

We also have to place an upper bound as to the number of networks that may be traversed, since failure to do so could result in an infinite network path. With RIP, this limit is 15. Indeed, a metric of 16 (normally referred to as infinity) is taken to mean *network unreachable*. We should note here that this assumes traversal of a network has an associated *cost* (metric) of 1, the normal way in which RIP is configured. Where we wish to administratively define best routes, we are normally able to do this by assigning a higher cost to least attractive routes. Here however, our 15 hop limit may well become a problem. Figure 10-2 shows a simple, although possibly not practical, example of this scenario.

In this example then, we see that by assigning a metric of 7 to each of the WAN links, a total metric of 16 exists between the source and destination networks using the left hand route. Since this value is out of the allowable range for RIP, the left hand route cannot be our favored route. Most importantly however, if the link on the right hand side of the figure should fail, the left hand route still cannot be used, rendering the destination network unreachable as far as stations on the source network are concerned.

The Routing Information Protocol (RIP)

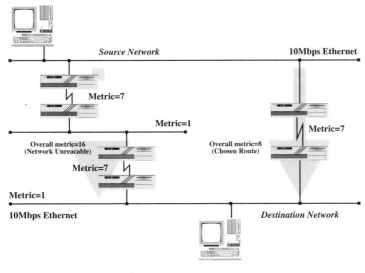

Figure 10-2: Assigning Higher Metrics

10.2 Protocol Operation

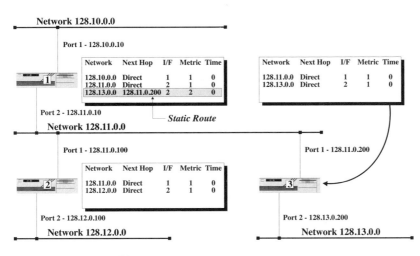

Figure 10-3: Routing Tables at Start-up

At start-up, routers will have limited information available. They will of course know the addresses of their interfaces, and they may also be pre-configured with *static* routes. This information is held in tables called *routing tables,* and is shown in Figure 10-3. In addition to network reachability information (the network ID, and the metric), the routing table also holds other, vital information. This additional information includes, to how to get to the destination network (Next Hop), the interface through which packets must pass (I/F), and a timer indicating how old the entry is. The timer itself is key to the operation of the protocol and will be discussed shortly however, in our example overleaf, a value of zero is taken to mean that the entry will not be aged out.

As you will see from Figure 10-3, we have three routers interconnecting four networks. In the figure, each routing table contains the directly connected networks of the router, and router 1 has a static route to network 128.13.0.0. Router 2 has no knowledge of networks 128.13.0.0, or 128.10.0.0, and equally, router 3 has no knowledge of networks 128.10.0.0 or 128.12.0.0. Finally, in our example each network represents a cost (metric) of 1.

With RIP, routers exchange information with their neighbors. Where a router is connected to a broadcast network (such as Ethernet), this exchange is performed through a broadcast frame. Where we have non-broadcast networks (such as X.25), either exchanges take place between *pre-configured* neighbors, or static routes are used instead.

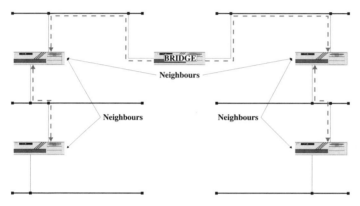

Figure 10-4: RIP Neighbour Routers

From Figure 10-4, you will notice that the two upper routers are considered neighbors since the networks on their uppermost ports are connected via a bridge. Since routers do not pass broadcast frames, updates from one router cannot automatically be propagated throughout the entire internetwork. A bridge, being a Layer 2 device however, is transparent to the routers and will pass broadcast update frames. Thus, the updates between the two upper routers will be passed, allowing them to consider each other neighbors. Periodically, routers broadcast routing updates to each of their neighbors. The update itself is a set of messages[1] containing an entry for each destination in the routing table, and its associated metric. If we now return to our example of Figure 10-3, we see in Figure 10-5 the state of the routing tables after the initial RIP updates have taken place, and the network is stable.

1. The Routing update may comprise a number of messages due to limitations of network MTU. In general, the larger the routing table is, the more messages will be required.

The Routing Information Protocol (RIP)

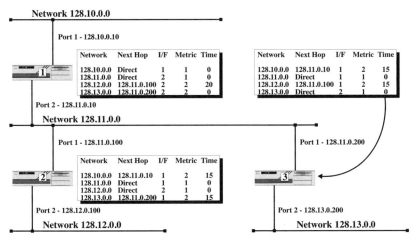

Network 128.10.0.0

Port 1 - 128.10.0.10

Network	Next Hop	I/F	Metric	Time
128.10.0.0	Direct	1	1	0
128.11.0.0	Direct	2	1	0
128.12.0.0	128.11.0.100	2	2	20
128.13.0.0	128.11.0.200	2	2	0

Network	Next Hop	I/F	Metric	Time
128.10.0.0	128.11.0.10	1	2	15
128.11.0.0	Direct	1	1	0
128.12.0.0	128.11.0.100	1	2	15
128.13.0.0	Direct	2	1	0

Port 2 - 128.11.0.10

Network 128.11.0.0

Port 1 - 128.11.0.100   Port 1 - 128.11.0.200

Network	Next Hop	I/F	Metric	Time
128.10.0.0	128.11.0.10	1	2	15
128.11.0.0	Direct	1	1	0
128.12.0.0	Direct	2	1	0
128.13.0.0	128.11.0.200	1	2	15

Port 2 - 128.12.0.100   Port 2 - 128.13.0.200

Network 128.12.0.0   Network 128.13.0.0

Figure 10-5: Routing Tables with Network Stability

Routing advertisements contain the contents of the routers routing table. Looking now from the perspective of a router receiving an update from its neighbor, we shall examine how routes are actually selected. When an update is received from a neighbor, the cost of the network over which the update was received is added to the advertised metric, and this new value is then used when comparing routes. Obviously if we have no prior knowledge of the advertised network, the information is stored immediately. If the advertised network is already known to us, then the metric (cost) of the existing route is compared with the metric associated with the route received. Where the cost is lower, the new route is adopted immediately. Where the router advertising the network is the same as that which originally provided it, the route is adopted even where the metric is larger.

10.2.1 Handling Topology Changes

So, by periodically broadcasting the contents of the routing tables over the router interfaces, do we achieve a stable network in a timely manner as we have shown above, or are there other factors to be considered? Certainly in real networks, although it is hoped that the topology remains stable over long periods of time, routers and links do fail causing topology changes. With routing algorithms therefore, the ability to time-out failed routes is crucial to the convergence[2] of the network, and it is for this reason that the routing tables contain a *time-to-live* value for each entry. In RIP, each router typically sends a routing table update every 30 seconds. Therefore a router, detecting that a link has failed, can inform its neighbors. Equally, if a router fails, its neighbors will not receive a routing update from it, and will therefore assume that either the router or an interconnecting link has failed. Unfortunately, it is possible for packets to be lost on networks. Thus, just because we have not heard from a neighboring router for 30 seconds, does not necessarily

2. A network is said to converge when a stable topology is achieved.

mean that it is down. In order to be sure then, we typically wait for between three and six update times before marking the route as invalid, a long time in networking terms.

To discuss this further, we must now consider the slightly more complex network comprising four routers, and six networks, shown in Figure 10-6.

Notice in the figure that each network has an associated cost of 1, except for the network that joins routers 3, and 4. If we now consider the state of the routing tables with reference to the *Target Network*, we see the following:

Table 10-1: Routing Table for Each Router

Router	Route via	Metric
1	Router 2	3
2	Router 4	2
3	Router 2	3
4	Direct Connection	1

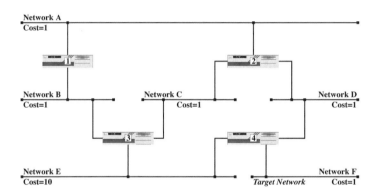

Figure 10-6: Handling Topology Changes

Next we shall consider what happens if the connection between router 2, and 4 (Network D) fails. Obviously a path does exist (albeit high cost) over Network E. However, it will take time for the routing tables to stabilize and the overall network topology to converge.

Router 2 will determine that the route to router 4 is no longer available and, via the timeout mechanism, will inform routers 1, and 3 in its next update. In turn, the other routers will send updates that will eventually result in the network finally stabilizing again. Routers, we have said, advertise their routing tables to their neighbors. Therefore, router 3 will have been advertising to routers 1, 2, and 4 that it also has a route (without using network E) to the target network (although this was through router 2). Likewise, router 1 will have been advertising a route to the target network to routers 2, and 3 (again, in reality this was also through router 2). When router 2 times out its route then, it will believe that a route exists via router 1, or 3.

Of course, the routes advertised by routers 1, and 3 no longer exist, and even when they discover this fact they will still initially believe that the other has a valid

The Routing Information Protocol (RIP)

route. Thus, since the failed route is not cleared throughout the network immediately, we have to go through several iterations of updates to achieve stability. In this way, routers 1, 2, and 3 are involved in a *mutual deception*, with each claiming that it has a route that actually no longer exists. Table 10-2 shows the initial state, and a number of iterations of routing table updates with respect to the Target Network for each router with respect to time. Here we have also assumed that each router sends its updates at the same time to make the example simpler.

Table 10-2: Acheiving Convergence

							TIME >						
	Initial State		*Iteration 1*		*Iteration 2*		*Iteration 3*		......	*Iteration 8*		*Iteration 9*	
Router	*via*	*metric*	*via*	*metric*	*via*	*metric*	*via*	*metric*	......	*via*	*metric*	*via*	*metric*
1	2	3	3	4	3	5	3	6	......	3	11	3	12
2	N/A	----	3	4	3	5	3	6	......	3	11	3	12
3	2	3	1	4	1	5	1	6	......	1	11	4	11
4	Direct	1	Direct	1	Direct	1	Direct	1	......	Direct	1	Direct	1

As you will see, we may have to wait a long time for network stability with the scenario outlined above. Indeed at worst, when a network becomes completely isolated from another part of the system, we may have to *count to infinity*. Figure 10-7 shows how this may occur:

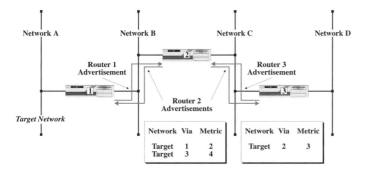

Figure 10-7: Counting to Infinity

Here, we shall assume that the cost of each network is 1, and that the topology is stable. In this case, the routing tables of routers 2, and 3 with respect to the target network will look like those shown in the figure. But what happens if router 1 fails? Router 2 will time out the route to the target network via router 1, and advertise the route via router 3. In turn, router 3 will advertise to router 2 that it has a route to the target network but that the metric is higher. Since it was router 3 that originally advertised this route, from our previous discussion, it must be adopted. Router 2 now advertises to router 3 again (but now with a higher metric) and so on. Eventually the metric reaches 16 (our *infinite* value), and the route is marked as invalid. This phenomenon is termed *counting to infinity*, and it for this reason that the overall diameter of the network (the number of hops) must be kept small.

10.2.2 Split Horizon

It should now be apparent that we must have a method of limiting RIP adver-tisements so that routers do not deceive each other in the way outlined above. A simple method of achieving this is to employ the principle known as *Simple Split Horizon*, where routers do not advertise routes on the interface over which they were learnt. Thus, in our example above, Router 1 will advertise a route to the target network to router 2. In turn, router 2 will advertise this route to router 3. Router 3 will not however advertise this route back to router 2 thereby limiting the possibility of deception.

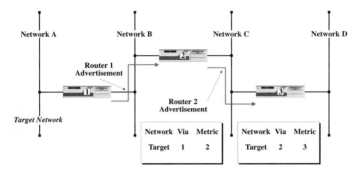

Figure 10-8: Simple Split Horizon

10.2.3 Poison Reverse

Poison Reverse is the process whereby routes that involve a measure of deception are advertised but *poisoned* with a metric of infinity (16). *Poison Reverse*, as it is normally implemented, involves routers advertising routes over the interfaces on which they were learnt, but indicating that the network is unreachable; i.e. with a metric of 16. For a point-to-point network, as we saw in the previous example, simply not advertising a reverse route immediately breaks routing loops. But what happens when there are other routers connected to the shared network? Here, more than two routers are involved in the loop, thus complicating routing updates.

Consider Figure 10-9 where, once again, the cost of each network is 1:

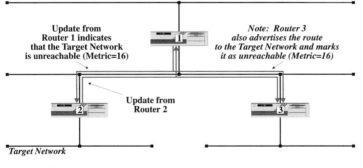

Figure 10-9: Poison Reverse

In this example, router 2 advertises that it can reach the Target Network with an associated cost of 1. Routers 1, and 3, update their routing tables indicating that the Target Network is reachable (via router 2), with a metric of 2. Routers 1, and 3 now advertise the route to the Target Network, but mark it as unreachable. If router 1 has a route through router 2, it should mark the route as unreachable whenever talking to other routers. After all, router 3 can reach router 2 by itself, and it would never have to route traffic destined for the Target Network via router 1.

Poison Reverse does have one major drawback, in that it makes the size of routing tables, and therefore routing updates, considerably larger. With Poison Reverse, routers must advertise both valid routes, and also routes that should not go via the router. So, if we have a large, Star topology network as shown in Figure 10-10, we may pass very large routing updates that consist mainly of routes that should not pass through the advertising router. This could be seen as making extremely inefficient use of available bandwidth. This figure shows such an example, where each of the *branch routers* (routers 1 to 8), advertise a valid route to their local network, and then advertise each of the other seven networks as being unreachable. An overhead of seven to one!

So what does Poison Reverse actually give us? Certainly where routes are static, we might argue that Poison Reverse is an overhead that we can ill afford. However, where routes fail, it is useful to mention routes that should not go through the router as well as those that should. In this way, routes that become unusable, will be eliminated immediately rather than waiting for them to be timed out, and thus may speed convergence. Generally, network administrators must weigh the cost of extra bandwidth against convergence speed in an effort to maximize overall network performance.

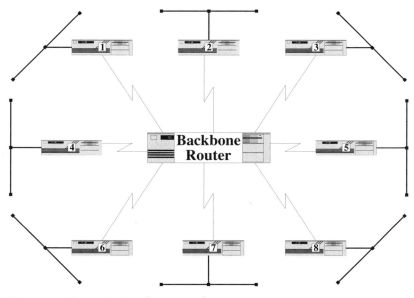

Figure 10-10: Large, Star Topology Network

10.2.4 Triggered Updates

Split Horizon and Poison Reverse attempt to resolve routing problems that involve two routers in a pattern of mutual deception. But what happens where there are three (or more) routers involved in such a pattern? For example, if we have three routers (routers 1, 2, and 3) and the network is constructed so that router 1 believes that it has a route via router 2, router 2 believes that the route is via router 3, and router 3 believes that the route is via router 1? Neither Split Horizon, nor Poison Reverse will overcome this problem, so we must find another way.

Triggered Updates attempt to break this loop by changing the rules regarding when updates actually occur. We have said that RIP uses a timed update method whereby routers advertise their entire routing table to their neighbors at regular intervals. When Triggered Updates are implemented, each time that a router changes a metric for a stored route (or receives information regarding a route to a new network), it sends an update immediately. These Triggered Updates are sent even if the router has an standard update pending, or if it has just sent such an update. In this way dynamic behaviour is generally improved.

We cannot guarantee that by using Triggered Updates, failed routes will be removed immediately. Since each router will send its standard updates at a different time, while a set of Triggered Updates are percolating through the system, standard updates will also be occurring. Therefore, it is possible that after a router has received a Triggered Update from a neighbor, it might then receive a normal update from elsewhere that revives the route.

10.2.5 Route States and Timers

Generally RIP updates are sent every 30 seconds. Where we have many routers sharing a broadcast network there is a possibility that, due to processing loads, these updates could synchronize over a period of time. This would result in all of the routers sending their updates at the same time, a scenario undesirable at the best of times. However, since RIP uses broadcasts to advertise its routes, it is even more so. To overcome this situation, implementations generally employ a method of timing that requires the router to add a small, random, amount of time to the 30 second update interval, or use a clock source unaffected by router loading.

In addition to the 30 second update timer, RIP also has two timers associated with each route. Firstly a timer (typically three to six update times) is used to *time-out* routes for which no update has been received. This timer is initialized each time an update for the route is received. On the expiration of this timer (i.e. if we have received no information about it for 180 seconds), the route is declared invalid but is not removed immediately. Instead, the route is retained in the routing table and marked as invalid by associating a metric of 16 with it. Of course, since a material change has occurred in the routing table, a triggered update would be initiated if these were used. Routes marked in this way are also included in regular updates, since this continues to inform neighboring routers that the route should no longer be used.

When a route is timed out, a second timer, the so called *Garbage Collection* timer, is started. This timer is normally set to the equivalent of four update times (120 seconds) and, on its expiration, the route is removed from the routing table.

Once a route is removed from the routing table, it is no longer included in any updates. Thus, whilst the Garbage Collection timer is running, this is considered the final phase of the routes life. Should an update for this route be received during this time, the timer is cleared and the route re-instated. Equally, if a new route for this network is received while the *Garbage Collection* timer is running, the new route will replace the existing one, and the timer will again be cleared. As before, the re-instatement of the route, or the reception of a new route to the network in question, would cause a triggered update to be sent to the neighboring routers.

10.3 RIP Protocol Format and Operation

RIP travels encapsulated in UDP datagrams, and uses the UDP port 520_{10}. All updates are both sent, and received over this port resulting in port 520 being used as both the source and destination ports of the UDP header when regular, *timed*, updates are sent. Although most updates are unsolicited, as we shall see later in this section, RIP also supports a *query/response* mechanism where a station can request an update from a router. In this case, the requesting station will generate a request from some arbitrary UDP port, but the response will always be returned to UDP port 520 on the requesting machine.

The actual protocol format, as shown in Figure 10-11, includes information about networks, and the distance to them (the metric). Update messages can be up to 512 octets in length thus, for large updates, multiple UDP datagrams may be required. You will notice that there are no flags indicating partial information. However, although we would not make best use of network bandwidth, in theory routes could be handled singly with no problems. From the figure, you will see that each route requires 20 octets and, since we have a 4 octet fixed header, we are able to carry information regarding 25 routes in each datagram.

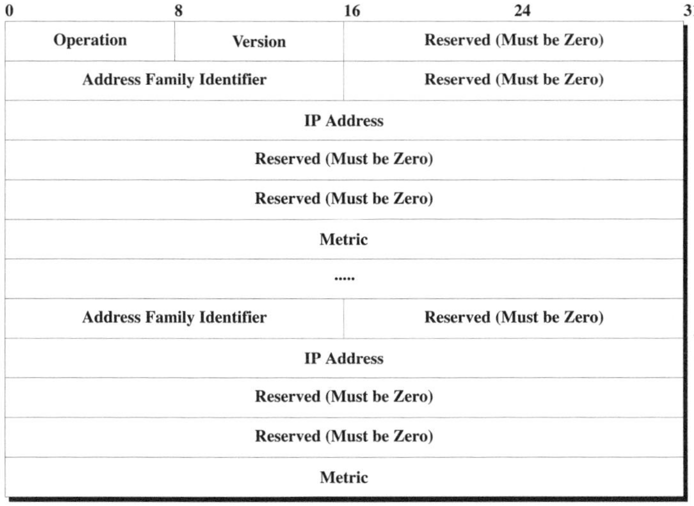

0	8	16	24	31
Operation	Version	Reserved (Must be Zero)		
Address Family Identifier		Reserved (Must be Zero)		
IP Address				
Reserved (Must be Zero)				
Reserved (Must be Zero)				
Metric				
.....				
Address Family Identifier		Reserved (Must be Zero)		
IP Address				
Reserved (Must be Zero)				
Reserved (Must be Zero)				
Metric				

Figure 10-11: RIP Protocol Format

You will see from Figure 10-11 that each route entry has an *Address Family Identifier* used to identify the format of the route itself. For IP this value is 2, however RIP is a general purpose routing protocol that can, and is, used for protocols other than IP. As such, each route entry allows for addresses of up to 12 octets in length, and uses the *Address Family Identifier* to indicate the actual address type. Obviously for routes to IP networks, only four octets are used, leaving the remaining eight octets reserved as indicated.

The one octet *Operation* field identifies the type of operation being performed. There are five such operations of which only two are currently valid. Table 10-3 lists possible operation type codes.

Table 10-3: RIP Operation Codes

Code	Meaning	Description
1	Request	Requests that the router sends all or part of its routing table.
2	Response	This is a message that contains all or part of the routers routing table. This type of message is sent either in response to a request, or as a normal timed update.
3	Trace On	Obsolete function. Any datagrams containing this operation are ignored.
4	Trace Off	Obsolete function. Any datagrams containing this operation are ignored.
5	Reserved	Reserved for Sun Microsystems for internal use. Messages containing this operation code are ignored by other systems.

The *Version* field is interpreted as follows:

Any datagram with a version number of zero is discarded without further processing. Datagrams that have a version number of 1, are discarded if any of the *Must be Zero* fields contain a non-zero value. If the version number is greater than 1, the datagram will not be discarded. Instead, route entries that can be correctly interpreted are still processed. Thus, any future enhancements to the protocol[3] should be fully backward compatible.

If the message is a *Request* type, this indicates that a device is being asked to supply all or part of its routing table. Requests are normally sent as broadcasts from UDP port 520 however it is possible to send such requests from any source port. Where the source port is 520, only those hosts actively participating in RIP will respond.[4] Where the source port is anything other than 520, all RIP processes receiving the request will respond, a feature extremely useful for management purposes.

When a request is received, the entries contained in the datagram are processed sequentially. If there is only a single entry with an *Address Family Identifier* of zero (meaning unspecified) and a metric of 16 (infinity), the entire routing table is returned.[5] Where there are between 1 and 25 entries, each entry is compared with the routing table and, if a route exists, that route's metric is placed in the metric field. Where there is no route to the destination network, a metric of 16 (infinity)

3. See the discussion on RIP II (RFC 1723) in section 10.5.
4. Many end stations are passive, RIP listeners. In these cases the end station acts promiscuously listening to RIP activity and amends its routing tables accordingly. These devices do not however send routing updates to neighboring hosts.
5. This is obviously subject to the restrictions regarding Source Port mentioned earlier.

is used. Once information regarding each of the requested routes has been updated, the *Operation* field is changed to *Response*, and the datagram is returned to the requesting station. The UDP Source Port used in the original request is of course then used as the Destination Port in the returned datagram. Finally, if there are no entries in the request, it is ignored and no response is generated.

Typically, where a complete routing table is requested, Split Horizon rules will be applied. Where specific routes are requested, no Split Horizon is used and the information contained in the routing table is used directly. The rationale behind this, is that if information is being specifically requested, the requester is assumed to want to know exact details and would therefore not wish anything to be hidden.

10.3.1 RIP Datagram Processing

A *Response* is generated, and therefore received, as either a response to a specific *Request*, a regular Update, or a Triggered update resulting from a metric change being detected elsewhere in the network. *Response* datagrams received from ports other than 520 are ignored by receiving stations. Where the *Response* is valid, each entry is examined and the receiver's routing tables are updated according to the flow chart shown in Figure 10-12.

As you will see in the figure, processing of the incoming datagram is aborted if the Source UDP Port is anything other than 520. Where the datagram is valid, processing of route entries then progresses sequentially through the datagram with routes containing invalid Address Family Identifiers being ignored. A route entry could contain either the address of a distant network, or an end system. RIP makes no distinction between these and also has no way of communicating Subnet Mask information. Thus, in internets using the RIP protocol, each network is assumed to use the same mask value.

The metric is updated such that the new value is the advertised metric plus the cost associated with the network over which the response was received. In practice, the cost associated with networks is generally assumed to be 1, thereby gently incrementing the metric each time that the route is advertised to successive routers throughout the internet. An exception to this, is where the advertised metric is 16 (infinity). In this case, there is no point in incrementing the value since the network is already unreachable.

Where we do not already have a route to the advertised network in the routing table, we learn it from the update. An exception to this is where the advertised metric is infinity since there is no point in learning about routes to unreachable networks. Assuming that the route is valid, and that we already have a route to the destination, we test whether this advertisement came from the router that originally provided the route. In fact, all routes contained in this update will have originated from the same neighboring router, therefore whether we make this test here or at some other point is broadly irrelevant. What is important however, is that we will only adopt new routes to existing destinations where they are *better* than those that we are already aware of, or where the new route (even if it is worse) is advertised by the original router. Where we receive an update that contains a route to an existing destination and is no better than the route we already have, we will use the oldest route (i.e. that which was learnt first). Thus, where an existing route is advertised by the same router from which we originally learnt it, we will adopt that route regardless.

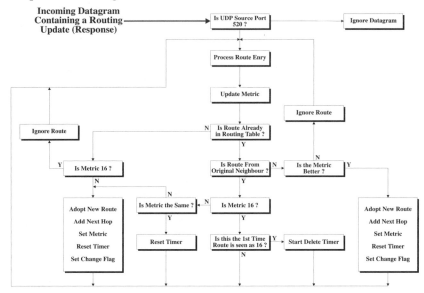

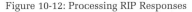

Figure 10-12: Processing RIP Responses

If the route is from the router that originally supplied the route and has the same metric, we merely reset the timer indicating that the route is still valid. Where we learn a route to a new destination, or where the metric for an existing route changes, you will see that we also set a *change flag* to indicate that we must send a *triggered update*. When an existing route becomes unreachable, we start a delete timer that will eventually lead to the route being deleted. Here, although not shown, we would also set the *change flag* to indicate that we must send an update to inform our neighbors of the changed route status.

Where a route does become invalid, you will see that we test to see whether this is the first time the route has been flagged as unreachable, and thus only start the delete timer once. This is important, since it is likely that we shall receive updates from other sources telling us that the destination has become unreachable. After all, we do not wish to reset this timer each time we receive such an update, as this would mean that the route would potentially never be timed out.

To examine RIP operation in detail, let us consider the network in Figure 10-13.

From this network we have taken three traces. In the first trace (Figure 10-14) the analyser was positioned on network 172.17.0.0 and views network traffic while router 4 is power cycled. In this trace, we begin by seeing Router 2 advertise that routes to networks 172.19.0.0 and beyond are unreachable. As Router 4 returns to its operational state, we then see all routes re-appear in the routing updates.

The second trace (Figure 10-15) shows the exchanges taking place between Routers 3 and 4 across network 172.18.0.0. This trace is significant since it shows Poison Reverse in operation. Both routers (3 and 4) are providing Poisoned updates so both are poisoning those routes that were learnt over network 172.18.0.0.

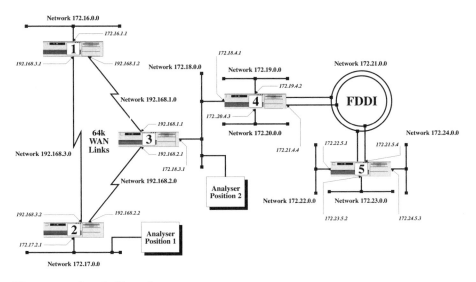

Figure 10-13: Sample Network

In the final trace (Figure 10-16) shows the effects of running a mixed Split Horizon/Poison Reverse environment. In this example, Router 3 is running Poison Reverse, while Router 4 is running Split Horizon. Here, the size of routing updates is significant since those originating from Router 4 are 100 octets smaller (5 routes are not advertised).

```
μSCOPE                  PACKET TRACE DECODE REPORT           (c) T.Kenyon 1995


=========================μscope=========================================
Frame     : 1              Len     : 270           Error    : None
T Elapsed: 18:54:38:999    T Delta : 00:03:17:879
-----------------------------[mac]-------------------------------------
Dest Mac : ffffffffffff   Sourc Mac: Xyplex123e66   Type     : IP
-----------------------------[ip]--------------------------------------
IP Ver    : 4              IP HLen : 20 Bytes
TOS       : 0x00           Pkt Len : 252            Seg ID   : 0x0046
Flags     : FRAG:*.LAST    Frag Ptr : 0      (8 Octet)  TTL   : 64
PID       : UDP  ( 17)     Checksum : 0xcb99 (Good)
Dst IP    : 255.255.255.255  Src IP <B: 172.17.2.1
-----------------------------[udp]-------------------------------------
Dest Port: RIP [   520]              Src Port : RIP [   520]
Length    : 232                      Checksum : 0x0000 (NoCheck)
-----------------------------[rip]-------------------------------------
Command   : RESPonse       Version : 1             Reserved : 00
-----------------------------[routes: 11]------------------------------
Family: 2  {172. 16.  0.  0} Hops: 2    Family: 2  {172. 18.  0.  0} Hops: 2
Family: 2  {172. 19.  0.  0} Hops: 16   Family: 2  {172. 20.  0.  0} Hops: 16
Family: 2  {172. 21.  0.  0} Hops: 16   Family: 2  {172. 22.  0.  0} Hops: 16
Family: 2  {172. 23.  0.  0} Hops: 16   Family: 2  {172. 24.  0.  0} Hops: 16
Family: 2  {192.168.  1.  0} Hops: 2    Family: 2  {192.168.  2.  0} Hops: 1
Family: 2  {192.168.  3.  0} Hops: 1
===========================[data:    4]================================
010A  A2 A4 14 27                       ...'
```

Routing Update (Response) from Router 2 (IP Address 172.17.2.1).

Router 2 does not advertise a route to Network 172.17.0.0 on this interface since this update originates from interface 172.17.2.1.

Router 4 is off-line and the routes that it was advertising have timed-out. Thus, routes to networks 172.19.0.0 and beyond are marked as unreachable.

```
===============================µscope==================================
Frame    : 2              Len     : 150           Error    : None
T Elapsed: 18:55:09:596   T Delta : 00:00:30:597
-------------------------------[mac]-----------------------------------
Dest Mac : ffffffffffff   Sourc Mac: Xyplex123e66    Type     : IP
-------------------------------[ip]------------------------------------
IP Ver   : 4              IP HLen  : 20 Bytes
TOS      : 0x00           Pkt Len  : 132           Seg ID   : 0x0049
Flags    : FRAG:*.LAST    Frag Ptr : 0     (8 Octet)  TTL      : 64
PID      : UDP  ( 17)     Checksum : 0xcc0e (Good)
Dst IP   : 255.255.255.255  Src IP <B: 172.17.2.1
-------------------------------[udp]-----------------------------------
Dest Port: RIP [   520]              Src Port : RIP [   520]
Length   : 112                       Checksum : 0x0000 (NoCheck)
-------------------------------[rip]-----------------------------------
Command  : RESPonse       Version  : 1            Reserved : 00
-----------------------------[routes:   5]----------------------------
Family: 2 {172. 16.  0.  0} Hops: 2  Family: 2 {172. 18.  0.  0} Hops: 2
Family: 2 {192.168.  1.  0} Hops: 2  Family: 2 {192.168.  2.  0} Hops: 1
Family: 2 {192.168.  3.  0} Hops: 1
============================[data:   4]===============================
0092   A9 EA DE A2                          ....
```

```
===============================µscope==================================
Frame    : 3              Len     : 150           Error    : None
T Elapsed: 18:55:40:197   T Delta : 00:00:30:601
-------------------------------[mac]-----------------------------------
Dest Mac : ffffffffffff   Sourc Mac: Xyplex123e66    Type     : IP
-------------------------------[ip]------------------------------------
IP Ver   : 4              IP HLen  : 20 Bytes
TOS      : 0x00           Pkt Len  : 132           Seg ID   : 0x004c
Flags    : FRAG:*.LAST    Frag Ptr : 0     (8 Octet)  TTL      : 64
PID      : UDP  ( 17)     Checksum : 0xcc0b (Good)
Dst IP   : 255.255.255.255  Src IP <B: 172.17.2.1
-------------------------------[udp]-----------------------------------
Dest Port: RIP [   520]              Src Port : RIP [   520]
Length   : 112                       Checksum : 0x0000 (NoCheck)
-------------------------------[rip]-----------------------------------
Command  : RESPonse       Version  : 1            Reserved : 00
-----------------------------[routes:   5]----------------------------
Family: 2 {172. 16.  0.  0} Hops: 2  Family: 2 {172. 18.  0.  0} Hops: 2
Family: 2 {192.168.  1.  0} Hops: 2  Family: 2 {192.168.  2.  0} Hops: 1
Family: 2 {192.168.  3.  0} Hops: 1
============================[data:   4]===============================
0092   98 6A AC F2                          .j..
```

*Frames 4 and 5 Removed
Similar to Frame 3*

```
===============================µscope==================================
Frame    : 6              Len     : 270           Error    : None
T Elapsed: 18:56:55:678   T Delta : 00:00:30:598
-------------------------------[mac]-----------------------------------
Dest Mac : ffffffffffff   Sourc Mac: Xyplex123e66    Type     : IP
-------------------------------[ip]------------------------------------
IP Ver   : 4              IP HLen  : 20 Bytes
TOS      : 0x00           Pkt Len  : 252           Seg ID   : 0x0056
Flags    : FRAG:*.LAST    Frag Ptr : 0     (8 Octet)  TTL      : 64
PID      : UDP  ( 17)     Checksum : 0xcb89 (Good)
Dst IP   : 255.255.255.255  Src IP <B: 172.17.2.1
-------------------------------[udp]-----------------------------------
Dest Port: RIP [   520]              Src Port : RIP [   520]
Length   : 232                       Checksum : 0x0000 (NoCheck)
-------------------------------[rip]-----------------------------------
Command  : RESPonse       Version  : 1            Reserved : 00
-----------------------------[routes:  11]----------------------------
Family: 2 {172. 16.  0.  0} Hops: 2  Family: 2 {172. 18.  0.  0} Hops: 2
Family: 2 {172. 19.  0.  0} Hops: 3  Family: 2 {172. 20.  0.  0} Hops: 3
Family: 2 {172. 21.  0.  0} Hops: 3  Family: 2 {172. 22.  0.  0} Hops: 4
Family: 2 {172. 23.  0.  0} Hops: 4  Family: 2 {172. 24.  0.  0} Hops: 4
Family: 2 {192.168.  1.  0} Hops: 2  Family: 2 {192.168.  2.  0} Hops: 1
Family: 2 {192.168.  3.  0} Hops: 1
============================[data:   4]===============================
010A   D8 DB 52 42                          ..RB
```

Figure 10-14: Trace Showing Update Traffic on Network 172.17.0.0

The Routing Information Protocol (RIP)

```
====================================μscope==========================================
Frame     : 1              Len      : 270           Error     : None
T Elapsed: 18:59:18:536    T Delta  : 00:02:04:114
---------------------------------[mac]----------------------------------------------
Dest Mac : ffffffffffff    Sourc Mac: Xyplex156806  Type      : IP
----------------------------------[ip]----------------------------------------------
IP Ver   : 4               IP HLen  : 20 Bytes
TOS      : 0x00            Pkt Len  : 252            Seg ID    : 0x0024
Flags    : FRAG:*.LAST     Frag Ptr : 0    (8 Octet) TTL       : 64
PID      : UDP  ( 17)      Checksum : 0xc9ba (Good)
Dst IP   : 255.255.255.255 Src IP <B: 172.18.4.1
---------------------------------[udp]----------------------------------------------
Dest Port: RIP [  520]                 Src Port : RIP [  520]
Length   : 232                         Checksum : 0x0000 (NoCheck)
---------------------------------[rip]----------------------------------------------
Command  : RESPonse        Version  : 1             Reserved : 00
-------------------------------[routes: 11]----------------------------------------
Family: 2  {172. 16.  0.  0} Hops: 16   Family: 2  {172. 17.  0.  0} Hops: 16
Family: 2  {172. 19.  0.  0} Hops: 1    Family: 2  {172. 20.  0.  0} Hops: 1
Family: 2  {172. 21.  0.  0} Hops: 1    Family: 2  {172. 22.  0.  0} Hops: 2
Family: 2  {172. 23.  0.  0} Hops: 2    Family: 2  {172. 24.  0.  0} Hops: 2
Family: 2  {192.168.  1.  0} Hops: 16   Family: 2  {192.168.  2.  0} Hops: 16
Family: 2  {192.168.  3.  0} Hops: 16
==============================[data:    4]==========================================
010A  30 E2 BB 8C                                0...
```

Router 4 (IP Address 172.18.4.1) advertises its routing table indicating that it has routes to networks 172.19.0.0, 172.20.0.0, 172.21.0.0, 172.22.0.0, 172.23.0.0, and 172.24.0.0. Since it would have learnt about networks 172.16.0.0, 172.17.0.0, 192.168.1.0, 192.168.2.0, and 192.168.3.0 over this interface, the metrics for these networks are set to infinity. As before, since this advertisement originates on network 172.18.0.0, this network is not advertised at all.

```
====================================μscope==========================================
Frame     : 2              Len      : 270           Error     : None
T Elapsed: 18:59:20:245    T Delta  : 00:00:01:709
---------------------------------[mac]----------------------------------------------
Dest Mac : ffffffffffff    Sourc Mac: Xyplex135b7e  Type      : IP
----------------------------------[ip]----------------------------------------------
IP Ver   : 4               IP HLen  : 20 Bytes
TOS      : 0x00            Pkt Len  : 252            Seg ID    : 0x00bd
Flags    : FRAG:*.LAST     Frag Ptr : 0    (8 Octet) TTL       : 64
PID      : UDP  ( 17)      Checksum : 0xca21 (Good)
Dst IP   : 255.255.255.255 Src IP <B: 172.18.3.1
---------------------------------[udp]----------------------------------------------
Dest Port: RIP [  520]                 Src Port : RIP [  520]
Length   : 232                         Checksum : 0x0000 (NoCheck)
---------------------------------[rip]----------------------------------------------
Command  : RESPonse        Version  : 1             Reserved : 00
-------------------------------[routes: 11]----------------------------------------
Family: 2  {172. 16.  0.  0} Hops: 2    Family: 2  {172. 17.  0.  0} Hops: 2
Family: 2  {172. 19.  0.  0} Hops: 16   Family: 2  {172. 20.  0.  0} Hops: 16
Family: 2  {172. 21.  0.  0} Hops: 16   Family: 2  {172. 22.  0.  0} Hops: 16
Family: 2  {172. 23.  0.  0} Hops: 16   Family: 2  {172. 24.  0.  0} Hops: 16
Family: 2  {192.168.  1.  0} Hops: 1    Family: 2  {192.168.  2.  0} Hops: 1
Family: 2  {192.168.  3.  0} Hops: 2
==============================[data:    4]==========================================
010A  3D 8A 8B 5E                                =..^
```

Router 3 (IP Address 172.18.3.1) advertises its routing table indicating that it has routes to networks 172.16.0.0, 172.17.0.0, 192.168.1.0, 192.168.2.0, and 192.168.3.0. Since it would have learnt about networks 172.19.0.0, 172.20.0.0, 172.21.0.0, 172.22.0.0, 172.23.0.0, and 172.24.0.0 over this interface, the metrics for these networks are set to infinity. Again, since this advertisement originates on network 172.18.0.0, this network is not advertised at all.

Figure 10-15: Sample Trace Showing Poison Reverse Updates Across Network 172.18.0.0

μSCOPE   PACKET TRACE DECODE REPORT   (c) T.Kenyon 1995

```
====================================μscope==========================================
Frame     : 1              Len      : 170           Error     : None
T Elapsed: 19:02:58:795    T Delta  : 00:00:29:575
---------------------------------[mac]----------------------------------------------
Dest Mac : ffffffffffff    Sourc Mac: Xyplex156806  Type      : IP
----------------------------------[ip]----------------------------------------------
IP Ver   : 4               IP HLen  : 20 Bytes
TOS      : 0x00            Pkt Len  : 152            Seg ID    : 0x0051
Flags    : FRAG:*.LAST     Frag Ptr : 0    (8 Octet) TTL       : 64
PID      : UDP  ( 17)      Checksum : 0xc9f1 (Good)
Dst IP   : 255.255.255.255 Src IP <B: 172.18.4.1
---------------------------------[udp]----------------------------------------------
Dest Port: RIP [  520]                 Src Port : RIP [  520]
Length   : 132                         Checksum : 0x0000 (NoCheck)
---------------------------------[rip]----------------------------------------------
Command  : RESPonse        Version  : 1             Reserved : 00
-------------------------------[routes:  6]----------------------------------------
Family: 2  {172. 19.  0.  0} Hops: 1    Family: 2  {172. 20.  0.  0} Hops: 1
Family: 2  {172. 21.  0.  0} Hops: 1    Family: 2  {172. 22.  0.  0} Hops: 2
Family: 2  {172. 23.  0.  0} Hops: 2    Family: 2  {172. 24.  0.  0} Hops: 2
==============================[data:    4]==========================================
00A6  55 BF CF F3                                U...
```

Router 4 advertises its routing table over network 172.18.0.0. Since this router is running RIP in Split Horizon mode, it does not advertise routes learnt over this interface. Thus, routes to networks 172.16.0.0, 172.17.0.0, 192.168.1.0, 192.168.2.0, and 192.168.3.0 are not included in the update. Since this advertisement is sent across network 172.18.0.0, this network is not advertised at all.

```
============================μscope============================
Frame    : 2              Len      : 270           Error     : None
T Elapsed: 19:02:59:825   T Delta  : 00:00:01:030
----------------------------[mac]----------------------------
Dest Mac : ffffffffffff   Sourc Mac: Xyplex135b7e  Type      : IP
----------------------------[ip]-----------------------------
IP Ver   : 4              IP HLen  : 20 Bytes
TOS      : 0x00           Pkt Len  : 252           Seg ID    : 0x00d7
Flags    : FRAG:*.LAST    Frag Ptr : 0    (8 Octet) TTL      : 64
PID      : UDP ( 17)      Checksum : 0xca07 (Good)
Dst IP   : 255.255.255.255 Src IP <B: 172.18.3.1
----------------------------[udp]----------------------------
Dest Port: RIP [  520]              Src Port : RIP [  520]
Length   : 232                      Checksum : 0x0000 (NoCheck)
----------------------------[rip]----------------------------
Command  : RESPonse       Version  : 1             Reserved : 00
-----------------------[routes: 11]--------------------------
Family: 2 {172. 16.  0.  0} Hops: 2   Family: 2 {172. 17.  0.  0} Hops: 2
Family: 2 {172. 19.  0.  0} Hops: 16  Family: 2 {172. 20.  0.  0} Hops: 16
Family: 2 {172. 21.  0.  0} Hops: 16  Family: 2 {172. 22.  0.  0} Hops: 16
Family: 2 {172. 23.  0.  0} Hops: 16  Family: 2 {172. 24.  0.  0} Hops: 16
Family: 2 {192.168.  1.  0} Hops: 1   Family: 2 {192.168.  2.  0} Hops: 1
Family: 2 {192.168.  3.  0} Hops: 2
=============================[data:    4]=====================
010A  4B E8 25 7B                           K.%{
```

Router 3 advertises its routing table over network 172.18.0.0. This router is running RIP in Poison Reverse mode thus, it advertises routes learnt over this interface. Here, routes to networks 172.19.0.0, 172.20.0.0, 172.24.0.0 are poisoned but those to 172.21.0.0, 172.22.0.0, 172.23.0.0, and 172.16.0.0, 172.16.0.0, 192.168.1.0, 192.168.2.0, and 192.168.3.0 have metrics that reflect their true distance from Router 3. Once again, network 172.18.0.0, is not advertised.

Figure 10-16: Sample Trace Showing the Effects of Split Horizon

10.3.2 Router Operation at Start-up

As we have already seen, when routers are first powered on, they have only minimal routing information. Through their configuration, they are aware of the IP Addresses of their various interfaces and therefore the networks (and Subnetworks) to which they connect. In addition, they may also be configured with certain *Static* routes, but apart from these routes they will know nothing of the internet of which they form a part.

Routers then, often broadcast *Requests* on each of their interfaces when they are first powered on. These *Requests* ask neighboring routers to supply their entire routing tables (i.e. the request contains only a single, zero, entry with a metric of 16). In this way, a full routing table can be built in a minimum of time.

10.4 The Arguments Surrounding RIP

From our previous discussions, clearly RIP is a simple, yet effective, routing protocol for small to medium sized networks. Perfect it certainly is not, since RIP does have a significant number of drawbacks. However, it is standardized, widely implemented, and being compact, has certain advantages to host systems.

10.4.1 RIP Limitations

RIP has many drawbacks as a routing protocol capable of taking us into the 21st Century. However, while not wishing to paint a picture that is too bleak, it is only fair to highlight the shortcomings of the protocol as follows:

• The maximum network diameter is 15 *hops*. This limitation does not come from a desire to limit network sizes, but instead from the need to reduce the time taken for the network to converge. By limiting the overall diameter in this way, where routing loops exist they will be overcome in the shortest timeframe possible.

- Routing updates occur regularly (typically every 30 seconds) and require that the router sends its entire routing table. In addition, an update (again consisting of the entire routing table) will be sent whenever a change has been detected (a *Triggered Update*). In reality, we only *need* to send updates when requested, when a metric changes, or when a topology change has been noted. Sadly RIP does not allow us to do this.

  Naturally, if we did only send updates when a change had been detected, we would need to employ some means of detecting whether our neighbors were still alive. This however could be achieved with a simple *Hello* type protocol that would only consume a small amount of network bandwidth and thus make RIP a far better protocol overall.

- One method of reducing the convergence time that we have discussed is to employ *Poison Reverse*. Here, you will recall, that we advertise those routes for which the router both should, and should not, be used. Thus the size of our routing tables, and subsequent routing updates are increased.

- RIP uses broadcasts to relay information between neighbors. While it is true that the amount of network bandwidth consumed is unaffected by this transmission method, all hosts attached to the network must process the datagram whether they are involved in the routing process or not. This then leads to a higher overhead on all attached devices and potentially results in wasted CPU cycles.

- RIP uses a simple hop count mechanism to determine the quality of a route. While this method is perfectly valid, it fails to take into account the actual interface speed of the links employed. Figure 10-1 showed us that although one path may contain more networks than another, due to the speed of the interconnecting links, this still represented the better route.

  Of course, administrators can normally change metrics manually. This however leads to a greater administrative overhead, and makes the process of routing generally less adaptive.

- RIP makes no distinction between Subnets. As we have seen, we cannot advertise a Subnet mask which means that all networks that make up our internet must use the same mask. This can lead to problems where we wish to employ variable length Subnet masks[6] throughout our internet.

  Sadly this limitation does not stop with variable length masks, since even when using the same Subnet Mask throughout our internet we may still have problems. RFC 1058 tells us that routers will potentially send different information to different neighbors when subnets are in use. For neighbors connected to the subnetted network, it advertises all subnets to which it is directly connected, using the subnet number. For neighbors connected to other networks however, it advertises only a single route to the network as a whole.

- RIP provides no authentication mechanism. In other words, a RIP router will accept updates from any RIP compliant device.

  Some vendors have implemented RIP *Trusted Routers* in their software. In these, Network Administrators program from which RIP neighbors to accept

---

6. See section 9.2.1 for a discussion of Variable Length Subnet Masks.

updates. However, this solution is restrictive since it is implemented on a per-router basis thus increasing the administration task enormously for large internets.

10.4.2 RIP Strengths

The major strengths of RIP lie in the number of networks that employ it and the fact that, being small, many hosts have RIP *Listener* tasks that listen to router activity and amend their own routing tables accordingly. RIP is an old protocol that has served the Internet community well. True, it has its drawbacks, but it is well understood, robust, and easy to implement. Generally, Network Administrators like it and continue to implement it even though there are better protocols available to them. Overall, RIP will be with us in either its current, or in a modified form for many years to come and has been the blueprint for all current routing technology. RIP is certainly not obsolete, and with enhancements currently being applied to the protocol (particularly with RIP II discussed next), it will provide us with the levels of functionality demanded by the Internet community today.

10.5 RIP II

RIP II, as described in RFC 1723[7], specifies extensions to the RIP protocol that expands on the amount of useful information carried in a RIP message. In particular, RIP II provides for an authentication scheme, allows for updates to be transmitted as either broadcasts or multicasts, and introduces the ability to carry Subnet masks. This latter feature is key where our internet comprises many networks each with a different mask value. Since, without this information, the router is unable to determine whether the route entry is to a network, or to a host. Unfortunately, in order to preserve backward compatibility, the diameter of networks using RIP II has not been increased.

10.5.1 RIP II Protocol Format

RIP II uses the same basic protocol format as RIP, redefining certain of the fields. As with RIP, the message size prohibits the carrying of more than 25 routes, and UDP port 520 is used. The complete protocol format is shown in Figure 10-17.

Here you will see that the format has a four octet header as before. With RIP II however, the information carried in each route entry is changed. The Address Family Identifier remains, as does the IP Address, and Metric. The interpretation is also as before. The two octets immediately following the Address Family Identifier that were previously unused are now employed as a *Route Tag*. This field is intended to be used as a method of distinguishing between routes that belong to either the local RIP domain, or an external autonomous system. As an example of *Route Tag* usage, where we import a route from say EGP or BGP, we may choose to place the Autonomous System Number from which the route was learnt in this

7. Note that RFC 1723 is not an Internet standard. At the time of writing, RIP II is still in the process of ratification by the Internet community.

field. Exactly how this field is used is undefined, however provided that all routers within the domain agree on a common interpretation, this fact is broadly irrelevant.

0	8	16	24	31
Operation	Version	Reserved (Must be Zero)		
Address Family Identifier		Route Tag		
IP Address				
Subnet Mask				
Next Hop				
Metric				
.....				
Address Family Identifier		Route Tag		
IP Address				
Subnet Mask				
Next Hop				
Metric				

Figure 10-17: RIP II Protocol Format

The *Subnet Mask* field is the mask applied to the IP Address supplied in the route entry. RIP II allows for this field to be empty for compatibility with RIP I routers that do not advertise Subnet masks. However, in order to provide complete backwards compatibility, it is important that we adhere to a few simple rules:

- If RIP I routers share the same network as RIP II routers, it is important that the RIP II routers do not advertise information that relates to a more specific Subnet. If this were to happen, confusion as to whether the route applies to a network or host would arise. For example, if a RIP II router advertised a route to 193.129.45.129, would the RIP I router consider this host 129 on network 193.129.45.0, or as host 1 on Subnetwork 4 of network 193.129.45? Obviously, unless it knows that the Subnet mask is 255.255.255.224, it cannot tell!

- Supernet routes (i.e. Those that have a Subnet mask that is less specific than the natural Subnet mask) must not be advertised where they may be received by RIP I routers. Again, if our RIP II router were to advertise the route to 193.129.45.129, we might wish to interpret it as host 129.45.129 on network 193.0.0.0. Obviously without the Subnet mask we cannot make this judgement.

The *Next Hop* field is used to inform recipients of the IP Address of the next router en-route to the destination. If the originating router is providing the best route to the destination, then this field is set to 0.0.0.0. Obviously, since the recipient must be able to send packets to the next hop directly, where this field is non-zero, then the next hop router must be attached to the same network as the recipient of the update. This field is of particular importance where we wish to eliminate packets being routed via a less than optimal route in networks where RIP is not the only routing protocol in use, as shown in Figure 10-18.

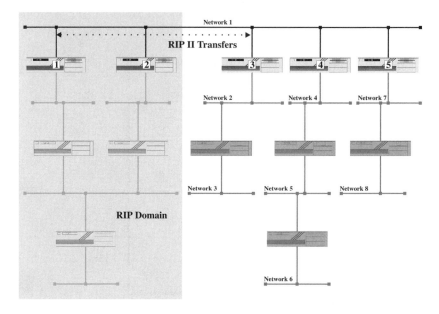

Figure 10-18: RIP II and Other IGPs

Consider the effects of routers 1, and 2 running RIP II, while routers 3, 4, and 5 are running some other IGP such as OSPF. Here, routers 3, 4, and 5 are exchanging information so we can assume that each know that Networks 2, and 3 are reachable via router 3, Networks 4, 5, and 6 are reachable via router 4, and Networks 7, and 8 are reachable via router 5. By ensuring that the Next Hop router is correctly represented, only one of these routers (router 3, 4, or 5) needs to run RIP II in addition to OSPF. Thus routers 1, and 2 will then learn that Networks 2, and 3 are reachable via router 3, Networks 4, 5, and 6 are reachable via router 4, and Networks 7, and 8 are reachable via router 5. If the Next Hop field were not available, then all routers would have to participate in both RIP II, and OSPF.

10.5.2 RIP II Authentication

RIP II allows authentication on a *per-message* basis. That is to say that each message sent, may be individually authenticated. Authentication requires a complete route entry and allows an authentication string of up to 16 octets. An authenticated message is signalled by the first (and only first) route entry in a RIP II message containing a special, previously unused, Address Family Identifier value ($FFFF_{16}$). This entry then contains a two octet Authentication Type field (currently only type 2, *simple password*, is defined), and a password of up to sixteen octets in length. A typical RIP II message may then look as in Figure 10-19.

Since RIP I will process all route entries that can be correctly interpreted, authenticated messages will be accepted by RIP I processes, thus compatibility is assured.

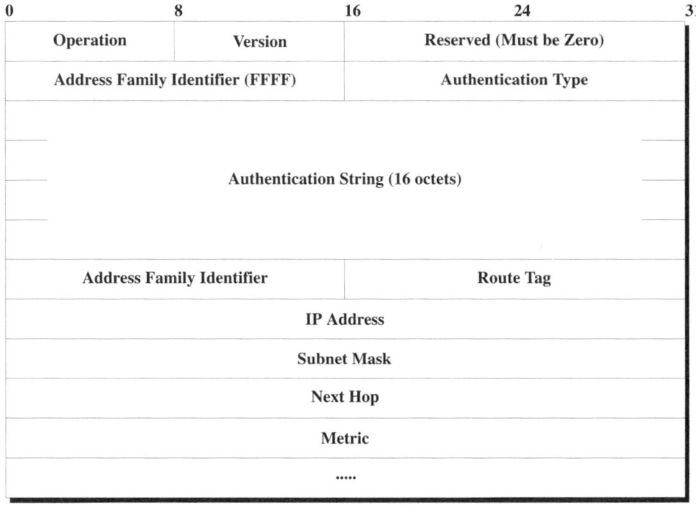

0	8	16	24	31

Operation	Version	Reserved (Must be Zero)	
Address Family Identifier (FFFF)		Authentication Type	
Authentication String (16 octets)			
Address Family Identifier		Route Tag	
IP Address			
Subnet Mask			
Next Hop			
Metric			
.....			

Figure 10-19: RIP II Authentication

10.5.3 RIP II and Multicasting

We saw that with RIP I being a broadcast based protocol, network hosts that are not participating in RIP would waste valuable CPU cycles processing irrelevant information. RIP II attempts to overcome this by using multicasts[8] by default, with an assigned Multicast address of 224.0.0.9. Obvious care must be taken when we mix RIP I and RIP II routers, since a RIP II Response that has been Multicast would be ignored by a RIP I router. RFC 1723 therefore suggests that the use of multicasts should be configurable in order to maintain backwards compatibility with RIP I.

10.5.4 Compatibility with RIP I

RIP II is totally backward compatible with RIP I, due to the fact that any message received with a Version greater than 1 should not be rejected solely on the grounds that a reserved field contains a non-zero value. Instead, processing should continue, with the RIP I process ignoring those route entries that cannot be correctly interpreted.

RFC 1723 suggests that RIP routers should incorporate a per-interface *compatibility switch*. In this way, each interface could be configured with one of the following four settings:

- None: The router will not participate in RIP I or II.

- RIP I: The router sends only RIP I messages (via broadcasts).

- RIP I Compatibility: The router participates fully, except that RIP II messages are broadcast.

8. See Chapter 14 for a complete discussion on Multicasting.

- RIP II: The router participates fully with RIP II messages sent as
                             multicasts.

In addition, all routers should be able to be configured such that, on a per-interface basis, the router can accept RIP I only, RIP II only, both RIP I, and RIP II, or no messages. Thus, where desired, all RIP II routers should be able to participate fully in RIP I. For example, if a properly configured RIP II router receives a RIP I *Request*, it should respond with a RIP I *Response*. If however it is configured to only respond to RIP II, then it should ignore the request.

10.6 Summary

In this chapter we have examined what is probably one of the most significant protocols in the entire Internet Protocol Suite. The Routing Information Protocol embodies the very essence of IP in that it enables data to be routed to distant networks. It is significant because it was the first of such protocols to be standardized and it's use is widespread. True, it is not the best protocol when we consider others such as OSPF (discussed in Chapter 11) but it does have strengths apart from the base of devices that use it.

Firstly, because of it's age, it has an extremely wide following and for small to moderate internets it is certainly more than adequate. Secondly, host machines (particularly Unix devices) can *listen* to routers exchanging information and modfiy their own routing tables dynamically rather than relying on redirects from routers. Sadly RIP does tend to be slow to converge due to the Distance Vector Algorithm that is used. However, with the reliability inherent in most devices today and high speed digital lines, we have to ask if this really is such a problem overall.

RIP II brings with it an attempt at making RIP more acceptable in todays networks. Firstly, RIP II provides authentication and the ability to use variable length subnets throughout the internet. Secondly, and possibly most importantly though, RIP II uses multicasts to exchange information.

Sadly, RIP II cannot extend the allowable diameter of the internet because of the limitations on Distance Vector Algorithms generally. It is however receiving great publicity at the present time and vendors are now implementing it. Whether users will convert remains to be seen, it does however provide a more flexible protocol that can only be for the good after all.

The Open Shortest Path First Protocol (OSPF)

Like the *Routing Information Protocol* (RIP) discussed in the previous chapter, the *Open Shortest Path First* (OSPF) protocol is one of the family of *Interior Gateway Protocols* (IGPs). OSPF however, represents the latest thinking in this particular area of networking and as such, is poised to become the routing protocol of choice for major vendors of internetworking equipment.

As we saw previously, RIP uses a distance-vector algorithm in order gauge the quality of routing information received. With this type of algorithm, any router within an internet will learn of all reachable networks, but will know of only the next hop router en-route to the final destination, and the relative cost involved. Conversely, OSPF, uses a *Link-State* protocol. Here, each router within a particular *Area* of the internet maintains an identical database describing the topology of the enitre Autonomous System[1] in terms of reachable networks, the routers that inter-connect them, and the costs involved with the use of each link. OSPF then uses this information to construct what is known as a *Shortest Path Tree* that describes the topology from its own perspective, and from this determines the routes that should be placed in the routing table.

Since OSPF routers know the exact topology of the Autonomous System, when topology changes occur these routers are able to adapt quickly thus greatly reducing the time taken for convergence. OSPF also allows the Autonomous System to be split into administrative areas. This has the effect of reducing the amount of traffic generated by the routing protocol itself, further reduces convergence time, and provides greater protection from routing failures. Furthermore, OSPF optionally allows the cost of using any link to be administratively defined, and we are able to assign multiple costs to links based upon the *Type of Service*[2] desired. Finally, OSPF also allows multiple, equal cost paths to be utilized simultaneously, uses Multicasts[3] to relay routing information, and can authenticate all router exchanges. These features then make OSPF a practical and flexible routing protocol that uses available links to the full, and guards against rogue information from being propagated throughout an Autonomous System.

OSPF, as described by RFC 1583, is an Internet *Draft* Standard with the status of *Elective*. RIP however, despite its short comings, is a Standard protocol (Std 34).

---

1. An Autonomous System is defined by OSPF as an internet having a common routing policy.

2. Type of Service is discussed in Chapter 5, The Internet Protocol (IP).

3. See Chapter 14 for a complete discussion on Multicasting.

In this chapter we shall examine OSPF in detail and, by considering a simple network, show how routing is achieved with a minimum of overhead.

11.1 Metrics

As we have said, OSPF allows link costs to be administratively configured. This means that the actual cost of using links, and therefore particular routes, can be controlled more closely and allows administrators to regulate which routes should be used.

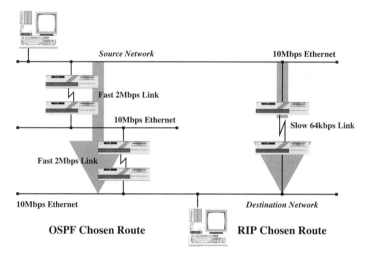

Figure 11-1: OSPF Link Costs

While it is true that vendors generally allow metrics to be manually configured for most routing protocols, OSPF makes greatest use of this flexibility. By default, OSPF, calculates a link cost based upon the actual speed of the link whereas distance vector algorithms generally ignore this.[4] Thus, where two routes exist between source and destination networks, the route used would be that which represents the lowest accumulated cost in terms of link speed. Considering Figure 11-1 which compares the operation of RIP and OSPF, if we assume that all costs are set to their default values, we see that OSPF chooses the real least cost path. This is because although our path on the left takes more hops and is potentially longer, the links in use are faster, resulting in greater traffic throughput.

Of course the actual selection of routes based upon link costs does not take into account router performance, nor the reliability of links or hardware. Thus, where these factors are an issue, administratively assigned costs must be used.

---

4. IP based Distance Vector algorithms such as RIP ignore link cost, but RIP in an IPX environment does take this into consideration.

11.1.1 Type of Service Routing

You will recall from our discussions of the Internet Protocol, that the IP header contains a Type-of-Service (TOS) field used to describe how the Datagram should be handled by the routing process. The field, shown below, is a single octet containing three bits that specify the *Precedence* of the Datagram, and four bits describing the TOS. These bits then have the values and meanings shown in Table 11-1 when used by the OSPF routing protocol:

Table 11-1: IP Type of Service Field Values

OSPF Value	D	T	R	M	Description as per RFC 1700
0	0	0	0	0	Normal (default) Service.
2	0	0	0	1	Minimize Monetary Cost.
4	0	0	1	0	Maximize Reliability.
8	0	1	0	0	Maximize Throughput.
14	1	0	0	0	Minimize Delay.
30	1	1	1	1	Maximize Security.

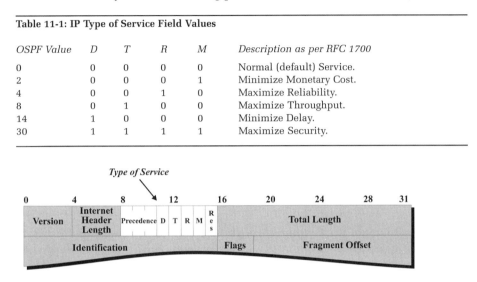

Figure 11-2: The IP Datagram Header

Administrators can specify different costs associated with links based upon a particular *Type-of-Service*. For example, where multiple paths exist between a source and destination network, an administrator could define different link costs based upon the *Type-of-Service* requested by the application. Here, if we had File Transfer and Virtual Terminal applications and paths via terrestrial and satellite links, we could apply different link costs based upon the throughput or delay desired. Consider Figure 11-3.

Terrestrial links provide good response with little delay. Satellite links though, while being excellent for carrying large volumes of data, introduce large delays making them unacceptable for interactive applications. Thus, assuming that we were able to specify a desired *Type-of-Service*, we would send our File Transfers across the satellite link, and the Virtual Terminal data over the terrestrial path. In this way, we are able to make best use of the paths available to us.

Type-of-Service routing is not without expense. In order to accommodate many paths based upon multiple costs, the router must derive multiple routing table entries from the information it holds. As such, since there may be as many as 16 possible combinations for the four TOS bits, the router may therefore need to calculate and use 16 routing tables. All OSPF routers must be able to calculate routes based upon Type-of-Service, and it is a requirement that all router links must be configured with cost for Type-of-Service zero. Beyond this, there is no requirement for a router to either use or to route data on any non-zero path thus conserving routing table space and processing cycles within the router.

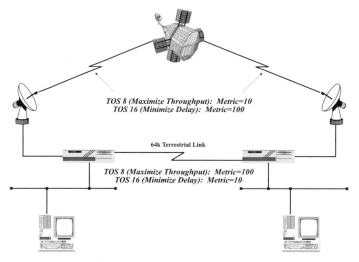

Figure 11-3: Type-of-Service Routing

For any route, it is wholly possible that there may not be a non-zero Type-of-Service path available. In these instances, since a zero Type-of-Service path must exist, datagrams requiring the non-zero Type-of-Service will be routed via a TOS-0 path. Because of this, routers that use only Type-of-Service zero (referred to as *TOS-0-only* routers) can be freely mixed with other routers supporting all 16 potential service types. When routers are mixed in this way, the *TOS-0-only* routers will be avoided as much as possible when forwarding traffic that has requested a specific (non-zero) Type-of-Service.

11.1.2 Equal Cost Paths

OSPF routers will discover all routes to all destinations thus, they will be able to store and use multiple paths where they exist. OSPF does not demand that multiple paths are used nor does it dictate how such routes are stored internally. Instead, an implementation may choose to maintain only a fixed number of routes and use only the best route to any given target. The important point however, is that the router will know about the routes regardless of whether it actually chooses to use them or not.

11.2 An Overview of OSPF

OSPF is a complex protocol when compared to other IGPs such as RIP. OSPF also introduces many new concepts and a whole new set of terms that must be understood if we are to fully appreciate the way in which it operates. As such, it is worth

The Open Shortest Path First Protocol (OSPF)

spending a few moments considering these terms and then taking an overall view of the protocol before discussing it in detail.

11.2.1 OSPF Terminology

- **Autonomous System (AS)**
  The traditional interpretation of this term is an internet that is controlled by a single administrative authority. However within the context of OSPF, an AS can be considered as a group of routers that share a common routing policy. For example, an internet where one group of routers runs say RIP and another runs OSPF may be split into two Autonomous Systems.

- **Router ID**
  OSPF introduces the concept of an identifier used to uniquely identify each router within an Autonomous System. This identifier is actually a 32 bit number and is the highest IP Address assigned to any of the router's interfaces by default.

- **Interface**
  An interface (sometimes also referred to as a Link) is the connection between a router and one of the networks to which it attaches. Associated with an interface are the IP Address, Subnet Mask, and a Metric. It is important to note however, that OSPF allows the use of Un-numbered Point-to-Point links. Where these are used, no IP Address or Subnet Information is required.

- **Adjacency**
  An adjacency is a relationship that is formed between selected routers (Neighbors) that share a common network. As we shall see when we discuss the protocol in detail, by forming adjacencies we can reduce the overall network traffic when routing information is exchanged.

- **Hello Protocol**
  The Hello Protocol is a simple, yet important, part of OSPF used to establish and maintain a Neighbor relationship and Adjacency. On multi-access networks such as Ethernet, this protocol is also used to automatically discover such neighboring routers.

- **Database Description (DD) Packets**
  Routers exchange these packets as part of the database sychronization process. The database description packet itself contains summary information about reachable Networks and routers, from which routers determine what additional information is required to update their own database.

- **Link State Request (LSR) Packets**
  A Link State Request is used to request additional information required by a router to update its' own database.

- **Link State Update (LSU) Packets and Link State Advertisements (LSAs)**
  LSU packets contain Link State Advertisements which, in turn, contain full information about a particular router or network. Indeed, it is through these packets that routers eventually find the information required to allow database synchronization. Figure 11-4 shows us a simplified view of database synchronization.

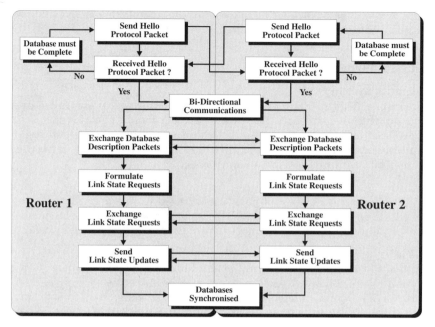

Figure 11-4: Database Synchronization (Simplified)

- **Areas**

  As we have already said, OSPF allows an internet to be divided into administrative areas. Where Areas are used however, a basic restriction applies in that
  all Areas must attach to a special Area called the *Backbone Area*. All Inter-Area
  traffic must then be routed via the backbone. Where the topology of the network
  does not allow for a direct connection, special paths known as *Virtual Links* are
  established to carry the Inter-Area routing traffic.

  Where Areas are used, we can no longer say that each router within the internet will have an identical database. Routers within an *area* share a common
  view of their *Area* through their individual databases, but the databases of
  routers from different areas will not be the same.

- **Internal Routers**

  These are routers that have all directly connected networks belonging to the
  same Area. Thus, where we have chosen not to split our internet into Areas, all
  routers will fall into this category.

- **Area Border Routers (ABRs)**

  An ABR is a router that attaches to multiple Areas. In simple terms, these
  routers will actually have multiple databases each describing a different area to
  which the router is attached. ABRs, by their definition, must also attach to the
  Backbone Area either directly or through *Virtual Links*.

- **Backbone Routers**

  A Backbone Router is one that has an interface to the Backbone Area. ABRs, by
  this definition are therefore Backbone Routers. However, it is not only ABRs

The Open Shortest Path First Protocol (OSPF)

that fall into this category since it is possible that some routers may have all interfaces connected only to the Backbone. In this case these routers can also be considered to be Internal Routers.

- **Autonomous System Boundary Routers (ASBRs)**
  ASBRs are responsible for exchanging information with routers in other Autonomous Systems. Such routers can be ABRs, or Internal Routers and may or may not participate in Backbone operations. Typically, these routers will have a database of information held about each Area to which they connect, and will also run a second routing protocol that may be another IGP or an EGP.

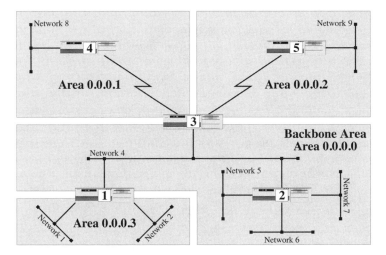

Figure 11-5: Simplified Example of OSPF Areas

In Figure 11-5, we see an example of an internet divided into Areas. By examining a much simplified internet such as this, we can identify many of the router types previously discussed. For example, Routers 1 and 3 are acting as ABRs. Routers 1, 2, and 3 are Backbone Routers but, since Router 2 has all interfaces within a single Area, it is therefore also an Internal Router. In this particular example there are no ASBRs. However if one of the routers (say router 2) were to be connected to an Autonomous System running a different routing protocol, then this router would become an ASBR and in so doing would run two routing protocols.

The ABRs will of course have multiple databases, one for each of the areas to which they connect. Router 1 will have two databases, one describing Areas 0.0.0.0 and the other 0.0.0.3. Router 3 will have three databases describing Areas 0.0.0.0, 0.0.0.1 and 0.0.0.2. Routers 4 and 5 will have only a single database describing Area 0.0.0.1, and 0.0.0.2 respectively. Finally, assuming that it is not running as an ASBR, Router 2 will have just one database that describes Area 0.0.0.0.

11.2.2 Network and Area Types

OSPF defines several different types of Network and Area, each with it's own particular characteristics. As far as the Network types are concerned, the type of network is purely dependant upon the number of routers attached. For Areas however, the choice is less clear and generally router manufacturers allow administrators to configure the area type required. Where the area type is unspecified, it is considered to be a *plain* area and flooding of all Link State Advertisements both into and throughout the area is normal.

- **Stub Network**
  Stub Networks are those networks that have only a single OSPF router attached. In Figure 11-5, all networks with the exception of Network 4 would fall into this category.

- **Transit Network**
  These are networks with two or more OSPF routers attached. As such, in addition to locally generated or addressed traffic, these networks are also able to forward traffic that is in transit. Network 4 in Figure 11-5 is an example of such a network.

- **Stub Area**
  Stub Areas can be configured where there is only a single ABR, or when the choice of exit point is such that we need not make decisions on a per-external destination basis. For example, we may have two ABRs that share a common network within the Stub Area, and link to a common network in the backbone. Thus, all traffic that is to be routed external to the area must pass through a single exit point. In Figure 11-5, areas 0.0.0.1, 0.0.0.2, and 0.0.0.3 could all be configured as Stub Areas.

  One restriction on Stub Areas is that ASBRs cannot be placed in them, because we cannot flood External Route Advertisements through these areas. The advantages of configuring an area in this way however, is that we can reduce the size of the database and therefore the memory requirements of the router. External Route Advertisements are discussed later.

- **Not So Stubby Area (NSSA)**
  RFC 1587 defines the Not So Stubby Area as being similar to the Stub Area but having the capability of importing and flooding AS External Routes through the Area and therefore allowing ASBRs to be used. ABRs can then take the routes imported from the ASBRs and summarize them for transmission across the backbone.

- **Stub – No Summary**
  Not supported by all vendors, ABRs connecting this type of area will not propagate summary LSAs into the area. Instead, Routers internal to the area rely solely on a Default Route to forward data to networks in other areas.

11.2.3 Designated and Backup Designated Routers

In common with other routing protocols, it is neighboring OSPF routers that exchange routing information. At variance with other protocols, OSPF routers use IP Multicast packets for these exchanges in order to reduce the load on hosts that are not participating with them. This however presents other problems such as how to reduce the traffic generated by these exchanges. As an example of this, consider the following figure where 9 routers share a common broadcast network.

Figure 11-6: Router Adjacency (1)

If each of the routers were to exchange information with each of the others, a total of 36 (or [n(n-1)]/2) exchanges would have to take place. By limiting the number of routers with which we exchange information, we are able to greatly reduce this figure. Thus, in OSPF, each router forms what is termed an *adjacency* with a maximum of only two neighbors as Figure 11-7 shows.

The routers with which adjacencies are formed are termed the *Designated Router* (DR) and the *Backup Designated Router* (BDR). These routers assume particular responsibility in that it is they who are responsible for the eventual dissemination of routing information amongst all routers on the shared network. As can be seen, by operating in this way the amount of routing traffic is now greatly reduced to only 15 (or 2[n-1]) exchanges.

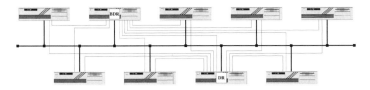

Figure 11-7: Router Adjacency (2)

Both the Designated Router and the Backup Designated Router form adjacencies with each of the other routers and each other, in order to provide a measure of resilience. If the Designated Router should fail, since the Backup Designated Router holds identical information, the transition to a stable topology can be achieved in the shortest possible timeframe.

The adjacency itself is formed and maintained through the *Hello* protocol, a simple protocol used to elect the Designated and Backup Designated Routers and to also test whether adjacent routers are alive.

OSPF does not use timed updates that involve entire routing tables to be exchanged at regular intervals. Instead, OSPF routers exchange their databases at start-up. This means that after an initial flurry of activity to synchronize databases, the routers then only need exchange routing information on an as needed basis. While this reduces the traffic generated from routing information, it neither ensures that neighboring routers are alive, nor does it report which networks are reachable. The Hello protocol is therefore critical to the operation of OSPF. Without it we would have no means of detecting new or failed routers, and consequently we would not be able to identify new or failed routes. The Hello protocol itself is discussed in section 11.3.

11.2.4 Router Adjacency and Network Types

In today's internets it is important that protocols are able to use all network types. With OSPF then, routers can form adjacencies over the following networks:

- **Point-to-Point Networks**
  These are networks that join a single pair of routers over say a 64k leased line. These networks do not have to be assigned an IP address and, when configured in this way, such links are referred to as being *un-numbered*.

- **Broadcast Networks**
  Broadcast networks are where many attached routers are supported and there is a capability to address a single packet to all units simultaneously (broadcast). In actual fact, OSPF uses a Multicast to communicate with adjacent devices, however, the principles of communicating with multiple devices simultaneously remain the same. Ethernet is an example of such a network type.

- **Non-Broadcast Networks**
  Non-Broadcast, multi-access networks such as ISDN, X.25, and Frame Relay, allow the simultaneous connection of multiple routers but have no broadcast (multicast) capability. In these networks, packets that would otherwise be sent to all neighbors simultaneously are therefore sent as unicasts to each adjacent neighbor in turn. This then requires some measure of pre-configuration, however it is unavoidable on this type of network.

11.3 Protocol Operation

OSPF, unlike RIP, uses IP directly and is identified by protocol ID 89_{10}. Consequently, OSPF is encapsulated only in IP and the underlying network headers associated with Layer 2. Furthermore, over multi-access networks, OSPF messages are sent as either unicasts or multicasts.[5] Where multicasts are used, two IP Addresses have been allocated which are described in Table 11-2.

Table 11-2: OSPF Multicast IP Addresses

Multicast Name	Address	Description
AllSPFRouters	224.0.0.5	All routers must be able to receive packets sent to this address. Hello and certain other packets are sent to this address.
AllDRouters	224.0.0.6	The Designated and Backup Designated Routers must be able to receive this address. Some protocol packets use this as the destination address.

Packets sent to these multicast addresses are not meant to travel over multiple networks. Consequently, the packets should not be forwarded by routers. In order to ensure this, the *Time-to-Live* field of the IP header is set to 1. Similarly, although OSPF is capable of performing *Type-of-Service* routing, OSPF packets are sent using TOS zero although the *Precedence* field should reflect *Internetwork Control*.

5. Multicasting is described in detail in Chapter 14.

Although we have said that OSPF is a complex protocol, much is done to simplify the actual packet formats. As such, all OSPF packets share the common header format shown below:

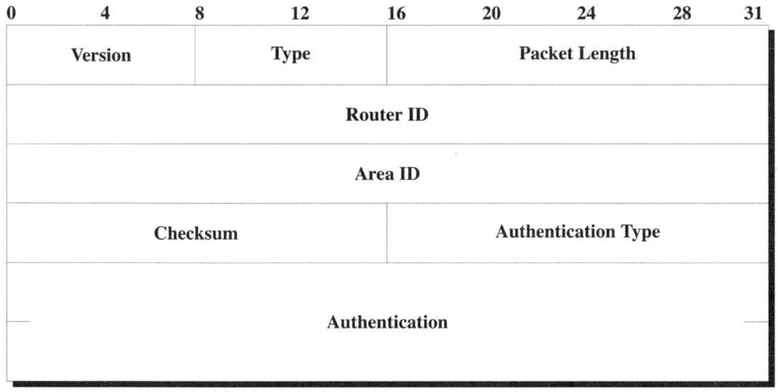

0 4 8 12	16 20 24 28 31
Version	Type	Packet Length
Router ID	
Area ID	
Checksum	Authentication Type
Authentication	

Figure 11-8: The OSPF Header

The *Version* field contains the 8 bit version number of the protocol (currently 2), and the *Type* field (8 bits) contains a value reflecting the packet type. Valid types are shown in Table 11-3.

Table 11-3: OSPF Type Values

Type Code (Decimal)	Description
1	Hello
2	Database Description
3	Link State Request
4	Link State Update
5	Link State Acknowledgement

The 16 bit *Packet Length* field defines the length of the packet in octets. This value includes the length of the OSPF header but excludes the IP header. In theory, the length could be up to 65,535 octets and thus rely on the fragmentation capabilities of IP to fragment the datagram where necessary. In practice, OSPF routers attempt to limit the size of packets to 576 octets and thereby avoid fragmentation particularly where the packet is to travel over *Virtual Links*.[6]

The 32 bit *Router ID* field is used to convey the Router ID of the packet's source. This ID, which is the highest assigned IP Address by default, is used to identify the end of an adjacency when it exists. The *Area ID* (again 32 bits) is used to identify the area to which the sender of this packet belongs. Routing information is contained within a single area in an effort to reduce the overall amount of routing information that travels throughout an Autonomous System. As we have said though, an AS may be split into multiple areas typically where large numbers of routers and networks exist. This concept, since it is an important feature of OSPF, is discussed in detail in section 11.5.

6. Virtual Links are used to link OSPF Areas to the Backbone where a direct connection would otherwise be impossible. This is discussed later in the chapter.

The 16 bit Checksum field ensures that the packet arrives intact. The checksum is calculated in the normal manner amongst IP hosts in that it is the 16 bit one's compliment of the one's compliment sum of all 16 bit words including any bits carried during the calculation. The checksum itself is calculated on the entire OSPF packet from the start of the header to the end of the data, but excludes the 64 bit *Authentication* field. Where the packet is an odd number of octets, the packet is padded with an octet of zero before the checksum process commences.

The 16 bit *Authentication Type* identifies the authentication scheme in use, and the 64 bit *Authentication* field the actual authentication data. Currently, OSPF supports two authentication types namely *No Authentication* (Type 0), and *Simple Password* (Type 1). Where there is no authentication, routing exchanges in the area are not authenticated and the Authentication field can contain any data since it is not examined by receiving routers. Where simple password authentication is employed, the Authentication field contains the actual password itself.

Authentication is configured on a per-Area basis. Thus, all routers within a given area must use the same authentication type. Where password authentication is selected however, the actual password in use is configurable on a per-interface basis. Thus, a different password may be configured for each network within an area.

Turning our attention now to the actual operation of OSPF, we shall base our discussions on the simple internet shown in Figure 11-9. As we proceed through the description of OSPF, we will then add further routers that provide both a measure of resilience when connecting to our remote sites, and also serve to further demonstrate the main features and benefits of the protocol in general.

The Addresses, Subnet Masks, and Metrics assigned to the components of the diagram are as shown in Table 11-4. Notice that here, we will use only Natural Subnet Masks and we will use a consistent metric of 10 throughout for all of our LAN interfaces. In addition, only TOS 0 will be used.

Table 11-4: IP Addresses Associated with Figure 11-9

Network	Router and Interface	IP Address	Subnet Mask	TOS-0 Metric
Network 1	Router 1, Interface 1	192.168.1.1	255.255.255.0	10
Network 2	Router 1, Interface 2	192.168.2.1	255.255.255.0	10
Network 3	Router 1, Interface 3	192.168.3.1	255.255.255.0	10
	Router 1, Interface 4	192.168.4.1	255.255.255.0	10
Network 4	Router 2, Interface 4	192.168.4.2	255.255.255.0	10
	Router 3, Interface 1	192.168.4.3	255.255.255.0	10
Network 5	Router 2, Interface 1	192.168.5.2	255.255.255.0	10
Network 6	Router 2, Interface 2	192.168.6.2	255.255.255.0	10
Network 7	Router 2, Interface 3	192.168.7.2	255.255.255.0	10
Network 8	Router 4, Interface 1	192.168.8.4	255.255.255.0	10
Network 9	Router 5, Interface 1	192.168.9.5	255.255.255.0	10

You will see from Figure 11-9 and Table 11-4, that the wide-area links in use (those linking Routers 3, and 4, and Routers 3, and 5) make use of the *Un-Numbered* facility of OSPF. Whilst this is not mandatory, it is made possible because the links in question are Point-to-Point. Thus, IP address space is conserved and overall router configuration is simplified.

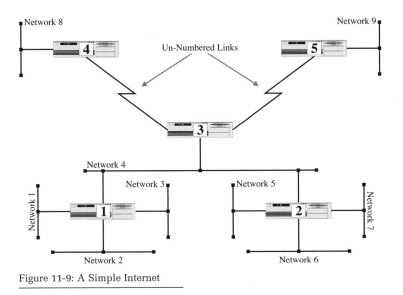

Figure 11-9: A Simple Internet

11.3.1 The Hello Protocol

As we have already said, Adjacency forming commences through the *Hello Protocol* operating over links that are common to multiple routers. In order to study this more closely we shall consider how the adjacencies are formed and maintained over a single network, in this case Network 4. This section of the network is shown in Figure 11-10.

When an OSPF router first comes on-line, it will issue a Hello packet to indicate to other routers on the network that it is available and to determine whether a Designated Router and Backup Designated Router already exist. These Designated and Backup Designated routers are elected through a configurable parameter called the *Router Priority*. Of course, it is highly probable that two (or more) routers could have the same priority value assigned. In this case the *Router ID*, which by default is normally taken to be the highest IP Address assigned to the router, is used to break potential deadlock. In the event that no such routers have currently been chosen, the DR and BDR router will be elected based upon these fields contained in the Hello packet.

Where other, *operational*, routers already exist on the network, the router will receive Hello packets from them indicating their existence and, where applicable, the address(es) of the routers that have assumed the Designated and Backup Designated roles. The responses also contain a list of all routers from which hello packets have been recently received. Thus, when a router sees its own address in this list, *bi-directional* communications is said to have been established although at this point, it cannot be said to be adjacent to any of the other routers.

Adjacency is established with only the Designated and Backup Designated routers on the network. Routers are said to be adjacent when their databases are synchronized, a process that itself follows a well defined sequence of events and which is covered in the next sections.

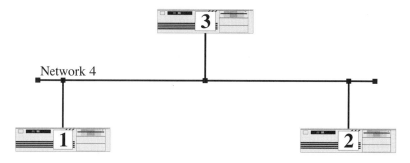

Network 4

Figure 11-10: Forming Adjacencies

Returning to the Hello protocol, Hello packets are also used to maintain the bi-directional relationship once established. Periodically, routers issue Hello packets and, in turn, expect to receive similar packets from their neighbors. Where a Hello packet has not been seen from a neighbor within a timeout interval (the *Router Dead Interval*), that neighbor is assumed down and causes a topology change which will be communicated by the Designated (and Backup Designated) router.

As you will now appreciate, the Hello protocol is critical to the proper operation of OSPF, and it is in no small part due to this simple protocol, that OSPF is extremely responsive to topology changes. The format of Hello packets (excluding the OSPF Header previously described) is shown in Figure 11-11.

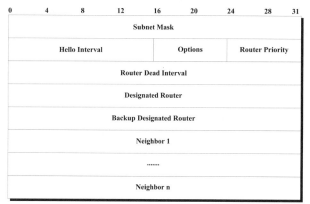

Figure 11-11: The Hello Protocol

With this protocol, the *Subnet Mask* field directly follows the Authentication field of the header and identifies the mask in use on this network. Obviously, all routers that share a common network must use the same mask or routing would not be possible.

The 16 bit *Hello Interval* defines the interval (in seconds) at which the router originating the packet will send Hellos. The *Options* field specifies options that the router is either capable of supporting or will support. The field, as in Figure 11-12,

The Open Shortest Path First Protocol (OSPF)

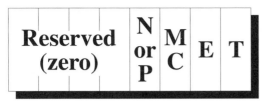

Reserved (zero)	N or P	M C	E	T

Figure 11-12: The Options Field

uses only the four least ignificant bits referred to a *T, E, MC,* and *N or P*. The T bit defines the routers TOS capability. When set to zero, this indicates that the router is capable of supporting only TOS 0 (a TOS-0-only router). As such, other routers capable of non TOS 0 routing will ignore this router wherever possible when routing non-TOS 0 data. The E bit is used to reflect the area's external routing capability and whether External Link Advertisements[7] are flooded through a Stub area. The MC bit describes the router's Multicast Capability as defined by RFC 1584 – *MOSPF*.[8] Finally, the N or P bit is used to describe the router's *NSSA*[9] capability. The bit is referred to as being N when in a Hello Packet and is used to ensure that all routers within the area agree on what type area this is.

The *Router Priority* field is used to convey the priority used in the determination of the Designated and Backup Designated routers. This single octet field can therefore assume a value of between zero and 255. Where the value zero is used though, the router sending the packet indicates that it is ineligible to assume the Designated or Backup Designated roles and will therefore not be chosen.

The 32 bit *Router Dead Interval* defines the number of seconds that the router will wait for a Hello packet from a neighbor before declaring that it is down. The 32 bit *Designated Router* and *Backup Designated Router* fields are used to convey this routers perception of who the Designated and Backup Designated routers are. These fields then contain the IP Addresses of those routers.

Finally the *Neighbor List* (Neighbor 1 to Neighbor n) identifies all routers from whom Hellos have been received within the Router Dead Interval. Thus, a router sending Hello packets will know when bi-directional communication has been established with its neighbors when it sees itself in Hello packets received from them.

The trace in Figure 11-13 shows the Hello traffic on the sample network (Network 4) introduced in Figures 11-9, and 11-10. In this trace, the first two frames show the Hello packets from Router 3 when it is the only active router on Network 4. In frame 3, Router 1 sends its first Hello indicating that it does not know if a Designated Router and Backup Designated Router have been elected. Finally, in frame 4, Router 3 sends it's regular Hello packet indicating that it has seen Router 1 by including it in it's Neighbor list. At this point, both routers now know that *Bi-Directional* communication is possible.

7. External Link Advertisements are *Link State Advertisements* (LSAs) that describe networks in other Autonomous Systems. LSAs are discussed in section 11.3.6.

8. Chapter 14 contains a detailed description of OSPF when used in a Multicast environment.

9. The NSSA (Not-so-Stubby-Area) describes the router's capabilities when dealing with External Link Advertisements within Stub Areas. This was discussed in section 11.2.

```
======================================µscope======================================
Frame    : 1                  Len     : 82           Error     : None
T Elapsed: 13:37:28:084       T Delta : 00:03:39:643
--------------------------------[mac]---------------------------------
Dest Mac : 01005e000005       Sourc Mac: Xyplex135b7e    Type    : IP
---------------------------------[ip]---------------------------------
IP Ver   : 4                  IP HLen  : 20 Bytes
TOS      : 0xc0               Pkt Len  : 64           Seg ID   : 0x0088
Flags    : FRAG:*.LAST        Frag Ptr : 0    (8 Octet)  TTL    : 1 (Low)
PID      : OSPF ( 89)         Checksum : 0x136d (Good)
Dst IP <D: 224.0.0.5          Src IP <C: 192.168.4.3
--------------------------------[ospf]--------------------------------
OSPF Ver : 2                  Type     : HELLO         Length   : 44
Router ID: 192.168.4.3        Area  ID : 0.0.0.0       Checksum : 0x7347
AU Type  : 00                 AU Key   : {          }
--------------------------------[hello]-------------------------------
Hello Msk: 255.255.255.0      Hello Int: 10           Hello Pri: 1
Options  : 02                 Dead Int : 40
DR       : 192.168.4.3        BDR      : 0.0.0.0
=================================[data:   4]==============================
004E  86 4C 5E 1A                                     .L^.
```

Destination Address used is the Multicast Address *AllSPFRouters*.

Time-to-Live=1. This frame should not travel over multiple networks.

No Authentication in use.

Hello Interval=10s, and the *Router Dead Interval*=40s.

R3, being the only active Router elects itself as the *DR*. No *BDR* has been elected at this time.

```
======================================µscope======================================
Frame    : 2                  Len     : 82           Error     : None
T Elapsed: 13:37:38:284       T Delta : 00:00:10:200
--------------------------------[mac]---------------------------------
Dest Mac : 01005e000005       Sourc Mac: Xyplex135b7e    Type    : IP
---------------------------------[ip]---------------------------------
IP Ver   : 4                  IP HLen  : 20 Bytes
TOS      : 0xc0               Pkt Len  : 64           Seg ID   : 0x0089
Flags    : FRAG:*.LAST        Frag Ptr : 0    (8 Octet)  TTL    : 1 (Low)
PID      : OSPF ( 89)         Checksum : 0x136c (Good)
Dst IP <D: 224.0.0.5          Src IP <C: 192.168.4.3
--------------------------------[ospf]--------------------------------
OSPF Ver : 2                  Type     : HELLO         Length   : 44
Router ID: 192.168.4.3        Area  ID : 0.0.0.0       Checksum : 0x7347
AU Type  : 00                 AU Key   : {          }
--------------------------------[hello]-------------------------------
Hello Msk: 255.255.255.0      Hello Int: 10           Hello Pri: 1
Options  : 02                 Dead Int : 40
DR       : 192.168.4.3        BDR      : 0.0.0.0
=================================[data:   4]==============================
004E  36 F9 CA 0D                                     6...
```

The *Options* field indicates that this router is *TOS-0-Only* and is willing to send and accept External Links Advertisements being flooded through the Area.

```
======================================µscope======================================
Frame    : 3                  Len     : 82           Error     : None
T Elapsed: 13:37:39:133       T Delta : 00:00:00:849
--------------------------------[mac]---------------------------------
Dest Mac : 01005e000005       Sourc Mac: Xyplex456866    Type    : IP
---------------------------------[ip]---------------------------------
IP Ver   : 4                  IP HLen  : 20 Bytes
TOS      : 0xc0               Pkt Len  : 64           Seg ID   : 0x006b
Flags    : FRAG:*.LAST        Frag Ptr : 0    (8 Octet)  TTL    : 1 (Low)
PID      : OSPF ( 89)         Checksum : 0x138c (Good)
Dst IP <D: 224.0.0.5          Src IP <C: 192.168.4.1
--------------------------------[ospf]--------------------------------
OSPF Ver : 2                  Type     : HELLO         Length   : 44
Router ID: 192.168.4.1        Area  ID : 0.0.0.0       Checksum : 0x37f5
AU Type  : 00                 AU Key   : {          }
--------------------------------[hello]-------------------------------
Hello Msk: 255.255.255.0      Hello Int: 10           Hello Pri: 1
Options  : 02                 Dead Int : 40
DR       : 0.0.0.0            BDR      : 0.0.0.0
=================================[data:   4]==============================
004E  8C 83 07 9E                                     ....
```

Router R1 comes on-line.

R1 does not know which, if any, routers are elected as *DR* or *BDR*.

```
======================================µscope======================================
Frame    : 4                  Len     : 86           Error     : None
T Elapsed: 13:37:48:489       T Delta : 00:00:09:356
--------------------------------[mac]---------------------------------
Dest Mac : 01005e000005       Sourc Mac: Xyplex135b7e    Type    : IP
---------------------------------[ip]---------------------------------
IP Ver   : 4                  IP HLen  : 20 Bytes
TOS      : 0xc0               Pkt Len  : 68           Seg ID   : 0x008e
Flags    : FRAG:*.LAST        Frag Ptr : 0    (8 Octet)  TTL    : 1 (Low)
PID      : OSPF ( 89)         Checksum : 0x1363 (Good)
Dst IP <D: 224.0.0.5          Src IP <C: 192.168.4.3
--------------------------------[ospf]--------------------------------
OSPF Ver : 2                  Type     : HELLO         Length   : 48
Router ID: 192.168.4.3        Area  ID : 0.0.0.0       Checksum : 0xae99
AU Type  : 00                 AU Key   : {          }
--------------------------------[hello]-------------------------------
Hello Msk: 255.255.255.0      Hello Int: 10           Hello Pri: 1
Options  : 02                 Dead Int : 40
DR       : 192.168.4.3        BDR      : 0.0.0.0
Neighbour: 192.168.4.1
=================================[data:   4]==============================
0052  AE B3 10 2A                                     ...*
```

Hello packet from Router R3.

Router R3 indicates that it has seen Router R1 within the *Router Dead Interval*, therefore *bi-directional* communication has been established.

Figure 11-13: Hello Protocol Exchanges

       The Open Shortest Path First Protocol (OSPF)

In the next trace, (Figure 11-14) we examine what happens when Router 2 comes on-line. Remember that two routers (Routers 1 and 3) are already active on Network 4. As such, the Designated Router and Backup Designated Router are now already established.

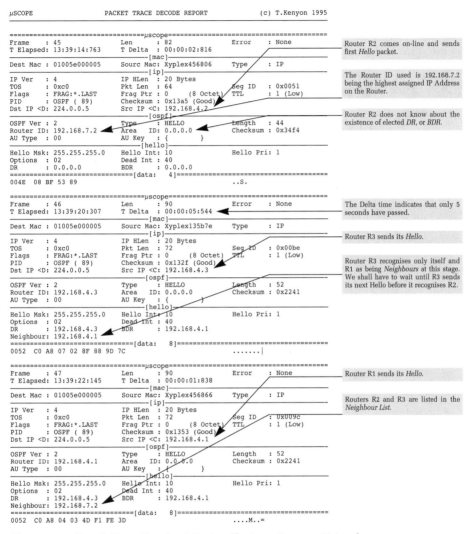

Figure 11-14: Sample Trace Showing 3 Routers Sharing a Common Network

Frame 45 shows Router 2 coming on-line and sending it's first Hello packet. In this frame, as in frame 3 from the previous trace, the router does not know of the elected *DR* and *BDR* and therefore leaves these fields blank. Frame 46 shows the Hello packet from Router 3, and indicates in this that it has seen only Router R1 and suggesting that bi-directional communication with this unit is possible. Until it's next Hello packet (when it will acknowledge R2) bi-directional communication between R2 and R3 will not be possible. Finally, frame 47 shows the Hello packet from router R1 which lists routers R2 and R3 as *Neighbors*.

Notice that thoughout this exchange, Router 2, and subsequently the other routers, consider router R2 as having a Router ID of 192.168.7.2. This is because the default Router ID is always the same as the highest assigned IP Address of the unit. In the case of R1 and R3 the highest Address assigned is that used by the interface that connects them to Network 4. In the case of R2 however, this unit has an interface with a higher value IP Address.

11.3.2 Exchanging Database Information and Creating Adjacencies

Once bi-directional communication has been established, the neighboring routers will exchange Database information. The process starts with neighboring routers exchanging *Database Description* packets in a *poll-response*[10] (*Master/ Slave*) manner. These packets describe the contents of the router's topological database as a series of *Link State Advertisement* (LSA) headers – Summarized information describing part of the actual database itself.

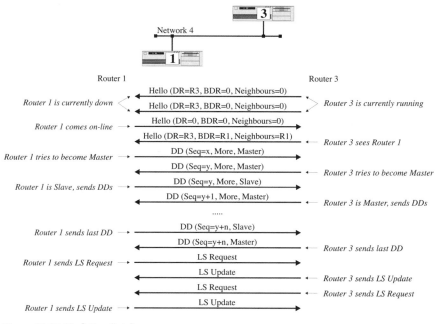

Figure 11-15: Updating Databases

Based upon this information, each router then builds a list of *Link State Requests* (or LSRs) that it needs to send in order to bring its own database up to date. For example, the router may receive a Database Description packet that identifies a LSA

---

10. The actual operation of this Master/Slave relationship is discussed in section 11.3.3 next.

The Open Shortest Path First Protocol (OSPF)

that it does not have (or the Database Description may indicate that the neighbor has a later copy). Thus, the list of requests is built, and then sent to the neighbor.

When a LSR is received, the router sends *Link State Update* (LSU) packets containing the full *Link State Advertisements* (LSAs) requested. Hence, the routers involved will eventually have identical databases at which time they are said to be adjacent.

Figure 11-15 shows how these exchanges take place. Since there may be multiple *Database Description* packets exchanged, routers involved in this stage of adjacency forming operate in a *poll-response* mode. During this phase, one of the routers will become the *Master* and send a Database Description packet (poll), which is then acknowledged by a Database Description packet sent by the *Slave* (response). This then continues until each side has sent all Database Descriptions. The Master will be the router with the highest Router ID of the pair and will therefore force it's neighbor to assume the role of Slave.

As the figure shows, polls and responses are linked through a packet sequence number (called the *Database Description Sequence Number*). During the initial establishment of this phase, each neighbor suggests a Sequence Number to be used. It is that suggested by the Master however which is actually implemented during the exchange.

11.3.3 Exchanging Database Description Packets

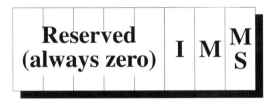

Figure 11-16: Database Description flags

The partial packet format shown in Figure 11-17 describes the format of the Database Description packet (excluding the OSPF Header) that , as before, follows directly after the *Authen-tication* field in the OSPF header.

The Options field has the same meaning as in the Hello packet and was described previously in Figure 11-12. The 8 bit *Flags* field (shown in Figure 11-16) indicates the following: The *I* (Init) bit denotes that this is the first in a sequence of Database Description packets. The *M* (More) bit indicates that more Database Description packets will follow, and the *MS* (Master/Slave) bit the role of this router. When this last bit is set, the router is acting as the Master during the Database Description exchange. Otherwise, the router is acting as the Slave.

The Database Description Sequence Number is used to sequence the exchange of Database Description packets. The initial value of this field is determined when the I bit is set in the Flags field and is then incremented for each packet sent until the transfer is complete. The Link State Advertisement Header(s) that then occupy the remainder of the packet contain all of the information needed to uniquely identify the actual advertisement itself. This is shown in Figure 11-18.

The 16 bit *Link State Age* field indicates the time (in seconds) since the Link State Advertisement was originated. The *Options* field is again as described in the Hello packet format, and describes the capabilities of the router. The 8 bit *Link State Type* field identifies the type of Link State Advertisement presented. In actual fact there are six different types of LSA each starting with the header shown in Figure 11-18. The six LSA types and the associated values for this field are shown in Table 11-5.

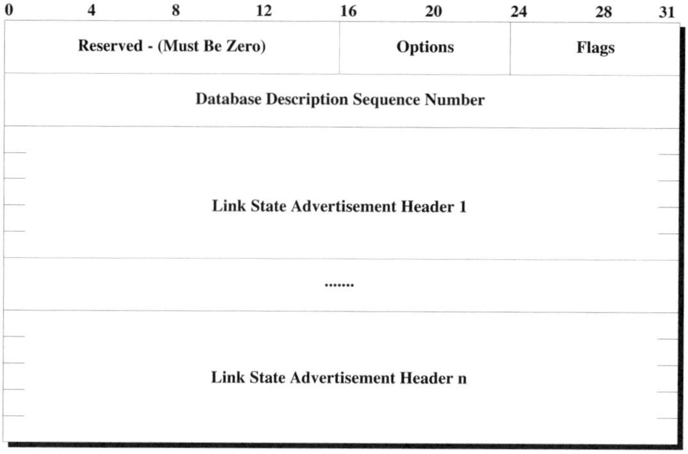

Figure 11-17: The Database Description Packet

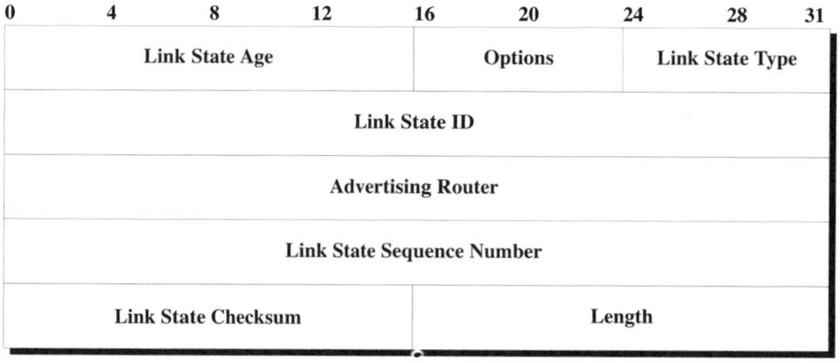

Figure 11-18: The Link State Advertisement (LSA) Header

Table 11-5: LSA Types

Value	Type	Description
1	Router Links	Describes the State (and cost) of the routers interfaces
2	Network Links	Indicates Transit Networks with more than one router attached.
3	Summary Link (IP Network)	Originated by Area Border Routers (ABRs), these
4	Summary Link (ASBR)	indicate networks in the AS but outside the Area.
5	AS External Link	Originated by ASBRs, to advertise destinations outside the AS.
7	Not-so-Stubby-Area (NSSA) Advertisement	Allows the transmission of AS External Link. Advertisements throughout a Not-so-Stubby Area (NSSA).[11]

The 32 bit *Link State ID* field is used to identify the environment that is being described. For *Network Links Advertisements*, this field contains the IP Address of the interface of the *Designated Router* and for *Router Links Advertisements*, the field contains the Router's ID. Where this is a *Summary Link Advertisement*, it will

11. See Section 11.2 for a discussion of the NSSA.

The Open Shortest Path First Protocol (OSPF)

contain the IP Address of the destination network or the Router ID of the *ASBR*, and where this LSA describes an *External Link*, the IP Address of the destination network. These latter two types will be discussed more fully when we consider the whole Link State Advertisement and routing to another Autonomous System.

The 32 bit *Advertising Router* field contains the *Router ID* of the router that orig-inated this Database Description packet and therefore holds the original LSA. The *Link State Sequence Number* (32 bits) is the unique sequence number applied to this Database Description packet. This sequence number can then be used to detect old or duplicate information.

The 16 bit *Checksum* field contains the checksum of the entire LSA including the header but excluding the Link State Age. Finally, the *Length* field (16 bits) indi-cates the length of the LSA including the 20 octet header.

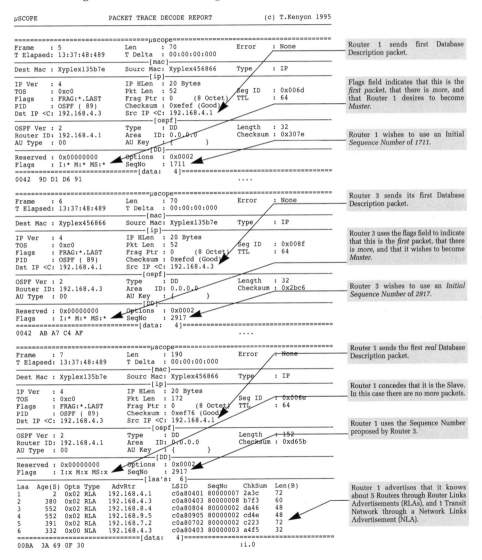

```
µSCOPE              PACKET TRACE DECODE REPORT        (c) T.Kenyon 1995


========================µscope========================================
Frame   : 5                 Len    : 70          Error    : None
T Elapsed: 13:37:48:489     T Delta : 00:00:00:000
                            ----[mac]----
Dest Mac : Xyplex135b7e     Sourc Mac: Xyplex456866    Type    : IP
                            ----[ip]----
IP Ver  : 4                 IP HLen : 20 Bytes
TOS     : 0xc0              Pkt Len : 52         Seg ID   : 0x006d
Flags   : FRAG:*.LAST       Frag Ptr : 0   (8 Octet) TTL    : 64
PID     : OSPF ( 89)        Checksum : 0xefef (Good)
Dst IP <C: 192.168.4.3      Src IP <C: 192.168.4.1
                            ----[ospf]----
OSPF Ver : 2                Type   : DD          Length   : 32
Router ID: 192.168.4.1      Area   ID: 0.0.0.0   Checksum : 0x307e
AU Type  : 00               AU Key   :  {        }
                            ----[DD]----
Reserved : 0x00000000       Options  : 0x0002
Flags    : I:* M:* MS:*     SeqNo    : 1711
========================[data:   4]====================================
0042  9D D1 D6 91                         ....


========================µscope========================================
Frame   : 6                 Len    : 70          Error    : None
T Elapsed: 13:37:48:489     T Delta : 00:00:00:000
                            ----[mac]----
Dest Mac : Xyplex456866     Sourc Mac: Xyplex135b7e    Type    : IP
                            ----[ip]----
IP Ver  : 4                 IP HLen : 20 Bytes
TOS     : 0xc0              Pkt Len : 52         Seg ID   : 0x008f
Flags   : FRAG:*.LAST       Frag Ptr : 0   (8 Octet) TTL    : 64
PID     : OSPF ( 89)        Checksum : 0xefcd (Good)
Dst IP <C: 192.168.4.1      Src IP <C: 192.168.4.3
                            ----[ospf]----
OSPF Ver : 2                Type   : DD          Length   : 32
Router ID: 192.168.4.3      Area   ID: 0.0.0.0   Checksum : 0x2bc6
AU Type  : 00               AU Key   :  {        }
                            ----[DD]----
Reserved : 0x00000000       Options  : 0x0002
Flags    : I:* M:* MS:*     SeqNo    : 2917
========================[data:   4]====================================
0042  AB A7 C4 AF                         ....


========================µscope========================================
Frame   : 7                 Len    : 190         Error    : None
T Elapsed: 13:37:48:489     T Delta : 00:00:00:000
                            ----[mac]----
Dest Mac : Xyplex135b7e     Sourc Mac: Xyplex456866    Type    : IP
                            ----[ip]----
IP Ver  : 4                 IP HLen : 20 Bytes
TOS     : 0xc0              Pkt Len : 172        Seg ID   : 0x006e
Flags   : FRAG:*.LAST       Frag Ptr : 0   (8 Octet) TTL    : 64
PID     : OSPF ( 89)        Checksum : 0xef76 (Good)
Dst IP <C: 192.168.4.3      Src IP <C: 192.168.4.1
                            ----[ospf]----
OSPF Ver : 2                Type   : DD          Length   : 152
Router ID: 192.168.4.1      Area   ID: 0.0.0.0   Checksum : 0xd65b
AU Type  : 00               AU Key   :  {        }
                            ----[DD]----
Reserved : 0x00000000       Options  : 0x0002
Flags    : I:x M:x MS:x     SeqNo    : 2917
                            ----[lsa's:  6]----
Lsa  Age(S) Opts Type  AdvRtr        LSID      SeqNo     ChkSum  Len(B)
1      2   0x02 RLA  192.168.4.1   c0a80401  80000007   2a3c     72
2    380   0x02 RLA  192.168.4.3   c0a80403  80000008   b7f3     60
3    552   0x02 RLA  192.168.8.4   c0a80804  80000002   da46     48
4    552   0x02 RLA  192.168.9.5   c0a80905  80000002   cd4e     48
5    391   0x02 RLA  192.168.7.2   c0a80702  80000002   c223     72
6    332   0x00 NLA  192.168.4.3   c0a80403  80000003   a4f5     32
========================[data:   4]====================================
00BA  3A 69 0F 30                         :i.0
```

Router 1 sends first Database Description packet.

Flags field indicates that this is the *first packet*, that there is *more*, and that Router 1 desires to become *Master*.

Router 1 wishes to use an Initial *Sequence Number* of *1711*.

Router 3 sends its first Database Description packet.

Router 3 uses the flags field to indicate that this is the *first* packet, that there is *more*, and that it wishes to become *Master*.

Router 3 wishes to use an *Initial Sequence Number* of *2917*.

Router 1 sends the first *real* Database Description packet.

Router 1 concedes that it is the Slave. In this case there are no more packets.

Router 1 uses the Sequence Number proposed by Router 3.

Router 1 advertises that it knows about 5 Routers through Router Links Advertisements (RLAs), and 1 Transit Network through a Network Links Advertisement (NLA).

```
============================================μscope============================================
Frame    : 8              Len      : 170            Error     : None
T Elapsed: 13:37:48:498   T Delta  : 00:00:00:009
                          ----------[mac]-------
Dest Mac : Xyplex456866   Sourc Mac: Xyplex135b7e   Type      : IP
                          ----------[ip]--------
IP Ver   : 4              IP HLen  : 20 Bytes
TOS      : 0xc0           Pkt Len  : 152            Seg ID    : 0x0090
Flags    : FRAG:*.LAST    Frag Ptr : 0     (8 Octet) TTL      : 64
PID      : OSPF ( 89)     Checksum : 0xef68 (Good)
Dst IP <C: 192.168.4.1    Src IP <C: 192.168.4.3
                          ----------[ospf]------
OSPF Ver : 2              Type     : DD             Length    : 132
Router ID: 192.168.4.3    Area   ID: 0.0.0.0        Checksum  : 0x880f
AU Type  : 00             AU Key     {         }
                          ----------[DD]--------
Reserved : 0x00000000     Options  : 0x0002
Flags    : I:x M:x MS:*   SeqNo    : 2918
                          ----------[lsa's:  5]-----
Lsa Age(S) Opts Type   AdvRtr        LSID       SeqNo     ChkSum  Len(B)
1   338    0x02 RLA    192.168.4.1   c0a80401 80000004 8177    72
2   326    0x02 RLA    192.168.4.3   c0a80403 80000009 5dbf    60
3   550    0x02 RLA    192.168.8.4   c0a80804 80000002 da46    48
4   550    0x02 RLA    192.168.9.5   c0a80905 80000002 cd4e    48
5   391    0x02 RLA    192.168.7.2   c0a80702 80000002 c223    72
============================================[data:   4]============================================
00A6  27 3B 55 57                               ';UW
```

Router 3 sends its own Database Description packet.

Router 3 indicates that it is the Master.

Sequence Number is now incremented by 1.

Links Advertisements from Router 3.

Figure 11-19: Exchanging Database Description Packets

As we have said, the exchange of Database Description packets follows a *poll-response* procedure and the previous trace (Figure 11-19) shows such an exchange between routers 3, and 1. In this case, Router 3 is elected *Master* in the initial exchanges (frames 5 and 6) since this router has a higher *Router ID*. Router 1 then commences its sending of Database Descriptions using the sequence number chosen by Router 3. If the trace were to be continued, we would see Router 2 also exchange Database Description information. In this case however, although Router 1 is the BDR, Router 2 would become Master due to it's higher Router ID.

11.3.4 Requesting Additional Information Through Link State Requests (LSRs)

Once the Database Description packets have been successfully exchanged, each router compares the information received with that currently held and from this, generates a list of Link State Requests (LSRs). These LSRs are designed to allow the router to ensure that it is holding the most up-to-date information in its database and thus allow for full database synchronisation.

These requests are sent to the neighbor who, in turn, responds with full Link State Advertisements through Link State Update (LSU) packets. When the neighbor has responded with the proper LSU packet, it is acknowledged and the request is removed from the list and another LSR is then sent. This then continues until all the requests are satisfied.

The format of the Link State Request (without the OSPF header) is shown in Figure 11-20.

From the figure, it can be seen that a single Link State Request packet can carry multiple LSRs each uniquely identified by their *Type* (32 bits), *ID* (32 bits), and the *Router ID* of the router advertising them (32 bits). A request therefore is used to identify the advertisement but not a particular instance. Instead, requests imply that the most recent instance should be supplied. Once again, applying this to a practical example, the trace of Figure 11-21 shows the process of Link State Requests immediately following the Database Description exchange that we saw in the previous trace.

0	4	8	12	16	20	24	28	31
Link State Type 1								
Link State ID 1								
Advertising Router 1								
.....								
Link State Type n								
Link State ID n								
Advertising Router n								

Figure 11-20: Link State Request Packets

```
µSCOPE                   PACKET TRACE DECODE REPORT          (c) T.Kenyon 1995


==============================µscope=================================
Frame     : 9             Len     : 86            Error    : None        Router 3 sends its LSR to Router 1.
T Elapsed: 13:37:48:498   T Delta : 00:00:00:000
------------------------------[mac]----------------------------------
Dest Mac : Xyplex456866   Sourc Mac: Xyplex135b7e  Type     : IP         Router 3 requests further information
------------------------------[ip]-----------------------------------   about     the    Network   Links
IP Ver    : 4             IP HLen  : 20 Bytes                            Advertisement (NLA) for 192.168.4.3,
TOS       : 0xc0          Pkt Len  : 68             Seg ID  : 0x0091     and the Router Links Advertisement
Flags     : FRAG:*.LAST   Frag Ptr : 0   (8 Octet) TTL     : 64         (RLA) for the router with Router ID
PID       : OSPF ( 89)    Checksum : 0xefbb (Good)                      192.168.4.1.
Dst IP <C: 192.168.4.1    Src IP <C: 192.168.4.3
------------------------------[ospf]---------------------------------
OSPF Ver : 2              Type     : LSReq          Length  : 48
Router ID: 192.168.4.3    Area  ID: 0.0.0.0         Checksum : 0x2673
AU Type  : 00             AU Key   : {        }
------------------------------[lsr's: 2]-----------------------------
Lsa  Type  Rtr ID        Adv Rtr
1    NLA   192.168.4.3   192.168.4.3
2    RLA   192.168.4.1   192.168.4.1
==============================[data:   4]============================
0052  45 A1 E7 E8                            E...


==============================µscope=================================
Frame     : 10            Len     : 70            Error    : None        This is the last Database Description
T Elapsed: 13:37:48:498   T Delta : 00:00:00:000                         Packet acknowledging frame 8 in
------------------------------[mac]----------------------------------    figure 11-19.
Dest Mac : Xyplex135b7e   Sourc Mac: Xyplex456866  Type     : IP
------------------------------[ip]-----------------------------------    The Flags indicate that the source of
IP Ver    : 4             IP HLen  : 20 Bytes                            this packet is the Slave, and that this
TOS       : 0xc0          Pkt Len  : 52             Seg ID  : 0x006f     is the last DD packet.
Flags     : FRAG:*.LAST   Frag Ptr : 0   (8 Octet) TTL     : 64
PID       : OSPF ( 89)    Checksum : 0xefed (Good)
Dst IP <C: 192.168.4.3    Src IP <C: 192.168.4.1
------------------------------[ospf]---------------------------------
OSPF Ver : 2              Type     : DD             Length  : 32
Router ID: 192.168.4.1    Area  ID: 0.0.0.0         Checksum : 0x2bce
AU Type  : 00             AU Key   : {        }
------------------------------[DD]-----------------------------------
Reserved : 0x00000000     Options  : 0x0002
Flags    : I:x M:x MS:x   SeqNo    : 2918
==============================[data:   4]============================
0042  0E 9D 2F D0                            ../.


==============================µscope=================================
Frame     : 11            Len     : 74            Error    : None        Router 1 requests information about
T Elapsed: 13:37:48:498   T Delta : 00:00:00:000                         the Router Links Advertisement (RLA)
------------------------------[mac]----------------------------------    for the Router with ID 192.168.4.3.
Dest Mac : Xyplex135b7e   Sourc Mac: Xyplex456866  Type     : IP
------------------------------[ip]-----------------------------------
IP Ver    : 4             IP HLen  : 20 Bytes
TOS       : 0xc0          Pkt Len  : 56             Seg ID  : 0x0070
Flags     : FRAG:Ā.LAST   Frag Ptr : 0   (8 Octet) TTL     : 64
PID       : OSPF ( 89)    Checksum : 0xefe8 (Good)
Dst IP <C: 192.168.4.3    Src IP <C: 192.168.4.1
------------------------------[ospf]---------------------------------
OSPF Ver : 2              Type     : LSReq          Length  : 36
Router ID: 192.168.4.1    Area  ID: 0.0.0.0         Checksum : 0xafd6
AU Type  : 00             AU Key   : {        }
------------------------------[lsr's: 1]-----------------------------
Lsa  Type  Rtr ID        Adv Rtr
1    RLA   192.168.4.3   192.168.4.3
==============================[data:   4]============================
0046  CA 29 E0 B9                            .)..
```

Figure 11-21: Link State Requests

11.3.5 Link State Updates

Link State Update (LSU) packets contain an OSPF header followed by a number of Link State Advertisements (LSAs) as shown in Figure 11-22. In this figure, the entire packet is displayed with the Header itself shown shaded.

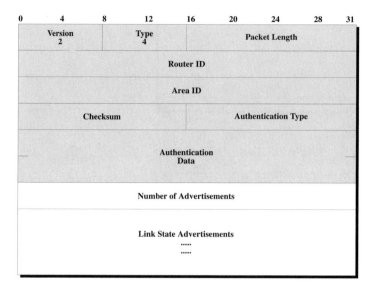

Figure 11-22: Link State Updates

These packets are sent in response to Link State Requests and must be acknowledged by the receiving router through Link State Acknowledgements. Acknowledgements, are simply OSPF Headers with a number of Link State Advertisement Headers immediately following the *Authentication* field. Acknowledgements may be either directed to the router that originated the update as a unicast or alternatively, may be sent to the *AllSPFRouters* Multicast address.

Many acknowledgements may be grouped together in a single Link State Acknowledgement packet. Directed Acknowledgements (those sent as unicasts) are sent immediately in response to a received *duplicate* LSA. Multicast Acknowledgements are delayed to allow for two things. Firstly, by delaying an acknowledgement, we are able to potentially acknowledge many LSAs at one time. Secondly, by multicasting, we can acknowledge LSAs received from several neighbors simultaneously.

11.3.6 Link State Advertisements

In all, there are six separate types of Link State Advertisement each starting with a common 20 octet Link State Advertisement header. These LSAs then describe a specific piece of information about the actual internet to which the router is connected.

All routers generate what is known as a Router Links Advertisement that describes both the number and types of links that the router has. This advertisement will tell neighbors the metrics for the links when various Types of Service (especially TOS-0[12]) are requested. Where the router is elected as the Designated Router, it will also generate a Network Links Advertisement. This tells neighbors about other routers that share the common network. Other advertisement types are also generated by ABRs and ASBRs, and are covered later.

The Link State Advertisement header (shown previously in Figure 11-18) contains a *Link State Type* field, used to define the type of advertisement and an *Options* field that is used to describe the capabilities of the router. Other fields then include the *Age* of the advertisement, it's *ID*, the ID of the router advertising it, and a *Sequence Number*.

Router Links Advertisements

Router Links Advertisements (Type 1) are generated by each router in an area and are used to describe the state and associated cost of each of the router's links to the area. All of the links and their associated metrics for each Type-of-Service supported must be described by a single router links advertisement potentially making these packets extremely large. The actual format of these packets (following the Link State Advertisement Header) is shown in Figure 11-23.

In the Advertisements, the flags V, E, and B describe additional information about the router and the actual link. The *V* flag is set when the router is the endpoint of an active *Virtual Link*[13], the *E* flag is set when the router is acting as an *Autonomous System Boundary Router*[14] (ASBR), and the *B* flag is set when the router is acting as an *Area Border Router*[15] (ABR).

The *Number of Links* Field (16 bits) is used to define the number of links that this router supports and therefore the overall size of this advertisement. The remaining fields then describe each router link.

The 8 bit *Type* field, the 32 bit *Link ID* and 32 bit *Link Data* fields are all connected. The Type field describes the type of link being described and the *Link ID* field describes what the router connects to. The actual value of this latter field will naturally depend upon the type of link however, where this itself would also originate a Link State Advertisement, the IDs from each will be identical. The *Link Data* again depends upon the type of link being described. Table 11-6 shows the values of each of these fields and how they interact.

The 8 bit *Number of Types-of-Service* field identifies how many different TOS metrics are included in the advertisement of this link. This figure excludes the metric for Type-of-Service zero since all links must have a metric associated with TOS-0 to make them compatible with TOS-0 only routers. For example, if the link advertisement supported only TOS-0, then this value would be 0.

12. All links must be configured with a metric for TOS-0 although they do not need to maintain metrics relating to other Types-of-Service – See Section 11.1.1.

13. Virtual Links are used only where an Autonomous System (AS) as divided into Areas and a distinct Area cannot be directly connected to the Backbone. This concept and its application is discussed in Section 11.5.2.

14. An Autonomous System Border Router is one that connects Autonomous Systems together. These routers by their definition, must run multiple routing protocols.

15. An Area Border Router is used to link Areas within an Autonomous System. Areas are discussed in Section 11.5.

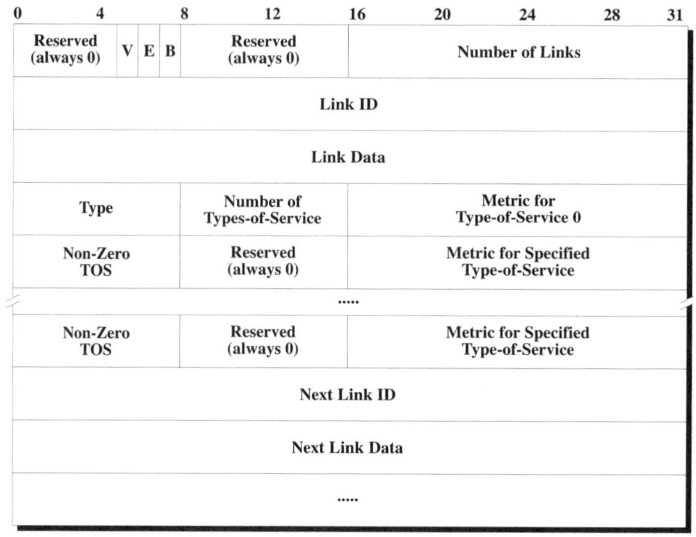

Figure 11-23: Router Links Advertisements

Table 11-6: Link ID and LSA Data Interaction

Type	Description	Link ID	Link Data
1	Point-to-Point Connection to another	The neighboring router's Router ID.	The interface's MIB II IfIndex value.
2	Connection to a Transit Network.[16]	The IP Address of the Designated Router.	The IP Address of the router interface.
3.	Connection to a Stub Network.[17]	The IP Network/ Subnet number.	The Network's IP Subnet Mask.
4.	Virtual Link.	The Neighboring router's Router ID.	The IP Address of the router interface.

The *Metric for Type-of-Service 0* field provides the 16 bit metric associated with routing a packet requesting TOS-0, or when no non-zero TOS route is available. This field must always be present. If applicable to this link, there may also be a number of *Non-Zero TOS* fields (8 bits) and associated *Metrics* (16 bits). Finally, the remaining links are described in the same way.

Network Links Advertisements

Network Links Advertisements (Type 2), are only originated by the Designated Router for the multi-access network. This packet lists the Subnet Mask (32 bits) and all of the routers attached to the network (including itself and all routers that are fully adjacent to it). In this way, all routers attached to the network are advertised through this single packet. The format of the packet (much simpler than that

16. A Transit Network is a Multi-Access (broadcast) network where more than one router is attached and therefore a DR exists.
17. A Stub Network is one where only a single router exists.

of the *Router Links Advertisement*) is shown below (excluding the *Link State Advertisement* Header):

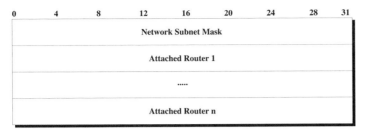

Figure 11-24: The Network Links Advertisement

Summary Links Advertisements

Summary Links Advertisements are generated by Area Border Routers to advertise destinations that belong to the Autonomous System but which are outside of the Area. Link State Type 3 advertisements, those relating to *IP Networks*, use the network address as the Link State ID. Type 4 advertisements, those from *Autonomous System Boundary Routers* (ASBRs) and therefore relating to a different AS, have the Router ID of the advertising router as the Link State ID. Other than this, the format of the advertisement packet is identical and (excluding the *Link State Advertisement* Header) is shown in Figure 11-25.

The Network Subnet Mask indicates the Subnet Mask that is associated with the advertised network. This is valid for Type 3 Link State Advertisements (those from ABRs) but has no meaning when generated by ASBRs (i.e. Type 4 LSAs). In the case of the ASBR then, this field is set to all zeroes.

The remainder of the packet then comprises an 8 bit Type-of-Service followed by a 12 bit metric associated with it. The only rules applied here are that the Types-of-Service must be listed in ascending order of magnitude, and that TOS-0 must be present (and listed first).

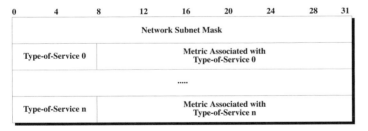

Figure 11-25: The Summary Links Advertisement

AS External Link Advertisements

Two types of advertisement are used as AS External Link State Advertisements. Both are generated by Autonomous System Boundary Routers (ASBRs) and use

LSA Types 5, and 7. The first, (Type 5) are generated as normal advertisements into an AS through a *plain* Area (i.e. not a Stub Area or NSSA). The second, (Type 7) are generated when the ASBR is connected to a NSSA.

The ASBR generates a separate LSA for each destination that is external to the Autonomous System with the Link State ID containing the network address of the destination network. Additionally, this advertisement type can be used to describe a Default Route.[18] In this case the Link State ID in the header, and Network Subnet Mask field in the LSA itself will both be set to 0.0.0.0.

The format of both AS External Link State Advertisement types is the same and is shown in Figure 11-26. The way in which the two types are handled and some of the fields however, are subtly different:

- You recall from our discussions surrounding Figure 11-12 that the *Options* field of OSPF Headers contains a bit called *N or P*. In Hello packets this bit is referred to as N and is used to describe the router's capability in a NSSA. This ensures that all routers in the NSSA will agree on the area's configuration. For example, if the bit is set off (0), the router will not generate nor accept Type 7 LSAs (NSSA Advertisements). This bit by it's definition then, works together with the E bit in these packets. Thus if it is set on, the E bit must be reset (0).

- Where the packet is a LSA Type 7, the bit is called the P bit. In these types of packet, when the bit is set, it indicates that NSSA Border Routers should translate the Type 7 LSA into a Type 5 (AS External Links Advertisement) LSA. In this way, Type 7 LSAs are only advertised within a single NSSA and are not flooded into the Backbone.

- A Type 7 LSA may be originated within a NSSA and also propagated thoughout it. In common with Stub Areas though, NSSAs will neither originate nor receive Type 5 LSAs.

The Network Subnet Mask field contains the subnet mask for the destination network provided that this is not a default route. Each route can then have a number of Types-of-Service associated with it which are described in the remainder of the packet.

For each TOS, the E bit specifies the *Type* of metric. Where this bit is on (i.e. 1), the metric is referred to as being of *Type 2* implying that it is the same as the metric stored in the routing table. Typically, this metric will be associated with another protocol. If the E bit is off (i.e. 0), the metric is referred to as being of *Type 1* and the size of the metric is comparable to the Link State metric. In other words, a Type 1 metric includes the costs associated with traversing the AS as well as the external cost.

One major advantage of Type 2 metrics is that they ignore the costs associated with traversing the AS, and therefore the cost of reaching the ASBR. Where the cost of reaching the ASBR, or the total cost of reaching the target network is the main criteria however, Type 1 metrics should be used.

The Forwarding Address (32 bits) is the address to which data for this destination will be forwarded. Where the address is 0.0.0.0 (i.e. a Default Route), the data is

18. Default Routes are used when no specific routes exist to a destination. For more information see Chapter 9.

forwarded to the advertising router instead (i.e. the ASBR responsible for delivery outside the AS).

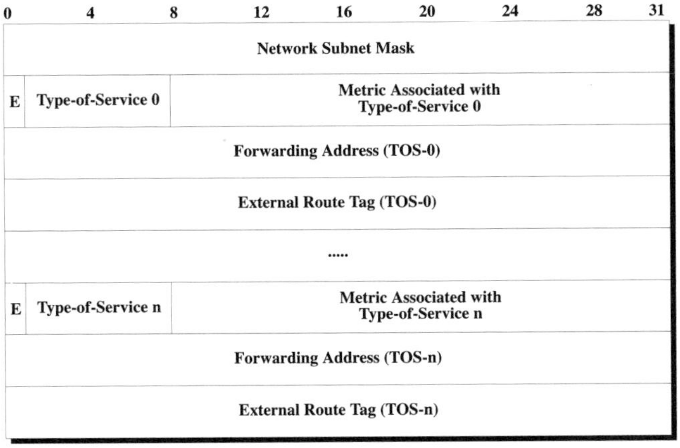

0	4	8	12	16	20	24	28	31

Network Subnet Mask

| E | Type-of-Service 0 | Metric Associated with Type-of-Service 0 |

Forwarding Address (TOS-0)

External Route Tag (TOS-0)

.....

| E | Type-of-Service n | Metric Associated with Type-of-Service n |

Forwarding Address (TOS-n)

External Route Tag (TOS-n)

Figure 11-26: The AS External Link Advertisement

The 32 bit External Route Tag is not actually used by OSPF but may be used to communicate information between ASBRs. The actual implementation of this field is not defined within RFC 1583 and is implementation specific.

Returning to our sample internet, the next trace shows how routers 1 and 3 exchange Link State Updates in response to the Link State Requests seen in Figure 11-21. Once this exchange is complete the databases will be synchronized and the routers will then be said to be *adjacent*.

```
µSCOPE                    PACKET TRACE DECODE REPORT         (c) T.Kenyon 1995

==============================µscope==============================
Frame    : 12              Len     : 170          Error    : None
T Elapsed: 13:37:48:498    T Delta : 00:00:00:000
                              -[mac]-
Dest Mac : Xyplex135b7e    Sourc Mac: Xyplex456866    Type     : IP
                              -[ip]-
IP Ver   : 4               IP HLen : 20 Bytes
TOS      : 0xc0            Pkt Len : 152          Seg ID    : 0x0071
Flags    : FRAG:*.LAST     Frag Ptr : 0    (8 Octet) TTL      : 64
PID      : OSPF ( 89)      Checksum : 0xef87 (Good)
Dst IP <C: 192.168.4.3     Src IP <C: 192.168.4.1
                              -[ospf]-
OSPF Ver : 2               Type    : LSUpd         Length   : 132
Router ID: 192.168.4.1     Area  ID: 0.0.0.0       Checksum : 0xb3ff
AU Type  : 00              AU Key  : {       }
                              -[lsu's: 2]-
Lsu  Age(S) Opts Type   AdvRtr      LSID     SeqNo   ChkSum  Len(B)
1    333   0x00 NLA    192.168.4.3  c0a80403 80000003 a4f5    32
2    3     0x02 RLA    192.168.4.1  c0a80401 80000007 2a3c    72
==============================[data:   0]==============================

==============================µscope==============================
Frame    : 13              Len     : 126          Error    : None
T Elapsed: 13:37:48:498    T Delta : 00:00:00:000
                              -[mac]-
Dest Mac : Xyplex456866    Sourc Mac: Xyplex135b7e    Type     : IP
                              -[ip]-
IP Ver   : 4               IP HLen : 20 Bytes
TOS      : 0xc0            Pkt Len : 108          Seg ID    : 0x0092
Flags    : FRAG:*.LAST     Frag Ptr : 0    (8 Octet) TTL      : 64
PID      : OSPF ( 89)      Checksum : 0xef92 (Good)
Dst IP <C: 192.168.4.1     Src IP <C: 192.168.4.3
                              -[ospf]-
OSPF Ver : 2               Type    : LSUpd         Length   : 88
Router ID: 192.168.4.3     Area  ID: 0.0.0.0       Checksum : 0x6582
AU Type  : 00              AU Key  : {       }
                              -[lsu's: 1]-
Lsu  Age(S) Opts Type   AdvRtr      LSID     SeqNo   ChkSum  Len(B)
1    327   0x02 RLA    192.168.4.3  c0a80403 80000009 5dbf    60
==============================[data:   0]==============================
```

Router 1 responds to Frame 9 (previous trace) and provides LSAs for the NLA 192.168.4.3, and the RLA 192.168.4.1.

Router 3 responds to frame 11 (previous trace) and provides the RLA for 192.168.4.3.

```
==============================μscope==============================
Frame    : 14              Len     : 98              Error    : None
T Elapsed: 13:37:48:509    T Delta : 00:00:00:011
------------------------------[mac]------------------------------
Dest Mac : 01005e000005    Sourc Mac: Xyplex135b7e   Type     : IP
------------------------------[ip]-------------------------------
IP Ver   : 4               IP HLen : 20 Bytes
TOS      : 0xc0            Pkt Len  : 80             Seg ID   : 0x0097
Flags    : FRAG:*.LAST     Frag Ptr : 0    (8 Octet) TTL      : 1 (Low)
PID      : OSPF ( 89)      Checksum : 0x134e (Good)
Dst IP <D: 224.0.0.5       Src IP <C: 192.168.4.3
------------------------------[ospf]-----------------------------
OSPF Ver : 2               Type     : LSUpd          Length   : 60
Router ID: 192.168.4.3     Area  ID : 0.0.0.0        Checksum : 0xf439
AU Type  : 00              AU Key   : {        }
------------------------------[lsu's: 1]-------------------------
Lsu  Age(S) Opts Type  AdvRtr       LSID      SeqNo    ChkSum  Len(B)
1    3600   0x00 NLA   192.168.4.3  c0a80403  80000003 a4f5    32
==============================[data:  0]==========================
```

Router 3 (the DR) sends a Multicast to flood the Transit Network 192.168.4.0 with a NLA relating to 192.168.

The Age of this advertisement is 3600 seconds (the maximum age allowed). Thus, this advertisement has been prematurely aged and then sent to Age-Out all instances of this LSA. This is done primarily to erase the entry held by router 192.168.4.1 who has no real claim to advertise the NLA in the first place.

```
==============================μscope==============================
Frame    : 15              Len     : 126             Error    : None
T Elapsed: 13:37:49:234    T Delta : 00:00:00:725
------------------------------[mac]------------------------------
Dest Mac : 01005e000005    Sourc Mac: Xyplex135b7e   Type     : IP
------------------------------[ip]-------------------------------
IP Ver   : 4               IP HLen : 20 Bytes
TOS      : 0xc0            Pkt Len  : 108            Seg ID   : 0x009a
Flags    : FRAG:*.LAST     Frag Ptr : 0    (8 Octet) TTL      : 1 (Low)
PID      : OSPF ( 89)      Checksum : 0x132f (Good)
Dst IP <D: 224.0.0.5       Src IP <C: 192.168.4.3
------------------------------[ospf]-----------------------------
OSPF Ver : 2               Type     : LSUpd          Length   : 88
Router ID: 192.168.4.3     Area  ID : 0.0.0.0        Checksum : 0x4be3
AU Type  : 00              AU Key   : {        }
------------------------------[lsu's: 1]-------------------------
Lsu  Age(S) Opts Type  AdvRtr       LSID      SeqNo    ChkSum  Len(B)
1    1      0x02 RLA   192.168.4.3  c0a80403  8000000a b3f5    60
==============================[data:  0]==========================
```

Router 3 generates and advertises a new RLA for itself. The Sequence number has been incremented 80000009 to 8000000a, and the Age has been set to 1 second.

```
==============================μscope==============================
Frame    : 16              Len     : 102             Error    : None
T Elapsed: 13:37:49:322    T Delta : 00:00:00:088
------------------------------[mac]------------------------------
Dest Mac : 01005e000005    Sourc Mac: Xyplex456866   Type     : IP
------------------------------[ip]-------------------------------
IP Ver   : 4               IP HLen : 20 Bytes
TOS      : 0xc0            Pkt Len  : 84             Seg ID   : 0x0072
Flags    : FRAG:*.LAST     Frag Ptr : 0    (8 Octet) TTL      : 1 (Low)
PID      : OSPF ( 89)      Checksum : 0x1371 (Good)
Dst IP <D: 224.0.0.5       Src IP <C: 192.168.4.1
------------------------------[ospf]-----------------------------
OSPF Ver : 2               Type     : LSAck          Length   : 64
Router ID: 192.168.4.1     Area  ID : 0.0.0.0        Checksum : 0x11ea
AU Type  : 00              AU Key   : {        }
------------------------------[lsa's: 2]-------------------------
Lsa  Age(S) Opts Type  AdvRtr       LSID      SeqNo    ChkSum  Len(B)
1    3600   0x00 NLA   192.168.4.3  c0a80403  80000003 a4f5    32
2    327    0x02 RLA   192.168.4.3  c0a80403  80000009 5dbf    60
==============================[data:  4]==========================
0062  AB 00 BD F8                                    ....
```

Router 1 acknowledges the *old* NLA for 192.168.4.0, and the *old* RLA for 192.168.4.3. This is a *Delayed Acknowledgement* so that multiple LSAs can be acknowledged simultaneously.

```
==============================μscope==============================
Frame    : 17              Len     : 82              Error    : None
T Elapsed: 13:37:49:503    T Delta : 00:00:00:181
------------------------------[mac]------------------------------
Dest Mac : 01005e000005    Sourc Mac: Xyplex135b7e   Type     : IP
------------------------------[ip]-------------------------------
IP Ver   : 4               IP HLen : 20 Bytes
TOS      : 0xc0            Pkt Len  : 64             Seg ID   : 0x009b
Flags    : FRAG:*.LAST     Frag Ptr : 0    (8 Octet) TTL      : 1 (Low)
PID      : OSPF ( 89)      Checksum : 0x135a (Good)
Dst IP <D: 224.0.0.5       Src IP <C: 192.168.4.3
------------------------------[ospf]-----------------------------
OSPF Ver : 2               Type     : LSAck          Length   : 44
Router ID: 192.168.4.3     Area  ID : 0.0.0.0        Checksum : 0x0340
AU Type  : 00              AU Key   : {        }
------------------------------[lsa's: 1]-------------------------
Lsa  Age(S) Opts Type  AdvRtr       LSID      SeqNo    ChkSum  Len(B)
1    3      0x02 RLA   192.168.4.1  c0a80401  80000007 2a3c    72
==============================[data:  4]==========================
004E  C6 16 81 7E                                    ...~
```

Router 3 sends a Delayed Ack, acknowledging the RLA for 192.168.4.1.

The Open Shortest Path First Protocol (OSPF)

```
===========================μscope============================
Frame    : 18          Len    : 86          Error    : None
T Elapsed: 13:37:50:345 T Delta  : 00:00:00:842
----------------------------[mac]----------------------------
Dest Mac : 01005e000005  Sourc Mac: Xyplex456866  Type    : IP
----------------------------[ip]-----------------------------
IP Ver  : 4            IP HLen  : 20 Bytes
TOS     : 0xc0         Pkt Len  : 68           Seg ID  : 0x0076
Flags   : FRAG:*.LAST  Frag Ptr : 0    (8 Octet) TTL     : 1 (Low)
PID     : OSPF ( 89)   Checksum : 0x137d (Good)
Dst IP <D: 224.0.0.5   Src IP <C: 192.168.4.1
----------------------------[ospf]---------------------------
OSPF Ver : 2           Type   : HELLO        Length   : 48
Router ID: 192.168.4.1 Area   ID: 0.0.0.0    Checksum : 0xe9ef
AU Type  : 00          AU Key   : {       }
----------------------------[hello]--------------------------
Hello Msk: 255.255.255.0  Hello Int: 10       Hello Pri: 1
Options  : 02          Dead Int : 40
DR       : 192.168.4.3 BDR      : 192.168.4.1
Neighbour: 192.168.4.3
============================[data:   4]=======================
0052  FE E6 99 38                         ...8


===========================μscope============================
Frame    : 19          Len    : 98          Error    : None
T Elapsed: 13:37:50:353 T Delta  : 00:00:00:008
----------------------------[mac]----------------------------
Dest Mac : 01005e000005  Sourc Mac: Xyplex135b7e  Type    : IP
----------------------------[ip]-----------------------------
IP Ver  : 4            IP HLen  : 20 Bytes
TOS     : 0xc0         Pkt Len  : 80           Seg ID  : 0x009e
Flags   : FRAG:*.LAST  Frag Ptr : 0    (8 Octet) TTL     : 1 (Low)
PID     : OSPF ( 89)   Checksum : 0x1347 (Good)
Dst IP <D: 224.0.0.5   Src IP <C: 192.168.4.3
----------------------------[ospf]---------------------------
OSPF Ver : 2           Type   : LSUpd        Length   : 60
Router ID: 192.168.4.3 Area   ID: 0.0.0.0    Checksum : 0x0447
AU Type  : 00          AU Key   : {       }
----------------------------[lsu's:  1]----------------------
Lsu Age(S) Opts Type   AdvRtr      LSID    SeqNo     ChkSum  Len(B)
1     1   0x00 NLA    192.168.4.3  c0a80403 80000004 a2f6    32
============================[data:   0]=======================


===========================μscope============================
Frame    : 20          Len    : 138         Error    : None
T Elapsed: 13:37:51:369 T Delta  : 00:00:01:016
----------------------------[mac]----------------------------
Dest Mac : 01005e000005  Sourc Mac: Xyplex456866  Type    : IP
----------------------------[ip]-----------------------------
IP Ver  : 4            IP HLen  : 20 Bytes
TOS     : 0xc0         Pkt Len  : 120          Seg ID  : 0x0077
Flags   : FRAG:*.LAST  Frag Ptr : 0    (8 Octet) TTL     : 1 (Low)
PID     : OSPF ( 89)   Checksum : 0x1348 (Good)
Dst IP <D: 224.0.0.5   Src IP <C: 192.168.4.1
----------------------------[ospf]---------------------------
OSPF Ver : 2           Type   : LSUpd        Length   : 100
Router ID: 192.168.4.1 Area   ID: 0.0.0.0    Checksum : 0xd84c
AU Type  : 00          AU Key   : {       }
----------------------------[lsu's:  1]----------------------
Lsu Age(S) Opts Type   AdvRtr      LSID    SeqNo     ChkSum  Len(B)
1     1   0x02 RLA    192.168.4.1  c0a80401 80000008 797b    72
============================[data:   0]=======================


===========================μscope============================
Frame    : 21          Len    : 126         Error    : None
T Elapsed: 13:37:55:630 T Delta  : 00:00:04:261
----------------------------[mac]----------------------------
Dest Mac : 01005e000005  Sourc Mac: Xyplex135b7e  Type    : IP
----------------------------[ip]-----------------------------
IP Ver  : 4            IP HLen  : 20 Bytes
TOS     : 0xc0         Pkt Len  : 108          Seg ID  : 0x00a1
Flags   : FRAG:*.LAST  Frag Ptr : 0    (8 Octet) TTL     : 1 (Low)
PID     : OSPF ( 89)   Checksum : 0x1328 (Good)
Dst IP <D: 224.0.0.5   Src IP <C: 192.168.4.3
----------------------------[ospf]---------------------------
OSPF Ver : 2           Type   : LSUpd        Length   : 88
Router ID: 192.168.4.3 Area   ID: 0.0.0.0    Checksum : 0x4de1
AU Type  : 00          AU Key   : {       }
----------------------------[lsu's:  1]----------------------
Lsu Age(S) Opts Type   AdvRtr      LSID    SeqNo     ChkSum  Len(B)
1     1   0x02 RLA    192.168.4.3  c0a80403 8000000b b1f6    60
============================[data:   0]=======================
```

Standard Hello packet sent from Router 1. This acknowledges that Router 3 is the DR, that it is the BDR, and that it has seen Router 3 within the last *Router Dead Interval.*

A new NLA for 192.168.4.0 has been created by Router 3. Again the Sequence Number has been incremented 80000003 (frame 14) to 80000004, and the Age has been reset to 1 second. This is then Multicast to Network 192.168.4.0 to flood the transit network.

Router 1 creates a new RLA for 192.168.4.1.

Router 3 creates a new RLA for 192.168.4.3.

```
===========================================µscope========================================
Frame    : 22              Len     : 82              Error     : None
T Elapsed: 13:37:56:464    T Delta : 00:00:00:834
-------------------------------------------[mac]-----------------------------------------
Dest Mac : 01005e000005    Sourc Mac: Xyplex456866    Type      : IP
-------------------------------------------[ip]------------------------------------------
IP Ver   : 4               IP HLen : 20 Bytes
TOS      : 0xc0            Pkt Len : 64              Seg ID    : 0x0078
Flags    : FRAG:*.LAST     Frag Ptr: 0      (8 Octet)  TTL       : 1 (Low)
PID      : OSPF ( 89)      Checksum : 0x137f (Good)
Dst IP <D: 224.0.0.5       Src IP <C: 192.168.4.1
-------------------------------------------[ospf]---------------------------------------
OSPF Ver : 2               Type     : LSAck           Length    : 44
Router ID: 192.168.4.1     Area   ID: 0.0.0.0         Checksum  : 0x7b8d
AU Type  : 00              AU Key   : {        }
-------------------------------------------[lsa's:  1]---------------------------------
Lsa  Age(S) Opts Type  AdvRtr        LSID     SeqNo    ChkSum  Len(B)
1      1   0x02 RLA   192.168.4.3   c0a80403 8000000b b1f6     60
==========================================[data:   4]===================================
004E  A6 21 01 EF                                     .!..
```

Router 1 acknowledges the new RLA for 192.168.4.1 (frame 21).

```
===========================================µscope========================================
Frame    : 23              Len     : 98              Error     : None
T Elapsed: 13:37:58:685    T Delta : 00:00:02:221
-------------------------------------------[mac]-----------------------------------------
Dest Mac : Xyplex456866    Sourc Mac: Xyplex135b7e    Type      : IP
-------------------------------------------[ip]------------------------------------------
IP Ver   : 4               IP HLen : 20 Bytes
TOS      : 0xc0            Pkt Len : 80              Seg ID    : 0x00a2
Flags    : FRAG:*.LAST     Frag Ptr: 0      (8 Octet)  TTL       : 64
PID      : OSPF ( 89)      Checksum : 0xef9e (Good)
Dst IP <C: 192.168.4.1     Src IP <C: 192.168.4.3
-------------------------------------------[ospf]---------------------------------------
OSPF Ver : 2               Type     : LSUpd           Length    : 60
Router ID: 192.168.4.3     Area   ID: 0.0.0.0         Checksum  : 0x043f
AU Type  : 00              AU Key   : {        }
-------------------------------------------[lsu's:  1]---------------------------------
Lsu  Age(S) Opts Type  AdvRtr        LSID     SeqNo    ChkSum  Len(B)
1      9   0x00 NLA   192.168.4.3   c0a80403 80000004 a2f6     32
==========================================[data:   0]===================================
```

Router 3 sends an Update to Router 1 advertising NLA for 192.168.4.0.

```
===========================================µscope========================================
Frame    : 24              Len     : 86              Error     : None
T Elapsed: 13:37:58:685    T Delta : 00:00:00:000
-------------------------------------------[mac]-----------------------------------------
Dest Mac : 01005e000005    Sourc Mac: Xyplex135b7e    Type      : IP
-------------------------------------------[ip]------------------------------------------
IP Ver   : 4               IP HLen : 20 Bytes
TOS      : 0xc0            Pkt Len : 68              Seg ID    : 0x00a3
Flags    : FRAG:*.LAST     Frag Ptr: 0      (8 Octet)  TTL       : 1 (Low)
PID      : OSPF ( 89)      Checksum : 0x134e (Good)
Dst IP <D: 224.0.0.5       Src IP <C: 192.168.4.3
-------------------------------------------[ospf]---------------------------------------
OSPF Ver : 2               Type     : HELLO           Length    : 48
Router ID: 192.168.4.3     Area   ID: 0.0.0.0         Checksum  : 0xe9ef
AU Type  : 00              AU Key   : {        }
-------------------------------------------[hello]-------------------------------------
Hello Msk: 255.255.255.0   Hello Int: 10             Hello Pri: 1
Options  : 02              Dead Int : 40
DR       : 192.168.4.3     BDR      : 192.168.4.1
Neighbour: 192.168.4.1
==========================================[data:   4]===================================
0052  78 AA 3E 3E                                     x.>>
```

Standard Hello packet from Router 3 declaring itself as DR, Router 1 as BDR, and indicating that it has seen Router 1 within the last Router Dead Interval.

```
===========================================µscope========================================
Frame    : 25              Len     : 82              Error     : None
T Elapsed: 13:37:59:526    T Delta : 00:00:00:841
-------------------------------------------[mac]-----------------------------------------
Dest Mac : 01005e000005    Sourc Mac: Xyplex456866    Type      : IP
-------------------------------------------[ip]------------------------------------------
IP Ver   : 4               IP HLen : 20 Bytes
TOS      : 0xc0            Pkt Len : 64              Seg ID    : 0x0079
Flags    : FRAG:*.LAST     Frag Ptr: 0      (8 Octet)  TTL       : 1 (Low)
PID      : OSPF ( 89)      Checksum : 0x137e (Good)
Dst IP <D: 224.0.0.5       Src IP <C: 192.168.4.1
-------------------------------------------[ospf]---------------------------------------
OSPF Ver : 2               Type     : LSAck           Length    : 44
Router ID: 192.168.4.1     Area   ID: 0.0.0.0         Checksum  : 0x8ca7
AU Type  : 00              AU Key   : {        }
-------------------------------------------[lsa's:  1]---------------------------------
Lsa  Age(S) Opts Type  AdvRtr        LSID     SeqNo    ChkSum  Len(B)
1      9   0x00 NLA   192.168.4.3   c0a80403 80000004 a2f6     32
==========================================[data:   4]===================================
004E  72 6C 2B 1E                                     rl+.
```

Acknowledgement sent to the Multicast address from Router 1 acknowledging the NLA for 192.168.4.0 (frames 19 and 23).

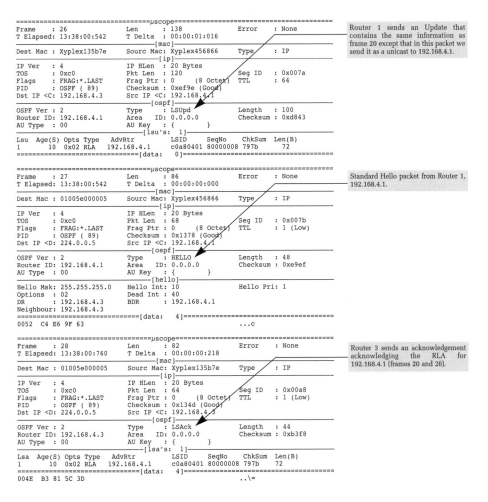

```
=========================================μscope=========================================
Frame    : 26              Len      : 138          Error    : None
T Elapsed: 13:38:00:542    T Delta  : 00:00:01:016
                                    -[mac]-
Dest Mac : Xyplex135b7e    Sourc Mac: Xyplex456866  Type     : IP
                                    -[ip]-
IP Ver   : 4               IP HLen  : 20 Bytes
TOS      : 0xc0            Pkt Len  : 120          Seg ID   : 0x007a
Flags    : FRAG:*.LAST     Frag Ptr : 0      (8 Octet)  TTL      : 64
PID      : OSPF ( 89)      Checksum : 0xef9e (Good)
Dst IP <C: 192.168.4.3     Src IP <C: 192.168.4.1
                                    -[ospf]-
OSPF Ver : 2               Type     : LSUpd        Length   : 100
Router ID: 192.168.4.1     Area   ID: 0.0.0.0      Checksum : 0xd843
AU Type  : 00              AU Key   : {         }
                                    -[lsu's:  1]-
Lsu  Age(S) Opts Type  AdvRtr       LSID      SeqNo     ChkSum  Len(B)
1       10  0x02 RLA   192.168.4.1  c0a80401  80000008  797b      72
=========================================[data:    0]=========================================
```

Router 1 sends an Update that contains the same information as frame 20 except that in this packet we send it as a unicast to 192.168.4.1.

```
=========================================μscope=========================================
Frame    : 27              Len      : 86           Error    : None
T Elapsed: 13:38:00:542    T Delta  : 00:00:00:000
                                    -[mac]-
Dest Mac : 01005e000005    Sourc Mac: Xyplex456866  Type     : IP
                                    -[ip]-
IP Ver   : 4               IP HLen  : 20 Bytes
TOS      : 0xc0            Pkt Len  : 68           Seg ID   : 0x007b
Flags    : FRAG:*.LAST     Frag Ptr : 0      (8 Octet)  TTL      : 1 (Low)
PID      : OSPF ( 89)      Checksum : 0x1378 (Good)
Dst IP <D: 224.0.0.5       Src IP <C: 192.168.4.1
                                    -[ospf]-
OSPF Ver : 2               Type     : HELLO        Length   : 48
Router ID: 192.168.4.1     Area   ID: 0.0.0.0      Checksum : 0xe9ef
AU Type  : 00              AU Key   : {         }
                                    -[hello]-
Hello Msk: 255.255.255.0   Hello Int: 10           Hello Pri: 1
Options  : 02              Dead Int : 40
DR       : 192.168.4.3     BDR      : 192.168.4.1
Neighbour: 192.168.4.3
=========================================[data:    4]=========================================
0052  C4 E6 9F 63                              ...c
```

Standard Hello packet from Router 1, 192.168.4.1.

```
=========================================μscope=========================================
Frame    : 28              Len      : 82           Error    : None
T Elapsed: 13:38:00:760    T Delta  : 00:00:00:218
                                    -[mac]-
Dest Mac : 01005e000005    Sourc Mac: Xyplex135b7e  Type     : IP
                                    -[ip]-
IP Ver   : 4               IP HLen  : 20 Bytes
TOS      : 0xc0            Pkt Len  : 64           Seg ID   : 0x00a8
Flags    : FRAG:*.LAST     Frag Ptr : 0      (8 Octet)  TTL      : 1 (Low)
PID      : OSPF ( 89)      Checksum : 0x134d (Good)
Dst IP <D: 224.0.0.5       Src IP <C: 192.168.4.3
                                    -[ospf]-
OSPF Ver : 2               Type     : LSAck        Length   : 44
Router ID: 192.168.4.3     Area   ID: 0.0.0.0      Checksum : 0xb3f8
AU Type  : 00              AU Key   : {         }
                                    -[lsa's:  1]-
Lsa  Age(S) Opts Type  AdvRtr       LSID      SeqNo     ChkSum  Len(B)
1       10  0x02 RLA   192.168.4.1  c0a80401  80000008  797b      72
=========================================[data:    4]=========================================
004E  B3 81 5C 3D                              ..\=
```

Router 3 sends an acknowledgement acknowledging the RLA for 192.168.4.1 (frames 20 and 26).

Figure 11-27: Sample Trace Showing Link State Updates

11.4 Creating the Shortest Path Tree

Once the databases within neighboring routers have been synchronized and the router has achieved adjacency with the DR (and potentially BDR), each router then creates what is known as a *Shortest Path Tree* (SPT) from it's newly synchronized database. Once created, this tree is then used as the basis for the creation of the router's routing table. Where multiple *Types of Service* are supported, one SPT must be created for each TOS thereby increasing the overhead on the router. In any event, a SPT *must* be created for TOS-0, since all routers must support this as a minimum. When creating the SPT, the router places itself at the root of a chart that maps routes to all networks and routers within the internet. In this way, the router will now know the best possible routes to all networks. This process is best described with

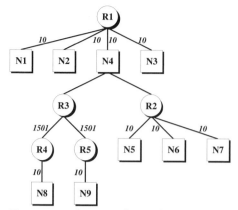

Figure 11-28: Shortest Path Tree for Router 1

Figure 11-28 which examines our sample network and looks at the SPT created by Router 1. Notice that the metric assigned to the WAN interfaces of Router 3 is 1501 (broadly equivalent to a 64k link). In actual fact, the metric assigned to the other ends of these links (at Routers 4 and 5) is 1602 although this is not shown in the preceding figure since the links are un-numbered, and are therefore shown direct. Should the links have been numbered, the router would have included a route to each interface connected to the link, a concept that can serve to confuse the unwary. Indeed if this were the case, our SPT would now appear as shown in Figure 11-29.

Having constructed the Shortest Path Tree (and we shall assume un-numbered links), the router is now able to create a routing table that identifies routes to every network within the internet based upon best possible paths.

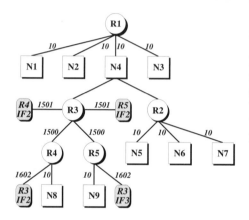

Figure 11-29: Shortest Path Tree for Router 1 Using Numbered Links

11.4.1 The Routing Table

Once the Shortest Path Tree has been created, we will be in a position to create the routing table. Again with reference to Router 1 from our sample network, the figure below shows such a table. Notice that some routes have an asterisk (*) next to them indicating a preferred route. This is of particular relevance where multiple, equal cost, routes exist.

```
08-00-87-05-68-66 (X056866)            BR/410         9 Feb 1996 20:35:55

Destination   Mask           Next Hop      Intf    Prot Pref   Metric Typ
192.168.1.0   255.255.255.0                 1      Local  *
192.168.2.0   255.255.255.0                 2      Local  *
192.168.3.0   255.255.255.0                 3      Local  *
192.168.4.0   255.255.255.0                 4      Local  *
192.168.5.0   255.255.255.0  192.168.4.2    4      Ospf   1*       20
192.168.6.0   255.255.255.0  192.168.4.2    4      Ospf   1*       20
192.168.7.0   255.255.255.0  192.168.4.2    4      Ospf   1*       20
192.168.8.0   255.255.255.0  192.168.4.3    4      Ospf   1*     1521
192.168.9.0   255.255.255.0  192.168.4.3    4      Ospf   1*     1521
```

Figure 11-30: Routing Table for Router 1

11.5 Using Areas

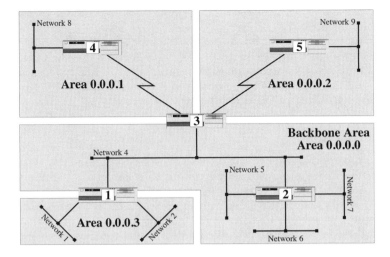

Figure 11-31: An Example of Areas

OSPF, as we have already said, allows you to group contiguous networks together into what are known as *Areas*. An area itself contains the networks (and of course the hosts) together with the routers that interconnect them. This then means that each area within the Autonomous System will run its own routing algorithm,[19] and routers within the area will therefore share a common view of the area's topology through their databases. Thus, when areas are used, we can no longer say that *all* routers within an AS will have identical databases. In actual fact, the topology of an area is invisible from the outside of that area. Equally, *Internal Routers* within an area will know nothing of the detailed topology external to the area. So what are the advantages of using areas, and when would we typically need them?

The main advantages of using areas lies in the fact that by splitting the AS in this way, we can achieve a significant reduction in the actual amount of routing traffic. Secondly, we effect some measure of protection against bad information and routing failures. For example, a potentially catastrophic failure in one area of our internet need not affect the entire AS. However, as to when areas are required, this is generally less clear. As a rule, where an AS incorporates more than say 30 routers, we should consider using areas. This is not to say that improvements will not be seen with less, but it is true to say that with around 30 routers we will almost certainly benefit.

Routers that interconnect areas have multiple databases, one for each area to which they connect. These routers, known as *Area Border Routers* (ABRs), then summarize information from one area and pass this summarized information into the others. Figure 11-31 shows a simple example of how we might split an AS into areas. The IP Addresses assigned to the networks are the same as were used

19. Do not confuse the term routing algorithm with routing protocol as all Areas will run OSPF.

throughout this chapter (see section 11.3, Figure 11-9) with the exception that in this example, Router 1 has only three interfaces in use (IF 1, 2, and 4). While not essential to this model, it does show that interfaces can be disabled without affecting the overall operation of OSPF.

Areas are identified by a unique 32 bit identifier called the *Area ID*. The choice of a 32 bit ID is not accidental. In fact the original thinking behind this, was that if an internet is split into areas based around Subnets, the Area ID could reflect the Subnets in use. There are not however any hard and fast rules, and indeed any Area ID could be used provided that it is *unique* within the internet.

11.5.1 The Backbone Area

Where an AS is divided into areas, one *special* area must be configured that will be responsible for the distribution of routing information and traffic between areas. This area, known as the Backbone, consists of all networks that are not part of any other area, the routers that interconnect them, the hosts that exist on these networks, and any routers that are connected to multiple areas (Area Border Routers). All ABRs therefore naturally connect to the backbone since it is through these routers that all inter-area data must pass. In actual fact, where we do not have areas configured, all networks, hosts, and routers will exist (typically transparently) within this area. So regardless of the OSPF configuration, a backbone *must* always exist, and it exhibits all of the properties of any other area as we have previously described.

ABRs run multiple copies of the OSPF algorithm, one for each area to which they connect. Each non-backbone interface will then accept information from other routers that are members of the area. Another copy then runs on the interface that connects to the backbone. This other copy does not flood the backbone with information learnt from the other area(s) however. Instead, the interface that connects to the backbone sends Summary Link Advertisements. Similarly, the other (non-backbone) interfaces send Summary Links Advertisements back to the connected area rather than flood them with backbone information. In this way, a reduction in routing traffic and a level of protection against routing failures are achieved.

11.5.2 Virtual Links

One difference between the Backbone and other areas is that the area does not need to be physically contiguous. In other words, the backbone itself can exist in two physical areas, logically linked by what is known as a *Virtual Link*.

This facility is important since it is sometimes impossible to connect an area to the backbone, simply due to geographical constraints. For example, if we consider the internet shown in Figure 11-32, it is possible that the topology of all areas could be complex enough to justify them being areas in their own right. The geography of the internet and the WAN links available however may dictate that Area 0.0.0.3 must be remote.

The Open Shortest Path First Protocol (OSPF)

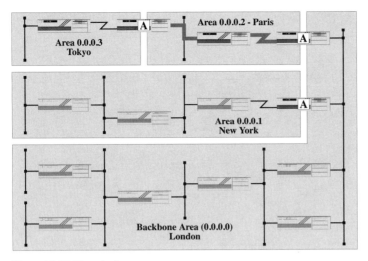

Figure 11-32: Remote Areas

In this example, all ABRs are identified with the letter A. Here we see that the backbone is made contiguous by configuring a Virtual Link between the Backbone and Area 0.0.0.3 (shown by the thick shaded line). This allows the ABR connected to the backbone to provide connectivity to the ABR at the far end of the link, with the virtual link then being treated in a similar manner to Point-to-Point links.

Inter-area routes that are flooded across the backbone are sent to the far ABR just as if it were to be connected directly to the backbone. In turn, the far ABR summarizes the routes advertised internally to Area 0.0.0.3, and passes these back to the backbone. All virtual links must be configured (normally manually) between ABRs using the Router ID to identify them rather than the IP Address of any one interface. One rule about ABRs however, is that (with the exception of the ABR connected to the backbone) all ABRs must belong to at least one non-backbone area. This area is then known as a *virtual link transit area*.

While this example is valid, it is not the most common implementation of Virtual Links. Remember that all inter-area traffic must pass through the backbone area. Thus, a scenario involving a *detached* backbone is often used to increase resilience. Consider Figure 11-33.

In this example we are attempting to achieve a measure of resilience so that we could afford for one WAN link to fail, while still maintaining connectivity to all networks. One might reasonably assume that we could take the upper WAN link and join it in such a way that it was part of Area 0.0.0.1 thereby making Router 7 an ABR and leaving Router 6 as an Internal Router. By the same argument of course, one might think that this link could become part of Area 0.0.0.2 making Router 6 the ABR. Neither of these scenarios would provide the resilience that we need however.

Consider for a moment what would happen if Router 7 was an ABR, and the upper WAN link was part of Area 0.0.0.1. Next, think what would happen if the WAN link between Routers 3 and 4 went down. Could we reach Network 8? Sadly no, because all inter-area traffic must pass through the Backbone. Thus our only alternative to provide the resilience required is to make both Router 6 and

Router 7 ABRs, and to configure Virtual Links between them and Router 3 as shown Figure 11-33.

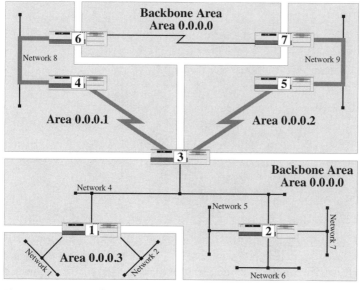

Figure 11-33: A Detached Backbone

When designing complex OSPF internets that will incorporate areas, care must be taken to provide the correct level of resilience. OSPF does not repair areas. Thus, if an area becomes isolated, OSPF will not attempt to reconstruct the overall topology. Routes will therefore only remain available where sufficient thought is given to resilience as the internet is designed.

11.5.3 Intra-Area and Inter-Area Routing

Where areas are configured, routing within the AS takes place on two levels depending upon whether the source and destination stations reside in the same area. Where they do, *intra-area* routing is used, using information available solely within the area. No information regarding external areas is required.

Where data needs to be routed between areas, a three stage process is used where the data traverses three distinct intra-area paths, with the routing algorithm choosing those with the least cost for the TOS requested. These paths can then be described as:

- A path that takes our data from the source host to the ABR. This path takes our data across the source area to the best exit point (the ABR).

- A path that routes our data across the backbone between the source and destination areas. From the ABR that links our source area to the backbone, to the ABR that links the backbone to the destination area.

The Open Shortest Path First Protocol (OSPF)

- A path that delivers our data to the destination host. In other words, a path from the destination ABR to the destination host.

For example, with our internet described in Figure 11-31, the Shortest Path Tree for Router 2 (assuming un-numbered links were used) would now look like that shown in Figure 11-34.

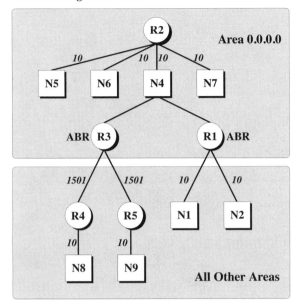

Figure 11-34: Shortest Path Tree for Router 2

Again with reference to Figure 11-31, the following trace (Figure 11-35) shows the start of routers 1 and 3 becoming adjacent and the types of advertisements exchanged. For this trace we begin with only Router 3 running, and then power on Router 1. We then see Summary Links Advertisements are sent for networks that exist outside of the backbone, while standard advertisements are used for the backbone area itself.

```
µSCOPE                    PACKET TRACE DECODE REPORT           (c) T.Kenyon 1995
                          ---------------------------------------------------

===============================µscope===========================================
Frame    : 1              Len     : 82              Error    : None          Router 3 sends a Hello packet to the
T Elapsed: 18:59:36:609   T Delta : 00:00:41:931                             AllSPFRouters Multicast Address.
                                    -[mac]-
Dest Mac : 01005e000005   Sourc Mac: Xyplex135b7e   Type      : IP
                                    -[ip]-
IP Ver   : 4              IP HLen  : 20 Bytes
TOS      : 0xc0           Pkt Len  : 64             Seg ID   : 0x0013
Flags    : FRAG:*.LAST    Frag Ptr : 0     (8 Octet) TTL      : 1
PID      : OSPF ( 89)     Checksum : 0x13e2 (Good)
Dst IP <D: 224.0.0.5      Src IP <C: 192.168.4.3
                                    -[ospf]-
OSPF Ver : 2              Type     : HELLO           Length   : 44
Router ID: 192.168.4.3    Area  ID: 0.0.0.0          Checksum : 0x7347
AU Type  : 00             AU Key   : {        }
                                    -[hello]-
Hello Msk: 255.255.255.0  Hello Int: 10              Hello Pri: 1
Options  : 02             Dead Int : 40
DR       : 192.168.4.3    BDR      : 0.0.0.0
==============================[data:   4]=======================================
004E  09 41 A5 8D                                    .A..
```

```
=============================μscope=============================
Frame   : 2                 Len     : 82              Error   : None
T Elapsed: 18:59:46:804     T Delta : 00:00:10:195
-----------------------------[mac]------------------------------
Dest Mac : 01005e000005     Sourc Mac: Xyplex135b7e   Type    : IP
-----------------------------[ip]-------------------------------
IP Ver   : 4                IP HLen  : 20 Bytes
TOS      : 0xc0             Pkt Len  : 64             Seg ID   : 0x0014
Flags    : FRAG:*.LAST      Frag Ptr : 0    (8 Octet) TTL      : 1
PID      : OSPF ( 89)       Checksum : 0x13e1 (Good)
Dst IP <D: 224.0.0.5        Src IP <C: 192.168.4.3
-----------------------------[ospf]-----------------------------
OSPF Ver : 2                Type     : HELLO          Length   : 44
Router ID: 192.168.4.3      Area  ID: 0.0.0.0         Checksum : 0x7347
AU Type  : 00               AU Key   : {       }
-----------------------------[hello]----------------------------
Hello Msk: 255.255.255.0    Hello Int: 10             Hello Pri: 1
Options  : 02               Dead Int : 40
DR       : 192.168.4.3      BDR      : 0.0.0.0
============================[data:   4]=========================
004E  5C 8E 59 CB                                     \.Y.


=============================μscope=============================
Frame   : 3                 Len     : 82              Error   : None
T Elapsed: 18:59:47:937     T Delta : 00:00:01:133
-----------------------------[mac]------------------------------
Dest Mac : 01005e000005     Sourc Mac: Xyplex456866   Type    : IP
-----------------------------[ip]-------------------------------
IP Ver   : 4                IP HLen  : 20 Bytes
TOS      : 0xc0             Pkt Len  : 64             Seg ID   : 0x0002
Flags    : FRAG:*.LAST      Frag Ptr : 0    (8 Octet) TTL      : 1
PID      : OSPF ( 89)       Checksum : 0x13f5 (Good)
Dst IP <D: 224.0.0.5        Src IP <C: 192.168.4.1
-----------------------------[ospf]-----------------------------
OSPF Ver : 2                Type     : HELLO          Length   : 44
Router ID: 192.168.4.1      Area  ID: 0.0.0.0         Checksum : 0x37f5
AU Type  : 00               AU Key   : {       }
-----------------------------[hello]----------------------------
Hello Msk: 255.255.255.0    Hello Int: 10             Hello Pri: 1
Options  : 02               Dead Int : 40
DR       : 0.0.0.0          BDR      : 0.0.0.0
============================[data:   4]=========================
004E  AC 45 06 CF                                     .E..


=============================μscope=============================
Frame   : 4                 Len     : 64              Error   : None
T Elapsed: 18:59:47:937     T Delta : 00:00:00:000
-----------------------------[mac]------------------------------
Dest Mac : ffffffffffff     Sourc Mac: Xyplex135b7e   Type    : ARP
-----------------------------[arp]------------------------------
HW Type  : 10Mb Ethernet    Protocol : IP             Opcode  : ARP REQuest
HW AddLen: 6   Bytes        PR AddLen: 4    Bytes

SrHW Addr: 080087135b7e
SrPR Addr: 192 168 4 3

DeHW Addr: ffffffffffff
DePR Addr: 192 168 4 1
============================[data:  22]=========================
002A  02 E1 00 03 00 06 00 00 00 00 00 00 04 00 02 3C  ..............<
003A  00 05 B6 5A 60 09                                 ...Z`.


=============================μscope=============================
Frame   : 5                 Len     : 64              Error   : None
T Elapsed: 18:59:47:977     T Delta : 00:00:00:040
-----------------------------[mac]------------------------------
Dest Mac : Xyplex135b7e     Sourc Mac: Xyplex456866   Type    : ARP
-----------------------------[arp]------------------------------
HW Type  : 10Mb Ethernet    Protocol : IP             Opcode  : ARP RESPonse
HW AddLen: 6   Bytes        PR AddLen: 4    Bytes

SrHW Addr: 080087456866
SrPR Addr: 192 168 4 1

DeHW Addr: 080087135b7e
DePR Addr: 192 168 4 3
============================[data:  22]=========================
002A  02 E1 00 03 00 06 00 00 00 00 00 00 04 00 02 3C  ..............<
003A  00 05 94 6C B9 E8                                 ...l..


=============================μscope=============================
Frame   : 6                 Len     : 86              Error   : None
T Elapsed: 18:59:57:003     T Delta : 00:00:09:026
-----------------------------[mac]------------------------------
Dest Mac : 01005e000005     Sourc Mac: Xyplex135b7e   Type    : IP
-----------------------------[ip]-------------------------------
IP Ver   : 4                IP HLen  : 20 Bytes
TOS      : 0xc0             Pkt Len  : 68             Seg ID   : 0x0015
Flags    : FRAG:*.LAST      Frag Ptr : 0    (8 Octet) TTL      : 1
PID      : OSPF ( 89)       Checksum : 0x13dc (Good)
Dst IP <D: 224.0.0.5        Src IP <C: 192.168.4.3
-----------------------------[ospf]-----------------------------
OSPF Ver : 2                Type     : HELLO          Length   : 48
Router ID: 192.168.4.3      Area  ID: 0.0.0.0         Checksum : 0xae99
AU Type  : 00               AU Key   : {       }
-----------------------------[hello]----------------------------
Hello Msk: 255.255.255.0    Hello Int: 10             Hello Pri: 1
Options  : 02               Dead Int : 40
DR       : 192.168.4.3      BDR      : 0.0.0.0
----------------------------[neighbors: 1]----------------------
192.168.4.1
============================[data:   4]=========================
0052  02 D8 B5 FC                                      ....
```

Router 3 sends another Hello but is still currently the only router on.

Router 1 comes on-line and sends its first Hello packet. The DR and BDR fields are blank since it does not know of any other routers on Network 4.

Router 3 sends an ARP Request to Router 1 to obtain its MAC Address.

Router 1 responds with an ARP Response.

Router 3 sends its regular Hello and indicates that it has now seen Router 1

The Open Shortest Path First Protocol (OSPF)

```
==============================μscope==============================
Frame   : 7            Len     : 70          Error    : None
T Elapsed: 18:59:57:011    T Delta : 00:00:00:008
----------------------------[mac]----------------------------
Dest Mac : Xyplex135b7e    Sourc Mac: Xyplex456866    Type     : IP
----------------------------[ip]-----------------------------
IP Ver  : 4            IP HLen : 20 Bytes
TOS     : 0xc0         Pkt Len : 52          Seg ID   : 0x0005
Flags   : FRAG:*.LAST  Frag Ptr: 0    (8 Octet)    TTL      : 64
PID     : OSPF ( 89)   Checksum: 0xf057 (Good)
Dst IP <C: 192.168.4.3    Src IP <C: 192.168.4.1
----------------------------[ospf]---------------------------
OSPF Ver : 2           Type    : DD          Length   : 32
Router ID: 192.168.4.1    Area  ID: 0.0.0.0    Checksum : 0x3723
AU Type  : 00          AU Key  : {       }
----------------------------[DD]-----------------------------
Reserved : 0x0000      Options : 0x0002
Flags    : I:* M:* MS:*    SeqNo   : 10
=============================[data:   4]==========================
0042 D0 B0 70 61                             ..pa
```

Router 1 commences the sending of Database Description packets by starting negotiation.

The Flags field indicates Router 1's desire to become Master, that there are More packets to follow, and that this is the Initial packet.

```
==============================μscope==============================
Frame   : 8            Len     : 70          Error    : None
T Elapsed: 18:59:57:011    T Delta : 00:00:00:000
----------------------------[mac]----------------------------
Dest Mac : Xyplex456866    Sourc Mac: Xyplex135b7e    Type     : IP
----------------------------[ip]-----------------------------
IP Ver  : 4            IP HLen : 20 Bytes
TOS     : 0xc0         Pkt Len : 52          Seg ID   : 0x0016
Flags   : FRAG:*.LAST  Frag Ptr: 0    (8 Octet)    TTL      : 64
PID     : OSPF ( 89)   Checksum: 0xf046 (Good)
Dst IP <C: 192.168.4.1    Src IP <C: 192.168.4.3
----------------------------[ospf]---------------------------
OSPF Ver : 2           Type    : DD          Length   : 32
Router ID: 192.168.4.3    Area  ID: 0.0.0.0    Checksum : 0x366c
AU Type  : 00          AU Key  : {       }
----------------------------[DD]-----------------------------
Reserved : 0x0000      Options : 0x0002
Flags    : I:* M:* MS:*    SeqNo   : 191
=============================[data:   4]==========================
0042 5D C8 C3 65                             ]..e
```

Router 3 starts negotiation over who will be Master in the exchange of Database Description packets.

Router 1 believes that it should be Master. The Flags field also indicates that this is the initial packet, and that more packets are to follow.

```
==============================μscope==============================
Frame   : 9            Len     : 130         Error    : None
T Elapsed: 18:59:57:011    T Delta : 00:00:00:000
----------------------------[mac]----------------------------
Dest Mac : Xyplex135b7e    Sourc Mac: Xyplex456866    Type     : IP
----------------------------[ip]-----------------------------
IP Ver  : 4            IP HLen : 20 Bytes
TOS     : 0xc0         Pkt Len : 112         Seg ID   : 0x0006
Flags   : FRAG:*.LAST  Frag Ptr: 0    (8 Octet)    TTL      : 64
PID     : OSPF ( 89)   Checksum: 0xf01a (Good)
Dst IP <C: 192.168.4.3    Src IP <C: 192.168.4.1
----------------------------[ospf]---------------------------
OSPF Ver : 2           Type    : DD          Length   : 92
Router ID: 192.168.4.1    Area  ID: 0.0.0.0    Checksum : 0x01f0
AU Type  : 00          AU Key  : {       }
----------------------------[DD]-----------------------------
Reserved : 0x0000      Options : 0x0002
Flags    : I:x M:x MS:x    SeqNo   : 191
----------------------------[lsa's: 3]-----------------------
Lsa Age(S) Opts Type  AdvRtr       LSID      SeqNo     ChkSum Len(B)
1    4    0x02 RLA    192.168.4.1   c0a80401  80000002  1fdb   36
2    6    0x00 SLnA   192.168.4.1   c0a80100  80000001  0379   28
3    6    0x00 SLnA   192.168.4.1   c0a80200  80000001  f783   28
=============================[data:   4]==========================
007E 50 05 B9 A6                             P...
```

Router 1 sends its first real Database Description packet and concedes that it is the Slave.

The Database Description includes the following:
A Router Links Advertisement with an LSID that contains the ID of the router (C0A80401 or 192.168.4.1). Two Summary Network Links Advertisements with LSIDs that contain the Network Address of the Networks being summarised (C0A80100, and C0A80200 which translate to 192.168.1.0, and 192.168.2.0).

```
==============================μscope==============================
Frame   : 10           Len     : 90          Error    : None
T Elapsed: 18:59:57:020    T Delta : 00:00:00:009
----------------------------[mac]----------------------------
Dest Mac : Xyplex456866    Sourc Mac: Xyplex135b7e    Type     : IP
----------------------------[ip]-----------------------------
IP Ver  : 4            IP HLen : 20 Bytes
TOS     : 0xc0         Pkt Len : 72          Seg ID   : 0x0017
Flags   : FRAG:*.LAST  Frag Ptr: 0    (8 Octet)    TTL      : 64
PID     : OSPF ( 89)   Checksum: 0xf031 (Good)
Dst IP <C: 192.168.4.1    Src IP <C: 192.168.4.3
----------------------------[ospf]---------------------------
OSPF Ver : 2           Type    : DD          Length   : 52
Router ID: 192.168.4.3    Area  ID: 0.0.0.0    Checksum : 0x2b2d
AU Type  : 00          AU Key  : {       }
----------------------------[DD]-----------------------------
Reserved : 0x0000      Options : 0x0002
Flags    : I:x M:x MS:*    SeqNo   : 192
----------------------------[lsa's: 1]-----------------------
Lsa Age(S) Opts Type  AdvRtr       LSID      SeqNo     ChkSum Len(B)
1    185  0x02 RLA    192.168.4.3   c0a80403  80000002  fef7   36
=============================[data:   4]==========================
0056 D1 B5 00 70                             ...p
```

Router 3 sends a Database Description that contains only a RLA describing itself (LSID equal to C0A80403, that translates to 192.168.4.3).

Using Areas

```
=============================μscope=============================
Frame    : 11            Len    : 70           Error    : None
T Elapsed: 18:59:57:020   T Delta  : 00:00:00:000
-----------------------------[mac]-----------------------------
Dest Mac : Xyplex135b7e   Sourc Mac: Xyplex456866   Type   : IP
-----------------------------[ip]------------------------------
IP Ver   : 4             IP HLen  : 20 Bytes
TOS      : 0xc0          Pkt Len  : 52
Flags    : FRAG:*.LAST   Frag Ptr : 0      (8 Octet)  Seg ID   : 0x0007
PID      : OSPF ( 89)    Checksum : 0xf055 (Good)     TTL      : 64
Dst IP <C: 192.168.4.3   Src IP <C: 192.168.4.1
-----------------------------[ospf]----------------------------
OSPF Ver : 2             Type     : DD          Length   : 32
Router ID: 192.168.4.1   Area  ID: 0.0.0.0      Checksum : 0x3674
AU Type  : 00            AU Key   : {        }
-----------------------------[DD]------------------------------
Reserved : 0x0000        Options  : 0x0002
Flags    : I:x M:x MS:x  SeqNo    : 192
=============================[data:   4]=======================
0042  88 11 5E 00                        ..^.
```

Router 1 has completed sending its Database Description packets.

```
=============================μscope=============================
Frame    : 12            Len    : 98           Error    : None
T Elapsed: 18:59:57:020   T Delta  : 00:00:00:000
-----------------------------[mac]-----------------------------
Dest Mac : Xyplex456866   Sourc Mac: Xyplex135b7e   Type   : IP
-----------------------------[ip]------------------------------
IP Ver   : 4             IP HLen  : 20 Bytes
TOS      : 0xc0          Pkt Len  : 80
Flags    : FRAG:*.LAST   Frag Ptr : 0      (8 Octet)  Seg ID   : 0x0018
PID      : OSPF ( 89)    Checksum : 0xf028 (Good)     TTL      : 64
Dst IP <C: 192.168.4.1   Src IP <C: 192.168.4.3
-----------------------------[ospf]----------------------------
OSPF Ver : 2             Type     : LSReq       Length   : 60
Router ID: 192.168.4.3   Area  ID: 0.0.0.0      Checksum : 0xa215
AU Type  : 00            AU Key   : {        }
-----------------------------[lsr's:  3]-----------------------
Lsa  Type  LSID      Adv Rtr
1    SLnA  c0a80200   192.168.4.1
2    SLnA  c0a80100   192.168.4.1
3    RLA   c0a80401   192.168.4.1
=============================[data:   4]=======================
005E  2C 10 1B 6F                        ,..o
```

Router 3 sends a LSR requesting information about the RLA for Router 1, and the Summary Network Links C0A80200 and C0A80100 (192.168.2.0, and 192.168.1.0).

```
=============================μscope=============================
Frame    : 13            Len    : 74           Error    : None
T Elapsed: 18:59:57:020   T Delta  : 00:00:00:000
-----------------------------[mac]-----------------------------
Dest Mac : Xyplex135b7e   Sourc Mac: Xyplex456866   Type   : IP
-----------------------------[ip]------------------------------
IP Ver   : 4             IP HLen  : 20 Bytes
TOS      : 0xc0          Pkt Len  : 56
Flags    : FRAG:*.LAST   Frag Ptr : 0      (8 Octet)  Seg ID   : 0x0008
PID      : OSPF ( 89)    Checksum : 0xf050 (Good)     TTL      : 64
Dst IP <C: 192.168.4.3   Src IP <C: 192.168.4.1
-----------------------------[ospf]----------------------------
OSPF Ver : 2             Type     : LSReq       Length   : 36
Router ID: 192.168.4.1   Area  ID: 0.0.0.0      Checksum : 0xafd6
AU Type  : 00            AU Key   : {        }
-----------------------------[lsr's:  1]-----------------------
Lsa  Type  LSID      Adv Rtr
1    RLA   c0a80403   192.168.4.3
=============================[data:   4]=======================
0046  24 B3 37 09                        $.7.
```

Router 1 sends its LSR asking for information about the RLA for router C0A80403 (192.168.4.3).

```
=============================μscope=============================
Frame    : 14            Len    : 158          Error    : None
T Elapsed: 18:59:57:020   T Delta  : 00:00:00:000
-----------------------------[mac]-----------------------------
Dest Mac : Xyplex135b7e   Sourc Mac: Xyplex456866   Type   : IP
-----------------------------[ip]------------------------------
IP Ver   : 4             IP HLen  : 20 Bytes
TOS      : 0xc0          Pkt Len  : 140
Flags    : FRAG:*.LAST   Frag Ptr : 0      (8 Octet)  Seg ID   : 0x0009
PID      : OSPF ( 89)    Checksum : 0xeffb (Good)     TTL      : 64
Dst IP <C: 192.168.4.3   Src IP <C: 192.168.4.1
-----------------------------[ospf]----------------------------
OSPF Ver : 2             Type     : LSUpd       Length   : 120
Router ID: 192.168.4.1   Area  ID: 0.0.0.0      Checksum : 0x3cc0
AU Type  : 00            AU Key   : {        }
-----------------------------[lsu's:  3]-----------------------
Lsu  Age(S) Opts Type   AdvRtr        LSID      SeqNo     ChkSum  Len(B)
1      7    0x00 SLnA   192.168.4.1   c0a80200  80000001  f783    28
2      7    0x00 SLnA   192.168.4.1   c0a80100  80000001  0379    28
3      5    0x02 RLA    192.168.4.1   c0a80401  80000002  1fdb    36
=============================[data:   0]=======================
```

Router 1 sends its Link Stat Update (LSU) in response to Router 3's request.

```
=============================μscope=============================
Frame    : 15            Len    : 102          Error    : None
T Elapsed: 18:59:57:020   T Delta  : 00:00:00:000
-----------------------------[mac]-----------------------------
Dest Mac : Xyplex456866   Sourc Mac: Xyplex135b7e   Type   : IP
-----------------------------[ip]------------------------------
IP Ver   : 4             IP HLen  : 20 Bytes
TOS      : 0xc0          Pkt Len  : 84
Flags    : FRAG:*.LAST   Frag Ptr : 0      (8 Octet)  Seg ID   : 0x0019
PID      : OSPF ( 89)    Checksum : 0xf023 (Good)     TTL      : 64
Dst IP <C: 192.168.4.1   Src IP <C: 192.168.4.3
-----------------------------[ospf]----------------------------
OSPF Ver : 2             Type     : LSUpd       Length   : 64
Router ID: 192.168.4.3   Area  ID: 0.0.0.0      Checksum : 0x6429
AU Type  : 00            AU Key   : {        }
-----------------------------[lsu's:  1]-----------------------
Lsu  Age(S) Opts Type   AdvRtr        LSID      SeqNo     ChkSum  Len(B)
1     186   0x02 RLA    192.168.4.3   c0a80403  80000002  fef7    36
=============================[data:   0]=======================
```

Router 3 sends its LSU in response to Router 1's request.

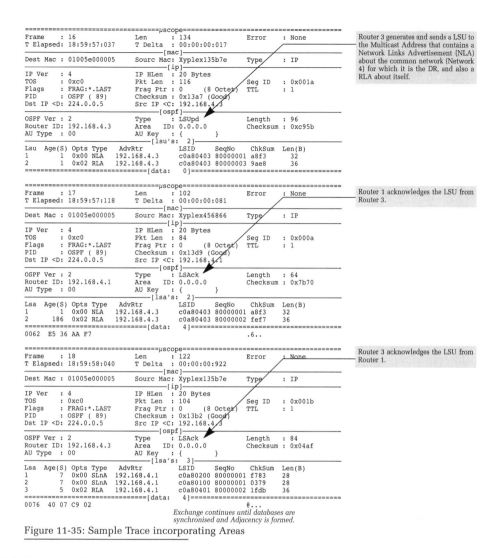

```
=============================μscope=============================
Frame    : 16            Len    : 134           Error    : None
T Elapsed: 18:59:57:037  T Delta : 00:00:00:017
-----------------------------[mac]-----------------------------
Dest Mac : 01005e000005  Sourc Mac: Xyplex135b7e    Type    : IP
-----------------------------[ip]------------------------------
IP Ver   : 4             IP HLen  : 20 Bytes
TOS      : 0xc0          Pkt Len  : 116           Seg ID  : 0x001a
Flags    : FRAG:*.LAST   Frag Ptr : 0    (8 Octet) TTL     : 1
PID      : OSPF ( 89)    Checksum : 0x13a7 (Good)
Dst IP <D: 224.0.0.5     Src IP <C: 192.168.4.3
-----------------------------[ospf]----------------------------
OSPF Ver : 2             Type     : LSUpd         Length  : 96
Router ID: 192.168.4.3   Area  ID: 0.0.0.0        Checksum : 0xc95b
AU Type  : 00            AU Key   : {        }
-----------------------------[lsu's:  2]-----------------------
Lsu Age(S) Opts Type  AdvRtr      LSID     SeqNo     ChkSum  Len(B)
1      1 0x00 NLA  192.168.4.3  c0a80403 80000001 a8f3    32
2      1 0x02 RLA  192.168.4.3  c0a80403 80000003 9ae8    36
=============================[data:   0]=======================

=============================μscope=============================
Frame    : 17            Len    : 102           Error    : None
T Elapsed: 18:59:57:118  T Delta : 00:00:00:081
-----------------------------[mac]-----------------------------
Dest Mac : 01005e000005  Sourc Mac: Xyplex456866    Type    : IP
-----------------------------[ip]------------------------------
IP Ver   : 4             IP HLen  : 20 Bytes
TOS      : 0xc0          Pkt Len  : 84            Seg ID  : 0x000a
Flags    : FRAG:*.LAST   Frag Ptr : 0    (8 Octet) TTL     : 1
PID      : OSPF ( 89)    Checksum : 0x13d9 (Good)
Dst IP <D: 224.0.0.5     Src IP <C: 192.168.4.1
-----------------------------[ospf]----------------------------
OSPF Ver : 2             Type     : LSAck         Length  : 64
Router ID: 192.168.4.1   Area  ID: 0.0.0.0        Checksum : 0x7b70
AU Type  : 00            AU Key   : {        }
-----------------------------[lsa's:  2]-----------------------
Lsa Age(S) Opts Type  AdvRtr      LSID     SeqNo     ChkSum  Len(B)
1      1 0x00 NLA  192.168.4.3  c0a80403 80000001 a8f3    32
2    186 0x02 RLA  192.168.4.3  c0a80403 80000002 fef7    36
=============================[data:   4]=======================
0062  E5 36 AA F7                           .6..

=============================μscope=============================
Frame    : 18            Len    : 122           Error    : None
T Elapsed: 18:59:58:040  T Delta : 00:00:00:922
-----------------------------[mac]-----------------------------
Dest Mac : 01005e000005  Sourc Mac: Xyplex135b7e    Type    : IP
-----------------------------[ip]------------------------------
IP Ver   : 4             IP HLen  : 20 Bytes
TOS      : 0xc0          Pkt Len  : 104           Seg ID  : 0x001b
Flags    : FRAG:*.LAST   Frag Ptr : 0    (8 Octet) TTL     : 1
PID      : OSPF ( 89)    Checksum : 0x13b2 (Good)
Dst IP <D: 224.0.0.5     Src IP <C: 192.168.4.3
-----------------------------[ospf]----------------------------
OSPF Ver : 2             Type     : LSAck         Length  : 84
Router ID: 192.168.4.3   Area  ID: 0.0.0.0        Checksum : 0x04af
AU Type  : 00            AU Key   : {        }
-----------------------------[lsa's:  3]-----------------------
Lsa Age(S) Opts Type  AdvRtr      LSID     SeqNo     ChkSum  Len(B)
1      7 0x00 SLnA 192.168.4.1  c0a80200 80000001 f783    28
2      7 0x00 SLnA 192.168.4.1  c0a80100 80000001 0379    28
3      5 0x02 RLA  192.168.4.1  c0a80401 80000002 1fdb    36
=============================[data:   4]=======================
0076  40 07 C9 02                           @...
```

Router 3 generates and sends a LSU to the Multicast Address that contains a Network Links Advertisement (NLA) about the common network (Network 4) for which it is the DR, and also a RLA about itself.

Router 1 acknowledges the LSU from Router 3.

Router 3 acknowledges the LSU from Router 1.

Exchange continues until databases are synchronised and Adjacency is formed.

Figure 11-35: Sample Trace incorporating Areas

11.6 Joining Autonomous Systems Together

Autonomous System Boundary Routers (ASBRs) are used to link to one or more routers in another Autonomous System. As such, these routers will run both OSPF, and at least one other routing protocol. This *other* protocol could be an EGP such as the Exterior Gateway Protocol or the Border Gateway Protocol. Alternatively, since OSPF considers an AS to be an internet that uses a common routing policy, the other protocol could easily be another IGP such as RIP.

ASBRs send Autonomous System External Link Advertisements into the OSPF Autonomous System, that are derived from the external protocol and describe routes to networks external to the OSPF AS. Alternatively, AS External LSAs can be used to describe a static or default route. As with other LSAs, one advertisement is generated for each reachable network. Unlike other LSAs however, AS External Link State Advertisements are flooded throughout an entire AS without regard for areas (except Stub Areas). Indeed, the AS External Link State Advertisement is the only LSA that is not confined to the area in which it originated.

Since AS External LSAs are not flooded through a Stub Area, ASBRs cannot be placed in them. As we have said, if we do not flood these advertisements throughout the area, the size of the database held by the router is reduced together with it's memory requirements. For Stub Areas to operate then, one (or more) ABR must advertise a default route into the Stub Area via a Summary Link Advertisement. This advertisement for the default route is then flooded throughout the area, but no further. Hosts and routers contained within the Stub Area that wish to send data to an external network, then use this default route.

Not-so-Stubby Areas do not have this restriction. In NSSAs, Type 7 LSAs are used which are then translated to Type 5 LSAs at NSSA border routers. As such ASBRs that support the generation of Type 7 LSAs can be placed in NSSAs.

Routing to another AS, as with inter-area routing, can be a multi-stage process.

- An intra-area route taking the data from the source network to an ABR.

- A second intra-area route taking our data across the backbone. This part takes us from the ABR linking the source area to the backbone, to the ABR that links the backbone to the area that contains the ASBR.

- A final intra-area route within this AS that takes us to the ASBR.

- Lastly our data travels inter-AS across the ASBR. Of course, this may not be the end of the journey as the data may now have to traverse the far AS before it finally reaches it's destination.

11.7 Summary

OSPF represents the very latest in thinking as far as Interior Gateway Protocols (IGPs) is concerned. Complex it certainly is, however the convergence times (the time that it takes to acheive a stable topology after a link or router state change) is significantly shorter than it's older counterpart RIP.

OSPF uses a Link State Algorithm and as such each router works from a database that is identical to others within the area. This database contains more than simple reachability information with all routers being listed and the status and costs associated with their links. In addition OSPF, through a multicast extension, allows the propogation of multicast group information and this MOSPF as it is known is discussed in Chapter 14.

It is true that although OPSF is now becoming the de-facto protocol used for routing, it does have one major drawback in that hosts cannot generally listen to OSPF transmissions. So, Unix and other machines are unable to take advantage of the routing traffic on the networks to which they attach and are therefore not able to maintain dynamic routing tables as they are with say RIP. To overcome this, ICMP has been extended with the addition of the Router Discovery Protocol (RDP). In this, discussed in Chapter 6, routers are able to advertise their existence to locally attached hosts, and hosts are able to query the network to assertain where their nearest router is located.

The Exterior Gateway Protocol (EGP)

CHAPTER 12

So far we have discussed how routers within an internet exchange network reachability information. In so doing, we have considered the Routing Information Protocol (RIP), and the Open Shortest Path First Protocol (OSPF). But what if we wish to join multiple internets from multiple authorities, that each run different Interior Gateway Protocols? Here we will have some form of *Backbone* network that will link our various internets together. But how will we pass reachability information between them?

The Exterior Gateway Protocol (EGP) is used to convey network reachability information between neighboring routers that reside within different administrative authorities. These administrative authorities, or Autonomous Systems as they are known, are then free to decide both what routing information is to be propagated, and how this should be achieved. If we were to have a simple architecture such as that shown in Figure 12-1, our task would be simple. For example, depending upon the overall diameter of the internet, either RIP, or OSPF would suffice.

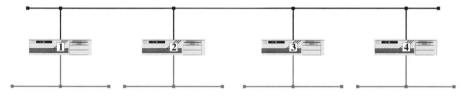

Figure 12-1: A Simple Internet

However, an Autonomous System can, and normally does, contain a number of routers that form a complete, complex, internet in its own right. The problems that EGP addresses then are those that surround what information to advertise, and to whom. Consider the following scenario shown in Figure 12-2.

In this example, we have four sites (maybe university campuses or even large buildings within a corporate end user) each with its own internet. Obviously, if these internets are large, then it would be impractical for all routers to hold network reachability information about all available networks. Thus, we would program the routers in each of the Autonomous Systems with default routes[1] that point to the main router for that Autonomous System (routers 1 to 4). In this way, assuming that routers 1 to 4 are exchanging routing information, hosts that reside

1. The concept of Default Routes is discussed in Section 9.1.2.

within any one Autonomous System can communicate with hosts in any of the other Autonomous Systems.

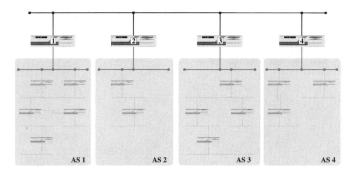

Figure 12-2: A Complex Internet

Where we wish to exchange information with another Autonomous System, we use an Exterior Gateway Protocol (an EGP[2]). The original protocol developed for this purpose was *the* Exterior Gateway Protocol (EGP) as defined in RFC 904 and, although now dated, is widely used today. True, few private internets are large enough to require the use of an EGP at all, however in order to fully understand all of the issues involved in routing, it is desirable to understand how EGP operates.

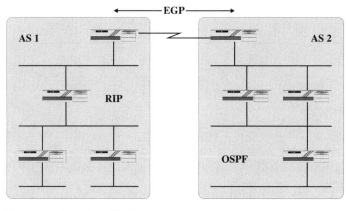

Figure 12-3: The Use of EGP

Of course, our overall view of Autonomous Systems can be much simplified. We may have only two Autonomous systems that need to be linked as shown in Figure 12-3. Here, each Autonomous System runs its own IGP, and exchanges reachability information with the other using the Exterior Gateway Protocol (EGP). This is shown in Figure 12-3.

2. The Exterior Gateway Protocol is one example of an EGP. Another, newer protocol, the Border Gateway Protocol (BGP) is discussed in the next chapter.

In this example, we see two Autonomous Systems, each with a unique Autonomous System Number (ASN). This numbering is no accident, since in order that our routing algorithms can make routing decisions, each Autonomous System is assigned a unique number or ASN.[3] Therefore, our *core* routers are now able to route information between Autonomous Systems successfully.

In fact, the routers joining our two Autonomous Systems actually run two distinct routing protocols. Firstly, they run the Interior Gateway Protocol in use within the Autonomous System (RIP, or OSPF, etc.), and secondly an Exterior Gateway Protocol (such as EGP). Thus, our core devices will know about the reachability of networks within the AS (through the IGP), and be able to convey this information to routers in a neighboring AS (through EGP).

12.1 The EGP Protocol Format and Operation

The Exterior Gateway Protocol is a direct user of IP, identified by an IP protocol identifier of 8. EGP messages are therefore passed directly to the IP layer and encapsulated within an IP datagram. While this method of transmission allows the overhead of using such a protocol to be reduced, it does mean that EGP is totally reliant on those services provided by IP. For example, depending upon the MTU of the underlying network technology, IP may be required to fragment the datagram before transmission. Indeed, this would not be uncommon in an environment large enough to require the use of EGP. However, since IP has no retransmission capability, if a single fragment is lost the entire datagram will need to be re-transmitted.

There are three distinct parts to the operation of the Exterior Gateway Protocol as follows:

- Firstly, EGP relies on neighbors (peers) exchanging information. Thus, at start-up, an EGP router will attempt to *acquire* one or more neighbors with which to exchange routing information.

- Secondly, once the EGP neighbor relationship is established, our neighbors will test reachability to each other through a simple *Hello* protocol, thereby ensuring that the relationship is still valid. Obviously should a router crash, it will have no way of informing its neighbor(s) that it has gone down. Thus, this test of *reachability* is essential.

- Finally, our neighbors exchange network reachability information, listing the networks that they can reach, and the associated metrics.

In order to support these various phases, EGP uses a number of message formats briefly described in Table 12-1. In this section, we shall examine these message formats, and the protocol operation for each of the phases.

---

3. ASNs are assigned by the Internet Assigned Numbers Authority (IANA).

Table 12-1: EGP Message Types

Message Type	Description
Request	Requests the acquisition of a neighbor and/or the initialization of polling variables
Confirm	Confirms the acquisition of a neighbor and/or the initialization of polling variables
Refuse	Used to refuse the acquisition of a neighbor and/or the initialization of polling variables
Cease	Used to request the de-activation of a neighbor
Cease-Ack	Confirms the de-activation of a neighbor
Hello	Used to test neighbor reachability
I Heard You (I-H-U)	Confirms neighbor reachability
Poll	Used to request a network reachability update from a neighbor
Update	Provides network reachability information
Error	Used to convey error information

12.1.1 EGP Message Header

As we have said, EGP uses a large number of messages, to support it's three main functions. In order to maintain relative simplicity however, all EGP messages use the fixed length header shown in Figure 12-4.

The one octet *Version* field identifies the version of the protocol (currently 2). The single octet *Type* field is used to define the type of EGP message that is being conveyed. Table 12-2 identifies valid values for this field in each of the various message types.

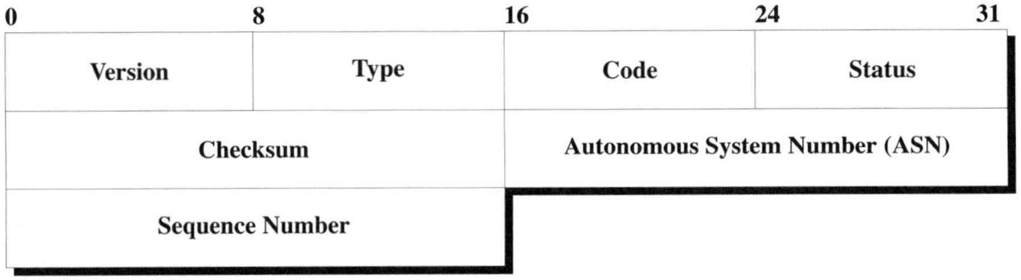

0	8	16	24	31
Version	Type	Code	Status	
Checksum		Autonomous System Number (ASN)		
Sequence Number				

Figure 12-4: EGP Message Header

Table 12-2: EGP Type Field Values

Type	EGP Message
1	Update Response/Indication
2	Poll Command
3	Neighbor Acquisition Message
5	Neighbor Reachability Message
8	Error Response/Indication

The single octet *Code* field (sometimes referred to as being the *sub-type*) further defines the message type. The *Status* field (again one octet), contains status information that is dependent upon the actual message type itself. The 16 bit *Checksum* field is used to validate the integrity of the EGP message. The value contained in this field is computed by first breaking the entire EGP message down into a series of 16 bit words. These words are then summed using one's compliment arithmetic, with any carry added in, and the one's compliment of the result finally taken. This method of checksum calculation is therefore consistent with all of the Internet protocols.

The two octet *Autonomous System Number (ASN)*, is the number that identifies the Autonomous System from which the message was sent. Finally, the Sequence Number (two octets) is used to synchronize messages between EGP neighbors. Synchronization occurs in a similar fashion to that of TCP. When acquiring a neighbor, an initial sequence number (ISN) is established, which is then incremented each time the host transmits an EGP message. Where the neighbor replies, it does so with the last sequence number received, thereby allowing the transmission and reception of packets to be matched.

12.1.2   Neighbor Acquisition/Cease

The initial phase of EGP operation is for the router to become, or acquire one or more neighbors. When in this state, the router periodically transmits *Request* commands until it receives a *Confirm* response from a neighboring router. A router may refuse to become a neighbor by issuing a *Refuse* response. For example, the router may be prohibited from communicating with the specific Autonomous System indicated in the Request command, or it may have a temporary resource shortage. In these cases, the *Refuse* response, rather than a *Confirm* response, would be transmitted.

Upon receipt of a *Confirm* response, the routers will negotiate certain parameters and transition to the next phase of operation, that of Neighbor Reachability. Part of this negotiation phase is to determine the intervals at which the neighbors will exchange *Hello* messages in the *Reachability* phase, and how often they will exchange Network Reachability information. Neighbors assume either an *Active*, or *Passive* role. As an *Active* neighbor, the router will send *Hello* messages, and expect to receive *I-Heard-You* responses. As a *Passive* neighbor, the router will expect to receive *Hello* messages, and will transmit *I-Heard-You* messages in response to them. These exchanges though are described more fully later.

Another part of *Neighbor Acquisition*, is the *Cease* command, where one neighbor wishes to cease participation in EGP. In this case, one neighbor will issue a *Cease* command, and expect a *Cease Acknowledge* response (the only valid response to this command).

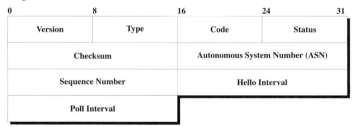

Figure 12-5: EGP Neighbor Acquisition

For Neighbor Acquisition messages such as this, the Type field is always set to 3. The Code field that then further defines the message will contain one of the values shown in Table 12-3.

Table 12-3: EGP Neighbor Acquisition Codes

Code	Description
0	Request Command: The router is attempting to acquire neighbor(s).
1	Confirm Response: The router transmitting this message agrees to become a neighbor.
2	Refuse Response: The router refuses to become a neighbor.
3	Cease Command: The router wishes to cease participation in EGP.
4	Cease Acknowledge: The router agrees to EGP operation ceasing.

The Status field contains one of the values from Table 12-4 used as either negotiated parameters, or to identify problems:

Table 12-4: EGP Neighbor Acquisition Status Values

Status	Description
0	Unspecified: Used when none of the other Statuses apply.[4]
1	Active Mode: Used in a Request/Confirm, this identifies the neighbor as being Active.
2	Passive Mode: Used in a Request/Confirm, this identifies the neighbor as being Passive.
3	Insufficient Resources: The router is reporting that its resources are exhausted. This may be due to insufficient table space, or a general resource problem in the router.
4	Administratively Prohibited: This may indicate that the Autonomous System presented is unknown to the receiver. In this case, an alternative router must be sought.
5	Going Down: Caused by either an operator initiated stop, or an Abort timeout.
6	Parameter Problem: The router has detected a problem such as an invalid Poll timer, or it is unable to assume the role requested (Active/Passive).
7	Protocol Violation: An invalid command has been received for the current state of the router.

From the preceding discussions, it is apparent that one of the neighbors must operate in the Active mode, and one Passive. During the acquisition phase, the neighbors will elect to be either Active, Passive, or *Don't Care*. In the case where the neighbor has no preference as to the role it should assume, the Status field is set to 0 indicating that none of the statuses apply. Of course, it is highly possible that both neighbors will elect to assume the same role. In EGP this situation has to be resolved, and Table 12-5 indicates the eventual outcome for this situation:

Table 12-5: EGP Neighbor Mode Selection

Sender	Receiver	Result
Active	Passive	The Sender becomes the Active neighbor and the Receiver Passive.
Passive	Passive	This is an illegal state and the receiver will send a Refuse Response.
Active	Active	The router from the lower Autonomous System will become Active, and the other Passive.

4. Typically, we may also use a Status of 0 to indicate that we wish to negotiate the *Mode* (Active/Passive).

The Exterior Gateway Protocol (EGP)

Sender	Receiver	Result
Don't Care	Active	The Receiver will assume the role of the Active neighbor and the sender the Passive role.
Don't Care	Passive	The Sender will become the Active neighbor and the Receiver Passive.
Don't Care	Don't Care	The router from the lower Autonomous System will become Active, and the other Passive.

The 16 bit *Hello Interval* is used to communicate the minimum acceptable *Hello* polling interval in seconds, and the 16 bit *Poll Interval*, the minimum acceptable time (in seconds) between successive *Network Reachability* polls. By defining these minimum acceptable intervals, we therefore guard against excessive polling by adjacent neighbors.

Figure 12-6 shows an example of routers in two Autonomous Systems firstly becoming neighbors, and then ceasing EGP activity. In the upper example, Router 1 issues a Request command (Type 3, Code 0) and indicates that it has no preference as to whether it should become the Active, or Passive neighbor (Status 0). For this example, we also see that Router 1 suggests a Hello interval of 45 seconds, and a Poll Interval of 180 seconds.

Router 2 responds with a Confirm response (Code 1) and also indicates that it has no preference as to its role (Status 0). This router though, suggests a Hello Interval of 30 seconds, and a Poll Interval of 90 seconds. Thus, based upon this exchange, Router 1 will become the Active router (since it is from the lower of the two Autonomous Systems) and Router 2 the Passive. Finally, we will use a Hello Interval of 30 seconds, and a Poll Interval of 90 seconds since these values were suggested by the Passive neighbor – A normal conclusion to this phase.

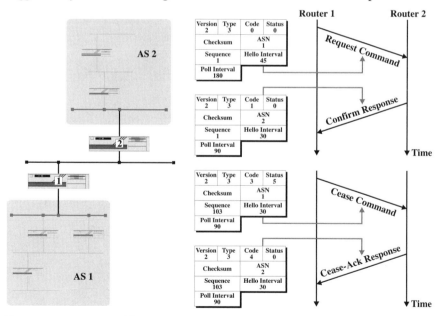

Figure 12-6: An EGP Neighbor Acquisition/Cease Example

The lower example shows us a typical exchange where a neighbor wishes to cease participation in EGP. Here, Router 1 transmits a Cease command with a Status of 5 (Going Down). Router 2 then responds with a Cease Acknowledgement. There can be no other response to a Cease request. Once one party indicates its desire to cease participation, its neighbor(s) *must* agree.

Finally, we must consider the case where we have more than two Autonomous Systems sharing a common network. Where this is the case, although each of the routers connecting these Autonomous Systems to the shared network are neighbors, we find that they actually have different relationships.

Neighbors are said to be either direct, or indirect. Where neighbors are direct, they have a direct neighbor relationship as we have already described, operate the Hello protocol, and exchange Network Reachability messages. Where the relationship is indirect, as shown in Figure 12-7, the indirect neighbors learn about distant networks reachable through the third party, from their direct neighbor.

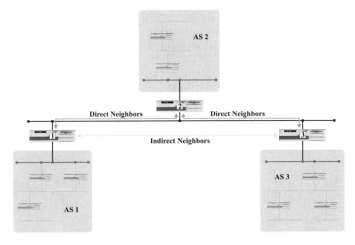

Figure 12-7: Direct and Indirect Neighbors

12.1.3 Neighbor Reachability

During Neighbor Reachability, the direct neighbors exchange small messages designed to ensure that the other party is up, and able to reliably exchange Network Reachability information. The frequency with which these messages are expected is defined during the *Neighbor Acquisition* phase, and is equal to the negotiated *Hello Time*. These messages use only the EGP message header (Figure 12-8) with the *Type* field set to 5.

As we have already mentioned, the Hello protocol relies on the active neighbor sending *Hello*s, and the Passive (receiver) to respond with *I-Heard-You*s. With this message type, the Code field is set to 0 for a *Hello* message, and 1, for an *I-Heard-You* response. The Status field then indicates the status of the EGP protocol with a value of 0 for indeterminate, 1 for Up, and 2 for Down. Note that these statuses do not indicate the physical state of the link, but instead are used to indicate the status of the protocol as defined by the EGP *State Machine* described later.

The Exterior Gateway Protocol (EGP)

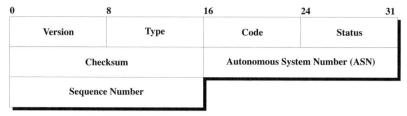

0		8		16		24		31
Version		Type		Code		Status	
Checksum				Autonomous System Number (ASN)			
Sequence Number							

Figure 12-8: EGP Neighbor Reachability Messages

Whether we can reliably exchange Network Reachability information is determined by the *I-Heard-You* response received from the Passive neighbor. The Active party will send Hellos and *receive I-Heard-You*s but will not attempt to Poll for Network Reachability information until the *I-Heard-You* response contains an Up status (1).

One important point to consider is that Neighbor Acquisition messages define the *Minimum* time at which Hellos should be expected. Therefore, a Passive neighbor should expect to receive Hellos at a rate no higher than that specified during the *Neighbor Acquisition* phase. Indeed, where the Hello rate exceeds that negotiated, an error is sent. Equally, we negotiate no Maximum time between successive Hellos. Thus, our Active neighbor may legitimately send Hellos at a lower rate than that requested by the Passive neighbor. For a full discussion of the implications surrounding the rate at which *Hello/I-Heard-You* messages are sent, please refer to the section on the EGP Finite State Machine later in this chapter.

12.1.4   Poll Command

Once our routers have either acquired a neighbor, or agreed to become a neighbor, and reachability is assured through *Hello/I-Heard-You* exchanges, network reachability information is exchanged through a *Poll/Response* mechanism. The *Active* neighbor begins the exchange by polling the *Passive* neighbor that then responds with an Update Response. The Active neighbor then sends its own Update Response to the Passive neighbor thereby ensuring that both routers in the pair are updated.

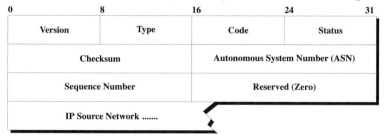

0		8		16		24		31
Version		Type		Code		Status	
Checksum				Autonomous System Number (ASN)			
Sequence Number				Reserved (Zero)			
IP Source Network							

Figure 12-9: EGP Poll Command

For Poll commands, the *Type* field is always set to 2, and the *Code* field is unused (zero). As with *Neighbor Reachability* messages, the *Status* field is then used to indicate the status of the EGP protocol with 0 used to indicate Indeterminate, 1 to indicate Up, and 2 to indicate Down.

In EGP, all reachability measurements are taken from a known network (that which is common to both neighbors and therefore also common to both Autonomous Systems). Thus, the *IP Source Network* field contains this Network ID, as a left justified field of 1, 2, or 3 octets with trailing zeroes (as determined by the Class of network).

The actual *Minimum* time interval at which polling occurs, is determined during the *Neighbor Acquisition* phase. This is suggested by each neighbor and indicated by the *Poll Interval* field of the Neighbor Acquisition message.[5] Thus, both parties receive updated information within agreed timescales.

12.1.5 Update Response/Indication Messages

An EGP *Update Response/Indication* message is sent by the *Passive* neighbor in response to a *Poll Request*, and by an *Active* neighbor upon receipt of the *Update Response* from it's passive partner as Figure 12-11 shows. Depending upon the size of the Autonomous System being reported, these messages can be extremely large. Their format (as described in Figure 12-10) can also be extremely complex depending upon the number of routes that have to be reported.

With the Update Response/Indication message, the *Type* field is always set to 1, and the *Code* field is unused (zero). The Status field, in common with other messages is used to inform the partner of the status of the EGP protocol with 0 used to indicate an Indeterminate state, 1 to indicate the Up state, and 2 to indicate the Down state. In addition to these statuses however, the Update Response/ Indication message also uses the high order 8 bit of the octet to signify that this message is unsolicited.

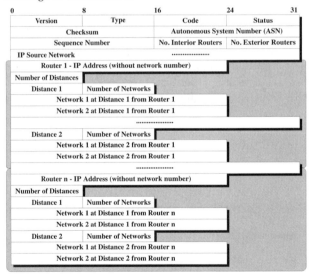

Figure 12-10: EGP Update Response/Indication Message

---

5. The actual time interval adopted is that suggested by the passive neighbor as discussed earlier in this chapter.

EGP actually allows each of the neighbors to transmit one unsolicited update between successive polls. Generally, this unsolicited update is then used when either the neighbor transitions to the Up state, or when the unit detects a change in the routing information being provided. Polling at a rate higher than this results in an error condition (Excessive Polling Rate) being reported to the other neighbor.

The two 8 bit fields *Number of Interior Routers*, and *Number of Exterior Routers*, are used to indicate the number of interior and exterior routers for which routes appear in this message respectively. The *IP Source Network*, is the left justified 1, 2, or 3 octet Network ID from which all distances are measured. This Network ID has the same meaning as in the *Poll Command* message and represents the network common to both neighbors. The *Router IP Address* fields (*Router 1 ... Router n*) contain the 1, 2, or 3 octet Host IDs of the router(s) being reported. Addresses in these fields will be either the router sending the update, or one of the routers neighbors. Thus, since these will reside on the *IP Source Network,* no indication of Network ID is required.

The *Number of Distances* field is used to indicate the number of different distances (the metrics) that are reachable through this router. Each *Distance* field then provides the metric for those networks that are reachable through the router as reported in the *Network at Distance from Router* fields. The total number of networks being reported at this distance is then indicated by the *Number of Networks* field for each distance quoted. Since these messages can become extremely large, the network fields themselves provide only the Network ID and are therefore 1, 2, or 3 octets in length. By reporting reachable networks in this way, we are therefore able to conserve space within these messages, and thus make better use of available network bandwidth.

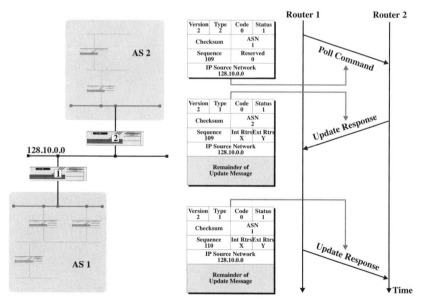

Figure 12-11: EGP Poll/Update Exchange

From a practical standpoint, not all routers that share a common network need to run an EGP. In practice we find that we may have multiple routers running an IGP, with only a single device that also runs EGP. Figure 12-12 demonstrates this point.

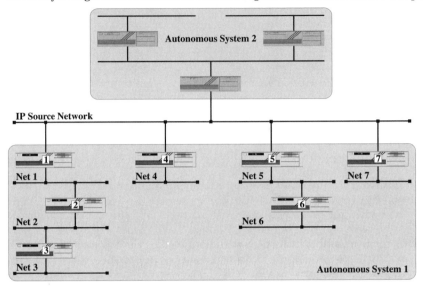

Figure 12-12: A Sample EGP Internet

In this example, router 4 runs EGP and passes network reachability information to Autonomous System 2 on behalf of all other routers. Here, Router 4 advertises those networks reachable within its Autonomous System as shown in Table 12-6:

Table 12-6: Network Reachability Information

Network	Reachable Via	Network	Reachable Via
Net 1	Router 1	Net 2	Router 1
Net 3	Router 1	Net 4	Router 4
Net 5	Router 5	Net 6	Router 5
Net 7	Router 7		

12.1.6 Error Response/Indication

Either neighbor may send an Error message in response to a command or response in which an error has been detected. The one rule restricting these messages however, is that Error messages are never sent in response to a received Error message. As Figure 12-13 shows, the message format is simple and, in an effort to aid the diagnosis of potential faults, contains the first 12 octets of the EGP header that caused this condition.

The *Type* field for this message type has a value of 8, and the *Code* field is unused (zero). The Status field, again used to inform the partner of the status of the EGP protocol uses the values 0, 1, and 2 to indicate an Indeterminate state, the Up state, and

The Exterior Gateway Protocol (EGP)

Down state respectively. Also, as with the *Update Response/Indication* message, the high order 8 bit of the octet (128_{10}) is to signify that this message is unsolicited.

The *Reason* field is used to convey why the Error message was sent as detailed in Table 12-7.

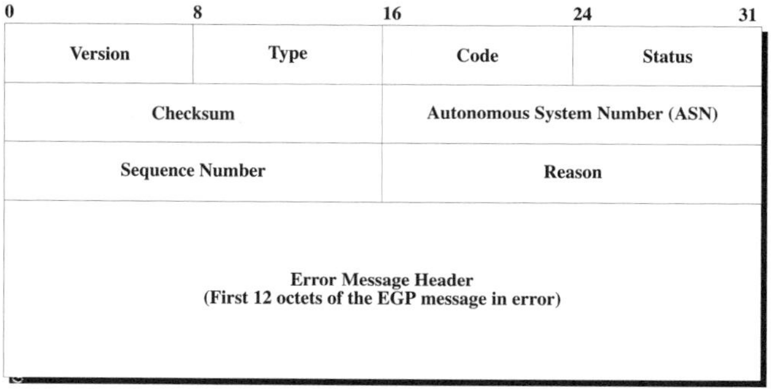

0	8	16	24	31
Version	Type	Code		Status
Checksum		Autonomous System Number (ASN)		
Sequence Number		Reason		
Error Message Header (First 12 octets of the EGP message in error)				

Figure 12-13: EGP Error Response/Indication

Table 12-7: EGP Error Message Reason Fields

Reason Code	Reason	Description
0	Unspecified	Used when no other Reason Code applies.
1	Bad EGP Header Format	Indicates one of the following: • A bad message length. • An invalid *Type*, *Code*, or *Status* field.
2	Bad EGP Data field Format	Used when one of the following is detected: • A nonsense polling rate specified during the *Neighbor Acquisition* phase. • An invalid *Update Response/Indication* message format. • The *IP Source Network* address in an *Update Response/Indication* did not match that in the corresponding *Poll* command.
3	Reachability Information Unavailable	No information is available for the network. Specified in the *IP Source Network* field of a Poll command.
4	Excessive Polling Rate	Used when the neighbor detects one of the following conditions: Two or more *Hello*, or *Poll*, commands within the minimum specified intervals, or two or more *Request* commands received within an unreasonably short time period during the *Neighbor Acquisition* phase.
5	No Response	No Response was received for a *Poll* after some unspecified timeout interval. This interval is implementation specific.

The first 12 octets of the EGP header that caused the Error condition are included so that the receiver can determine which of the Reasons applies in the case of Codes 1, 2, or 4. Since these codes could have different meanings depending upon the circumstances in which they are used, this additional information is, of course, imperative.

12.2 EGP Metrics

EGP uses a single octet to specify the distance to any particular network, thus we are limited such that no reachable network can have an associated metric of more than 255. In actual fact, a metric of 255 is normally deemed to mean unreachable, therefore our maximum allowable metric for reachable networks is 254.

This limitation of metrics is, in itself, not normally a problem. What does become a problem however, is where we wish to advertise (import) reachable networks *into* an Autonomous System running an IGP such as RIP. Here we cannot advertise networks with metrics greater than 15, since to do so would render them unreachable. Equally, if we wish to advertise (export) networks *from* an IGP such as OSPF, the metric may be larger than 254 making them unreachable as far as EGP is concerned. The answer then is to scale the metric used. This scaling however is not standardised and is therefore implementation specific. Thus, care must be taken when creating networks with routers from multiple vendors to ensure that inter-operability does not become an issue.

12.3 The EGP Finite State Machine

We have now discussed all of the phases involved in EGP, and touched upon certain states within these phases. In order to fully understand how these states affect the operation of EGP however, it is necessary to examine these in slightly more detail. Figure 12-14 shows a simplified model of the EGP Finite State Machine, and shows how we transition between these states.

When in the *Idle* state, the router does not generate any EGP messages except to respond to a *Request Command*. On receipt of a *Request*, our router sends a *Confirm Acknowledgement* and then transitions to the *Down* state. Alternatively, the router may transition from *Idle* to the *Acquisition* state due to a System or Operator initiated event, labelled *Start* in the figure.

From the *Acquisition* state, the router begins to transmit *Requests*, and waits for a *Confirm* to be received. Again, when the *Confirm* is received, the router transitions to the *Down* state. Of course, the router could receive a *Refuse* in response to a transmitted *Request*. In this case, the router will transition to back to the *Idle* state and again wait to be restarted, or to receive a *Request*.

Once in the Down state, the protocol has either received a Request command to which it has responded with a Confirm Acknowledgement, or it has received a Confirm Acknowledgement in response to a Request that it has sent. In essence, the protocol has now moved to the Neighbor Reachability phase of operation and processes Cease, Hello, and further Request commands. In addition, if this router is the Active neighbor, it will also send Hello messages itself. At this time, the router will not send Poll commands, although, unsolicited updates that are received may optionally be processed.

During the *Neighbor Reachability* phase, the router will move from the *Down* state to the *Up* state or vice versa when the following conditions are met:

- A router acting as an *Active* neighbor will transition from the *Down* state to the *Up* state provided that it receives three *I-Heard-Yous* within four *Hello*

Intervals. A *Passive* neighbor will transition to the *Up* state on reception of the first *Hello.*

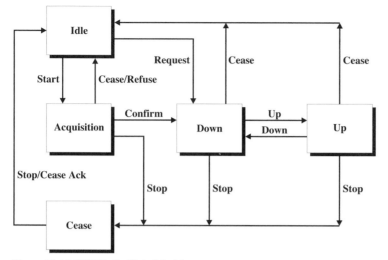

Figure 12-14: EGP Finite State Machine

- If the router is the *Active* neighbor, it will transition from the *Up* state to the *Down* state when it receives one or less *I-Heard-You* responses from four consecutive *Hellos* transmitted within the proper times. A *Passive* neighbor however, will transition to the *Down* state only when it has heard no *Hellos* within four consecutive *Hello Intervals.*

In the *Up* state, the router processes and responds to *all* commands. If it is an *Active* neighbor it will transmit *Hellos*, and will send *Poll* commands to solicit network reachability updates. As a *Passive* neighbor, the router will send network reachability updates in response to *Poll* commands, and *I-Heard You* responses when *Hello* messages are received.

Finally, in the Cease state, the router is assumed to have received a Stop event from either a local operator or a system generated event. In this state, the router will continually send Cease commands and then return to the Idle state upon reception of a Cease Acknowledgement response, or a further Stop event. In this way, the designers of the protocol have tried to ensure that any neighbor(s) of the router receive the Cease command and stop the protocol.

12.4 EGP, an Example

Figure 12-15 and the trace that follows show two routers (193.128.104.20 and 193.128.104.36) exchanging EGP information in a simple internet. The network itself is shown first, and in the trace we see the routers progressing through the startup phase of EGP. This example is significant since it firstly shows EGP operation as the routers progress through the Neighbor Acquisition, and Neighbour Reachability phases, and then exchange routing information. Secondly it shows that, although the two Autonomous Systems use different Interior Gateway Protocols, EGP operates without any problems.

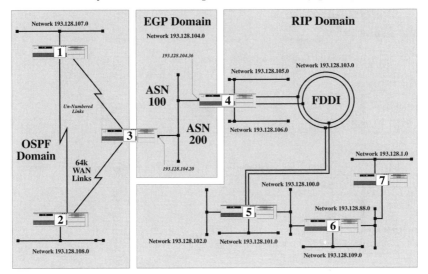

Figure 12-15: A Simple Internet Using EGP

```
µSCOPE                     PACKET TRACE DECODE REPORT            (c) T.Kenyon 1995
-----------------------------------------------------------------------------
```

Packet decodes as follows:
```
02        Version
03        Neighbour Acquisition
00        Request Command
00        Unspecified Status
FD01      Checksum
0064      ASN – Value 100₁₀
0001      Sequence Number
001E      Hello Interval – Value 30₁₀
0078      Poll Interval – Value 120₁₀
```
The remainder is Padding and the 4 octet Ethernet FCS.

```
=======================µscope=======================
Frame    : 1              Len      : 64             Error     : None
T Elapsed: 17:13:48:153   T Delta  : 00:09:10:803
-------------------------[mac]-------------------------
Dest Mac : Xyplex156806   Sourc Mac: Xyplex135b7e    Type      : IP
-------------------------[ip]--------------------------
IP Ver   : 4              IP HLen  : 20 Bytes
TOS      : 0x00           Pkt Len  : 34              Seq ID    : 0x0058
Flags    : FRAG:*.LAST    Frag Ptr : 0      (8 Octet) TTL      : 64
PID      : 8              Checksum : 0x2743 (Good)
Dst IP <C: 193.128.104.36 Src IP <C: 193.128.104.20
========================[data: 30]=====================
0022  02 03 00 00 FD 01 00 64 00 01 00 1E 00 78 02 08    .......d.....x..
0032  02 08 00 C0 00 00 02 01 00 00 E9 77 94 B2          ..........w..
```

Packet decodes as follows:
```
02        Version
03        Neighbour Acquisition
01        Confirm Response
02        Passive Mode
FB9B      Checksum
00C8      ASN – Value 200₁₀
0001      Sequence Number
001E      Hello Interval – Value 30₁₀
0078      Poll Interval – Value 120₁₀
```
The remainder is Padding and the 4 octet Ethernet FCS.

```
=======================µscope=======================
Frame    : 2              Len      : 64             Error     : None
T Elapsed: 17:13:48:153   T Delta  : 00:00:00:000
-------------------------[mac]-------------------------
Dest Mac : Xyplex135b7e   Sourc Mac: Xyplex156806    Type      : IP
-------------------------[ip]--------------------------
IP Ver   : 4              IP HLen  : 20 Bytes
TOS      : 0x00           Pkt Len  : 34              Seq ID    : 0x00dd
Flags    : FRAG:*.LAST    Frag Ptr : 0      (8 Octet) TTL      : 64
PID      : 8              Checksum : 0x26be (Good)
Dst IP <C: 193.128.104.20 Src IP <C: 193.128.104.36
========================[data: 30]=====================
0022  02 03 01 02 FB 9B 00 C8 00 01 00 1E 00 78 76 0C    .............xv.
0032  FD FF 07 A0 91 8B 0A 95 07 D5 FB 23 A3 01          ...........#..
```

Packet decodes as follows:
```
02        Version
05        Neighbour Acquisition
00        Hello Message
02        Down Status
FD93      Checksum
0064      ASN – Value 100₁₀
0001      Sequence Number
```
The remainder is Padding and the 4 octet Ethernet FCS.

```
=======================µscope=======================
Frame    : 3              Len      : 64             Error     : None
T Elapsed: 17:13:48:153   T Delta  : 00:00:00:000
-------------------------[mac]-------------------------
Dest Mac : Xyplex156806   Sourc Mac: Xyplex135b7e    Type      : IP
-------------------------[ip]--------------------------
IP Ver   : 4              IP HLen  : 20 Bytes
TOS      : 0x00           Pkt Len  : 30              Seq ID    : 0x0059
Flags    : FRAG:*.LAST    Frag Ptr : 0      (8 Octet) TTL      : 64
PID      : 8              Checksum : 0x2746 (Good)
Dst IP <C: 193.128.104.36 Src IP <C: 193.128.104.20
========================[data: 30]=====================
0022  02 05 00 02 FD 93 00 64 00 01 00 1E 00 78 76 0C    .......d.....xv.
0032  FD FF 07 A0 91 8B 0A 95 07 D5 7A 43 5D 22          .........zC]"
```

```
=============================μscope=============================
Frame    : 4            Len      : 64          Error    : None
T Elapsed: 17:13:48:153  T Delta  : 00:00:00:000
                        -[mac]-
Dest Mac : Xyplex135b7e   Sourc Mac: Xyplex156806   Type     : IP
                        -[ip]-
IP Ver   : 4            IP HLen  : 20 Bytes
TOS      : 0x00         Pkt Len  : 30              Seg ID   : 0x00de
Flags    : FRAG:*.LAST  Frag Ptr : 0    (8 Octet)  TTL      : 64
PID      : 8            Checksum : 0x26c1 (Good)
Dst IP <C: 193.128.104.20   Src IP <C: 193.128.104.36
============================[data:   30]============================
0022   02 05 01 02 FC 2F 00 C8 00 01 00 07 00 00 00 00   ...../..........
0032   00 00 00 00 00 00 00 00 00 00 00 B9 B9 F4 95       ..............
```

Packet decodes as follows:
02	Version
05	Neighbour Acquisition
01	I-Heard-You Response
02	Down Status
FC2F	Checksum
00C8	ASN – Value 200_{10}
0001	Sequence Number

The remainder is Padding and the 4 octet Ethernet FCS.

```
=============================μscope=============================
Frame    : 5            Len      : 64          Error    : None
T Elapsed: 17:13:48:153  T Delta  : 00:00:00:000
                        -[mac]-
Dest Mac : Xyplex135b7e   Sourc Mac: Xyplex156806   Type     : IP
                        -[ip]-
IP Ver   : 4            IP HLen  : 20 Bytes
TOS      : 0x00         Pkt Len  : 36              Seg ID   : 0x00df
Flags    : FRAG:*.LAST  Frag Ptr : 0    (8 Octet)  TTL      : 64
PID      : 8            Checksum : 0x26ba (Good)
Dst IP <C: 193.128.104.20   Src IP <C: 193.128.104.36
============================[data:   30]============================
0022   02 02 00 01 D3 93 00 C8 00 02 00 1E C1 80 68 00   ..............h.
0032   FD FF 07 A0 91 8B 0A 95 07 D5 9A 92 EA 2E          ..............
```

Packet decodes as follows:
02	Version
02	Poll Command
00	Unused
01	Up State
D393	Checksum
00C8	ASN – Value 200_{10}
0002	Sequence Number
001E	Reserved octets
C18068	Source Network 193.128.104.0

The remainder is Padding and the 4 octet Ethernet FCS.

```
=============================μscope=============================
Frame    : 6            Len      : 91          Error    : None
T Elapsed: 17:13:48:153  T Delta  : 00:00:00:000
                        -[mac]-
Dest Mac : Xyplex135b7e   Sourc Mac: Xyplex156806   Type     : IP
                        -[ip]-
IP Ver   : 4            IP HLen  : 20 Bytes
TOS      : 0x00         Pkt Len  : 73              Seg ID   : 0x00e0
Flags    : FRAG:*.LAST  Frag Ptr : 0    (8 Octet)  TTL      : 64
PID      : 8            Checksum : 0x2694 (Good)
Dst IP <C: 193.128.104.20   Src IP <C: 193.128.104.36
============================[data:   57]============================
0022   02 01 00 81 33 11 00 C8 00 01 01 00 C1 80 68 00   ....3.........h.
0032   24 04 01 03 C1 80 6A C1 80 69 C1 80 67 02 03 C1   $.....j..i..g...
0042   80 66 C1 80 65 C1 80 64 03 02 C1 80 6D C1 80 58   .f..e..d....m..X
0052   04 01 C1 80 01 13 60 F1 E5                         ......`..
```

Packet decodes as follows:
02	Version
01	Update Response
00	Unused
81	Up Status (Unsolicited Message)
3311	Checksum
00C8	ASN – Value 200_{10}
0001	Sequence Number
01	Number of Interior Routers – Value 1
00	Number of Exterior Routers – Value 0
C1806800	Source Network – 193.128.104.0
24	Router 1 (Host ID) – Value 36
04	Number of Distances – Value 4
0103	Distance 1 Hop, Number of Networks 3
C1806A	193.128.106
C18069	193.128.105
C18067	193.128.103
0203	Distance 2 Hops, Number of Networks 3
C18066	193.128.102
C18065	193.128.101
C18064	193.128.100
0302	Distance 3 Hops, Number of Networks 2
C1806D	193.128.109
C18058	193.128.88
0401	Distance 4 Hops, Number of Networks 1
C18001	193.128.1

The remainder is Padding and the 4 octet Ethernet FCS.

```
=============================μscope=============================
Frame    : 7            Len      : 64          Error    : None
T Elapsed: 17:14:18:753  T Delta  : 00:00:30:600
                        -[mac]-
Dest Mac : Xyplex156806   Sourc Mac: Xyplex135b7e   Type     : IP
                        -[ip]-
IP Ver   : 4            IP HLen  : 20 Bytes
TOS      : 0x00         Pkt Len  : 30              Seg ID   : 0x0060
Flags    : FRAG:*.LAST  Frag Ptr : 0    (8 Octet)  TTL      : 64
PID      : 8            Checksum : 0x273f (Good)
Dst IP <C: 193.128.104.36   Src IP <C: 193.128.104.20
============================[data:   30]============================
0022   02 05 00 02 FD 93 00 64 00 01 00 00 A5 75 00 00   .......d.....u..
0032   00 00 00 00 00 00 00 00 00 00 D1 7D 8A 00          ...........}..
```

Packet decodes as follows:
02	Version
05	Neighbour Reachability
00	Hello
02	Down Status
FD93	Checksum
0064	ASN – Value 100_{10}
0001	Sequence Number

The remainder is Padding and the 4 octet Ethernet FCS.

```
=============================μscope=============================
Frame    : 8            Len      : 64          Error    : None
T Elapsed: 17:14:18:753  T Delta  : 00:00:00:000
                        -[mac]-
Dest Mac : Xyplex135b7e   Sourc Mac: Xyplex156806   Type     : IP
                        -[ip]-
IP Ver   : 4            IP HLen  : 20 Bytes
TOS      : 0x00         Pkt Len  : 30              Seg ID   : 0x00e4
Flags    : FRAG:*.LAST  Frag Ptr : 0    (8 Octet)  TTL      : 64
PID      : 8            Checksum : 0x26bb (Good)
Dst IP <C: 193.128.104.20   Src IP <C: 193.128.104.36
============================[data:   30]============================
0022   02 05 01 01 FC 30 00 C8 00 01 00 02 00 04 00 01   .....0..........
0032   02 00 00 03 00 04 00 00 30 00 4B EC 20 BA          ........0.K. .
```

Packet decodes as follows:
02	Version
05	Neighbour Reachability
01	I-Heard-You
01	Up Status
FC30	Checksum
00C8	ASN – Value 200_{10}
0002	Sequence Number

The remainder is Padding and the 4 octet Ethernet FCS.

EGP, an Example

```
=============================µscope=============================
Frame    : 9            Len      : 64           Error    : None
T Elapsed: 17:14:49:353  T Delta  : 00:00:30:600
                         [mac]
Dest Mac : Xyplex156806  Sourc Mac: Xyplex135b7e  Type      : IP
                         [ip]
IP Ver   : 4            IP HLen  : 20 Bytes
TOS      : 0x00         Pkt Len  : 30             Seg ID   : 0x0067
Flags    : FRAG:*.LAST  Frag Ptr : 0    (8 Octet) TTL      : 64
PID      : 8            Checksum : 0x2738 (Good)
Dst IP <C: 193.128.104.36  Src IP <C: 193.128.104.20
=============================[data:   30]=============================
0022  02 05 00 02 FD 93 00 64 00 01 87 32 3E 66 04 53    .......d...2>f.S
0032  00 02 00 00 01 08 00 01 00 02 DB F5 6B 48          ...........kH
```

Packet decodes as follows:
02   Version
05   Neighbour Reachability
00   Hello
02   Down Status
FD93   Checksum
0064   ASN – Value 100₁₀
0001   Sequence Number
The remainder is Padding and the 4 octet Ethernet
FCS.

```
=============================µscope=============================
Frame    : 10           Len      : 64           Error    : None
T Elapsed: 17:14:49:353  T Delta  : 00:00:00:000
                         [mac]
Dest Mac : Xyplex135b7e  Sourc Mac: Xyplex156806  Type      : IP
                         [ip]
IP Ver   : 4            IP HLen  : 20 Bytes
TOS      : 0x00         Pkt Len  : 30             Seg ID   : 0x00e8
Flags    : FRAG:*.LAST  Frag Ptr : 0    (8 Octet) TTL      : 64
PID      : 8            Checksum : 0x26b7 (Good)
Dst IP <C: 193.128.104.20  Src IP <C: 193.128.104.36
=============================[data:   30]=============================
0022  02 05 01 01 FC 30 00 C8 00 01 00 02 00 04 00 01    .....0..........
0032  02 00 00 03 00 04 00 00 30 00 E6 CC 3B C3          ........0...;.
```

Packet decodes as follows:
02   Version
05   Neighbour Reachability
01   I-Heard-You
01   Up Status
FC30   Checksum
00C8   ASN – Value 200₁₀
0001   Sequence Number
The remainder is Padding and the 4 octet Ethernet
FCS.

```
=============================µscope=============================
Frame    : 11           Len      : 64           Error    : None
T Elapsed: 17:14:49:353  T Delta  : 00:00:00:000
                         [mac]
Dest Mac : Xyplex156806  Sourc Mac: Xyplex135b7e  Type      : IP
                         [ip]
IP Ver   : 4            IP HLen  : 20 Bytes
TOS      : 0x00         Pkt Len  : 36             Seg ID   : 0x0068
Flags    : FRAG:*.LAST  Frag Ptr : 0    (8 Octet) TTL      : 64
PID      : 8            Checksum : 0x2731 (Good)
Dst IP <C: 193.128.104.36  Src IP <C: 193.128.104.20
=============================[data:   30]=============================
0022  02 02 00 01 D4 13 00 64 00 02 00 02 C1 80 68 00    .......d......h.
0032  02 00 00 03 00 04 00 00 30 00 AA 2A BA 21          ........0..*.!
```

Packet decodes as follows:
02   Version
02   Poll Command
00   Unused
01   Up Status
D413   Checksum
0064   ASN – Value 100₁₀
0002   Sequence Number
0002   Reserved octets
C18068   Source Network 193.128.104.0
The remainder is Padding and the 4 octet Ethernet
FCS.

```
=============================µscope=============================
Frame    : 12           Len      : 64           Error    : None
T Elapsed: 17:14:49:353  T Delta  : 00:00:00:000
                         [mac]
Dest Mac : Xyplex156806  Sourc Mac: Xyplex135b7e  Type      : IP
                         [ip]
IP Ver   : 4            IP HLen  : 20 Bytes
TOS      : 0x00         Pkt Len  : 46             Seg ID   : 0x0069
Flags    : FRAG:*.LAST  Frag Ptr : 0    (8 Octet) TTL      : 64
PID      : 8            Checksum : 0x2726 (Good)
Dst IP <C: 193.128.104.36  Src IP <C: 193.128.104.20
=============================[data:   30]=============================
0022  02 01 00 81 0E E6 00 64 00 02 01 00 C1 80 68 00    .......d......h.
0032  14 01 01 02 C1 80 6C C1 80 6B 8E 57 44 5C          ......l..k.WD\
```

Packet decodes as follows:
02   Version
01   Update Response
00   Unused
81   Up Status (Unsolicited Message)
0EE6   Checksum
0064   ASN – Value 100₁₀
0002   Sequence Number
01   Number of Interior Routers – Value 1
00   Number of Exterior Routers – Value 0
C1806800   Source Network – 193.128.104.0
14   Router 1 (Host ID) – Value 20
01   Number od Distances – Value 1
0102   Distance 1 Hop, Number of Networks 2
C1806C   193.128.108
C1806B   193.128.107
The remainder is the 4 octet Ethernet FCS.

```
=============================µscope=============================
Frame    : 13           Len      : 91           Error    : None
T Elapsed: 17:14:49:353  T Delta  : 00:00:00:000
                         [mac]
Dest Mac : Xyplex135b7e  Sourc Mac: Xyplex156806  Type      : IP
                         [ip]
IP Ver   : 4            IP HLen  : 20 Bytes
TOS      : 0x00         Pkt Len  : 73             Seg ID   : 0x00e9
Flags    : FRAG:*.LAST  Frag Ptr : 0    (8 Octet) TTL      : 64
PID      : 8            Checksum : 0x268b (Good)
Dst IP <C: 193.128.104.20  Src IP <C: 193.128.104.36
=============================[data:   57]=============================
0022  02 01 00 01 33 90 00 C8 00 02 01 00 C1 80 68 00    ....3.........h.
0032  24 04 01 03 C1 80 6A C1 80 69 C1 80 67 02 03 C1    $.....j..i..g...
0042  80 66 C1 80 65 C1 80 64 03 02 C1 80 6D C1 80 58    .f..e..d....m..X
0052  04 01 C1 80 01 B8 98 53 91                         .......S.
```

Packet decodes as follows:
02   Version
01   Update Response
00   Unused
01   Up Status (Unsolicited Message)
3390   Checksum
00C8   ASN – Value 200₁₀
0002   Sequence Number
01   Number of Interior Routers – Value 1
00   Number of Exterior Routers – Value 0
C1806800   Source Network – 193.128.104.0
24   Router 1 (Host ID) – Value 20
04   Number od Distances – Value 4
0103   Distance 1 Hop, Number of Networks 3
C1806A   193.128.106
C18069   193.128.105
C18067   193.128.103
0203   Distance 2 Hops, Number of Networks 3
C18066   193.128.102
C18065   193.128.101
C18064   193.128.100
0302   Distance 3 Hops, Number of Networks 2
C1806D   193.128.109
C18058   193.128.88
0401   Distance 4 Hops, Number of Networks 1
C18001   193.128.1
The remainder is the 4 octet Ethernet FCS.

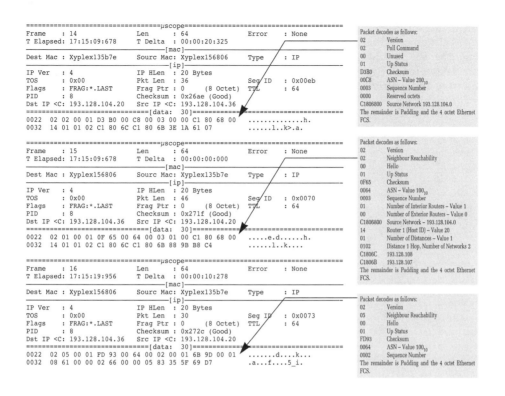

```
=================================μscope=================================
Frame    : 14              Len    : 64              Error    : None
T Elapsed: 17:15:09:678    T Delta : 00:00:20:325
--------------------------[mac]--------------------------
Dest Mac : Xyplex135b7e    Sourc Mac: Xyplex156806   Type     : IP
---------------------------[ip]---------------------------
IP Ver   : 4              IP HLen : 20 Bytes
TOS      : 0x00           Pkt Len : 36             Seq ID   : 0x00eb
Flags    : FRAG:*.LAST    Frag Ptr : 0    (8 Octet) TTL      : 64
PID      : 8              Checksum : 0x26ae (Good)
Dst IP <C: 193.128.104.20 Src IP <C: 193.128.104.36
===========================[data:  30]===========================
0022  02 02 00 01 D3 B0 00 C8 00 03 00 00 C1 80 68 00    ..............h.
0032  14 01 01 02 C1 80 6C C1 80 6B 3E 1A 61 07          ......l..k>.a.

=================================μscope=================================
Frame    : 15              Len    : 64              Error    : None
T Elapsed: 17:15:09:678    T Delta : 00:00:00:000
--------------------------[mac]--------------------------
Dest Mac : Xyplex156806    Sourc Mac: Xyplex135b7e   Type     : IP
---------------------------[ip]---------------------------
IP Ver   : 4              IP HLen : 20 Bytes
TOS      : 0x00           Pkt Len : 46             Seq ID   : 0x0070
Flags    : FRAG:*.LAST    Frag Ptr : 0    (8 Octet) TTL      : 64
PID      : 8              Checksum : 0x271f (Good)
Dst IP <C: 193.128.104.36 Src IP <C: 193.128.104.20
===========================[data:  30]===========================
0022  02 01 00 01 0F 65 00 64 00 03 01 00 C1 80 68 00    .....e.d......h.
0032  14 01 01 02 C1 80 6C C1 80 6B 88 9B B8 C4          ......l..k....

=================================μscope=================================
Frame    : 16              Len    : 64              Error    : None
T Elapsed: 17:15:19:956    T Delta : 00:00:10:278
--------------------------[mac]--------------------------
Dest Mac : Xyplex156806    Sourc Mac: Xyplex135b7e   Type     : IP
---------------------------[ip]---------------------------
IP Ver   : 4              IP HLen : 20 Bytes
TOS      : 0x00           Pkt Len : 30             Seq ID   : 0x0073
Flags    : FRAG:*.LAST    Frag Ptr : 0    (8 Octet) TTL      : 64
PID      : 8              Checksum : 0x272c (Good)
Dst IP <C: 193.128.104.36 Src IP <C: 193.128.104.20
===========================[data:  30]===========================
0022  02 05 00 01 FD 93 00 64 00 02 00 01 6B 9D 00 01    .......d....k...
0032  08 61 00 00 02 66 00 00 05 83 35 5F 69 D7          .a...f....5_i.
```

Packet decodes as follows:
```
02        Version
02        Poll Command
00        Unused
01        Up Status
D3B0      Checksum
00C8      ASN – Value 200₁₀
0003      Sequence Number
0000      Reserved octets
C1806800  Source Network 193.128.104.0
The remainder is Padding and the 4 octet Ethernet
FCS.
```

Packet decodes as follows:
```
02        Version
02        Neighbour Reachability
00        Hello
0F65      Checksum
0064      ASN – Value 100₁₀
0003      Sequence Number
01        Number of Interior Routers – Value 1
00        Number of Exterior Routers – Value 0
C1806800  Source Network – 193.128.104.0
14        Router 1 (Host ID) – Value 20
01        Number of Distances – Value 1
0102      Distance 1 Hop. Number of Networks 2
C1806C    193.128.108
C1806B    193.128.107
The remainder is Padding and the 4 octet Ethernet
FCS.
```

Packet decodes as follows:
```
02        Version
05        Neighbour Reachability
00        Hello
01        Up Status
FD93      Checksum
0064      ASN – Value 100₁₀
0002      Sequence Number
The remainder is Padding and the 4 octet Ethernet
FCS.
```

Figure 12-16: Sample EGP Trace

12.5 Summary

In practice, few internets are large enough to warrant the use of an EGP. Indeed, even nation-wide or global corporate networks would seldom require its use since with these internets, every router would probably require information about all routes. Where multiple organizations wish to join together however, a protocol such as EGP is used.

EGP itself is now relatively old. The RFC through which it is defined (RFC 904) dates back to 1984 although EGP has served the internet community well and has been the only such protocol for many years.

Today, the choice is a little less limited in that we now have an updated EGP available to us in the form of the Border Gateway Protocol (BGP) which is discussed in the next chapter. EGP though is robust and, by directly using IP presents us with very little overhead. True, it is at the mercy of IP which we have already said is an unreliable communications method. Equally, EGP is fairly intolerant of packet loss with partners expecting 75% reception or better. Also, EGP will require that an entire update is re-transmitted if a single packet from an update is lost. This latter point can then become significant where we have a very large internet with many routes to be advertised.

Finally, EGP does not have a very flexible approach to metrics and scales badly in environments that also run an IGP such as RIP. EGP metrics can be between 1 and 254. RIP metrics allow only a maximum of 15. Importing exterior routes into an Autonomous System must therefore be performed carefully with appropriate filtering and metric conversion where necessary.

The Border Gateway Protocol (BGP)

Like EGP discussed in the previous chapter, the Border Gateway Protocol (BGP) is used to exchange routing information between Autonomous Systems (ASs). BGP then is the latest member of the Exterior Gateway Protocol family. The classic definition of an Autonomous System is one that is under the control of a single administrative authority, uses a single, common, Interior Gateway Protocol (IGP), and a common set of metrics. Today, this definition no longer fits. Many Autonomous Systems now use several IGPs and several sets of metrics. However, provided that the AS appears to use a coherent routing policy, BGP can be used.

BGP has undergone many changes in recent years and, as such, it epitomizes the way in which the Internet community operates, with change being the only constant factor within the networking industry. Certainly it is true to say that, like EGP, few internets will require its use. Moreover, considering the potentially small operational base of the protocol, it is interesting to note that the current version is 4!

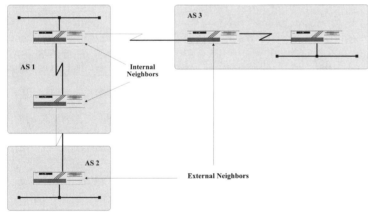

Figure 13-1: Internal and External Neighbors

BGP version 4 is defined by RFC 1771, and with it several new definitions are used. BGP supports two neighbor types known as *Internal* and *External*. An Internal Neighbor resides in the same AS, while External Neighbors reside in other ASs. Figure 13-1 shows an example of Internal and External Neighbors in a BGP environment.

As in OSPF, a connection between two BGP devices residing in different AS's is referred to as an *external link*, and a connection to BGP devices within the same AS as *internal links*. One definition that is new to BGP however is that of the *BGP Speaker*, the term applied to a device that is running BGP and conversing with another BGP device. You will notice also, that we have avoided using the term *router*. This is because devices that run BGP need not be routers. Non-routing hosts can exchange routing information with routers through any applicable routing protocol, and then use BGP to exchange information with a router in another AS. For the purposes of our discussion however we will assume that it is only routers that implement BGP.

13.1 BGP Operation

BGP uses TCP as its transport, thereby eliminating the need to provide additional sequencing or retransmission techniques, and the port number used is 179_{10}. BGP routers then maintain *Routing Information Bases* (RIBs) that contain the routing information learnt and/or advertised as defined by the individual router's routing policies.

Pairs of routers exchange information in what are called *Update* messages. These messages can also be used to mark a previously advertised route as being no longer available. Before any such information can be sent however, the routers involved in the exchange must first open the connection and confirm the connection parameters. Initially, the routers then exchange their entire BGP routing tables however, unlike some other routing protocols, BGP does not require that all information is exchanged on a regular basis. Instead, incremental information is exchanged only as the routing tables change. To ensure that partners are alive though, a *KeepAlive* message is used in a similar fashion to the *Hello* message used by OSPF. The simplified diagram of Figure 13-2 and the text following, shows how BGP operates. A complete example together with an associated trace, is then shown in section 13.3.

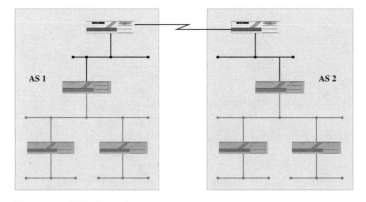

Figure 13-2: BGP Operations

The Border Gateway Protocol (BGP)

The two routers that are to exchange BGP information (shown at the top) firstly open a TCP connection using port 179. Once opened, the routers then exchange BGP *Open* packets that allows the protocol to exchange information. The response to which (apart from the normal Transport Layer Acknowledgements) is a *KeepAlive* packet. The routers now exchange *Update* packets advertising routes from within their Autonomous Systems and then exchange only KeepAlives that ensure their neighbor is reachable.

Should existing routes become unavailable, an *Update* packet is sent withdrawing them. The protocol then reverts to exchanging only *KeepAlives* once more. Equally where new routes become available, these too are advertised through *Update* packets.

Finally, when the connection is to be closed (due to a normal shutdown or through an error condition), the router initiating the closure sends a *Notification* packet indicating the reason, and the TCP connection itself is closed.

13.2 BGP Message Formats

From the previous section it is clear that, like other protocols, there are a number of different message formats associated with BGP. These messages each share the common header format that is shown in Figure 13-3. BGP messages then can be between 19 octets (the minimum size where a header is sent without any data) and 4096 octets maximum.

13.2.1 The BGP Message Header

Each BGP message consists of a fixed length header of 19 octets. Variable length data may then follow this header depending upon the type of BGP message. The message header format is then shown in Figure 13-3.

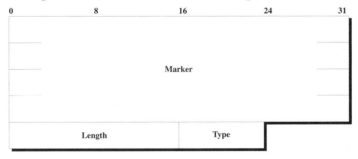

Figure 13-3: BGP Message Header Format

The *Marker* field is 16 octets in length and contains a value that can be predicted by the receiver. Where authentication is used for example, the Marker may carry information that the receiver can compute, based upon the authentication algorithm. If the Type of message is an Open, or if the Open contains no authentication information, then the marker must be all ones (FFFFFFFF$_{16}$). Thus, the

Marker field itself has a dual purpose, to both detect loss of synchronization, and to authenticate incoming messages.

The 16 bit *Length* field is used to define the overall length of the message (including the header) in octets. As we have already established, the minimum BGP message is one that consists of only a header. Thus the minimum value of this field must be 19. Equally, since the maximum BGP message size cannot exceed 4096 octets, this represents the highest value that the field can contain.

The 8 bit *Type* field is used to indicate the type of message that is being transmitted. Four message types are defined as identified in Table 13-1.

Table 13-1: BGP Message Types

Value	Type	Description
1	Open	Used to Open the BGP connection so that routing information can be passed between BGP routers.
2	Update	Used to exchange routing information between BGP routers.
3	Notification	Sent whenever an error condition is detected. The BGP connection is closed immediately after a Notification message is sent.
4	KeepAlive	Used to determine whether BGP a partner is alive.

13.2.2 Open Messages

Each end of the connection sends an Open message immediately after a transport connection has been established by TCP. Assuming that the information contained in the Open is then acceptable, the connection partner responds with a KeepAlive message and the connection is declared open for the exchange of routing information. Update, KeepAlive, and Notification messages can then be exchanged across the link.

The format of the Open message (excluding the BGP Message Header shown in Figure 13-3) is shown in Figure 13-4 with the Version field immediately following the Type field of the header.

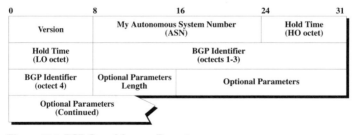

Figure 13-4: BGP Open Message Format

The 8 bit *Version* field defines the version of the protocol and therefore the format of the packet. Currently, the version number is 4. The 16 bit *My Autonomous System Number* field indicates the Autonomous System Number (ASN) of the router sending the packet.

The *Hold Time* field is 16 bits long and is used to determine the maximum amount of time (in seconds) that can elapse between the receipt of successive

KeepAlive and/or Update messages. The Hold Time is an administrative variable that must be configured on each router. When a router receives an Open message, it then uses the smaller of its own configured value and that received in the Open message, as the Hold Time.

The BGP Identifier field is a 4 octet (32 bit) value used to identify the sending router. All BGP routers set the value of the BGP Identifier to an IP Address that has been assigned to one of its interfaces. Since all IP Addresses must be unique, this method of selection ensures that a unique BGP Identifier is chosen.

BGP Open messages may also contain a number of optional parameters. The existence of these parameters is communicated through the *Optional Parameters Length* field that is 8 bits long. Where this field is zero, no optional parameters are present and the Optional Parameters field is omitted. Where the Optional Parameters Length field is non-zero, Optional Parameters (as described below) are present.

The *Optional Parameters* field contains a variable length list of optional parameters each following the format shown in Figure 13-5. The 8 bit *Parameter Type* field contains a code that identifies the type of parameter being described. Currently only one such parameter is defined, that of Authentication Information (Type 1). The *Parameter Length* field (again 8 bits in length) then contains the length of the variable *Parameter Value* field.

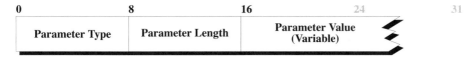

Figure 13-5: BGP Open Optional Parameters

The only optional parameter currently defined is that of Authentication Information (Parameter Type 1). In this case, the variable length Parameter Value contains the following data format.

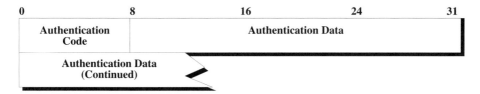

Figure 13-6: BGP Open Authentication Information

The *Authentication Code* field is used to identify the authentication mechanism in use. Broadly, this value will indicate the mechanism itself, the meaning of the *Authentication Data*, and also the algorithm that should be used when computing the value of the *Marker* field of the BGP header. The actual *Authentication Data* field is therefore dependent upon the Authentication Code used.

The trace in Figure 13-7 shows a typical Open sequence.

```
====================================µSCOPE===================================
Frame     : 3                Len      : 64              Error    : None
T Elapsed: 15:15:45:811      T Delta  : 00:00:00:480
--------------------------------[mac]----------------------------------------
Dest Mac : Xyplex456866      Sourc Mac: Xyplex456806    Type     : IP
---------------------------------[ip]----------------------------------------
IP Ver   : 4                 IP HLen  : 20 Bytes
TOS      : 0x00              Pkt Len  : 44              Seg ID   : 0x006e
Flags    : FRAG:*.LAST       Frag Ptr : 0    (8 Octet)  TTL      : 64
PID      : TCP  ( 6)         Checksum : 0x310a (Good)
Dst IP <C: 192.168.100.1     Src IP <C: 192.168.100.2
---------------------------------[tcp]---------------------------------------
Src Port : 4000              Dst Port : 179
Seq No   : 0x0000014f        Ack No   : 0x00000001
Head Len : 6   words         Flags    : ....S.          Window   : 0x0100
Checksum : 0x3c2f (Good)     Urg Ptr  : 0x0000          Options  : Present
-------------------------------[options]-------------------------------------
Option   : MaxSegSize        Length   : 4               Value    : 05b4
==============================[data:   6]====================================
003A   00 00 66 34 5C A8                      ..f4\.
```

Router 192.168.100.2 sends a *Syn* Segment to port 179 to open the connection.

```
====================================µSCOPE===================================
Frame     : 4                Len      : 64              Error    : None
T Elapsed: 15:15:45:811      T Delta  : 00:00:00:000
--------------------------------[mac]----------------------------------------
Dest Mac : Xyplex456806      Sourc Mac: Xyplex456866    Type     : IP
---------------------------------[ip]----------------------------------------
IP Ver   : 4                 IP HLen  : 20 Bytes
TOS      : 0x00              Pkt Len  : 44              Seg ID   : 0x0098
Flags    : FRAG:*.LAST       Frag Ptr : 0    (8 Octet)  TTL      : 64
PID      : TCP  ( 6)         Checksum : 0x30e0 (Good)
Dst IP <C: 192.168.100.2     Src IP <C: 192.168.100.1
---------------------------------[tcp]---------------------------------------
Src Port : 179               Dst Port : 4000
Seq No   : 0x000001a8        Ack No   : 0x00000000
Head Len : 6   words         Flags    : .A..S.          Window   : 0x0100
Checksum : 0x3a77 (Good)     Urg Ptr  : 0x0000          Options  : Present
-------------------------------[options]-------------------------------------
Option   : MaxSegSize        Length   : 4               Value    : 05b4
==============================[data:   6]====================================
003A   FF FF C0 AE 86 89                      ......
```

Router 192.168.100.1 responds with a *Syn/Ack*.

```
====================================µSCOPE===================================
Frame     : 5                Len      : 64              Error    : None
T Elapsed: 15:15:45:811      T Delta  : 00:00:00:000
--------------------------------[mac]----------------------------------------
Dest Mac : Xyplex456866      Sourc Mac: Xyplex456806    Type     : IP
---------------------------------[ip]----------------------------------------
IP Ver   : 4                 IP HLen  : 20 Bytes
TOS      : 0x00              Pkt Len  : 40              Seg ID   : 0x006f
Flags    : FRAG:*.LAST       Frag Ptr : 0    (8 Octet)  TTL      : 64
PID      : TCP  ( 6)         Checksum : 0x310d (Good)
Dst IP <C: 192.168.100.1     Src IP <C: 192.168.100.2
---------------------------------[tcp]---------------------------------------
Src Port : 4000              Dst Port : 179
Seq No   : 0x00000150        Ack No   : 0x000000a9
Head Len : 5   words         Flags    : .A....          Window   : 0x0100
Checksum : 0x5234 (Good)     Urg Ptr  : 0x0000          Options  : None
==============================[data:  10]====================================
0036   02 04 05 B4 FF FF 93 87 52 53          ........RS
```

Router 192.168.100.2 sends an *ACK* – The connection is now open.

```
====================================µSCOPE===================================
Frame     : 6                Len      : 64              Error    : None
T Elapsed: 15:15:45:811      T Delta  : 00:00:00:000
--------------------------------[mac]----------------------------------------
Dest Mac : Xyplex456806      Sourc Mac: Xyplex456866    Type     : IP
---------------------------------[ip]----------------------------------------
IP Ver   : 4                 IP HLen  : 20 Bytes
TOS      : 0x00              Pkt Len  : 40              Seg ID   : 0x0099
Flags    : FRAG:*.LAST       Frag Ptr : 0    (8 Octet)  TTL      : 64
PID      : TCP  ( 6)         Checksum : 0x30e3 (Good)
Dst IP <C: 192.168.100.2     Src IP <C: 192.168.100.1
---------------------------------[tcp]---------------------------------------
Src Port : 179               Dst Port : 4000
Seq No   : 0x000001a9        Ack No   : 0x00000150
Head Len : 5   words         Flags    : .A....          Window   : 0x0100
Checksum : 0x5234 (Good)     Urg Ptr  : 0x0000          Options  : None
==============================[data:  10]====================================
0036   02 04 05 B4 FF FF 34 D7 3B 14          ......4.;.
```

```
====================================µSCOPE===================================
Frame     : 7                Len      : 87              Error    : None
T Elapsed: 15:15:45:811      T Delta  : 00:00:00:000
--------------------------------[mac]----------------------------------------
Dest Mac : Xyplex456866      Sourc Mac: Xyplex456806    Type     : IP
---------------------------------[ip]----------------------------------------
IP Ver   : 4                 IP HLen  : 20 Bytes
TOS      : 0x00              Pkt Len  : 69              Seg ID   : 0x0070
Flags    : FRAG:*.LAST       Frag Ptr : 0    (8 Octet)  TTL      : 64
PID      : TCP  ( 6)         Checksum : 0x30ef (Good)
Dst IP <C: 192.168.100.1     Src IP <C: 192.168.100.2
---------------------------------[tcp]---------------------------------------
Src Port : 4000              Dst Port : 179
Seq No   : 0x00000150        Ack No   : 0x000001a9
Head Len : 5   words         Flags    : .AP...          Window   : 0x0100
Checksum : 0x2b21 (Good)     Urg Ptr  : 0x0000          Options  : None
==============================[data:  33]====================================
0036   FF FF FF FF FF FF FF FF FF FF FF FF FF FF FF FF   ................
0046   00 1D 01 04 00 C8 00 5A C0 A8 64 02 00 20 CB A2   .......Z..d.. ..
0056   93                                                .
```

Router 192.168.100.2 Sends an *Ack* and a BGP *Open*.

Packet decode as follows:

FF..FF	Market – 16 octets of all ones
001D	Length 29 octets
01	Type – Value 1 (Open)
04	Version – Value 4
00C8	ASN – Value 200
005A	Hold Time – Value 90 seconds
C0A86402	Router ID – Value 192.168.100.2
00	Option Length – No options present

Figure 13-7: Sample BGP Open

13.2.3 Update Messages

Update messages are used to advertise a single route and/or withdraw multiple unfeasible routes from service. Using this information, a router can then update its Routing Information Base (RIB) or routing tables accordingly. One point should be noted though concerning the interaction of BGP with IGPs. RFC 1772 (*Application of the Border Gateway Protocol in the Internet*) tells us that BGP will never advertise a route until it has learnt it through an IGP. Thus, simply connecting two routers together will not always acheive the desired result.

As with Open messages, the Update message includes the fixed length BGP message header previously described, and then optionally contains other fields as shown in Figure 13-8. These mesages contain optional information because they can be used to advertise a new route, and/or withdraw multiple routes that have become unuseable. Obviously at startup, the message contains only those routes that are available. However, during the lifetime of the connection, it is highly likely that they would be used to either withdraw routes or to install new ones.

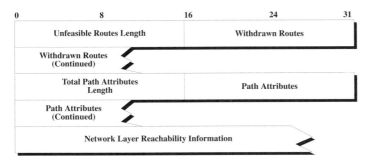

Figure 13-8: BGP Update Message Format

The *Unfeasible Routes Length* field is used to indicate the total length (in octets) of the *Withdrawn Routes* field. A value of zero here indicates that no routes are being withdrawn, and that the Withdrawn Routes field is therefore not present.

The *Withdrawn Routes* field is of variable length as defined by the *Withdrawn Routes Length* field. This then contains a list of encoded IP Address prefixes as shown in Figure 13-9. Here, each address prefix is encoded with a 1 octet *Length* field followed by the IP Address prefix itself. The length field defines the length of the IP Address prefix in bits. Where this length is zero, it indicates that the prefix matches all IP Addresses and that all routes are withdrawn.

0	8	16	24	31
Length		Prefix		

Figure 13-9: BGP Withdrawn Routes

The *Total Path Attribute Length* field is used to indicate the total length of the *Path Attributes* field (in octets). A value of zero in this field indicates that no Path

Attributes exist in the Update and that the *Path Attributes*, and *Network Layer Reachability Information* fields have been omitted from the packet.

The Path Attributes field then contains a list of attributes that further define the path being advertised. Each attribute is made up of three pieces of information; a 2 octet *Attribute Type*, a 1 or 2 octet *Attribute Length*, and a variable length *Attribute Value*. The 2 octet Attribute Type field, shown in Figure 13-10 is used to describe the type of attribute and various other information. Bit 0 is referred to as the *Optional* bit and defines whether the attribute is optional. Bit 1, the *Transitive* bit, defines whether an optional attribute is transitive. That is whether it is used as part of the Path description of a route that is being advertised through this AS. Where the attribute is non-optional however, this bit must be set on. Bit 2 is called the *Partial* bit and is used to define whether the information was included by the originator. In the case of non-optional attributes this bit must be off. Bit 3 is the *Extended* bit and defines whether the Attribute Length field is 1 octet or 2 octets long. When this bit is set, the length field is 2 octets. The second octet of the Type field then describes the type of attribute which is then followed by the Length field and the actual attribute value.

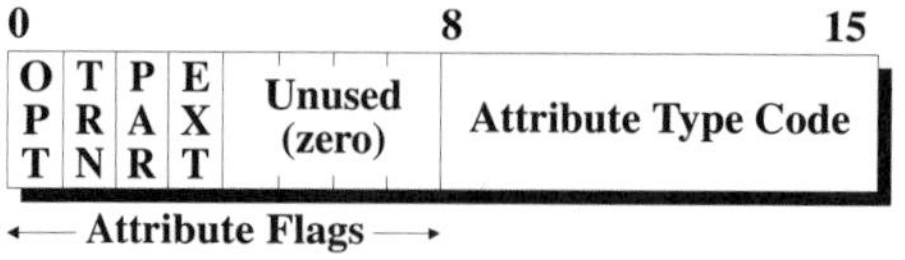

Figure 13-10: Path Attributes Type Field

Attributes themselves then fall into two distinct categories:

- **Well Known Attributes**
  These must be recognized by all BGP hosts. Two types of Well Known Attribute exist, namely Mandatory and Discretionary:
  - Mandatory Well Known Attributes must be included in every Update message. All of these attributes must also be passed to other BGP peers (after updating if appropriate).
  - Discretionary Well Known Attributes, although they must be recognized by all BGP hosts, do not need to be present in every update message.

- **Optional Attributes**
  Paths can contain one or more of these attributes, however it is not required that they be recognized by all BGP hosts. As with the Well Known attributes, two types of Optional attributes also exist:
  - Transitive Optional Attributes are passed between Autonomous Systems. This type of attribute is defined as one where the Transitive bit is set in the Attributes Flags field.
  - Non-Transitive Optional Attributes are not passed between Autonomous Systems. The Transitive bit in the Attribute Flags field is not set for this type of attribute.

RFC 1771 then defines the following attributes:

- **ORIGIN – Attribute Type Code 1**
  This is a *Well Known Mandatory* attribute that is generated by the Autonomous System that originated the routing information. Being mandatory, this attribute

The Border Gateway Protocol (BGP)

must be included in all Update messages if the BGP Speaker[1] is propagating information about this route. In this, the Attribute value is 1 octet in length and contains one of the values shown in Table 13-2.

Table 13-2: BGP Origin Attributes

Value	Description
0	IGP – The Network Layer Reachability Information is interior to the originating Autonomous System.
1	EGP – The Network Layer Reachability Information was learnt through EGP.
2	Incomplete – The Network Layer Reachability Information was learnt by some other means.

- **AS_PATH – Attribute Type Code 2**

  AS_PATH is a *Mandatory, Well Known* attribute that identifies the Autonomous Systems through which routing information carried in this Update message has passed. This information is then represented by the three pieces of information shown in Figure 13-11.

  The *Path Segment Type* field is 8 bits long and can contain either the value 1 or 2. Where the value is 1, the Segment Type is said to be an AS_SET, an unordered set of the ASs that this route has traversed in the Update message. Where the value is 2, the Type is referred to as an AS_SEQUENCE which is an ordered set of ASs traversed. The 8 bit *Path Segment Length* field contains the number of ASs traversed. The *Path Segment Value* field then contains one or more 16 bit fields that each contain an Autonomous System Number.

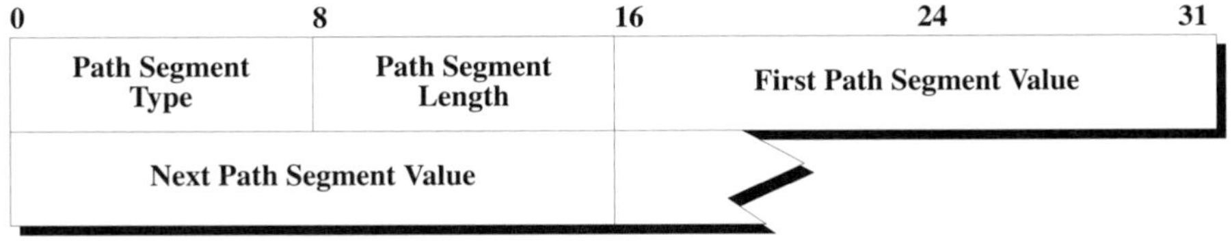

Figure 13-11: AS_PATH Attribute

When the Speaker originates the route and it is propagating the information to another device in a neighboring AS, it includes its own AS number in an AS_PATH Attribute. Where the Speaker originates the route and it is propagating the information to another device within the same AS, it includes an empty AS_PATH Attribute. Additionally, when the BGP Speaker propagates a route learnt from another device, it modifies the attribute by placing its own AS number in the path. In this way, the receiver can determine the path over which the update came. However, if the Speaker is advertising the route to another device within the same Autonomous System no modification takes place. This is because the attribute relates to the ASs through which the routing information has passed. Obviously if the information is to stay within the same AS, this attribute must therefore remain the same.

1. A BGP Speaker is a device that is participating in BGP.

- **NEXT_HOP – Attribute Type Code 3**

  This is a *Well Known, Mandatory* attribute that defines the IP Address of the router that should be used as the next hop to the destination(s) listed in the Network Layer Reachability field of the Update.

- **MULTI_EXIT_DISC – Attribute Type Code 4**

  This is a 4 octet *Optional, Non-Transitive* attribute that contains a metric value used to discriminate among possible multiple entry and exit points to the same neighboring AS. As with all routing protocols the lower the value of the metric, the greater the chance of being chosen. Thus where multiple possible entry/exit routes exist, the one with the lower metric will be chosen provided that it is available.

- **LOCAL_PREF – Attribute Type Code 5**

  As its name suggests, this attribute is used only within an Autonomous System (hence Local). The attribute itself contains a 4 octet value that is used to indicate to peers internal to the AS, a degree of preference for each external route advertised. This is a *Well Known, Discretionary* attribute.

- **ATOMIC_AGGREGATE – Attribute Type Code 6**

  Again *Well Known*, and *Discretionary*, this attribute is of zero length. To understand how this attribute works however, we must first appreciate what information is actually carried in the *Network Layer Reachability Information* (NLRI) fields of Update messages. NLRI is carried as a set of IP prefixes. Thus, what is known as overlap can occur where we have two (or more) similar prefixes. For example, prefixes of aaa.bbb.0.0 and aaa.bbb.ccc.0 could be said to overlap although the latter would be more specific. The ATOMIC_AGGREGATE attribute is then used by a BGP Speaker to inform other BGP devices that the local system has chosen a less specific route over that which is more specific.

- **AGGREGATOR – Attribute Type Code 7**

  Aggregation is defined by RFC 1771 as being "*the process of combining the characteristics of several different routes in such a way that a single route can be advertised.*" Aggregating routes therefore allows us to reduce the amount of information that BGP Speakers need to store and exchange.

  Aggregator, is an *Optional, Transitive* attribute of six octets in length. The makeup of this attribute is the last AS that formed the aggregate route (encoded as 2 octets) and the 4 octet IP Address of the Speaker that actually formed the aggregate route. Obviously this attribute is only ever applied to routes that have been formed by aggregation.

The final field of the Update message is the Network Layer Reachability Information (NLRI) which is encoded as the dual field shown in Figure 13-12. The *Length* field is used to indicate the length (in bits) of the IP Address prefix contained in the *Prefix* field.

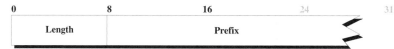

Figure 13-12: Network Layer Reachability Information

The NLRI field is of variable length. We have said that each Update message can advertise at most only one route, however, this single route can be described by multiple attributes. Where multiple attributes are provided, these must all relate to the information contained in the NLRI field.

The partial trace Figure 13-13 shows a simple update message.

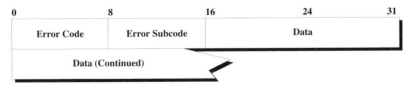

```
μSCOPE                    PACKET TRACE DECODE REPORT        (c) T.Kenyon 1995
```

```
=============================μscope=================================
Frame    : 11          Len    : 103       Error    : None
T Elapsed: 12:04:30:598  T Delta : 00:00:00:918
                         ----[mac]----
Dest Mac : Xyplex456806   Sourc Mac: Xyplex456866   Type   : IP
                         ----[ip]----
IP Ver  : 4          IP HLen : 20 Bytes
TOS     : 0x00       Pkt Len : 85                Seq ID  : 0x0037
Flags   : FRAG:*.LAST  Frag Ptr : 0    (8 Octet)  TTL     : 64
PID     : TCP ( 6)    Checksum : 0x3118 (Good)
Dst IP <C: 192.168.100.2  Src IP <C: 192.168.100.1
                         ----[tcp]----
Src Port : 4002        Dst Port : 179
Seq No   : 0x00000537   Ack No   : 0x000006fa
Head Len : 5   words    Flags    : .AP...        Window  : 0x2000
Checksum : 0x53c5 (Good)  Urg Ptr  : 0x0000       Options :  None
======================[data:  49]===========================
0036  FF FF FF FF FF FF FF FF FF FF FF FF FF FF FF FF  ................
0046  00 2D 02 00 00 00 12 40 01 01 00 40 02 04 02 01  .-.....@...@....
0056  00 64 40 03 04 C0 A8 64 01 18 C0 A8 0D 68 A7 CB  .d@....d.....h..
0066  14
```

Packet decodes as follows:	
FF..FF	Marker – 16 octets of all ones
002D	Length – Value 45
02	Type – Value 2 – Update
0000	Unfeasible Routes Length – Value 0 – No unfeasible routes
0012	Total Path Attributes Length – Value 18_{10}
4001	Transitive Attrib (Type Code 1-Origin)
01	Attribute 1 octet long
00	Derived from an IGP
4002	Transitive Attrib (Type Code 2-AS_Path)
04	Attribute 4 octets long
02	Path Segment Type – Value AS_Sequence
01	Path Segment Length – Value 1 AS
0064	Path Segment Value – Value 100
4003	Transitive Attrib (Type Code 3-Next_Hop)
04	Attribute 4 octets long
C0A86401	Next Hop Address – Value 192.168.100.1
18	NLRI Length – Value 24 bits
C0A80D	NLRI – Value 192.168.13

Figure 13-13: Simple Update Packet

13.2.4 KeepAlive Messages

KeepAlive messages are exchanged between BGP peers to ensure that they are reachable. BGP does not use any transport layer keep-alive mechanism thus, as with OSPF, we must use some other method. With BGP, peers exchange headers with a Type field of 4, and with no other information.

13.2.5 Notification Messages

Notification messages are sent when an error condition is detected or where we wish to close the connection. In BGP though, there is no chance for recovery and the connection is closed immediately after a Notification Message is sent. The actual format of such messages is the BGP Header followed immediately by the Notification format as shown in Figure 13-14.

```
0              8              16             24            31
┌───────────────┬───────────────┬──────────────────────────┐
│  Error Code   │ Error Subcode │           Data           │
├───────────────┴───────────────┴──────────────────────────┘
│       Data (Continued)        │
└───────────────────────────────┘
```

Figure 13-14: BGP Notification Message Format (excluding Header)

The 8 bit *Error Code* field is used to indicate the type of *Notification* message being conveyed, and the 8 bit *Error Subcode* field then further defines this by providing more specific information about the error. Table 13-3 details the Error codes and their associated subcodes. The text that follows then describes the errors in further detail. Finally, the Data field carries diagnostic information to identify the reason for the Notification. The actual contents of this field are therefore dependent upon the Error code and Sub-Code and is described later.

Table 13-3: BGP Notification Error Codes

Error Code	Error Code Name	Sub Code(s)	Sub-Code Name
1	Message Header Error	1	Connection not Synchronized
		2	Bad Message Length
		3	Bad Message Type
2	OPEN Message Error	1	Unsupported Version Number
		2	Bad Peer AS
		3	Bad BGP Identifier
		4	Unsupported Optional Parameter
		5	Authentication Failure
		6	Unacceptable Hold Time
3	UPDATE Message Error	1	Malformed attribute list
		2	Unrecognized Well-Known Attribute
		3	Missing Well-Known Attribute
		4	Attribute Flags Error
		5	Attribute Length Error
		6	Invalid ORIGIN Attribute
		7	AS Routing Loop
		8	Invalid NEXT_HOP Attribute
		9	Optional Attribute Error
		10	Invalid Network Field
		11	Malformed AS_PATH
4	Hold Timer Expired		
5	Finite State Machine Error		No Sub-Codes defined for these Errors
6	Cease		

- **Message Header Errors**

   Where we have a Message Header error reported, the Connection not Synchronized sub-code (sub code 1) is used to indicate that the contents of the Marker field are not as expected. You will recall that for an Open message, the Marker field should be all ones, and for all other types of messages, the value is determined by the optional Authentication information.

   Where the Message Header error indicates a length error (sub code 2), the length of a message is deemed to be incorrect. The Data field then contains the length field thought to be in error. Equally, if a bad Type field is detected in a message, then a Notification of Bad Message Type is used and the Data field contains a copy of the bad Type field.

- **Open Message Errors**

   Open Message errors are used to report errors detected during the Open phase of BGP. Where an unsupported Version number is detected (sub code 1), the Data field contains a two octet value that represents the largest locally supported version number less than that bid by the remote BGP peer.

The Bad Peer AS error (sub code 2) is used to indicate that the receiver is not prepared to accept the Autonomous System number proposed by the peer. A Bad BGP Identifier error (sub code 3) is posted if the Open message contains an incorrect IP Address in the BGP Identifier field. Equally, the Authentication Failure error (sub code 5) is posted where the Open message contains authentication information that is unacceptable to the receiver.

Where the Open message contains an Attribute that is unsupported, the Unsupported Optional Parameter (sub code 4) error is sent. Finally, the receiver will reject an Open message if it contains an illegal Hold Timer value (sub code 6). To be legal, the Hold Time value must be at least 3 seconds however, BGP Speakers can reject any time that they consider to be unacceptable if they are configured to do so.

- **Update Message Errors**
  Whenever an Update message is received, it is checked to ensure that there are no errors. If the Unfeasible Routes Length or Total Attribute Length is too large, an error of Malformed Attribute List is sent (sub code 1). This error is also used where an attribute appears more than once.

  If any attribute has a Flags field that does not agree with the Attribute Type code, then an Attribute Flags Error (sub code 4) is sent in the Notification message. Similarly, if any attribute is found to have a length that does not agree with the Type of attribute being described, the Attribute Length error (sub code 5) is used. The Data field then contains the attribute thought to be in error in both of these cases.

  As we saw, certain of the Well-Known attributes are mandatory. If any are found to be missing, the Missing Well-Known Attribute error (sub code 3) is sent and the Data field contains the Attribute Type code of the missing attribute. If a Well-Known attribute is not recognized, then the Data field contains the unrecognized attribute and the Unrecognized Well-Known attribute error (sub code 2) is sent.

  The Well-Known attribute ORIGIN must be present and in a form that can be understood by the receiver. Where this is not the case, the Data field will contain the unrecognized attribute and the Invalid Origin attribute error (sub code 6) is used to inform the peer.

  The NEXT_HOP attribute must be correct for external links or an Invalid Next-Hop attribute error (sub code 8) is sent. In particular, the Next-Hop must contain a valid IP Address and this address must be on the same subnet as the receiver.

  Optional attributes contained in an Update message are checked, and an error condition is sent where errors are detected. In this case the error code Optional attribute error (sub code 9) is used and the Data field then contains the attribute in error.

  If the NRLI field is in error, the Invalid Network Field error (sub code 10) is used. Finally, if an error is detected in the AS_PATH, the Malformed AS_PATH error (sub code 11) is posted.

- **Hold Timer Expired**
  When a peer does not receive a KeepAlive or Update message within the time specified in the Hold Time field of an Open message, a Notification is sent with

a Hold Timer Expired error code. No sub codes are defined for this error type, and the connection is immediately closed.

- **Finite State Machine Error**
  This error is used to indicate that an unexpected event has occurred. Again no sub codes exist for this error type.

- **Cease**
  This is not an error condition. Instead, a BGP peer may use this Notification message to close a connection gracefully at any time. As an example, a peer may choose to send this message when the BGP processes are being closed down. Figure 13-15 shows a sample trace of a cease message.

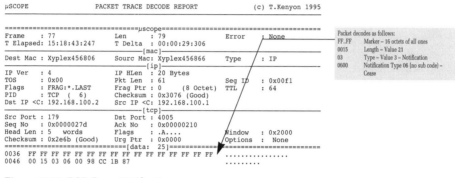

Figure 13-15: BGP Cease Notification

13.3 A Simple BGP Example

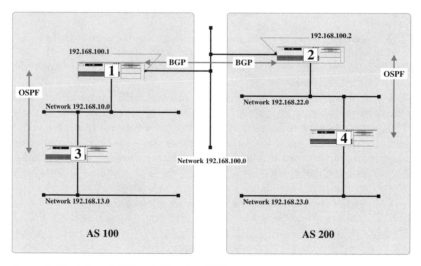

Figure 13-16: A Simple Network Running BGP

The Border Gateway Protocol (BGP)

In order to see the whole picture of the operation of BGP, we can consider the network shown in Figure 13-16. Here we see two routers (Routers 1 and 2) joined by a common network, exchanging BGP information. Two other routers (Routers 3 and 4) also exchange information with these two, but via OSPF. The interfaces joining the Autonomous Systems then run only BGP, while those within each AS run only OSPF.

In the example, each router (1 and 2) will learn about the *remote* networks in the opposite Autonomous System as the following trace shows.

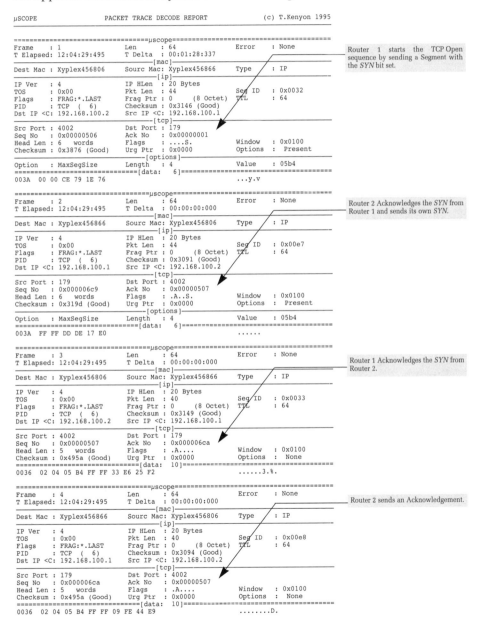

```
μSCOPE              PACKET TRACE DECODE REPORT        (c) T.Kenyon 1995


=========================μscope==========================
Frame    : 1              Len      : 64           Error    : None          Router 1 starts the TCP Open
T Elapsed: 12:04:29;495   T Delta  : 00:01:28;337                          sequence by sending a Segment with
                             -[mac]-                                        the SYN bit set.
Dest Mac : Xyplex456806   Sourc Mac: Xyplex456866  Type     : IP
                             -[ip]-
IP Ver   : 4              IP HLen  : 20 Bytes
TOS      : 0x00           Pkt Len  : 44            Seq ID   : 0x0032
Flags    : FRAG:*.LAST    Frag Ptr : 0   (8 Octet) TTL      : 64
PID      : TCP ( 6)       Checksum : 0x3146 (Good)
Dst IP <C: 192.168.100.2  Src IP <C: 192.168.100.1
                             -[tcp]-
Src Port : 4002           Dst Port : 179
Seq No   : 0x00000506     Ack No   : 0x00000001
Head Len : 6   words      Flags    : ....S.        Window   : 0x0100
Checksum : 0x3876 (Good)  Urg Ptr  : 0x0000        Options  : Present
                             -[options]-
Option   : MaxSegSize     Length   : 4             Value    : 05b4
=========================[data:    6]====================
003A  00 00 CE 79 1E 76                    ...y.v

=========================μscope==========================
Frame    : 2              Len      : 64           Error    : None          Router 2 Acknowledges the SYN from
T Elapsed: 12:04:29;495   T Delta  : 00:00:00;000                          Router 1 and sends its own SYN.
                             -[mac]-
Dest Mac : Xyplex456866   Sourc Mac: Xyplex456806  Type     : IP
                             -[ip]-
IP Ver   : 4              IP HLen  : 20 Bytes
TOS      : 0x00           Pkt Len  : 44            Seq ID   : 0x00e7
Flags    : FRAG:*.LAST    Frag Ptr : 0   (8 Octet) TTL      : 64
PID      : TCP ( 6)       Checksum : 0x3091 (Good)
Dst IP <C: 192.168.100.1  Src IP <C: 192.168.100.2
                             -[tcp]-
Src Port : 179            Dst Port : 4002
Seq No   : 0x000006c9     Ack No   : 0x00000507
Head Len : 6   words      Flags    : .A..S.        Window   : 0x0100
Checksum : 0x319d (Good)  Urg Ptr  : 0x0000        Options  : Present
                             -[options]-
Option   : MaxSegSize     Length   : 4             Value    : 05b4
=========================[data:    6]====================
003A  FF FF DD DE 17 E0                    ......

=========================μscope==========================
Frame    : 3              Len      : 64           Error    : None          Router 1 Acknowledges the SYN from
T Elapsed: 12:04:29;495   T Delta  : 00:00:00;000                          Router 2.
                             -[mac]-
Dest Mac : Xyplex456806   Sourc Mac: Xyplex456866  Type     : IP
                             -[ip]-
IP Ver   : 4              IP HLen  : 20 Bytes
TOS      : 0x00           Pkt Len  : 40            Seq ID   : 0x0033
Flags    : FRAG:*.LAST    Frag Ptr : 0   (8 Octet) TTL      : 64
PID      : TCP ( 6)       Checksum : 0x3149 (Good)
Dst IP <C: 192.168.100.2  Src IP <C: 192.168.100.1
                             -[tcp]-
Src Port : 4002           Dst Port : 179
Seq No   : 0x00000507     Ack No   : 0x000006ca
Head Len : 5   words      Flags    : .A....        Window   : 0x0100
Checksum : 0x495a (Good)  Urg Ptr  : 0x0000        Options  : None
=========================[data:   10]====================
0036  02 04 05 B4 FF FF 33 E6 25 F2        ......3.%.

=========================μscope==========================
Frame    : 4              Len      : 64           Error    : None          Router 2 sends an Acknowledgement.
T Elapsed: 12:04:29;495   T Delta  : 00:00:00;000
                             -[mac]-
Dest Mac : Xyplex456866   Sourc Mac: Xyplex456806  Type     : IP
                             -[ip]-
IP Ver   : 4              IP HLen  : 20 Bytes
TOS      : 0x00           Pkt Len  : 40            Seq ID   : 0x00e8
Flags    : FRAG:*.LAST    Frag Ptr : 0   (8 Octet) TTL      : 64
PID      : TCP ( 6)       Checksum : 0x3094 (Good)
Dst IP <C: 192.168.100.1  Src IP <C: 192.168.100.2
                             -[tcp]-
Src Port : 179            Dst Port : 4002
Seq No   : 0x000006ca     Ack No   : 0x00000507
Head Len : 5   words      Flags    : .A....        Window   : 0x0100
Checksum : 0x495a (Good)  Urg Ptr  : 0x0000        Options  : None
=========================[data:   10]====================
0036  02 04 05 B4 FF FF 09 FE 44 E9        ........D.
```

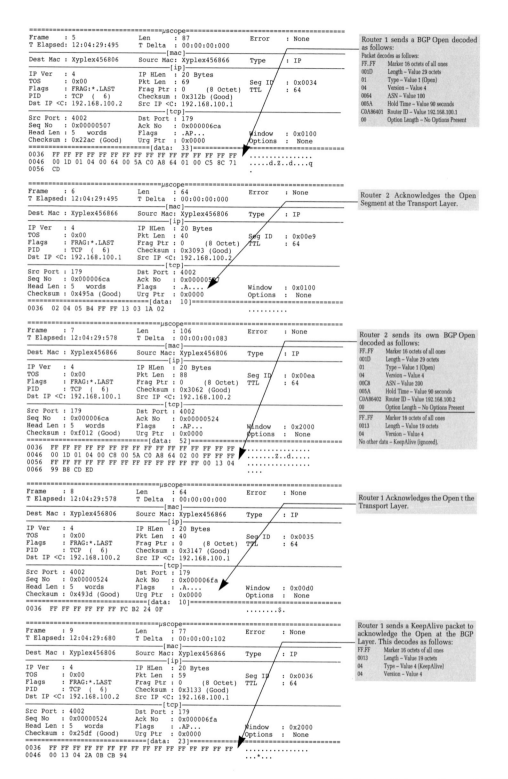

The Border Gateway Protocol (BGP)

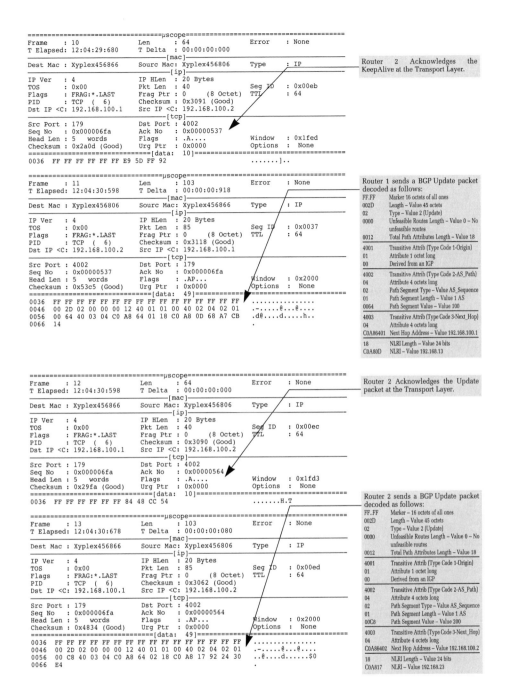

```
===============================µscope================================
Frame     : 10              Len      : 64           Error    : None
T Elapsed: 12:04:29:680     T Delta  : 00:00:00:000
------------------------------[mac]-
Dest Mac : Xyplex456866     Sourc Mac: Xyplex456806     Type        : IP
------------------------------[ip]-
IP Ver   : 4                IP HLen  : 20 Bytes
TOS      : 0x00             Pkt Len  : 40              Seg ID    : 0x00eb
Flags    : FRAG:*.LAST      Frag Ptr : 0    (8 Octet) TTL       : 64
PID      : TCP  ( 6)        Checksum : 0x3091 (Good)
Dst IP <C: 192.168.100.1    Src IP <C: 192.168.100.2
------------------------------[tcp]-
Src Port : 179              Dst Port : 4002
Seq No   : 0x000006fa       Ack No   : 0x00000537
Head Len : 5   words        Flags    : .A....         Window    : 0x1fed
Checksum : 0x2a0d (Good)    Urg Ptr  : 0x0000         Options   : None
=============================[data:  10]=============================
0036  FF FF FF FF FF FF E9 5D FF 92              .......]..
```

Router 2 Acknowledges the KeepAlive at the Transport Layer.

```
===============================µscope================================
Frame     : 11              Len      : 103          Error    : None
T Elapsed: 12:04:30:598     T Delta  : 00:00:00:918
------------------------------[mac]-
Dest Mac : Xyplex456806     Sourc Mac: Xyplex456866     Type        : IP
------------------------------[ip]-
IP Ver   : 4                IP HLen  : 20 Bytes
TOS      : 0x00             Pkt Len  : 85              Seg ID    : 0x0037
Flags    : FRAG:*.LAST      Frag Ptr : 0    (8 Octet) TTL       : 64
PID      : TCP  ( 6)        Checksum : 0x3118 (Good)
Dst IP <C: 192.168.100.2    Src IP <C: 192.168.100.1
------------------------------[tcp]-
Src Port : 4002             Dst Port : 179
Seq No   : 0x00000537       Ack No   : 0x000006fa
Head Len : 5   words        Flags    : .AP...         Window    : 0x2000
Checksum : 0x53c5 (Good)    Urg Ptr  : 0x0000         Options   : None
=============================[data:  49]=============================
0036  FF FF FF FF FF FF FF FF FF FF FF FF FF FF FF FF   ................
0046  00 2D 02 00 00 00 12 40 01 01 00 40 02 04 02 01   .-.....@...@....
0056  00 64 40 03 04 C0 A8 64 01 18 C0 A8 0D 68 A7 CB   .d@....d.....h..
0066  14                                                .
```

Router 1 sends a BGP Update packet decoded as follows:

FF.FF	Marker 16 octets of all ones
002D	Length – Value 45 octets
02	Type – Value 2 (Update)
0000	Unfeasible Routes Length – Value 0 – No unfeasible routes
0012	Total Path Attributes Length – Value 18
4001	Transitive Attrib (Type Code 1-Origin)
01	Attribute 1 octet long
00	Derived from an IGP
4002	Transitive Attrib (Type Code 2-AS_Path)
04	Attribute 4 octets long
02	Path Segment Type – Value AS_Sequence
01	Path Segment Length – Value 1 AS
0064	Path Segment Value – Value 100
4003	Transitive Attrib (Type Code 3-Next_Hop)
04	Attribute 4 octets long
C0A86401	Next Hop Address – Value 192.168.100.1
18	NLRI Length – Value 24 bits
C0A80D	NLRI – Value 192.168.13

```
===============================µscope================================
Frame     : 12              Len      : 64           Error    : None
T Elapsed: 12:04:30:598     T Delta  : 00:00:00:000
------------------------------[mac]-
Dest Mac : Xyplex456866     Sourc Mac: Xyplex456806     Type        : IP
------------------------------[ip]-
IP Ver   : 4                IP HLen  : 20 Bytes
TOS      : 0x00             Pkt Len  : 40              Seg ID    : 0x00ec
Flags    : FRAG:*.LAST      Frag Ptr : 0    (8 Octet) TTL       : 64
PID      : TCP  ( 6)        Checksum : 0x3090 (Good)
Dst IP <C: 192.168.100.1    Src IP <C: 192.168.100.2
------------------------------[tcp]-
Src Port : 179              Dst Port : 4002
Seq No   : 0x000006fa       Ack No   : 0x00000564
Head Len : 5   words        Flags    : .A....         Window    : 0x1fd3
Checksum : 0x29fa (Good)    Urg Ptr  : 0x0000         Options   : None
=============================[data:  10]=============================
0036  FF FF FF FF FF FF 84 48 CC 54              .......H.T
```

Router 2 Acknowledges the Update packet at the Transport Layer.

```
===============================µscope================================
Frame     : 13              Len      : 103          Error    : None
T Elapsed: 12:04:30:678     T Delta  : 00:00:00:080
------------------------------[mac]-
Dest Mac : Xyplex456866     Sourc Mac: Xyplex456806     Type        : IP
------------------------------[ip]-
IP Ver   : 4                IP HLen  : 20 Bytes
TOS      : 0x00             Pkt Len  : 85              Seg ID    : 0x00ed
Flags    : FRAG:*.LAST      Frag Ptr : 0    (8 Octet) TTL       : 64
PID      : TCP  ( 6)        Checksum : 0x3062 (Good)
Dst IP <C: 192.168.100.1    Src IP <C: 192.168.100.2
------------------------------[tcp]-
Src Port : 179              Dst Port : 4002
Seq No   : 0x000006fa       Ack No   : 0x00000564
Head Len : 5   words        Flags    : .AP...         Window    : 0x2000
Checksum : 0x4834 (Good)    Urg Ptr  : 0x0000         Options   : None
=============================[data:  49]=============================
0036  FF FF FF FF FF FF FF FF FF FF FF FF FF FF FF FF   ................
0046  00 2D 02 00 00 00 12 40 01 01 00 40 02 04 02 01   .-.....@...@....
0056  00 C8 40 03 04 C0 A8 64 02 18 C0 A8 17 92 24 30   ..@....d......$0
0066  E4                                                .
```

Router 2 sends a BGP Update packet decoded as follows:

FF.FF	Marker – 16 octets of all ones
002D	Length – Value 45 octets
02	Type – Value 2 (Update)
0000	Unfeasible Routes Length – Value 0 – No unfeasible routes
0012	Total Path Attributes Length – Value 18
4001	Transitive Attrib (Type Code 1-Origin)
01	Attribute 1 octet long
00	Derived from an IGP
4002	Transitive Attrib (Type Code 2-AS_Path)
04	Attribute 4 octets long
02	Path Segment Type – Value AS_Sequence
01	Path Segment Length – Value 1 AS
00C8	Path Segment Value – Value 200
4003	Transitive Attrib (Type Code 3-Next_Hop)
04	Attribute 4 octets long
C0A86402	Next Hop Address – Value 192.168.100.2
18	NLRI Length – Value 24 bits
C0A817	NLRI – Value 192.168.23

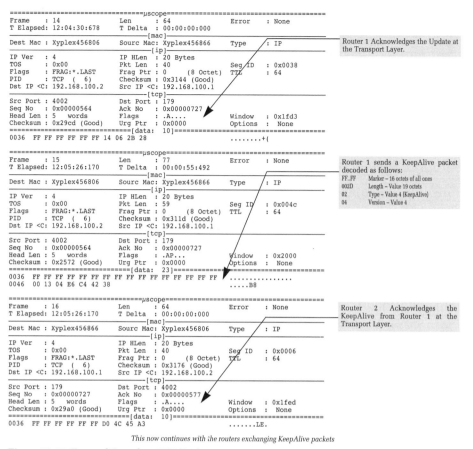

```
=============================μscope=============================
Frame    : 14            Len      : 64            Error    : None
T Elapsed: 12:04:30:678  T Delta  : 00:00:00:000
                              [mac]
Dest Mac : Xyplex456806  Sourc Mac: Xyplex456866  Type     : IP
                              [ip]
IP Ver   : 4             IP HLen  : 20 Bytes
TOS      : 0x00          Pkt Len  : 40            Seg ID   : 0x0038
Flags    : FRAG:*.LAST   Frag Ptr : 0    (8 Octet) TTL      : 64
PID      : TCP ( 6)      Checksum : 0x3144 (Good)
Dst IP <C: 192.168.100.2 Src IP <C: 192.168.100.1
                              [tcp]
Src Port : 4002          Dst Port : 179
Seq No   : 0x00000564    Ack No   : 0x00000727
Head Len : 5   words     Flags    : .A....        Window   : 0x1fd3
Checksum : 0x29cd (Good) Urg Ptr  : 0x0000        Options  : None
=============================[data:  10]========================
0036  FF FF FF FF FF FF 14 06 2B 28              ........+(
```

Router 1 Acknowledges the Update at the Transport Layer.

```
=============================μscope=============================
Frame    : 15            Len      : 77            Error    : None
T Elapsed: 12:05:26:170  T Delta  : 00:00:55:492
                              [mac]
Dest Mac : Xyplex456806  Sourc Mac: Xyplex456866  Type     : IP
                              [ip]
IP Ver   : 4             IP HLen  : 20 Bytes
TOS      : 0x00          Pkt Len  : 59            Seg ID   : 0x004c
Flags    : FRAG:*.LAST   Frag Ptr : 0    (8 Octet) TTL      : 64
PID      : TCP ( 6)      Checksum : 0x311d (Good)
Dst IP <C: 192.168.100.2 Src IP <C: 192.168.100.1
                              [tcp]
Src Port : 4002          Dst Port : 179
Seq No   : 0x00000564    Ack No   : 0x00000727
Head Len : 5   words     Flags    : .AP...        Window   : 0x2000
Checksum : 0x2572 (Good) Urg Ptr  : 0x0000        Options  : None
=============================[data:  23]========================
0036  FF FF FF FF FF FF FF FF FF FF FF FF FF FF FF  ...............
0046  00 13 04 E6 C4 42 38                         .....B8
```

Router 1 sends a KeepAlive packet decoded as follows:

FF..FF	Marker – 16 octets of all ones
002D	Length – Value 19 octets
02	Type – Value 4 (KeepAlive)
04	Version – Value 4

```
=============================μscope=============================
Frame    : 16            Len      : 64            Error    : None
T Elapsed: 12:05:26:170  T Delta  : 00:00:00:000
                              [mac]
Dest Mac : Xyplex456866  Sourc Mac: Xyplex456806  Type     : IP
                              [ip]
IP Ver   : 4             IP HLen  : 20 Bytes
TOS      : 0x00          Pkt Len  : 40            Seg ID   : 0x0006
Flags    : FRAG:*.LAST   Frag Ptr : 0    (8 Octet) TTL      : 64
PID      : TCP ( 6)      Checksum : 0x3176 (Good)
Dst IP <C: 192.168.100.1 Src IP <C: 192.168.100.2
                              [tcp]
Src Port : 179           Dst Port : 4002
Seq No   : 0x00000727    Ack No   : 0x00000577
Head Len : 5   words     Flags    : .A....        Window   : 0x1fed
Checksum : 0x29a0 (Good) Urg Ptr  : 0x0000        Options  : None
=============================[data:  10]========================
0036  FF FF FF FF FF FF D0 4C 45 A3              .......LE.
```

Router 2 Acknowledges the KeepAlive from Router 1 at the Transport Layer.

This now continues with the routers exchanging KeepAlive packets

Figure 13-17: Trace of Complete BGP Exchange

13.4 Summary

It is probably true to say that BGP, like it's older counterpart EGP, will never receive the wide acceptance of the Interior Gateway Protocols (IGPs). As we said at the outset, few networks are large enough to require the use of an exterior gateway protocol at all although BGP does provide significant advantages over EGP for those that do.

BGP uses the reliable Transport Control Protocol as its transport and therefore requires no further sequencing mechanism. Synchronization however is deemed necessary although this is reasonably unique in the IP suite. This syncronization is then provided through the Marker field of the BGP header.

BGP is now being implemented by vendors although it should be noted that generally this has been slow. Whether it is because few can see its usage will be high enough to warrant the development costs involved or whether it is because BGP itself is still undergoing change is difficult to determine. What is clear is that at version 4 we possibly still do not have a protocol that will stand the tests of time in the way that EGP has.

Broadcasting and Multicasting with IP

C H A P T E R   14

The practice of Broadcasting has long been used in the IP world as a means of informing many hosts about certain information. We saw in Chapter 10, that RIP uses broadcasts to exchange routing information. Also, many other protocols make use of this simple technique to communicate information to many hosts with a single packet. Broadcasting then can be an attractive method of transmission, simple to understand, easy to implement, and one that has been with us since the dawn of networking itself. But broadcasting is not some magical method for data delivery, it does have its associated costs. IP Broadcasts are sent as broadcasts at layer 2 which can cause hosts to consume many CPU cycles. For example, hosts that have no interest in the information being conveyed, have to service an interrupt from the lower layers and decode the data, only to discard it when they find out what the packet contains.

Multicasting is similar in that this too allows information from a single packet to be conveyed to multiple hosts simultaneously. Multicast packets though, are addressed to groups of stations at both the IP layer and at Layer 2 rather than to everyone. Thus, those hosts that are not part of the multicast group will discard the frame at Layer 2 and therefore conserve cycles within the host itself.

The Internet community is dedicated to moving to an environment where multicasting should replace broadcasting and much work is being done in this area. In this chapter then we will discuss the merits of Broadcasting and Multicasting and see how these operate in an IP environment.

14.1 Broadcasting

We said in Chapter 4 that certain IP address combinations are reserved for Broadcasting and Multicasting. For example, a host address of either all 0's or all 1's represents the broadcast address, but routers will not pass broadcast packets. So, in a routed environment who will receive the broadcasts?

Broadcasts can be useful if a station wishes to find out some information but is unsure of which device(s) can supply it. For example, a station may wish to find the current name of a host name table. Equally, a station may wish to exchange information with a large subset of other stations quickly, as in the case of routing table updates. It must be remembered however, that broadcasting is costly to stations that had no need of the broadcast in the first place, and that broadcasting is only a substitute for multicasting, which is generally by far the better choice. But what are the alternatives for stations that do not implement multicasting or for network technologies that have no multicast capability?

Firstly, stations could maintain a *hard-wired* list of all neighbors that it might ask when it requires information. This however would provide administrators with severe problems on networks that are likely to change. Secondly, the station in question could poll all of its possible neighbors. It would then be impossible to achieve fast responses though, and the polling operation itself could consume a vast amount of network bandwidth.

RFC 919 addresses the issue of broadcasting, and in so doing defines four distinct classes of IP broadcasting as follows:

- **Single destination broadcasts on the local IP network**
  A station sends a packet that is destined for a specific IP host but the sending station broadcasts it at the Data Link layer, maybe to avoid routing. Since this is not an IP broadcast, no IP layer involvement is required by the sending station. Receiving stations however, must be able to discard such packets where they are not required – this then does nothing to conserve CPU cycles within hosts to which the broadcast is not directed.

- **Broadcasts to all stations on the local IP network**
  In this case, a particular value (either all 0's or all 1's) is used in the Host ID section of the address. This is then taken to mean broadcast to all stations and not a transmission to a particular network host. All stations, must be able to recognize both this address and their own, unique, IP address.

  Such a broadcast method, referred to as a *Local* broadcast, can be used to determine Name Servers, Time Servers and other hosts on the network. Similarly, a router receiving a Local broadcast, must consider that the data contained is destined for itself and act on it accordingly. After all, this could be a routing table update. The important thing is, devices receiving this packet must be resident on the local network.

- **Broadcasts to all stations on a remote IP network**
  It may be useful to broadcast to all stations on some remote IP network; for example, to load an image file from a boot server on a remote network when we do not know its complete IP address. In this particular case, the packet is routed from router to router in the normal way until it eventually arrives at a router with a direct connection to the target network. This last router will then broadcast the packet on that target network. These are called *Directed* broadcasts.

- **Broadcasting to the entire Internet**
  This type of broadcast has little use and is certainly undesirable. For this reason, routers will typically choose not to forward these broadcasts. Therefore, where the Network and Host IDs of the IP address is set to all 0's or all 1's, (that is 255.255.255.255) the address will be considered as a Limited broadcast and remain on the local network.

In a *Local* broadcast, both the Network and Host identifiers are either all 0's or all 1's,[1] therefore an address of 255.255.255.255 or 0.0.0.0 is considered a Limited Broadcast and is therefore restricted to the network on which it originated. Should

---

1. Remember that older IP implementations used all 0's broadcasts while later implementations use all 1's.

the LANs be interconnected through either Repeaters or Bridges though, then the broadcast would be communicated to all attached LANs.

In the case of a *Directed* Broadcast, the Network Identifier will contain a valid network address, and the Host Identifier either all 1's or all 0's. An address of 172.16.255.255 or 172.16.0.0 however would be unclear since this could be considered a *directed* broadcast to all stations on network 172.16.0.0, or a local broadcast. It would then depend on the address of the station sending the packet in the first place. For example, if the station sending the broadcast was actually on network 172.16.0.0, then this would be a *local* broadcast. Let us consider Figure 14-1 in which we will assume that each of the routers have valid routes to all of the networks and that station A is broadcasting. Table 14-1 then shows the results using different broadcast addresses.

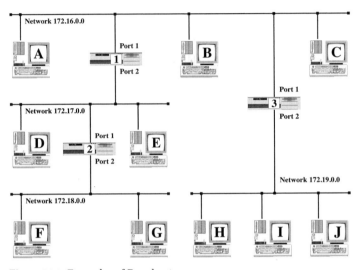

Figure 14-1: Examples of Broadcasts

Table 14-1: Different Broadcast Addresses and the Resulting Actions

Broadcast Address	Recipients	Broadcast Type
0.0.0.0	Stations A, B, & C Router 1 Port 1, Router 3 Port 1	Local
255.255.255.255	Stations A, B, & C Router 1 Port 1, Router 3 Port 1	Local
172.16.0.0	Stations A, B, & C Router 1 Port 1, Router 3 Port 1	Local
172.16.255.255	Stations A, B, & C Router 1 Port 1, Router 3 Port 1	Local
172.17.0.0	Stations D, & E Router 1 Port 2, Router 2 Port 1	Directed
172.17.255.255	Stations D, & E Router 1 Port 2, Router 2 Port 1	Directed
172.18.0.0	Stations F, & G Router 2 Port 2	Directed
172.18.255.255	Stations F, & G Router 2 Port 2	Directed
172.19.0.0	Stations H, I, & J Router 3 Port 2	Directed
172.19.255.255	Stations H, I, & J Router 3 Port 2	Directed

14.1.1 Broadcasting in the Presence of Subnets

We saw in the previous discussion that a *Directed* broadcast is used to send a packet to all hosts on a specific remote network and that it could not be used to transmit a packet to more than one network at a time. In a subnetted environment the situation is similar in that, a Directed Broadcast cannot be used to send a packet to all subnets – remember that we are restricted from using a Subnet where the subnet address would be either all 0's or all 1's. A Subnetted environment therefore behaves in exactly the same way as our previous example, the only way that we could possibly broadcast to all hosts on all subnets would be to modify the way that a *Local* broadcast operates, a scenario that is generally thought undesirable.

In Figure 14-2 we have now applied subnets. We shall again assume that all routers have routes to all networks and that station A is broadcasting. The results of various broadcast packets are then shown in Table 14-2.

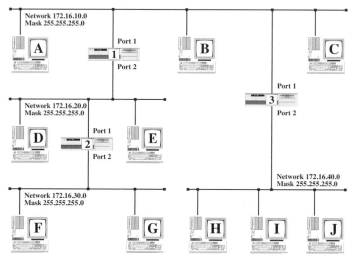

Figure 14-2: Broadcasting with Subnets

Table 14-2: Broadcast Types and Subnets

Broadcast Address	Recipients	Broadcast Type
0.0.0.0	Stations A, B, & C Router 1 Port 1, Router 3 Port 1	Local
255.255.255.255	Stations A, B, & C Router 1 Port 1, Router 3 Port 1	Local
172.16.10.0	Stations A, B, & C Router 1 Port 1, Router 3 Port 1	Local
172.16.10.255	Stations A, B, & C Router 1 Port 1, Router 3 Port 1	Local
172.16.20.0	Stations D, & E Router 1 Port 2, Router 2 Port 1	Directed
172.16.20.255	Stations D, & E Router 1 Port 2, Router 2 Port 1	Directed
172.16.30.0	Stations F, & G Router 2 Port 2	Directed
172.16.30.255	Stations F, & G Router 2 Port 2	Directed
172.16.40.0	Stations H, I, & J Router 3 Port 2	Directed
172.16.40.255	Stations H, I, & J Router 3 Port 2	Directed

14.2 Multicasting

RFC 1112 defines the term *Multicasting* as "...*the transmission of an IP Datagram*[2] *to a host group, a set of zero or more hosts identified by a single IP destination address.*" Most network technologies, Ethernet, and most IEEE 802.x networks for example, support multicasting by a modification of the physical or MAC address. Also, at the IP layer you will recall, a special class of address (Class D) is reserved for this purpose.

Membership of a host group is dynamic, that is, members may join or leave groups at any time. There is no restriction on either the location of such groups nor on the numbers of hosts in any group at any time. Similarly, a host may be a member of multiple groups or alternatively may choose not to be a member of any group at all. In addition, there is no requirement that the host must be a member of a group before it can send datagrams to it.

Host groups can be permanent or transient. A permanent group has a well-known IP address but it is the address and not the membership of the group that is permanent. Transient groups on the other hand, have dynamically assigned addresses that exist only as long as they have members.

Any forwarding of IP multicasts are handled by IP *multicast routers* that in most cases are integrated with standard IP routers. Any IP multicast transmitted on the local network will be received by all attached network hosts. Should this multicast have an IP *Time-to-Live*[3] greater than 1, it will then be forwarded by attached multicast routers to other networks that contain members of the multicast group. Forwarding takes place in the normal fashion (and within the Time-to-Live specified) with the multicast routers completing delivery by the transmission of the packet as a local multicast.

To date, there are three levels of conformance to the IP multicast specification:

- **Level 0 – No support for IP Multicasting**
  At this time there is no requirement that all IP implementations should support the process of IP multicasts. RFC 1112 has a status of *Recommended* meaning that whilst it is desirable, it is not mandatory. Level 0 hosts are generally unaffected by multicast activity on the local network. The only exception may arise where a multicast is received and must be discarded without reporting an error. These packets can be easily identified by the presence of a Class D address.

- **Level 1 – The support for the transmission but not reception of IP Multicasting**
  Level 1 hosts may participate in some multicast activity maybe by the reporting of status or other information. In this case the host may periodically generate multicast packets for transmission to other hosts but will act as a Level 0 host for the purposes of multicast reception.

- **Level 2 – Full support for IP Multicasting**
  These hosts fully participate in IP Multicasts. They join and leave host groups, as well as send and receive multicast packets. These hosts require full imple-

---

2. The Datagram is the basic element of transmission within an IP environment. A Datagram is also sometimes called an IP packet.

3. The IP Time-to-Live is described in Chapter 5.

mentation of the Internet Group Management Protocol (IGMP) plus any extensions to the local IP implementation that are required.

14.2.1 Host Group Addresses

You will recall that all IP Multicast addresses are Class D. This means that the leading four bits of the 32 bit address are 1110 meaning, that in *dotted decimal notation*, the range of addresses will be 224.0.0.0 to 239.255.255.255. RFC 1700 (Internet Assigned Numbers) also states that the addresses shown in Table 14-3 should be allocated.

Table 14-3: Standard IP Multicast Addresses

Address	Service Type
224.0.0.0	Reserved
224.0.0.1	All Systems on this Subnet
224.0.0.2	All Routers on this Subnet
224.0.0.3	Unassigned
224.0.0.4	Distance Vector Multicast Routing Protocol (DVMRP) Routers
224.0.0.5	All Open Shortest Path First (OSPFIGP) Routers
224.0.0.6	All Open Shortest Path First (OSPFIGP) Designated Routers
224.0.0.7	ST Routers
224.0.0.8	ST Hosts
224.0.0.9	RIP2 Routers
224.0.0.10-224.0.0.255	Unassigned
224.0.1.0	Versatile Message Transaction Protocol (VMTP) Managers Group
224.0.1.1	NTP Network Time Protocol
224.0.1.2	SGI-Dogfight
224.0.1.3	RWhod
224.0.1.4	VNP
224.0.1.5	Artificial Horizons – Aviator
224.0.1.6	NSS – Name Service Server
224.0.1.7	AUDIONEWS – Audio News Service
224.0.1.8	SUN NIS+ Information Service
224.0.1.9	MTP Multicast Transport Protocol
224.0.1.10-224.0.1.255	Unassigned
224.0.2.1	"rwho" Group (BSD) – Unofficial
224.0.2.2	SUN RPC PMAPPROC_CALLIT
224.0.3.0-224.0.3.255	RFE Generic Service
224.0.4.0-224.0.4.255	RFE Individual Conferences
224.1.0.0-224.1.255.255	ST Multicast Groups
224.2.0.0-224.2.255.255	Multimedia Conference Calls
232.x.x.x	Versatile Message Transaction Protocol (VMTP) Transient Groups

14.2.2 Mapping IP Multicasts to Local Network Multicasts

Network technologies such as Ethernet and those using the IEEE 802.x standard, directly support the use of multicasting. For example, to specify a multicast address, the assigned MAC address is modified by turning on the least significant bit of the most significant octet (the *Individual or Group Address bit*). The Internet Assigned Numbers Authority (IANA) has an assigned block of Ethernet addresses

(00-00-5E-xx-xx-xx) that may be used for the purpose of multicasting which, through the use of the I/G bit, becomes 01-00-5E-xx-xx-xx.

When mapping IP multicasts to physical or MAC addresses, the low 23 bits of the IP address are placed over the low 23 bits of the MAC address. The IANA address range is therefore 01-00-5E-00-00-00 to 01-00-5E-7F-FF-FF. Since there are 28 significant bits in an IP multicast address however, this means that more than one IP host address group may map to the same Ethernet address. Figure 14-3 shows how this mapping is achieved.

Network technologies that do not have a multicast capability, will map the IP multicast address to a broadcast address and then broadcast the frame. This is obviously less desirable than multicasting, however it does provide for the transmission to groups of stations at the IP level.

Level 1 compliance (support for the transmission but not reception of IP Multicasts) is easily achieved. Stations that comply with this category of service must be able to send packets to a host group address and therefore be able to map the host group to a MAC level multicast address.

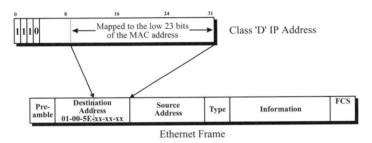

Figure 14-3: Mapping IP Multicasts to Ethernet Addresses

Achieving compliance at Level 2 (Full support for IP Multicasting) is more complex since a host that operates with this level of conformity must maintain a list of host group memberships associated with each of its network interface(s). This stems from the basic premise that a host will join specific multicast groups that exist on particular networks.

As an example, consider the following rules for a host that has multiple network interfaces:

- All incoming packets that have a destination address of a group to which this host does not belong should be discarded.

- A packet that arrives on one interface but destined for a group to which the host only belongs on another interface should be discarded.

- Reception of a packet that contains a multicast address as the source address must be discarded without reporting an error. This is considered as an illegal packet.

- Reception of a packet that has a destination address of a group to which this host belongs on that interface, but with an IP Time-to-Live of 1 should not be discarded. Reception of the packet and membership of that group is taken to mean that the packet has reached a valid destination host.

14.3 The Internet Group Management Protocol (IGMP)

To make optimum use of local network bandwidth, multicast routers require information about which host groups, local hosts are members of. Without this information, such devices would need to propagate all IP multicasts to all networks making multicasting no better than broadcasting.

The Internet Group Management Protocol (IGMP) is used by IP hosts and multicast routers to request and report individual host group memberships. Like ICMP, IGMP is considered an integral part of the IP layer of Level 2 compliant devices, and uses the IP protocol identifier '2' to identify it. Figure 14-4 shows the IGMP message format applicable for host to multicast router communication.

0	4	8	16	31
Version	Type	Unused	Checksum	
Group Address				

Figure 14-4: IGMP Message Format

The 4 bit *Version* field identifies the version of the protocol which is currently 1. The *Type* field (also 4 bits) specifies which of the two types of IGMP message this is. IGMP Type 1 messages are referred to as *Query* messages and allow multicast routers to query hosts attached to the local network to determine which host groups have members. IGMP Type 2 messages are *Host Membership Reports* and allow local hosts to respond to Query messages. The *Unused* field, as its name suggests, is unused and will always be set to zero on transmission of the message. Receiving hosts then ignore this field. The *Checksum* field is the one's compliment of the one's compliment sum of the entire (8 octet) IGMP message. For the purposes of computing the checksum, this field is assumed to be zero, as is normal in IP protocols. The *Group Address* field is zeroed and therefore ignored in the case of a *Group Membership Query* message. In the case of the *Group Membership Report* message though, this field holds the group address of the group being reported by the locally attached host.

14.3.1 IGMP Operation

Multicast routers send Host Query Messages to discover which host groups have members on their locally attached networks. These queries are sent via the *All Hosts Group* multicast address (224.0.0.1) and each carry an IP Time-to-Live of 1, thus ensuring that they are not forwarded.

Hosts respond to these query messages by generating *Host Membership Reports* to report each host group to which they belong on the interface through which the query was received. Obviously this could produce large peaks in network traffic on the local network if all attached hosts were to immediately respond to such queries. To overcome this two methods are suggested by RFC 1112:

- On reception of a Query, the hosts will start random a timer (using one of its IP addresses as a *seed*) for each of its group memberships on the network interface through which it received the query. As each of these timers then expires, a report will be generated for the corresponding host group. This ensures a steady flow of traffic across the local network and therefore reduces the risk of traffic peaks. The use of an IP address as a seed to the random timer further reduces the chance that multiple hosts will generate reports simultaneously.

  An exception to this would be where a timer for a particular host group was already running when the query was received. In this case the host will not reset its timer but will instead allow the time to continue in the normal way and transmit the report when it expires.

- Reports are sent with an IP destination address equal to the host group being reported and with an IP Time-to-Live equal to 1. This allows other members of the same host group to hear the transmissions of neighboring stations and therefore to stop their timers if they too are a member of the same group. Remember that the multicast router has no interest in the number of group members, but merely that at least one group member exists on the locally attached network.

An exception to both of the above scenarios, is that the All Hosts Group (224.0.0.1) is never reported to multicast routers. Reception of a Query message and subsequent reports, is proof that at least one host is a member of a host group.

Multicast routers send queries relatively infrequently (typically no more than once per minute) to refresh their knowledge of host group memberships. Infrequent queries then keeps IGMP traffic to a minimum. When a multicast router first powers up however, it is normal for such devices to issue many queries in a short space of time thereby allowing them to build their knowledge of memberships quickly. Hosts wishing to join new host groups, transmit a report immediately (through the appropriate interface and with an IP Time-to-Live of 1) for the host group that it wishes to join. They do not wait for a query, since this host may be the first member of the group on that particular local network. Typically this report is transmitted two or three times in order to overcome the possibility that the report could be lost or corrupted. The trace in Figure 14-5 shows an IGMP Query sent from a router.

Hosts may be in one of three states with respect to any host group on any interface. Figure 14-6 shows these states and the possible transitions between them.

- **Non-Member State**

  In this state, the host does not belong to the specified host group on that interface. With the exception of the *AllHosts* group, this is the initial state for all host groups. The *AllHosts* group is a special group of which all Level 2 hosts are members. It is from this state (and this state alone) that a host may join a group by issuing a *Report*.

- **Delaying Member State**

  In this state, a host is a member of the group and has a random timer running (normally as a result of receiving a query) but has yet to send a report. From this state, either a report will be sent (at the expiration of the timer), the timer will be stopped (on reception of a report from another host), or the host will elect to leave the group. In any of these cases, the host will change state.

Where the host either sends a report (on the expiration of the timer) or receives a report from another host, it will transition to the Idle Member State. In the case where the host wishes to leave the host group, it will transition to the Non-Member state.

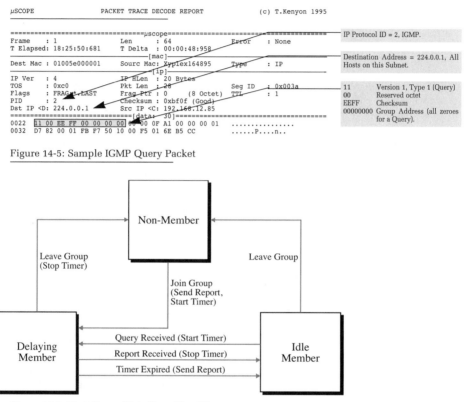

Figure 14-5: Sample IGMP Query Packet

Figure 14-6: Host Group State Transition Diagram

- **Idle Member State**

  The Idle Member State is where the host is a member of the group on this interface but does not have a random timer running. For example, where the host has not received a query from a multicast router. Should a query arrive while in this state, the host will transition to the *Delaying Member State*. Alternatively, the host may choose to leave the group whilst in this state. In this case it will transition to the *Non-Member* State directly.

14.3.2 The Allocation of Transient Host Group Addresses

The ways in which transient host group addresses may be allocated is implementation specific. From the table at the start of this section you will see that while many address blocks are allocated, there is more than enough space for other groups to be designated as the need arises.

Protocols such as the *Versatile Message Transaction Protocol* (VMTP) generate their own groups and then map these to a subset of the group 232.x.x.x. Another allocation technique is to have multiple servers available on the network that can be contacted and then asked to issue a new transient group. Finally, RFC 1112 suggests that since transmission of a multicast cannot be guaranteed to reach only the intended hosts, it may be possible for a host to randomly allocate a host group address and then move should this allocation already be in use. Typically though, since hosts capable of multicasting will generally be Level 2 devices, the host itself should, through time, have an idea of which addresses are currently occupied.

14.4 The Propagation of Multicast Routing Information

In order for multicast datagrams to be effectively routed through an internet, it is important that all routers know where multicast host groups exist. We have seen how both unicast and broadcast datagram delivery relies upon routers having knowledge of each reachable network. This is insufficient though where multicasts are concerned since it is undesirable to transmit multicasts onto local networks where no hosts exist for that particular group.

Unfortunately, although multicasting at the IP level is now standardized, there is no real standard for the propagation of multicast routes. Two such protocols do exist however. Firstly, there is the *Distance Vector Multicast Routing Protocol* (DVMRP) which is specified in RFC 1075 and is defined as experimental. Being experimental, it has limited use although it is the multicast propagation protocol used within the *Mbone*.[4] In addition to the propagation of routes over which multicast packets can travel, DVMRP also supports a feature called *tunnelling* where networks or routers that do not have a multicast capability may be traversed.

The other protocol utilizes extensions to OSPF and is referred to as Multicast OSPF or MOSPF. MOSPF, described by RFC 1584, is a *Standards Track* protocol and is now fast becoming the accepted protocol for the propagation of this information. In terms of end results however, MOSPF and DVMRP both perform similar functions and, while MOSPF is fast gaining popularity in this field, for the sake of completion both protocols are described in this chapter.

14.5 The Distance Vector Multicast Routing Protocol (DVMRP)

DVMRP uses a modification of IGMP to pass information. Essentially DVMRP introduces a new Type code and makes use of the *Unused* field as a *Sub-Type* that is then used to specify the type of DVMRP message. DVMRP is an *Interior Gateway Protocol* (IGP) for use in a multicast environment only. Routers that route both multicast and unicast datagrams and wish to use DVMRP, must implement both DVMRP and some other IGP such as either RIP or OSPF.

4. The MBone is the part of the Internet used to convey live music amongst other things. The MBone is also probably the only place where DVMRP is used.

Figure 14-7 shows the general DVMRP format.

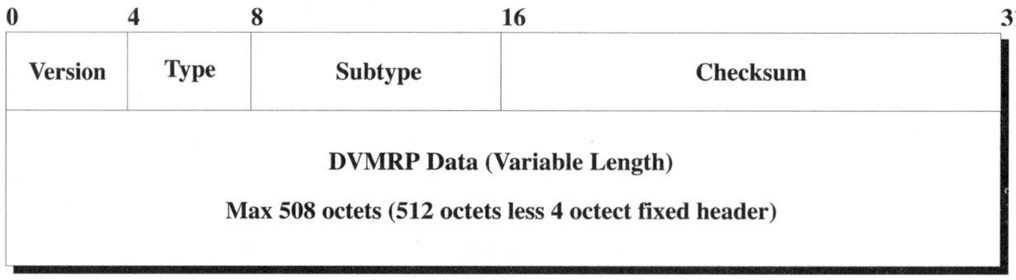

0	4	8	16	31
Version	Type	Subtype	Checksum	

DVMRP Data (Variable Length)

Max 508 octets (512 octets less 4 octect fixed header)

Figure 14-7: DVMRP General Message Format

The 4 bit *Version* field defines the protocol version which is currently 1, and the *Type* field is always 3 for DVMRP packets. The *Subtype* field then identifies the type of DVMRP message. Table 14-4 identifies each valid Subtype code:

Table 14-4: DVMRP Subtype Codes

Subtype	Description
1	Response – The message contains one (or more) routes to destination(s)
2	Request – The message requests routes to one (or more) destination(s)
3	Non-Membership Report – The message provides non-membership report(s)
4	Non-Membership Cancellation – The message cancels previously issued non-membership report(s)

The *Checksum* is calculated in the normal manner for IP hosts. The remainder of the message is then taken up with a stream of *tagged* data in which each element is preceded by its own operation code or identifier. Each of these tagged data fields is always a multiple of sixteen bits with an eight bit numeric command code and at least an eight bit data portion. Sixteen bit alignment is therefore required for all elements, the format of which is shown in Figure 14-8.

DVMRP Commands:

- **Null Command (Command Code 0)**

  The Null command has an eight bit Data field that is ignored. The Null command is used for padding where alignment to 32 bits is required. No additional data fields are used.

- **Address Family Indicator (AFI) Command (Command Code 2)**

  Used to identify the family or address class that, in turn, will identify the length of address used. The AFI then sets the address class until the next AFI in the data stream is read. By default the data field will be set to 2 indicating IP and hence 32 bit addresses. No additional data fields are required.

Broadcasting and Multicasting with IP

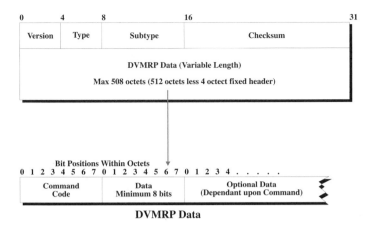

DVMRP Data

Figure 14-8: DVMRP Command Format

- **Subnet Mask Command (Command Code 3)**

  This command identifies the subnet mask that should be used. The Data field will have a value of 0 or 1 where 0 means that no subnet mask applies and 1 that the subnet mask (of a length defined by the AFI) follows in the next field. For an AFI of 2 (IP), the next field would therefore be 32 bits in length and would contain the subnet mask in use for that network address.

- **Metric Command (Command Code 4)**

  DVMRP is loosely based upon RIP and therefore uses a metric based upon hop counts from the router that sent the update. The Data field then contains the value of the metric (between 1 and 255). There are no additional data fields.

- **Flags0 Command (Command Code 5)**

  The Flags0 command provides a means of supplying more information about a route that has an infinite metric. With this command, the bits of the data field represent eight possible flags of which only two are currently defined (the two least significant, bits 6 and 7). Where bit 7 is set, the destination is unreachable and where bit 6 is set, Split Horizon has concealed the route.

- **Infinity Command (Command Code 6)**

  The Data field in this case is the infinity metric and may assume any value between 1 and 255. By default this is 16 as with RIP. Once issued, this command then defines the infinity metric for all other metrics in the data stream.

- **Destination Address (DA) Command (Command Code 7)**

  The DA command allows the description of a list of destination networks (and sub-networks). In this case the Data field will contain a count of the number of destinations (1 to 255) that will be specified in the Optional Data field(s). In the case of IP, each of these optional data fields will be 32 bits in length as defined by the Address Family Indicator (AFI) command. The maximum number of destinations that may be carried is subject to the overall message length limitation however, and no message may exceed 512 octets. The currently set metric, infinity, flags0, and subnet mask together define the actual route.

- **Requested Destination Address (RDA) Command (Command Code 8)**
  RDA provides a list of destinations for which routes are requested. In this form, the Data field contains a count of the number of addresses supplied (from 0 to 255) with a count of zero indicating that a request for all routes has been encoded. Where individual routes are requested, each of the routes is represented in an Optional data field of 32 bits for IP addresses.

  As with the previous command, the number of routes that may actually be encoded is restricted by the maximum message length, and is therefore dependent upon the AFI specified.

- **Non-Membership Report (NMR) Command (Command Code 9)**
  This command tells receivers that the sending router has no hosts using the particular host group and that the receiving router can cease sending datagrams for the specified group(s).

  Here, the Data field contains the number (1 to 255) of multicast address and hold down timer pairs. Following the Data field there will then be pairs of optional data fields (of length specified by the AFI command) containing these multicast addresses and hold down timers. The multicast address fields are then used to indicate which host groups are no longer required and the Hold Down Timer (the time in seconds) for which this Non-Membership Report is valid.

- **Non-Membership Report Cancel (NMR Cancel) Command (Command Code 10)**
  The NMR Cancel command allows the cancellation of previously issued NMRs. With this, the Data field contains a number which is interpreted as a count of multicast addresses that follow in Optional Data fields. Each of these Optional data fields is of a length indicated by the current AFI command.

14.5.1 DVMRP in Operation

As we have said, DVMRP is based upon RIP. However unlike RIP, which is concerned with routes to a particular destination network, DVMRP is concerned with how return routes to the local network should be managed. In this way routers pass information among themselves to ensure that, on reception of a multicast datagram, a copy may be passed to every member of the host group.

You will recall that multicast routers must maintain tables of host group memberships on their attached networks. As such, the router may send IGMP Requests, with an IP Time-to-Live of 1, to the All Hosts group (224.0.0.1) and await responses. As we have previously said, the reasoning for such a short TTL is to ensure that these requests are not forwarded throughout the internet since the object of this phase is to determine local membership only. Where we have multiple multicast routers attached to a common network, there is little point in each router sending these requests. Instead, multicast routers on a network will elect a single, *Designated*, router (the router with the lowest IP address) to perform all queries. Each router, when first powered on, will assume itself to be this Designated router until it receives information to the contrary by hearing either

Queries or Reports from another router. However, since each router must be capable of receiving all possible multicasts, routers will build their own tables from responses received across the common network.

All inter-router traffic is performed using IGMP and the destination multicast address 224.0.0.4 (All DVMRP routers). Where traffic must traverse a network incapable of multicasting, tunnels are established between the two end points. This traffic is then sent via unicast datagrams between the end point routers. Consider the following examples:

1. A request for all routes to all IP destinations:

0	4	8	12	16	20	24	28	31
Version (1)	Type (3) DVMRP	Subtype (2) Request			Checksum			
Command (AFI) Value 02		Data (IP) Value 02		Command (RDA) Value 08		Data (All Destinations) Value 00		

Figure 14-9: Sample DVMRP Packet (1)

2. Supplying a Non-Membership report for groups 224.2.3.1 ($E0020301_{16}$) with a hold down timer of 30 ($1E_{16}$) seconds and 224.2.4.6 ($E0020406_{16}$) with a hold down timer of 20 (14_{16}) seconds.

0	4	8	12	16	20	24	28	31
Version (1)	Type (3) DVMRP	Subtype (3) Non Membership Rpt			Checksum			
Command (AFI) Value 02		Data (IP) Value 02		Command (NMR) Value 0A		Data (Count) Value 02		
Optional Data (Multicast Address 1) Value E0 02 03 01								
Optional Data (Hold Down Timer 1) Value 00 00 00 1E								
Optional Data (Multicast Address 2) Value E0 02 04 06								
Optional Data (Hold Down Timer 2) Value 00 00 00 14								

Figure 14-10: Sample DVMRP Packet (2)

14.6 Multicast OSPF

RFC 1584 describes extensions to OSPF[5] that allows Host Group information to be propagated throughout an internet. To examine this in detail we will consider the example shown in Figure 14-11. Although much the following description is applicable to both DVMRP and MOSPF, since MOSPF is by far the most popular protocol, we will consider this example with reference to MOSPF only.

5. In order to fully understand the operation of MOSPF, a good knowledge of OSPF is required. The reader is therefore urged to study Chapter 11 first.

In the figure we see several hosts. Those labelled Ha, Hb, and Hc are hosts capable of generating multicasts and those labelled as Ma, Mb, and Mc are members of host groups a, b, and c respectively. Thus, if host Hb were to generate a packet destined for host group b, it would be routed via routers 3, 4, and 2 to arrive at network 2. Equally, if host Hc was to generate a packet destined for host group a, it would be routed via routers 5, 4, and 1 to reach network 1. Obviously, no further routing would be required to reach the host which is part of that group resident on network 6.

In common with OSPF, the delivery of a datagram (although in this case a multicast datagram) takes place by forwarding it along a *Shortest Path Tree*. Certain differences between OSPF and MOSPF do exist however, and these are discussed here.

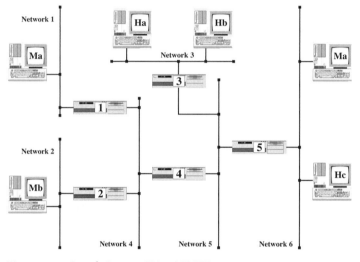

Figure 14-11: Sample internet Using MOSPF

- Unlike OSPF routers where routing is based solely upon the destination address of a datagram, the actual path taken by a datagram in a MOSPF internet is based upon both the datagram's source address and the multicast destination.

- Unlike unicast routers running OSPF, it is sometimes necessary for multicast routers to replicate a datagram when group members lie in different directions. For example in Figure 14-11, if host Ha was to generate a multicast to group a, router 3 would forward it to network 5 where routers 4 and 5 would then each need to forward it. Router 5 would forward its copy to network 6, while router 4 would forward its copy to network 4 where router 1 would then onward route it to network 1. Two identical copies of the datagram would therefore be made.

- For a given multicast datagram, all routers will calculate an identical *Shortest Path Tree* on demand. That is, when the first datagram for any given source network/multicast destination pairing is received, the router will build a Shortest Path Tree for that datagram. Since all routers calculate an identical Shortest

Broadcasting and Multicasting with IP

Path Tree, there will only ever be one shortest path between the source and any group member. Therefore there is no provision for equal-cost multi-path as there is with OSPF.

• OSPF is used to forward only unicast datagrams, and MOSPF only multicasts. MOSPF then normally forwards IP multicasts as data-link multicasts as previously described. Two exceptions however do exist. Firstly, MOSPF can be used over networks that have no multicast/broadcast capability. In this case the datagram is forwarded to specific MOSPF neighbors as a unicast. Secondly, the configuration of MOSPF is normally such that the router can also be configured to forward an IP multicast as a data-link unicast. This would then avoid the replication of the datagram where say we wished to exclude the multicast group member on network 6 from receiving the multicast sent from host Ha.

14.6.1 MOSPF Operation

As we have already said, MOSPF routers base their forwarding decision on both the source addresses of the datagram and the multicast address. Multicast routers therefore maintain a cache that contains an entry for each source address/multicast destination pair. This cache is actually built from two distinct parts. Firstly, the group membership(s) of hosts on the locally attached networks obtained from IGMP, and secondly, the datagram's shortest path tree that, as described previously, is built on demand for each source address/multicast destination pairing.

IGMP plays a vital role in MOSPF since it is through this, that MOSPF routers learn about group memberships of hosts connected to their locally attached networks. In practice, the MOSPF router is unconcerned with the number of hosts that are members of any particular host group. Instead the router needs only to be aware that at least one host is a member of a group, because it will then multicast the datagram to complete the delivery process.

One important point however, is that it is only the *Designated Router* that participates in IGMP, sending queries and listening for responses. MOSPF routers that have not been elected as the Designated Router then ignore all IGMP activity. This ensures that there is only one router performing the IGMP function, and that the unnecessary replication of datagrams is prevented. For example, with reference to Figure 14-11, routers 1 to 5 would maintain the information shown in Table 14-5 about the multicast host groups connected to their locally attached networks. Notice that since there are no multicast hosts on networks 3, 4, and 5, there are no IGMP membership reports, and therefore routers 3 and 4 do not keep any records.

Table 14-5: Multicast host groups on each router.

Router	Network and Host Group(s)
1	Network 1/Host Group A
2	Network 2/Host Group B
3	None
4	None
5	Network 6/Host Group A

MOSPF capability is communicated amongst routers in the Headers of all OSPF packets. OSPF Hello packets are sent at regular intervals which, you will recall from our discussions of the OSPF protocol, are sent to inform a router's neighbors both that it is alive, and also to inform them which other routers have been heard within the *Router Dead Interval*. It is the *MC* bit in the *Options* field of this Header that conveys this capability. If set, the router is capable of performing multicast routing using MOSPF. If this bit is not set however, no MOSPF capability exists. When calculating the route over which multicasts must travel then, routers only consider those paths that have MOSPF capability. Figure 14-12 shows two OSPF Hello packets from the same router. In the first, the router has no MOSPF capability and in the second, MOSPF has been enabled.

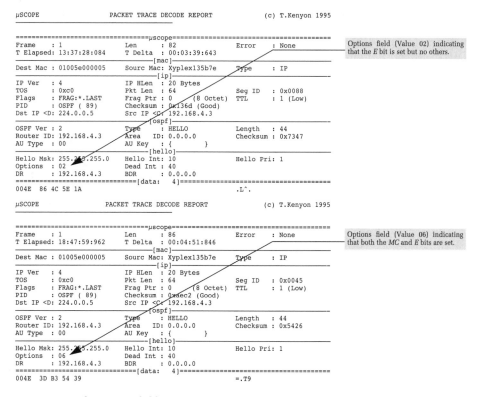

Figure 14-12: The Options field in MOSPF Headers

Once a router has established that group members exist on one or more of its attached network(s), MOSPF must communicate this to the rest of the routers within the Autonomous System. This will then ensure that a remotely generated multicast datagram will be forwarded to the router for eventual delivery to its attached host(s). MOSPF accomplishes this through a slight modification of the Router Links Advertisement, and the introduction of a new Link State Advertisement (Type 6) called a *Group Membership LSA*.

You will recall that a Router Links Advertisement is generated into each of a router's attached areas, and that it is this information that describes the state and cost of the router's interfaces to that area. The modification to make this LSA compliant with MOSPF is simple and requires that only one extra bit is defined. This bit, the so called *W* bit in the *Router Type* field, indicates that the router is a *Wildcard Multicast Receiver*, and that all multicast datagrams should be sent to it regardless of host group memberships. The Router Links Advertisement (excluding the Link State Header) is shown in Figure 14-13.

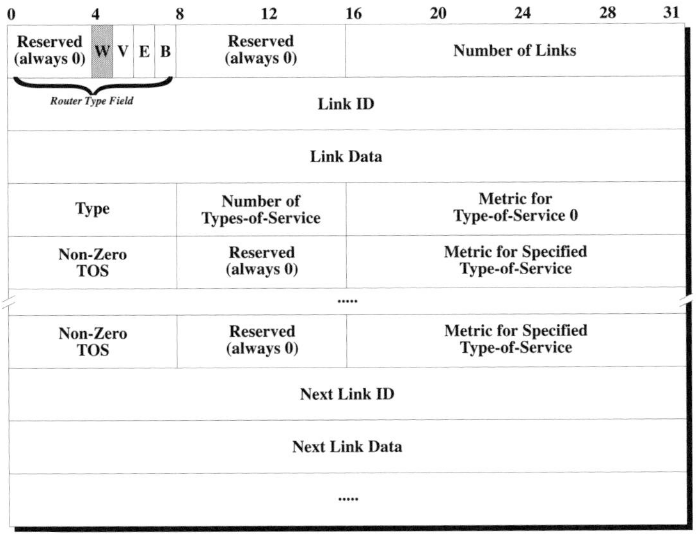

Figure 14-13: The Router Links Advertisement for MOSPF

The reason why the Wildcard option is important, is that Group Membership LSAs are specific to a particular OSPF area and are never flooded beyond the area in which they were originated. A router's Group Membership LSA for an area therefore indicates its directly attached networks belonging to that area and containing members of a particular multicast group. Thus, Inter-Area and Inter-AS multicast forwarding routers are normally configured to issue Router LSAs with the Wildcard bit set.

With reference to the Group Membership LSA, one such advertisement is generated for each multicast group that has one or more members. However, since only Designated Routers participate in IGMP, it would seem natural that only Designated Routers generate Group Membership LSAs. This assumption though, is not strictly true. Certainly, DRs will generate these LSAs, but other routers may do so too. For example, an Area Border Router (ABR) originates these LSAs into the Backbone Area where it has group members in its non-backbone attached areas. In addition, routers who themselves have internal applications that are part of a specific host group will also generate group membership LSAs. The format of the Group Membership LSA with the Link State Header (shaded in the figure) is shown in Figure 14-14.

As Figure 14-14 shows, the Group Membership LSA comprises the standard 20 octet Link State Header using a Link State Type of 6, and a Link State ID that identifies the Destination Host Group. The list of *vertices* (the *Vertex Type* and *Vertex ID* fields) then identify the type of information being conveyed and its identity. The 32 bit *Vertex Type* field will be equal to 1 where the LSA is describing a router, or 2 where a transit network is being described. The 32 bit *Vertex ID* field then contains the Router ID for a Vertex Type indicating a router, or the IP Address of the

Designated Router where the Vertex Type indicates a *transit network*. Of course, where the Vertex Type field indicates a router, the only legal Router ID allowed in the Vertex ID field is that of the Advertising Router itself.

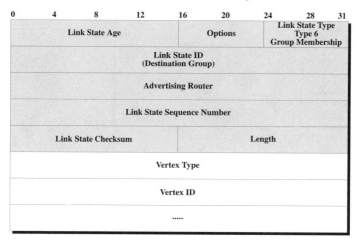

Figure 14-14: MOSPF Group Membership LSA

14.6.2 *Pruned* Shortest Path Trees

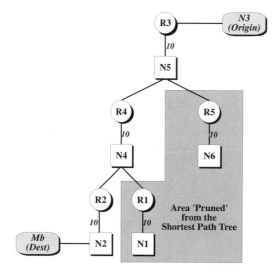

Figure 14-15: Shortest Path Tree for a Multicast Datagram

Once all MOSPF routers have synchronized their databases and adjacency is achieved, they are ready to forward multicast datagrams to hosts that are members of specific groups. As we have already said though, unlike OSPF, the router creates a shortest path tree *on demand* as multicast datagrams are received. This Shortest Path Tree also differs from that of OSPF in that an identical tree (the so-called Pruned Shortest Path Tree) is created by all routers on the path of the datagram.

The shortest path tree for MOSPF is said to be *pruned* because routers that do not participate in the delivery of this *specific* datagram are excluded from it. For example in Figure 14-11, if Host Hb sends a multicast datagram to host group b, it will need to be delivered to only the host that resides on network 2. The pruned shortest path tree for all routers would

Broadcasting and Multicasting with IP

therefore look similar to that shown in Figure 14-15. Note that in this example, we have assumed that the metric associated with all router interfaces is 10.

For this example, Router 3 would be the Designated Router for Network 3, and Router 2 would be the Designated Router for Network 2. It is these routers then (and these alone) that participate in IGMP activity related to this particular datagram. All the while that Host Mb advertises its membership of host group b, any datagrams sent to this group that originate on Network 3 will follow the path outlined by the tree. Once host Mb leaves the group (assuming that there are no further members on Network 2), the tree can then be destroyed.

If Network 6 was placed within a different OSPF Area, then Router 5 would naturally become an Area Border Router (ABR). If Router 5 advertised itself as a Wildcard Multicast Receiver, it too would receive this particular multicast even though it has no hosts that are part of host group b. Now, only Router 1 and Network 1 would be excluded (or pruned).

14.7 Summary

The Internet community is dedicated to moving towards an environment where Unicasts and Multicasts are used almost exclusively. This trend can be seen in the newer protocols such as RIP II and OSPF, and provides a means to reduce the amount of unnecessary broadcast traffic. MOSPF is certainly the most popular of all the routing protocols in a multicast environment and, working with IGMP as it does, provides an excellant companion.

Unquestionably, if we were to look at normal traffic on any network, we would see a large number of broadcasts. When we now consider that most hosts are interrupt driven, this can place a large overhead on CPUs processing information about which they have no interest. Multicasts on the other hand can be discarded at the Data Link layer when the host has no interest in the information conveyed, and it is this that makes multicasting so attractive. As the Internet community matures still further it is unlikely that we shall see new protocols that broadcast as freely as their older counterparts. Indeed, in truth although there will always be a need for some local broadcast traffic, protocols such as RIP will find that their life is limited as much through their traffic type as their functionality.

The Domain Name System (DNS)

As humans, we naturally find it difficult to remember long (seemingly meaningless) strings of numbers to represent host addresses. Thus, alphanumeric names that are more akin to our native language seem a far better alternative. But what form should this naming (or more correctly, high level addressing) scheme take? Should we allow a single level name to be mapped to a single IP Address? And if we did, would this not serve to only give us the same problems as those outlined in Chapter 4 when we discussed the possibilities of a centralized Internet addressing authority?

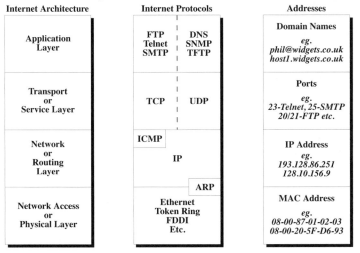

Internet Architecture	Internet Protocols	Addresses
Application Layer	FTP DNS Telnet SNMP SMTP TFTP	**Domain Names** *eg.* *phil@widgets.co.uk* *host1.widgets.co.uk*
Transport or Service Layer	TCP UDP	**Ports** *eg.* *23-Telnet, 25-SMTP* *20/21-FTP etc.*
Network or Routing Layer	ICMP IP	**IP Address** *eg.* *193.128.86.251* *128.10.156.9*
Network Access or Physical Layer	ARP Ethernet Token Ring FDDI Etc.	**MAC Address** *eg.* *08-00-87-01-02-03* *08-00-20-5F-D6-93*

Figsure 15-1: Addressing with the Internet Protocols

Clearly, when discussing addressing at all, we need to be able to propose a scheme that provides us with answers not only to our current requirements, but also those of the future. For example, a world-wide, single level, hierarchy would require a single, central, authority to allocate and administer names. A daunting task regardless of the size of administration, that would not even allow the flexibility demanded by the Internet community. In this instance then, a hierarchical naming scheme is required where we are able to delegate the responsibility for name allocation. Equally, since we cannot insist that all sites use names, this system must compliment rather than attempt to replace the IP Address. In addition, we need to be able to map any names used, to the IP addresses understood throughout the Internet community itself.

Within the Internet protocols then, we find a naming convention and resolution system called the *Domain Name System* or DNS. This Application layer protocol uses the User Datagram Protocol (UDP) which of course in turn uses IP. Figure 15-1 shows the relationship of these protocols and also serves to demonstrate the connection between this level of addressing and those below it.

This scheme naturally requires that we employ *Servers* (Name Servers) whose job it is to respond to address resolution requests received from *Resolvers*, and thus provide the link between a name (provided by a host), and an IP Address. In real terms, the Name Server, and the Resolver can be either a single, or multiple machines and DNS itself can operate in either a *Recursive or Iterative* mode, the differences and relative merits of which will be discussed later.

15.1 The Domain Name Space

The *Domain Name Space* is a specification for a *distributed, tree structured* hierarchical name space with associated data. It is *distributed* because we have a single, (un-named) root and then areas (or domains) that are locally administered. The phrase *tree-structured*, then defines the overall look of the name space. At its simplest level, the name space itself describes a number of nodes or *leafs* that are each used to describe a single host system. Users then query this information by calling on the services of *Resolvers* (typically a process running on the host) wherein the domain of interest and the type of *resource* information is requested. For example, the user may provide a name[1] to the Resolver, and the corresponding IP address is then returned.

It would of course be impractical to expect all servers to contain information about the entire hierarchy. Thus, name servers generally hold information about only a small subset of the name space and then pointers to other name servers that can be used where additional information is required. Name servers know for which parts of the name space they hold complete information and are then said to be an *Authority* for that part of the hierarchy. This data, held by the server, is referred to as being a *zone* and can be considered a *subtree* of the total domain name space. The server, through a timeout mechanism, then checks to make sure that the data it is holding is up to date and, where it is not, obtains a new copy from either local storage or another name server. This point is important since DNS expects all zones to be sustained by at least two Name Servers. This then provides redundancy by allowing the secondary server(s) to acquire zone information from the primary server through zone transfers.

Resolvers, those processes responsible for querying servers and therefore performing actual DNS lookups, cache the information received. This data is not as complete as the server zone information would be, and is discarded after a time-out period. It does however reduce network traffic and improve performance by locally storing frequently used information.

---

1. We shall see later that the resolution of IP addresses from names is a small part of the Domain Name System functionality.

The Domain Name System refers to the records held about a host as *Resource Records* each of which contains specific information. Each node then could be said to have a corresponding resource set (a set of records) and, in addition, a *label* (that can be up to 63 octets in length) to uniquely identify it. The actual Domain Name of a node, is therefore a list of labels on the path from itself to the root – an unnamed node at the head of the hierarchy – which can be no more than 255 octets in length. By convention, this name is then a null terminated string, read from left to right, with the left most label being the most specific (or that of the host), and the right most being the least specific (that closest to the root). These labels, when written, are then separated by dots (.) thus forming our domain name.

Domain Names are unique since, although a label may be repeated elsewhere in the hierarchy, brothers (those leafs at the same level) may not be given the same label. In addition, although we may wish to represent our names as mixed case, the Domain Name System performs all comparisons in a case-insensitive manner. Figure 15-2 demonstrates a simple Domain Name hierarchy and shows these facilities.

The concept of a *domain* – that part of the domain name space at or below the domain name specifying the domain itself, and a *sub-domain*, where it is wholly contained within another *domain* should now be clear from the figure. For example, in the figure, the domain "*widgets.co.uk*" is contained within the "*co.uk*" domain and is therefore a sub-domain of it. Equally, when specifying names, these may be specified as either absolute or relative to a particular domain. For example, we could specify the complete name for our host "*host1*" as an absolute "*host1. widgets.co.uk*". However, if we reside within the same domain, "*widgets.co.uk*", we may choose to provide only the relative name of "*host1*".

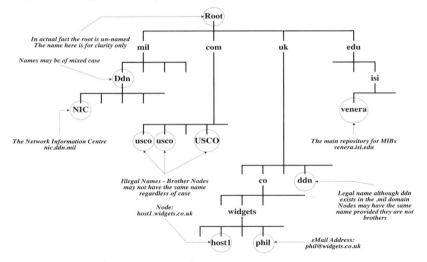

Figure 15-2: A Simple Domain Hierarchy

15.1.1 Aliases

Within the Domain Name System, allowance is made for a host to assume multiple names. For example, while a host will normally have only a single IP Address to identify it, it may be known by a number of different names. Such additional names, or *aliases* as they are called, must therefore present no problems to DNS.

Aliases are accommodated through special Resource Records such that where one of these records exists, no other data is present. Thus, data held concerning any particular name cannot be different to that of its aliases.

15.1.2 The Internet Mail System and DNS

So far we have discussed the implications of host naming in a distributed, hierarchical, name tree. But what about one of the most used features for naming, that of Internet Mail?[2] For mailboxes, mapping is slightly more complex since addresses are normally formed from a local portion, and a mail domain such as <local portion>@<mail domain>. In this case, a typical mail address might therefore be "*phil@widgets.co.uk*". However, since there may be more than one *phil* working for *widgets*, it is not uncommon to find underscores, and even dots, embedded in our local portion such as "*phil.miller@widgets.co.uk*" or "*phil_miller@widgets.co.uk*". Consequently, for the purposes of the Domain Name System, the entire local portion is converted to a single local portion resulting in "*phil@widgets.co.uk*" becoming "*phil.wigets.co.uk*" as shown in our previous diagram, Figure 15-2.

15.2 Resource Records

As we have said, each node may have a number of associated resource records, the order of which is neither significant, nor need to be preserved by name servers or any other parts of the Domain Name System. In general, each Resource Record will have the information shown in Table 15-1.

Table 15-1: Resource Record Types and Associated Data

Class	Description
Owner	The Domain Name where the Resource Record is found.
Type	The type of the resource stored in this record. This value is an encoded 16 bit field as follows:

A	A Host Address – Value 1.
CNAME	The canonical name of an alias – Value 5.
HINFO	The CPU and Operating System type used by the host – Value 13.
MB	Specifies the host that has the specified mailbox – Value 7.
MD	Defines the host with a mail agent for the domain – Value 3.
MF	Defines a host able to forward mail for the domain – Value 4.
MG	Specifies a mailbox that is a member of the mail group – Value 8.
MINFO	The mailbox responsible for a mailing list – Value 14.
MR	The Domain Name of a rename mailbox – Value 9.
MX	The Mail Exchange for the domain – Value 15.
NS	The authoritative name server for the domain – Value 2.
NULL	Further information – Value 10.

2. The most common Internet Mail system (the Simple Mail Transfer Protocol or SMTP) is discussed in Chapter 18.

Class		Description
	PTR	A pointer to another part of the Domain Name space – Value 12.
	SOA	The start of the Zone of Authority – Value 6.
	TXT	Simple text strings – Value 16
	WKS	A Well Known Service Description – Value 11.
Class		Used to identify the protocol family and represented as a 16 bit encoded value, the following protocols are identified:
	IN	The Internet System – Value 1.
	CH	The Chaos System – Value 3.
TTL		A 32 bit integer that represents the number of seconds that Resolvers should hold the resource record in theirs caches before being discarded.
RDATA		The type and class dependent data describing the actual resource: For the IN class, this contains a 32 bit IP Address.
RDATA	A	For the Chaos (CH) class, this contains a domain name followed by a 16 bit octal chaos address.
	CNAME	A Domain Name.
	HINFO	Host Information defining the CPU, and Operating System Types.
	MB	The Domain Name of the host that has the specified mailbox.
	MD	The Domain Name of a host that has a mail agent for the domain and is therefore able to deliver mail for the domain.
	MF	The Domain Name of a host capable of forwarding mail to the domain.
	MG	A Domain Name specifying a mailbox that is a member of the mail group.
	MINFO	The Domain Name of a mailbox responsible for the mailing list followed by a second Domain Name, that of the mailbox to receive error messages.
	MR	A Domain Name specifying a mail redirection.
	MX	A 16 bit preference value followed by a the name of a host willing to act as a mail exchange. In this, the lower the preference value, the better.
	NS	A host name.
	NULL	Any other RR data up to 65535 octets in length.
	PTR	A domain name.
	SOA	This can contain many fields of information identifying the start of the authority.
	TXT	A simple textural description of the host.
	WKS	Contains Address and Protocol information, and a bit mask to specify the ports used.

This can then be shown diagramatically as follows:

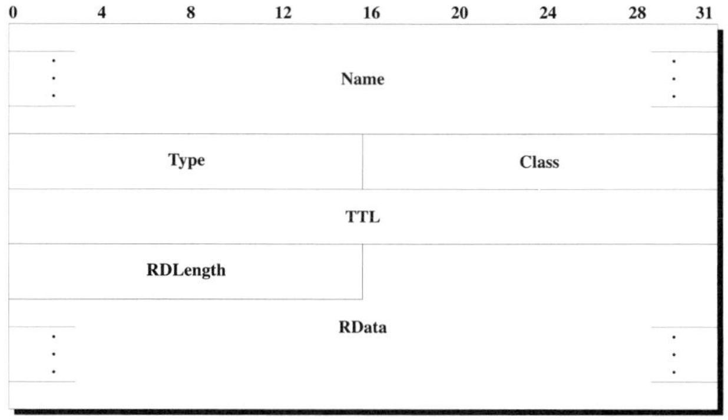

Figure 15-3: Resource Record Format

From this figure, it can be seen that the *Name* and *RData* fields are of variable length. As we have said, a name can be up to 255 octets in length, and is read from the left (the most significant octet) to the right (that nearest the root). Also, as the root is un-named, this string is terminated with a null character and no corresponding length field is required.

The *RData* field is different since, depending upon the data carried in the record, this field can be of variable length with no immediate termination characters. The *RDLength* field is therefore used to explicitly define the length of *Rdata*. In Addition to the Resource Record *Type* and *Class* Codes which were defined in Table 15-1, additional codes may also be seen in Queries. These codes, referred to as *QType* and *QClass* are then defined in Table 15-2.

Table 15-2: QType Codes

QType	Value (decimal)	Description
AXFR	252	A Request to transfer an entire zone – A Zone Transfer.
MAILB	254	A Request for all Mailbox related records.
*	255	A Request for all records.

With the *QClass*, only one additional class exists namely the asterisk (*) which has a value of 255. In this case the class is taken to mean *any class*.

15.2.1 The *A* (Address) Type Resource Record

With the *A* Type record, the Type has a value of 1 (A), and the *RData* field contains the 32 bit IP Address of the host. Should the host have multiple IP Addresses, then multiple A Type records will exist.

15.2.2 The *CName* (Canonical Name) Type Resource Record

The *CName* Type record's *RData* field contains the Canonical or Primary name of the owner of the record. The *Owner* field in this instance then contains the alias by which this host is also known. As with the real owner, the alias can be up to 255 octets. Thus the *RData* field will be up to 255 octets in length to accommodate this. Normal DNS rules as to the reading of this field apply whereby it is read from left to right with the most significant octet being that on the left.

Where a *CName* record is encountered, servers resolving client queries may choose to restart the query with the Canonical name specified. This however is dependent upon the implementation at the server and is discussed in Section 15.3.

15.2.3 The *HInfo* (Host Information) Type Resource Record

The *HInfo* record is used where we wish to appropriate further information about a host. Principally, this would be used for protocols such as FTP where hosts with the same operating system types could use special procedures. These procedures might then allow the task to be performed either quicker or simpler.

In this type of record, the *RData* field contains two character strings to represent the CPU and Operating System type respectively. These strings may be up to 40 octets in length and are defined in the current Internet Assigned Number Document.[3]

15.2.4 The *MB, MD, MF, MG, MInfo, MR,* and *MX* (Mail) Type Resource Records

While much work has been completed in the area of mail delivery, much more still continues. Thus, the mail Resource Records possibly represent a major area of current DNS research and therefore constitute the largest subset of Resource Record types.

MX type records are the main record type and define the domain name of a host that will act as a mail exchange for the host specified in the *Owner* field. In this case, the *RData* field contains a 16 bit *Preference* field, and the domain name of the mail exchange host. The *Preference* field is then used to indicate the preference of this Record over others from the same owner, with lower values being preferred. As before, the Domain Name of the mail exchange host can be up to 255 octets in length.

For example, where we wish to send mail to a user such as "*phil@widgets.co.uk*", a Mail Exchange (*MX*) Query will be sent to look up the *MX* type Resource Record for "*widgets.co.uk*". With this information returned, an Address (*A*) Query is then sent to determine the IP Address of the Mail Exchange host.

Other Mail Type records exist and although these have the status of being either experimental or obsolete, they are described below for completeness.

MB type records (officially experimental) can be used to specify a host that incorporates a specified mailbox. In these records, the *RData* field then contains the Domain Name of that host.

MD type records (officially obsolete) were used to identify a host that included an agent for the domain, and was therefore able to deliver mail for it. Again, the *RData* field contained the Domain Name for that host. This type has now been superseded by the *MX* (Mail Exchange) type record. Where *MD* records are found in master files, it is recommended that they either be rejected, or converted to *MX* records with a preference of zero.

MF type records (again obsolete) were used to define the Domain Name of a mail agent prepared to accept mail items to be forwarded to the particular domain. Here, the *RData* field would contain the Domain Name of this host. Where these records are now found, it is recommended that they be converted to *MX* records with preference value of 10.

MG type records (officially experimental) can be used to specify the Domain Name of a mailbox that is a member of a mail group. Here, the *RData* field contains the Domain Name of the mailbox.

MInfo type records (again experimental) can be used to identify the Domain Name of the mailbox responsible for a mailing list, and the Domain Name of the mailbox that should receive any related error messages. In this record type, the

3. For example: RFC1700 (Reynolds & Postel) October 1994.

RData field contains these two Domain Names.

MR type records (experimental) can be used to hold the Domain Name of a mailbox that is the proper *rename* of an existing mailbox. For example, if a user moves to a different mailbox, the MR type record can be used to redirect mail. In this case the *RData* field holds this new Domain Name only.

15.2.5 The *NS* (Name Server) Type Resource Record

Name Server (*NS*) records are used to specify the name of the host from which *authoritative* information should be expected. Previously we said that a host that held all of the information about a particular area of the name space was said to be an *Authority*. Thus it is the name of this host that is returned in the *RData* field of this record type.

With the *NS* record, the named host will have complete zone information that starts at the name specified in the *Owner* field. By organizing the name space in this way, redundant name servers are therefore easily updated by performing zone transfers. Here, potentially large, portions of the name space can be copied between servers and thus Name Server redundancy can be achieved.

15.2.6 The *PTR* (Pointer) Type Resource Record

These records are used to simply point to other areas of the name space. In this case, the *RData* field contains the domain name of the target name space zone.

15.2.7 The *SOA* (Start of Authority) Type Resource Record

The *SOA* record is used to define zone management parameters. The actual *RData* field of these records, while not particularly complex, is large and is best illustrated with Figure 15-4.

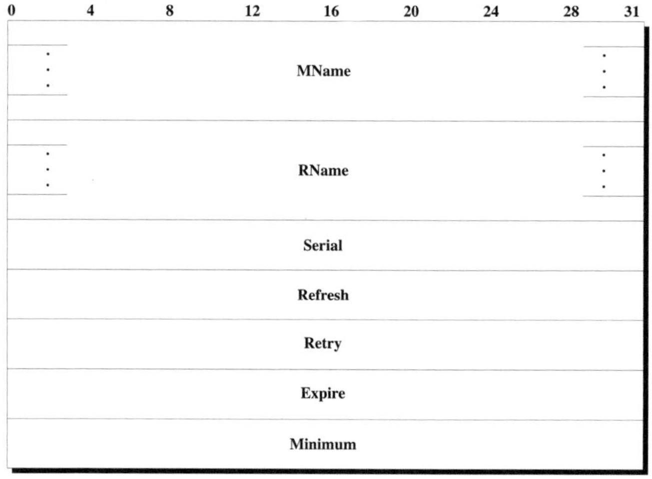

Figure 15-4: The SOA RData Format

The *MName* field is used to specify the domain name of the name server that was the original or primary source of data for this zone. The *RName* field specifies the mailbox address of the person responsible for the zone. The *Serial* field is used to convey the 32 bit version number of the original copy of the zone information. The *Refresh* field, represented as a 32 bit integer, defines the time (in seconds) before the zone information should be refreshed. The *Retry* field (also 32 bits) defines the time (in seconds) that should elapse before a failed refresh is re-tried. The 32 bit *Expire* field specifies the time (in seconds) after which the zone is no longer authoritative. Finally, the 32 bit *Minimum* field specifies the minimum TTL (Time-to-Live) that should be exported with any Resource Records from this zone.

15.2.8   The *TXT* (Text) Type Resource Record

Text records are used only to hold descriptive data, the actual format of which will depend upon the domain in which it is found.

15.2.9   The *WKS* (Well Known Service) Type Resource Record

WKS records are used to supply additional information about hosts by providing information about the *well known services* supported by a protocol on a particular host. In the case of the *WKS* record, the *RData* field contains three fields as shown in Figure 15-5. In this figure, the 32 bit *Address* field specifies the IP Address of the host and the *Protocol* field defines the 8 bit IP protocol number as identified in the Internet Assigned Number document. The *Bit Map* field is of variable length (in multiples of 8 bits) and is used to define which port(s) are used by the protocol. Here, the first bit corresponds to port 0, the second to port 1, the third to port 2 and so on. Thus, where the bit in the *Bit Map* is set, that port is in use and the server should be listening on it.

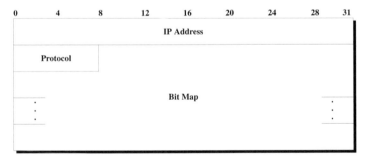

Figure 15-5: The WKS RData Format

For example, if the protocol field has the value 6, this indicates that TCP is used. If the 26th bit in the Bit Map is then set to 1 (indicating port 25 or SMTP), then the server will be listening on TCP port 25. Obviously the converse is also true. Where the bit in the *Bit Map* is 0, the server will not be listening on the corresponding port.

If the server supports multiple protocols (such as TCP, and UDP), then multiple *WKS* records will be used. Equally if he host has multiple IP Addresses, since the *socket* is the concatenation of the IP Address and Port number, again multiple *WKS* records will be required.

15.2.10 The *NULL* Type Resource Record

Null type records, which are officially experimental, allow any data of up to 65535 octets to be held in a Resource Record. Null records are not allowed in master files, however they may be used as placeholders in certain, experimental, extensions to DNS.

15.3 DNS Operation

From the perspective of the Resolver, DNS is a distributed database spread among multiple servers. DNS operates in a Client-Server mode, with client hosts being pre-configured with the address of one or more name servers through which the Resolver process then pursues requests. Since DNS is a distributed system though, it is highly likely that servers will receive requests that can only be satisfied by another server. Consequently, DNS can operate in two distinct modes namely *Iterative*, or *Recursive*.

In the Iterative mode, when the client presents a query, it may receive a response referring it to another server. The client must then pursue the request possibly getting referred time and time again. When a server is operating in the Recursive mode however, it will proceed with the query at other servers on behalf of the client. Recursive operation therefore reduces the loading on simpler host systems in that they do not need to implement a full Resolver function. By using recursive systems, we also find that network loading can be reduced. Using larger and fewer, centrally located caches in this way increases our hit ratio thereby reducing network load particularly where large distances and potentially slow links are involved.

Whether we use an Iterative or Recursive method, the result of any requests will then either provide the information requested, or alternatively will refer the client to another server. The operation of clients can then be described by the following steps:

- Examine the local cache to see if the information required is already held. If it is found then we assume that it is valid, since if this was not the case, it would have been discarded after being timed out.

- Assuming that the information is not available locally, determine which server(s) should be queried by examining the cache of name servers. Hosts will be pre-configured with the address of at least one server thus providing a starting point for all queries. Servers may also return information regarding better sources for information regarding certain domains. Where additional information is received as a result of standard queries in this way, this information is cached along with those pre-configured servers.

- Transmit the query to the primary or first choice server and await a response. If no response is received within the timeout period, send queries to the configured secondary or other name servers and again await a response. This continues until we have exhausted all known name servers after which we will report the condition and give up.

- If a response is received, it will contain one of the following:
  - An answer to the requested query. In this case the response will be cached and the information used.
  - An error or some type of non-sensible response. In the event that the response contains a bona-fide error message, the result will be conveyed to the requesting process. This could indicate an invalid name or name format, a non-existent domain, or any other error condition.

    If the response shows a potential server failure, the server will be deleted from the cache and we will attempt to resolve the query through another server (if available) as indicated in the third step above.

- The name of a server that can better answer the query. Here, although we have not received a direct answer to the query, we have learnt of another server that may be able to assist with this and other queries. The server information returned will be cached and the server then queried to resolve the query as in the second step above.

- A Canonical Name. If a canonical name is returned, the cache is queried to determine whether the required information about the name is already held locally. In effect then, the real name is cached and then the process starts again.

The actual operation can therefore be demonstrated by the simplified diagram of Figure 15-6.

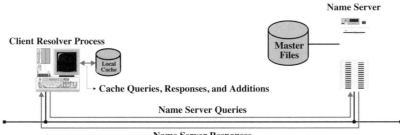

Figure 15-6: Simple DNS Operation

Although this figure shows only a single server and a single client, in practice we would require at least two servers and of course many clients would typically be involved. In addition, the client may need to make many queries to name servers to resolve a single query. Thus, the actual time taken for resolution cannot be easily specified.

15.3.1 Name Server Operation

Depending upon the desired functionality, a Name Server can either be a dedicated machine operating in a stand-alone fashion as indicated in the previous figure, or it could also incorporate its own client Resolver as well. In this latter case the server could then also be used to run user applications.

As we have already said, DNS requires that each zone is supported by at least two servers and that zone information is transferred between them. Thus, periodically, the primary and secondary servers will communicate to ensure that the information held is current or to exchange zone information. Figure 15-7 shows a typical example of this.

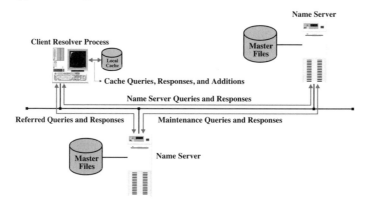

Figure 15-7: Multiple Name Servers

Where we have a host system supporting both Name Server and Resolver features, certain elements are naturally shared to conserve host resources. Figure 15-8 shows a simplified block diagram of such a host interacting with other client Resolvers and Name Servers:

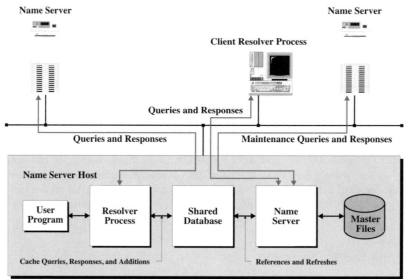

Figure 15-8: A Name Server Host

The Domain Name System (DNS)

In Figure 15-8, we see our host (represented by the block diagram) using another name server to resolve queries, resolving queries from other Resolvers, and exchanging zone information with maintenance queries and responses. This is possibly the most common use of name servers since only extremely large organizations are able to justify hosts dedicated to the name serving function alone.

Earlier we mentioned the use of Recursive servers to reduce the load on simple hosts and we noted that centralized caching potentially reduced network loading. Here, the client Resolver is referred to as a *Stub Resolver* and issues *Recursive Requests* to the server. Figure 15-9 shows an example of such a system where our end user hosts are simple devices incapable of Iterative operation.

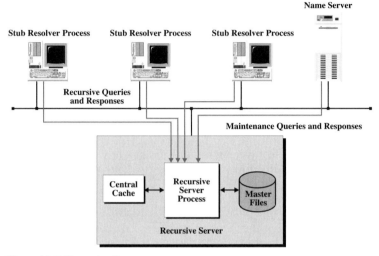

Figure 15-9: Recursive Servers

15.4 DNS Protocol Format

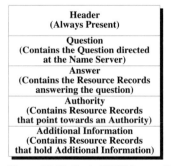

Figure 15-10: Basic DNS Message Format

Most DNS messages are carried within the UDP protocol[4] using Port 53_{10}, and are divided into 5 sections some of which may be empty, depending upon the type of message itself. Figure 15-10 shows the overall format of DNS messages, which is further described in the following sections.

As the figure shows, the *Header* is always present. This section contains an *Operation Code* that describes the type of operation, and a series of *Flags* and *Counters* that then describe which other sections are present, and the number of Resource Records contained in each.

4. UDP is not considered reliable enough for Zone Transfers thus, for these operations TCP is used. Again, Port 53 is utilized for this purpose.

The *Question* section contains fields that describe the actual query posed to the name server. The *Answer*, *Authority*, and *Additional* sections then contain Resource Records that contain the answer to the query, where an *Authoritative* Name Server can be found, and any additional information relating to the query.

15.4.1   The Header Section

The format of the Header is shown in Figure 15-11. This section is always present regardless of DNS message type and contains the fields and flags that describe the type of query and the data contained within the message itself.

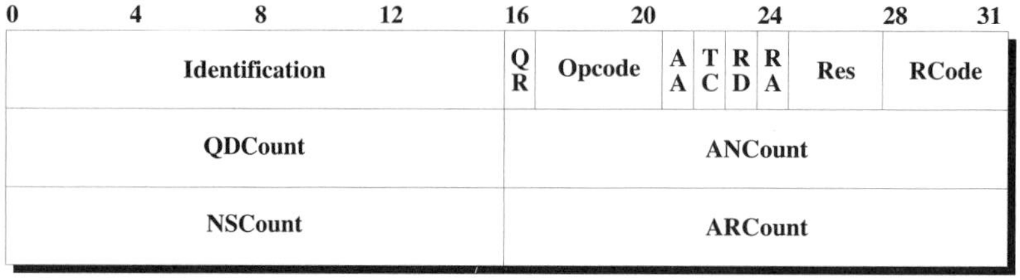

0	4	8	12	16	20	24	28	31

Identification	QR	Opcode	AA	TC	RD	RA	Res	RCode
QDCount				ANCount				
NSCount				ARCount				

Figure 15-11: The DNS Message Header

The 16 bit *Identification* field is a unique number assigned by the system generating the query. This field is then copied to any response so that the requesting host can match queries with responses. The single bit *QR* flag is used to indicate whether this message is a Query, or a Response. When set (value 1), the message contains a response and when not set (value 0), the message contains a query. The *Opcode* field contains a 4 bit value that identifies the type of query the message contains based upon the values shown in Table 15-3.

Table 15-3: Query Message Types

Value	Operation
0	A Standard Query (QUERY).
1	An Inverse Query (IQUERY).[5]
2	A Server Status Request (STATUS).
3-15	Reserved for future use.

The single bit flags *AA*, *TC*, *RD*, and *RA* are used to qualify either the Query or Response. The *AA* flag indicates that the response is Authoritative and that the name server that responded was therefore an authority for the domain name requested in the Query. The *TC* flag indicates that the message has been truncated. UDP allows a maximum message size of 512 octets (excluding the IP and UDP headers) thus, where the message length is greater than this, the message is truncated and the TC flag is set.

The *RD*, and *RA* flags relate to recursion. The *RD* flag, set in a Query, indicates that the querying host would like the name server to recursively persue the query.

5. The Inverse Query (IQUERY) is discussed in section 15.5.

The Domain Name System (DNS)

The *RA* flag, set in responses, indicates if the name server is able to provide a recursive service. The 3 bit *Reserved* field is reserved for future use and must be zero in all DNS messages. The 4 bit *RCode* field is set in responses to qualify the reply. The values are then shown in Table 15-4.

Table 15-4: RCode Field Values

Value	Description
0	No Error.
1	Format Error. The Name Server was unable to interpret the Query.
2	Server Failure. The Name Server was unable to process the QUERY due to a problem.
3	Name Error. The Domain Name specified does not exist. This error condition is applicable only to Authoritative responses.
4	Not Implemented. The Name Server does not support the requested Query type.
5	Refused. The Name Server has refused to perform the specified operation for some reason. This type of error can exist if the Name Server has refused to perform the operation for say, policy reasons. For example, the Name Server may not be allowed to provide information to the requester.
6-15	Reserved for future use.

The 16 bit *QDCount*, *ANCount*, *NSCount*, and *ARCount* fields specify the number of entries in the *Question*, *Answer*, *Authority* and *Additional* sections respectively. In the case of the *NSCount* field, this identifies the number of Name Server (NS) Resource Records.

15.4.2 The Question Section

The Question section carries the parameters about the question being asked in the Query. While it is normal to only present a single question in a Query, the QDCount field in the header defines the actual number of questions posed. Figure 15-12 shows the format of this section.

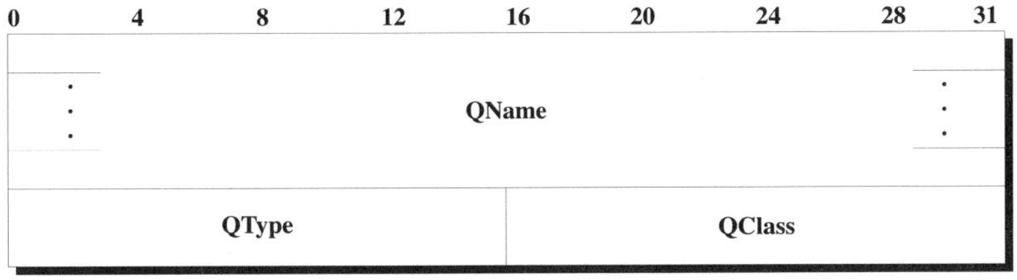

Figure 15-12: The Question Section

The variable length *QName* field is the Domain Name at which the *Query* is directed. The name is represented as a series of labels each of which comprises a single length octet followed by the actual label. The field then terminates with a single length octet of zero representing the *Null* label of the root. Each label can be up to 63 octets long, and the entire name up to 255 octets. This field can therefore be of any length (up to the permitted maximum) and can contain an odd number of octets. No padding is ever used.

The 16 bit *QType* field is used to specify the type of query. The values here will be the same as those shown in the table in section 15.2. The *QClass* field, again 16 bits, specifies the class of the *Query* and will contain the value 1 for the Internet system.

15.4.3 The Answer, Authority, and Additional Information Sections

These sections contain Resource Records, the format of which was described in section 15.2. In these sections, the actual numbers of records appearing are communicated through the ANCount, NSCount, and ARCount fields of the message header.

15.4.4 Message Compression

As we have seen, Domain Names can be very long and Datagram size is limited. Thus, to reduce message sizes, DNS provides a facility whereby repetition of names can be eliminated. Where used, this optional feature allows an entire Domain Name to be replaced by a partial name, or label list, and a pointer to a prior occurrence of the same name. This pointer (shown in Figure 15-13) is a two octet string with the two most significant bits set to 1. This pattern is chosen so as to avoid confusion with standard labels that must be preceded with single octet length field and whose maximum length is restricted to 63 octets. Thus, with standard labels, these two bits would be set to zero. The remaining 14 bits are then used as an Offset field to identify where (with respect to the start of the message), the remaining labels of the name can be found.

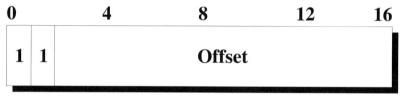

Figure 15-13: DNS Compression Pointer

Consider the following simplified example of Figure 15-14 where we wish to represent two Domain Names, "*host1.widgets.co.uk*", and "*server.widgets.co.uk*".

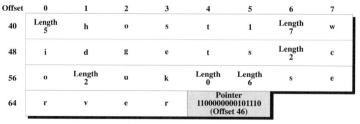

Figure 15-14: DNS Compression Example

Here, assuming all offsets to be in decimal and ignoring all other associated fields, we see that at offset 40 the name "*host1.widgets.co.uk*" is stored. At offset

The Domain Name System (DNS)

60, the *Null* length field signifies the root and hence the termination of this name. At offset 61, we see the name *"server.widgets.co.uk"* represented as the label *server*, and a pointer to offset 46 for the remaining labels *"widgets.co.uk"*. In actual fact, this diagram represents a significant over-simplification since it is unlikely that we would find two domain names next to each other in the same message. In reality, the name containing the pointer will generally be elsewhere within the message body, maybe many octets apart.

15.5 Inverse Queries

The Inverse Query is an optional feature of the Domain Name System allowing a resource to be mapped to a Domain Name. For example, a standard query may be used to map an address to a Domain Name, while an Inverse Query is used to map a Domain Name to an address.

Where an Inverse Query is used, the message will contain a single Resource Record in the *Answer* section of the message with the *Question* section empty. A valid response to such a message is for the Name Server to either return an error response with the *"Not Implemented"* error indicated, or to return a message containing a number of questions in the *Question* section. Where the response does not indicate an error (i.e. the server supports Inverse Queries), the *Question* section will contain *all* names that the Name Server knows about, that match the Query Resource Record. However, since no Name Server will ever have knowledge of the entire name-space, such responses can never be assumed to be complete.

For example, if we wish to determine the Domain Name(s) for the address 192.168.87.62, the transactions shown in Figure 15-15 may take place.

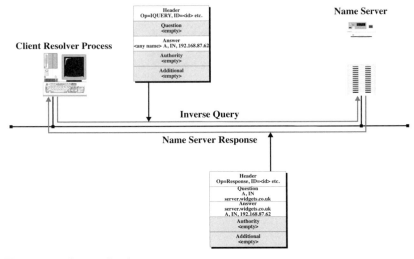

Figure 15-15: Inverse Queries

Notice how in the request, the Answer field contains a dummy Resource Record that comprises any name, a Type of A (Address), a Class of IN (Internet), and the

IP Address of the host for which resolution is required. The name specified here can be any properly formed name however, since the Root comprises a single Null length field, the Root is generally used to minimize the length of the message.

In the Response, the name in the Answer section will be the name contained within the first Resource Record found. Obviously, the example shown above is simplified in that it contains only a single Question section. Indeed, in many real instances several Queries would be contained here.

15.6 Looking up DNS Information

One useful utility available on many hosts is the *nslookup* program. This program allows the user to obtain information such as Name to Address mappings, Mail Exchanger, Mail Rename, Host Information, Mailbox, Host Information etc. Figure 15-16 shows a simple nslookup session where the user is obtaining IP Address and Mail Exchanger information.

```
phil >nslookup
Default Server:  sun.widgets.co.uk
Address: 192.168.12.173
> ?
Commands:     (identifiers are shown in uppercase. [] means optional)
NAME                     - print info about the host/domain NAME using default server
NAME1  NAME 2- as above, but use NAME2 as server
help or ?     - print help information
exit                     - exit the program
set OPTION    - set an option
    all       - print options, current server and host
    [no]debug- print debugging information
    [no]d2    - print exhaustive debugging information
    [no]defname      - append domain name to each query
    [no]recurse      - ask for recursive answer to query
    [no]vc    - always use a virtual circuit
    domain=NAME          - set default domain name to NAME
    root=NAME- set root server to NAME
    retry=X   - set number of retries to X
    timeout=X- set time-out interval to X
    querytype=X         - set query type to one of A,CNAME,HINFO,MB,MG,MINFO,MR,MX
    type=X    - set query type to one of A,CNAME,HINFO,MB,MG,MINFO,MR,MX
server NAME   - set default server to NAME, using current default server
lserver NAME  - set default server to NAME, using initial server
finger [NAME] - finger the optional NAME
root                     - set current default server to the root
is NAME [> FILE]- list the domain NAME, with output optionally going to FILE
view FILE     - sort an 'ls' output file and view it with more
> venera.isi.edu
Server:  sun.widgets.co.uk
Address:  192.168.12.173
Non-authoritative answer:
Name:  venera.isi.edu
Address: 128.9.0.32
> set querytype=mx
> venera.isi.edu
Server:  sun.widgets.co.uk
Address:  192.168.12.173
venera.isi.edu preference = 10, mail exchanger = quark.ISI.EDU
venera.isi.edu preference = 0, mail exchanger = venera.ISI.EDU
quark.ISI.EDU inet address = 128.9.208.208
venera.ISI.EDU inet address = 128.9.0.32
> set querytype=a
> ds.internic.net
Server:  sun.widgets.co.uk
Address:  192.168.12.173
Name: ds.internic.net
Address: 198.49.45.10
> exit
phil >
```

Figure 15-16: The nslookup Utility

The Domain Name System (DNS)

15.7 A DNS Example

The trace in Figure 15-17 shows an example of a Domain Name Query and the associated Response. In this example, we see a simple request from a client host requesting a Name to Address mapping. Although the simplest of examples, this exchange shows what is possibly the most typical use of the Domain Name System, and what certainly accounts for much DNS traffic.

In this example, the first two packets show a station (193.128.88.21) querying the DNS Server (193.128.88.173) and then, this server contacting another server (204.70.128.1) for further information. In packet 3, the second server responds to the first and, if we were then to view further frames we would see the first server responding to the client station.

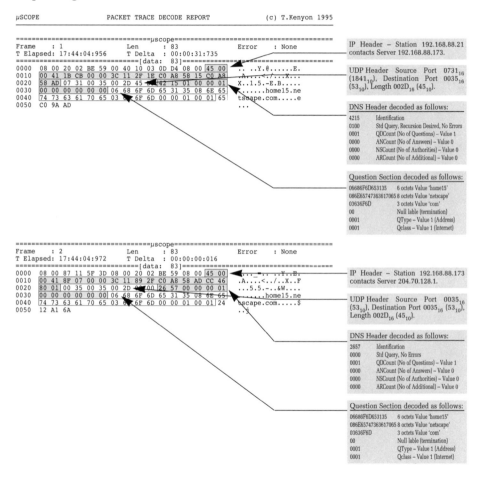

```
=============================μscope=============================
Frame   : 3              Len     : 204              Error  : None
T Elapsed: 17:44:05:388  T Delta : 00:00:00:416
=============================[data: 204]=============================
0000  08 00 20 02 BE 59 08 00 87 11 5F 3D 08 00 45 00   .. .Y...._=..E.
0010  00 BA F2 47 40 00 F3 11 2E 75 CC 46 80 01 C0 A8   ...G@....u.F....
0020  58 AD 00 35 00 35 00 A6 3F 1C 26 57 84 80 00 01   X..5.5..?.&W....
0030  00 02 00 02 00 02 06 68 6F 6D 65 31 35 08 6E 65   .......home15.ne
0040  74 73 63 61 70 65 03 63 6F 6D 00 00 01 00 01 C0   tscape.com......
0050  0C 00 05 00 01 00 00 0E 10 00 14 05 77 77 77 31   ............www1
0060  35 08 6E 65 74 73 63 61 70 65 03 63 6F 6D 00 C0   5.netscape.com..
0070  31 00 01 00 01 00 00 0E 10 00 04 C6 5F FB 20 C0   1..........._. .
0080  37 00 02 00 01 00 00 0E 10 00 05 02 6E 73 C0 37   7...........ns.7
0090  C0 37 00 02 00 01 00 00 0E 10 00 0C 02 6E 73 03   .7...........ns.
00A0  6D 63 69 03 6E 65 74 00 C0 61 00 01 00 01 00 00   mci.net..a......
00B0  0E 10 00 04 C6 5F FB 0A C0 72 00 01 00 01 00 00   ....._...r......
00C0  0E 10 00 04 CC 46 80 01 F1 83 50 86               .....F....P.
```

Figure 15-17: DNS Trace

DNS Header decoded as follows:

2657	Identification
0000	Std Query, No Errors
0001	QDCount (No of Questions) – Value 1
0002	ANCount (No of Answers) – Value 2
0002	NSCount (No of Authorities) – Value 2
0002	ARCount (No of Additional) – Value 2

Question Section decoded as follows:

06686F6D653135	6 octets Value 'home15'
086E65747363617065	8 octets Value 'netscape'
03636F6D	3 octets Value 'com'
00	Null lable (termination)
0001	QType – Value 1 (Address)
0001	Qclass – Value 1 (Internet)

Answer Section decoded as follows:

Answer 1

C00C	Compressed data same as Off 12 'home15.netscape.com'
0005	Cannonical Name of Alias
0001	Class Internet
00000E10	TTL – Value 3600 Seconds
0014	Length of Resource data – Value 20
057777773135	5 octets Value 'www15'
086E65747363617065	8 octets Value 'netscape'
03636F6D	3 octets Value 'com'
00	Null Lable (termination)

Answer 2

C031	Compressed data same as Off 49 'www15.netscape.com'
0001	Address
0001	Class Internet
00000E10	TTL – Value 3600 Seconds
0004	Length of Resource data – Value 4
C65FFB20	IP Address – Value 198.95.251.32

Authority Section decoded as follows:

Authority 1

C037	Compressed data same as Off 55 'netscape.com'
0002	Authoritative Name Server for Domain
0001	Class Internet
00000E10	TTL – Value 3600 Seconds
0005	Length of Resource data – Value 5
026E73	2 octets Value 'ns'
C037	Compressed data same as Off 55

Authority 2

C037	Compressed data same as Off 55 'netscape.com'
0002	Authoritative Name Server for Domain
0001	Class Internet
00000E10	TTL – Value 3600 Seconds
000C	Length of Resource data – Value 4
026E73	2 octets value 'ns'
036D6369	3 octets Value 'mci'
036E6574	3 octets Value 'net'
00	Null Label (termination)

Additional Info decoded as follows:

Additional Information 1

C061	Compressed data same as Off 97 'ns.netscape.com'
0001	Host Address
0001	Class Internet
00000E10	TTL – Value 3600 Seconds
0004	Length of Resource data – Value 4
C65FFB0A	IP Address – Value 198.95.251.10

Additional Information 2

C037	Compressed data same as Off 112 'ns.mci.net'
0001	Host Address
0001	Class Internet
00000E10	TTL – Value 3600 Seconds
0004	Length of Resource data – Value 4
CC468001	IP Address – Value 204.70.128.1.

The Domain Name System (DNS)

15.8 Summary

In this chapter we have seen the operation of the Domain Name System (DNS). Arguably, this is one of the major protocols used within an IP environment since it is through co-operation with DNS, that most users gain access to Internet hosts. DNS works in a client server mode that allows end stations (users or clients) to contact servers for DNS resolutions. Such resolution may be simply Name to Address, or can include mail address to mail exchanger. In this latter case, the server is used to resolve the name of the mail server responsible for mail delivery to a particular domain.

Like the IP Address, DNS uses a heirarchical address space called the *Name Space*. This allows our system to scale well as it grows and also allows a great deal of local control. With such a potentially large space however, it is impossible for all servers to contain information about the whole space. Thus, two modes of operation are used namely *Iterative* and *Recursive*. In the iterative model of operation, a server that is unable to answer a request directly will refer the requestor to another server. In the Recursive model however, the server will perform the search itself on behalf of the client.

The main design criteria of the protocol are well met in that it is unobtrusive to normal operation and operates almost seamlessly to provide this service. RFCs 1034 and 1035 define the protocol and its operation and that it works over both UDP and TCP. Where a client resolver process requests information, this is normally perfomed using the lower overhead UDP implementation. The down side to this of course is that no inherent reliability exist, and indeed DNS does nothing to improve on this. Where more critical transfers are needed, such as the transfer of information between servers to update tables, the more reliable TCP is used. Zone transfers as they are known, are less frequent than ordinary resolution requests so this is more than acceptable.

Telnet and Rlogin

The primary goal of any network is to provide a mechanism for the sharing of resources and/or data. The sharing of resources such as printers is a subject in its own right and will typically be dependant upon the operating systems in use at both the host and client sites. The sharing of data however, generally falls into two distinct groups, namely, the wholesale copying of files, and on-line access. Files may be copied in their entirety through the implementation of the File Transfer Protocol (FTP), or the Trivial File Transfer Protocol (TFTP). These are discussed in detail in Chapters 17, and 19 respectively. On-line access to host resources though is the subject of this chapter.

The Telnet and Rlogin protocols provide a general bi-directional communications path that interfaces terminal devices to a terminal oriented process on a host machine, thus providing the illusion that the user has a local connection. Rlogin (available with Berkeley BSD UNIX systems) is built upon the ideas of Telnet but introduces an idea of trusted hosts thus eliminating the necessity for the user to identify himself when accessing a remote system. With these ideas in mind, we shall look at the Telnet protocol, and then examine how Rlogin modifies this to create what is a much simpler user interface.

16.1 The Telnet Protocol

Telnet (defined by RFC 854) uses a TCP connection (using port 23_{10}) over which it transmits data interspersed (where required) with control characters. The protocol itself assumes that each end of the connection is an imaginary *Network Virtual Terminal* (NVT) that incorporates the minimum functionality required for a simple terminal to connect to a host system. Where this is insufficient for user needs, certain options may then be negotiated. In this way users with advanced terminals can enjoy added functionality, without penalizing those who have only modest terminals. A user at a remote terminal therefore, should be offered exactly the same services and functionality, as those provided to local users.

The process of option negotiation is through four distinct command/response pairs termed *DO*, *DON'T*, *WILL*, and *WON'T*. By using this structure, described below, clients and servers can use any locally agreed or standardized option. At the start of the session, each end is assumed to terminate at an NVT, and either party may then initiate option negotiation at any time during the session. The method of negotiation is to have either party (or both) initiate a request that some specified option takes effect. The receiver may then either accept the request or reject it depending upon local conditions and/or support for the requested option. Whilst certain options are standardized and must be implemented, there exists a number of options that have meaning only between certain host types. One party requesting that an option takes effect for the duration of the session does not guarantee acceptance by the peer process. However, if one process wishes to disable an option, refusal by the peer is not allowed. Where an option is accepted, that option takes effect immediately. Where an option is rejected, the associated set of connection parameters remain as those specified for an NVT.

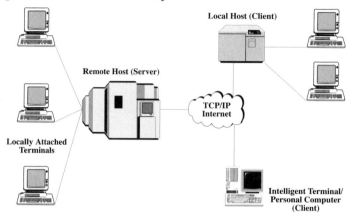

Figure 16-1: A Telnet Example

16.1.1   Option Command/Responses

The option command/response pairs; DO, DON'T, WILL, and WON'T, can best be described as follows: A process that wishes the receiver to implement an option will send a DO. In response, the receiver will send a WILL (affirmative response), or a WON'T (negative response). Where a process wishes to start using an option, it will send a WILL. In response, the receiver will send either a DO (affirmative response), or a DON'T (negative response). Table 16-1 summarizes this:

Table 16-1: Telnet Option Commands and Responses

Command	Meaning	Response	Meaning
DO	The sender wishes the receiver to implement the specified option.	WILL	The receiver agrees, and the option is enabled at the receiver.
		WON'T	The receiver disagrees. The option is not enabled at the receiver.
WILL	The sender wishes to commence using the specified option.	DO	The receiver agrees. The option is enabled by the sender.
		DON'T	The receiver disagrees. The option is not enabled by the sender.
DON'T	The sender wishes the receiver to disable the specified option.	WON'T	The receiver MUST agree and indicates this with WON'T.
WON'T	The sender will stop using the specified option.	DON'T	The receiver MUST agree and indicates this with DON'T.

For example, if the sender wishes the receiver to commence option ABC, it will send a DO ABC. The receiver will respond with WILL ABC (if it will implement the option), or WON'T ABC (if it will not implement the option). If the sender wishes to start using option XYZ, it will send WILL XYZ. The receiver will respond with either DO XYZ (if the receiver agrees), or DON'T XYZ (if the receiver disagrees). Notice that the last two commands (DON'T, and WON'T) are used when options are to be disabled. The only allowable responses to a request to disable an option is affirmative, indicated in these cases by WON'T, and DON'T.

Since either party may initiate a request, it would seem entirely possible to enter a loop of requests/acknowledgements that would never terminate. To overcome this situation, a few simple rules are always followed:

- A sender only ever sends a command to request a change in option status. A sender never advertises the mode in which it is currently working.

- Where a recipient receives a request to enter a mode that is already in use, the request will not be acknowledged. If the request is for a change in option status it will always be acknowledged even if that acknowledgement is a refusal.

- Whenever a request to change the status of an option is sent, the sender inserts the request at the point at which the change should take effect. This may result in the receiver buffering data without displaying it until it has determined what option has been requested. Indication of the presence of an imbedded option is therefore normally through the use of the TCP *Urgent Pointer*.

- Rejected requests are never repeated unless something changes. This overcomes the situation where a host, having had a request rejected once, continually re-requests the option.

- Where both hosts simultaneously request the same option be used, neither is acknowledged. Instead, each request from the other host is taken as a positive acknowledgement of the local hosts desire to instigate the option.

If the receiver receives a request to use an option that it does not support, it will refuse the request. This eliminates the situation that might otherwise arise where the two ends of the connection negotiate about an option that is foreign to one host. For example, the sender wishes to activate the PQR option which is unknown to the receiver. The sender transmits DO PQR, the receiver responds with WON'T PQR.

16.1.2 Telnet Control Functions

As we have already said, the primary purpose of Telnet is to provide a general purpose protocol that interfaces terminal devices with a terminal oriented process. While it is true that host systems will implement control functions in different ways, Telnet attempts to standardize the major functions found on many terminals. These functions are as follows:

Are You There (AYT): When a system or task appears to have crashed, the remote user has no way of telling. In this case, the user will note an unexpectedly quiet system and will have no way of telling what, if anything has gone wrong. Telnet therefore incorporates a method for determining that the remote system is still alive through the AYT function. When this function is received, the receiving host sends back an audible or visual signal to the user indicating that it is.

Erase Character (EC): Local terminals incorporate a Character Erase character (normally the backspace key) that erases the last character sent. If we are to emulate such a local terminal and provide at least the same minimal functionality, then it is important that the Telnet protocol also implements this function. The EC function is the standard method for transmitting such a character, however its use can create a data stream that has the following appearance:

<char 1> <char 2> <char 3> *<EC>* *<EC>* <new char 2> <new char 3>

Erase Line (EL): As with the Erase Character command, many terminals offer an Erase Line command to erase all input on the current line. In Telnet, the EL function is used to achieve this.

Interrupt Process (IP): This is used where a user wishes to suspend, interrupt, or abort an operation.

Abort Output (AO): This allows the user to request that the output that would normally be displayed on the screen or printing device is suppressed. Remember that data may be in transit at the time that the AO is received. Such data could actually be in transit and buffered in internetworking devices, or it could be held in local buffers on the receiving host – in either case, this data will not be flushed by the Abort Output function but must instead be cleared with the *Synch* function.

"*Synch*" Signal: The Telnet Synch signal is used to attempt to regain control over a runaway task. In much the same way that a local terminal would have a Break key, Telnet uses the Synch signal to indicate the user's desire to cease the current task and reset the link. Unlike a local terminal however, a network connection may buffer data en-route between the server and the client, so how can we assure that all data is flushed? Simply, we rely on the TCP Urgent Data function that is not subject to flow controls. Here, the TCP Urgent (URG) flag is set and the TCP data contains only a Telnet DATA MARK command.

The effect of receiving a Telnet Synch is to discard all characters (except Telnet commands between the sender and the recipient. This method is therefore the standard way to clear the data path, and is used in conjunction with the AO function.

16.1.3 Standard NVT Characters

A Network Virtual Terminal operates with the standard 7 bit ASCII character set. An NVT is therefore able to display all 95 USASCII characters (codes $32\text{-}126_{10}$). In addition, the following standard characters (shown in Table 16-2) are defined for an NVT.

Table 16-2: Standard Telnet Characters

Code Decimal	Name	Meaning	Code Decimal	Name	Meaning
0	NUL	Null Character No-Op	10	LF	Linefeed
7	BEL	Bell Character	11	VT	Vertical Tab
8	BS	Backspace Character	12	FF	Formfeed
9	HT	Horizontal Tab	13	CR	Carriage Return

16.1.4 Telnet Commands and Options

Since Telnet uses a single TCP connection over which both commands and data must be passed, the designers of the protocol devised a method by which commands, and option negotiation, could be embedded in the data stream. Telnet commands consist of sequences at least two octets in length. Each command sequence starts with a single octet *escape* character called *Interpret As Command* (IAC) which is then followed by the relevant code for the command in question. Where an option is to be negotiated, a third octet is then used to represent the actual option value. The Figure 16-2 shows a simple command/response sequence for command *ABC*:

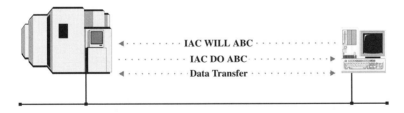

Figure 16-2: Telnet Command/Response Sequence

Some options are relatively complex in nature requiring more than a single octet value. In these cases a *Sub-negotiation* phase is employed. The standard method of negotiation remains unchanged, firstly one party requests that the option be invoked with the DO, or WILL command. If the response is positive, the response will be WILL, or DO as normal. At this time both parties have agreed that the option should be used and may now enter a sub-negotiation phase to work out the fine detail. Here, the command *Sub-negotiation Begin* (SB) is used followed by the option code, the parameters, and finally the *Sub-negotiation End* (SE). Since both parties have agreed to use the option in the first phase of this exchange, it is assumed that each will support all parameters. Where this is not the case, the receiver can send a WON'T, or DON'T at any time to cancel further sub-negotiation. The example in Figure 16-3 shows a simple sub-negotiation for the option XYZ:

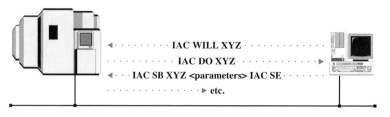

```
◄· · · · · · · · · · IAC WILL XYZ · · · · · · · · · · ·
· · · · · · · · · · · · IAC DO XYZ · · · · · · · · · · · ►
◄· · · IAC SB XYZ <parameters> IAC SE · · · · · ·
· · · · · · · · · · · · · · · · · ► etc.
```

Figure 16-3: Telnet Option Sub-negotiation

16.1.5   RFCs Related to Telnet Options

Unlike many other protocols, Telnet does not rely on a single RFC to define all of its functions. Instead, the range of Telnet options has grown as new functionality has been demanded by users. All commands and options however, use characters outside the normal USASCII range of printable and control characters. Listed in Table 16-3 are the major commands and options together with their decimal (and hexadecimal) values.

Table 16-3: Telnet Commands and Options

Name	Value Decimal	Value Hex	RFC	Meaning
Options				
Transmit Binary	0	00	856	When the binary transmission option is used, the receiver interprets non IAC characters received from the sender as 8 bit binary data. (See Note 1)
Echo	1	01	857	Using this option, the end systems agree to echo data over the Telnet connection rather than (or in addition to) local echo.
Suppress Go Ahead	3	03	858	When in use, this option suppresses Telnet Go-Ahead characters from being transmitted. (See Note 2)
Telnet Status Option	5	05	859	Allows the user or process to view the current status of the Telnet options as viewed from the remote end of the connection.
Telnet Timing Mark	6	06	860	Requests that the receiver issue a timing mark that indicates all previously received data has been processed.
Terminal Type	24	18	1091	Allows the sender and receiver to exchange terminal type information thereby allowing

Name	Value Decimal	Value Hex	RFC	Meaning
Options (continued)				
				the most appropriate type to be selected. (See Note 3)
End of Record	25	19	885	Terminates data sent with an End-of-Record (EOR) character.
Telnet Line Mode	34	22	1184	Reduces the amount of network bandwidth consumed by allowing the user local editing and the transmission of complete lines of text. (See Note 4)
X-Display Location	35	23	1096	When a user is running Telnet from X-Windows, it allows the receiver to know the location of the windows in use.
Extended Option List	255	FF	861	Allows the available option space to be increased by a further 256. (See Note 5)
Commands				
Sub-negotiation End	240	F0	854	The end of sub-negotiation Parameters.
No Operation	241	F1	854	No operation. The receiver ignores this code.
Data Mark	242	F2	854	Used in the Telnet Synch and always in a TCP segment with the Urgent Pointer and Urgent Flag set accordingly.
Break	243	F3	854	The NVT Break character.
Interrupt Process	244	F4	854	Used where a user wishes to suspend, interrupt, or abort an operation.
Abort Output	245	F5	854	Allows the user to request that the output that would normally be displayed on the screen or printing device is suppressed.
Are You There	246	F6	854	When received, the receiving host sends back an audible or visual signal to the user indicating that it is alive.
Erase Character	247	F7	854	Indicates that the last character should be erased.
Erase Line	248	F8	854	Indicates that the last line should be erased.
Go Ahead	249	F9	854	Used to indicate to the receiver that it should transmit. (See Note 2)
Sub-negotiation Begin	250	FA	854	The start of the sub-negotiation phase.
WILL <option>	251	FB	854	Indicates a desire to commence using an option, or confirmation that the option is now being used.
WON'T <option>	252	FC	854	Indicates a refusal to use, or continue to use an option.
DO <option>	253	FD	854	Indicates a desire that the receiver should start performing the indicated option, or a confirmation that the sender is using the option.
DON'T <option>	254	FE	854	Indicates that the receiver should stop using the indicated option, or that the sender no longer expects the receiver to be using the option.
Interpret as Command	255	FF	854	Used as the Telnet Escape character meaning that the next octet should be treated as a command. (See Note 1)

Note 1:

It is useful to have a *Binary Transmission Mode* available to Telnet users allowing them to transmit 8 bit binary data directly over the connection without the need to employ other higher level protocols such as the File Transfer Protocol (FTP). This is of particular relevance when the Telnet user in question is a process rather than a human operator.

In normal use, Telnet is restricted to using the 95 printable characters as defined by the USASCII code set, plus a number of control characters. By using this option though, the receiver will interpret all octets received as eight bit binary data except for the IAC octet. This restriction is key to the operation of the protocol since, as we have seen, Telnet relies upon embedded commands in the data stream itself. Hence, where we wish to transmit the code FF_{16} (255_{10}) the data octet is first *escaped* using the IAC octet. Therefore to transmit a single octet of value FF_{16}, we actually transmit FFFF. On reception, the receiving host then strips one of these octets, leaving the data stream as it was originally intended. No further restrictions are placed on the protocol since the transmission of all commands (always preceded by IAC) will, by their very definition, be interpreted correctly.

Note 2:

The theoretical NVT that terminates each end of the Telnet connection is a Half Duplex device that uses a *Go Ahead* signal as an invitation for the remote end of the link (as viewed by the sender) to transmit. In practice however, since Telnet operates over TCP, a Full Duplex connection is established that obviously does not require such transmission etiquette. For this reason the *Suppress Go-Ahead* option may be negotiated. Where Suppress Go-Ahead is in effect, the command string IAC GA, is treated as a *No Operation*, and is therefore ignored.

Note 3:

Today, many terminal devices are actually PCs running an emulation package to emulate simple ASCII devices. Most of these emulation packages have multiple emulation modes with vastly differing characteristics. Equally, many of todays host systems are able to control a similarly large variety of terminal types. It therefore follows, that if we have some method by which the server can interrogate the client to determine which emulation(s) are available, we shall be able to select the emulation offering the richest functionality supported by both machines.

The *Terminal Type* option allows the selection of the most applicable terminal type through sub-negotiation and has two sub options, namely, *Send* (value 1), and *Is* (value 0). In use, the server requests an emulation mode with the *Send* option which is responded to with an *Is*. Should the server then wish to continue to determine other available emulations, it will send a further *Send* option to which the response will again be an *Is*. This time however, the response will contain the next available emulation. The following exchange serves to demonstrate this point:

IAC DO *Terminal-Type*   *The server requests the client to accept the option.*

IAC WILL *Terminal-Type*   *The client responds positively –*

	sub-negotiation may now begin at any time.
IAC SB *Terminal-Type* SEND IAC SE	*The server requests the first emulation mode.*
IAC SB *Terminal-Type* IS DEC-VT100 IAC SE	*The client sends its emulation mode.*

Note 4:

When operating in *character* mode, a large amount of network bandwidth is consumed. When placed in context, to transmit a single character using TCP and IP over an Ethernet network there is an overhead of some 63 octets in headers and padding. In addition, if this character is echoed, then the overhead is obviously doubled resulting in possibly 128 octets being transmitted to transfer a single character.

The Telnet Line Mode option allows complete lines of text to be composed at the client terminal and then transmitted as a whole. However, although this results in a reduction in network bandwidth consumed, it also raises other important issues. Firstly, the local terminal must be capable of echoing locally. Secondly, and of equal importance, the terminal must be capable of performing all editing functions. Finally, the client must be able to translate the Telnet commands IP, BRK, AYT, AO, etc. to their local equivalents since these could arrive at any time. Thus, although the Line Mode option has certain benefits, clearly its use places much responsibility at the client process itself.

Note 5:

Currently, Telnet supports a total of 256 options (00_{16} to FF_{16}). The Extended Option List option, although currently unused, is intended to reserve a further 256 option codes that may be used at some later date. The general mechanics of the option are that machines will negotiate whether to use the Extended Option List, and then use sub-negotiation to determine which extended option is to be used. The following perceived exchange illustrates this point:

IAC DO *Extended Option List*
IAC WILL *Extended Option List*
IAC SB *Extended Option List* DO/DON'T/WILL/WON'T *<option>* IAC SE

As will be appreciated, this is for future use and has little relevance today when there is ample option space available.

16.1.6 A Sample Telnet Session

The trace shown in Figure 16-4 shows a Telnet Session between a station and the management port of a router and illustrates option negotiation and simple data transfer. The ARP and TCP session establishment phases have been removed for clarity.

```
============================μscope============================
Frame    : 7              Len      : 67           Error    : None
T Elapsed: 19:04:01:249   T Delta  : 00:00:00:000
----------------------------[mac]----------------------------
Dest Mac : 0000e80f04af   Sourc Mac: Xyplex064892  Type     : IP
-----------------------------[ip]----------------------------
IP Ver   : 4              IP HLen  : 20 Bytes
TOS      : 0x00           Pkt Len  : 49            Seg ID   : 0x004e
Flags    : FRAG:*.LAST    Frag Ptr : 0    (8 Octet) TTL     : 192
PID      : TCP  ( 6)      Checksum : 0x20a1  (Good)
Dst IP <C: 192.168.12.36  Src IP <C: 192.168.12.99
----------------------------[tcp]----------------------------
Src Port : TELNET         Dst Port : 1273
Seq No   : 0x000098ab     Ack No   : 0x00000001
Head Len : 5  words       Flags    : .AP...       Window   : 0x0100
Checksum : 0x7534 (Good)  Urg Ptr  : 0x0000       Options  : None
----------------------[telnet options: 3]--------------------
WILL ECHO ,  DO SUPRESS_GO_AHEAD ,  WILL SUPRESS_GO_AHEAD
=========================[data:   4]=========================
003F  C5 CC 52 85                                  ..R.
```

The router indicates its desire to Echo and to Supress Go Ahead. It also asks that the station Supresses Go Ahead.

```
============================μscope============================
Frame    : 8              Len      : 64           Error    : None
T Elapsed: 19:04:01:277   T Delta  : 00:00:00:028
----------------------------[mac]----------------------------
Dest Mac : Xyplex064892   Sourc Mac: 0000e80f04af  Type     : IP
-----------------------------[ip]----------------------------
IP Ver   : 4              IP HLen  : 20 Bytes
TOS      : 0x00           Pkt Len  : 40            Seg ID   : 0x0003
Flags    : FRAG:*.LAST    Frag Ptr : 0    (8 Octet) TTL     : 32
PID      : TCP  ( 6)      Checksum : 0xf6   (Good)
Dst IP <C: 192.168.12.99  Src IP <C: 192.168.12.36
----------------------------[tcp]----------------------------
Src Port : 1273           Dst Port : TELNET
Seq No   : 0x00000001     Ack No   : 0x000098b4
Head Len : 5  words       Flags    : .AP...       Window   : 0x01f7
Checksum : 0x7638 (Good)  Urg Ptr  : 0x0000       Options  : None
=========================[data:  10]=========================
0036  00 00 00 00 00 00 D8 25 56 A0               .......%V.
```

The station acknowledges the Telnet Negotiation packet.

The station's Window Size dropts to $017F_{16}$.

```
============================μscope============================
Frame    : 9              Len      : 64           Error    : None
T Elapsed: 19:04:01:321   T Delta  : 00:00:00:044
----------------------------[mac]----------------------------
Dest Mac : Xyplex064892   Sourc Mac: 0000e80f04af  Type     : IP
-----------------------------[ip]----------------------------
IP Ver   : 4              IP HLen  : 20 Bytes
TOS      : 0x00           Pkt Len  : 40            Seg ID   : 0x0004
Flags    : FRAG:*.LAST    Frag Ptr : 0    (8 Octet) TTL     : 32
PID      : TCP  ( 6)      Checksum : 0xf5   (Good)
Dst IP <C: 192.168.12.99  Src IP <C: 192.168.12.36
----------------------------[tcp]----------------------------
Src Port : 1273           Dst Port : TELNET
Seq No   : 0x00000001     Ack No   : 0x000098b4
Head Len : 5  words       Flags    : .AP...       Window   : 0x0200
Checksum : 0x762f (Good)  Urg Ptr  : 0x0000       Options  : None
=========================[data:  10]=========================
0036  00 00 00 00 00 00 C2 6D B7 C1               .......m..
```

The station sends a further Acknowledgement segment recovering its Window Size to 0200_{16}.

```
============================μscope============================
Frame    : 10             Len      : 64           Error    : None
T Elapsed: 19:04:01:321   T Delta  : 00:00:00:000
----------------------------[mac]----------------------------
Dest Mac : Xyplex064892   Sourc Mac: 0000e80f04af  Type     : IP
-----------------------------[ip]----------------------------
IP Ver   : 4              IP HLen  : 20 Bytes
TOS      : 0x00           Pkt Len  : 43            Seg ID   : 0x0005
Flags    : FRAG:*.LAST    Frag Ptr : 0    (8 Octet) TTL     : 32
PID      : TCP  ( 6)      Checksum : 0xf1   (Good)
Dst IP <C: 192.168.12.99  Src IP <C: 192.168.12.36
----------------------------[tcp]----------------------------
Src Port : 1273           Dst Port : TELNET
Seq No   : 0x00000001     Ack No   : 0x000098b4
Head Len : 5  words       Flags    : .AP...       Window   : 0x0200
Checksum : 0x752e (Good)  Urg Ptr  : 0x0000       Options  : None
----------------------[telnet options: 1]--------------------
DO ECHO
=========================[data:   7]=========================
0039  00 00 00 C9 42 9E 78                        ....B.x
```

The station acknowledges the routers desire to Echo by issuing a Do Echo.

```
============================μscope============================
Frame    : 11             Len      : 64           Error    : None
T Elapsed: 19:04:01:321   T Delta  : 00:00:00:000
----------------------------[mac]----------------------------
Dest Mac : 0000e80f04af   Sourc Mac: Xyplex064892  Type     : IP
-----------------------------[ip]----------------------------
IP Ver   : 4              IP HLen  : 20 Bytes
TOS      : 0x00           Pkt Len  : 40            Seg ID   : 0x004f
Flags    : FRAG:*.LAST    Frag Ptr : 0    (8 Octet) TTL     : 192
PID      : TCP  ( 6)      Checksum : 0x20a9 (Good)
Dst IP <C: 192.168.12.36  Src IP <C: 192.168.12.99
----------------------------[tcp]----------------------------
Src Port : TELNET         Dst Port : 1273
Seq No   : 0x000098b4     Ack No   : 0x00000004
Head Len : 5  words       Flags    : .A....       Window   : 0x00fd
Checksum : 0x7737 (Good)  Urg Ptr  : 0x0000       Options  : None
=========================[data:  10]=========================
0036  FF FD 01 00 00 00 D9 2A 97 80               .......*..
```

The router acknowledges the Negotiation Segment from the station.

```
```

```
===========================μscope===========================
Frame    : 12              Len      : 64           Error    : None
T Elapsed: 19:04:01:321    T Delta  : 00:00:00:000
---------------------------[mac]---------------------------
Dest Mac : Xyplex064892    Sourc Mac: 0000e80f04af   Type     : IP
---------------------------[ip]----------------------------
IP Ver   : 4               IP HLen  : 20 Bytes
TOS      : 0x00            Pkt Len  : 43            Seg ID   : 0x0006
Flags    : FRAG:*.LAST     Frag Ptr : 0    (8 Octet) TTL     : 32
PID      : TCP ( 6)        Checksum : 0xf0    (Good)
Dst IP <C: 192.168.12.99   Src IP <C: 192.168.12.36
---------------------------[tcp]---------------------------
Src Port : 1273            Dst Port : TELNET
Seq No   : 0x00000004      Ack No   : 0x000098b4
Head Len : 5  words        Flags    : .AP...         Window   : 0x0200
Checksum : 0x732d (Good)   Urg Ptr  : 0x0000         Options  : None
                          -[telnet options: 1]-
WILL SUPRESS_GO_AHEAD
===========================[data:    7]=====================
0039  00 00 00 B0 1E 19 7B                   ......{
```

The station indicates its willingness to Supress Go Ahead as requested by the router.

```
===========================μscope===========================
Frame    : 13              Len      : 64           Error    : None
T Elapsed: 19:04:01:321    T Delta  : 00:00:00:000
---------------------------[mac]---------------------------
Dest Mac : 0000e80f04af    Sourc Mac: Xyplex064892   Type     : IP
---------------------------[ip]----------------------------
IP Ver   : 4               IP HLen  : 20 Bytes
TOS      : 0x00            Pkt Len  : 40            Seg ID   : 0x0050
Flags    : FRAG:*.LAST     Frag Ptr : 0    (8 Octet) TTL     : 192
PID      : TCP ( 6)        Checksum : 0x20a8 (Good)
Dst IP <C: 192.168.12.36   Src IP <C: 192.168.12.99
---------------------------[tcp]---------------------------
Src Port : TELNET          Dst Port : 1273
Seq No   : 0x000098b4      Ack No   : 0x00000007
Head Len : 5  words        Flags    : .A....         Window   : 0x00fd
Checksum : 0x7734 (Good)   Urg Ptr  : 0x0000         Options  : None
===========================[data:   10]=====================
0036  FF FB 03 00 00 00 36 0B CC C0           ......6...
```

The router sends an Acknowledgement to the station's segment.

The router's Window has shrunk to $00FD_{16}$.

```
===========================μscope===========================
Frame    : 14              Len      : 64           Error    : None
T Elapsed: 19:04:01:331    T Delta  : 00:00:00:010
---------------------------[mac]---------------------------
Dest Mac : Xyplex064892    Sourc Mac: 0000e80f04af   Type     : IP
---------------------------[ip]----------------------------
IP Ver   : 4               IP HLen  : 20 Bytes
TOS      : 0x00            Pkt Len  : 43            Seg ID   : 0x0007
Flags    : FRAG:*.LAST     Frag Ptr : 0    (8 Octet) TTL     : 32
PID      : TCP ( 6)        Checksum : 0xef    (Good)
Dst IP <C: 192.168.12.99   Src IP <C: 192.168.12.36
---------------------------[tcp]---------------------------
Src Port : 1273            Dst Port : TELNET
Seq No   : 0x00000007      Ack No   : 0x000098b4
Head Len : 5  words        Flags    : .AP...         Window   : 0x0200
Checksum : 0x7328 (Good)   Urg Ptr  : 0x0000         Options  : None
                          -[telnet options: 1]-
DO SUPRESS_GO_AHEAD
===========================[data:    7]=====================
0039  00 00 00 A2 30 79 73                   ....0ys
```

The station acknowledges that the router should Supress Go Ahead.

```
===========================μscope===========================
Frame    : 15              Len      : 64           Error    : None
T Elapsed: 19:04:01:331    T Delta  : 00:00:00:000
---------------------------[mac]---------------------------
Dest Mac : 0000e80f04af    Sourc Mac: Xyplex064892   Type     : IP
---------------------------[ip]----------------------------
IP Ver   : 4               IP HLen  : 20 Bytes
TOS      : 0x00            Pkt Len  : 40            Seg ID   : 0x0051
Flags    : FRAG:*.LAST     Frag Ptr : 0    (8 Octet) TTL     : 192
PID      : TCP ( 6)        Checksum : 0x20a7 (Good)
Dst IP <C: 192.168.12.36   Src IP <C: 192.168.12.99
---------------------------[tcp]---------------------------
Src Port : TELNET          Dst Port : 1273
Seq No   : 0x000098b4      Ack No   : 0x0000000a
Head Len : 5  words        Flags    : .A....         Window   : 0x00fd
Checksum : 0x7731 (Good)   Urg Ptr  : 0x0000         Options  : None
===========================[data:   10]=====================
0036  FF FD 03 00 00 00 CA 95 0E D8           .........
```

The router Acknowledges the station's segment.

The router's Window remains at $00FD_{16}$.

```
===========================μscope===========================
Frame    : 16              Len      : 64           Error    : None
T Elapsed: 19:04:05:600    T Delta  : 00:00:04:269
---------------------------[mac]---------------------------
Dest Mac : Xyplex064892    Sourc Mac: 0000e80f04af   Type     : IP
---------------------------[ip]----------------------------
IP Ver   : 4               IP HLen  : 20 Bytes
TOS      : 0x00            Pkt Len  : 41            Seg ID   : 0x0008
Flags    : FRAG:*.LAST     Frag Ptr : 0    (8 Octet) TTL     : 32
PID      : TCP ( 6)        Checksum : 0xf0    (Good)
Dst IP <C: 192.168.12.99   Src IP <C: 192.168.12.36
---------------------------[tcp]---------------------------
Src Port : 1273            Dst Port : TELNET
Seq No   : 0x0000000a      Ack No   : 0x000098b4
Head Len : 5  words        Flags    : .AP...         Window   : 0x0200
Checksum : 0x6925 (Good)   Urg Ptr  : 0x0000         Options  : None
===========================[data:   10]=====================
0036  0D 00 00 00 00 00 50 D5 86 AF           ......P...
```

The station sends an Acknowledgement.

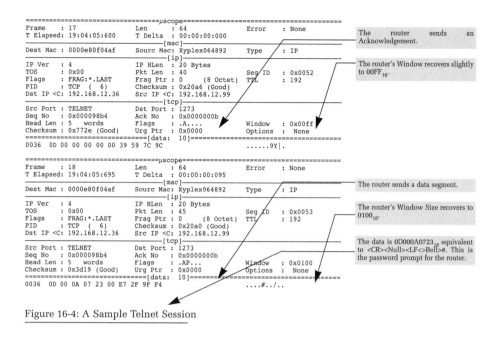

```
========================================μscope=======================================
Frame   : 17        Len     : 64          Error    : None
T Elapsed: 19:04:05:600   T Delta : 00:00:00:000
                              ----[mac]----
Dest Mac : 0000e80f04af   Sourc Mac: Xyplex064892   Type    : IP
                              ----[ip]----
IP Ver  : 4          IP HLen : 20 Bytes
TOS     : 0x00       Pkt Len : 40         Seg ID   : 0x0052
Flags   : FRAG:*.LAST   Frag Ptr : 0      (8 Octet)  TTL      : 192
PID     : TCP  ( 6)  Checksum : 0x20a6 (Good)
Dst IP <C: 192.168.12.36   Src IP <C: 192.168.12.99
                              ----[tcp]----
Src Port : TELNET    Dst Port : 1273
Seq No   : 0x000098b4   Ack No   : 0x0000000b
Head Len : 5   words   Flags    : .A....      Window   : 0x00ff
Checksum : 0x772e (Good)   Urg Ptr  : 0x0000      Options  : None
=============================[data: 10]=============================
0036  0D 00 00 00 00 00 39 59 7C 9C              ......9Y|.

========================================μscope=======================================
Frame   : 18        Len     : 64          Error    : None
T Elapsed: 19:04:05:695   T Delta : 00:00:00:095
                              ----[mac]----
Dest Mac : 0000e80f04af   Sourc Mac: Xyplex064892   Type    : IP
                              ----[ip]----
IP Ver  : 4          IP HLen : 20 Bytes
TOS     : 0x00       Pkt Len : 45         Seg ID   : 0x0053
Flags   : FRAG:*.LAST   Frag Ptr : 0      (8 Octet)  TTL      : 192
PID     : TCP  ( 6)  Checksum : 0x20a0 (Good)
Dst IP <C: 192.168.12.36   Src IP <C: 192.168.12.99
                              ----[tcp]----
Src Port : TELNET    Dst Port : 1273
Seq No   : 0x000098b4   Ack No   : 0x0000000b
Head Len : 5   words   Flags    : .AP...      Window   : 0x0100
Checksum : 0x3d19 (Good)   Urg Ptr  : 0x0000      Options  : None
=============================[data: 10]=============================
0036  0D 00 0A 07 23 00 E7 2F 9F F4              ....#../..
```

The router sends an Acknowledgement.

The router's Window recovers slightly to $00FF_{16}$.

The router sends a data segment.

The router's Window Size recovers to 0100_{16}.

The data is $0D000A0723_{16}$ equivalent to <CR><Null><LF><>Bell>#. This is the password prompt for the router.

Figure 16-4: A Sample Telnet Session

16.2 Rlogin

Rlogin, it should be noted is not an Internet *Standard* protocol, but instead is offered in Berkeley BSD 4 UNIX systems. Due to the wide implementation of BSD 4, the protocol is used extensively in networks that have a predominance of UNIX hosts. In short, the protocol provides a Telnet like environment that relies on both remote echo and local flow control, but most importantly makes use of more of the UNIX terminal environment than its sister protocol. Finally, since Rlogin introduces a concept of *trusted hosts*, many UNIX systems can be configured in such a way that users do not need to enter passwords when connecting to a remote host with this protocol.

Rlogin connections, like their Telnet counterparts, use a TCP connection. However, with Rlogin the listener port used is 513_{10} (0201_{16}). After a connection has been established to this port, the client then sends four null terminated strings as follows:

*<null>*client-user-name*<null>*server-user-name*<null>*terminal-type/speed*<null>*

You will notice that the first of these strings is, in fact, empty. The other strings then contain the name of the user on the local (client) system, the name that should be used to access the server, and finally the terminal type and speed. In response, the server sends a single null character to indicate that it has received the initial information, and enters data transfer mode. The negotiation of window[1]

1. The window size negotiated here has nothing to do with flow control but instead refers to the size of window displayed at the client terminal.

size may now follow. This facility is discussed in the next section.

16.2.1 Rlogin Commands

As with Telnet, data is normally sent as a stream to the client's screen. Some processing, such as the expansion of tabs, may be required before the data can actually be displayed, however since this is a *local issue*, we shall ignore it for the purposes of our discussion. Within this data stream, the server can imbed control octets that require the client to take some action. In contrast to Telnet though, clients never enter into negotiation over *options*.

Where the server wishes the client to take an action, it will imbed a single octet control character into the data stream, set the TCP *Urgent* flag (URG) and, use the *Urgent Pointer* to indicate the position of the control octet. The client should then act upon this information before processing the rest of the data stream as defined by TCP. The four control octets are defined in Table 16-4.

Table 16-4: Rlogin Control Octets

Code Decimal	Code Hex	Description
02	02	Causes the client to discard all buffered data received from the server that has not been written to the screen.
16	10	Instructs the client to switch to raw mode. In this mode, the Start and Stop flow control characters are not handled locally but are instead treated as raw data.
32	20	Instructs the client to switch to cooked mode. In this mode, the Start and Stop flow control characters are processed locally. This is the default mode of operation.
128	80	Requests that the client sends its current window size – see below.

If the server has signalled that it is happy to accept client window size changes, the client can then send a special string of 12 octets whenever such screen or window size changes occur. This special string, always starting with the sequence FFFF, is shown below:

FF FF s s rr cc xp yp

The two octets FFFF are followed by two octets (16 bits) each containing a single ASCII lower-case 's'. It is envisaged that, should the need arise, further control sequences could be used by replacing these 's' characters. The remaining fields are then each two octets (16 bits) in length as follows: 'rr' indicates the number of character rows available. 'cc' indicates the number of character columns. 'xp' indicates the number of pixels in the X direction, and 'yp' the number of pixels in the Y direction.

16.2.2 Rlogin Security Considerations

While Rlogin has achieved great popularity based upon its ease of use, it must be stressed that the penalty for such ease is at the expense of security. As we mentioned at the start of this section, many implementations of Rlogin allow users to connect from trusted hosts without the need to enter a password. This has the disadvantage that should one system become compromised, ALL systems will equally be open to potential attack.

16.3 Summary

The Telnet protocol defines a standardized method for connecting systems together using a virtual terminal emulation, or Network Virtual Terminal (NVT) and normally an application of the same name. In the early days of the Internet, there was really only Telnet and the File Transfer Protocol, (FTP) of course today, many more protocols exist. The very essence of the Internet Protocol Suite relies on the easy connection of Internet host. Telnet (and it's BSD 4 enhancement Rlogin) epitomizes this premise and allows users to gain access to network hosts as if connected locally. In truth, Telnet, FTP, and Mail could be said to be the major application protocols in use or at the very least the starting points for such things as the Hyper Text Transfer Protocol (HTTP) as used on the World Wide Web.

Telnet is not simply defined by a single document. Unlike other protocols that have evolved as a single entity, Telnet has had functionality added as time has passed. Many RFCs have been written that have added functionality as we have seen although in truth, Telnet has also been the victim of some jokes.

For example, RFC 1097 (Telnet Subliminal Message Option) is dated 1 April 1989 and pokes fun at Telnet option negotiation. In reality of course, any protocol that uses commands such as Do, Don't, Will, and Won't must deserve some comment. However, the designers of the Telnet protocol have certainly produced a reliable and robust protocol that uses the minimum of host resource yet provides a maximum of functionality.

Finally, Telnet (and indeed Rlogin) provides for *in-band* option negotiation at any time during the life of the connection and, by using a flow controlled, reliable TCP connection, ensures that no data is lost. In all, when we consider the age of Telnet, it has to be considered an elder statesman of application protocols.

The File Transfer Protocol (FTP)

CHAPTER 17

The File Transfer Protocol (FTP) is one of the original protocols in the Internet Protocol Suite. It was developed to allow the sharing of files and to encourage the use of remote computers by a reliable and efficient means. Ideas that, at least on the surface, would seem fairly obvious. What may not be immediately apparent however, is that the protocol must shield the user from the vast differences in file storage methods, and provide a simple set of universally agreed commands. Likewise, the protocol must honor the security of the end systems in terms of file ownership, and access protection.

The first proposal for a file transfer mechanism appeared in 1971 (RFC 114). The current RFC, RFC 959 expands greatly on these original ideas and provides us with an application protocol that uses the robust and reliable Transmission Control Protocol (TCP). In addition, FTP uses many principles found in other protocols. For example, FTP uses a *Control connection* over which the Telnet protocol is used.

17.1 FTP Basic Operation

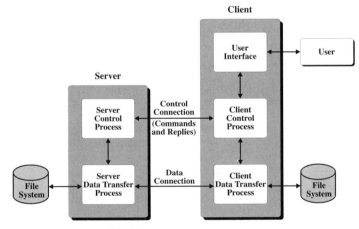

Figure 17-1: FTP Model of Operation

FTP is based upon a client-server model with clients transferring files to (*PUT*ting) and from (*GET*ting) the server. Two connections are in use during an FTP session.

One to convey standard FTP commands and responses (the *Control* connection), and one for the actual transfer of data (the *Data* connection). Figure 17-1 shows this in operation.

In our model then, the Client Control Process, at the user's instigation, establishes the Control Connection over which standard FTP commands and responses are sent. The Control connection must remain open at all times that commands and/or data are being transferred. Failure to maintain this connection results in the FTP Data connection being closed and the session aborted.

FTP commands specify the parameters for the data transfer (transfer mode, data representation, and file structure), and the actual operation to be performed (store, retrieve, etc.). Once the operation and the associated parameters have been conveyed, the Client then listens on a pre-defined TCP port and the Server initiates the data connection. At this point though it is worth noting two important variations.

Firstly, FTP does not require the Data Connection to be established between the server and the host that initiated the FTP commands. A user FTP process must however ensure that one of the third-party machines listens on a designated port, and that the other initiates the Data Connection. Here, the user establishes a Control connection with both servers, and then arranges for the establishment of a Data connection between them. Figure 17-2 demonstrates this particular scenario.

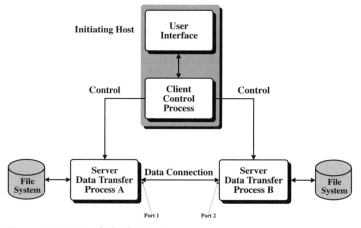

Figure 17-2: FTP and Third Party Hosts

Secondly, with security high on the agenda of most companies today, there exists a variant that allows the client to initiate the data connection. In this way the client machine is in control of the port numbers in use over both the control and data connections, and thereby provides the network administrator with greater control. This is referred to as a FTP Passive Open.

17.2 Data Transfer Functions

As we have said, data is only ever transferred over the Data connection with the Control connection being used solely for the transfer of commands, their associated replies, and any other status information necessary. Data is transferred from the File System on the sending host, however it is often necessary to perform transformations on the data at the receiving host depending upon its representation. Commands are used that specify the *Mode* (the number of bits that should be transmitted), the *STRU*ture of the file, and whether or not the data is stored in a compressed format. Equally, where binary data is to be transferred, this causes its own problems since it will not be immediately clear how the data should be represented.

17.2.1 Data Types

FTP supports a multitude of different data types that describe the code set used to represent the stored data. Of all those specified, by far the two most common are the *ASCII* representation and the *IMAGE*, or *BINARY* representation and it is these that we shall discuss in detail here. Other representations that may be found for example include *LOCAL* where data is transferred in an octet size specified by the user, and EBCDIC which is intended for the efficient transfer of data between hosts that employ EBCDIC character representation.

ASCII representation is the default mode and all FTP implementation must support this. Here, where appropriate, the sender converts the stored data from its internal representation to standard NVT-ASCII as used by the TELNET protocol. On receipt, the receiving host will then convert the data from this standard form to whatever format is required. In adhering to the NVT-ASCII standard,[1] the <CRLF> sequence is used to denote the end of a line of text, and all data is represented in 8 bit octets. The IMAGE type (sometimes referred to as BINARY) demands that all data is transferred as contiguous bits and, as with ASCII, all FTP implementations must support this type. With the IMAGE type, the storage system structure may require that the records, or indeed the file, be padded. Where this is the case, the padding used must be all zeroes, and the method of padding must be known to the host that is storing the data.

With ASCII (and EBCDIC) types, a further parameter that defines the vertical format control may be specified. However, to understand the motivation for this, we should first consider the reasons why files are transferred between hosts in the first place.

A file will be transferred for either printing, storage (and subsequent retrieval), or for processing. If we are transferring a file for printing, then it is imperative that we know how vertical format control characters are represented. If we are transferring the file for storage, it is assumed that we shall wish to retrieve it at some time in the future in exactly the same form. Finally, where we are transferring the file for processing, the target host should be able to process the file without undue problems. Merely specifying that the file is represented by the ASCII or EBCDIC codes will not, in itself, satisfy these requirements. Thus FTP defines three formats as follows:

- **Non-Print**: The default format and one that must be accepted by all implementations of FTP. In this case, the file is assumed to have no vertical format

---

1. See Chapter 16 Telnet and Rlogin for a discussion of the NVT-ASCII standard.

information and when it is passed to a printer process, standard spacing, tab, and margin values should be used. This format is normally used for all files that are transferred for either processing or storage.

- **Telnet Format Controls**: In this case the file will be assumed to contain standard ASCII/EBCDIC vertical format controls such as <CR>, <LF>, <NL>, <FF>, etc. and should be interpreted by any printer process accordingly. In addition the sequence <CRLF>, is used to denote the end-of-line sequence.

- **Carriage Control (ASA)**: Here the file will contain ASA (FORTRAN) vertical format control sequences and vertical movement should be interpreted in accordance with the ASA standard. In this particular case, the first character of the record is used to determine the vertical movement of the paper before the rest of the record is printed. Within the ASA standard, a blank specifies that the paper should be moved up one line, a '0' specifies that the paper should be moved two lines, a '1', that the paper should be moved to the top of the next page, and a '+' that no movement should take place.

  Clearly where printing is record oriented in this way, there has to be some way that a printer can distinguish between these records. FTP defines three explicit data structures. One of these is the *Record Structure* where each record is marked during transfer thus keeping logical records together. Where no formal internal file structure exists, we then rely on the <CRLF> sequence to define ends of lines, however any format control characters as defined above would then take precedence.

17.2.2 Data Structures

As we have just seen, FTP allows the structure of a file to be specified. In total three such file structures are defined allowing us to distinguish the way in which data is actual stored:

- **File Structure**: This is the default specifying that no internal structure exists and that the file should be considered as a continuous stream of data octets.

- **Record Structure**: Identifies that the file comprises a number of sequential records.

- **Page Structure**: This is used to describe files that are discontinuous or random access. Normally associated with files of this type, there is further information that describes the file as a whole (a *file descriptor*), or a section of the file (typically known as a *page descriptor*). In order to accommodate the multitude of possible *page sizes*, each *page* is transmitted with a page header that is defined as shown in Figure 17-3.

Header Length	Page Index	Data Length	Page Type	Optional Fields

Figure 17-3: The Page Header

The File Transfer Protocol (FTP)

The *Header Length* contains the number of logical octets that comprise the page header including this octet. The *Page Index* is the logical page number of this section of the file. This is not necessarily the transmission sequence but is used to identify this page of the file. The *Data Length* provides the number of logical octets in this data page. The *Page Type* indicates what type of page is being transmitted:

Page Type 0: Indicates that this is the last page. In this case, the Header Length is 4, and the Data Length is zero.

Page Type 1: Indicates that a Simple Page is being transmitted and that no page level control information is required. Here, as with the last page, no Optional field(s) will be present.

Page Type 2: A Descriptor page is transmitted that describes the whole file.

Page Type 3: The Page being transmitted is Access Controlled. In this case, an Optional field will be present indicating the Access Control of the transmitted page. Thus the Header Length field must indicate at least 5 octets.

17.3 FTP Transmission Modes

FTP supports three modes for the efficient transmission of data. One formats the data, a second also compresses the data, and a third passes data with little or no processing at all. Whatever mode is employed, all transfers are terminated with an End-of-file (EOF) that is either explicitly stated (as in the case of the last page for files with Page Structure), or is implicit with the closing of the data connection. In order to allow for standardized data transfer, the transmitting host will translate its own internal end of line (or end of record) designation to that required by the transfer mode and structure. On receipt, the receiving host performs an inverse operation substituting the standard delimiter for that required by its own file system.

17.3.1 Stream Mode

In this case, the data is transmitted as a stream of octets. No restrictions are placed on the representation type used and, where required, record structures are allowed. Where a record structured file is to be transmitted, the ends of records (EORs) and the end of the file (EOF) are indicated by a simple two octet control code. In this control code, the first octet will have all bits set *on* indicating the Escape character. Then, for an EOR, the second octet will have the low order 1 bit *on* to indicate an EOR (value 01), and the low order 2 bit *on* to indicate EOF (value 02). To indicate both EOR and EOF together, both the low order 1 and 2 bits are turned *on* (value 03) however, this is only allowable as the last octet of data.

So what happens when we wish to transmit a legitimate FF as a data octet? Here we use the control octets again but this time both are set with all bits on (FFFF).

If the file is of structure type *File Structure*, no EOR is required but EOF must be indicated. In this case, EOF is implied by simply closing the data connection and no control octets are used at all.

17.3.2 Block Mode

In this mode, data is transferred as a series of data blocks that are preceded by three header octets. The header, shown in Figure 17-4, comprises a *Count* field to indicate the total length of the block and therefore where the next block starts, and a descriptor code that defines EOR, EOF, a Restart Marker, and whether or not the data contained should be considered as being suspect. Equally, any other pertinent information could be described here. As with the Stream Mode, Record Structures are allowed, and any representation type can be used. The descriptor codes (specified in decimal to represent the corresponding bit in the octet) are indicated through flag bits as follows. Note that by using bits in this way, any combination of codes may also be expressed.

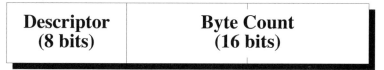

Descriptor (8 bits)	Byte Count (16 bits)

Figure 17-4: Block Mode Header

128   An End of Record is indicated. Here, the EOR is at the end of this data block.

64   The End of this data block is to be treated as the End-of-File (EOF).

32   Suspected errors in the data. This is not used to detect errors in the transmitted data stream, since this function is part of TCP. Instead, where this flag is set, it indicates that the transmitting host believes that the data retrieved from its file system may be unreliable.

16   This data block is a *Restart marker*. A Restart Marker is embedded into the data stream as a number of 8 bit octets that represent printable (but not space) characters. The marker itself could represent an octet or record count, or any other information that a system could use to identify a checkpoint. When the receiver receives this string, it then marks the corresponding position of this checkpoint in the received data stream and informs the user. In the event of failure, the user can then use this information to identify where the transfer had reached, and recommence data transfer from this point. For example, to transmit a three octet marker, the block would be as shown in Figure 17-5.

Descriptor (8 bits Value=16)	Byte Count (16 bits, Value=6)	Marker (8 bits)	Marker (8 bits)	Marker (8 bits)

Figure 17-5: Markers

17.3.3 Compressed Mode

Compressed mode is useful for obtaining increased bandwidth (particularly for large transmissions over slow links) with only little CPU overhead. In this mode we must consider three distinct types of data that may be sent, namely *regular* (uncompressible) data that is sent in octet strings, *compressed* data, and *control* information sent in escape sequences. Where we wish to transmit 0 to 127 octets of standard (non compressible) data, we precede the data with a single octet with its highest order bit set to zero, and the remaining seven bits set to reflect the number of octets that follow. Figure 17-6 shows this.

The File Transfer Protocol (FTP)

Figure 17-6: Standard (non compressed) Data

Where data can be compressed, we are able to compress up to 63 octets of the same data into two octets as shown in Figure 17-7. In this case a single octet of data that represents the string to be compressed is preceded by an octet with the highest order two bits set to 10, and the remaining six bits set to indicate how many replications are required.

Figure 17-7: Compressed and Filler Data

Equally, if we are to transmit filler, then we may compress up to 63 octets of this in a single octet with the two highest order bits set on, and the remaining six bits set to represent the number of filler octets required. The actual filler octet used will vary with the representation selected. For example, ASCII and EBCDIC, use the space character, and IMAGE uses the zero byte.

17.4 File Transfer Functions

Communications between the User Control Process, and the Server Control Process is over the Control connection that is established as a standard TCP connection and uses the Telnet protocol. Some of the most common commands[2] are listed in the following sections, together with brief descriptions.

17.4.1 Access Control Commands

To gain access to the transfer environment, a number of commands are used. These commands are shown in Table 17-1 together with a brief description.

Table 17-1: Access Control Commands

Command	Meaning	Description
USER	Enter a username	Allows the user to identify him/herself and thereby gain access to the servers file system. Typically, the actual username will be supplied as an argument to the USER command. Many implementations allow the user to change the username in use thus allowing different privileges and accounting information.

2. Most FTP implementations today are based on a graphical user interface (GUI). Thus, these commands generally tend to be hidden from the user. When using a *command line* implementation however, it is these commands (or similar) and responses that are used.

Command	Meaning	Description
PASS	Enter a password	Allows the user to enter a password that authenticates the USER information previously entered. Some implementations automatically ask for a password immediately after the user has entered the USER command and suppresses echo at this time.
ACCT	Enter Account information	This command (sometimes entered in full – ACCOUNT) identifies the users account. For instance many anonymous FTP sites on the Internet allow only restricted access to general users however, those that identify themselves with the ACCT command are then able to access private directories.
CWD	Change Working Directory	Allows the user to navigate to a different directory. This command requires an argument that then specifies the target directory. In some implementations this command is abbreviated to the UNIX cd command.
CDUP	Change to Parent Directory	This allows the user to easily change to the Parent directory.
SMNT	Structure Mount	Allows the user to mount a different file system data structure. Many implementations use the command STRUCT for this. In all cases, the command takes an argument that defines the actual structure name.
REIN	Reinitialize	This command terminates the current user and resets the control connection to the state that it was in immediately after the control connection was initialised. The USER command should be the next command issued.
LOGOUT	Logs the user out	This command terminates the user, the control connection and the data connection.

17.4.2 Transfer Parameters

Unlike the access control parameters, most transfer parameters have default values and any arguments are only required where the default is *not* to be used. Standard values are defined by Table 17-2.

Table 17-2: FTP Transfer Parameters

Command	Meaning	Default	Description
PORT	Defines the Host port for the data connection		Under normal use, this command is not required since default TCP listener ports are defined for both the user and server data ports. These can be changed, with the PORT command.
PASV	Defines a Passive listener port		Requests that the server data transfer process listens on a specified port rather than initiate a data connection. This is used where a third party host is used (see Fig. 17-2).
TYPE	Specify the representation of the data	ASCII	This allows the user to specify a particular representation of data. As we have seen, a representation on its own is not necessarily sufficient, therefore a second parameter (the vertical format) may also be specified.

The File Transfer Protocol (FTP)

Command	Meaning	Default	Description
STRU	Define the file structure	FILE	The argument supplied with this command is a single character as follows: F – File (no internal structure) R – Record structure P – Page structure
MODE	Specify the transfer mode	STREAM	This command, together with its associated argument, defines the transfer mode: S – Stream B – Block C – Compressed

17.4.3 FTP Service Commands

It is through the Service Commands that the actual transfer is initiated. All data transfer takes place over the data connection and normally requires arguments that define the filename and, optional, pathname. These are described in Table 17-3.

Table 17-3: FTP Service Commands

Command	Description
RETR	This command retrieves (GETs) a copy of the file from the servers file system and stores it on the client file system. On many implementations, this command is replaced with GET. Equally some implementations support a multiple GET function (mget) that allows the retrieval of multiple files.
STOR	Using this command causes the client to transfer a copy of the named file to the server. Many implementations use the PUT command in preference to this.
STOU	This command behaves in a similar fashion to the STOR command except that in this case the file is stored with a name that is unique within the directory.
APPE	Again operating in a similar manner to STOR, this command causes a copy of the file specified to be transferred to the server. In this instance however, if a file of that name already exists, the data from the transferred file is appended to it.
ALLO	Only required by some servers, this command is used to allocate sufficient space to accommodate the new file. This command requires an argument defining a decimal integer that then represents the number of octets that should be reserved.
REST	Where markers have been used in a data stream, the argument associated with this command (the marker pattern) causes the server to skip over the file to the relevant position. The command is followed by relevant transfer commands to resume transfer.
RNFR	This command specifies a path and filename of a file that is to be renamed. By itself, this command has no immediate effect, instead it is followed by a RNTO (rename to) command that specifies the new name.
RNTO	Used with the RNFR (rename from) command, this command changes the name of a file.
ABOR	The Abort command informs the server that it should abort the previous FTP command and any associated data transfer.
DELE	This command causes the specified file to be deleted at the server site.
RMD	This command (actually remove directory) removes the directory at the server site.
MKD	Causes the directory specified in the pathname to be created.
PWD	The Print Working Directory command causes the name of the current working directory to be returned in the reply.
LIST	The list command (also known as ls, or dir) lists the contents of the current directory or returns information about the file if a filename is specified as an argument.

Command	Description
NLST	This command causes a directory listing to be sent from the server to the client site. With this command, only filenames are returned.
SITE	Used with site specific commands that may be essential for data transfer but are not part of the FTP specification.
SYST	This command is used to determine the operating system in use at the server.
STAT	This command is used to solicit a status response from the server. If the command is sent during a transfer, the reply will indicate the status of that transfer. If the command is sent between transfers, an argument may also be supplied such as a partial filename. In this case, depending upon the implementation, the response may be a complete list of all files that match the partial name.
HELP	Causes a list of FTP commands to be displayed.
NOOP	This command has no effect on any parameters or previously entered commands. Instead, the No-Operation merely causes the server to send an OK response.

17.5 FTP Responses

All FTP commands generate responses that are numeric and, normally, textual. The reason for this dual approach to command responses is that the numeric response is designed for automated processes, while the associated text is for human operators. Most FTP responses comprise a three digit code, followed by a space and a single line of text. This is then delimited by a TELNET end-of-line code. The FTP recommendations do allow for multiple line responses however, in this case the initial space is replaced by a hyphen that is then followed by multiple text lines. To signal to the receiver that the text has finished, the last line will also contain the response code, a space, and finally the last line of text. Since the textual response is, to some extent, implementation specific, we shall discuss the numeric responses and examine these in detail.

Each position within our three digit response code has significance. For example, the first digit of the reply code has five possible values. These values are then listed below:

- **1yz**   Positive Preliminary Reply
  The command that was requested is being actioned. The user should expect another reply before issuing any further commands.

- **2yz**   Positive Completion Reply
  The requested action has been successfully completed and a new command may now be issued.

- **3yz**   Positive Intermediate Reply
  The last command has been accepted, however it is currently not being actioned since further information is required. In this instance, the user is expected to issue a further command that specifies the required information.

- **4yz**   Transient Negative Completion Reply
  The command has not been accepted and therefore the requested action has not taken place. A response of this type neither indicates a problem nor an error in the syntax of the command. In this case, the error is considered transitory and the user process should re-commence sending the last command sequence.

- **5yz**   Permanent Negative Completion Reply

The command has not been accepted and therefore the requested action has not taken place. 5 series responses are normally the result of a permanent error either within the syntax of the command, or a hard error at the server or client site. In any event, the user should remedy the fault before attempting the command sequence again.

The second digit is used to further specify the types of error. Again five such digits are specified although please note that x4z is currently undefined.

- **x0z**   Syntax

Replies with the second digit set to 0 relate to syntax errors, syntactically correct commands that do not fit any functional category, un-implemented, and suplerfluous commands.

- **x1z**   Information

Replies of this type are responses to requests for information such as Status, or Help.

- **x2z**   Connections

These replies relate solely to control and data connections.

- **x3z**   Authentication and Accounting

These are replies to the login process and accounting procedures.

- **x5z**   File System

These replies indicate the status of the servers file system. Typically these responses may be received after requesting a file transfer or other action.

The third digit provides yet further information regarding the response as expanded upon with the second digit. To see how these function, it is better to look at a complete list of FTP responses as shown Table 17-4.

Table 17-4: FTP Responses

Reply Code	Meaning
110	Restart Marker reply. In this case the textual response will be of the form MARK ssss = cccc where ssss is the server's data stream marker, and cccc is the data stream marker for the client.
120	Service ready in nnn minutes.
125	Data connection already open, transfer commencing.
150	File status OK, about to open data connection.
200	Command OK.
202	Command not implemented, or superfluous at this site.
211	System Status or System Help reply.
212	Directory status.
213	File status.
214	Help message. This reply is only useful to human operators since it is in response to a specific help request on a particular command.
215	NAME system type where NAME is an official system name from the list in the assigned numbers document.
220	Service ready for new user.

Reply Code	Meaning
221	Service closing control connection. The user will be logged out if appropriate.
225	Data connection open, no transfer in progress.
226	Closing data connection. Requested file action successful.
227	Entering Passive mode.
230	User logged in – proceed.
250	Requested file action OK – completed.
257	"Pathname" created.
331	User name OK, need password.
332	Need account for login.
350	Requested file action pending further information.
421	Service not available, closing control connection. This is allowable as a response to any command where the service knows that it must shut down.
425	Cannot open data connection.
426	Connection closed, transfer aborted.
450	Requested file action not taken – file unavailable (i.e. busy).
451	Requested action aborted, local error in processing.
452	Requested action not taken, insufficient storage space.
500	Syntax error – command unrecognized.
501	Syntax error in parameters or arguments.
502	Command not implemented.
503	Bad sequence of commands.
504	Command not implemented for that parameter.
530	Not logged in.
532	Need account for storing files.
550	Requested action not taken – file unavailable (e.g. File not found, insufficient privilege).
551	Requested action aborted, page type unknown.
552	Requested file action aborted – storage allocation exceeded.
553	Requested action not taken – file name not allowed.

17.6 A Complete FTP Example

The trace of Figure 17-8 shows a typical FTP session that lists the contents of the target directory. In this example we have a station at IP Address 192.168.12.36, and a server at 192.168.12.171. This trace is important since it demontstrates all of the features of FTP, with Control and Data Session establishment and Data Session termination.

```
µSCOPE              PACKET TRACE DECODE REPORT          (c) T.Kenyon 1995


=============================µscope=============================
Frame     : 3           Len     : 64          Error    : None
T Elapsed: 19:34:58:100  T Delta  : 00:00:00:008
                          ------[mac]------
Dest Mac : Sun   1bc95a  Sourc Mac: 0000e80f04af   Type    : IP
                          ------[ip]------
IP Ver    : 4            IP HLen  : 20 Bytes
TOS       : 0x00         Pkt Len  : 44           Seg ID   : 0x0001
Flags     : FRAG:Ä.LAST  Frag Ptr : 0    (8 Octet)  TTL      : 32
PID       : TCP ( 6)     Checksum : 0xac   (Good)
Dst IP <C: 192.168.12.171 Src IP <C: 192.168.12.36
                          ------[tcp]------
Src Port : 1300          Dst Port : FTP.Ctrl
Seq No   : 0x00000000    Ack No   : 0x00000000
Head Len : 6  words      Flags    : ....S.       Window   : 0x1000
Checksum : 0xe8dd (Good) Urg Ptr  : 0x0000       Options  : Present
                          ----[options]----
Option    : MaxSegSize   Length   : 4            Value    : 05b4
=========================[data:   6]=============================
003A  00 00 6A 5A C6 86                    ..jZ..
```

The Station needs a SYN segment to the server's FTP Control Port (21_{10}).

Maximum Segment Size set to $5B4_{16}$.

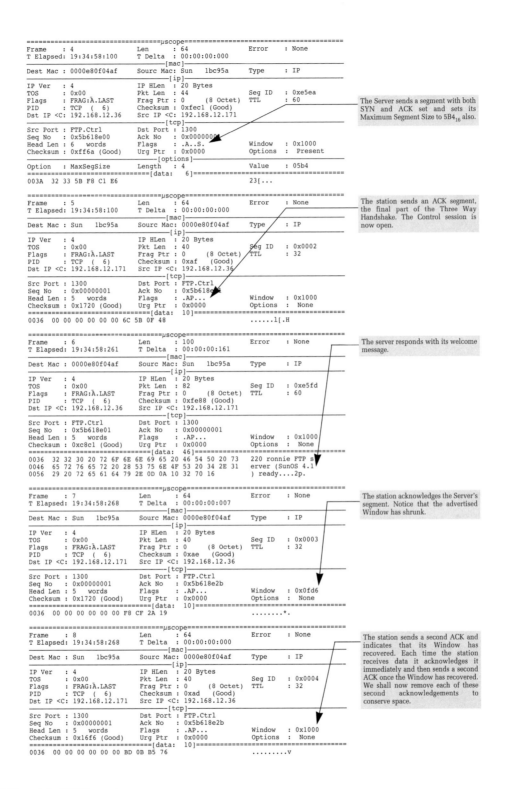

```
=========================================μscope=========================================
Frame    : 4               Len      : 64           Error      : None
T Elapsed: 19:34:58:100    T Delta  : 00:00:00:000
------------------------------------[mac]-----------------------------------
Dest Mac : 0000e80f04af    Sourc Mac: Sun   1bc95a  Type      : IP
------------------------------------[ip]------------------------------------
IP Ver   : 4               IP HLen  : 20 Bytes
TOS      : 0x00            Pkt Len  : 44            Seg ID    : 0xe5ea
Flags    : FRAG:À.LAST     Frag Ptr : 0     (8 Octet) TTL       : 60
PID      : TCP  ( 6)       Checksum : 0xfec1 (Good)
Dst IP <C: 192.168.12.36   Src IP <C: 192.168.12.171
------------------------------------[tcp]-----------------------------------
Src Port : FTP.Ctrl        Dst Port : 1300
Seq No   : 0x5b618e00      Ack No   : 0x00000000
Head Len : 6    words      Flags    : .A..S.         Window    : 0x1000
Checksum : 0xff6a (Good)   Urg Ptr  : 0x0000         Options   : Present
-----------------------------------[options]--------------------------------
Option   : MaxSegSize      Length   : 4             Value     : 05b4
=================================[data:    6]===============================
003A  32 33 5B F8 C1 E6                              23[...
```

The Server sends a segment with both SYN and ACK set and sets its Maximum Segment Size to 5B4_16 also.

```
=========================================μscope=========================================
Frame    : 5               Len      : 64           Error      : None
T Elapsed: 19:34:58:100    T Delta  : 00:00:00:000
------------------------------------[mac]-----------------------------------
Dest Mac : Sun   1bc95a    Sourc Mac: 0000e80f04af  Type      : IP
------------------------------------[ip]------------------------------------
IP Ver   : 4               IP HLen  : 20 Bytes
TOS      : 0x00            Pkt Len  : 40            Seg ID    : 0x0002
Flags    : FRAG:À.LAST     Frag Ptr : 0     (8 Octet) TTL       : 32
PID      : TCP  ( 6)       Checksum : 0xaf   (Good)
Dst IP <C: 192.168.12.171  Src IP <C: 192.168.12.36
------------------------------------[tcp]-----------------------------------
Src Port : 1300            Dst Port : FTP.Ctrl
Seq No   : 0x00000001      Ack No   : 0x5b618e01
Head Len : 5    words      Flags    : .AP...         Window    : 0x1000
Checksum : 0x1720 (Good)   Urg Ptr  : 0x0000         Options   : None
=================================[data:   10]===============================
0036  00 00 00 00 00 00 6C 5B 0F 48                  ......l[.H
```

The station sends an ACK segment, the final part of the Three Way Handshake. The Control session is now open.

```
=========================================μscope=========================================
Frame    : 6               Len      : 100          Error      : None
T Elapsed: 19:34:58:261    T Delta  : 00:00:00:161
------------------------------------[mac]-----------------------------------
Dest Mac : 0000e80f04af    Sourc Mac: Sun   1bc95a  Type      : IP
------------------------------------[ip]------------------------------------
IP Ver   : 4               IP HLen  : 20 Bytes
TOS      : 0x00            Pkt Len  : 82            Seg ID    : 0xe5fd
Flags    : FRAG:À.LAST     Frag Ptr : 0     (8 Octet) TTL       : 60
PID      : TCP  ( 6)       Checksum : 0xfe88 (Good)
Dst IP <C: 192.168.12.36   Src IP <C: 192.168.12.171
------------------------------------[tcp]-----------------------------------
Src Port : FTP.Ctrl        Dst Port : 1300
Seq No   : 0x5b618e01      Ack No   : 0x00000001
Head Len : 5    words      Flags    : .AP...         Window    : 0x1000
Checksum : 0xc8c1 (Good)   Urg Ptr  : 0x0000         Options   : None
=================================[data:   46]===============================
0036  32 32 30 20 72 6F 6E 6E 69 65 20 46 54 50 20 73  220 ronnie FTP s
0046  65 72 76 65 72 20 28 53 75 6E 4F 53 20 34 2E 31  erver (SunOS 4.1
0056  29 20 72 65 61 64 79 2E 0D 0A 10 32 70 16        ) ready....2p.
```

The server responds with its welcome message.

```
=========================================μscope=========================================
Frame    : 7               Len      : 64           Error      : None
T Elapsed: 19:34:58:268    T Delta  : 00:00:00:007
------------------------------------[mac]-----------------------------------
Dest Mac : Sun   1bc95a    Sourc Mac: 0000e80f04af  Type      : IP
------------------------------------[ip]------------------------------------
IP Ver   : 4               IP HLen  : 20 Bytes
TOS      : 0x00            Pkt Len  : 40            Seg ID    : 0x0003
Flags    : FRAG:À.LAST     Frag Ptr : 0     (8 Octet) TTL       : 32
PID      : TCP  ( 6)       Checksum : 0xae   (Good)
Dst IP <C: 192.168.12.171  Src IP <C: 192.168.12.36
------------------------------------[tcp]-----------------------------------
Src Port : 1300            Dst Port : FTP.Ctrl
Seq No   : 0x00000001      Ack No   : 0x5b618e2b
Head Len : 5    words      Flags    : .AP...         Window    : 0x0fd6
Checksum : 0x1720 (Good)   Urg Ptr  : 0x0000         Options   : None
=================================[data:   10]===============================
0036  00 00 00 00 00 00 F8 CF 2A 19                  ........*.
```

The station acknowledges the Server's segment. Notice that the advertised Window has shrunk.

```
=========================================μscope=========================================
Frame    : 8               Len      : 64           Error      : None
T Elapsed: 19:34:58:268    T Delta  : 00:00:00:000
------------------------------------[mac]-----------------------------------
Dest Mac : Sun   1bc95a    Sourc Mac: 0000e80f04af  Type      : IP
------------------------------------[ip]------------------------------------
IP Ver   : 4               IP HLen  : 20 Bytes
TOS      : 0x00            Pkt Len  : 40            Seg ID    : 0x0004
Flags    : FRAG:À.LAST     Frag Ptr : 0     (8 Octet) TTL       : 32
PID      : TCP  ( 6)       Checksum : 0xad   (Good)
Dst IP <C: 192.168.12.171  Src IP <C: 192.168.12.36
------------------------------------[tcp]-----------------------------------
Src Port : 1300            Dst Port : FTP.Ctrl
Seq No   : 0x00000001      Ack No   : 0x5b618e2b
Head Len : 5    words      Flags    : .AP...         Window    : 0x1000
Checksum : 0x16f6 (Good)   Urg Ptr  : 0x0000         Options   : None
=================================[data:   10]===============================
0036  00 00 00 00 00 00 BD 0B B5 76                  ........v
```

The station sends a second ACK and indicates that its Window has recovered. Each time the station receives data it acknowledges it immediately and then sends a second ACK once the Window has recovered. We shall now remove each of these second acknowledgements to conserve space.

A Complete FTP Example

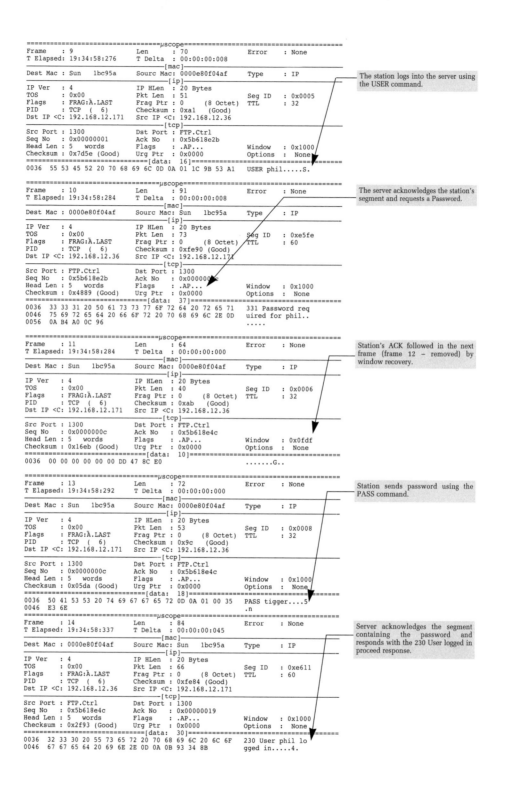

```
=======================================μscope=======================================
Frame     : 9              Len      : 70            Error     : None
T Elapsed: 19:34:58:276    T Delta  : 00:00:00:008
-------------------------------[mac]-------------------------------
Dest Mac : Sun   1bc95a    Sourc Mac: 0000e80f04af   Type      : IP
-------------------------------[ip]-------------------------------
IP Ver   : 4               IP HLen  : 20 Bytes
TOS      : 0x00            Pkt Len  : 51             Seg ID    : 0x0005
Flags    : FRAG:Ā.LAST     Frag Ptr : 0    (8 Octet) TTL       : 32
PID      : TCP  ( 6)       Checksum : 0xa1   (Good)
Dst IP <C: 192.168.12.171  Src IP <C: 192.168.12.36
-------------------------------[tcp]-------------------------------
Src Port : 1300            Dst Port : FTP.Ctrl
Seq No   : 0x00000001      Ack No   : 0x5b618e2b
Head Len : 5    words      Flags    : .AP...         Window    : 0x1000
Checksum : 0x7d5e (Good)   Urg Ptr  : 0x0000         Options   : None
==============================[data:  16]==============================
0036  55 53 45 52 20 70 68 69 6C 0D 0A 01 1C 9B 53 A1   USER phil.....S.
```

The station logs into the server using the USER command.

```
=======================================μscope=======================================
Frame     : 10             Len      : 91            Error     : None
T Elapsed: 19:34:58:284    T Delta  : 00:00:00:008
-------------------------------[mac]-------------------------------
Dest Mac : 0000e80f04af    Sourc Mac: Sun   1bc95a   Type      : IP
-------------------------------[ip]-------------------------------
IP Ver   : 4               IP HLen  : 20 Bytes
TOS      : 0x00            Pkt Len  : 73             Seg ID    : 0xe5fe
Flags    : FRAG:Ā.LAST     Frag Ptr : 0    (8 Octet) TTL       : 60
PID      : TCP  ( 6)       Checksum : 0xfe90 (Good)
Dst IP <C: 192.168.12.36   Src IP <C: 192.168.12.171
-------------------------------[tcp]-------------------------------
Src Port : FTP.Ctrl        Dst Port : 1300
Seq No   : 0x5b618e2b      Ack No   : 0x0000000c
Head Len : 5    words      Flags    : .AP...         Window    : 0x1000
Checksum : 0x4889 (Good)   Urg Ptr  : 0x0000         Options   : None
==============================[data:  37]==============================
0036  33 33 31 20 50 61 73 73 77 6F 72 64 20 72 65 71   331 Password req
0046  75 69 72 65 64 20 66 6F 72 20 70 68 69 6C 2E 0D   uired for phil..
0056  0A B4 A0 0C 96                                     .....
```

The server acknowledges the station's segment and requests a Password.

```
=======================================μscope=======================================
Frame     : 11             Len      : 64            Error     : None
T Elapsed: 19:34:58:284    T Delta  : 00:00:00:000
-------------------------------[mac]-------------------------------
Dest Mac : Sun   1bc95a    Sourc Mac: 0000e80f04af   Type      : IP
-------------------------------[ip]-------------------------------
IP Ver   : 4               IP HLen  : 20 Bytes
TOS      : 0x00            Pkt Len  : 40             Seg ID    : 0x0006
Flags    : FRAG:Ā.LAST     Frag Ptr : 0    (8 Octet) TTL       : 32
PID      : TCP  ( 6)       Checksum : 0xab    (Good)
Dst IP <C: 192.168.12.171  Src IP <C: 192.168.12.36
-------------------------------[tcp]-------------------------------
Src Port : 1300            Dst Port : FTP.Ctrl
Seq No   : 0x0000000c      Ack No   : 0x5b618e4c
Head Len : 5    words      Flags    : .AP...         Window    : 0x0fdf
Checksum : 0x16eb (Good)   Urg Ptr  : 0x0000         Options   : None
==============================[data:  10]==============================
0036  00 00 00 00 00 00 DD 47 8C E0                     .......G..
```

Station's ACK followed in the next frame (frame 12 – removed) by window recovery.

```
=======================================μscope=======================================
Frame     : 13             Len      : 72            Error     : None
T Elapsed: 19:34:58:292    T Delta  : 00:00:00:000
-------------------------------[mac]-------------------------------
Dest Mac : Sun   1bc95a    Sourc Mac: 0000e80f04af   Type      : IP
-------------------------------[ip]-------------------------------
IP Ver   : 4               IP HLen  : 20 Bytes
TOS      : 0x00            Pkt Len  : 53             Seg ID    : 0x0008
Flags    : FRAG:Ā.LAST     Frag Ptr : 0    (8 Octet) TTL       : 32
PID      : TCP  ( 6)       Checksum : 0x9c    (Good)
Dst IP <C: 192.168.12.171  Src IP <C: 192.168.12.36
-------------------------------[tcp]-------------------------------
Src Port : 1300            Dst Port : FTP.Ctrl
Seq No   : 0x0000000c      Ack No   : 0x5b618e4c
Head Len : 5    words      Flags    : .AP...         Window    : 0x1000
Checksum : 0x05da (Good)   Urg Ptr  : 0x0000         Options   : None
==============================[data:  18]==============================
0036  50 41 53 53 20 74 69 67 67 65 72 0D 0A 01 00 35   PASS tigger....5
0046  E3 6E                                             .n
```

Station sends password using the PASS command.

```
=======================================μscope=======================================
Frame     : 14             Len      : 84            Error     : None
T Elapsed: 19:34:58:337    T Delta  : 00:00:00:045
-------------------------------[mac]-------------------------------
Dest Mac : 0000e80f04af    Sourc Mac: Sun   1bc95a   Type      : IP
-------------------------------[ip]-------------------------------
IP Ver   : 4               IP HLen  : 20 Bytes
TOS      : 0x00            Pkt Len  : 66             Seg ID    : 0xe611
Flags    : FRAG:Ā.LAST     Frag Ptr : 0    (8 Octet) TTL       : 60
PID      : TCP  ( 6)       Checksum : 0xfe84 (Good)
Dst IP <C: 192.168.12.36   Src IP <C: 192.168.12.171
-------------------------------[tcp]-------------------------------
Src Port : FTP.Ctrl        Dst Port : 1300
Seq No   : 0x5b618e4c      Ack No   : 0x00000019
Head Len : 5    words      Flags    : .AP...         Window    : 0x1000
Checksum : 0x2f93 (Good)   Urg Ptr  : 0x0000         Options   : None
==============================[data:  30]==============================
0036  32 33 30 20 55 73 65 72 20 70 68 69 6C 20 6C 6F   230 User phil lo
0046  67 67 65 64 20 69 6E 2E 0D 0A 0B 93 34 8B         gged in.....4.
```

Server acknowledges the segment containing the password and responds with the 230 User logged in proceed response.

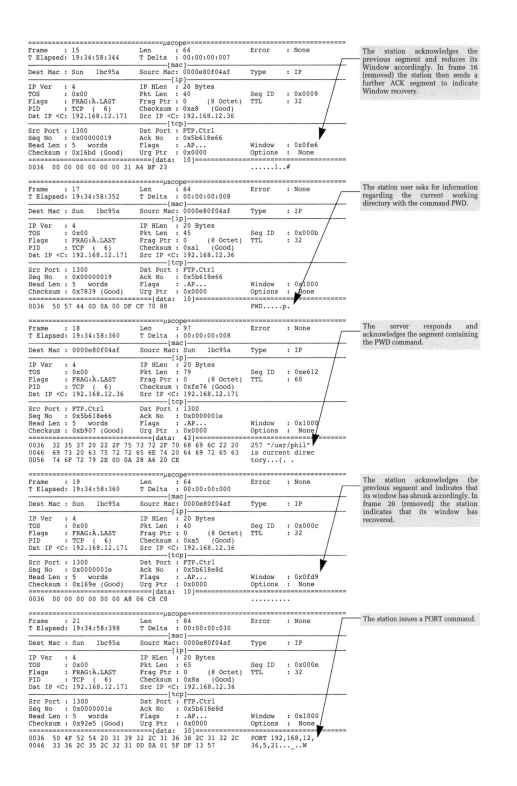

```
=========================μscope=========================
Frame   : 15              Len    : 64            Error    : None
T Elapsed: 19:34:58:344   T Delta : 00:00:00:007
-------------------------[mac]-------------------------
Dest Mac : Sun   1bc95a   Sourc Mac: 0000e80f04af   Type    : IP
-------------------------[ip]--------------------------
IP Ver   : 4              IP HLen : 20 Bytes
TOS      : 0x00           Pkt Len : 40             Seg ID  : 0x0009
Flags    : FRAG:Ā.LAST    Frag Ptr : 0    (8 Octet)  TTL     : 32
PID      : TCP  ( 6)      Checksum : 0xa8    (Good)
Dst IP <C: 192.168.12.171 Src IP <C: 192.168.12.36
-------------------------[tcp]-------------------------
Src Port : 1300           Dst Port : FTP.Ctrl
Seq No   : 0x00000019     Ack No   : 0x5b618e66      Window  : 0x0fe6
Head Len : 5  words       Flags    : .AP...           Options : None
Checksum : 0x16bd (Good)  Urg Ptr  : 0x0000
=========================[data:  10]=========================
0036   00 00 00 00 00 00 31 A4 BF 23                ......1..#
```

The station acknowledges the previous segment and reduces its Window accordingly. In frame 16 (removed) the station then sends a further ACK segment to indicate Window recovery.

```
=========================μscope=========================
Frame   : 17              Len    : 64            Error    : None
T Elapsed: 19:34:58:352   T Delta : 00:00:00:008
-------------------------[mac]-------------------------
Dest Mac : Sun   1bc95a   Sourc Mac: 0000e80f04af   Type    : IP
-------------------------[ip]--------------------------
IP Ver   : 4              IP HLen : 20 Bytes
TOS      : 0x00           Pkt Len : 45             Seg ID  : 0x000b
Flags    : FRAG:Ā.LAST    Frag Ptr : 0    (8 Octet)  TTL     : 32
PID      : TCP  ( 6)      Checksum : 0xa1    (Good)
Dst IP <C: 192.168.12.171 Src IP <C: 192.168.12.36
-------------------------[tcp]-------------------------
Src Port : 1300           Dst Port : FTP.Ctrl
Seq No   : 0x00000019     Ack No   : 0x5b618e66      Window  : 0x1000
Head Len : 5  words       Flags    : .AP...           Options : None
Checksum : 0x7839 (Good)  Urg Ptr  : 0x0000
=========================[data:  10]=========================
0036   50 57 44 0D 0A 00 DF CF 70 88                PWD.....p.
```

The station user asks for information regarding the current working directory with the command PWD.

```
=========================μscope=========================
Frame   : 18              Len    : 97            Error    : None
T Elapsed: 19:34:58:360   T Delta : 00:00:00:008
-------------------------[mac]-------------------------
Dest Mac : 0000e80f04af   Sourc Mac: Sun   1bc95a   Type    : IP
-------------------------[ip]--------------------------
IP Ver   : 4              IP HLen : 20 Bytes
TOS      : 0x00           Pkt Len : 79             Seg ID  : 0xe612
Flags    : FRAG:Ā.LAST    Frag Ptr : 0    (8 Octet)  TTL     : 60
PID      : TCP  ( 6)      Checksum : 0xfe76   (Good)
Dst IP <C: 192.168.12.36  Src IP <C: 192.168.12.171
-------------------------[tcp]-------------------------
Src Port : FTP.Ctrl       Dst Port : 1300
Seq No   : 0x5b618e66     Ack No   : 0x0000001e      Window  : 0x1000
Head Len : 5  words       Flags    : .AP...           Options : None
Checksum : 0xb907 (Good)  Urg Ptr  : 0x0000
=========================[data:  43]=========================
0036   32 35 37 20 22 2F 75 73 72 2F 70 68 69 6C 22 20  257 "/usr/phil"
0046   69 73 20 63 75 72 72 65 6E 74 20 64 69 72 65 63  is current direc
0056   74 6F 72 79 2E 0D 0A 28 A6 20 CE                 tory...(. .
```

The server responds and acknowledges the segment containing the PWD command.

```
=========================μscope=========================
Frame   : 19              Len    : 64            Error    : None
T Elapsed: 19:34:58:360   T Delta : 00:00:00:000
-------------------------[mac]-------------------------
Dest Mac : Sun   1bc95a   Sourc Mac: 0000e80f04af   Type    : IP
-------------------------[ip]--------------------------
IP Ver   : 4              IP HLen : 20 Bytes
TOS      : 0x00           Pkt Len : 40             Seg ID  : 0x000c
Flags    : FRAG:Ā.LAST    Frag Ptr : 0    (8 Octet)  TTL     : 32
PID      : TCP  ( 6)      Checksum : 0xa5    (Good)
Dst IP <C: 192.168.12.171 Src IP <C: 192.168.12.36
-------------------------[tcp]-------------------------
Src Port : 1300           Dst Port : FTP.Ctrl
Seq No   : 0x0000001e     Ack No   : 0x5b618e8d      Window  : 0x0fd9
Head Len : 5  words       Flags    : .AP...           Options : None
Checksum : 0x169e (Good)  Urg Ptr  : 0x0000
=========================[data:  10]=========================
0036   00 00 00 00 00 00 A8 06 C8 C8                .........
```

The station acknowledges the previous segment and indicates that its window has shrunk accordingly. In frame 20 (removed) the station indicates that its window has recovered.

```
=========================μscope=========================
Frame   : 21              Len    : 84            Error    : None
T Elapsed: 19:34:58:398   T Delta : 00:00:00:030
-------------------------[mac]-------------------------
Dest Mac : Sun   1bc95a   Sourc Mac: 0000e80f04af   Type    : IP
-------------------------[ip]--------------------------
IP Ver   : 4              IP HLen : 20 Bytes
TOS      : 0x00           Pkt Len : 65             Seg ID  : 0x000e
Flags    : FRAG:Ā.LAST    Frag Ptr : 0    (8 Octet)  TTL     : 32
PID      : TCP  ( 6)      Checksum : 0x8a    (Good)
Dst IP <C: 192.168.12.171 Src IP <C: 192.168.12.36
-------------------------[tcp]-------------------------
Src Port : 1300           Dst Port : FTP.Ctrl
Seq No   : 0x0000001e     Ack No   : 0x5b618e8d      Window  : 0x1000
Head Len : 5  words       Flags    : .AP...           Options : None
Checksum : 0x92e5 (Good)  Urg Ptr  : 0x0000
=========================[data:  30]=========================
0036   50 4F 52 54 20 31 39 32 2C 31 36 38 2C 31 32 2C  PORT 192,168,12,
0046   33 36 2C 35 2C 32 31 0D 0A 01 5F DF 13 57        36,5,21..._..W
```

The station issues a PORT command.

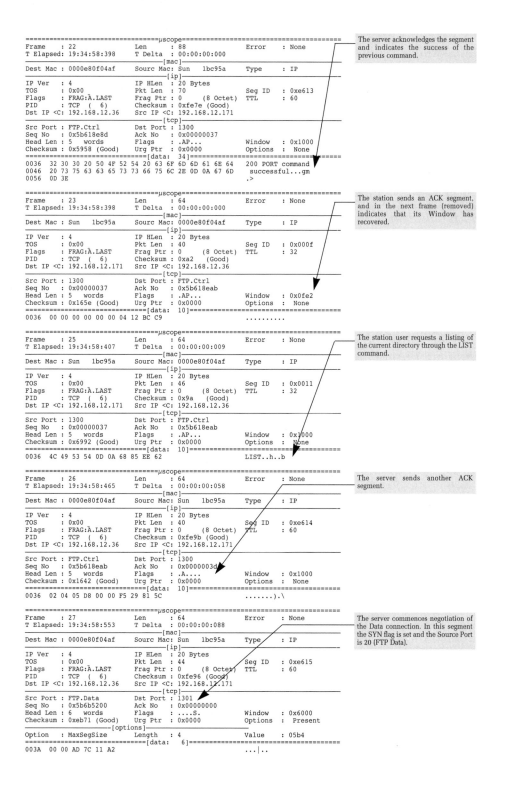

```
=======================================μscope========================================
Frame    : 22              Len      : 88            Error    : None
T Elapsed: 19:34:58:398    T Delta  : 00:00:00:000
---------------------------------[mac]-----------------------------------------------
Dest Mac : 0000e80f04af    Sourc Mac: Sun    1bc95a    Type     : IP
---------------------------------[ip]------------------------------------------------
IP Ver   : 4               IP HLen  : 20 Bytes
TOS      : 0x00            Pkt Len  : 70           Seg ID   : 0xe613
Flags    : FRAG:Ä.LAST     Frag Ptr : 0     (8 Octet)  TTL      : 60
PID      : TCP  ( 6)       Checksum : 0xfe7e (Good)
Dst IP <C: 192.168.12.36   Src IP <C: 192.168.12.171
---------------------------------[tcp]-----------------------------------------------
Src Port : FTP.Ctrl        Dst Port : 1300
Seq No   : 0x5b618e8d      Ack No   : 0x00000037
Head Len : 5   words       Flags    : .AP...        Window   : 0x1000
Checksum : 0x5958 (Good)   Urg Ptr  : 0x0000        Options  : None
=================================[data:  34]=========================================
0036   32 30 30 20 50 4F 52 54 20 63 6F 6D 6D 61 6E 64   200 PORT command
0046   20 73 75 63 63 65 73 73 66 75 6C 2E 0D 0A 67 6D    successful...gm
0056   0D 3E                                             .>
```

The server acknowledges the segment and indicates the success of the previous command.

```
=======================================μscope========================================
Frame    : 23              Len      : 64            Error    : None
T Elapsed: 19:34:58:398    T Delta  : 00:00:00:000
---------------------------------[mac]-----------------------------------------------
Dest Mac : Sun    1bc95a   Sourc Mac: 0000e80f04af   Type     : IP
---------------------------------[ip]------------------------------------------------
IP Ver   : 4               IP HLen  : 20 Bytes
TOS      : 0x00            Pkt Len  : 40           Seg ID   : 0x000f
Flags    : FRAG:Ä.LAST     Frag Ptr : 0     (8 Octet)  TTL      : 32
PID      : TCP  ( 6)       Checksum : 0xa2    (Good)
Dst IP <C: 192.168.12.171  Src IP <C: 192.168.12.36
---------------------------------[tcp]-----------------------------------------------
Src Port : 1300            Dst Port : FTP.Ctrl
Seq No   : 0x00000037      Ack No   : 0x5b618eab
Head Len : 5   words       Flags    : .AP...        Window   : 0x0fe2
Checksum : 0x165e (Good)   Urg Ptr  : 0x0000        Options  : None
=================================[data:  10]=========================================
0036   00 00 00 00 00 00 04 12 BC C9                     .........
```

The station sends an ACK segment, and in the next frame (removed) indicates that its Window has recovered.

```
=======================================μscope========================================
Frame    : 25              Len      : 64            Error    : None
T Elapsed: 19:34:58:407    T Delta  : 00:00:00:009
---------------------------------[mac]-----------------------------------------------
Dest Mac : Sun    1bc95a   Sourc Mac: 0000e80f04af   Type     : IP
---------------------------------[ip]------------------------------------------------
IP Ver   : 4               IP HLen  : 20 Bytes
TOS      : 0x00            Pkt Len  : 46           Seg ID   : 0x0011
Flags    : FRAG:Ä.LAST     Frag Ptr : 0     (8 Octet)  TTL      : 32
PID      : TCP  ( 6)       Checksum : 0x9a   (Good)
Dst IP <C: 192.168.12.171  Src IP <C: 192.168.12.36
---------------------------------[tcp]-----------------------------------------------
Src Port : 1300            Dst Port : FTP.Ctrl
Seq No   : 0x00000037      Ack No   : 0x5b618eab
Head Len : 5   words       Flags    : .AP...        Window   : 0x1000
Checksum : 0x6992 (Good)   Urg Ptr  : 0x0000        Options  : None
=================================[data:  10]=========================================
0036   4C 49 53 54 0D 0A 68 85 EE 62                     LIST..h..b
```

The station user requests a listing of the current directory through the LIST command.

```
=======================================μscope========================================
Frame    : 26              Len      : 64            Error    : None
T Elapsed: 19:34:58:465    T Delta  : 00:00:00:058
---------------------------------[mac]-----------------------------------------------
Dest Mac : 0000e80f04af    Sourc Mac: Sun    1bc95a    Type     : IP
---------------------------------[ip]------------------------------------------------
IP Ver   : 4               IP HLen  : 20 Bytes
TOS      : 0x00            Pkt Len  : 40           Seg ID   : 0xe614
Flags    : FRAG:Ä.LAST     Frag Ptr : 0     (8 Octet)  TTL      : 60
PID      : TCP  ( 6)       Checksum : 0xfe9b (Good)
Dst IP <C: 192.168.12.36   Src IP <C: 192.168.12.171
---------------------------------[tcp]-----------------------------------------------
Src Port : FTP.Ctrl        Dst Port : 1300
Seq No   : 0x5b618eab      Ack No   : 0x0000003d
Head Len : 5   words       Flags    : .A....        Window   : 0x1000
Checksum : 0x1642 (Good)   Urg Ptr  : 0x0000        Options  : None
=================================[data:  10]=========================================
0036   02 04 05 D8 00 00 F5 29 81 5C                     .......).\
```

The server sends another ACK segment.

```
=======================================μscope========================================
Frame    : 27              Len      : 64            Error    : None
T Elapsed: 19:34:58:553    T Delta  : 00:00:00:088
---------------------------------[mac]-----------------------------------------------
Dest Mac : 0000e80f04af    Sourc Mac: Sun    1bc95a    Type     : IP
---------------------------------[ip]------------------------------------------------
IP Ver   : 4               IP HLen  : 20 Bytes
TOS      : 0x00            Pkt Len  : 44           Seg ID   : 0xe615
Flags    : FRAG:Ä.LAST     Frag Ptr : 0     (8 Octet)  TTL      : 60
PID      : TCP  ( 6)       Checksum : 0xfe96 (Good)
Dst IP <C: 192.168.12.36   Src IP <C: 192.168.12.171
---------------------------------[tcp]-----------------------------------------------
Src Port : FTP.Data        Dst Port : 1301
Seq No   : 0x5b6b5200      Ack No   : 0x00000000
Head Len : 6   words       Flags    : ....S.        Window   : 0x6000
Checksum : 0xeb71 (Good)   Urg Ptr  : 0x0000        Options  : Present
-------------------------------[options]---------------------------------------------
Option   : MaxSegSize      Length   : 4             Value    : 05b4
=================================[data:   6]=========================================
003A   00 00 AD 7C 11 A2                                 ...|..
```

The server commences negotiation of the Data connection. In this segment the SYN flag is set and the Source Port is 20 (FTP Data).

```
==============================μscope==============================
Frame    : 28              Len      : 64            Error    : None
T Elapsed: 19:34:58:560    T Delta  : 00:00:00:007
------------------------------[mac]-------------------------------
Dest Mac : Sun    1bc95a   Sourc Mac: 0000e80f04af   Type     : IP
------------------------------[ip]--------------------------------
IP Ver   : 4               IP HLen  : 20 Bytes
TOS      : 0x00            Pkt Len  : 44            Seg ID   : 0x0012
Flags    : FRAG:À.LAST     Frag Ptr : 0     (8 Octet) TTL      : 32
PID      : TCP  ( 6)       Checksum : 0x9b    (Good)
Dst IP <C: 192.168.12.171  Src IP <C: 192.168.12.36
------------------------------[tcp]-------------------------------
Src Port : 1301            Dst Port : FTP.Data
Seq No   : 0x00000000      Ack No   : 0x5b6b51
Head Len : 6   words       Flags    : .AP.S.        Window   : 0x1000
Checksum : 0x3b59 (Good)   Urg Ptr  : 0x0000        Options  : Present
----------------------------[options]-----------------------------
Option   : MaxSegSize      Length   : 4             Value    : 05b4
==============================[data:    6]========================
003A  00 00 3F 34 CE EA                              ..?4..
```

The station responds with a segment containing SYN and ACK.

```
==============================μscope==============================
Frame    : 29              Len      : 64            Error    : None
T Elapsed: 19:34:58:560    T Delta  : 00:00:00:000
------------------------------[mac]-------------------------------
Dest Mac : 0000e80f04af    Sourc Mac: Sun    1bc95a  Type     : IP
------------------------------[ip]--------------------------------
IP Ver   : 4               IP HLen  : 20 Bytes
TOS      : 0x00            Pkt Len  : 40            Seg ID   : 0xe616
Flags    : FRAG:À.LAST     Frag Ptr : 0     (8 Octet) TTL      : 60
PID      : TCP  ( 6)       Checksum : 0xfe99 (Good)
Dst IP <C: 192.168.12.36   Src IP <C: 192.168.12.171
------------------------------[tcp]-------------------------------
Src Port : FTP.Data        Dst Port : 1301
Seq No   : 0x5b6b5201      Ack No   : 0x000001
Head Len : 5   words       Flags    : .A....        Window   : 0x6000
Checksum : 0x031e (Good)   Urg Ptr  : 0x0000        Options  : None
==============================[data:   10]========================
0036  02 04 05 B4 00 00 79 D5 11 F9                  ......y...
```

The server responds with the third part of the handshake (ACK) and the data connection is now open.

```
==============================μscope==============================
Frame    : 30              Len      : 129           Error    : None
T Elapsed: 19:34:58:560    T Delta  : 00:00:00:000
------------------------------[mac]-------------------------------
Dest Mac : 0000e80f04af    Sourc Mac: Sun    1bc95a  Type     : IP
------------------------------[ip]--------------------------------
IP Ver   : 4               IP HLen  : 20 Bytes
TOS      : 0x00            Pkt Len  : 111           Seg ID   : 0xe617
Flags    : FRAG:À.LAST     Frag Ptr : 0     (8 Octet) TTL      : 60
PID      : TCP  ( 6)       Checksum : 0xfe51 (Good)
Dst IP <C: 192.168.12.36   Src IP <C: 192.168.12.171
------------------------------[tcp]-------------------------------
Src Port : FTP.Ctrl        Dst Port : 1300
Seq No   : 0x5b618eab      Ack No   : 0x0000003d
Head Len : 5   words       Flags    : .AP...        Window   : 0x1000
Checksum : 0x04ab (Good)   Urg Ptr  : 0x0000        Options  : None
==============================[data:   75]========================
0036  31 35 30 20 41 53 43 49 49 20 64 61 74 61 20 63  150 ASCII data c
0046  6F 6E 6E 65 63 74 69 6F 6E 20 66 6F 72 20 2F 62  onnection for /b
0056  69 6E 2F 6C 73 20 28 31 39 32 2E 31 36 38 2E 31  in/ls (192.168.1
0066  32 2E 33 36 2C 31 33 30 31 29 20 28 30 20 62 79  2.36,1301) (0 by
0076  74 65 73 29 2E 2E 0D 0A 9A CE 74 3C              tes).....t<
```

The server indicates that the data connection is open by posting a message to the station over the Control connection.

```
==============================μscope==============================
Frame    : 31              Len      : 64            Error    : None
T Elapsed: 19:34:58:560    T Delta  : 00:00:00:000
------------------------------[mac]-------------------------------
Dest Mac : Sun    1bc95a   Sourc Mac: 0000e80f04af   Type     : IP
------------------------------[ip]--------------------------------
IP Ver   : 4               IP HLen  : 20 Bytes
TOS      : 0x00            Pkt Len  : 40            Seg ID   : 0x0013
Flags    : FRAG:À.LAST     Frag Ptr : 0     (8 Octet) TTL      : 32
PID      : TCP  ( 6)       Checksum : 0x9e    (Good)
Dst IP <C: 192.168.12.171  Src IP <C: 192.168.12.36
------------------------------[tcp]-------------------------------
Src Port : 1300            Dst Port : FTP.Ctrl
Seq No   : 0x0000003d      Ack No   : 0x5b618ef2
Head Len : 5   words       Flags    : .AP...        Window   : 0x0fb9
Checksum : 0x163a (Good)   Urg Ptr  : 0x0000        Options  : None
==============================[data:   10]========================
0036  00 00 00 00 00 00 8D A4 B6 E5                  .........
```

The station acknowledgdes the message over the Control connection. In the next frame (removed) the Window recovers.

A Complete FTP Example

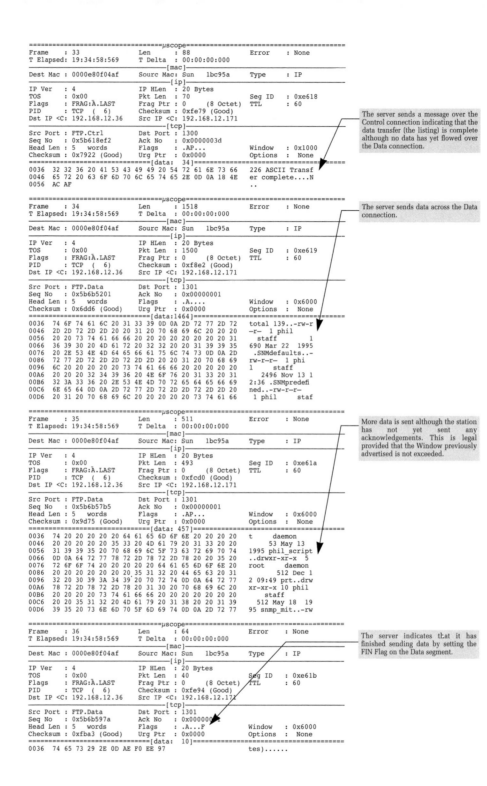

```
=================================μscope=========================================
Frame    : 33              Len      : 88               Error   : None
T Elapsed: 19:34:58:569    T Delta  : 00:00:00:000
--------------------------------[mac]-------------------------------------------
Dest Mac: 0000e80f04af     Sourc Mac: Sun  1bc95a      Type    : IP
--------------------------------[ip]--------------------------------------------
IP Ver   : 4               IP HLen  : 20 Bytes
TOS      : 0x00            Pkt Len  : 70               Seg ID  : 0xe618
Flags    : FRAG:Ā.LAST     Frag Ptr : 0     (8 Octet)  TTL     : 60
PID      : TCP  ( 6)       Checksum : 0xfe79 (Good)
Dst IP <C: 192.168.12.36   Src IP <C: 192.168.12.171
--------------------------------[tcp]-------------------------------------------
Src Port : FTP.Ctrl        Dst Port : 1300
Seq No   : 0x5b618ef2      Ack No   : 0x0000003d
Head Len : 5   words       Flags    : .AP...           Window  : 0x1000
Checksum : 0x7922 (Good)   Urg Ptr  : 0x0000           Options : None
=================================[data:  34]====================================
0036  32 32 36 20 41 53 43 49 49 20 54 72 61 6E 73 66   226 ASCII Transf
0046  65 72 20 63 6F 6D 70 6C 65 74 65 2E 0D 0A 18 4E   er complete....N
0056  AC AF                                             ..
```

The server sends a message over the Control connection indicating that the data transfer (the listing) is complete although no data has yet flowed over the Data connection.

```
=================================μscope=========================================
Frame    : 34              Len      : 1518             Error   : None
T Elapsed: 19:34:58:569    T Delta  : 00:00:00:000
--------------------------------[mac]-------------------------------------------
Dest Mac: 0000e80f04af     Sourc Mac: Sun  1bc95a      Type    : IP
--------------------------------[ip]--------------------------------------------
IP Ver   : 4               IP HLen  : 20 Bytes
TOS      : 0x00            Pkt Len  : 1500             Seg ID  : 0xe619
Flags    : FRAG:Ā.LAST     Frag Ptr : 0     (8 Octet)  TTL     : 60
PID      : TCP  ( 6)       Checksum : 0xf8e2 (Good)
Dst IP <C: 192.168.12.36   Src IP <C: 192.168.12.171
--------------------------------[tcp]-------------------------------------------
Src Port : FTP.Data        Dst Port : 1301
Seq No   : 0x5b6b5201      Ack No   : 0x00000001
Head Len : 5   words       Flags    : .A....           Window  : 0x6000
Checksum : 0x6dd6 (Good)   Urg Ptr  : 0x0000           Options : None
=================================[data:1464]====================================
0036  74 6F 74 61 6C 20 31 33 39 0D 0A 2D 72 77 2D 72   total 139..-rw-r
0046  2D 2D 72 2D 2D 20 20 31 20 70 68 69 6C 20 20 20   -r-- 1 phil
0056  20 20 73 74 61 66 66 20 20 20 20 20 20 20 31 20   staff         1
0066  36 39 30 20 4D 61 72 20 32 32 20 20 31 39 39 35   690 Mar 22  1995
0076  20 2E 53 4E 4D 64 65 66 61 75 6C 74 73 0D 0A 2D   .SNMdefaults..-
0086  72 77 2D 72 2D 2D 72 2D 2D 20 31 20 70 68 69      rw-r-- 1 phi
0096  6C 20 20 20 20 20 20 73 74 61 66 66 20 20 20 20   l    staff
00A6  20 20 20 32 34 39 36 20 4E 6F 76 20 31 33 20 31   2496 Nov 13 1
00B6  32 3A 33 36 20 2E 53 4E 4D 70 72 65 64 65 66 69   2:36 .SNMpredefi
00C6  6E 65 64 0D 0A 2D 72 77 2D 72 2D 2D 72 2D 2D 20   ned..-rw-r-r--
00D6  20 31 20 70 68 69 6C 20 20 20 20 20 73 74 61 66   1 phil    staf
```

The server sends data across the Data connection.

```
=================================μscope=========================================
Frame    : 35              Len      : 511              Error   : None
T Elapsed: 19:34:58:569    T Delta  : 00:00:00:000
--------------------------------[mac]-------------------------------------------
Dest Mac: 0000e80f04af     Sourc Mac: Sun  1bc95a      Type    : IP
--------------------------------[ip]--------------------------------------------
IP Ver   : 4               IP HLen  : 20 Bytes
TOS      : 0x00            Pkt Len  : 493              Seg ID  : 0xe61a
Flags    : FRAG:Ā.LAST     Frag Ptr : 0     (8 Octet)  TTL     : 60
PID      : TCP  ( 6)       Checksum : 0xfcd0 (Good)
Dst IP <C: 192.168.12.36   Src IP <C: 192.168.12.171
--------------------------------[tcp]-------------------------------------------
Src Port : FTP.Data        Dst Port : 1301
Seq No   : 0x5b6b57b5      Ack No   : 0x00000001
Head Len : 5   words       Flags    : .AP...           Window  : 0x6000
Checksum : 0x9d75 (Good)   Urg Ptr  : 0x0000           Options : None
=================================[data: 457]====================================
0036  74 20 20 20 20 20 20 64 61 65 6D 6F 6E 20 20 20   t    daemon
0046  20 20 20 20 20 35 33 20 4D 61 79 20 31 33 20 20   53 May 13
0056  31 39 39 35 20 70 68 69 6C 5F 73 63 72 69 70 74   1995 phil_script
0066  0D 0A 64 72 77 78 72 2D 78 72 2D 78 20 20 35 20   ..drwxr-xr-x  5
0076  72 6F 6F 74 20 20 20 20 64 61 65 6D 6F 6E 20 20   root    daemon
0086  20 20 20 20 20 20 20 35 31 32 20 44 65 63 20 31   512 Dec 1
0096  32 20 30 39 3A 34 39 20 70 72 74 0D 0A 64 72 77   2 09:49 prt..drw
00A6  78 72 2D 78 72 2D 78 20 31 30 20 70 68 69 6C 20   xr-xr-x 10 phil
00B6  20 20 20 20 73 74 61 66 66 20 20 20 20 20 20 20   staff
00C6  20 20 35 31 32 20 4D 61 79 20 31 38 20 20 31 39   512 May 18  19
00D6  39 35 20 73 6E 6D 70 5F 6D 69 74 0D 0A 2D 72 77   95 snmp_mit..-rw
```

More data is sent although the station has not yet sent any acknowledgements. This is legal provided that the Window previously advertised is not exceeded.

```
=================================μscope=========================================
Frame    : 36              Len      : 64               Error   : None
T Elapsed: 19:34:58:569    T Delta  : 00:00:00:000
--------------------------------[mac]-------------------------------------------
Dest Mac: 0000e80f04af     Sourc Mac: Sun  1bc95a      Type    : IP
--------------------------------[ip]--------------------------------------------
IP Ver   : 4               IP HLen  : 20 Bytes
TOS      : 0x00            Pkt Len  : 40               Seg ID  : 0xe61b
Flags    : FRAG:Ā.LAST     Frag Ptr : 0     (8 Octet)  TTL     : 60
PID      : TCP  ( 6)       Checksum : 0xfe94 (Good)
Dst IP <C: 192.168.12.36   Src IP <C: 192.168.12.171
--------------------------------[tcp]-------------------------------------------
Src Port : FTP.Data        Dst Port : 1301
Seq No   : 0x5b6b597a      Ack No   : 0x00000001
Head Len : 5   words       Flags    : .A...F           Window  : 0x6000
Checksum : 0xfba3 (Good)   Urg Ptr  : 0x0000           Options : None
=================================[data:  10]====================================
0036  74 65 73 29 2E 0D AE F0 EE 97                     tes)......
```

The server indicates that it has finished sending data by setting the FIN Flag on the Data segment.

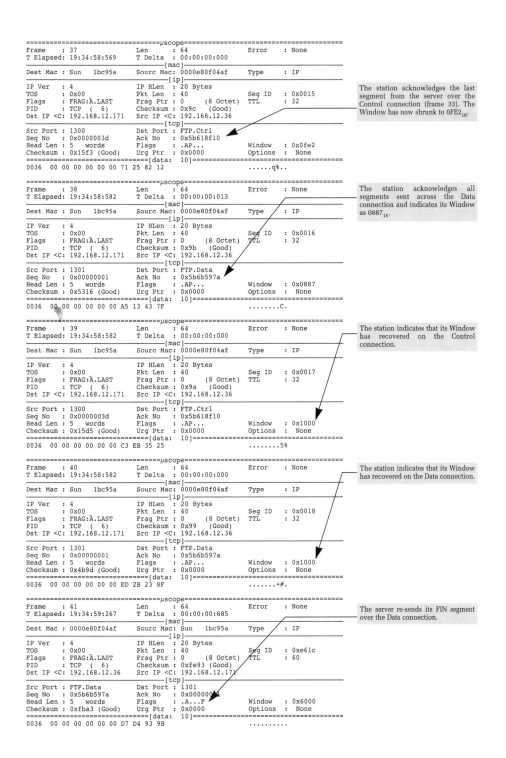

```
===========================μscope============================
Frame    : 37                Len      : 64              Error    : None
T Elapsed: 19:34:58:569      T Delta  : 00:00:00:000
---------------------------[mac]----------------------------
Dest Mac : Sun    1bc95a     Sourc Mac: 0000e80f04af    Type     : IP
----------------------------[ip]----------------------------
IP Ver   : 4                 IP HLen  : 20 Bytes
TOS      : 0x00              Pkt Len  : 40              Seg ID   : 0x0015
Flags    : FRAG:Ā.LAST      Frag Ptr : 0     (8 Octet) TTL      : 32
PID      : TCP  ( 6)         Checksum : 0x9c   (Good)
Dst IP <C: 192.168.12.171    Src IP <C: 192.168.12.36
---------------------------[tcp]----------------------------
Src Port : 1300              Dst Port : FTP.Ctrl
Seq No   : 0x0000003d        Ack No   : 0x5b618f10
Head Len : 5    words        Flags    : .AP...          Window   : 0x0fe2
Checksum : 0x15f3 (Good)     Urg Ptr  : 0x0000          Options  : None
===========================[data:  10]=======================
0036  00 00 00 00 00 00 71 25 82 12              ......q%..
```

The station acknowledges the last segment from the server over the Control connection (frame 33). The Window has now shrunk to 0FE2₁₆.

```
===========================μscope============================
Frame    : 38                Len      : 64              Error    : None
T Elapsed: 19:34:58:582      T Delta  : 00:00:00:013
---------------------------[mac]----------------------------
Dest Mac : Sun    1bc95a     Sourc Mac: 0000e80f04af    Type     : IP
----------------------------[ip]----------------------------
IP Ver   : 4                 IP HLen  : 20 Bytes
TOS      : 0x00              Pkt Len  : 40              Seg ID   : 0x0016
Flags    : FRAG:Ā.LAST      Frag Ptr : 0     (8 Octet) TTL      : 32
PID      : TCP  ( 6)         Checksum : 0x9b   (Good)
Dst IP <C: 192.168.12.171    Src IP <C: 192.168.12.36
---------------------------[tcp]----------------------------
Src Port : 1301              Dst Port : FTP.Data
Seq No   : 0x00000001        Ack No   : 0x5b6b597a
Head Len : 5    words        Flags    : .AP...          Window   : 0x0887
Checksum : 0x5316 (Good)     Urg Ptr  : 0x0000          Options  : None
===========================[data:  10]=======================
0036  00 00 00 00 00 00 A5 13 43 7F              ........C.
```

The station acknowledges all segments sent across the Data connection and indicates its Window as 0887₁₆.

```
===========================μscope============================
Frame    : 39                Len      : 64              Error    : None
T Elapsed: 19:34:58:582      T Delta  : 00:00:00:000
---------------------------[mac]----------------------------
Dest Mac : Sun    1bc95a     Sourc Mac: 0000e80f04af    Type     : IP
----------------------------[ip]----------------------------
IP Ver   : 4                 IP HLen  : 20 Bytes
TOS      : 0x00              Pkt Len  : 40              Seg ID   : 0x0017
Flags    : FRAG:Ā.LAST      Frag Ptr : 0     (8 Octet) TTL      : 32
PID      : TCP  ( 6)         Checksum : 0x9a   (Good)
Dst IP <C: 192.168.12.171    Src IP <C: 192.168.12.36
---------------------------[tcp]----------------------------
Src Port : 1300              Dst Port : FTP.Ctrl
Seq No   : 0x0000003d        Ack No   : 0x5b618f10
Head Len : 5    words        Flags    : .AP...          Window   : 0x1000
Checksum : 0x15d5 (Good)     Urg Ptr  : 0x0000          Options  : None
===========================[data:  10]=======================
0036  00 00 00 00 00 00 C3 EB 35 25              ........5%
```

The station indicates that its Window has recovered on the Control connection.

```
===========================μscope============================
Frame    : 40                Len      : 64              Error    : None
T Elapsed: 19:34:58:582      T Delta  : 00:00:00:000
---------------------------[mac]----------------------------
Dest Mac : Sun    1bc95a     Sourc Mac: 0000e80f04af    Type     : IP
----------------------------[ip]----------------------------
IP Ver   : 4                 IP HLen  : 20 Bytes
TOS      : 0x00              Pkt Len  : 40              Seg ID   : 0x0018
Flags    : FRAG:Ā.LAST      Frag Ptr : 0     (8 Octet) TTL      : 32
PID      : TCP  ( 6)         Checksum : 0x99   (Good)
Dst IP <C: 192.168.12.171    Src IP <C: 192.168.12.36
---------------------------[tcp]----------------------------
Src Port : 1301              Dst Port : FTP.Data
Seq No   : 0x00000001        Ack No   : 0x5b6b597a
Head Len : 5    words        Flags    : .AP...          Window   : 0x1000
Checksum : 0x4b9d (Good)     Urg Ptr  : 0x0000          Options  : None
===========================[data:  10]=======================
0036  00 00 00 00 00 00 ED 2B 23 8F              .......+#.
```

The station indicates that its Window has recovered on the Data connection.

```
===========================μscope============================
Frame    : 41                Len      : 64              Error    : None
T Elapsed: 19:34:59:267      T Delta  : 00:00:00:685
---------------------------[mac]----------------------------
Dest Mac : 0000e80f04af      Sourc Mac: Sun    1bc95a   Type     : IP
----------------------------[ip]----------------------------
IP Ver   : 4                 IP HLen  : 20 Bytes
TOS      : 0x00              Pkt Len  : 40              Seg ID   : 0xe61c
Flags    : FRAG:Ā.LAST      Frag Ptr : 0     (8 Octet) TTL      : 60
PID      : TCP  ( 6)         Checksum : 0xfe93 (Good)
Dst IP <C: 192.168.12.36     Src IP <C: 192.168.12.171
---------------------------[tcp]----------------------------
Src Port : FTP.Data          Dst Port : 1301
Seq No   : 0x5b6b597a        Ack No   : 0x0000000
Head Len : 5    words        Flags    : .A...F          Window   : 0x6000
Checksum : 0xfba3 (Good)     Urg Ptr  : 0x0000          Options  : None
===========================[data:  10]=======================
0036  00 00 00 00 00 00 D7 D4 93 9B              ..........
```

The server re-sends its FIN segment over the Data connection.

```
=========================================μscope=========================================
Frame    : 42            Len      : 64                Error    : None
T Elapsed: 19:34:59:267  T Delta  : 00:00:00:000
-----------------------------------[mac]------------------------------------------------
Dest Mac : Sun  1bc95a   Sourc Mac: 0000e80f04af       Type     : IP
-----------------------------------[ip]-------------------------------------------------
IP Ver   : 4             IP HLen  : 20 Bytes
TOS      : 0x00          Pkt Len  : 40                 Seg ID   : 0x0019
Flags    : FRAG:Ä.LAST   Frag Ptr : 0      (8 Octet)   TTL      : 32
PID      : TCP  ( 6)     Checksum : 0x98    (Good)
Dst IP <C: 192.168.12.171  Src IP <C: 192.168.12.36
-----------------------------------[tcp]------------------------------------------------
Src Port : 1301          Dst Port : FTP.Data
Seq No   : 0x00000001    Ack No   : 0x5b6b597b
Head Len : 5   words     Flags    : .A....             Window   : 0x1000
Checksum : 0x4ba4 (Good) Urg Ptr  : 0x0000             Options  : None
=====================================[data:  10]========================================
0036  00 00 00 00 00 00 88 D2 C0 C9                .........
```

The station acknowledges the server's Data connection FIN segment.

```
=========================================μscope=========================================
Frame    : 43            Len      : 64                Error    : None
T Elapsed: 19:34:59:275  T Delta  : 00:00:00:008
-----------------------------------[mac]------------------------------------------------
Dest Mac : Sun  1bc95a   Sourc Mac: 0000e80f04af       Type     : IP
-----------------------------------[ip]-------------------------------------------------
IP Ver   : 4             IP HLen  : 20 Bytes
TOS      : 0x00          Pkt Len  : 40                 Seg ID   : 0x001a
Flags    : FRAG:Ä.LAST   Frag Ptr : 0      (8 Octet)   TTL      : 32
PID      : TCP  ( 6)     Checksum : 0x97    (Good)
Dst IP <C: 192.168.12.171  Src IP <C: 192.168.12.36
-----------------------------------[tcp]------------------------------------------------
Src Port : 1301          Dst Port : FTP.Data
Seq No   : 0x00000001    Ack No   : 0x5b6b597b
Head Len : 5   words     Flags    : .A...F             Window   : 0x1000
Checksum : 0x4ba3 (Good) Urg Ptr  : 0x0000             Options  : None
=====================================[data:  10]========================================
0036  00 00 00 00 00 00 D8 1D 72 5A                ........rZ
```

The station sends its own FIN segment over the Data connection.

```
=========================================μscope=========================================
Frame    : 44            Len      : 64                Error    : None
T Elapsed: 19:34:59:275  T Delta  : 00:00:00:000
-----------------------------------[mac]------------------------------------------------
Dest Mac : 0000e80f04af  Sourc Mac: Sun  1bc95a        Type     : IP
-----------------------------------[ip]-------------------------------------------------
IP Ver   : 4             IP HLen  : 20 Bytes
TOS      : 0x00          Pkt Len  : 40                 Seg ID   : 0xe61d
Flags    : FRAG:Ä.LAST   Frag Ptr : 0      (8 Octet)   TTL      : 60
PID      : TCP  ( 6)     Checksum : 0xfe92 (Good)
Dst IP <C: 192.168.12.36   Src IP <C: 192.168.12.171
-----------------------------------[tcp]------------------------------------------------
Src Port : FTP.Data      Dst Port : 1301
Seq No   : 0x5b6b597b    Ack No   : 0x00000002
Head Len : 5   words     Flags    : .A....             Window   : 0x6000
Checksum : 0xfba2 (Good) Urg Ptr  : 0x0000             Options  : None
=====================================[data:  10]========================================
0036  00 00 00 00 00 00 59 74 68 B0                ......Yth.
```

The server acknowledges the station's FIN segment over the Data connection closing this connection. If any further data is to be sent, a new Data connection must now be established.

```
=========================================μscope=========================================
Frame    : 45            Len      : 66                Error    : None
T Elapsed: 19:35:35:967  T Delta  : 00:00:36:692
-----------------------------------[mac]------------------------------------------------
Dest Mac : Sun  1bc95a   Sourc Mac: 0000e80f04af       Type     : IP
-----------------------------------[ip]-------------------------------------------------
IP Ver   : 4             IP HLen  : 20 Bytes
TOS      : 0x00          Pkt Len  : 48                 Seg ID   : 0x001b
Flags    : FRAG:Ä.LAST   Frag Ptr : 0      (8 Octet)   TTL      : 32
PID      : TCP  ( 6)     Checksum : 0x8e    (Good)
Dst IP <C: 192.168.12.171  Src IP <C: 192.168.12.36
-----------------------------------[tcp]------------------------------------------------
Src Port : 1300          Dst Port : FTP.Ctrl
Seq No   : 0x0000003d    Ack No   : 0x5b618f10
Head Len : 5   words     Flags    : .AP...             Window   : 0x1000
Checksum : 0x43db (Good) Urg Ptr  : 0x0000             Options  : None
=====================================[data:  12]========================================
0036  54 59 50 45 20 49 0D 0A B4 C4 2F DD          TYPE I..../.
```

The station sends the TYPE IMAGE command to set the server to Binary transfer mode in preparation for the next transfer.

```
=========================================μscope=========================================
Frame    : 46            Len      : 78                Error    : None
T Elapsed: 19:35:35:975  T Delta  : 00:00:00:008
-----------------------------------[mac]------------------------------------------------
Dest Mac : 0000e80f04af  Sourc Mac: Sun  1bc95a        Type     : IP
-----------------------------------[ip]-------------------------------------------------
IP Ver   : 4             IP HLen  : 20 Bytes
TOS      : 0x00          Pkt Len  : 60                 Seg ID   : 0xe61e
Flags    : FRAG:Ä.LAST   Frag Ptr : 0      (8 Octet)   TTL      : 60
PID      : TCP  ( 6)     Checksum : 0xfe7d (Good)
Dst IP <C: 192.168.12.36   Src IP <C: 192.168.12.171
-----------------------------------[tcp]------------------------------------------------
Src Port : FTP.Ctrl      Dst Port : 1300
Seq No   : 0x5b618f10    Ack No   : 0x00000045
Head Len : 5   words     Flags    : .AP...             Window   : 0x1000
Checksum : 0x82d5 (Good) Urg Ptr  : 0x0000             Options  : None
=====================================[data:  24]========================================
0036  32 30 30 20 54 79 70 65 20 73 65 74 20 74 6F 20   200 Type set to
0046  49 2E 0D 0A B9 75 E0 45                           I....u.E
```

The server acknowledges the stations desire to enter Binary mode.

The File Transfer Protocol (FTP)

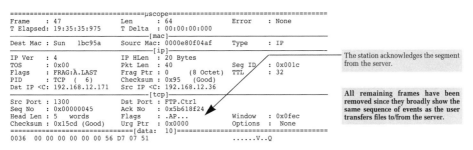

```
=================================μscope=============================================
Frame    : 47              Len       : 64              Error    : None
T Elapsed: 19:35:35:975    T Delta   : 00:00:00:000
                                         -[mac]-
Dest Mac : Sun    1bc95a   Sourc Mac: 0000e80f04af     Type     : IP
                                         -[ip]-
IP Ver   : 4               IP HLen   : 20 Bytes
TOS      : 0x00            Pkt Len   : 40               Seg ID   : 0x001c
Flags    : FRAG:À.LAST     Frag Ptr  : 0     (8 Octet)  TTL      : 32
PID      : TCP  ( 6)       Checksum  : 0x95   (Good)
Dst IP <C: 192.168.12.171  Src IP <C: 192.168.12.36
                                         -[tcp]-
Src Port : 1300            Dst Port  : FTP.Ctrl
Seq No   : 0x00000045      Ack No    : 0x5b618f24
Head Len : 5    words      Flags     : .AP...           Window   : 0x0fec
Checksum : 0x15cd (Good)   Urg Ptr   : 0x0000           Options  : None
==============================[data:   10]===========================================
0036   00 00 00 00 00 00 56 D7 07 51                     ......V..Q
```

The station acknowledges the segment from the server.

All remaining frames have been removed since they broadly show the same sequence of events as the user transfers files to/from the server.

Figure 17-8: A Sample FTP Session Trace

17.7 Summary

FTP provides us with a reliable method of transferring files between machines. It is built upon TCP and accommodates multiple file types and data representations. FTP itself is possibly one of the most widely used protocols and generally the application has the same name. On the Internet, a vast number of FTP servers are available. Where we have Internet servers of this kind, most administrators use an *anonymous* account that allows access by anyone. This type of access (generally referred to as anonymous FTP) then requests the eMail address of the user as a password before access is finally granted.

FTP applications have undergone a number of changes in recent years. To an extent, the days of the command line are gone in most applications however, in FTP this is particularly true. Today, most applications use a *point and click* graphical interface that allows the user to select which file(s) are to be either stored or retreived. FTP itself provides the user with a consistent and simple to understand interface whether graphical or command line based. The actual operation of FTP as a protocol however is less simple. Using two concurrent TCP connections is fairly unique and, as we said in the introduction, the protocol has to accommodate multiple file system types seamlessly

The Simple Mail Transfer Protocol (SMTP)

The Simple Mail Transfer Protocol (SMTP) as defined by RFC 821 serves to provide a reliable and efficient mail delivery service. In operation, as a result of a user mail request, the SMTP sender (the client) establishes a TCP connection with listener port 25_{10} (19_{16}) on a SMTP recipient (server). Then, through a defined set of commands/responses, transfers mail items to the receiver in much the same way as the FTP control channel. Unlike FTP however, all transactions take place over a single connection.

Where both the sender and recipient reside on the same network (or in the same domain), the sender establishes a direct connection with the receiving host as demonstrated Figure 18-1. Here, a user at the sending host requests a mail service to be established with the receiver and mail items are either delivered to remote mailbox(s) or directly to remote users if they are available.

Figure 18-1: A Simple SMTP Exchange

The delivery of such local mail is of course extremely necessary, however the strength of SMTP lies in its ability to deliver mail messages to any user on any co-operating machine globally. Where the sender is unable to directly deliver mail as in the example above, intermediate systems are employed that forward mail to the intended recipient(s). Indeed, we should be able to direct mail messages to any number of recipients on many systems as Figure 18-2 shows.

In this example, we see that a single user directs mail to two remote users via intermediate systems (mail servers). Mail servers such as these are what are termed *store and forward* hosts where mail arriving will be stored locally and either forwarded immediately, or more commonly at some pre-determined time in the future. A mail server therefore, is merely another SMTP host. As such it may also have its own local users in much the same way as the sender and recipient hosts do.

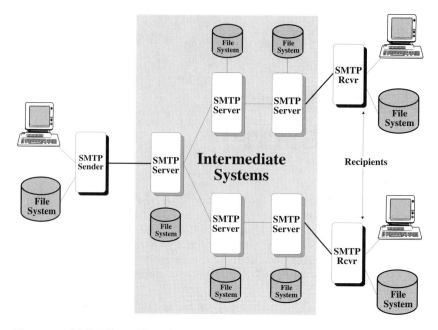

Figure 18-2: Mail Delivery Through Intermediate Systems

18.1 Defining Senders and Recipients

We saw in Chapter 15 (the Domain Name System (DNS)) how a name can be used to define an internet host. Therefore, since we have a hierarchical naming system, any host must have a unique name. Here we shall further refine that concept so that any user, on any host may also be uniquely identifiable in much the same way that both TCP and UDP uniquely identify processes through the use of *ports*.

You will recall that with TCP and UDP, the concept of sockets was introduced as a concatenation of the unique IP address and the port. Here we concatenate the unique user account with the domain name in much the same way, so as to provide a unique user account anywhere on our internet as follows:

The account name is separated from the fully specified domain name with an '@' symbol. Thus user *phil* on the machine *mercury.acmemkt.co.uk* would be specified as *phil@mercury.acmemkt.co.uk.*

18.2 Sending Mail Messages

Once the connection is established, the two ends of the link start a simple exchange that verifies that the hosts are communicating with who they think they are. The recipient normally starts this exchange with a simple welcome message indicating that the service is ready. The sender then sends the HELO message and identifies itself. This message is then acknowledged by the receiving host.

The actual process of sending a mail message comprises three parts. The process is started by issuing a MAIL or SEND command, used to identify the sender of the message. Once accepted, the sender specifies each of the recipients in turn and awaits a response from the host to which it is connected. These responses may be positive, in which case the server is able to deliver or forward the message to the intended recipient, or negative, in which case the server is unable or not prepared to deliver the message. Finally the sender sends the body of the message (the data) to the server process.

Identifying the sender of the message is also required to provide a *reverse path* over which replies may be sent and/or errors reported. The *reverse path* then always contains the source mailbox (the address of the sender's mailbox). The specification of recipients is provided through the RCPT command which will then specify a *forward path* that identifies a single recipient. Where multiple recipients of the message are desired, the RCPT command is issued as many times as required. The *forward path* may be more than a simple mailbox and can be a source routing list of hosts and the destination mailbox.

The data transferred then comprises a number of lines of text that ends in a specific character sequence. Normally a full stop entered alone on a line is used. This may of course change legitimately from implementation to implementation though.

Closing the connection can be initiated from either end, although in practice the receiving host rarely originates such a request. The closure sequence is started with the QUIT command that is then acknowledged by the receiver, and the TCP connection closed. The exchange below shows a simple mail interchange after the TCP connection is established to port 25. Note that the indented lines in this example then represent responses from the server.

```
            Sat,28 Jan 95 16:43:54 GMT acmemkt.co.uk
HELO millers.co.uk
            250 post — welcome millers.co.uk
MAIL FROM phil@post.flyers.co.uk
            250 OK
RCPT TO j.smith@ins.co.uk
            250 Recipient OK
RCPT TO george@acmemkt.co.uk
            550 No such user
RCPT TO harry.stott@acmemkt.co.uk
            250 Recipient OK
DATA
            354 Start mail input; end with <CRLF>.<CRLF>
lines of text
lines of text
lines of text
lines of text
.
            250 submitted and queued (msg.abc012582)
QUIT
            221 acmemkt.co.uk closing transmission channel
```

Where mail is forwarded, it generally relies on the recipient information being correct. Where the information is incorrect but the server knows the correct destination, the reply to the RCPT command could be one of either *251 User not local; will forward to <forward path>*, or *551 User not local; please try <forward path>*. In either case, the server is providing a warning which, in the second case, would then require further input.

We said previously that a mail message could be sent to a user's mailbox, or directly to the user. Obviously messages can only be sent directly to a user a) if the user is currently logged in, and b) if the user is prepared to accept mail at this time. SMTP has two distinct commands namely the MAIL and SEND commands. The MAIL command tells the receiver to deposit the incoming mail message in the users mailbox while the SEND command instructs the receiver to deliver the mail message directly to the user if possible. In addition, two further commands, the SAML, and SOML commands instruct the receiver to SEND *and* MAIL the user, and SEND *or* MAIL the user respectively.

18.2.1 Verifying and Expanding

SMTP allows the facilities of verifying user names and expanding mailing lists with the VRFY and EXPN commands. Whether the SMTP application actually implements these commands is implementation specific however where the commands are implemented, the sender sends the command with the user name to be verified or mailing list to be expanded. In the case of the VRFY command, the server then responds with the users full name or, with an error where the name is ambiguous. For example; VRFY Smith, could produce a response of 250 John Smith <j.smith@acmemkt.co.uk>. Equally the EXPN command could be used as follows:

```
EXPN mailing-list
        250 Niel Ambrose <nambrose@acmemkt.co.uk>
        250 Finbar Grey <grey@acmemkt.co.uk>
        250 Joan Brown <j.brown@acmemkt.co.uk>
```

18.3 SMTP Commands and Responses

The SMTP commands are used to define the mail transfer function requested by the user. All commands are character strings terminated by the <CRLF> characters and may contain several arguments.

18.3.1 SMTP Commands

Table 18-1 shows the commands used by SMTP together with any arguments required, and a brief description. There is no need for any particular implementation to support all commands however certain commads such as *HELO, MAIL, RCPT* etc. are generally considered mandatory.

Table 18-1: SMTP Commands

Command	Argument(s)	Description
HELO	The sender's host name.	This command identifies the sender's host name to the recipient. The recipient is identified in the connection greeting.
MAIL	The sender of the message.	Used to identify the sender of the mail message and therefore define the reverse path that should be used.
RCPT	The intended recipient of the message.	By defining the recipient, the forward path to that recipient is recorded. The RCPT command may be used as many times that there are recipients of the message.
DATA	The body of the mail message.	The receiver treats all lines that follow the DATA command as the mail message itself. The message is then terminated with a single full stop on a line by itself typically.
SEND	The intended recipient of the message.	This is used to initiate a mail message that should be delivered directly to a user if the user is currently logged in to the host system and is prepared to accept mail messages.
SOML	The intended recipient of the message.	Used to initiate a mail message that should be delivered directly to the user, if he is logged in and prepared to accept messages. Alternatively, the message should be delivered to the user's mailbox.
SAML	The intended recipient of the message.	Here the command specifies that the message should be delivered directly AND that a copy should be placed in the user's mailbox.
RSET		This command signifies that the current mail transaction should be aborted, that any stored senders, recipients, and mail data be deleted, and that the connection should be reset.
VRFY	The name of the recipient to be verified.	Used to confirm the identity of the user that was passed as an argument. The response to this command is the user's fully specified mailbox if the user exists.
EXPN	Mailing List to be expanded.	Asks the receiver to confirm the existence of the mailing list and return the fully specified mailboxes of the users that comprise the list.
HELP	The command name.	Asks the recipient server to send information regarding the command specified as the argument.
NOOP		Used to solicit an OK response from the recipient server.
QUIT		Specifies that the receiving host should send an OK response and then close the communication channel.
TURN		Commands the receiver to send an OK reply and then reverse the roles of the machines such that the receiver becomes the sending host.[1]

1. The TURN command is rarely used in SMTP implementations and normally results in a refusal. In this case the roles are not reversed and each end of the connection retains its original role.

18.3.2 SMTP Replies

Replies to SMTP commands are devised in such a way as to generate one, and only one, reply for each and any command. As with FTP, SMTP replies consist of a three digit number potentially followed by a text string. As before with FTP, the numeric response is designed for automatic processes while the textual string is designed for human operators. Table 18-2 shows typical response codes together with their textual meaning.

Table 18-2: SMTP Reply Codes and Meanings

Code	Description
211	System status or system help reply.
214	Help message. This contains information on a particular command.
220	Service ready.
221	Service closing transmission channel.
250	Requested action taken.
251	User not local will forward to *<forward path>*.
354	Start mail input. The message will normally be terminated with a single full stop alone on a line.
421	Service not available – closing communication channel.
450	Requested action not taken – mailbox unavailable.
451	Requested action not taken – local error in processing.
452	Requested action not taken – insufficient storage.
500	Syntax error – command unrecognized.
501	Syntax error in parameters or arguments.
502	Command not implemented.
503	Bad sequence of commands.
504	Command parameter not implemented.
550	Requested action not taken – mailbox unavailable.
551	User not local; please try *<forward path>*.
552	Requested action aborted – exceeded storage allocation.
553	Requested action not taken – mailbox name not allowed.
554	Transaction failed.

18.3.3 Returning Mail to the Sender

When we discussed the MAIL and SEND commands, we stated that the argument passed (who the message was from) was important since this provided a reverse path back to the sender. Certainly, if you wish to reply to a mail message received, the task will be made simpler if a reverse path exists as an integral part of the message itself. But what of errors? What will happen if the message cannot be delivered for any reason? Obviously here too the *reverse path* is important since an intermediate server is able to send back information as to what has gone wrong.

A problem exists here though, when the error message cannot be delivered back to the originator. Now non-delivery messages could potentially bounce backwards and forwards between hosts indefinitely!

The solution here is simple. Any message sent as a non-delivery reason contains no return address. Therefore should the non-delivery message itself be undeliverable, no error messages about error messages are produced. Our problem of non-delivery messages now no longer exists and errors are simply lost where they cannot be delivered.

18.4 Message Header Format

SMTP uses what is commonly termed an 822 header so named after the RFC (RFC 822) that defines it. This document is no more than a simple set of observed conventions which are rarely adhered to rigidly though. The reasons for such deviations are twofold. Firstly most of the information contained in mail messages is intended solely for human consumption and humans are able to tolerate a high degree of deviation. Secondly, while RFC 822 defines a simple framework, it also accepts that extensions may be applied.

Overall, the 822 message format is simple, a message header followed by an unrestricted area of message text, with the text area separated from the header by a simple blank line. Header lines then consist of a keyword delimited by a colon and any arguments associated with that keyword. Keywords such as *To*, *From*, *Date*, and *Subject* are common in this format although it should be noted that with modern application software the user may be unaware of their overall significance. This is because where they are not entered automatically, they will be prompted from the application and entered transparently into the mail message itself.

18.5 Summary

SMTP can be the very essence of Internet access and will certainly be the main reason why many organizations use the Internet at all. The protocol itself is, as we can see, simple in its operation and yet provides such major benefits. Most users are of course unaware of the underlying processes that take place during the sending of mail, taking the operation for granted since it is now so commonplace. Those interested in the underlying infrastructures however, must be aware of what is going on when mail is sent.

Mail is considered a key part of networking and as such uses the reliable services offered by TCP. Port 25_{10} is used and the actual connection is very similar to that used by say either Telnet or the FTP Control connection. All communications are based upon a client server model with our end stations (the clients) sending their mail to servers. Mail can then be passed from server to server (intermediate systems) until such time as the message is received by a server capable of delivering it. In many respects this can then be likened to the routing process discussed in Chapters 9 to 13.

While it is true that there are few hard and fast rules governing the transmittal of mail messages, most implementations adhere (if only losely) to the recommendations made in RFC 822. Today, the whole process of message preparation is automated, and this is then transparent to most users. Indeed, it is probably true to say that while mail remains the largest user of network resource, it is possibly the one that provides least visibility to the user.

Booting Internet Hosts with BootP and TFTP

Many network devices require that some form of image be loaded before they are able to perform their assigned function. *Basically dumb* devices such as repeaters, bridges, or even routers may need an image file downloaded to either participate in network management, or even to provide their basic function. The question is, that since the vendor will want to manufacture a large number of devices that will operate similarly (but not necessarily identically), how do they make them boot with potentially different images?

In Chapter 4, we saw that the RARP protocol, through co-operation with a server, allowed a device to determine its IP Address where it was in possession of only its physical or MAC Address. In this case, once in possession of it's IP Adrress, the device could then broadcast (using an IP file transfer protocol such as the Trivial File Transfer Protocol (TFTP)) to obtain an image file, again from a co-operating host. This, in part, is one of the major drawbacks of using RARP – that unless we now program our device, it will always need to broadcast for its image file, and will potentially load the same image to all devices. RFC 1084, (BOOTP Vendor Information Extensions) tells us that although RARP *"...can be used in conjunction with other supplemental protocols...a more integrated solution may be more desirable"*.

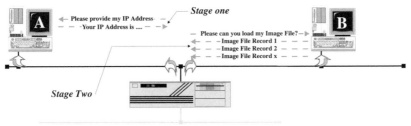

Figure 19-1: The Two Phase Boot Load Process

BootP, as defined by RFC 951, provides a means through which network hosts may achieve a higher level of autonomy. More specifically, it allows a device to determine its IP Address, the name of the image file to download, the IP Address of the server from which the file may be downloaded, and (where appropriate) the IP Address of the default router. An obvious advantage of such a system is the centralized management of network addresses, but most importantly we may now assign unique configuration files to each host on our network. BootP does not however load the image file itself. Instead, as with RARP, the process can be thought of as having two distinct phases: Firstly the acquisition of relevant information, and secondly the loading of the image file by a protocol such as TFTP. Figure 19-1 shows this two phase operation.

In Figure 19-1, the station on the left (Station A) acts as a RARP, or BootP server, and that on the right (Station B) as a TFTP server. Having previously looked at RARP, we shall now examine the use of the Bootstrap Protocol (BootP) and the Trivial File Transfer Protocol (TFTP) as a method of loading an image file. Note that the discussion of TFTP, is also applicable to where RARP/TFTP is used to load image or parameter information. Lets us not make the assumption that TFTP can only be used in this type of environment though. TFTP is a perfectly good stand-alone file transfer mechanism, albeit simple as it's name suggests.

19.1 The Bootstrap Protocol (BootP)

BootP operates over the User Datagram Protocol (UDP) and the Internet Protocol (IP), thereby providing significant advantages over RARP. Before discussing BootP then, it is useful to remind ourselves of the shortcomings that RARP has.

- RARP is a Link Layer protocol, and while we must assume that all network devices implement a Link Layer, not all devices implement RARP. RARP therefore may only be implemented on devices that have direct access to the Data Link layer, alternatively such devices would require considerable modification to allow access to the raw data required. On the other hand, BootP may be implemented on almost any device that supports an IP stack.

- RARP provides only the IP Address of the device, the actual file name that should be loaded (particularly in the case where RARP is used to start the load process of an image file) must be *hard coded* making it less flexible overall.

- With RARP, after successfully completing the operation, we shall be in possession of only our IP Address and some hard coded image file name. Since we will not know the addresses of the actual server, or any router that data may have to pass through, we are restricted to broadcasting our file load request that must then be serviced by a host on the local network. If the server is located on a distant network (maybe many hops away) we are therefore potentially prevented from using it.

19.1.1 BootP Basic Operation

RFC 951 suggests that, where used, the *client* device requesting the boot load service, implements the BootP protocol (and any other required protocol) in PROM or other non-volatile storage. This then ensures that no operator intervention is required, making BootP naturally simple in operation.

- BootP uses a simple, single packet exchange. The *client* sends a request (normally through an IP broadcast), and a response is generated by the *server*. If a response is not forthcoming, the client continually re-sends its request (after a suitable timeout period) until a reply is received.

- The same, *fixed length*, fields are used in both the request and reply. These fields are designed to be long enough to cover all eventualities and, by using the same request and reply formats, the overall operation is simplified.

- The request can optionally contain the name of the server that should respond. Thus, where multiple versions of the same bootfile exist, the client can specify the server explicitly. This provides a more flexible approach than RARP, however this is at the expense of simplicity since the server information would need to be pre-programmed into the device.

- The request can contain an optional *generic* filename. This allows further flexibility in the protocol, since the response would then contain a fully specified path name for the appropriate file. In this way, the client may request a *UNIX* type image file, but allow the BootP server, through its database, to determine the actual name of the file itself. Where the filename requested is a null string, or where the device has no knowledge of the file that should be loaded, the server returns the default filename instead.

- Clients may know their IP Address before commencement of the BootP process. Where this is the case, BootP will probably be used to determine the image filename only. If the client does not know its IP Address, then BootP will provide it, again based upon information stored in the server's database.

- We have said that one major advantage over RARP is that by using BootP, we are able to load an image file using TFTP or some other file transfer protocol from a server that may reside on a distant network. In this case, the client must be in possession of the servers IP Address, and the address of a default router. BootP again provides us with this functionality, in that replies can contain these pieces of information.

19.1.2 BootP Protocol Format

As we have seen, the underlying principle of the BootP protocol is that of simplicity. Figure 19-2 shows the packet format, which is then used for both requests and responses.

The single octet *Operation* has two possible values; 1 for a boot request, or 2 for a reply. The *Hardware Address Type* field is filled in by the client device, and is used to specify the type of underlying network hardware in use. Values for this field are specified in the Assigned Numbers document, and are the same as those used for the ARP/RARP protocol. A value of 1 in this field indicates that the hardware type is 10Mb Ethernet for example. The *Hardware Address Length* is used to specify how long the physical address is. For Ethernet this will be 6. The *Hops* field is always set to zero by clients requesting a bootstrap load service, and is then incremented by routers[1] as the packet passes from network to network.

---

1. Using the BootP protocol in a routed environment introduces certain difficulties. These will be discussed in section 19.1.4.

Client devices generating requests place a randomly generated identifier in the *Transaction ID* field. Since the same fields are used by both the request and the response, this field then allows the client to match responses received with the requests that it generated. The *Seconds* field is again entered by the client when generating the request, and is used to convey to servers how long the client has waited for a response. In this way, a server that would not normally service a particular host, may send a response if the client had waited an inordinate amount of time.

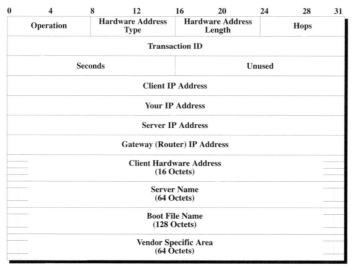

0	4	8	12	16	20	24	28	31
Operation		Hardware Address Type		Hardware Address Length		Hops		
Transaction ID								
Seconds				Unused				
Client IP Address								
Your IP Address								
Server IP Address								
Gateway (Router) IP Address								
Client Hardware Address (16 Octets)								
Server Name (64 Octets)								
Boot File Name (128 Octets)								
Vendor Specific Area (64 Octets)								

Figure 19-2: BootP Packet Format

The *Client IP Address* field is entered in a request by the client device only where it is already in possession of this information. If the client does not know its address, this field is left as nulls indicating that the server should provide this information. The server will however not adjust this field. Instead, the *Your IP Address* field is used by servers in responses. The *Gateway IP Address* field contains the IP address of the router that the client device should use when loading its image file. Where a router is not required during the loading phase, this field will normally be left blank by the server. The 16 octet *Client Hardware Address* field is filled in by the client device creating the request. This field is never truncated, but is instead padded with zeroes where the underlying network hardware uses a shorter addressing scheme as in Ethernet.

The 64 octet null-terminated *Server Name* field is optional, but allows the required server to be named. Since most BootP requests are broadcast by client devices, potentially many CPU cycles could be wasted by the receipt of requests that the server cannot service. By naming the server, it is hoped that some of this wastage can be avoided by the request packet being rejected as it is received. The *Boot File Name* field is the fully specified filename that the client should request from the load server. Requests can contain generic names, such as *"UNIX"*, that identifies the type of image requested. Upon receipt of such a request, the server is then able to interrogate its database to find the fully specified filename required, and then return this to the client. Finally, the 64 octet *Vendor Specific Area,* as its name suggests, was designed to convey information specific to the device requesting the BootP service. In the request form, this area may be used to convey information such as the serial number of the device, or hardware type. The only real restriction is that the operation of BootP must not rely on any information that may be contained here. Since the original introduction of BootP, through RFC 951, this area has been defined more formally. Most significantly, RFC 1084 *BOOTP Vendor Information Extensions* defines the following:

The first four octets are used to define the mode in which succeeding data is interpreted. This value, known as the *magic cookie,* is 99.130.83.99 (in dotted decimal notation). The remainder of the area is then implemented as free format with *extendible* tagged fields. Two major data types then exist, namely fixed and variable length. Two fixed length data types exist, those that have no data and comprise a single tag and are implicitly one octet in length, and those that contain specific data. The variable length fields comprise, by implication, a tag field, a length field, and the actual data being conveyed. Table 19-1 shows these data types:

Table 19-1: BootP Vendor Specific Area Variable Length Data Types

Tag	Data Type	Length	Description
0	Padding	-	Used to align subsequent fields to word boundaries.
1	Subnet Mask	4	Specifies the Subnet mask for the local network.
2	Time of Day	4	Provides the time offset of the local net in seconds and specified in Co-ordinated Universal Time (UTC) as a signed 32 bit integer.
3	Gateways	Variable	The field is X octets long and specifies the IP Addresses of X/4 routers. The first router specified should be considered preferred.
4	Time Servers	Variable	The field is X octets long and specifies the IP Addresses of X/4 time servers.
5	IEN-116 Servers	Variable	The field is X octets long and specifies the IP Addresses of X/4 IEN-116 type Name Servers.
6	Domain Servers	Variable	The field is X octets long and specifies the IP Addresses of X/4 Domain Name Servers.
7	Log Servers	Variable	The field is X octets long and specifies the IP Addresses of X/4 Log Servers.
8	Quote/Cookie Servers	Variable	The field is X octets long and specifies the IP Addresses of X/4 Quote of the Day Servers.
9	LPR Servers	Variable	The field is X octets long and specifies the IP Addresses of X/4 BSD Printer Servers.
10	Impress Servers	Variable	The field is X octets long and specifies the IP Addresses of X/4 Impress Network Image Servers.
11	RLP Servers	Variable	The field is X octets long and specifies the IP Addresses of X/4 Resource Location Protocol (RLP) Servers.
12	Host Names	Variable	Specifies the name of the client. This name may, or may not, be domain qualified.
13	Boot File Size	2	A 2 octet value that specifies the size of the boot file expressed in 512 octet blocks.

Tag	Data Type	Length	Description
128-254	Reserved	-	Specifies additional site-specific information. This is interpreted on a site, or implementation specific basis.
255	End of List	-	Identifies the end of useable data in the Vendor Specific Area. Remaining space in this 64 octet area is then padded with zeroes.

19.1.3 Constructing the BootP Request

When creating a BootP request, the client will fill in the *Source IP Address* field in the IP Header (if this is known) or will alternatively enter all zeroes. If the BootP server address is known, this will be entered into the *Destination Address* field of the IP Header. However, where the destination is not known, the client will enter the broadcast address 255.255.255.255, indicating that a local broadcast should be used.

BootP uses two reserved port numbers (67_{10}, and 68_{10}) to identify the Server and Client processes respectively. The client will therefore enter those port numbers in the UDP Header; 67_{10} (43_{16}) in the *Destination Port* field, and 68_{10} (44_{16}) in the *Source Port* field. Finally, the client device enters any information that it knows into the BootP packet, and then transmits the request. Unlike many applications that use a dynamically allocated Source Port, the BootP port must be reserved to ensure that responses are received.

One of the primary reasons for using BootP in the first place is for the client to determine its IP Address. Since it is unlikely to have any information other than its physical address, the need to broadcast the request is apparent. But, what is not necessarily quite so obvious is that the response will almost certainly also have to be broadcast back! The client machine will not know its own IP Address at the time that the response is generated. It will therefore be unable to respond to ARP frames generated by the server. One alternative method, available in BSD 4.2 UNIX systems, is for the server to "manually" construct an ARP cache entry from the *Client Hardware Address* field without actually sending an ARP frame. However since this is implementation specific, it cannot be considered a guaranteed method, and broadcasting the response may be the only sure way to guarantee that the response will be received by the client device. The port number, together with the randomly generated Transaction ID will then identify a response destined for any particular device on the network.

19.1.4 Using BootP with Routers

We have said that, most likely, the client device will broadcast its request across the local network. So what happens when the BootP server is several network hops away? We have seen that routers will not forward broadcast messages, so how will our request ever get to the BootP server?

RFC 951 suggests a simple modification to router code that allows them to listen to BootP broadcasts and then re-transmit these packets over their other interfaces. Obviously it would be extremely wasteful if the router were to re-broadcast each packet received, especially if it were to be the first packet sent. So the RFC recommends that re-broadcast only takes place when the *Seconds* field reaches some pre-determined value, indicating that the packet has been re-transmitted at least once. This *Helper* or *UDP Broadcast Forwarding* function, as it is generally called, then provides another advantage of BootP, in that BootP requests may traverse multiple networks whereas RARP packets certainly cannot.

19.1.5 BootP Configuration

Any configuration of network hosts is implementation specific, however because of the nature of this protocol, it may be useful to examine the BootP configuration file found on a Sun workstation. The file, ***/etc/bootptab***, may look something like this:

`LR1-s6:\`	*A Label to uniquely identify this record in the file*
`:ht=ethernet:\`	*The Hardware Type of the client devices interface*
`:ha=0800874208e6:\`	*The Hardware Address of the client device*
`:ip=192.168.89.62:\`	*The IP Address that should be assigned to the client*
`:sm=255.255.255.0:\`	*The Subnet Mask that the client should use*
`:hd=/home/tftpboot:\`	*The Home Directory that contains the image file*
`:bf=x0208e6.img:`	*The name of the image file itself*
`xRR1-s4:\`	
`:ht=ethernet:\`	
`:ha=0800871208e4:\`	
`:ip=192.168.16.10:\`	
`:sm=255.255.255.0:\`	
`:hd=/home/tftpboot:\`	
`:gw=193.128.6.3:\`	*The IP Address of the Gateway (Router) to use*
`:bf=x0208e4.img:`	

It is obviously impossible to be specific about configuration files and many *flavours* of BootP configuration files exist. Typically however they all include a means of entering the the IP and physical addresses of the clients that they will service, and also information about the file that should be used and of course where that file is located.

19.1.6 Re-Transmitting BootP Requests

We have said that where a request is not answered within a certain time, the client will re-transmit its request. In order to ensure that the network does not become flooded with these requests however, re-transmissions generally take place at intervals of around 4 seconds. Where the request has not been answered in say, 4 minutes, re-transmission may then slow to only once in each 4 minute period.

An alternative method may be to use a random re-transmission timer that employs a *binary exponential back-off* similar to that used by Ethernet after a colission has been detected. The advantage of this system is that if a network with multiple BootP clients is attempting to recover from a power failure, recovery could be quicker since there would be fewer BootP response *collisions* where multiple servers might respond. The actual method employed will of course be implementation specific, however these methods are suggested by RFC 951 and are therefore quoted here.

Figure 19-3 shows a sample BootP *Request* packet based upon the information that we have discussed in the preceeding sections. The response (not shown here) would then have the missing information filled out and be returned to the requesting station using an identical message format with the Operation field set to indicate a response.

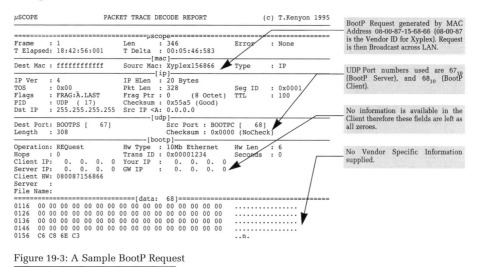

```
µSCOPE                  PACKET TRACE DECODE REPORT            (c) T.Kenyon 1995
==========================================µscope==================================
Frame   : 1                 Len     : 346           Error    : None
T Elapsed: 18:42:56:001     T Delta : 00:05:46:583
                            ─[mac]─
Dest Mac : ffffffffffff     Sourc Mac: Xyplex156866        Type    : IP
                            ─[ip]─
IP Ver   : 4                IP HLen : 20 Bytes
TOS      : 0x00             Pkt Len : 328          Seg ID   : 0x0001
Flags    : FRAG:Ã.LAST      Frag Ptr : 0    (8 Octet)  TTL     : 100
PID      : UDP  ( 17)       Checksum : 0x55a5 (Good)
Dst IP   : 255.255.255.255  Src IP <A: 0.0.0.0
                            ─[udp]─
Dest Port: BOOTPS [   67]        Src Port : BOOTPC [    68]
Length   : 308                   Checksum : 0x0000 (NoCheck)
                            ─[bootp]─
Operation: REQuest          Hw Type  : 10Mb Ethernet    Hw Len   : 6
Hops     : 0                Trans ID : 0x00001234       Seconds  : 0
Client IP:   0.  0.  0.  0  Your IP  :   0.  0.  0.  0
Server IP:   0.  0.  0.  0  GW IP    :   0.  0.  0.  0
Client HW: 080087156866
Server   :
File Name:
============================[data:  68]============================
0116   00 00 00 00 00 00 00 00 00 00 00 00 00 00 00 00   ................
0126   00 00 00 00 00 00 00 00 00 00 00 00 00 00 00 00   ................
0136   00 00 00 00 00 00 00 00 00 00 00 00 00 00 00 00   ................
0146   00 00 00 00 00 00 00 00 00 00 00 00 00 00 00 00   ................
0156   C6 C8 6E C3                                       ..n.
```

BootP Request generated by MAC Address 08-00-87-15-68-66 (08-00-87 is the Vendor ID for Xyplex). Request is then Broadcast across LAN.

UDP Port numbers used are 67_{10} (BootP Server), and 68_{10} (BootP Client).

No information is available in the Client therefore these fields are left as all zeroes.

No Vendor Specific Information supplied.

Figure 19-3: A Sample BootP Request

19.2 TFTP

Having considered two methods by which a device can obtain information about itself (RARP, and BootP) we now move to the second stage of the load process, that of loading the actual image file. To achieve this goal, some form of file transfer is required. It is conceivable that the device could use the File Transfer Protocol (FTP). However, this is an unlikely choice since FTP is a large and complex protocol that requires TCP, and cannot easily be programmed into PROM or other *static* memory. The much simpler Trivial File Transfer Protocol (TFTP), as defined by RFC 1350, uses UDP (in much the same way that BootP does), and it allows requests to be broadcast. TFTP therefore is an ideal choice.

TFTP, as its name suggests, is a simple protocol without many of the features and functions available in other file transfer protocols such as FTP. For example, TFTP supports only the reading and writing of files to or from a remote server. As such, it cannot list directories, and there is also no user authentication.

Because TFTP uses UDP, it works in a connectionless mode, and must provide any additional reliability (over that provided by IP/UDP) itself. TFTP accomplishes this by having receivers separately acknowledging every packet that they receive. Likewise, transmitting stations only transmit packets in response to requests, or on receipt of an acknowledgement relating to the previous packet. Finally, TFTP transfers always take place using a block size of between 0 and 512 octets each. Larger block sizes that would be available in say FTP are not supported at all.

19.2.1 TFTP Operation

A transfer always commences with a request to either read or write a file. Assuming that the server grants the request, it will then respond with an acknowledgement (in the case of a *write* request), or a block of data containing between 0 and 512 octets (in the case of a *read* request). The transfer of data now takes place one data block at a time, with the sender waiting to receive an acknowledgement from the receiver before the next block may be transmitted. In this way overhead is reduced, since the sender needs to maintain only one block in its buffers for retransmission purposes: This *lock/step* mechanism also ensures that all previous blocks must have been successfully received.

All data blocks are numbered from one, and acknowledgements (except for the initial acknowledgement following a *write* request) always carry the number of the data block that they are acknowledging. In this way there can be no confusion by either side as to how the transfer is progressing. Since an acknowledgement sent in response to a Write Request is not acknowledging data, it is considered a special case. Here, an acknowledgement of zero is used to signify to the requester that the transfer may proceed and this is the only time that an acknowledgement of zero is legal. Where a packet is lost, the recipient will timeout and re-transmit its last packet (acknowledgement or data). The sender will, on receipt of this retransmission, then re-transmit its own last packet thus re-establishing the link.

Although the operation of TFTP is simple, it is able to detect and report errors. Typically errors cause immediate termination of the transfer, and are always signalled by an error packet that is never acknowledged nor re-transmitted. No guarantees are made that error packets will ever arrive at their intended destination. Instead, time-outs are used to detect when termination should occur due to packet loss of this type.

As we said, TFTP transfers always use a block size of between 0 and 512 octets but, where a block is less than 512 octets long, termination of the transfer is implied. In this case, when the final block is received, it will be acknowledged by the receiving station and the host will then terminate its side of the transfer. This termination may occur immediately after the acknowledgement is sent, but most implementations will delay for a period of time to ensure that retransmission is not required. So what would happen if the file being transferred is an exact multiple of 512 octets? In this case the file is transferred using 512 octet blocks until all data has been sent, followed by a data block that contains zero octets of data to signal that the transfer should terminate.

19.2.2 TFTP Protocol Format

In all, TFTP uses four separate PDUs that are: *Read Request* (RRQ), *Write Request* (WRQ), *Data, Acknowledgement* (ACK), and *Error*. The Read Request and Write Request share the same format which is shown in Figure 19-4.

OP Code (2 Octets)	Filename (Variable)	Null (1 Octet)	Mode (Variable)	Null (1 Octet)

Figure 19-4: TFTP Read/Write Request

The two octet *OP Code* field defines the type of operation requested: 1 for Read Requests, and 2 for Write Requests. The *Filename* field is a variable length *Null Terminated, Netascii* string. Where Netascii is 8 bit USASCII with the modifications specified by the Telnet protocol (RFC 794). The first of the *Null* fields then represents the termination of this string.

The variable length *Mode* field is also a Null Terminated Netascii string, this time specifying the mode that should be used for the data transfer. The Mode field will contain one of the following strings:

- **netascii**

    In this mode, hosts must translate any data received into their own format.

- **octet**

    In this mode, the file is transferred in the format of the machine from which the file is being transferred.

- **mail**

    Although this mode is now rarely used, the name of the recipient must be used instead of the filename, and the transfer must begin with a Write Request. Apart from this, it is identical to the netascii mode.

    The name of the recipient may be either just the users name <username>, or it may be of the form <username>@<hostname>. In the latter case of course, the mail may then be forwarded by one or more mail relays.

Data is transferred in Data packets as described in Figure 19-5.

OP Code (2 Octets)	Block Number (2 Octets)	Data (0 - 512 Octets)

Figure 19-5: TFTP Data Format

For this PDU, the *OP Code* is always set to 3, indicating that it is carrying data, and the two octet *Block Number* field contains the number of the data block being carried. Blocks are always numbered from 1, and these numbers are incremented for each successive block sent. If the block contains 512 octets of data it cannot be the last block; where the block contains less than 512 octets of data, it signals that all data has been transferred, and that the transfer should terminate.

All packets other than duplicate Acknowledgements and Error packets are either acknowledged, or an Error packet is sent in place of an acknowledgement

OP Code (2 Octets)	Block Number (2 Octets)

Figure 19-6: TFTP Acknowledgement Format

after a suitable timeout period. An acknowledgement to a Write Request or Data packet is either an ACK packet, or an Error. An acknowledgement to an ACK or a Read Request, is either a Data packet or an Error. Figure 19-6 shows the format of the Acknowledgement packet: The *Op Code* for this type of packet is always 4, and the *Block Number* field contains the block number of the Data block that is actually being acknowledged. There are no other fields in this packet at all. Remember though that the next data block will not be sent by the transmitter until such time as the acknowledgement for the previous block has been received. Should the acknowledgement be lost, the transmitter will timeout and re-send the previous Data block. In normal operation, this will then force the receiver to re-send the acknowledgement, and thus re-establish the transfer from that point.

When Write Requests are granted by the server, these are acknowledged by an ACK packet. So what will be the value of the *Block Number* field given that no Data has been transferred yet? More specifically, Data packets are always numbered from 1, and the first Data packet must carry this number. Since we cannot allow any confusion that might arise from a delayed acknowledgement reaching the receiver, the value of the *Block Number* field for this type of ACK, is always zero. A positive acknowledgement of a Write Request is therefore the only time that an Acknowledgement packet may carry this value as its Block Number.

Finally, we must consider what happens when things go wrong, and how errors are reported. This task is performed by the Error packet shown in Figure 19-7. However, before considering this, remember that TFTP provides little possibility of recovery from error conditions. Indeed only one error will not cause the transfer to cease abruptly, and that is when a packet is received addressed to an unknown port. In this case since the port number is unknown, the receiver will discard the packet since it will be unaware that a transfer is taking place.

OP Code (2 Octets)	Error Code (2 Octets)	Error Message (Variable)	Null (1 Octet)

Figure 19-7: TFTP Error Format

The *OP Code* is always 5 for this type of packet. The two octet *Error Code* is an integer that defines the error that is being reported and Table 19-2 describes all possible values. The *Error Message* is a variable length, *Null Terminated*, *netascii* description of the error, intended only to ease the decoding of error conditions by human operators. Finally, the single octet *Null* field represents the null termination of the Error Message field.

Table 19-2: TFTP Error Codes

Error Code	Meaning
0	Not defined – See Error Message field (if present) for meaning
1	File not found
2	Access violation
3	Disk full or allocation exceeded
4	Illegal TFTP operation
5	Unknown Transfer ID (See section 19.2.3 – The determination of UDP Port Numbers)
6	File already exists
7	No such user

Should a request not be granted, or should an abnormal condition occur, an Error Message is sent. Error messages may be sent in response to any other packet type, but should be considered only a courtesy since they are neither re-transmitted nor acknowledged. It is partly because of this, and the designers' motivation to keep the protocol so simple, that no recovery can take place.

19.2.3 The Determination of UDP Port Numbers

As we have seen on several occasions, it is imperative that the processes at each end of the transfer know the ID of the other. In UDP, these processes are identified on a particular host, by unique *Ports*. We saw that with BootP we have two such reserved ports, so that both the server and client processes can be identified. With TFTP however, we have only a server port reserved (Port 69_{10}). So how can the TFTP server process cope with multiple simultaneous requests, and how do clients assign their own *source* ports?

With TFTP, the *Port* is referred to as a *Transfer ID*, and obviously since the source and destinations must be unique on their respective hosts we need to have some means of determining this. The way that TFTP deals with this problem is as follows:

- The host making the request (Read or Write) generates a Transaction ID (TID) between 0 and 65,535. This is normally generated randomly, to guard against the possibility of successive TIDs having the same value. Of course, any number eventually selected should not clash with another that may potentially be in use, or that may be selected by other processes.

  This TID then becomes the *Source Port* number used in the UDP header for all further packets generated for this transfer.

- The Request (Read or Write) is now sent to the server using the reserved port number 69 as the UDP *Destination Port*, and the TID previously generated as the UDP *Source Port*.

- On receipt, the server processes the request and it too generates a TID. The same restrictions regarding uniqueness still apply, only in this case, the server should of course also avoid selecting port 69.

- The server now responds using the client's TID as the UDP *Destination Port*, and its own TID (just generated) as the UDP *Source Port*. All further exchanges associated with this transfer now take place using these TIDs, which are then destroyed when the transfer terminates.

In this way, since the server *spawns* a new port number for each request, it is able to service multiple clients. Equally, by random generation, each client should always choose a unique port number that can be used.

19.2.4 Security and TFTP

We have already said that TFTP provides no authentication. This being the case, provided that the correct (or indeed incorrect) permissions are applied to files, any client process could conceivably read or write files on the server. In an effort to overcome this problem, many implementations now incorporate what is termed *Secure TFTP*, which prohibits a client from straying outside of a pre-defined directory structure.

In this implementation, TFTP considers the TFTP home directory; i.e. where TFTP loadable files exist, to be the *root* of the file system. This means that although it is still the permissions of files in this area that determine who can read or write them, TFTP users cannot stray from this particular directory tree as shown in Figure 19-8.

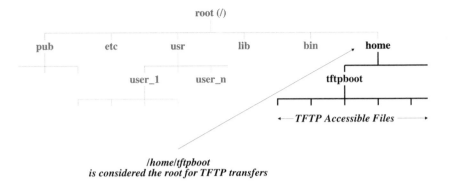

root (/)

pub   etc   usr   lib   bin   home

          user_1   user_n   tftpboot

                                          ◄—— *TFTP Accessible Files* ——►

/home/tftpboot
is considered the root for TFTP transfers

Figure 19-8: TFTP Security

19.2.5 Sample TFTP Traces

In this section we examine three TFTP traces. In the first (Figure 19-9) we see a simple Write Request that is terminated because the file to be transferred does not currently reside on the server. In the second (Figure 19-10) we see a TFTP *Get* (Read) operation that is used to transfer a file from the Server to the Client. In this example the transfer is successful and terminates normally. Finally, in our third example (Figure 19-11), we see the start of a TFTP Write operation. This is significant since it is the only time that an Acknowledgement of zero is used. A Read Request for example, is acknowledged simply by supplying the firt 512 octets of the requested file.

As with other examples however, the traces presented here represent only small transfers for the sake of clarity and where necessary data has been truncated.

```
μSCOPE                    PACKET TRACE DECODE REPORT          (c) T.Kenyon 1995      Request from station sent to UDP Port
                                                                                     69₁₀ (TFTP) of the Server.

===============================μscope==============================================
Frame    : 6              Len      : 70              Error    : None                Operation is Write Request.
T Elapsed: 19:38:38:538   T Delta  : 00:00:03:052
                          ───[mac]───
Dest Mac : Sun   1bc95a   Sourc Mac: 0000e80f04af    Type     : IP                  Filename "autoexec.bat".
                          ───[ip]───
IP Ver   : 4              IP HLen  : 20 Bytes
TOS      : 0x00           Pkt Len  : 52              Seg ID   : 0x0002              Null Terminator.
Flags    : FRAG:Ā.LAST    Frag Ptr : 0    (8 Octet)  TTL      : 32
PID      : UDP ( 17)      Checksum : 0x98    (Good)
Dst IP <C: 192.168.12.171 Src IP <C: 192.168.12.36                                 Transfer Mode is "netascii" followed
                          ───[udp]───                                              by a Null Terminator.
Dest Port: TFTP [  69]    Src Port : 1213
Length   : 32             Checksum : 0x9c33 (Good)
                          ───[tftp]───
Operation: WReq
===========================[data:   26]============================================
002C  61 75 74 6F 65 78 65 63 2E 62 61 74 00 6E 65 74  autoexec.bat.net
003C  61 73 63 69 69 00 B7 A7 12 77                    ascii....w

===============================μscope==============================================
Frame    : 7              Len      : 65              Error    : None
T Elapsed: 19:38:38:647   T Delta  : 00:00:00:109                                  Error (0005₁₆).
                          ───[mac]───
Dest Mac : 0000e80f04af   Sourc Mac: Sun   1bc95a    Type     : IP                 Code 0001₁₆ File Not Found.
                          ───[ip]───
IP Ver   : 4              IP HLen  : 20 Bytes
TOS      : 0x00           Pkt Len  : 47              Seg ID   : 0xe66c             Null Terminated Ascii message "File
Flags    : FRAG:Ā.LAST    Frag Ptr : 0    (8 Octet)  TTL      : 60                 not found".
PID      : UDP ( 17)      Checksum : 0xfe31 (Good)
Dst IP <C: 192.168.12.36  Src IP <C: 192.168.12.171
                          ───[udp]───
Dest Port: 1213           Src Port : 3964
Length   : 27             Checksum : 0x0000 (NoCheck)
===========================[data:   23]============================================
002A  00 05 00 01 46 69 6C 65 20 6E 6F 74 20 66 6F 75  ....File not fou
003A  6E 64 00 35 2A 38 E9                             nd.5*8.
```

Figure 19-9: A Sample TFTP Write Request Terminating in an Error

```
========================μscope========================
Frame    : 3          Len      : 66            Error    : None
T Elapsed: 19:42:59:717   T Delta  : 00:00:00:008
------------------------[mac]------------------------
Dest Mac : Sun    1bc95a  Sourc Mac: 0000e80f04af   Type     : IP
------------------------[ip]------------------------
IP Ver   : 4          IP HLen  : 20 Bytes
TOS      : 0x00       Pkt Len  : 48              Seg ID   : 0x0009
Flags    : FRAG:Ā.LAST Frag Ptr : 0    (8 Octet)  TTL      : 32
PID      : UDP ( 17)  Checksum : 0x95   (Good)
Dst IP <C: 192.168.12.171   Src IP <C: 192.168.12.36
------------------------[udp]------------------------
Dest Port: TFTP [  69]    Src Port : 1215
Length   : 28             Checksum : 0x4c14 (Good)
------------------------[tftp]------------------------
Operation: RReq
========================[data: 22]========================
002C  70 68 69 6C 2E 74 78 74 00 6E 65 74 61 73 63 69   phil.txt.netasci
003C  69 00 91 AB 29 4E                                 i...)N
```

The station contacts the server on UDP Port 69_{10}. The selection of the Source Port (1215_{10}) is implementation specific.

Operation is a Read Request.

Null terminated filename "phil.txt" followed by the Null terminated Mode "netascii".

```
========================μscope========================
Frame    : 4          Len      : 562           Error    : None
T Elapsed: 19:42:59:827   T Delta  : 00:00:00:110
------------------------[mac]------------------------
Dest Mac : 0000e80f04af   Sourc Mac: Sun    1bc95a   Type     : IP
------------------------[ip]------------------------
IP Ver   : 4          IP HLen  : 20 Bytes
TOS      : 0x00       Pkt Len  : 544             Seg ID   : 0xe673
Flags    : FRAG:Ā.LAST Frag Ptr : 0    (8 Octet)  TTL      : 60
PID      : UDP ( 17)  Checksum : 0xfc39 (Good)
Dst IP <C: 192.168.12.36    Src IP <C: 192.168.12.171
------------------------[udp]------------------------
Dest Port: 1215           Src Port : 3968
Length   : 524            Checksum : 0x0000 (NoCheck)
========================[data: 520]========================
002A  00 03 00 01 40 45 43 48 4F 20 4F 46 46 0D 0A 50   ....@ECHO OFF..P
003A  52 4F 4D 50 54 20 24 70 24 67 0D 0A 53 45 54 20   ROMPT $p$g..SET
004A  54 45 4D 50 3D 43 3A 5C 54 45 4D 50 0D 0A 49 46   TEMP=C:\TEMP..IF
005A  20 4E 4F 54 20 45 58 49 53 54 20 56 45 52 53 49   NOT EXIST VERSI
006A  4F 4E 2E 20 20 47 4F 54 4F 20 53 45 54 55 50 0D   ON.  GOTO SETUP.
007A  0A 43 4C 53 0D 0A 54 59 50 45 20 56 45 52 53 49   .CLS..TYPE VERSI
008A  4F 4E 0D 0A 0D 0A 43 3A 5C 44 4F 53 5C 53 48 41   ON....C:\DOS\SHA
009A  52 45 2E 45 58 45 20 2F 4C 3A 48 20 2F 4C 3A 30   RE.EXE .LH /L:0
00AA  43 3A 5C 44 4F 53 5C 53 4D 41 52 54 44 52 56 2E   C:\DOS\SMARTDRV.
00BA  45 58 45 20 43 3A 5C 44 4F 53 5C 44 4F 53 4B 42   EXE..C:\DOS\DOSK
00CA  45 59 0D 0A 50 41 54 48 20 43 3A 5C 4F 56 3B 43   EY..PATH C:\OV;C
00DA  3A 5C 58 43 50 3B 43 3A 5C 4E 45 54 4D 41 4E 41   :\XCP;C:\NETMANA
```

The packet length is 544 octets which comprises 512 octets data, 20 octets for the IP Header, 8 octets for the UDP Header, and 4 octets for the TFTP Header.

TFTP automatically re-negotiates the port through which it is operating. Requests arrive at Port 69_{10} however once successful, a new (random) port is selected. In this case the Server is now using 3968_{10}.

The positive response to a TFTP Read Request is to supply the first block (up to 512 octets) of the requested file. The data shown here has of course been truncated.

Opcode 0003 – Data Packet, Block Number 0001.

```
========================μscope========================
Frame    : 5          Len      : 64            Error    : None
T Elapsed: 19:42:59:835   T Delta  : 00:00:00:008
------------------------[mac]------------------------
Dest Mac : Sun    1bc95a  Sourc Mac: 0000e80f04af   Type     : IP
------------------------[ip]------------------------
IP Ver   : 4          IP HLen  : 20 Bytes
TOS      : 0x00       Pkt Len  : 32              Seg ID   : 0x000a
Flags    : FRAG:Ā.LAST Frag Ptr : 0    (8 Octet)  TTL      : 32
PID      : UDP ( 17)  Checksum : 0xa4   (Good)
Dst IP <C: 192.168.12.171   Src IP <C: 192.168.12.36
------------------------[udp]------------------------
Dest Port: 3968           Src Port : 1215
Length   : 12             Checksum : 0x5172 (Good)
========================[data: 22]========================
002A  00 04 00 01 00 00 00 00 00 00 00 00 00 00 00 00   ................
003A  00 00 B3 76 53 FA                                 ...vS.
```

Response from the station 192.168.12.36 Port 1215.

Opcode 0004 – Ack, acknowledging Block Number 0001. All other data in this frame is Padding.

```
========================μscope========================
Frame    : 6          Len      : 562           Error    : None
T Elapsed: 19:42:59:835   T Delta  : 00:00:00:000
------------------------[mac]------------------------
Dest Mac : 0000e80f04af   Sourc Mac: Sun    1bc95a   Type     : IP
------------------------[ip]------------------------
IP Ver   : 4          IP HLen  : 20 Bytes
TOS      : 0x00       Pkt Len  : 544             Seg ID   : 0xe674
Flags    : FRAG:Ā.LAST Frag Ptr : 0    (8 Octet)  TTL      : 60
PID      : UDP ( 17)  Checksum : 0xfc38 (Good)
Dst IP <C: 192.168.12.36    Src IP <C: 192.168.12.171
------------------------[udp]------------------------
Dest Port: 1215           Src Port : 3968
Length   : 524            Checksum : 0x0000 (NoCheck)
========================[data: 520]========================
002A  00 03 00 02 4F 43 4B 45 44 0D 0A 72 65 6D 20 20   ....OCKED..rem
003A  3D 3D 3D 3D 3D 3D 3D 3D 3D 3D 3D 3D 3D 3D 3D 3D   ================
004A  3D 3D 3D 3D 3D 3D 3D 3D 3D 3D 3D 3D 3D 3D 3D 3D   ================
005A  3D 3D 3D 3D 3D 3D 3D 3D 3D 3D 3D 3D 3D 3D 3D 3D   ================
006A  3D 3D 3D 3D 3D 3D 3D 3D 3D 3D 3D 3D 3D 3D 3D 3D   ================
007A  3D 3D 3D 3D 3D 3D 0D 0A 72 65 6D 20 20 41 64 64   =====..rem  Add
008A  61 6E 79 20 64 72 69 76 65 72 73 2C 20 65 74 63   any drivers, etc
009A  20 74 6F 20 74 68 69 73 20 73 65 63 74 69 6F 6E   to this section
00AA  20 77 68 69 63 68 20 61 72 65 20 75 6E 69 71 75   which are uniqu
00BA  65 20 74 6F 20 74 68 65 20 44 6F 63 6B 65 64 0D   e to the Docked.
00CA  0A 72 65 6D 20 20 43 6F 6E 66 69 67 75 72 61 74   .rem  Configurat
00DA  69 6F 6E 2E 0D 0A 72 65 6D 20 20 3D 3D 3D 3D 3D   ion...rem  =====
```

Opcode 0003 – Data Block, Block Number – 0002 followed by the next 512 octets of data (shown truncated).

```
============================μscope============================
Frame    : 7                 Len     : 64            Error    : None
T Elapsed: 19:42:59:835      T Delta : 00:00:00:000
----------------------------[mac]----------------------------
Dest Mac : Sun   1bc95a      Sourc Mac: 0000e80f04af  Type    : IP
----------------------------[ip]-----------------------------
IP Ver   : 4                 IP HLen  : 20 Bytes
TOS      : 0x00              Pkt Len  : 32            Seg ID   : 0x000b
Flags    : FRAG:Ā.LAST       Frag Ptr : 0    (8 Octet) TTL     : 32
PID      : UDP  ( 17)        Checksum : 0xa3  (Good)
Dst IP <C: 192.168.12.171    Src IP <C: 192.168.12.36
----------------------------[udp]----------------------------
Dest Port: 3968              Src Port : 1215
Length   : 12                Checksum : 0x5171 (Good)
========================[data:  22]==========================
002A  00 04 00 02 00 00 00 00 00 00 00 00 00 00 00 00   ................
003A  00 00 79 67 26 A3                                 ..yg&.
```

Opcode 0004 – Ack, acknowledging Block Number 0002. All other data in this frame is Padding.

```
============================μscope============================
Frame    : 8                 Len     : 562           Error    : None
T Elapsed: 19:42:59:835      T Delta : 00:00:00:000
----------------------------[mac]----------------------------
Dest Mac : 0000e80f04af      Sourc Mac: Sun   1bc95a  Type    : IP
----------------------------[ip]-----------------------------
IP Ver   : 4                 IP HLen  : 20 Bytes
TOS      : 0x00              Pkt Len  : 544           Seg ID   : 0xe675
Flags    : FRAG:Ā.LAST       Frag Ptr : 0    (8 Octet) TTL     : 60
PID      : UDP  ( 17)        Checksum : 0xfc37 (Good)
Dst IP <C: 192.168.12.36     Src IP <C: 192.168.12.171
----------------------------[udp]----------------------------
Dest Port: 1215              Src Port : 3968
Length   : 524               Checksum : 0x0000 (NoCheck)
========================[data: 520]==========================
002A  00 03 00 03 2A 2A 2A 2A 2A 2A 2A 2A 2A 2A 2A 2A   ....************
003A  2A 2A 2A 2A 2A 2A 2A 2A 2A 2A 2A 2A 2A 2A 2A 2A   ****************
004A  2A 0D 0A 72 65 6D 20 20 54 68 65 73 65 20 6C 69   *..rem  These li
005A  6E 65 73 20 61 64 64 20 74 68 65 20 4C 41 4E 54   nes add the LANT
006A  41 53 54 49 43 20 6E 65 74 77 6F 72 6B 20 61 6E   ASTIC network an
007A  64 20 74 68 65 20 73 6F 75 6E 64 20 63 61 72 64   d the sound card
008A  20 77 69 74 68 20 43 44 20 52 4F 4D 20 0D 0A 43    with CD ROM ..C
009A  41 4C 4C 20 43 3A 5C 4C 41 4E 54 41 53 54 49 5C   ALL C:\LANTASTI\
00AA  53 54 41 52 54 4E 45 54 2E 42 41 54 0D 0A 0D 0A   STARTNET.BAT....
00BA  53 45 54 20 53 4F 55 4E 44 3D 43 3A 5C 53 42 31   SET SOUND=C:\SB1
00CA  36 0D 0A 53 45 54 20 42 4C 41 53 54 45 52 3D 41   6..SET BLASTER=A
00DA  32 32 30 20 49 35 20 44 31 20 48 35 20 50 33 33   220 I5 D1 H5 P33
```

Opcode 0003 – Data Block, Block Number – 0003 followed by the next 512 octets of data (shown truncated).

```
============================μscope============================
Frame    : 9                 Len     : 64            Error    : None
T Elapsed: 19:42:59:846      T Delta : 00:00:00:011
----------------------------[mac]----------------------------
Dest Mac : Sun   1bc95a      Sourc Mac: 0000e80f04af  Type    : IP
----------------------------[ip]-----------------------------
IP Ver   : 4                 IP HLen  : 20 Bytes
TOS      : 0x00              Pkt Len  : 32            Seg ID   : 0x000c
Flags    : FRAG:Ā.LAST       Frag Ptr : 0    (8 Octet) TTL     : 32
PID      : UDP  ( 17)        Checksum : 0xa2  (Good)
Dst IP <C: 192.168.12.171    Src IP <C: 192.168.12.36
----------------------------[udp]----------------------------
Dest Port: 3968              Src Port : 1215
Length   : 12                Checksum : 0x5170 (Good)
========================[data:  22]==========================
002A  00 04 00 03 00 00 00 00 00 00 00 00 00 00 00 00   ................
003A  00 00 A5 D2 54 F7                                 ....T.
```

Opcode 0004 – Ack, acknowledging Block Number 0003. All other data in this frame is Padding.

```
============================μscope============================
Frame    : 10                Len     : 340           Error    : None
T Elapsed: 19:42:59:846      T Delta : 00:00:00:000
----------------------------[mac]----------------------------
Dest Mac : 0000e80f04af      Sourc Mac: Sun   1bc95a  Type    : IP
----------------------------[ip]-----------------------------
IP Ver   : 4                 IP HLen  : 20 Bytes
TOS      : 0x00              Pkt Len  : 322           Seg ID   : 0xe676
Flags    : FRAG:Ā.LAST       Frag Ptr : 0    (8 Octet) TTL     : 60
PID      : UDP  ( 17)        Checksum : 0xfd14 (Good)
Dst IP <C: 192.168.12.36     Src IP <C: 192.168.12.171
----------------------------[udp]----------------------------
Dest Port: 1215              Src Port : 3968
Length   : 302               Checksum : 0x0000 (NoCheck)
========================[data: 298]==========================
002A  00 03 00 04 6E 2E 0D 0A 72 65 6D 20 20 3D 3D 3D   ....n...rem  ===
003A  3D 3D 3D 3D 3D 3D 3D 3D 3D 3D 3D 3D 3D 3D 3D 3D   ================
004A  3D 3D 3D 3D 3D 3D 3D 3D 3D 3D 3D 3D 3D 3D 3D 3D   ================
005A  3D 3D 3D 3D 3D 3D 3D 3D 3D 3D 3D 3D 3D 3D 3D 3D   ================
006A  3D 3D 3D 3D 3D 3D 3D 3D 3D 3D 3D 3D 3D 3D          ==============
007A  3D 3D 0D 0A 72 65 6D 20 20 54 68 65 73 65 20 6C   ==..rem  These l
008A  69 6E 65 73 20 61 64 64 20 74 68 65 20 4F 44 49   ines add the ODI
009A  20 64 72 69 76 65 72 73 20 61 6E 64 20 74 68 65    drivers and the
00AA  20 43 68 61 6D 65 6C 65 6F 6E 20 54 43 50 2F 49    Chameleon TCP/I
00BA  50 20 53 74 61 63 6B 0D 0A 43 3A 5C 4E 45 43 55   P Stack..C:\NECU
00CA  54 49 4C 53 5C 42 41 43 4B 4C 49 54 45 20 46 55   TILS\BACKLITE FU
00DA  4C 4C 0D 0A 52 45 4D 20 45 43 48 4F 0D 0A 43 41   LL..REM ECHO..CA
```

The packet length is 322 octets which comprises 290 octets data, 20 octets for the IP Header, 8 octets for the UDP Header, and 4 octets for the TFTP Header. Since this is less than 512 octets, this must be the last packet.

Opcode 0003 – Data Block, Block Number – 0004 followed by the next 290 octets of data (shown truncated).

```
========================================μscope========================================
Frame    : 11              Len      : 64              Error    : None
T Elapsed: 19:42:59:854    T Delta  : 00:00:00:008
                              ----------[mac]----------
Dest Mac : Sun   1bc95a    Sourc Mac: 0000e80f04af    Type     : IP
                              ----------[ip]----------
IP Ver   : 4               IP HLen  : 20 Bytes
TOS      : 0x00            Pkt Len  : 32
Flags    : FRAG:Ā.LAST     Frag Ptr : 0    (8 Octet)  Seg ID   : 0x000d
PID      : UDP ( 17)       Checksum : 0xa1   (Good)    TTL      : 32
Dst IP <C: 192.168.12.171  Src IP <C: 192.168.12.36
                              ----------[udp]----------
Dest Port: 3968            Src Port : 1215
Length   : 12              Checksum : 0x516f (Good)
============================================[data:  22]===============================
002A  00 04 00 04 00 00 00 00 00 00 00 00 00 00 00 00   ....L...........
003A  00 00 C3 DE 4C 5F                                 ....L_
```

The Station (192.168.12.36) contacts
the Server (192.168.12.171) on UDP
Port 69_{10}.

Opcode 004 – Ack, acknowledging
Block Number 0004. All other data in
this frame is Padding.

Since the data block that this frame
acknowledges was less than 512
octets, this is the last frame in the
sequence. Data transfer is concluded.

Figure 19-10: A Successful TFTP Read

μSCOPE   PACKET TRACE DECODE REPORT   (c) T.Kenyon 1995

```
========================================μscope========================================
Frame    : 1               Len      : 66              Error    : None
T Elapsed: 19:40:49:218    T Delta  : 00:00:00:137
                              ----------[mac]----------
Dest Mac : Sun   1bc95a    Sourc Mac: 0000e80f04af    Type     : IP
                              ----------[ip]----------
IP Ver   : 4               IP HLen  : 20 Bytes
TOS      : 0x00            Pkt Len  : 48
Flags    : FRAG:Ā.LAST     Frag Ptr : 0    (8 Octet)  Seg ID   : 0x0004
PID      : UDP ( 17)       Checksum : 0x9a   (Good)    TTL      : 32
Dst IP <C: 192.168.12.171  Src IP <C: 192.168.12.36
                              ----------[udp]----------
Dest Port: TFTP [  69]     Src Port : 1214
Length   : 28              Checksum : 0x4c14 (Good)
                              ----------[tftp]----------
Operation: WReq
============================================[data:  22]===============================
002C  70 68 69 6C 2E 74 78 74 00 6E 65 74 61 73 63 69   phil.txt.netasci
003C  69 00 95 64 46 BE                                 i..dF.
```

Operation is Write Request.

Null terminated filename "phil.txt"
followed by Null terminated Mode
"netascii".

```
========================================μscope========================================
Frame    : 2               Len      : 64              Error    : None
T Elapsed: 19:40:49:320    T Delta  : 00:00:00:102
                              ----------[mac]----------
Dest Mac : 0000e80f04af    Sourc Mac: Sun   1bc95a    Type     : IP
                              ----------[ip]----------
IP Ver   : 4               IP HLen  : 20 Bytes
TOS      : 0x00            Pkt Len  : 32
Flags    : FRAG:Ā.LAST     Frag Ptr : 0    (8 Octet)  Seg ID   : 0xe66e
PID      : UDP ( 17)       Checksum : 0xfe3e (Good)    TTL      : 60
Dst IP <C: 192.168.12.36   Src IP <C: 192.168.12.171
                              ----------[udp]----------
Dest Port: 1214            Src Port : 3967
Length   : 12              Checksum : 0x0000 (NoCheck)
============================================[data:  22]===============================
002A  00 04 00 00 04 BD 00 1B 00 00 6F 74 20 66 6F 75   ..........ot fou
003A  6E 64 61 A1 99 01                                 nda...
```

Opcode 0004 – Ack, Block Number
0000. This is the standard positive
response to a Write Request.

```
========================================μscope========================================
Frame    : 3               Len      : 562             Error    : None
T Elapsed: 19:40:49:327    T Delta  : 00:00:00:007
                              ----------[mac]----------
Dest Mac : Sun   1bc95a    Sourc Mac: 0000e80f04af    Type     : IP
                              ----------[ip]----------
IP Ver   : 4               IP HLen  : 20 Bytes
TOS      : 0x00            Pkt Len  : 544
Flags    : FRAG:Ā.LAST     Frag Ptr : 0    (8 Octet)  Seg ID   : 0x0005
PID      : UDP ( 17)       Checksum : 0xfea8 (Good)    TTL      : 32
Dst IP <C: 192.168.12.171  Src <C: 192.168.12.36
                              ----------[udp]----------
Dest Port: 3967            Src Port : 1214
Length   : 524             Checksum : 0xcae8 (Good)
============================================[data: 520]===============================
002A  00 03 00 01 40 45 43 48 4F 20 4F 46 46 0D 0A 50   ....@ECHO OFF..P
003A  52 4F 4D 50 54 20 24 70 24 67 0D 0A 53 45 54 20   ROMPT $p$g..SET
004A  54 45 4D 50 3D 43 3A 5C 54 45 4D 50 0D 0A 49 46   TEMP=C:\TEMP..IF
005A  20 4E 4F 54 20 45 58 49 53 54 20 56 45 52 53 49   NOT EXIST VERSI
006A  4F 4E 2E 20 20 47 4F 54 4F 20 53 45 54 55 50 0D   ON.  GOTO SETUP.
007A  0A 43 4C 53 0D 0A 54 59 50 45 20 56 45 52 53 49   .CLS..TYPE VERSI
008A  4F 4E 0D 0A 0D 0A 43 3A 5C 44 4F 53 5C 53 48 41   ON....C:\DOS\SHA
009A  52 45 2E 45 58 45 0D 0A 4C 48 20 2F 4C 3A 30 20   RE.EXE..LH /L:0
00AA  43 3A 5C 44 4F 53 5C 53 4D 41 52 54 44 52 56 2E   C:\DOS\SMARTDRV.
00BA  45 58 45 0D 0A 43 3A 5C 44 4F 53 5C 44 4F 53 4B   EXE..C:\DOS\DOSK
00CA  45 59 0D 0A 50 41 54 48 20 43 3A 5C 4F 56 3B 43   EY..PATH C:\OV;C
00DA  3A 5C 58 43 50 3B 43 3A 5C 4E 45 54 4D 41 4E 41   :\XCP;C:\NETMANA
00EA  47 3B 43 3A 5C 44 4F 53 3B 43 3A 5C 57 49 4E 44   G;C:\DOS;C:\WIND
```

Total length is 544 octets comprising
512 octets of data, 20 octets of IP
Header, 8 octets of UDP Header, and 4
octets of TFTP Header.

Station sends first 512 octets of the file
(Opcode 0003 – Data Block), Block
Number 0001.

Figure 19-11: A TFTP Write Request

Booting Internet Hosts with BootP and TFTP

19.2.6 Directed TFTP

Our discussions to this point have centred on the need for a simple means through which we may load internet hosts. However, TFTP is a general purpose protocol whose implementations go much further than merely loading image files. True, where we wish to load an image and have obtained our own IP Address through say RARP, we will not be in possession of the IP Address of the server. We are then able to send requests by broadcasts. Nevertheless, where we are in possession of the IP Address of the server (such as with BootP), we can aim TFTP requests directly at the server thereby saving valuable processing cycles in all other local hosts.

Equally, TFTP can be used as a general purpose file transfer protocol performing many of the core functions of its larger, and somewhat more cumbersome counterpart FTP. This process is generally termed *Directed TFTP* and is used where we know the address of the host we wish to contact. Indeed the traces shown in Figures 19-9, 19-10, and 19-11 show this in operation since the client addresses the server directly rather than through a broadcast.

19.3 Summary

In this chapter we have now seen how both the Bootstrap and Trivial File Transfer Protocols operate, and looked at the two phases of loading network hosts in detail. In the first phase the host needs to obtain it's IP Address through either RARP or BootP. Of course if this information is pre-configured, then this phase can be omitted completely. In the second phase, the host then loads it's image through a transfer protocol such as TFTP.

TFTP though, is not only used to load hosts. Instead, TFTP is a general purpose file transfer protocol and can be used to transfer any files in an IP environment. Indeed some of the examples in this chapter showed just this.

TFTP also overcomes one major problem when talking about port numbers. It is important that TFTP is able to service multiple requests from different sources. As such it needs to spawn ports as required. TFTP accomodates this by selecting a random *Transaction ID* (TID) which it can then use as the source port. BootP on the other hand, uses distinct port numbers for both the Server and Client processes. In this way, requests from clients are always sent to the server listener port (from the client source port).

The Simple Network Management Protocol (SNMP)

C H A P T E R   20

The rapid growth of heterogeneous networks has led to a need for a simple system for managing IP based internets. In fact, the IAB now recommends that all IP and TCP implementations be network manageable, and that those implementations adopt the *Simple Network Management Protocol* (SNMP).

Before we describe SNMP, we should first look to its history: The Internet was, at its conception, a relatively high speed backbone that comprised many gateways (routers) from many vendors. The rapid growth of the Internet led to a need for a standards-based management system to control these gateways. This eventually became *The Simple Gateway Management Protocol* (SGMP). As the Internet matured and more systems were added, the need to manage *all* systems became even more apparent. Thus, it was logical to build upon the foundations laid by this protocol, and to develop it into a more generic management protocol that eventually became SNMP as we know it today.

SNMP is an Application protocol using the User Datagram Protocol (UDP), which in turn uses the Internet Protocol (IP). SNMP is not perfect. Indeed, it could be argued that it was never designed to be so, since it was always considered to be an interim measure that would fulfil the requirements of network managers until the OSI management protocols were ready. In practice of course, OSI management protocols failed to be delivered in a timely fashion and, are extremely difficult to implement.

20.1 The Management Task and SNMP

In real terms, the management task falls into five distinct areas:

- **Fault Management**

  This is concerned with the detection, and wherever possible, correction of faults in the network. Fault detection is possibly the single most important task of any management system, and as we shall see later, SNMP is ideally suited to this task. Correcting faults, particularly before they impact on network performance, is sadly rarely possible. Indeed in most circumstances, it is normally the users who alert managers when real problems occur.

- **Accounting Management**

  Accounting management is concerned with the gathering of statistics relating to network usage. These statistics can then be used to determine network access strategies and policies, charging policies, and future network needs.

361

- **Configuration Management**
  This is concerned with the control and monitoring of the configuration of the various networking systems that comprise the internet being managed. Centralized configuration management provides the administrator with ultimate control of his network, the ability to make modifications *on the fly*, and to immediately see the effects of such changes on other key networking resources.

- **Performance Management**
  Performance management is concerned with the gathering and analysis of network performance statistics. With this information, Network Administrators are able to identify (and possibly) rectify potential bottlenecks.

- **Security Management**
  This is concerned with controlling access to the various managed devices to ensure that the network is secure, and to generate alarms at the management station when intruders are detected. Many devices today are highly programmable, allowing the network manager to create secure network segments. As an example, consider an intelligent 10BaseT[1] hub that monitors the source addresses of packets arriving at its ports. Assuming that the device was intelligent enough, we could have the hub send a warning to a management station if a particular (or unknown) address is received.

SNMP, as its name suggests, is a relatively simple protocol by which management information for a network device may be inspected and/or altered by remote administrators. Operationally, SNMP treats a device as a number of statistical and configuration variables, or *Objects,* that may be manipulated. In practice, remote management stations poll the client device (the machine being managed) for appropriate information, which is then translated and displayed (normally through some graphical interface) as required. When we need to set the value of an object, we again poll the device but this time include the desired value of the object.

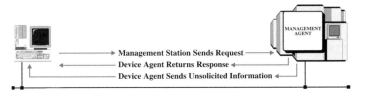

Figure 20-1: SNMP Basic Operation

In addition to the simple *Request/Response* mechanism just described, SNMP also supports a small number of unsolicited messages or *Traps* as they are known. These Traps allow the managed device to send information about significant events to (normally pre-configured) management stations. Thus, by manipulating management objects, we may gather statistics and/or change the configuration of the device. Additionally, through the reception of unsolicited information, we are

1. A 10BaseT hub refers to an Ethernet/IEEE 802.3 hub for twisted pair (UTP) wiring. See Chapter 3.

The Simple Network Management Protocol (SNMP)

able to log significant events and thereby warn managers of potential network failure. As a result, management of our network resources is achieved. Figure 20-1 shows the basic operation of SNMP.

The OSI protocols, namely *The Common Management Information Protocol* (CMIP), and *The Common Management Information System* (CMIS) take a different view of the management task to that presented by SNMP.

Firstly, SNMP uses the services of UDP, which you will remember, is connectionless in operation, whereas the OSI protocols rely on a connection oriented system. Each system has its merits. In the case of SNMP, the designers decided that where a device was having problems, it was better not to burden it with the overhead of a connection oriented protocol. It would (at least theoretically) therefore have more resources available, and would be more likely to respond to management requests. In the case of OSI, the rationale behind the connection oriented approach was that if the network was in trouble, an unacknowledged message would be resent several times. Therefore even in a congested network, the message would possibly get through.

Secondly, excluding the functionality provided by Traps, SNMP is a simple Request/Response or polling protocol. Any information required by the management station is requested, and a response is generated if the managed device is able to do so. This means that only a simple agent is required in the managed device, with the majority of the intelligence housed in the management station itself. OSI protocols, on the other hand, rely on a *reporting* mechanism where the device regularly sends information to the management station. This naturally places a need for greater intelligence at the device, a somewhat distasteful prospect to followers of SNMP.

What happens next in the battle for management supremacy is anybody's guess. One thing however is clear: vendors have now invested so much in SNMP based products, that we are unlikely to see a change in the short to medium term.

20.2 SNMP Architecture

To discuss SNMP, we should really discuss the three major elements of which it is comprised. There are of course many RFCs that relate to SNMP or its components and the most important are listed in section 20.4.1 and in Appendix B. Three RFCs however are of paramount importance, since these describe the operation of the protocol itself, the format that all management objects must follow, and a set of generic management objects that devices should support.

- RFC 1155   The Structure of Management Information (SMI)

  This document describes the way in which all information should be represented. In short, it formalizes the data types and structure that should be used for managed objects.

- RFC 1157   The Simple Network Management Protocol (SNMP)

  The document that details the actual protocol and operation of SNMP.

- RFC 1213   The Management Information Base (MIB-II)

  RFC 1156, introduced at the same time as SNMP and SMI, described 114 generic objects that SNMP compliant devices should support. These objects, generally referred to as MIB-I objects, were then increased to 171 by RFC 1213 one year later. RFC 1213 therefore provides a superset of objects generally referred to as MIB-II. In truth though, this set has now been superceeded with new objects being added all of the time.

Each of these is now discussed in detail in the following sections.

20.3 The Structure of Management Information (SMI)

SMI defines that all objects should be represented in the *Abstract Syntax Notation 1* (ASN.1), a formal ISO definition language. Each object has the following format:

- **OBJECT**

  A textural name (the *Object Descriptor*) for the object type, together with its *Object Identifier* (OID).

- **SYNTAX**

  This is the ASN.1 representation of the data type. Currently this may be one of the following:

Table 20-1: SNMP Data Types

Data Type	Description
Counter	Represents a non-negative integer with a maximum value of 2^{32}-1. When this value is exhausted, the counter will then wrap back to zero.
Display String	A string of octets restricted to those characters allowed with Telnet.
Gauge	Represents a non-negative integer that latches at a maximum value. The maximum value for a gauge is 2^{32}-1.
Integer	A whole numeric value such as the number of octets transmitted.
IP Address	Represents the 32 bit IP address as a 4 octet string.
List	A sequence of any other data types.
Network Address	An address from one of the protocol families. Currently only IP is supported.
Null	A string of Null octets normally used as a place holder.
Object Identifier	The name of an object specified as the string of numbers (the OID) used to traverse the MIB tree.
Octet String	A string of octets that may assume any value from 0 to 255_{10} such as a Community string.
Opaque	A method through which arbitrary data may be passed as an Octet String.
Physical Address	The physical address of a device expressed as an octet string (for Ethernet this would be 6 octets long).
Table	A sequence of lists.
Time Ticks	A counter representing time in hundredths of a second since some arbitrary time.

- **DEFINITION**

  A textural description of the object.

- **ACCESS**

  The access status of the object. This may be one of:

  Read-Only   The object may only be read regardless of the Access Mode employed.

  Read-Write   The object may be read and written depending on the Access Mode employed.

  Write-Only   The object may only be written by stations with the correct Access Mode.

  Not-Accessible   The object is unavailable regardless of Access Mode employed.

- **STATUS**

  The required status of the object.

  Mandatory   The object must be implemented where it is appropriate.

  Optional   The object may be implemented at the discretion of the vendor.

  Obsolete   The object is obsolete and has been superseded.

The following segment, taken from RFC 1213, shows a typical object formally specified as required by SMI.

```
sysObjectID OBJECT-TYPE
        SYNTAX OBJECT IDENTIFIER
        ACCESS read-only
        STATUS mandatory
        DESCRIPTION
                "The vendor's authoritative identification of the
                network management subsystem contained in the
                entity. This value is allocated within the SMI
                enterprises subtree (1.3.6.1.4.1) and provides an
                easy and unambiguous means for determining `what
                kind of box' is being managed. For example, if
                vendor `Flintstones, Inc.' was assigned the
                subtree 1.3.6.1.4.1.4242, it could assign the
                identifier 1.3.6.1.4.1.4242.1.1 to its `Fred
                Router'."
        ::= { system 2 }
```

20.4 The Management Information Base (MIB)

Management objects are defined in the Management Information Base (MIB), which uses a hierarchical naming scheme. Within this scheme, each object is identified by an Object Identifier (OID), a sequence of non-negative integers that uniquely describes the path taken through the hierarchical structure.

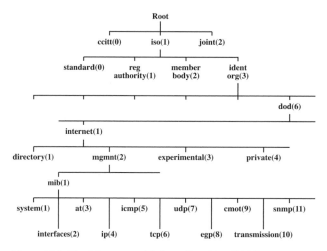

Figure 20-2: The Management Information Base (MIB)

MIB objects may then be specified either from the Root (which has no designator), or alternatively from anywhere within the hierarchical structure. For example:

```
1.3.6.1.2.1.1 is equivalent to {iso(1).org(3).dod(6).internet(1).mgmt(2).mib(1).system(1)}
{mgmt 1} is equivalent to {iso(1).org(3).dod(6).internet(1).mgmt(2).mib(1)}
```

In general, we are mainly concerned with just two groups that reside in the *internet* subtree, namely the *mgmt*, and *private* groups. For completeness however, the four major groups are discussed below:

- **directory**   {internet 1}   1.3.6.1.1
  This area was reserved to describe how the OSI directory structure may be used in the Internet. To date this has not been implemented and therefore is of little interest to us.

- **mgmt**   {internet 2}   1.3.6.1.2
  This area is used to define objects in the standard MIB. As RFCs defining new groups are ratified, the Internet Assigned Numbers Authority (IANA) assigns new group IDs.

- **experimental**   {internet 3}   1.3.6.1.3
  This subtree provides an area where experimentation is carried out. Only those organizations directly involved in the experiment have any interest in this subtree.

- **private**   {internet 4}   1.3.6.1.4
  This is possibly the most important area of the MIB, since it is within this subtree that vendors place objects specific to their particular devices. Beneath the private branch, there is a subtree called enterprises, beneath which each vendor may define its own structure. Vendors are assigned Private Enterprise Numbers (PENs) that uniquely identify them. They may then place all objects

The Simple Network Management Protocol (SNMP)

specific to their devices in this tree, provided of course that the object conforms to the format defined by SMI. Table 20-2 identifies some common PENs.

Table 20-2: Examples of Private Enterprise Numbers (PENs)

PEN	Vendor	PEN	Vendor	PEN	Vendor
2	IBM	33	Xyplex	63	Apple
7	Cayman	43	3Com	74	AT&T
9	Cisco	45	Synoptics	75	UB
18	Wellfleet	59	S. Graphics	79	ICL

Figure 20-2 showed the major part of the MIB, and identified the eleven groups of generic objects in the mib subtree at its base. Table 20-3 below describes the functions of these groups. A complete description of all objects contained within them (171 in total) can be found in Appendix C.

Table 20-3: MIB II Groups

Group Number	Group Name	Description
1	system	Returns generic configuration information.
2	interfaces	Defines the number of physical interfaces and additional parameters associated with the definition of the interface type and status.
3	at	Now marked as deprecated (these objects may also be found in the IP group), this group contains the address translation table for the device.
4	ip	These objects monitor the Internet Protocol (IP) used in the managed device.
5	icmp	Contains objects that return statistics on all aspects of ICMP.
6	tcp	Contains objects that monitor the Transmission Control Protocol (TCP).
7	udp	Provides statistical data on the User Datagram Protocol (UDP).
8	egp	These objects return statistics relating to the Exterior Gateway Protocol (EGP).
9	cmot	It was originally thought that this group would provide statistical and other information on CMOT as the transition to OSI protocols took place. This group however remains unused with no defined objects.
10	transmission	This group contains no directly defined objects. Instead, it contains a subtree of groups relating to network access methods.
11	snmp	Provides statistical data on the SNMP protocol. Although it was originally envisaged that the agent would be configured via this group, only statistical objects are currently defined.

20.4.1 RFCs Relating to Other MIBs

As we have already said, there are many RFCs that define MIB objects and indeed these are being added to all of the time. Table 20-4 lists just some of the most interesting of these documents together with their status.

Table 20-4: RFCs Defining MIBs

RFC Number	Description	Status
1253	OSPF MIB	Proposed Standard
1269	Border Gateway Protocol (BGP) Version 3	Proposed Standard
1353	Administration of the Simple Network Management Protocol (SNMP)	Proposed Standard
1354	IP Forwarding Table MIB	Proposed Standard
1381	SNMP MIB Extension for X.25 LAPB	Proposed Standard
1382	SNMP MIB Extension for X.25 Packet Layer Protocol	Proposed Standard
1406	DS1/E1 Interface Type MIB	Proposed Standard
1407	DS3/E3 Interface Type MIB	Proposed Standard
1414	Identification MIB	Proposed Standard
1461	Multi Protocol Interconnect over X.25	Proposed Standard
1471	Link Control Protocol of PPP	Proposed Standard
1472	Security Protocols of PPP	Proposed Standard
1473	IP Network Control of PPP	Proposed Standard
1474	Bridge Protocol of PPP	Proposed Standard
1493	Bridge MIB	Draft Standard
1512	FDDI Management MIB	Proposed Standard
1513	Token Ring Extensions to RMON	Proposed Standard
1514	Host Resources MIB	Proposed Standard
1515	IEEE 802.3 Medium Attachment Units (MAUs) MIB	Proposed Standard
1516	IEEE 802.3 Repeater MIB	Draft Standard
1525	Source Route Bridge MIB	Proposed Standard
1559	DECNet MIB	Draft Standard
1565	Network Services Monitoring MIB	Proposed Standard
1566	Mail Monitoring MIB	Proposed Standard
1567	X.500 Directory Monitoring MIB	Proposed Standard
1595	SONET/SDH Interface Type MIB	Proposed Standard
1604	Frame Relay MIB	Proposed Standard
1611	Domain Name System (DNS) Server MIB Extension	Proposed Standard
1612	Domain Name System (DNS) Resolver MIB Extension	Proposed Standard
1628	Uninterruptable Power Supply (UPS) MIB	Proposed Standard
1643	Ethernet MIB	Standard
1724	Routing Information Protocol (RIP) Version 2 MIB Extension	Draft Standard
1742	AppleTalk MIB	Proposed Standard
1743	Token Ring IEEE 802.5 MIB	No Status
1757	Remote Monitoring MIB (RMON)	Draft Standard

20.5 The Simple Network Management Protocol (SNMP)

SNMP defines a collection of network management stations and *network elements* (managed devices). The network management station is a complex device that runs the management application. Generally, this will comprise a graphical user interface (a GUI), a database of all devices that are being managed, a database of each of the objects that the devices support (the MIB), and of course the SNMP/IP stack. In all, these make the network management application extremely complex, and normally fairly large.

Each managed device, a terminal server, router, or even host system etc. will incorporate an *Agent* that performs the management function and the objects that may be requested and/or set by the management station. When compared to the management application, these agents are, by necessity, small. The entire philosophy upon which SNMP is built dictates the following:

- The number and complexity of management functions supported by the agent should be kept to a minimum. This naturally provides the following benefits:

  Development costs for management agent software is greatly reduced. Indeed, many agent implementations are freely available in the public domain.

  By increasing the burden of the remote management station, fewer restrictions are placed upon the level of sophistication or the form of management tools that can be developed. Equally, the development of new tools does not require changes to be made to the management agent itself, thereby protecting investment in network devices.

  Since the level of management functionality at the agent is reduced, the managed device is able to devote more resource to its primary function; that of passing internet traffic.

  As the management functionality of the agent is reduced, it is more easily understood by developers and those people implementing it. In fact, it is this simplicity that has made SNMP so popular today.

- The software architecture has to be independent from that of the devices that are managed.

- The protocol must be able to accommodate new, and potentially unanticipated, aspects of network management/operation.

SNMP endeavors to resist the introduction of support for imperative commands. To do so would render the protocol less robust and almost certainly more complex. The protocol must however allow any acceptable management functions to be performed. So how can this be achieved? Consider the desire to remotely reboot a device. It would be too easy to merely allow a new command to be added, and thereby open the protocol to vast extensions. Instead, by using the principle of setting objects, we are able to merely set the value of an object that will have the desired effect the next time it is read by the device.

We have also said that SNMP is built upon a Poll/Response architecture plus a limited number of *Traps*. This latter point of restricting unsolicited information that a device may provide, is wholly consistent with SNMPs goal of simplicity and minimizing the amount of network traffic generated by the protocol. In all SNMP uses only five Protocol Data Units (PDUs) called *Get Request*, *GetNextRequest*, *SetRequest*, *GetResponse*, and *Trap*. These will each be discussed in detail in section 20.5.2.

20.5.1 Authentication

RFC 1157 defines the permitted SNMP protocol exchanges themselves and the method by which each exchange is authenticated. It is obviously undesirable to allow just any management station to access any manageable device with no checks. SNMP therefore employs a simple, but potentially unsecure, authentication process in an attempt to ensure that only bona fide managers may make configuration changes. Before we discuss the protocol exchanges in detail, it would be logical to examine the authentication method employed.

SNMP defines the pairings of agents and management stations as an SNMP *Community,* identified by a simple octet string referred to as a *Community Name.* Each exchange between a management station and a manageable device is then accompanied by this string, in much the same way that a password is used to authenticate a user of a host system. Managed devices are normally programmed, such that a particular Community String allows a specific level of access (Read-Only, Read-Write etc.). In this way, the Community Name is used to define the level of access (the *Access Mode*) requested. Unfortunately, in the current implementation of SNMP, this *Community Name* is transmitted unencrypted, leading it to be described as employing only a *trivial* or *loose* authentication method.

From our discussion of the MIB, it is apparent that only a subset of objects are likely to be relevant to any single manageable device. For example, a repeater would not implement EGP, therefore making adoption of the EGP group pointless. In addition, each MIB object has an associated Access defining how the object may be manipulated. This *authenticated* subset, or *MIB View* as it is called, then defines which objects are available and their access, *Read-Only, Read-Write* etc. By combining this MIB View with the access requested through the Community Name, it is possible to determine what operations are allowed on any specific object. The resulting *Community Profile* as it is known, is shown in Table 20-5.

Table 20-5: The Community Profile

| Community | MIB View | | | |
Access Mode	Read-Only	Write-Only	Read-Write	No-Access
No Access	None	None	None	None
Read-Only	Read	None	Read	None
Read-Write	Read	Write	Write	None

From the table, a management station using a Community Name granting Read-Only access to a device will be able to read both Read-Only and Read-Write MIB objects, but will have no access to other objects. Equally, if a Community Name that allowed Read-Write access to the device was to be used, the management station would be able to perform more functions. For example, it would be able to read Read-Only objects, Read and Write those with an access mode of Read-Write, and write Write-Only objects. No level of access however will ever enable a management station to manipulate those objects with No-Access as their MIB View.

20.5.2   The SNMP Protocol Format

SNMP exchanges travel as totally independent messages within UDP datagrams. UDP port 161 is used for normal requests and responses, and port 162 is used to listen for Traps. Since SNMP uses ASN.1 encoding, PDUs do not have a fixed length header, they do however all follow the same basic pattern of a Version number,

Community String, and a Data area. The Data area then differs for each type of PDU. Written in ASN.1 format, a SNMP PDU would look like the one shown below:

```
Message ::=
SEQUENCE {
        version
                INTEGER {              The version number is currently 1
                        version-1 (0)  Version 1 is represented by 0
                },
        community
                OCTET STRING,
        data
                ANY                    The PDU itself is encoded as Data
}
```

It is interesting to note that although the version number is really only a single octet, due to the way that ASN.1 works, three octets are taken to encode it. Before proceeding, it is therefore probably best to see how this encoding method works. Although the method makes it hard to directly read, the structure of ASN.1 is relatively simple, since each data value is encoded in the following form:

[Identifier] [Data Length] [Data]

Table 20-6 shows the identifiers used for ASN.1 data types and their relevant hexadecimal values:

Table 20-6: ASN.1 Identifiers and Their Associated Values

Basic ASN.1 Types		Basic SNMP Types		SNMP Context-Specific Types	
Data Type	ID (Hex)	Data Type	ID (Hex)	Data Type	ID (Hex)
Integer	02	IP Address	40	GetRequest	A0
Octet String	04	Counter	41	GetNextRequest	A1
Null	05	Gauge	42	GetResponse	A2
Object Identifier	06	Time Ticks	43	SetRequest	A3
Sequence	30	Opaque	44	Trap	A4

Figure 20-3 then shows how a PDU may start:

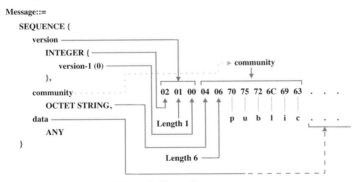

Figure 20-3: Basic SNMP Decode Example

The type of PDU is then represented by the following ASN.1 segment with two common constructs namely one for the Request/Response PDUs, and one for Traps.

```
PDUs ::=
        CHOICE {
        get-request
                GetRequest-PDU,         Value A0
        get-next-request
                GetNextRequest-PDU,     Value A1
        get-response
                GetResponse-PDU,        Value A2
        set-request
                SetRequest-PDU,         Value A3
        trap
                Trap-PDU                Value A4
        }
```

For Request/Response information the following is used:

```
RequestID ::=                   Used to match Responses to Requests
        INTEGER

ErrorStatus ::=                 Indicates if an error has been detected
        INTEGER {
                noError (0),
                tooBig (1),
                noSuchName (2),
                badValue (3),
                readOnly (4),
                genErr (5)
        }

ErrorIndex ::=                  Identifies where the error was detected
        INTEGER

VarBind ::=                     An instance of an OID/Value pair
        SEQUENCE {
                name
                        ObjectName,
                value
                        ObjectSyntax
        }

VarBindList ::=                 A list of Variable Bindings (VarBind)
        SEQUENCE OF
                VarBind
```

The *Request ID* is used to match requests (generated by the management station) with responses from the managed device. This is crucial to make best use of available network bandwidth, since it is most unlikely that a network management station would wish to issue a single request and then wait for a response before issuing the next. The *Error Status* is used to indicate the presence of an error in the requested *Variable Bindings*. Requests are sent with this equal to zero (*noError*), however the responses will have this set to a non-zero value where an error exists in the *Variable Bindings List*. It is inherent in the SNMP protocol that multiple objects may be requested. These requests though are treated as *atomic* in nature. That is to say that all requested objects must be available, and that the operation requested must be supported. In the event that any object is either not available, or that the request is not supported under the *Community View,* as derived from the *MIB View* and *Community Access*, NO data will be returned and an error will result. *ErrorStatus* has the following meanings:

- **tooBig**

  A *tooBig* error is where the resulting response would be too large for the management agent to construct. In this case the *ErrorIndex* will be set to a zero value.

- **noSuchName**

  The *noSuchName* error results from a name being specified in the Variable Bindings field that does not exist. In this case, the *Error Index* will identify the *Variable Binding* which is at fault.

- **badValue**

  badValue indicates that an object was requested but that the value specified is in an incorrect format. For example, a management station may have tried to set the value of an object that should contain an integer by using an octet string. In this case, as before, the *Error Index* will specify which object is at fault.

- **readOnly**

  This indicates that an attempt has been made to alter an object that, through its *MIB View*, is designated Read Only. The *Error Index* should then identify this object in the *Variable Bindings List*.

- **genErr**

  If any object cannot be retrieved, and the reason is not covered by any of the forgoing reasons, a general error, *genErr*, is reported, and the *Error Index* identifies the object in the *Variable Bindings List*.

As we have said, SNMP allows the setting and retrieval of multiple objects through a single PDU. However, since the entire PDU must be error free for any values to be returned, where an error exists, the *ErrorIndex* tells us which of the objects is in error. The *VarBindList* is a list of objects and their associated values. Where we are interrogating the objects, the request will contain the Object Identifier, *OID*, and a value of zero. The resultant response, assuming that no error is present, will then contain the value of the object. If we are attempting to set the value of an object, the value will contain the desired value after the operation has been successfully completed. The resulting response will then contain the same values as the request, with an ErrorStatus and ErrorIndex of 0 (noError), or a non-zero Status and Index where an error was present in the request.

The GetRequest PDU

The GetRequest PDU is generated by a management station in order to interrogate a managed device. The PDU may contain a number of requested objects, but as we have previously discussed, all objects must be available.

The response to a GetRequest is always a GetResponse PDU.

The GetNextRequset PDU

The GetNextRequest PDU is useful where you wish to traverse a table of unknown length, for example a routing table. As with the GetRequest, the only allowable response is the GetResponse. For example, suppose that the routing table in question contained the following:

Destination	Next Hop	Metric
128.10.5.99	26.10.36.121	7
43.25.10.1	19.32.12.10	5
10.23.121.6	26.10.36.121	7

The management station may issue a GetNextRequest that contains the OID values as the requested variables.

```
GetNextRequest {ipRouteDest, ipRouteNextHop, ipRouteMetric1}
```

The SNMP agent would respond with a GetResponse as follows:

```
GetResponse {(ipRouteDest.43.25.10.1="43.25.10.1"),
             (ipRouteNextHop.43.25.10.1="19.32.12.10"),
             (ipRouteMetric1.43.25.10.1=5)}
```

The management station might then continue with:

```
GetNextRequest {ipRouteDest.43.25.10.1, ipRouteNextHop.43.25.10.1,
   ipRouteMetric1.43.25.10.1}
```

The response would now be:

```
GetResponse {(ipRouteDest.10.23.121.6="10.23.121.6"),
             (ipRouteNextHop.10.23.121.6="26.10.36.121"),
             (ipRouteMetric1.10.23.121.6=7)}
```

Should the management station now attempt another GetNextRequest using the values just obtained, the response will be to return the first routing table entry. This now informs the management station that the table has been exhausted.

The GetResponse PDU

The GetResponse PDU is identical to that of the GetRequest, GetNextRequest, and SetRequest PDUs, except that the PDU Type will indicate that this is a response, and the *Error Status* and *Error Index* may contain a non-zero value.

The GetResponse is only ever generated by a managed device in response to a *GetRequest, GetNextRequest,* or *SetRequest* PDU. In the case of *Get* and *GetNext* requests, the values presented in the Variable Bindings will naturally be zero, along with the values in the ErrorStatus and ErrorIndex. In the case of the *SetRequest*, the values in the *Variable Bindings* will contain the desired values after the operation has completed successfully. Once again, the values of the ErrorStatus and ErrorIndex will be zero for a SetRequest.

The *GetResponse* PDU for *Get* and *GetNext* requests contain the values of the requested objects, provided that no object was incorrectly specified. In this case, the *ErrorStatus* and *ErrorIndex* will also be zero. Where the *GetResponse* is in response to a *SetRequest*, the values of the objects will be those that resulted from the operation. Again the *ErrorStatus* and *ErrorIndex* will contain zero where no error is reported.

The SetRequest PDU

As with the other *request* PDUs we have discussed in this section, the *SetRequest* is generated only by management stations. The difference being that in this case it is that the manager wishes to set the value of object(s). As with previous examples, multiple objects may be manipulated by this PDU. In the event that more than one such object is to be set, all modified objects are treated as if modified simultaneously even though in practice of course, this would not really be the case.

The Trap PDU

The *Trap* PDU differs from the other PDUs in two important areas. Firstly, the *Trap* is generated only by a managed device and does not require a response. Secondly the actual format of the PDU itself is different as shown by the ASN.1 construct below:

```
Trap-PDU ::=
        IMPLICIT SEQUENCE {
                enterprise          The type of object generating the trap
                                    as defined by sysObjectID
        agent-addr                  Address of the agent generating the trap
                NetworkAddress
        generic-trap                The generic trap type
                INTEGER {
                        coldStart (0),
                        warmstart (1),
                        linkDown (2),
                        linkUp (3),
                        authenticationFailure (4),
                        egpNeighborLoss (5),
                        enterpriseSpecific (6)
        }
        specific-trap               The code identifying the enterprise
                INTEGER,            specific trap itself
        time-stamp                  Elapsed time since the last
                TimeTicks,          initialization of the agent
        variable-bindings           Additional Information
                VarBindList
        }
```

SNMP defines six generic trap types as indicated above. *coldStart*, is used to signify that the agent is reinitializing and that, as a result, the configuration is liable to change. *warmStart*, indicates that the agent is reinitializing, but that the configuration is not changing. *linkDown*, alerts the management station(s) that a transition has occurred, resulting in the link going from the up to the down state. The first element of the Variable Bindings will contain the name and values of the *ifIndex* (from the *interfaces* group) of the affected interface. *linkUp* informs the management station(s) that an interface has transitioned from the down to the up state. As with the *linkDown* trap, the first element of the variable bindings will contain the name and value of the *ifIndex* of the affected interface. *authenticationFailure*, indicates to the management station(s) that an SNMP request has not been correctly authenticated. *egpNeighborLoss* signifies that the sending management agent has detected that one of its EGP neighbors has been marked as being down. With this trap, the first element of the Variable Bindings contains the name and value of the *egp NeighbourAddr* instance for the affected neighbor.

A seventh trap, the *enterpriseSpecific* Trap, exists to allow vendors to create their own traps. Where this is used, the *specific-trap* field is used to identify the particular trap that occurred. Note that excessive use of such traps is contrary to the premise upon which SNMP is built, namely that the predominant management task should be in the management station rather than the agent. Implementors should therefore resist the temptation to over complicate agents by developing too many enterprise specific traps.

Figure 20-4 shows the PDUs used in SNMP.

SNMP Requesst/Response PDUs

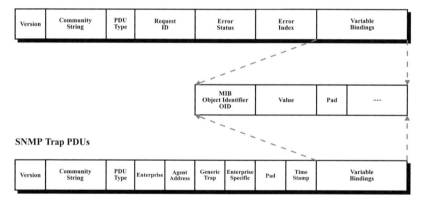

Figure 20-4: SNMP PDUs

20.6 SNMP Examples

The following figures show typical SNMP traces. The first, Figure 20-5, shows the GetRequest/GetResponse exchange when the OID 1.3.6.1.2.1.1.3 (SysUpTime) is requested, and the second figure (20-6) shows a Trap resulting from an authenti-

The Simple Network Management Protocol (SNMP)

cation failure. Both traces are shown in their *raw* state and are then decoded within the figure. Since SNMP uses ASN.1 encoding (which is not necessarily easy to decode), it is hoped that these figures will make SNMP packets a little clearer.

```
==================================µscope==================================
Frame    : 1              Len     : 86              Error    : None
T Elapsed: 18:32:52:487   T Delta : 00:15:59:611
=================================[data:   86]=============================
0000  08 00 87 05 68 66 08 00 20 1B C9 5A 08 00 45 00   ....hf.. ..Z..E.
0010  00 44 EF 28 00 00 3C 11 42 DA C1 80 64 AB C1 80   .D.(..<.B...d...
0020  64 FA 07 D0 00 A1 00 30 00 00 30 26 02 01 00 04   d......0..0&....
0030  06 70 75 62 6C 69 63 A0 19 02 01 00 02 01 00 02   .public.........
0040  01 00 30 0E 30 0C 06 08 2B 06 01 02 01 01 03 00   ..0.0...+.......
0050  04 00 10 92 0B 05                                  ......
```

Layer 2 (Ethernet) Header.

UDP Header.

IP Header.

SNMP Packet decoded as follows:
3026
Sequence 26_{16} (38_{10}) octets long
020100
Integer, length 1, Value 0 – Version Number 1
04067075626C6963
Octet String, length 6, Value 7075626C6963 ("public")
A019
GetRequest, Length 19_{16} (25_{10}) octets
020100
Integer, Length 1, Value 0 – Error Index 0
3011300F06082B06010201010300
Sequence, Length 11_{16} (17_{10})
Sequence, Length OF$_{16}$ (15_{10})
Object Identifier 2B06010201010300 – 1.3.6.1.2.1.1.3.0
0400
[Note: 2B decodes to 1.3]
Octet String, Length 0 – Place holder for GetResponse

Ethernet Frame Check Sequence.

```
==================================µscope==================================
Frame    : 2              Len     : 89              Error    : None
T Elapsed: 18:32:52:494   T Delta : 00:00:00:007
=================================[data:   89]=============================
0000  08 00 20 1B C9 5A 08 00 87 05 68 66 08 00 45 00   .. ..Z....hf..E.
0010  00 47 00 41 00 00 40 11 2D BF C1 80 64 FA C1 80   .G.A..@.-...d...
0020  64 AB 00 A1 07 D0 00 33 00 00 30 29 02 01 00 04   d......3..0)....
0030  06 70 75 62 6C 69 63 A2 1C 02 01 00 02 01 00 02   .public.........
0040  01 00 30 11 30 0F 06 08 2B 06 01 02 01 01 03 00   ..0.0...+.......
0050  43 03 23 8D 32 03 0F 79 E3                         C.#.2..y.
```

Layer 2 (Ethernet) Header.

IP and UDP Headers.

SNMP Packet decoded as follows:
3029
Sequence 29_{16} (41_{10}) octets long
020100
Integer, length 1, Value 0 – Version Number 1
04067075626C6963
Octet String, length 6, Value 7075626C6963 ("public")
A21C
GetRequest, Length $1C_{16}$ (28_{10}) octets
020100
Integer, Length 1, Value 0 – Request ID 0
020100
Integer, Length 1, Value 0 – Error Status 0
020100
Integer, Length 1, Value 0 – Error Index 0
3011300F06082B06010201010300
Sequence, Length 11_{16} (17_{10})
Sequence, Length OF$_{16}$ (15_{10})
Object Identifier 2B06010201010300 – 1.3.6.1.2.1.1.3.0
4303
Time Ticks, Length 3, Value 238D32

Ethernet Frame Check Sequence.

Figure 20-5: Sample SNMP Trace of a GetRequest and Corresponding GetResponse

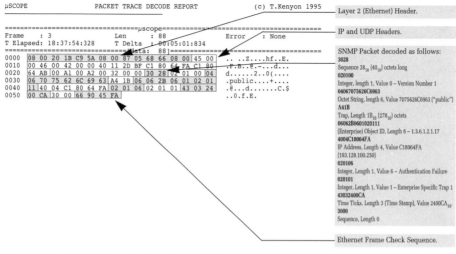

Figure 20-6: A SNMP Trap (Authentication Failure)

20.7 The Remote Monitoring MIB (RMON)

Much effort is being put into improving the functionality of SNMP, and nowhere more than in attempting to reduce the traffic generated by management itself. Polling all devices in an internet to gather statistics is a valid management method, but the traffic that this generates may become unacceptable where large numbers of devices are concerned. We have already said that excessive use of traps is undesirable since this will detract from the devices ability to perform its primary function. But what if we were to incorporate a dedicated device into our network with the sole purpose of monitoring traffic and errors?

The RMON MIB (RFC 1757) incorporates such monitoring devices into the framework of SNMP by allowing these to gather statistics and report back to management stations. Now, a management station needs only to poll the monitor to gather statistics about the devices around it, since its sole purpose is to *listen* to traffic and generate alarms when appropriate. There are currently nine groups of data defined for the RMON MIB:

Table 20-7: RMON Groups

RMON Group	Description
statistics	Records statistics based upon the number of frames seen.
history	Compiles statistics based upon the number of frames seen over a configured time interval.
alarms	Generates an Event if a programmed threshold is exceeded within a configured time interval.
host	Reports on hosts that have been detected (by address) and the number of frames transmitted.
hostTopN	Provides statistics based upon which of the detected hosts are transmitting most frames.

The Simple Network Management Protocol (SNMP)

RMON Group	Description
matrix	Reports on statistics based upon exchanges between pairs of host systems.
filter	Defines the criteria by which frames may be matched.
packet capture	Allows the capture of frames that satisfy a pre-defined filter condition. These frames are then stored by the device until requested by the Management Station.
event	Controls how events occur and how they are notified. An event may be triggered when a pre-defined threshold is exceeded. This may then, in turn, send an enterprise specific trap to a management station.

20.8 The Future of SNMP

We have so far described SNMP as it operates today. No discussion on this subject can be complete however, unless we discuss the future of such a useful protocol. Today, SNMP operates as a robust application protocol that satisfies the needs of most managers by providing statistical and configuration data on almost all network devices. Its failures must however be that it is not generic enough in nature, relying heavily on the Enterprise specific area of the MIB, and the fact that it is totally unsecure. It may be acceptable for any management station to gather operational statistics on a device, but it is almost certainly unacceptable to allow the configuration of these same devices to be tampered with.

To address the vendor or enterprise-specific nature of the MIB, we see more and more generic groups being added to report on the functionality of standard devices such as repeaters, bridges etc. Indeed, vendors who fail to implement these groups as they are ratified risk alienation in the management market, making their products little better than those proprietary products of the past.

Security is a different matter. In order to make SNMP secure, it is necessary that certain elements of the PDU be encrypted, a measure over which there is some debate. It is true that many papers have been written on the subject, and although not fully ratified, a newer version of SNMP, known simply as SNMP version II is available. The problem is that SNMP II is not backwards compatible with its original counterpart thus making it difficult to implement, and to therefore gain acceptance in the marketplace. We wait to see how the problem is to be eventually solved, but today we continue to use and develop what we know best.

20.9 Summary

SNMP is not perfect but it is a widely accepted method of managing IP devices. Having said that, it does scale extremely well and does provide for any amount of conceivable growth. As new device types are added, the structure of the Management Information Base lends itself perfectly to extension. New management functionality can be added almost seamlessly and, with ASN.1, we have a structure that can easily be converted to OSI management protocols when (if) they are needed.

We should however never lose track of the fact that the management function can be a large overhead on our networks and that 'keeping it simple' is the premise upon which SNMP is built. Users today demand graphical displays and with this the amount of information required to build these images is larger than it necessarily needs to be. At the simplest level, a simple command line interface could be used to gather information. The source code for such implementations is available in the public domain from sites at both the Massachusetts Institute of Technology (MIT), and the Carnegie Mellon University (CMU).

Most vendors offer a management solution that allows their products to be managed and true to their claims, their product will generally also manage devices from other vendors. These claims however must be regarded very closely. True, a level of management that involves the generic MIB II objects will be available but this will not provide the point and click graphical interface that we mentioned above. Firstly, very few such platforms will do this since few vendors would go to the trouble to provide the bit mapped pictures of competing devices necessary for the graphical interface.

Secondly, a vendor is unlikely to incorporate the Private area of the MIB tree from their competition, so information from another vendor will probably be missing. This latter point is less of a problem though because any reputable management software will normally allow other vendors MIBs to be imported, and these are generally available from the FTP site at *venera.isi.edu*.

Miscellaneous Protocols

In this chapter we shall deal with some of the protocols on the periphery of the Internet Protocol suite and those enjoying less publicity. Nevertheless, many protocols in this category are important as debugging and measurement tools, or provide information or connection methods unavailable elsewhere within the suite. Some are not actually considered to be *true protocols*, but instead *services* listening on specific TCP or UDP ports and taking action(s) when connections are established or when datagrams arrive. Nevertheless these can be important, well-known applications, that provide users with a great deal of information.

21.1 Echo Protocol

RFC 862 (Std 20) specifies a simple echo service useful for debugging and measurement. The principle of any such service is to simply return any data received to the sending host in much the same way as ICMP Echo Request/Reply. Here however, the protocol defines a service compatible with TCP and UDP.

With the TCP service, the server process listens on a well-known port (TCP port 7). When a connection is established, any data received is returned to the sender intact. This then continues until the calling host terminates the connection. In the UDP implementation, the server again listens on port 7 (albeit this time UDP). Since connections are not established with UDP though, the server process listens for datagrams arriving that specify this port number as the destination port, and again returns all received data intact.

21.2 Discard Protocol

Unlike the Echo protocol described above, Discard protocol packets are designed to be discarded by any host that receives them. This protocol therefore is useful where a network segment is to be loaded without unnecessarily impacting other host systems. RFC 863 (Std 21) defines two such services, one for TCP and the other for UDP. In the TCP service, once a connection is established on TCP port 9, all packets sent to this connection are discarded without any response being sent. This then continues until the sender terminates the connection. In the case of the UDP service, the host listens on UDP port 9 and discards any packets received, again without responding.

21.3 Time Protocol (Time)

The Time protocol is defined by RFC 868 (Std 26) which states that either TCP or UDP can be used. In practice though, most implementations use the much simpler UDP implementation since this requires less overhead on IP hosts. In addition, one advantage of using UDP is that the request can be broadcast whereas, with TCP it is impractical to broadcast a connection request.

The protocol is simple. In the first case (TCP), the client host creates a TCP connection to TCP port 37_{10} (25_{16}) of a server. The server then sends a TCP segment that contains the time as a 32 bit binary number representing the number of seconds that have elapsed since midnight 1st January 1900 (GMT). The client host then closes the connection. Should the server be unable to service the client with the correct time, then the connection is refused. In the more common UDP implementation, the server merely listens for an empty UDP datagram on UDP port 37_{10} and returns the time as described above. If the server is unable to provide the time, the datagram is ignored.

In using a 32 bit number, it is possible to inform hosts of any date and time up to the year 2036. For example, a value of $B4E6F2FE_{16}$ would correspond to 17:16:46 on 4 March 1996 GMT. The following trace shows an example of a client device broadcasting a query to determine the correct time.

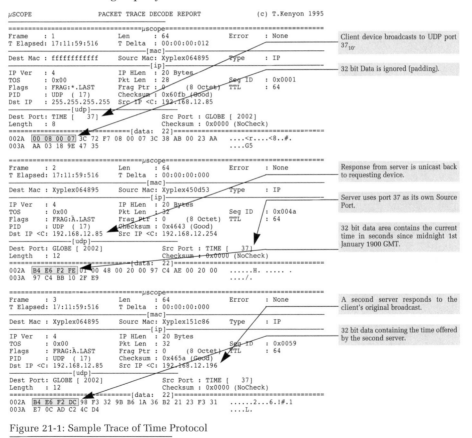

Figure 21-1: Sample Trace of Time Protocol

Using the Time Protocol, those devices that do not maintain clocks while powered off can easily determine the correct time. You will see from the trace in Figure 22-1 that two servers respond to our client's request and that each offers a different time (although only marginally). However, provided that an accurate time source is available on the network, any device can confirm (maybe at regular intervals) that the time it is holding is correct.

21.4 Daytime Protocol

A Daytime protocol simply sends the current date and time to a host that requests it. RFC 867 (Std 25) suggests that if such a protocol is to be implemented, then it should be this one. It is a simple service that is based upon either TCP or UDP and simply requires that a server responds to activity on port 13_{10}.

In the TCP based service, the server listens for a connection to be established on TCP port 13_{10} and then sends the current date and time out over the connection as an ASCII string. The connection is then closed by the service immediately. In the UDP service the server listens on port 13_{10}, however since UDP is connectionless, a string containing the current date and time is returned when a datagram is received.

In either case, there is no standard format for the ASCII string returned it is however recommended that only ASCII printing characters (plus spaces, carriage returns, and line feeds) are used, and that the response should occupy no more than one line. Suggested formats are:

- Weekday, Month Day, Year-Time Zone.

  For example: *Tuesday, March 5, 1996 12:05:23-GMT.*

- dd mmm yy hh:mm:ss zzz.

  For example: *05 MAR 96 12:05:23 GMT.*

21.5 Network Time Protocol (NTP)

The Network Time Protocol as defined in RFC 1119 is used to synchronize timekeeping among a number of distributed time servers and clients. The document itself defines all that is required in this context and includes, both the algorithms and architectures used. While much of the standard is beyond the scope of this book, the protocol itself is mentioned here since it is an Internet *standard* (Std 12) and has a status of recommended.

NTP is typically built on UDP using port 123_{10} although a TCP port of the same number is also reserved. In practice, much of the protocol is actually irrelevant to us since the protocol deals with areas of accuracy and synchronization. In practice, accuracy will of course depend heavily on the precision of the local clock hardware, the latency introduced by the various processes running on the unit, and the round trip delays introduced by the network itself. Thus, this protocol is not covered in any greater detail here.

21.6 Line Printer Daemon Protocol (LPD)

Unix systems and PC based IP hosts can both provide and use shared printer services through a number of programs such as lpr (used to assign a printjob to a queue), lpq (to display a queue), lprm (to remove a printjob from a queue), and lpc (to control a queue). These programs then interact with a daemon[1] process called the *line printer daemon* where the client makes requests to control printing.

LPR (the protocol used) is TCP based and listens on port 515_{10}. The protocol is simple with each command starting having a single octet code that represents the requested function, which is then followed by a number of operands each separated by white space. The end of the command is then indicated with the Line Feed character. These commands, as described in RFC 1179 are then described below:

- **Command Code 01 – Print any Waiting Jobs**
  Used to start the printing process if it is not already running and has a single operand that contains the print queue name.

- **Command Code 02 – Receive a Print Job**
  This command again contains a single operand that contains the queue name. Once issued, a second level of commands is then used to control the job itself. When the command has been issued, the client must then receive an acknowledgement that comprises either a single zero octet for a positive acknowledgement, or an octet containing any other value for a negative acknowledgement. The second level commands (sub commands), which must also be acknowledged in the same way, are described as follows:

  - **Sub-Command 01 – Abort Job**
    Used to remove any files that have so far been created during the current Receive Job. No operands are supplied therefore this sub command is simply two octets in length with a value of $010A_{16}$.

  - **Sub-Command 02 – Receive Control File**
    The control file is an ASCII stream of data with the ends of each line delimited by line feed characters. Two operands follow the command. The first specifies the count of octets in the control file. The second operand then defines the name of the control file and is always of the form *cfAxxx* where xxx is the three digit job number. Job numbers must be in the range 0-999, thus three digits is sufficient for this purpose. The sub-command itself is then terminated with a line feed, and must be acknowledged as before.

    The Control file represents a third level of commands that can be used to specify elements of the banner page and other items. Control file lines (always terminated by the line feed character) can therefore contain a number of commands, the most common of which are described below:

    - **Class for Banner Page – Code *C***
      This command starts with a command code of ASCII C followed by a string

1. A daemon process is an autonomous process that runs on a host. This term is most commonly used in a Unix environment.

of up to 31 octets that specifies the *Class* that will be printed in the banner.

- **Host Name – Code *H***
  Defines the host that was the source for the print job (up to 31 octets). This uses a command code, followed by the host name itself.

- **Indent Printing – Code *I***
  Defines by how many columns the output will be indented. The command is followed by a count of columns.

- **Job Name for Banner Page – *J***
  Most printouts have a Job Name in the banner page. This command then allows the job name to be specified (up to 99 octets). The command code is then followed by the name.

- **Print Banner Page – Code *L***
  This command causes the banner page to be printed (with an optional user name). The code is optionally followed by the name of the user.

- **Mail When Printed – Code *M***
  It is sometimes desirable to have the server mail the user on completion of the print job. This format then contains the code (M) followed by the user to whom the mail should be sent.

- **Name of Source File – Code *N***
  Used to specify the name of the file from which the data file was constructed. The format is the command followed by the name, which must be less than 132 octets.

- **User Identification – Code *P***
  Specifies the identity of the user that requested the print job. The command comprises the code followed by the name that must be no more than 31 octets in length.

- **Unlink Data File – Code *U***
  Using this command indicates that the file is no longer needed and should therefore only be used for data files. The command code itself is followed by the file name.

- **Print Formatted File – Code *f***
  This causes the data file to be printed as a plain text file providing page breaks as necessary.

- **Sub-Command 03 – Receive Data File**
  This sub-command like the Receive Control File, contains two operands. The first specifies the number of octets that will be transferred, and the second the name of the file itself. As before, the format of the data file name is set and must always be of the form *dfA* followed by a three digit number. Once acknowledged, the data file is then transferred followed by a TCP segment that contains a single octet of zero as an indication that the transfer is complete.

- **Command Code 03 – Send Queue State (Short)**

  The Send Queue State (Short) command is used to request that the server sends information regarding the contents of the queue. The command contains a number of operands the first of which is the queue name that is then followed by a list of user and/or job names. If both user names and job numbers are included then only those jobs specified for the user will be returned. If only user name(s) are supplied, then the returned data stream will contain those jobs applicable to those user(s).

- **Command Code 04 – Send Queue State (Long)**

  This command is similar to the Send Queue State (Short) except that more information is included.

- **Command Code 05 – Remove Jobs**

  The Remove Jobs command is used to delete jobs from the queue specified in the command. The command itself comprises the queue name, the name of the user making the request and then a list of users and/or job names that should be deleted. If the command has only the name of the user making the request and no corresponding list, then this is taken to mean delete the currently active job. However, if the user is not the owner of the job, the command will be ignored (unless the user is *root*). The command will be also be ignored if say, a user is identified in the list and the requesting user (not *root*) is not the owner of the job. Equally, if a job is specified in the list and the user (not *root*) is not the owner, the same would apply.

The following trace demonstrates the main components of a sample LPR transfer.

```
µSCOPE                  PACKET TRACE DECODE REPORT          (c) T.Kenyon 1995
```

The TCP Connection is opened with the normal Three-Way Handshake

```
===============================µscope=========================================
Frame   : 6               Len     : 67            Error    : None
T Elapsed: 19:06:27:210   T Delta : 00:00:00:000
-------------------------------[mac]------------------------------------------
Dest Mac : Xyplex050dc5   Sourc Mac: Xyplex150dc6  Type      : IP
-------------------------------[ip]-------------------------------------------
IP Ver   : 4              IP HLen  : 20 Bytes
TOS      : 0x00           Pkt Len  : 49            Seg ID   : 0x0f75
Flags    : FRAG:*.LAST    Frag Ptr : 0    (8 Octet) TTL      : 56
PID      : TCP ( 6)       Checksum : 0x2097 (Good)
Dst IP <C: 192.168.107.15 Src IP <C: 192.168.100.171
-------------------------------[tcp]------------------------------------------
Src Port : 1023           Dst Port : 515
Seq No   : 0x41171602     Ack No   : 0x000007e4
Head Len : 5   words      Flags    : .AP...        Window   : 0x1000
Checksum : 0x941a (Good)  Urg Ptr  : 0x0000        Options  : None
===============================[data:  13]====================================
0036  02 70 68 69 6C 70 72 74 0A 6F E7 55 87       .philprt.o.U.

===============================µscope=========================================
Frame   : 7               Len     : 64            Error    : None
T Elapsed: 19:06:27:210   T Delta : 00:00:00:000
-------------------------------[mac]------------------------------------------
Dest Mac : Xyplex150dc6   Sourc Mac: Xyplex050dc5  Type      : IP
-------------------------------[ip]-------------------------------------------
IP Ver   : 4              IP HLen  : 20 Bytes
TOS      : 0x00           Pkt Len  : 40            Seg ID   : 0x0098
Flags    : FRAG:*.LAST    Frag Ptr : 0    (8 Octet) TTL      : 64
PID      : TCP ( 6)       Checksum : 0x277d (Good)
Dst IP <C: 192.168.100.171 Src IP <C: 192.168.107.15
-------------------------------[tcp]------------------------------------------
Src Port : 515            Dst Port : 1023
Seq No   : 0x000007e4     Ack No   : 0x4117160b
Head Len : 5   words      Flags    : .A....        Window   : 0x0ff7
Checksum : 0xe819 (Good)  Urg Ptr  : 0x0000        Options  : None
===============================[data:  10]====================================
0036  00 00 00 00 00 00 14 E0 DB 57                ........W
```

The client sends a request to the server. LPR listens on TCP port 515.

Command Code 02 – Receive Printjob. Queue name – "philprt" End of command delimiter – 0A.

The server acknowledges the TCP segment of frame 6.

Miscellaneous Protocols

```
===============================µscope===============================
Frame   : 8                Len    : 64            Error    : None
T Elapsed: 19:06:27:210    T Delta : 00:00:00:000
-------------------------------[mac]-------------------------------
Dest Mac : Xyplex150dc6    Sourc Mac: Xyplex050dc5    Type    : IP
-------------------------------[ip]--------------------------------
IP Ver   : 4               IP HLen  : 20 Bytes
TOS      : 0x00            Pkt Len  : 41              Seg ID  : 0x0099
Flags    : FRAG:*.LAST     Frag Ptr : 0     (8 Octet) TTL     : 64
PID      : TCP  ( 6)       Checksum : 0x277b (Good)
Dst IP <C: 192.168.100.171  Src IP <C: 192.168.107.15
-------------------------------[tcp]-------------------------------
Src Port : 515             Dst Port : 1023
Seq No   : 0x000007e4      Ack No   : 0x4117160b
Head Len : 5   words       Flags    : .AP...          Window  : 0x1000
Checksum : 0xe807 (Good)   Urg Ptr  : 0x0000          Options : None
==============================[data:   10]=========================
0036  00 00 00 00 00 00 D1 B6 7D D4                 .......}.
```

The server sends a LPR acknowledgement, a single octet containing zero.

```
===============================µscope===============================
Frame   : 9                Len    : 76            Error    : None
T Elapsed: 19:06:27:257    T Delta : 00:00:00:047
-------------------------------[mac]-------------------------------
Dest Mac : Xyplex050dc5    Sourc Mac: Xyplex150dc6    Type    : IP
-------------------------------[ip]--------------------------------
IP Ver   : 4               IP HLen  : 20 Bytes
TOS      : 0x00            Pkt Len  : 58              Seg ID  : 0x0f76
Flags    : FRAG:*.LAST     Frag Ptr : 0     (8 Octet) TTL     : 56
PID      : TCP  ( 6)       Checksum : 0x208d (Good)
Dst IP <C: 192.168.107.15   Src IP <C: 192.168.100.171
-------------------------------[tcp]-------------------------------
Src Port : 1023            Dst Port : 515
Seq No   : 0x4117160b      Ack No   : 0x000007e5
Head Len : 5   words       Flags    : .AP...          Window  : 0x1000
Checksum : 0x8168 (Good)   Urg Ptr  : 0x0000          Options : None
==============================[data:   22]=========================
0036  03 31 39 30 20 64 66 41 30 32 30 72 6F 6E 6E 69  .190 dfA020ronni
0046  65 0A 01 F8 D1 E0                                e.....
```

The client acknowledges the LPR acknowledgement segment and sends the LPR command 03 – Receive Data File.
Command Code 03.
Count – 190 octets in length.
Filename – dfA020ronnie.

Frame 10   The server acknowledges the TCP segment of frame 9.
Frame 11   The server sends a segment containing a single octet of zero being an LPR
                  acknowledgement of the sub-command in frame 9.

```
===============================µscope===============================
Frame   : 12               Len    : 248           Error    : None
T Elapsed: 19:06:27:302    T Delta : 00:00:00:045
-------------------------------[mac]-------------------------------
Dest Mac : Xyplex050dc5    Sourc Mac: Xyplex150dc6    Type    : IP
-------------------------------[ip]--------------------------------
IP Ver   : 4               IP HLen  : 20 Bytes
TOS      : 0x00            Pkt Len  : 230             Seg ID  : 0x0f77
Flags    : FRAG:*.LAST     Frag Ptr : 0     (8 Octet) TTL     : 56
PID      : TCP  ( 6)       Checksum : 0x1fe0 (Good)
Dst IP <C: 192.168.107.15   Src IP <C: 192.168.100.171
-------------------------------[tcp]-------------------------------
Src Port : 1023            Dst Port : 515
Seq No   : 0x4117161d      Ack No   : 0x000007e6
Head Len : 5   words       Flags    : .AP...          Window  : 0x1000
Checksum : 0xc79c (Good)   Urg Ptr  : 0x0000          Options : None
==============================[data:  194]=========================
0036  54 68 69 73 20 69 73 20 61 20 74 65 73 74 20 70  This is a test p
0046  72 69 6E 74 20 66 69 6C 65 2E 61 62 63 64 65 66  rint file.abcdef
0056  67 68 69 6A 6B 6C 6D 6E 6F 70 71 72 73 74 75 76  ghijklmnopqrstuv
0066  77 78 79 7A 0A 62 63 64 65 66 67 68 69 6A 6B 6C  wxyz.bcdefghijkl
0076  6D 6E 6F 70 71 72 73 74 75 76 77 78 79 7A 61 0A  mnopqrstuvwxyza.
0086  63 64 65 66 67 68 69 6A 6B 6C 6D 6E 6F 70 71 72  cdefghijklmnopqr
0096  73 74 75 76 77 78 79 7A 61 62 0A 64 65 66 67 68  stuvwxyzab.defgh
00A6  69 6A 6B 6C 6D 6E 6F 70 71 72 73 74 75 76 77 78  ijklmnopqrstuvwx
00B6  79 7A 61 62 63 0A 65 66 67 68 69 6A 6B 6C 6D 6E  yzabc.efghijklmn
00C6  6F 70 71 72 73 74 75 76 77 78 79 7A 61 62 63 64  opqrstuvwxyzabcd
00D6  0A 54 68 69 73 20 69 73 20 74 68 65 20 65 6E 64  .This is the end
```

The client sends the data file to the server. No additional formatting takes place and no imbedded command codes are used.

Frame 13   The server acknowledges the TCP segment of frame 12.
Frame 14   The client sends a segment containing a single octet of zero indicating the End-of-File.
Frame 15   The server acknowledges the EOF octet of frame 14.
Frame 16   The server sends a LPR acknowledgement for the data file.

```
===============================µscope===============================
Frame   : 17               Len    : 75            Error    : None
T Elapsed: 19:06:27:748    T Delta : 00:00:00:015
-------------------------------[mac]-------------------------------
Dest Mac : Xyplex050dc5    Sourc Mac: Xyplex150dc6    Type    : IP
-------------------------------[ip]--------------------------------
IP Ver   : 4               IP HLen  : 20 Bytes
TOS      : 0x00            Pkt Len  : 57              Seg ID  : 0x0f7a
Flags    : FRAG:*.LAST     Frag Ptr : 0     (8 Octet) TTL     : 56
PID      : TCP  ( 6)       Checksum : 0x208a (Good)
Dst IP <C: 192.168.107.15   Src IP <C: 192.168.100.171
-------------------------------[tcp]-------------------------------
Src Port : 1023            Dst Port : 515
Seq No   : 0x411716dc      Ack No   : 0x000007e7
Head Len : 5   words       Flags    : .AP...          Window  : 0x1000
Checksum : 0x83c2 (Good)   Urg Ptr  : 0x0000          Options : None
==============================[data:   21]=========================
0036  02 37 36 20 63 66 41 30 32 30 72 6F 6E 6E 69 65  .76 cfA020ronnie
0046  0A 71 22 80 E7                                   .q"..
```

The client acknowledges the LPR acknowledgement segment and sends the LPR command 02 – Receive Control File.
Command Code 02.
Count – 76 octets in length.
Filename – cfA020ronnie.

Frame 18   The server acknowledges the segment of frame 17.
Frame 19   The server sends a LPR acknowledgement for the sub-command of frame 17.

Line Printer Daemon Protocol (LPD)

```
==============================μscope==============================
Frame    : 20                 Len      : 134            Error     : None
T Elapsed: 19:06:27:786       T Delta  : 00:00:00:030
------------------------------[mac]------------------------------
Dest Mac : Xyplex050dc5       Sourc Mac: Xyplex150dc6   Type      : IP
-------------------------------[ip]-------------------------------
IP Ver   : 4                  IP HLen  : 20 Bytes
TOS      : 0x00               Pkt Len  : 116            Seg ID    : 0x0f7b
Flags    : FRAG:*.LAST        Frag Ptr : 0     (8 Octet) TTL      : 56
PID      : TCP  ( 6)          Checksum : 0x204e (Good)
Dst IP <C: 192.168.107.15     Src IP <C: 192.168.100.171
------------------------------[tcp]------------------------------
Src Port : 1023               Dst Port : 515
Seq No   : 0x411716ed         Ack No   : 0x000007e8
Head Len : 5    words         Flags    : .AP...        Window    : 0x1000
Checksum : 0xaae6 (Good)      Urg Ptr  : 0x0000        Options   : None
==============================[data:   80]==============================
0036  48 72 6F 6E 6E 69 65 0A 50 70 68 69 6C 0A 4A 74    Hronnie.Pphil.Jt
0046  65 73 74 2E 70 72 74 0A 43 72 6F 6E 6E 69 65 0A    est.prt.Cronnie.
0056  4C 70 68 69 6C 0A 66 64 66 41 30 32 30 72 6F 6E    Lphil.fdfA020ron
0066  6E 69 65 0A 55 64 66 41 30 32 30 72 6F 6E 6E 69    nie.UdfA020ronni
0076  65 0A 4E 74 65 73 74 2E 70 72 74 0A 0E 7C 0C 85    e.Ntest.prt..|..
```

The client sends the control file decoded as follows:

H (Host Name)	"ronnie"	
P (User Id)	"phil"	
J (Job Name)	"test.prt"	
C (Class)	"ronnie"	
L (Print Banner)	"phil"	
f (Prt Formatted)	"dfA020ronnie"	
U (Unlink)	"dfA020ronnie"	
N (Name Src File)	"test.prt"	

Frame 21   The server acknowledges the segment of frame 20.
Frame 22   The server sends a further segment to indicate that its Window has recovered.
Frame 23   The client sends a single zero octet to indicate the end of the Control File.
Frame 24   The server acknowledges the segment sent in frame 23.
Frame 25   The server sends a LPR acknowledgement (single zero octet) to acknowledge receipt of the Control File.
Frame 26   The client acknowledges the segment in frame 25.

The TCP Connection is now closed in the normal way

Figure 21-2: Sample LPR Trace

21.7 SYSLOG

Syslog provides devices with the ability to log significant events at a central host. Many UNIX hosts run a syslog daemon process that listens on UDP port 514_{10} for messages. These messages are then logged to a file normally specified in the */etc/syslog.conf* file.

The messages generally have a priority associated with them based upon their severity. A priority zero message indicates a severe condition such as an abnormal system shutdown, while a priority six message indicates just status information. Since all messages are prioritized in this way, administrators can select the severity of message that a device sends based upon this priority. The host will then log only those messages that have a priority equal or below that specified. Table 21-1 lists the types of messages, their priority, and a brief description. Since the configuration of the Unix host is likely to be implementation specific however, the *man* pages for the host should be consulted for further information.

Table 21-1: SYSLOG Severities

Message Type	Priority	Description
LOG_EMERG	0	A severe condition.
LOG_ALERT	1	A condition that the system manager needs to correct immediately such as a corrupted system database.
LOG_CRIT	2	A critical condition such as a hard device error.
LOG_ERR	3	A software error condition.
LOG_WARNING	4	A warning message.
LOG_NOTICE	5	Conditions that are not error conditions, but may require specific procedures to adjust them.
LOG_INFO	6	Normal, informational messages.
LOG_DEBUG	7	Messages that contain information useful for testing only.

The partially decoded trace in Figure 21-3 shows a network device sending two syslog messages to a central host. In this particular case the device, a Terminal Server, firstly reports a user connection to a host using Telnet, and then the subsequent disconnection. The actual format of the message is implementation specific, thus it is highly likely that implementations from different vendors could produce different results.

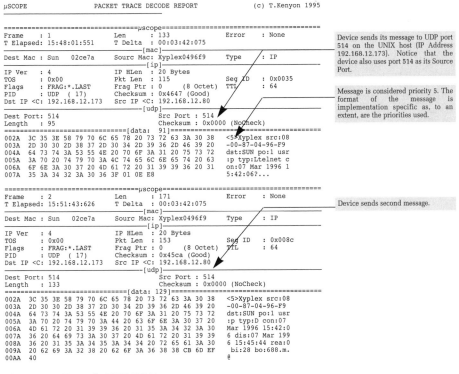

```
=============================μScope============================================
Frame    : 1                 Len      : 133           Error    : None
T Elapsed: 15:48:01:551      T Delta  : 00:03:42:075
                                     -[mac]-
Dest Mac : Sun   02ce7a      Sourc Mac: Xyplex0496f9   Type       : IP
                                     -[ip]-
IP Ver   : 4                 IP HLen  : 20 Bytes
TOS      : 0x00              Pkt Len  : 115            Seg ID   : 0x0035
Flags    : FRAG:*.LAST       Frag Ptr : 0     (8 Octet) TTL     : 64
PID      : UDP ( 17)         Checksum : 0x4647 (Good)
Dst IP <C: 192.168.12.173    Src IP <C: 192.168.12.80
                                     -[udp]-
Dest Port: 514               Src Port : 514
Length   : 95                Checksum : 0x0000 (NoCheck)
=============================[data:   91]======================================
002A  3C 35 3E 58 79 70 6C 65 78 20 73 72 63 3A 30 38   <5>Xyplex src:08
003A  2D 30 30 2D 38 37 2D 30 34 2D 39 36 2D 46 39 20   -00-87-04-96-F9
004A  64 73 74 3A 53 55 4E 20 70 6F 3A 31 20 75 73 72   dst:SUN po:1 usr
005A  3A 70 20 74 79 70 3A 4C 74 65 6C 6E 65 74 20 63   :p typ:Ltelnet c
006A  6F 6E 3A 30 37 20 4D 61 72 20 31 39 39 36 20 31   on:07 Mar 1996 1
007A  35 3A 34 32 3A 30 36 3F 01 0E E8                  5:42:06?...


=============================μScope============================================
Frame    : 2                 Len      : 171           Error    : None
T Elapsed: 15:51:43:626      T Delta  : 00:03:42:075
                                     -[mac]-
Dest Mac : Sun   02ce7a      Sourc Mac: Xyplex0496f9   Type       : IP
                                     -[ip]-
IP Ver   : 4                 IP HLen  : 20 Bytes
TOS      : 0x00              Pkt Len  : 153            Seg ID   : 0x008c
Flags    : FRAG:*.LAST       Frag Ptr : 0     (8 Octet) TTL     : 64
PID      : UDP ( 17)         Checksum : 0x45ca (Good)
Dst IP <C: 192.168.12.173    Src IP <C: 192.168.12.80
                                     -[udp]-
Dest Port: 514               Src Port : 514
Length   : 133               Checksum : 0x0000 (NoCheck)
=============================[data: 129]=======================================
002A  3C 35 3E 58 79 70 6C 65 78 20 73 72 63 3A 30 38   <5>Xyplex src:08
003A  2D 30 30 2D 38 37 2D 30 34 2D 39 36 2D 46 39 20   -00-87-04-96-F9
004A  64 73 74 3A 53 55 4E 20 70 6F 3A 31 20 75 73 72   dst:SUN po:1 usr
005A  3A 70 20 74 79 70 3A 44 20 63 6F 6E 3A 30 37 20   :p typ:D con:07
006A  4D 61 72 20 31 39 39 36 20 31 35 3A 34 32 3A 30   Mar 1996 15:42:0
007A  36 20 64 69 73 3A 30 37 20 4D 61 72 20 31 39 39   6 dis:07 Mar 199
008A  36 20 31 35 3A 34 35 3A 34 34 20 72 65 61 3A 30   6 15:45:44 rea:0
009A  20 62 69 3A 32 38 20 62 6F 3A 36 38 38 CB 6D EF   bi:28 bo:688.m.
00AA  40                                                @
```

Figure 21-3: Example SYSLOG Trace

Device sends its message to UDP port 514 on the UNIX host (IP Address 192.168.12.173). Notice that the device also uses port 514 as its Source Port.

Message is considered priority 5. The format of the message is implementation specific as, to an extent, are the priorities used.

Device sends second message.

21.8 Finger

Finger provides a service that allows hosts to interrogate devices to determine information about specific users. Defined as a service that can run over either TCP or UDP, most implementations tend to use TCP. In either case, port 79_{10} is always used, and the actual format of the data is implementation specific.

In the case of TCP, the device listens on port 79_{10} for a connection to be established, and then returns the requested information. The connection is then closed by the requester in the normal way by setting the *FIN* bit. No waiting is required for the TCP service since all data is acknowledged and flow control is achieved by standard TCP procedures. The trace below demonstrates the TCP implementation of the services and shows a host fingering a device (a Terminal Server) to determine the users logged in.

The connection is opened with the standard three-way handshake.

```
==============================µscope===============================
Frame   : 4              Len      : 64            Error   : None
T Elapsed: 19:10:53:288  T Delta  : 00:00:00:000
-----------------------------[mac]--------------------------------
Dest Mac : Xyplex150dc6  Sourc Mac: Xyplex050dc5  Type    : IP
-----------------------------[ip]---------------------------------
IP Ver  : 4              IP HLen  : 20 Bytes
TOS     : 0x00           Pkt Len  : 40            Seg ID  : 0x00bf
Flags   : FRAG:*.LAST    Frag Ptr : 0    (8 Octet) TTL     : 64
PID     : TCP  ( 6)      Checksum : 0x2756 (Good)
Dst IP <C: 192.168.100.171  Src IP <C: 192.168.107.15
-----------------------------[tcp]--------------------------------
Src Port : 79            Dst Port : 1232
Seq No   : 0x00000f18    Ack No   : 0x436bc402
Head Len : 5   words     Flags    : .A....        Window  : 0x0100
Checksum : 0x4074 (Good) Urg Ptr  : 0x0000        Options : None
==========================[data:  10]=============================
0036  00 00 00 00 00 00 1E 7F 2B A5                ........+.
```

```
==============================µscope===============================
Frame   : 5              Len      : 64            Error   : None
T Elapsed: 19:10:53:288  T Delta  : 00:00:00:000
-----------------------------[mac]--------------------------------
Dest Mac : Xyplex050dc5  Sourc Mac: Xyplex150dc6  Type    : IP
-----------------------------[ip]---------------------------------
IP Ver  : 4              IP HLen  : 20 Bytes
TOS     : 0x00           Pkt Len  : 42            Seg ID  : 0x0ffb
Flags   : FRAG:*.LAST    Frag Ptr : 0    (8 Octet) TTL     : 56
PID     : TCP  ( 6)      Checksum : 0x2018 (Good)
Dst IP <C: 192.168.107.15  Src IP <C: 192.168.100.171
-----------------------------[tcp]--------------------------------
Src Port : 1232          Dst Port : 79
Seq No   : 0x436bc402    Ack No   : 0x00000f18
Head Len : 5   words     Flags    : .AP...        Window  : 0x1000
Checksum : 0x2460 (Good) Urg Ptr  : 0x0000        Options : None
==========================[data:  10]=============================
0036  0D 0A 51 4F 00 00 24 38 81 DA                ..QO..$8..
```

```
==============================µscope===============================
Frame   : 6              Len      : 64            Error   : None
T Elapsed: 19:10:53:288  T Delta  : 00:00:00:000
-----------------------------[mac]--------------------------------
Dest Mac : Xyplex150dc6  Sourc Mac: Xyplex050dc5  Type    : IP
-----------------------------[ip]---------------------------------
IP Ver  : 4              IP HLen  : 20 Bytes
TOS     : 0x00           Pkt Len  : 40            Seg ID  : 0x00c0
Flags   : FRAG:*.LAST    Frag Ptr : 0    (8 Octet) TTL     : 64
PID     : TCP  ( 6)      Checksum : 0x2755 (Good)
Dst IP <C: 192.168.100.171  Src IP <C: 192.168.107.15
-----------------------------[tcp]--------------------------------
Src Port : 79            Dst Port : 1232
Seq No   : 0x00000f18    Ack No   : 0x436bc404
Head Len : 5   words     Flags    : .A....        Window  : 0x00fe
Checksum : 0x4074 (Good) Urg Ptr  : 0x0000        Options : None
==========================[data:  10]=============================
0036  00 00 00 00 00 00 51 5E 39 CB                ......Q^9.
```

```
==============================µscope===============================
Frame   : 7              Len      : 386           Error   : None
T Elapsed: 19:10:53:297  T Delta  : 00:00:00:009
-----------------------------[mac]--------------------------------
Dest Mac : Xyplex150dc6  Sourc Mac: Xyplex050dc5  Type    : IP
-----------------------------[ip]---------------------------------
IP Ver  : 4              IP HLen  : 20 Bytes
TOS     : 0x00           Pkt Len  : 368           Seg ID  : 0x00c1
Flags   : FRAG:*.LAST    Frag Ptr : 0    (8 Octet) TTL     : 64
PID     : TCP  ( 6)      Checksum : 0x260c (Good)
Dst IP <C: 192.168.100.171  Src IP <C: 192.168.107.15
-----------------------------[tcp]--------------------------------
Src Port : 79            Dst Port : 1232
Seq No   : 0x00000f18    Ack No   : 0x436bc404
Head Len : 5   words     Flags    : .AP...        Window  : 0x0100
Checksum : 0x1728 (Good) Urg Ptr  : 0x0000        Options : None
==========================[data: 332]=============================
0036  55 73 65 72 20 4E 61 6D 65 20 20 20 20 20 20  User Name
0046  20 50 6F 72 74 20 20 49 64 6C 65 20 20 20 4C  /Port  Idle   L
0056  6F 67 69 6E 20 20 20 20 20 20 50 6F 72 74      /ogin       Port
0066  20 4E 61 6D 65 20 20 20 20 20 20 20 20 53 74   Name       St
0076  61 74 75 73 20 20 20 20 20 20 20 20 20 20 20   atus
0086  0D 0A 28 52 65 6D 6F 74 65 29 20 20 20 20 20   ..(Remote)
0096  20 20 20 20 20 31 20 20 30 30 3A 30 34 3A 35 30     1 00:04:50
00A6  20 20 20 20 20 20 20 20 20 20 20 20 20 50 4F                 PO
00B6  52 54 5F 31 20 20 20 20 20 20 20 20 20 20 20   RT_1
00C6  41 76 61 69 6C 61 62 6C 65 20 20 20 20 20 20   Available
00D6  20 20 0D 0A 50 68 69 6C 20 4D 69 6C 6C 65 72 20  ..Phil Miller
```

Data shown truncated

Miscellaneous Protocols

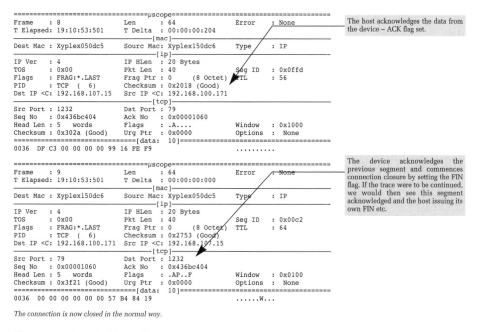

```
=============================μscope==========================================
Frame    : 8            Len     : 64              Error    : None
T Elapsed: 19:10:53:501  T Delta : 00:00:00:204
----------------------------[mac]-------------------------------
Dest Mac : Xyplex050dc5  Sourc Mac: Xyplex150dc6  Type     : IP
----------------------------[ip]--------------------------------
IP Ver   : 4            IP HLen : 20 Bytes
TOS      : 0x00          Pkt Len : 40            Seg ID   : 0x0ffd
Flags    : FRAG:*.LAST   Frag Ptr : 0    (8 Octet) TTL      : 56
PID      : TCP  ( 6)     Checksum : 0x2018 (Good)
Dst IP <C: 192.168.107.15  Src IP <C: 192.168.100.171
----------------------------[tcp]-------------------------------
Src Port : 1232          Dst Port : 79
Seq No   : 0x436bc404    Ack No   : 0x00001060
Head Len : 5  words      Flags    : .A....       Window   : 0x1000
Checksum : 0x302a (Good)  Urg Ptr  : 0x0000       Options  : None
=============================[data:  10]=====================================
0036  DF C3 00 00 00 00 99 16 FE F9            ..........

=============================μscope==========================================
Frame    : 9            Len     : 64              Error    : None
T Elapsed: 19:10:53:501  T Delta : 00:00:00:000
----------------------------[mac]-------------------------------
Dest Mac : Xyplex150dc6  Sourc Mac: Xyplex050dc5  Type     : IP
----------------------------[ip]--------------------------------
IP Ver   : 4            IP HLen : 20 Bytes
TOS      : 0x00          Pkt Len : 40            Seg ID   : 0x00c2
Flags    : FRAG:*.LAST   Frag Ptr : 0    (8 Octet) TTL      : 64
PID      : TCP  ( 6)     Checksum : 0x2753 (Good)
Dst IP <C: 192.168.100.171  Src IP <C: 192.168.107.15
----------------------------[tcp]-------------------------------
Src Port : 79            Dst Port : 1232
Seq No   : 0x00001060    Ack No   : 0x436bc404
Head Len : 5  words      Flags    : .AP..F       Window   : 0x0100
Checksum : 0x3f21 (Good)  Urg Ptr  : 0x0000       Options  : None
=============================[data:  10]=====================================
0036  00 00 00 00 00 00 57 B4 84 19            ......W...
```

The host acknowledges the data from the device – ACK flag set.

The device acknowledges the previous segment and commences connection closure by setting the FIN flag. If the trace were to be continued, we would then see this segment acknowledged and the host issuing its own FIN etc.

The connection is now closed in the normal way.

Figure 21-4: Sample Finger Trace

With UDP, the device merely listens on the port and returns the requested information in response to a received datagram. As with other services that use UDP though, since it is likely that the information will span multiple messages, the requesting host should wait for a period of time to elapse before processing the received data. This then ensures that all data has been received.

21.9 WHOIS/nickname

RFC 954 defines a simple query/response protocol used to interrogate centralized Internet servers to obtain network wide information about users, networks and domains in a human readable format. The service (known simply as whois or nickname) uses TCP port 43_{10} and is arranged such that the server listens and accepts connections on this port, and then responds to single line queries delimited with a Carriage Return/Line Feed sequence. The server then sends its response (based upon information contained within its database) and then immediately closes the connection.

WHOIS servers, of which there are relatively few, are designed to provide Internet registration information. Possibly the most used of these is *rs.internic.net* that will accept Telnet connections (login as user whois) or network connections using the whois service. Since most IP implementations today support a whois client though, Telnet*ing* to the host is generally unnecessary.

Generally the response from a whois server will contain some or all the following:

- The name and address of the organization that owns the domain or address.

- The name of the domain (where applicable).

- The technical and administrative contacts for the zone.

- The host names and addresses of machines and sites providing a name service for the domain.

The example below shows a typical whois session.

```
phil >whois-h rs.internic.net 192.168.0.0
IANA (IANA-CBLK-RESERVED)
    Internet Assigned Numbers Authority
    Information Sciences Institute
    University of Southern California
    4676 Admiralty Way, Suite 1001
    Marina del Rey, CA 90292-6695

    Netname: IANA-CBLK1
    Netblock: 192.168.0.0 - 192.168.255.0

    Coordinator:
        Reynolds, Joyce K.  (JKR1)  JKRey@ISI.EDU
        (310) 822-1511

    Domain System Inverse Mapping provided by:

    NS.ISI.EDU                      128.9.128.127
    RS0.INTERNIC.NET                198.41.0.5

    Record last updated on 14-June-95.

The InterNIC Registration Services Host contains ONLY Internet Information
(Networks, ASN's, Domains, and POC's).
Please use the whois server at nic.ddn.mil for MILNET Information.
```

Figure 21-5: Sample whois Session

The corresponding trace for this session is then shown in the following figure.

```
μSCOPE               PACKET TRACE DECODE REPORT          (c) T.Kenyon 1995
```

The connection is opened with the standard three-way handshake.

```
==============================μscope=============================================
Frame    : 17              Len    : 71            Error   : None
T Elapsed: 19:06:05:932    T Delta  : 00:00:00:000
-------------------------------[mac]--------------------------------------------
Dest Mac : Xyplex115f3d    Sourc Mac: Sun   02ce7a    Type    : IP
-------------------------------[ip]---------------------------------------------
IP Ver   : 4               IP HLen  : 20 Bytes
TOS      : 0x00            Pkt Len  : 53            Seq ID  : 0x231a
Flags    : FRAG:*.LAST     Frag Ptr : 0      (8 Octet)  TTL     : 60
PID      : TCP  ( 6)       Checksum : 0x7b4c (Good)
Dst IP <C: 198.41.0.6      Src IP <C: 172.16.88.173
-------------------------------[tcp]--------------------------------------------
Src Port : 3988            Dst Port : WHOIS
Seq No   : 0x13459801      Ack No   : 0x74b01201
Head Len : 5   words       Flags    : .AP...          Window  : 0x1000
Checksum : 0x46a4 (Good)   Urg Ptr  : 0x0000          Options : None
==============================[data:  17]=======================================
0036  31 39 32 2E 31 36 38 2E 30 2E 30 0D 0A E5 54 96    192.168.0.0...T.
0046  77                                                 w
```

The client sends its request to the server (port 43).

The request, delimited by the sequence 0D0A implies that the client is seeking information about the ownership of the network address block 192.168.0.0.

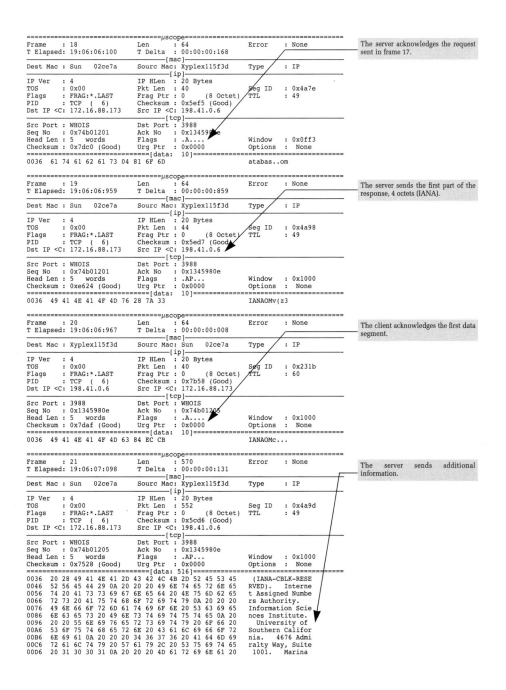

```
===============================μscope===============================
Frame    : 18              Len      : 64              Error    : None
T Elapsed: 19:06:06:100    T Delta  : 00:00:00:168
                                 ─[mac]─
Dest Mac : Sun   02ce7a    Sourc Mac: Xyplex115f3d    Type     : IP
                                 ─[ip]─
IP Ver   : 4               IP HLen  : 20 Bytes
TOS      : 0x00            Pkt Len  : 40              Seg ID   : 0x4a7e
Flags    : FRAG:*.LAST     Frag Ptr : 0     (8 Octet) TTL      : 49
PID      : TCP  ( 6)       Checksum : 0x5ef5 (Good)
Dst IP <C: 172.16.88.173   Src IP <C: 198.41.0.6
                                 ─[tcp]─
Src Port : WHOIS           Dst Port : 3988
Seq No   : 0x74b01201      Ack No   : 0x13459d3e
Head Len : 5   words       Flags    : .A....         Window   : 0x0ff3
Checksum : 0x7dc0 (Good)   Urg Ptr  : 0x0000         Options  : None
===============================[data:  10]===============================
0036   61 74 61 62 61 73 04 81 6F 6D           atabas..om
```

The server acknowledges the request sent in frame 17.

```
===============================μscope===============================
Frame    : 19              Len      : 64              Error    : None
T Elapsed: 19:06:06:959    T Delta  : 00:00:00:859
                                 ─[mac]─
Dest Mac : Sun   02ce7a    Sourc Mac: Xyplex115f3d    Type     : IP
                                 ─[ip]─
IP Ver   : 4               IP HLen  : 20 Bytes
TOS      : 0x00            Pkt Len  : 44              Seg ID   : 0x4a98
Flags    : FRAG:*.LAST     Frag Ptr : 0     (8 Octet) TTL      : 49
PID      : TCP  ( 6)       Checksum : 0x5ed7 (Good)
Dst IP <C: 172.16.88.173   Src IP <C: 198.41.0.6
                                 ─[tcp]─
Src Port : WHOIS           Dst Port : 3988
Seq No   : 0x74b01201      Ack No   : 0x1345980e
Head Len : 5   words       Flags    : .AP...         Window   : 0x1000
Checksum : 0xe624 (Good)   Urg Ptr  : 0x0000         Options  : None
===============================[data:  10]===============================
0036   49 41 4E 41 4F 4D 76 28 7A 33           IANAOMv(z3
```

The server sends the first part of the response, 4 octets (IANA).

```
===============================μscope===============================
Frame    : 20              Len      : 64              Error    : None
T Elapsed: 19:06:06:967    T Delta  : 00:00:00:008
                                 ─[mac]─
Dest Mac : Xyplex115f3d    Sourc Mac: Sun   02ce7a    Type     : IP
                                 ─[ip]─
IP Ver   : 4               IP HLen  : 20 Bytes
TOS      : 0x00            Pkt Len  : 40              Seg ID   : 0x231b
Flags    : FRAG:*.LAST     Frag Ptr : 0     (8 Octet) TTL      : 60
PID      : TCP  ( 6)       Checksum : 0x7b58 (Good)
Dst IP <C: 198.41.0.6      Src IP <C: 172.16.88.173
                                 ─[tcp]─
Src Port : 3988            Dst Port : WHOIS
Seq No   : 0x1345980e      Ack No   : 0x74b01205
Head Len : 5   words       Flags    : .A....         Window   : 0x1000
Checksum : 0x7daf (Good)   Urg Ptr  : 0x0000         Options  : None
===============================[data:  10]===============================
0036   49 41 4E 41 4F 4D 63 84 EC CB           IANAOMc...
```

The client acknowledges the first data segment.

```
===============================μscope===============================
Frame    : 21              Len      : 570             Error    : None
T Elapsed: 19:06:07:098    T Delta  : 00:00:00:131
                                 ─[mac]─
Dest Mac : Sun   02ce7a    Sourc Mac: Xyplex115f3d    Type     : IP
                                 ─[ip]─
IP Ver   : 4               IP HLen  : 20 Bytes
TOS      : 0x00            Pkt Len  : 552             Seg ID   : 0x4a9d
Flags    : FRAG:*.LAST     Frag Ptr : 0     (8 Octet) TTL      : 49
PID      : TCP  ( 6)       Checksum : 0x5cd6 (Good)
Dst IP <C: 172.16.88.173   Src IP <C: 198.41.0.6
                                 ─[tcp]─
Src Port : WHOIS           Dst Port : 3988
Seq No   : 0x74b01205      Ack No   : 0x1345980e
Head Len : 5   words       Flags    : .AP...         Window   : 0x1000
Checksum : 0x7528 (Good)   Urg Ptr  : 0x0000         Options  : None
===============================[data: 516]===============================
0036   20 28 49 41 4E 41 2D 43 42 4C 4B 2D 52 45 53 45   (IANA-CBLK-RESE
0046   52 56 45 44 29 0A 20 20 20 49 6E 74 65 72 6E 65   RVED).   Interne
0056   74 20 41 73 73 69 67 6E 65 64 20 4E 75 6D 62 65   t Assigned Numbe
0066   72 73 20 41 75 74 68 6F 72 69 74 79 0A 20 20 20   rs Authority.
0076   49 6E 66 6F 72 6D 61 74 69 6F 6E 20 53 63 69 65   Information Scie
0086   6E 63 65 73 20 49 6E 73 74 69 74 75 74 65 0A 20   nces Institute.
0096   20 20 55 6E 69 76 65 72 73 69 74 79 20 6F 66 20     University of
00A6   53 6F 75 74 68 65 72 6E 20 43 61 6C 69 66 6F 72   Southern Califor
00B6   6E 69 61 0A 20 20 20 20 34 36 37 36 20 41 64 6D 69  nia.    4676 Admi
00C6   72 61 6C 74 79 20 57 61 79 2C 20 53 75 69 74 65   ralty Way, Suite
00D6   20 31 30 30 31 0A 20 20 20 4D 61 72 69 6E 61 20   1001.   Marina
```

The server sends additional information.
```
```

```
=============================µscope==============================
Frame    : 22            Len      : 226          Error    : None
T Elapsed: 19:06:07:131  T Delta  : 00:00:00:033
---------------------------[mac]--------------------------------
Dest Mac : Sun   02ce7a  Sourc Mac: Xyplex115f3d  Type     : IP
---------------------------[ip]---------------------------------
IP Ver   : 4             IP HLen  : 20 Bytes
TOS      : 0x00          Pkt Len  : 208           Seg ID   : 0x4a9e
Flags    : FRAG:*.LAST   Frag Ptr : 0    (8 Octet) TTL      : 49
PID      : TCP  ( 6)     Checksum : 0x5e2d (Good)
Dst IP <C: 172.16.88.173 Src IP <C: 198.41.0.6
---------------------------[tcp]--------------------------------
Src Port : WHOIS         Dst Port : 3988
Seq No   : 0x74b01405    Ack No   : 0x1345980e
Head Len : 5   words     Flags    : .AP..F        Window   : 0x1000
Checksum : 0x4d80 (Good) Urg Ptr  : 0x0000        Options  : None
=============================[data: 172]=========================
0036  52 65 67 69 73 74 72 61 74 69 6F 6E 20 53 65 72   Registration Ser
0046  76 69 63 65 73 20 48 6F 73 74 20 63 6F 6E 74 61   vices Host conta
0056  69 6E 73 20 4F 4E 4C 59 20 49 6E 74 65 72 6E 65   ins ONLY Interne
0066  74 20 49 6E 66 6F 72 6D 61 74 69 6F 6E 0A 28 4E   t Information.(N
0076  65 74 77 6F 72 6B 73 2C 20 41 53 4E 27 73 2C 20   etworks, ASN's,
0086  44 6F 6D 61 69 6E 73 2C 20 61 6E 64 20 50 4F 43   Domains, and POC
0096  27 73 29 2E 0A 50 6C 65 61 73 65 20 75 73 65 20   's)..Please use
00A6  74 68 65 20 77 68 6F 69 73 20 73 65 72 76 65 72   the whois server
00B6  20 61 74 20 6E 69 63 2E 64 64 6E 2E 6D 69 6C 20   at nic.ddn.mil
00C6  66 6F 72 20 4D 49 4C 4E 45 54 20 49 6E 66 6F 72   for MILNET Infor
00D6  6D 61 74 69 6F 6E 2E 0A 53 35 20 89               mation..S5 .
```

The server sends the final segment of information and initiates the closure of the connection by setting the FIN bit.

The connection closure is completed in the normal way.

Figure 21-6: Trace of Sample whois Session

21.10 Character Generator Protocol (CHARGEN)

The Character Generator service is used to send data without regard to any input. RFC 864 (Std 22) then recommends that this simple service is implemented where such a system is required.

As with many of these protocols and services, Chargen can operate over both TCP and UDP. When used in a TCP environment, a server listens for a connection on TCP port 19_{10} and, when established, sends a stream of data. This data then continues until the connection is closed by the client. RFC 864 mentions that in this type of service, the server process must be prepared for an abrupt closure of the connection. This is because it is likely that the client will terminate the connection (potentially abruptly) when enough data has been sent. An advantage of the TCP service however is that data flow is constrained by the normal TCP flow control mechanisms and therefore we need not be concerned with a server sending data faster than it can be processed.

In the UDP implementation, the server again listens on port 19_{10} (although this time through UDP), and then sends a single datagram containing a random number (between 0 and 512) of characters. With UDP, there is no flow control mechanism. Thus, to ensure that the client does not receive more data than it can reasonably handle, only a single datagram is sent by the server in response to each one received. Because datagrams are exchanged only on a one-by-one basis and the UDP implementation is simple, no state information is maintained. Thus, data transmitted by a server does not need to exhibit any kind of continuity.

The data itself can be any printable character, however it is recommended that a recognizable pattern is used so that human operators can easily detect errors. One suggestion is that the data should be considered as 72 character lines (each ending with a carriage return and linefeed) that would display a scrolling pattern of the 95 printable characters in the ASCII character set. Figure 21-7 shows an example of this.

```
!"#$%&'()*+,-./0123456789:;<=>?@ABCDEFGHIJKLMNOPQRSTUVWXYZ[\]^_`abcdefgh
"#$%&'()*+,-./0123456789:;<=>?@ABCDEFGHIJKLMNOPQRSTUVWXYZ[\]^_`abcdefghi
#$%&'()*+,-./0123456789:;<=>?@ABCDEFGHIJKLMNOPQRSTUVWXYZ[\]^_`abcdefghij
$%&'()*+,-./0123456789:;<=>?@ABCDEFGHIJKLMNOPQRSTUVWXYZ[\]^_`abcdefghijk
%&'()*+,-./0123456789:;<=>?@ABCDEFGHIJKLMNOPQRSTUVWXYZ[\]^_`abcdefghijkl
&'()*+,-./0123456789:;<=>?@ABCDEFGHIJKLMNOPQRSTUVWXYZ[\]^_`abcdefghijklm
'()*+,-./0123456789:;<=>?@ABCDEFGHIJKLMNOPQRSTUVWXYZ[\]^_`abcdefghijklmn
()*+,-./0123456789:;<=>?@ABCDEFGHIJKLMNOPQRSTUVWXYZ[\]^_`abcdefghijklmno
)*+,-./0123456789:;<=>?@ABCDEFGHIJKLMNOPQRSTUVWXYZ[\]^_`abcdefghijklmnop
*+,-./0123456789:;<=>?@ABCDEFGHIJKLMNOPQRSTUVWXYZ[\]^_`abcdefghijklmnopq
```

Figure 21-7: Sample CHARGEN Output

21.11   Quote of the Day (Quote)

Like the Character Generation service described above, the Quote of the Day service can be implemented over either TCP or UDP, and returns ASCII readable text on receipt of either a connection (TCP service) or datagram (UDP service). The Quote of the Day service is defined by RFC 865 (Std 23).

In the TCP service, a server listens on TCP port 17_{10} for a connection. Once a connection is established, a short message is sent out, and the server then closes the connection immediately. In the case of UDP, the server listens on UDP port 17_{10}, and returns a datagram containing the short message for each datagram received. In both cases there is no specific syntax that must be used, but it is recommended that the message is limited to ASCII printable characters, spaces, carriage returns and line feeds, and that the message does not exceed 512 characters.

21.12   Users

Unlike Finger which can be used to interrogate a device for any user (active or not), this service reports only those users that are currently active (logged in).

RFC 866 (Std 24) defines two service types (TCP and UDP) both of which operate on port 11_{10}. In the TCP service, the server listens on port 11_{10} and, when a connection is established, returns a list of all currently active users. The connection is then closed by the server without waiting for the client to initiate the closure. In the UDP service, the server again listens on port 11_{10} and returns a list of active users in response to any received datagram at that port.

Users are not reported in any particular order and, where the entire list will not fit into a single datagram, the list of users is split subject to the condition that all information concerning any single user should travel together. In the UDP implementation then, a timeout period should be implemented so that the requesting station is sure that it has received all datagrams. Again, there is no required format for the data, but it is recommended that the message is limited to ASCII printable characters, spaces, carriage returns and line feeds, and that information regarding each user should be on a separate line.

21.13 Summary

In this chapter we have discussed some of the protocols and services that enjoy little publicity. You will note however, that many are in fact Internet standards and as such deserve mention. In addition, in highlighting just these few protocols we have not even started to scratch the surface of the Internet Protocol Suite. Indeed to fully document the protocols in use today would be a life's work which, although fulfilling, few of us could actually achieve.

This chapter then devotes time to just a few of the protocols and services in common use and is certainly not an all encompassing study. Certainly if we consider those protocols discussed, we find that there is a broad cross-section. We have a method of printing using the Line Printer Daemon Protocol (LPD), a method of centralized logging with SYSLOG and several management protocols and services such as Time, Finger, WHOIS, and Users. Finally we see other protocols primarily designed to exercise connections. So as this chapter shows, apart from the key protocols discussed elsewhere in this book, we have large numbers of others each with their own purpose and adding to the overall functionality of this feature rich suite.

Communications Over Wide Area Links

Today, many networks have dial-in ports that allow remote users to log in, transfer files, and send and receive electronic mail. Whether these users are travelling sales people, home workers, or network administration personnel that need to access the network out of hours, the need for remote access is here today, and is likely to grow dramatically in future years.

Remote Access has, to date, normally been achieved through Terminal or Access Servers. These devices take a raw bit stream from say, an RS232-C device, and convert it into a network session such as Telnet. This story though, is far from over. Nowadays, simple access to host systems through a virtual terminal emulator is far from acceptable and users require the ability to download files, and indeed to fully participate in network activities just as if they were local. So, although the device at the end of the telephone line is still a serial device, it now has intelligence. Gone are the days of the simple asynchronous device, we must now run a *Link Layer* protocol that is capable of carrying our upper layers, and therefore offer users the full functionality of the Internet protocol suite.

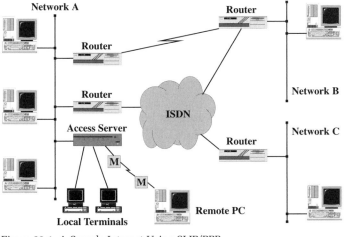

Figure 22-1: A Sample Internet Using SLIP/PPP

In this chapter we shall look at two such protocols namely Serial Line IP (or SLIP), and the Point-to-Point Protocol (PPP). One important point that must not be overlooked however, is that these protocols are far from restricted to remote users.

In the past, Bridge/Router vendors used proprietary protocols over Wide Area links. Today these manufacturers, in an effort to achieve inter-operability amongst themselves, are also turning to standardized protocols such as PPP. Today we find PPP used extensively over wide area links of all types due to its ability to carry multiple protocols. This then also makes it an ideal choice for interconnecting multi-protocol routers from different vendors.

Figure 22-1 shows an example of a network where remote access is used so that the remote PC can gain access to the network over a dial-in line via an Access (or Terminal) Server. If we assume that the PC merely runs a simple Terminal Emulation package, no Link Layer protocol will be required. Most commonly however, the PC would probably run either SLIP or PPP so that the user can run application protocols such as Telnet, FTP, and SMTP etc. At the network end of the connection, we see an Access Server that has a modem connected which, since it is connected to the PSTN, could be designated for purely incoming or outgoing calls. Alternatively, this modem could provide LAN users with bi-directional modem support enabling them to both make and receive calls to/from any other site.

The routers, we shall also assume, are connected using PPP as the Link Layer protocol since this is a feature rich protocol providing us with many advantages that will be discussed later. The actual configuration shown provides a leased line between networks A and B with ISDN backup, and an ISDN dial-on-demand link to Network C. Router configuration is unimportant at this stage, as is the actual type of connection. Instead, we must concern ourselves with exactly how connections are established, maintained, and finally closed.

22.1 Serial Line IP (SLIP)

Before looking at the Point-to-Point Protocol (PPP) in detail, let us first consider the dawn of time as far as IP remote connections are concerned. RFC 1055, the document defining SLIP is titled, "*A non-standard for transmission of IP datagrams over serial lines*," and this is possibly the best description of it. SLIP is a simple method of encapsulating IP Datagrams for transmission over serial lines, and provides nothing in terms of security, compression, protocol identification, or error detection. In all, although widely used, SLIP is merely a means of transporting IP Datagrams over these serial links.

22.1.1 SLIP Encapsulation

SLIP defines just two special characters to accomplish the task of encapsulation namely END and ESC (Escape). The END character is designated by the value $C0_{16}$ (192_{10}), and the ESC character by DB_{16} (219_{10}). IP datagrams are then transmitted directly over the serial link and the END character is appended immediately at the end of the packet as Figure 22-2 shows.

Some implementations differ slightly in that the END character is used as both a start and end delimiter. This means that immediately prior to transmitting the packet, we send an END. Spurious characters that have been received as a result of line noise are therefore rejected by the receiver without the need to reject the following packet.

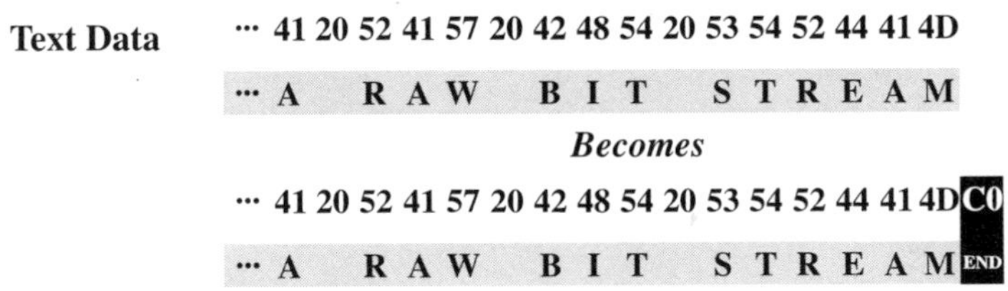

Text Data
··· 41 20 52 41 57 20 42 48 54 20 53 54 52 44 41 4D
··· A R A W B I T S T R E A M
Becomes
··· 41 20 52 41 57 20 42 48 54 20 53 54 52 44 41 4D C0
··· A R A W B I T S T R E A M END

Figure 22-2: SLIP Encapsulation

For example, where we have no spurious characters, the receiver merely receives two END characters back-to-back indicating a zero length IP packet. Either SLIP, or IP will now reject this. Where line noise has caused corruption between packets though, the receiver sees the spurious characters followed (maybe sometime later) by an END. These will then be rejected since they do not form a valid IP packet. The *uncorrupted* IP packet immediately following the END (assuming that it arrives without error), however will be accepted properly. Thus, on slow serial links (14.4kbps say), we will not need to retransmit a packet that would otherwise have been considered corrupt, and therefore discarded.

Obviously, if we are to introduce special control characters such as delimiters, we must take care to ensure that where these characters naturally occur within the data stream, there is no confusion. To achieve this, anywhere in the raw bit stream that we find an octet with value $C0_{16}$ (END), we replace it with the two octet string ESC END ($DBDC_{16}$). Similarly, to avoid confusion with the ESC character, anywhere that the octet DB_{16} (ESC) naturally occurs, we replace this with the string $DBDD_{16}$. The figure below shows how this translation of the bit stream takes place.

Raw Data
··· FC 05 A0 55 C0 23 69 77 21 38 DB 61 44 20 40 73 5C
··· U END # j w ! 8 a E @ c \
Becomes
··· FC 05 A0 55 DBDC 23 69 77 21 38 DBDD 61 44 20 40 73 5C C0
··· U ESC # j w ! 8 ESC a E @ c \ END

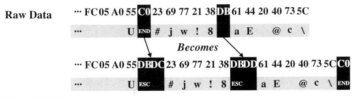

Figure 22-3: SLIP Bit Stream Translation

22.1.2 SLIP Packet Size

There is no defined maximum packet size for SLIP. In general though, most implementations adhere to the Berkeley UNIX SLIP driver architecture that uses a maximum packet size of 1006 octets. This number does not include the framing characters (END delimiters) but, since SLIP transmits IP datagrams directly, it does include the IP and TCP/UDP headers.

22.2 Compression

One of the problems associated with communications over slow serial links, is that we need to be able to squeeze as much usable bandwidth from them as possible.

For instance, if we consider the case of Internet access from remote locations over dial up lines, we will probably be using at best 14.4 or 28.8kbps modems. This would be the case for a home or mobile user. If we now consider that the user may wish to download large files (or graphics as in the case of World Wide Web access), the need to conserve bandwidth is apparent.

22.2.1 Van Jacobson Compression

To overcome some of the bandwidth that is consumed by bulk transfers, Van Jacobson suggested (in RFC 1144) a compression technique that is widely used today. Known simply as Van Jacobson or VJ Compression, or when associated with SLIP – CSLIP, the compression method is attractive through its simplicity.

While some of the actual mathematics behind Van Jacobson's arguments are extremely complex and beyond the scope of this book, Van Jacobson argues that it is possible to make significant savings in bandwidth by simply compressing the headers associated with common Internet protocols. In actual fact VJ Compression only works with TCP/IP headers. The argument here is that in the case of UDP/IP the datagrams are either less frequent, or the amount of data carried outweighs the usefulness of compression at all. In particular, to see the effects of overhead in an IP environment, we should look at a common application such as Telnet. Ignoring the Link Layer header for a Telnet packet, in order to carry a single octet of data we actually transmit 41 octets!

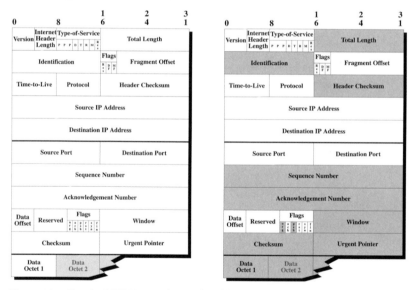

Figure 22-4: Standard IP/TCP Headers and Fields that Change

Figure 22-4 shows us that for any application using TCP and IP, we have 20 octets for the IP Header, and 20 octets for the TCP header[1] – all to carry one octet

---

1. The IP Header is fully described in Chapter 5, and the TCP Header is fully described in Chapter 7.

Communications Over Wide Area Links

of data. If we now consider the fields in these headers that actually change during the life of a connection (shown shaded on the right of the figure), we can appreciate that substantial savings can be made.

In fact, we can see that if we do not transmit those pieces of information that are constant throughout the life of the connection, we need only transmit 20 header octets and two flags. To achieve this near 2:1 header compression, all that we need do is to maintain a table of connections[2] at the sender and receiver, and ensure that the receiver keeps a copy of the header from the last packet it saw.

In practical terms we can actually make even better savings if we now consider those fields that we have just identified as changing. For example, the Total length field is redundant if we can assume that the Link Layer protocol will provide the length of the received packet. In a similar vein, the IP Header Checksum field is protecting only the IP Header. It is not logical though to transmit a checksum when we are not transmitting the header that it protects – so, the Header Checksum can be removed and reinstated when the Datagram is regenerated at the receiver. 16 octets of headers now remain, and again many of these can actually be removed.

If we consider how the fields change during a connection, we will see that in the sender to receiver direction, the *Identification*, *Sequence Number*, and *Check sum* fields will change. In the receiver to sender direction, the *Identification*, *Acknowledgement*, and *Checksum* fields change. So if the sender keeps a copy of the last packet sent, it can deduce which fields have changed and by how much. Now it merely needs to send a mask indicating the changed fields, and the amount by which they have changed. Figure 22-5 shows the header of a compressed TCP/IP Datagram.

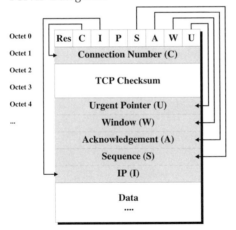

Figure 22-5: Compressed TCP/IP Header

As can be seen, the TCP Checksum is transmitted unchanged thereby ensuring that the end-to-end integrity of the connection is maintained. In addition, the first octet of the compressed TCP/IP header contains a bit mask that identifies which header fields have changed. Where the bit is set on, the corresponding field is included to indicate the amount by which the field has changed from the previous packet. If the bit is off, the field is not even present.

Changes are rarely negative, thus a positive change of between 1 and 255 can be represented by a single octet. Changes of zero are rare and would never be sent anyway. Therefore, where we do set a *changed* field to zero, we are representing a change greater than 255. In this case, the octet of zero represents that an extension follows and the next two octets are the high and low order octets of the changed value respectively. In the event that the actual change in a field is greater than could be represented by 16 bits (greater than 64k), the packet is sent uncompressed.

2. Entries in this *Connection Table* are referred to as *Slots*. We shall see later that the actual *Slot* (Connection) number does not actually need to be transmitted where the connection has not changed.

The first octet is key to the way in which the header now functions, so it is worth briefly describing each of the bits. The *C* bit is used to indicate that the *Connection Number* field is used. As we have already said, each end of the connection must maintain a table of connections for this compression scheme to work. We do not however need not transmit the connection number for each packet. This is of particular relevance if we consider a user communicating with a Telnet host through say a Terminal or Access Server. In this case, the user will probably not switch between sessions and therefore the connection number will remain static. One important point to note is that the Connection Number field is 1 octet long. This means that we can have up to 256 connections at any time – certainly more than would be required for normal operation.

The *I* bit indicates that the IP Identification field is included, and contains the change in the identification field from the last packet. Unlike other fields though, where the *I* bit is not set, we assume that the change is 1 not zero. In this way, for normal Datagram sequencing we do not have to include the Identification field at all.

The *P* bit indicates that the Push bit was set on in the original TCP Segment. No fields within the TCP header are associated with this field though, so there are no corresponding fields in the compressed header. The *S* and *A* bits indicate that changes have occurred in the TCP *Sequence* and *Acknowledgement* fields respectively and the changes to these fields are represented (in 2's compliment arithmetic) in the compressed header. The W bit indicates that there has been a change to the Window field. Changes to the Window can be positive or negative and as such this field is 16 bits long. Finally, the U bit indicates a change to the Urgent Pointer field. This field can contain zero since it is possible that the Urgent data is the first octet within the data. You will recall from our discussion in Chapter 7 the way in which Urgent Data is handled is implementation specific.

A single octet of compressed data from a Telnet session may then look like 0Cccccdd. Where $0C_{16}$ is the Mask representing a change to the Sequence Number and Acknowledgement fields (a change of 1 to the IP Identification field is not conveyed), *cccc* is the TCP Checksum, and *dd* is the single octet of data. Thus we have managed to compress 41 octets into just 4!

22.3 The Point-to-Point Protocol (PPP)

The major motivation behind the development of PPP was the desire to be able to transport datagrams of diferent protocols over Point-to-Point links. Unlike SLIP, PPP provides mechanisms to identify the protocol carried in any packet, to test the link itself, and to negotiate a variety of options. PPP then is composed of three parts as described by RFC 1661:

- A method of encapsulating Multi-Protocol datagrams. PPP can handle different protocols since it has a protocol identifier field. Thus, IP, IPX, DECnet, AppleTalk and many others can be carried over a single link. Each separate packet however must contain only one protocol.

- A Link Control Protocol (LCP) capable of establishing, configuring, and testing the link.

- A whole family of Network Control Protocols (NCPs) that are used to configure the link for the various network layer protocols that will use it. This configuration includes addressing and other protocol specific issues. The table below lists a number of NCPs together with the associated RFCs in which they are defined and the protocol ID used. For example, PPP uses the Protocol ID 8021_{16} to indicate that the IP Control Protocol is being carried during link configuration.

Table 22-1: PPP Network Control Protocols (NCPs)

Protocol Description	PPP Protocol ID	Protocol	RFC
Internet Protocol Control Protocol	8021	IPCP	1332
OSI Network Layer Control Protocol	8023	OSINLCP	1377
AppleTalk Control Protocol	8029	ATCP	1378
Internetwork Packet Exchange Control Protocol	802B	IPXCP	1552
Bridge Control Protocol	8031	BCP	1638
DecNet Phase IV Control Protocol	8027	DNCP	1762
Banyan Vines (Vines IP) Control Protocol	8035	BVCP	1763
XNS Internet Datagram Control Protocol	8025	XNSCP	1764

The Link Control Protocol (LCP) is designed to make the protocol as versatile as possible by automatically negotiating and agreeing on things such as the encapsulation format, the size of packet in use, and the detection of looped back links. In addition, PPP supports other standard *facilities* such as authentication, and a means of ensuring that the link remains operational. Finally, PPP allows vendors to develop their own extensions to LCP enabling such things as proprietary Encryption or, non-standard Authentication and Compression techniques.

22.3.1 PPP Encapsulation

PPP uses a simple encapsulation technique that is designed to identify the protocol being carried through the use of a protocol identification field. Obviously it is not sufficient to merely transmit this as-is, and a framing technique applicable to the type of link in use is also required. The most common of these, *HDLC-Like framing*, is discussed at the end of this chapter.

Figure 22-6 shows the basic format of PPP. The *Protocol* field (normally 16 bits) is used to identify the actual protocol being carried. Certain rules exist for protocol type numbering. For instance, all protocols must be an odd number. Thus, the least significant bit of the least significant octet must be 1. In addition, the least significant bit of the most significant octet must be 0, always making that octet even. Table 22-2 shows some of the supported protocols together with their associated IDs.

Protocol (16 Bits)	Information (Variable Length)	Padding (Varaible Length)

Figure 22-6: PPP Basic Format

The actual values of the Protocol field can be summarized as follows: Values in the 0*** to 3*** range are used to identify the network layer protocol in use. These are shown in Table 22-2. When IP is carried for example, the Protocol ID is

0021_{16}. Protocols in the range of $8***$ to $B***$ identify the Network Control Protocol and are listed in Table 22-1. Protocols in the range $4***$ to $7***$ are used for protocols that have only low traffic volumes and therefore no associated NCP. Finally, if the Protocol field contains a value in the range $C***$ to $F***$, then a Link Control Protocol is being carried and again these are listed in Table 22-2.

Table 22-2: Supported Protocols and Associated IDs

Protocol ID	Description	Protocol ID	Description
0001	Padding Protocol	C021	Link Control Protocol
0021	Internet Protocol	C023	Password Authentication Protocol
0023	OSI Network Protocol	C025	Link Quality Report
0025	Xerox NS IDP	C223	Challenge Handshake Authentication
0027	DecNet Phase IV		Protocol
0029	AppleTalk		
002B	Novell IPX		
002D	Van Jacobson Compressed TCP/IP		
002F	Van Jacobson Uncompressed TCP/IP		
0031	Bridging PDU		
0033	Stream Protocol (ST-II)		
0035	Banyan Vines		
0201	802.1d Hello Packets		
0231	Luxcom		
0233	Sigma Network Systems		

The *Information* field carries the actual data of the PPP frame. There will be between zero, and the what is termed the *Maximum Receive Unit* (MRU), of octets (including Padding but excluding the Protocol field). By default, the MRU is 1500 bytes however by negotiation, the two ends of the connection may agree on some other value. The *Padding* field may contain any number of octets up to the MRU. Where padding is used, it is the responsibility of the Network protocol to distinguish between real data and padding so that the padding can be discarded.

22.3.2 PPP Link Operation

Unlike SLIP, before any data is passed over the link, each end will send configuration packets, and test the link to ensure that it is operational. After each end is sure that the link is operational, the Network Control Protocols (NCPs) are used to configure the link for operation. As we have said, PPP is capable of carrying multiple protocols, thus multiple NCPs may be used. Figure 22-7 shows a simplified diagram of the phases that the link goes through and these are then described in more detail below.

In the *Dead* state, PPP is inactive waiting for the Physical layer to signal that it is ready. This may be a signal from some external event, or activation of the Data Carrier Detect signal in the case of a serial link coming up. At this time, the LCP will be in a state known as *Initial* or *Starting* since there cannot be any activity across the link. Once the physical layer has signalled that the link is ready, PPP transitions to the *Establish* state. In this state, LCP is used to establish the connection, by the two ends exchanging and acknowledging Configure packets.

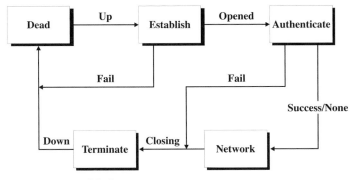

Figure 22-7: Simplified PPP State Diagram

If Authentication has been enabled, one of the ends of the connection will request the use of the authentication protocol during the *Establish* state. PPP supports two standard authentication protocols namely the *Password Authentication Protocol* (PAP) and the *Challenge Handshake Authentication Protocol* (CHAP). Other, proprietary protocols can be used, however both ends must agree on their usage.

Assuming that either no authentication was requested or that it was successful, PPP now transitions to the *Network* state. In this state each of the required Network Control Protocols (NCPs) will be used to configure the link for operation with that Network layer. NCPs can be used at any time that the link is open. This allows new Network protocols to be added to the link, and those that are no longer required to be removed. Once, the particular NCP has reached an Opened state, PPP is then able to carry the corresponding Network Layer protocol. If a particular NCP fails or the protocol was not opened in the first place, any packets for that protocol that are received will be returned to the sender in *Reject* packets.

The Link *Terminate* state is used to close the link through the exchange of Terminate packets and acknowledgements. Termination can occur at any time due to either a link failure or through some other event. In the case of Link failure, obviously no terminate acknowledgements will be received thus, termination normally occurs after some timeout value. In the case of a normal termination however, PPP ensures a graceful closure.

Once successfully terminated, the link then returns to the *Dead* state awaiting further requests to open the link or signals to indicate that the Physical Layer has been re-established.

22.3.3   Link Control Protocol (LCP) Packets General Format

LCP has three classes of packet each designed for a specific purpose:

- Link Configuration Packets, used to establish and configure the link.

- Link Termination Packets used to terminate the link.

- Link Maintenance Packets used to manage the link.

The general format of the LCP packet is shown in Figure 22-8.

Figure 22-8: LCP General Packet Format

Table 22-3: LCP Code Values

Code	Description
1	Configure Request
2	Configure Positive Acknowledgement (Ack)
3	Configure Negative Acknowledgement (Nak)
4	Configure Reject (Reject)
5	Terminate Request
6	Terminate Acknowledgement
7	Code Reject
8	Protocol Reject
9	Echo Request
10	Echo Reply
11	Discard Request
12	Identification
13	Time Remaining

The 8 bit *Code* field identifies the type of packet and will contain a value from Table 22-3. The 8 bit *Identifier* field is used to match requests with responses, and the 16 bit *Length* field is used to indicate the overall length of the LCP packet. This length includes the Code, Identifier, Length and Data fields and of course must not exceed the MRU of the link. The variable length *Data* field contains the data that the LCP packet is conveying. The actual data itself however is dependent upon the type of LCP packet and therefore the Code specified.

22.3.4 LCP Configure Request

A Configuration Request is always sent by a station when it wishes to change any of the link defaults or any parameter that the link is currently using. With this request, the *Code* field of the LCP Packet is set to 1, and the *Data* field contains a list of options, each formatted as detailed in Figure 22-9. Full descriptions of each of these options are also included.

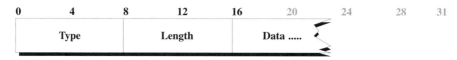

Figure 22-9: LCP Configuration Options – General Format

The *Type* field for the Request will contain one of the values in Table 22-4. The *Length* field identifies the overall length of the option including the Type, Length, and Data fields, and the Data field contains information specific to the configuration option being negotiated. All options specified are then negotiated and appropriate response(s) are sent back.

Communications Over Wide Area Links

Table 22-4: LCP Configure Request Type Values

Type	Description
0	Reserved
1	Maximum Receive Unit
3	Authentication Protocol
4	Quality Protocol
5	Magic Number
7	Protocol Field Compression
8	Address-and-Control-Field-Compression
9	FCS Alternatives
10	Self Describing Padding
13	Call Back
15	Compound Frames
17	Multi-Link MRRU
18	Multi-Link Short Sequence Number Header
19	Multi-Link Endpoint Discriminator

- **Maximum Receive Unit**

  This option is used to inform the remote peer that we require a change in the Maximum Receive Unit MRU. This indicates that we either wish a smaller packet size, or that we are capable of receiving a larger packet. The option is 4 octets long, uses a Type field with a value of 1, a 16 bit *MRU* size field, and no additional data.

  The option is, in a sense, for information purposes only. All implementations have to be capable of supporting a MRU of at least 1500 octets. Thus, where a peer requests a smaller MRU, the remote end can effectively ignore it. True, the peer must respond and, the requesting station may then send packets smaller than 1500 octets, but this is allowed. Similarly, in the event that the requesting station indicates that it can accept larger packet sizes, although the peer must respond, it need not make use of this facility. The peer can then continue to use a packet size of 1500 octets that the receiver must accommodate.

- **Authentication Protocol**

  Where it is desirable to have only trusted devices communicating, PPP allows the use of an authentication protocol. Two standardized options (PAP and CHAP) exist and either or both can be requested. The Configuration Request for this option uses a 16 bit Authentication Protocol field that is immediately followed by any additional data required such as the *hashing* or *encryption* algorithm used.

  By default, no authentication is required. Where it is desired, the requesting peer sends a LCP Configuration Request, requesting that specific protocol. Multiple protocols are not allowed in a single request. Thus where we were to allow both protocols, the first is requested and if it is negatively acknowledged, then the second is requested. Any device that requests authentication expects a positive acknowledgement (Configure Ack) from its peer. There is however, no requirement that both ends of the connection use the same protocol. For example, one end might use CHAP while the other uses PAP – this is perfectly legal provided that both peers agree on the authentication protocol(s) in use. The Authentication protocols themselves (PAP, and CHAP) as detailed in RFC 1334, are discussed in Section 22.4.

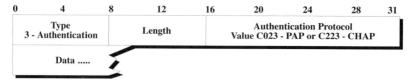

Figure 22-10: LCP Authentication Protocol Configuration

- **Quality Protocol**

  As with authentication, Link Quality Monitoring (LQM) is disabled by default. On some links however, particularly those with high error rates, it may be desirable to enable this facility in order to determine how often the link is dropped.

  The LCP Link Quality Protocol configuration packet (shown below) uses 16 bits to define the Quality protocol in use. The *Link Quality Report* protocol, standardized as part of PPP and detailed in RFC 1333 uses the code $C025_{16}$. The *Data* field then carries any additional information required by the protocol such as the reporting period. This is further described in Section 22.5.

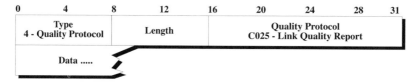

Figure 22-11: LCP Quality Protocol Configuration

- **Magic Number**

  A Magic Number is a unique identifier for the particular peer. Each peer will choose its own 32 bit number and then use the LCP to ensure that it is unique. Typically, the number can be based upon the Serial number or MAC address of the device however any value is acceptable provided that uniqueness can be assured.

  The Magic Number itself is used to detect looped back links and other anomalies. When a Configure Request is received with a Magic Number Configuration Option, the received Magic Number is compared with the Magic Number of the last Configure Request sent to the peer. Where these numbers are different, the link is not looped back and the request is positively acknowledged. If the two Magic Numbers are the same, it is possible that the link is looped so a Negative Acknowledgement is sent specifying a different Magic Number value. If we now receive a Negative Acknowledgement, then the link is not looped.

Figure 22-12: LCP Magic Number Negotiation

Once the Magic Number has been successfully negotiated, we can then check for a looped link during normal operation. For example, LCP Echo Request/Reply packets contain a Magic Number field that should be used. Thus through normal Echo packets, we can both ensure that the remote peer is alive, and detect looped links via the unique Magic Number.

- **Protocol Field Compression and Address-and-Control-Field Compression**
  Over slow links it is desirable to transmit data with as little overhead as possible. Thus, if there are any economies that can be made with PPP packets they should be exploited to the full. LCP allows us to negotiate compression of the PPP Protocol field (Protocol Field Compression – PFC), and compression of the Data Link Layer Address and Control Fields[3] (Address-and-Control-Field Compression – ACFC). In both cases, ACFC and PFC, compression takes place for normal data packets only and LCP packets are always be sent in an uncompressed form.
  The format for both LCP options is similar. The LCP Configure Request packet contains just an 8 bit *Type* field (value 7 for PFC, and 8 for ACFC), and an 8 bit Length field that should be set to 2. No *Data* field is ever present for either of these options.

- **FCS Alternatives**
  In January of 1994, PPP was enhanced by RFC 1570 which defined four extensions to the LCP configuration options. The provision of allowing different Frame Check Sequences (FCS) is one of these.
  FCS negotiation always takes place during the Establishment phase and the negotiated FCS can be used only during the Authentication and Network phases. At any other time, the default FCS must be used. Figure 22-13 shows the basic format of this LCP option.

Figure 22-13: LCP FCS Alternatives Negotiation

For this option the *Type* field is always 9, and the *Length* is always 3. The *Options* field is then used to define the type of FCS that is being negotiated. Options field values are the logical OR of the following:

---

3. See Section 22.8 for a complete discussion of the PPP Link Layer.

- 1 – Null FCS

For this, any FCS sent is considered to be padding and is removed.

- 2 – CCITT 16 bit FCS

This is the default FCS for most HDLC framed links.

- 4 – CCITT 32 bit FCS

This represents an optional FCS method using 32 bit check sequences.

- **Self Describing Padding**

  Some Network Layer and Compression protocols need to be able to detect and remove trailing padding. RFC 1570 introduced this option allowing peers to announce that they understand the principle of adding pad characters to the end of PPP Information fields and therefore that they can also remove them.

  With Self Describing Padding, the first padding octet must contain the value 1 indicating the Padding Protocol to the Compound Frames option (discussed below). Similarly, the last octet (excluding the FCS) must contain the number of octets to be removed. Equally, implementations must be aware of the Maximum Pad Value (MPV) defining the maximum value that a pad octet can have. Where we have a situation where no padding would normally be used but the last octet has a value of between 1 and the MPV, we must then append at least one octet of Self Describing Padding to the frame before the FCS.

  The Self Describing Padding option is used to negotiate the maximum number of padding octets that can be added to a frame (typically 2, 4, or 8) and is shown in Figure 22-14:

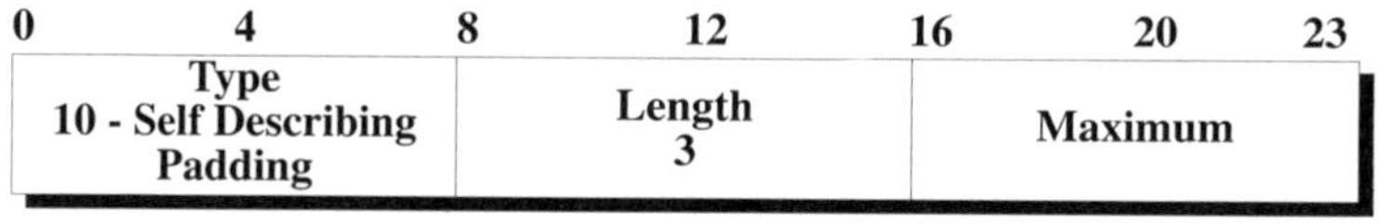

0	4	8	12	16	20	23
Type 10 - Self Describing Padding		Length 3		Maximum		

Figure 22-14: LCP Self Describing Padding (Maximum Pad Value) Negotiation

As with other options, this is of a fixed length with a value of 10 for the Type field, and 3 for the Length. The Maximum field then defines the maximum number of padding octets that can be added to a frame.

- **Call Back**

  RFC 1570 also defines a method that allows dial-up peers to request that they be called back. This option is particularly useful where we wish to incorporate either additional security, or where we desire centralized billing. Typically this option would be used in conjunction with an authentication protocol to gain user information, from which we could derive the user's location. The format of the Call Back option is shown in Figure 22-15:

Figure 22-15: LCP Call Back Negotiation

Communications Over Wide Area Links

In this option, the *Type* field is 13, and the *Length* field is always 3 or more. The Operation field is used to indicate the contents of the Message field with the following values:

- 0 – The location is determined through user authentication.

- 1 – *Dial string* to be used. It would be foolish to use this option if we were not certain of the identity of the user requesting the call back, thus authentication should be used. In addition, the receiving peer must have knowledge of the device that will actually be used to make the call.

- 2 – *Location Identifier*. This information (used in conjunction with the authentication information) can be used to interrogate a database to determine the call back location.

- 3 – A standardized (*E.164*) number that defines the call back location.

- 4 – A *Distinguished name* used to define the call back location.

The Message field is a variable length field whose meaning is determined by the Operation field. As an additional measure of security, the Message field itself is site or implementation specific. Thus, since only authorized callers should be in possession of this information, a measure of security is inherent in the system.

- **Compound Frames**
  To make better use of the bandwidth available, RFC 1570 introduced the concept of allowing multiple PPP encapsulated packets within the same frame. Where this is used, the sender adds additional packets to the frame by immediately following one packet with the Protocol field and associated Datagram of the next.

  Where padding has been added to a packet, it must follow the rules of Self Describing Padding outlined earlier. Thus, this option must always be negotiated with the Self Describing Padding option. The format of this option is simple. Two octets are used with the first, the *Type* field, having a value of 15, and the second, the *Length*, having a value of 2.

- **Multi-Link Maximum Receive Reconstructed Unit (MRRU)**
  PPP supports the simultaneous operation of multiple physical links to pass data between peers (known as PPP Multi-Link). When this option is successfully negotiated, it indicates that we are prepared to process incoming PPP packets from a peer along with any packets received from the same peer, but on a different physical link. In other words, the two (or more) links will be treated as a single *pipe* over which data flows. It also indicates the maximum *overall* payload that we can accept (1500 octets by default). Multi-Link operation is discussed in Section 22.6.

0	4	8	12	16	20	24	28	31
Type 17 - MRRU		Length 4		Maximum Receive Reconstructed Unit				

Figure 22-16: MRRU LCP Configuration Option

- **Multi-Link Short Sequence Number Header Format**
  As with the MRRU option, the Short Sequence Number option can be used to inform the peer that Multi-Link operation is supported. Where Multi-Link is in use, PPP packets are fragmented at the transmitter and reassembled at the receiver, thus a sequence number is required.
  The sequence number itself can be 24 bits long (the default) or, through this configuration option, 12 bits.[4] In use, the option contains only an 8 bit *Type* field of 18, and an 8 bit *Length* field of 2.

- **Multi-Link Endpoint Discriminator Option**
  This option is used to identify the end system that is transmitting the packet and therefore that this peer could be the same as the peer on another (existing) link. If the option distinguishes the peer from any other, then a new *bundle* of links is assumed and created. If the option identifies the peer as an existing peer, then the link will be joined to an existing *bundle*. Identification is achieved through a Class, and Address as shown in Figure 22-17.

0 4	8 12	16 20	24 28 31
Type 19 - Endpoint Discriminator	**Length Variable**	**Class**	**Address**

Figure 22-17: Multi-Link Endpoint Discriminator Option

The *Class* field is used to define the Class (type) of *Address* in use and therefore the Address length. Valid values are as follows:

0 Null Class indicating that the Address is 0 octets long.

1 Locally Assigned Address. This allows local addressing (such as a serial number) to be used. In this case the Address is up to 20 octets in length.

2 Internet Protocol. Here the Address field contains an IP Address and is therefore 4 octets in length.

3 IEEE 802.1 (Globally Assigned) MAC Address. In this instance, the Address field contains an 802.1 address in 802.3 (canonical) form with the Local/Global, and Multicast bits clear. Here, the Address field is 6 octets long.

4 PPP Magic Number. Now considered *deprecated*, this Class allows a block of up to 5, 32 bit Magic Numbers to be used. The maximum length of the Address field is therefore 20 octets.

5 Public Switched Network Directory Number. Here the Address field contains up to 15 octets that define the I.331 international telephone directory number used to access the peer over a public switched telephone network.

22.3.5 LCP Configure Acknowledgement and Rejection

The formats for the Configure Ack, Nak, and Reject are all the same and shown in Figure 22-18. A Configure Ack is sent to a peer if all options in a Configure Request

4. See Section 22.6.1 for the PPP fragment header.

are both recognizable and acceptable. In this case, the *Code* field contains the value 2, and the *Options* field contains the list of options that are being acknowledged, in the order that they were presented in the Configure Request packet. The *Identifier* field contains the same value as that in the Configure Request, and the *Length* field indicates the overall length of the packet.

A Configure Nak is sent when all options in the Configure Request are recognizable, but one or more option is unacceptable. The Configure Nak packet uses a *Code* field of 3, and the value of the *Identifier* field is again the same as that used in the original Configure Request. The *Options* field then contains a list of those options that are unacceptable, in the same order as they were presented. For those options with no value fields, the Configure Reject is used rather than the Nak if the option is unacceptable.

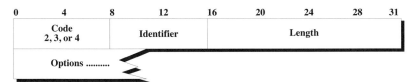

Figure 22-18: LCP Configure Ack, NAK, and Reject

The Configure Reject packet is sent both in the case where the unacceptable option has no value associated (as outlined above), and where received options are not recognizable. As before, the *Identifier* field will contain the identifier of the Configure Request packet, and the *Options* field will contain only those options that are not recognizable. The *Code* field in this instance always has a value of 4.

22.3.6 LCP Terminate Request and Terminate Ack

The LCP Terminate Request allows a peer to request that the link be closed gracefully. There can be no negotiation over termination, and a peer receiving a Terminate Request packet must send a Terminate Ack in response. Peers not receiving an acknowledgement to their first termination request will then continue to transmit requests until an acknowledgement is received or until some timeout value has elapsed. The general format for the Terminate Request/Ack packets is shown in Figure 22-19:

Figure 22-19: LCP Terminate Request/Ack

For the Terminate Request, the *Code* field will contain the value 5, and for the Ack, 6. The *Identifier* field in the Ack then contains the same value used in the Terminate Request packet sent by the peer.

22.3.7 LCP Code Reject

Unlike many other protocols, PPP does not use a *Version number* field to differentiate between versions of the protocol and therefore the format of the packet. This is deliberate in an attempt to reduce overhead, particularly on slow serial links. A problem however, now exists. What happens if a packet is received and we have no knowledge of the *Code* field in use?

In this case, the LCP Code Reject packet is used as shown in Figure 22-20. The *Code* field contains the value 7, and the *Identifier* field a unique value defined by the peer sending the Reject packet. The *Rejected Packet* field then contains a copy of the packet that is being rejected, possibly truncated to comply with the MRU of the peer.

Figure 22-20: LCP Code Reject

22.3.8 LCP Protocol Reject

If a peer receives a PPP packet with an unknown protocol, it will be rejected with a LCP Protocol Reject packet. The packet, shown in Figure 22-21, contains the Protocol ID that was found in the *PPP Protocol* field of the rejected packet, and a copy of the rejected packet in the *Rejected Information* field. As before, this field may need to be truncated in order to comply with the MRU of the peer. The Code field for this packet is always 8.

Figure 22-21: LCP Protocol Reject

22.3.9 LCP Echo Request/Reply

The LCP Echo Request/Reply is similar in operation to the ICMP Echo Request/Reply. These packets are used to test for loopback conditions, in the determination Link Quality, and to generally exercise the link in a bi-directional fashion. As with ICMP Echoes, if a peer receives a LCP Echo Request, it must respond with an Echo Reply. *Code* 9 is used for Requests and 10 for Replies and the *Identifier* field must be identical for both so that Requests and Replies can be matched.

The *Magic Number* is used in the detection of loopback conditions as previously discussed. If Magic Number negotiation has not taken place however, this field sent as zero. Finally, the *Data* field contains data for use by the sender, but it is not interpreted by the receiving peer.

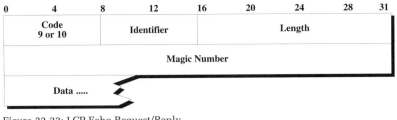

Figure 22-22: LCP Echo Request/Reply

22.3.10 LCP Discard Request

The LCP Discard Request again allows the peer to exercise the link. Like the Discard protocol described in Chapter 21, LCP Discard packets received are always discarded immediately. The Code field for this packet type is 11, and the Magic Number is again used to detect loopback conditions when they occur.

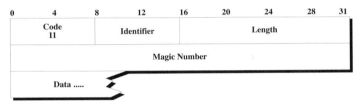

Figure 22-23: LCP Discard Request

22.3.11 LCP Identification

LCP Identification is an extension to the original specification for PPP and is again defined in RFC 1570. The LCP Identification packet can be used for many purposes including licence enforcement and general link problem identification. Since this can be used to learn the identification of a peer, it makes sense to allow it to be used at any time. As such, Identification packets can be sent even before the LCP has reached the Open state. Figure 22-24 (which is similar to 22-22) shows the format of the Identification packet.

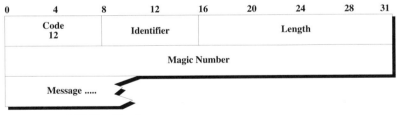

Figure 22-24: LCP Identification

The *Code* field is always 12 for this type of packet, and the *Identifier* field is a unique number that identifies this particular Identification packet. The *Magic Number* field is either set to the negotiated value for the Magic Number (as previously described), or is set to zero where Magic Number negotiation has not been completed. The *Message* field then contains the implementation specific identification message that is to be conveyed, the length of which can be determined from the *Length* field.

There is no required response to the Identification packet which in essence can be considered as informational. Instead, each end of the link can send Identifications as required to inform the peer who is at the remote end of the link.

22.3.12 LCP Time Remaining

This LCP packet is used to indicate to the peer how much time remains in this session. As with the Identification packet, the Time Remaining packet is an extension and is defined in RFC 1570. A Time Remaining of zero is not, in itself, sufficient to cause to the link to be terminated. The session can still only be terminated gracefully by the Terminate Request packet. Instead, this packet is advisory making the interpretation of it implementation specific to a great extent.

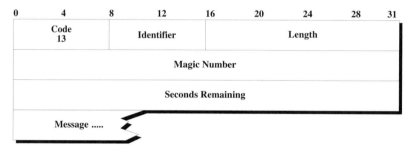

Figure 22-25: LCP Time Remaining

The Time Remaining packet is typically sent after the link has entered the Network phase, and then at regular intervals throughout the life of the session. No assumptions are made as to the actual regularity of these packets, however as the time remaining expires it would make sense to increase the frequency at which they are transmitted. Although this is implementation specific. The format of the Time Remaining LCP packet is standarized and is shown in Figure 22-25.

The *Code* field is always 13 for this type of packet, and the *Identifier* is again a unique 8 bit number. The *Magic Number* field contains the negotiated Magic Number (or zero where Magic Number negotiation has not completed). The 32 bit *Seconds Remaining* field indicates the (integral) number of seconds that remain for this session. Where this value is all ones, an infinite time remains.

The *Message* field contains a variable number of octets that are implementation specific. Where this field is used, its length is determined by interrogating the *Length* field (which by its definition must therefore be greater than 12).

22.3.13 Sample PPP Configuration Examples

In order to better understand the mechanics of LCP configuration, two sample traces follow. In the first (Figure 22-26), we see simple Magic Number negotiation

Communications Over Wide Area Links

taking place between two router peers and comprises 5 frames. The second trace (Figure 22-27) shows two exchanges. The first of these demonstrates the exchange of LCP Identification messages (2 frames), and the second a simple LCP Echo Request/Reply message exchange (also 2 frames).

```
µSCOPE              PACKET TRACE DECODE REPORT          (c) T.Kenyon 1995

=============================µscope=============================
Frame   : 1              Len   : 32        Error   : None
T Elapsed: 18:46:32:852  T Delta  : 00:00:32:001
                        ----------[WAN]----------
Dst Addr : DTE          Src Addr : DCE
                        ----------[ppp encap]----------
Address  : FF           Control  : 03
                        ----------[PPP]----------
Type    : LCP           Protocol : CTRL
Code    : CFG Req
Id      : 0x7e          Length   : 28 Bytes
                        ----------[Config]----------
Type    : 5-Magic-Number              Length   : 6 Bytes
Value   : 3c201c25
=============================[data:    0]=============================
```
The notion of *DTE* and *DCE* is introduced soley by the relative position of the WAN analysis equipment. Here, the DTE is the **local** router while the DCE is the **remote** router.

A LCP Magic Number Configuration Request is received from the WAN specifying a Magic Number of $3C201C25_{16}$.

```
=============================µscope=============================
Frame   : 2              Len   : 32        Error   : None
T Elapsed: 18:46:35:554  T Delta  : 00:00:02:702
                        ----------[WAN]----------
Dst Addr : DCE          Src Addr : DTE
                        ----------[ppp encap]----------
Address  : FF           Control  : 03
                        ----------[PPP]----------
Type    : LCP           Protocol : CTRL
Code    : CFG Req
Id      : 0x6c          Length   : 28 Bytes
                        ----------[Config]----------
Type    : 5-Magic-Number              Length   : 6 Bytes
Value   : b2a25a70
=============================[data:    0]=============================
```
The DTE (local router) requests that it uses a Magic Number of $B2A25A70_{16}$.

```
=============================µscope=============================
Frame   : 3              Len   : 32        Error   : None
T Elapsed: 18:46:35:561  T Delta  : 00:00:00:007
                        ----------[WAN]----------
Dst Addr : DTE          Src Addr : DCE
                        ----------[ppp encap]----------
Address  : FF           Control  : 03
                        ----------[PPP]----------
Type    : LCP           Protocol : CTRL
Code    : CFG Ack
Id      : 0x6c          Length   : 28 Bytes
                        ----------[Config]----------
Type    : 5-Magic-Number              Length   : 6 Bytes
Value   : b2a25a70
=============================[data:    0]=============================
```
The remote router positively acknowledges the Magic Number proposed by the local router.

```
=============================µscope=============================
Frame   : 4              Len   : 32        Error   : None
T Elapsed: 18:46:35:852  T Delta  : 00:00:00:291
                        ----------[WAN]----------
Dst Addr : DTE          Src Addr : DCE
                        ----------[ppp encap]----------
Address  : FF           Control  : 03
                        ----------[PPP]----------
Type    : LCP           Protocol : CTRL
Code    : CFG Req
Id      : 0x7f          Length   : 28 Bytes
                        ----------[Config]----------
Type    : 5-Magic-Number              Length   : 6 Bytes
Value   : 0aa27714
=============================[data:    0]=============================
```
Since the remote router is still awaiting an acknowledgement of its own Magic Number configuration request, it re-sends it, this time selecting another Number ($0AA27714_{16}$).

```
=============================µscope=============================
Frame   : 5              Len   : 32        Error   : None
T Elapsed: 18:46:35:859  T Delta  : 00:00:00:007
                        ----------[WAN]----------
Dst Addr : DCE          Src Addr : DTE
                        ----------[ppp encap]----------
Address  : FF           Control  : 03
                        ----------[PPP]----------
Type    : LCP           Protocol : CTRL
Code    : CFG Ack
Id      : 0x7f          Length   : 28 Bytes
                        ----------[Config]----------
Type    : 5-Magic-Number              Length   : 6 Bytes
Value   : 0aa27714
=============================[data:    0]=============================
```
The new number is acceptable to our local router, so it now positively acknowledges it.

Figure 22-26: Sample LCP Magic Number Negotiation

```
==============================μscope==============================
Frame   : 10                Len    : 40         Error    : None
T Elapsed: 18:46:35:883     T Delta : 00:00:00:004
------------------------------[WAN]-------------------------------
Dst Addr : DCE              Src Addr : DTE
------------------------------[ppp encap]-------------------------
Address  : FF               Control  : 03
------------------------------[PPP]-------------------------------
Type    : LCP              Protocol : CTRL
Code    : LCP Identification
Id      : 0x2e              Length   : 36 Bytes
==============================[data:  38]=========================
0002  C0 21 0C 2E 00 24 94 AA 16 62 58 59 50 4C 45 58   .!...$...bXYPLEX
0012  20 30 35 30 44 43 36 20 56 35 2E 30 2E 34 20 42    050DC6 V5.0.4 B
0022  52 2F 34 36 30 00                                 R/460.
```

The local router sends a LCP Identification packet. Such packets do not require acknowledgements thus, the remote router does not send one.

The Identification Message field is implementation specific.

```
==============================μscope==============================
Frame   : 11                Len    : 40         Error    : None
T Elapsed: 18:46:35:884     T Delta : 00:00:00:001
------------------------------[WAN]-------------------------------
Dst Addr : DTE              Src Addr : DCE
------------------------------[ppp encap]-------------------------
Address  : FF               Control  : 03
------------------------------[PPP]-------------------------------
Type    : LCP              Protocol : CTRL
Code    : LCP Identification
Id      : 0x31              Length   : 36 Bytes
==============================[data:  38]=========================
0002  C0 21 0C 31 00 24 0A A2 77 14 58 59 50 4C 45 58   .!.1.$..w.XYPLEX
0012  20 30 32 33 45 36 36 20 56 35 2E 30 2E 34 20 42    023E66 V5.0.4 B
0022  52 2F 34 36 30 00                                 R/460.
```

The remote router sends a LCP Identification packet.

The Magic Number is included in LCP Identification packets.

```
==============================μscope==============================
Frame   : 18                Len    : 12         Error    : None
T Elapsed: 18:46:37:727     T Delta : 00:00:01:843
------------------------------[WAN]-------------------------------
Dst Addr : DCE              Src Addr : DTE
------------------------------[ppp encap]-------------------------
Address  : FF               Control  : 03
------------------------------[PPP]-------------------------------
Type    : LCP              Protocol : CTRL
Code    : ECHO Request
Id      : 0xae              Length   : 8 Bytes
------------------------------[Echo]------------------------------
Magic No : 0x94aa1662
==============================[data:  10]=========================
0002  C0 21 09 AE 00 08 94 AA 16 62                     .!.......b
```

The local router sends a LCP Echo Request.

```
==============================μscope==============================
Frame   : 19                Len    : 12         Error    : None
T Elapsed: 18:46:37:730     T Delta : 00:00:00:003
------------------------------[WAN]-------------------------------
Dst Addr : DTE              Src Addr : DCE
------------------------------[ppp encap]-------------------------
Address  : FF               Control  : 03
------------------------------[PPP]-------------------------------
Type    : LCP              Protocol : CTRL
Code    : ECHO Reply
Id      : 0xae              Length   : 8 Bytes
------------------------------[Echo]------------------------------
Magic No : 0x0aa27714
==============================[data:  10]=========================
0002  C0 21 0A AE 00 08 0A A2 77 14                     .!.......w.
```

The remote router responds with a LCP Echo Reply.

The Magic Number is sent as part of either an Echo Request or Echo Reply.

Figure 22-27: Sample LCP Identification and Echo Request/Reply Exchanges

22.4 PPP Authentication Protocols

RFC 1334 defines two authentication protocols for use in a PPP environment, namely the Password Authentication Protocol (PAP), and the Challenge Handshake Authentication Protocol (CHAP). However, while these protocols are the most common in a PPP environment, due to the nature of PPP, other proprietary protocols (beyond the scope of this book) could also be used.

22.4.1 The Password Authentication Protocol (PAP)

The Password Authentication Protocol is a simple method by which a peer can learn the identity of its partner. The actual process takes place only after the initial Link Establishment phase has been completed, and takes the form of a two-way handshake. Essentially, after completion of the Link Establishment phase, the peer continually sends an Identification/Password pair until they are either acknowledged or the link is terminated.

As we saw in section 22.3.4, authentication is requested through a LCP option. For PAP the *Type* field contains a value of 3, the *Length* field 4, and the 16 bit *Authentication Protocol* field the value $C023_{16}$. The *Data* field is then unused. The PAP then travels in a PPP packet with a *Protocol* field value of $C023_{16}$. The general format of a PAP packet is shown in Figure 22-28.

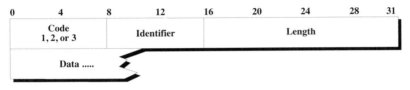

Figure 22-28: PAP Protocol General Format

The *Code* field can contain the values 1, 2, or 3 indicating an *Authenticate Request*, *Positive Acknowledgement* (Ack), or *Negative Acknowledgement* (Nak) respectively. The *Identifier* field is a unique 8 bit number used to associate replies with requests. The 16 bit *Length* field indicates the overall length of the PAP packet and includes the Code, Identifier, Length, and Data fields. Finally, the *Data* field is a variable number of octets, the format of which is determined by the operation to be performed and defined by the Code field.

- **Authenticate Request**

  An Authenticate Request is used to begin the authentication process. One peer (the requesting peer) will send a PAP request that contains its ID and Password during the Authenticate phase. This is then repeated at regular intervals until such time that either a valid reply is received, or the link is terminated through a Terminate Request LCP packet. The format for a PAP Request is shown in Figure 22-29.

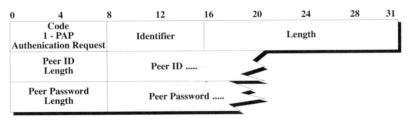

Figure 22-29: PAP Authentication Request

For this packet, the *Code* field is always set to 1, and the *Identifier* field is set to a unique value so that the eventual reply can be matched with this request. The *Peer ID* and *Password* Length fields then indicate the lengths of the ID and Password respectively and the *Length* field, the overall length of the packet.

- **Authenticate Ack and Authenticate Nak**

  The response to a PAP Authenticate Request is either positive (an Authenticate Ack), or negative (an Authenticate Nak). If the ID and Password pair sent by the requesting peer are acceptable, then the response will be positive. If the ID and/or Password are unacceptable, the response is negative, and the link is terminated with a *Terminate Request* LCP packet.

  The format for both of these packets is the same and is shown in Figure 22-30.

Figure 22-30: PAP Authenticate Ack/Nak

For these packets, the *Code* field will have a value of either 2 (Ack), or 3 (Nak). The 8 bit *Message Length* field then defines the length of an implementation specific message and the *Length* field, the overall length of the packet.

The following traces (Figures 22-31 and 22-32) show both a successful and an unsuccessful PAP negotiation. Notice that in the second trace (Figure 22-32), following the Authentication Nak, the link is terminated by the sequence Terminate Request/Terminate Acknowledgement.

```
µSCOPE                  PACKET TRACE DECODE REPORT            (c) T.Kenyon 1995

==================================µscope==================================
Frame    : 1                  Len     : 36        Error    : None        The DCE requests that the DTE
T Elapsed: 18:41:45:907       T Delta : 00:00:00:305                     identifies itself using PAP.
-----------------------------[WAN]-----------------------------
Dst Addr : DTE                Src Addr : DCE
------------------------------[ppp encap]-----------------------------
Address  : FF                 Control  : 03
------------------------------[ppp]-----------------------------
Type     : LCP                Protocol : CTRL
Code     : CFG Req
Id       : 0x4d               Length   : 32 Bytes
------------------------------[Config]-----------------------------
Type     : 3-Authentication-Protocol              Length   : 4 Bytes
Value    : PAP (c023)
=================================[data:  24]==================================
000C  05 06 6D F0 A1 20 15 12 58 59 50 4C 45 58 08 00   ..m.. ..XYPLEX..
001C  87 02 3E 66 00 03 00 00                           ..>f....

==================================µscope==================================
Frame    : 2                  Len     : 36        Error    : None        The DTE acknowledges the use of
T Elapsed: 18:41:45:915       T Delta : 00:00:00:008                     PAP.
-----------------------------[WAN]-----------------------------
Dst Addr : DCE                Src Addr : DTE
------------------------------[ppp encap]-----------------------------
Address  : FF                 Control  : 03
------------------------------[ppp]-----------------------------
Type     : LCP                Protocol : CTRL
Code     : CFG Ack
Id       : 0x4d               Length   : 32 Bytes
------------------------------[Config]-----------------------------
Type     : 3-Authentication-Protocol              Length   : 4 Bytes
Value    : PAP (c023)
=================================[data:  24]==================================
000C  05 06 6D F0 A1 20 15 12 58 59 50 4C 45 58 08 00   ..m.. ..XYPLEX..
001C  87 02 3E 66 00 03 00 00                           ..>f....
```

```
===============================µscope=======================================
Frame    : 3                 Len    : 26            Error   : None
T Elapsed: 18:41:46:762      T Delta : 00:00:00:847
-----------------------------[WAN]------
Dst Addr : DCE               Src Addr : DTE
-----------------------------[ppp encap]-
Address  : FF                Control  : 03
-----------------------------[PPP]-
Type     : LCP               Protocol : Password Auth
Code     : Auth Req
===============================[data:  18]==================================
0008   08 74 72 61 69 6E 69 6E 67 08 74 72 61 69 6E 69 69    .training.traini
0018   6E 67                                                 ng
```

The DTE sends an *Authentication Request.*

The DTE uses an eight octet ID of 'training', and an eight octet password of 'training'.

```
===============================µscope=======================================
Frame    : 4                 Len    : 9             Error   : None
T Elapsed: 18:41:46:764      T Delta : 00:00:00:002
-----------------------------[WAN]------
Dst Addr : DTE               Src Addr : DCE
-----------------------------[ppp encap]-
Address  : FF                Control  : 03
-----------------------------[PPP]-
Type     : LCP               Protocol : Password Auth
Code     : Auth Ack
===============================[data:   0]==================================
```

The DCE acknowledges the ID and Password with an *Authentication Ack.*

Figure 22-31: Sample PAP Exchange Resulting in Success

µSCOPE   PACKET TRACE DECODE REPORT   (c) T.Kenyon 1995

```
===============================µscope=======================================
Frame    : 23                Len    : 36            Error   : None
T Elapsed: 18:37:00:947      T Delta : 00:00:01:160
-----------------------------[WAN]------
Dst Addr : DCE               Src Addr : DTE
-----------------------------[ppp encap]-
Address  : FF                Control  : 03
-----------------------------[PPP]-
Type     : LCP               Protocol : CTRL
Code     : CFG Req
Id       : 0x0c              Length  : 32 Bytes
-----------------------------[Config]-
Type     : 3-Authentication-Protocol     Length  : 4 Bytes
Value    : PAP (c023)
===============================[data:  24]==================================
000C   05 06 0D 57 01 46 15 12 58 59 50 4C 45 58 08 00    ...W.F..XYPLEX..
001C   87 05 0D C6 00 02 00 00                             ........
```

The DTE requests that the DCE identifies itself through Authentication.

PAP is requested as the Authentication Protocol to be used.

```
===============================µscope=======================================
Frame    : 24                Len    : 36            Error   : None
T Elapsed: 18:37:00:954      T Delta : 00:00:00:007
-----------------------------[WAN]------
Dst Addr : DTE               Src Addr : DCE
-----------------------------[ppp encap]-
Address  : FF                Control  : 03
-----------------------------[PPP]-
Type     : LCP               Protocol : CTRL
Code     : CFG Ack
Id       : 0x0c              Length  : 32 Bytes
-----------------------------[Config]-
Type     : 3-Authentication-Protocol     Length  : 4 Bytes
Value    : PAP (c023)
===============================[data:  24]==================================
000C   05 06 0D 57 01 46 15 12 58 59 50 4C 45 58 08 00    ...W.F..XYPLEX..
001C   87 05 0D C6 00 02 00 00                             ........
```

The DCE acknowledges that it is prepared to use PAP.

```
===============================µscope=======================================
Frame    : 25                Len    : 19            Error   : None
T Elapsed: 18:37:00:958      T Delta : 00:00:00:004
-----------------------------[WAN]------
Dst Addr : DTE               Src Addr : DCE
-----------------------------[ppp encap]-
Address  : FF                Control  : 03
-----------------------------[PPP]-
Type     : LCP               Protocol : Password Auth
Code     : Auth Req
===============================[data:  11]==================================
0008   09 28 58 30 32 33 45 36 36 29 00                   .(X023E66).
```

The DCE sends its ID which is the nine octet string '(X023E66)'. No Password has been configured, so the DCE merely sends a *Password Length* field of zero.

```
===============================µscope=======================================
Frame    : 26                Len    : 9             Error   : None
T Elapsed: 18:37:00:960      T Delta : 00:00:00:002
-----------------------------[WAN]------
Dst Addr : DCE               Src Addr : DTE
-----------------------------[ppp encap]-
Address  : FF                Control  : 03
-----------------------------[PPP]-
Type     : LCP               Protocol : Password Auth
Code     : Auth Nak
===============================[data:   0]==================================
```

The Peer ID and/or Password are unacceptable to the DTE so it negatively acknowledges the PAP Authentication Request with a NAK.

```
=======================================μscope=======================================
Frame   : 27            Len    : 8              Error   : None        The DTE sends a Terminate Request
T Elapsed: 18:37:00:961 T Delta : 00:00:00:001                        to the DCE.
                        --------------[WAN]--------
Dst Addr : DCE          Src Addr : DTE
                        ------[ppp encap]-
Address  : FF           Control  : 03
                        -----[ppp]--
Type    : LCP           Protocol : CTRL
Code    : TERM Req
Id      : 0x02          Length   : 4 Bytes
=============================[data:   6]=============================================
0002  C0 21 05 02 00 04                                 .!....


=======================================μscope=======================================
Frame   : 28            Len    : 8              Error   : None        The DCE acknowledges the Terminate
T Elapsed: 18:37:00:963 T Delta : 00:00:00:002                        Request (the only allowable response
                        --------------[WAN]--------                   to a Terminate Request) with a
Dst Addr : DTE          Src Addr : DCE                                Terminate Ack.
                        ------[ppp encap]-
Address  : FF           Control  : 03
                        -----[ppp]--
Type    : LCP           Protocol : CTRL
Code    : TERM Ack
Id      : 0x02          Length   : 4 Bytes
=============================[data:   6]=============================================
0002  C0 21 06 02 00 04                                 .!....
```

Figure 22-32: Sample PAP Exchange Resulting in Failure

22.4.2   The Challenge Handshake Authentication Protocol (CHAP)

Unlike the Password Authentication Protocol that provides only a simple authentication system, CHAP provides a more secure scheme. Firstly, CHAP uses a three way handshake that employs a *secret* known only to the peers involved, and secondly, a *challenge* can be issued at any time during the life of the link. The secret itself is a minimum of 1 octet in length (although the preferred length is 16 octets), and is never transmitted over the link.

As with PAP, authentication is requested through a LCP option. For CHAP the *Code* field contains a value of 3, the *Length* field 4, and the 16 bit *Authentication Protocol* field the value C223$_{16}$. The *Data* field for a CHAP request then contains a single octet to indicate the one-way hashing method used. Values of 0 to 4 for this octet are reserved and therefore unused. A value of 5 indicates a desire to use the only standardized option at this time which is MD5.[5]

Figure 22-33 shows the general format of CHAP that then travels in a PPP packet with a *Protocol* field value of C223$_{16}$.

Figure 22-33: CHAP Packet – General Format

The *Code* field has a value of 1 for a *Challenge*, 2 for a *Response*, 3 for a *Success*, and 4 for a *Failure*. The *Identifier* field is then used to match commands with responses, and the *Length* field to indicate the total length of the packet. The *Data* field is of variable length and carries data as defined by the Code.

---

5. MD5 (*Message Digest Algorithm*) was developed by Massacheusetts Institute of Technology (MIT), and documented in RFC 1321.

- **Challenge and Response**

  CHAP begins with a peer sending a Challenge packet (*Code* field equal to 1). As with PAP, Challenge packets are then continually sent until either a response is received or the link is terminated. Challenge packets may be sent during the Authentication phase but, unlike PAP, a Challenge may also be sent at any time during the Network phase.

  The response to a Challenge is a CHAP Response (*Code* field equal to 2). Both packets have a similar format which is shown in Figure 22-34.

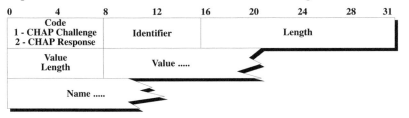

Figure 22-34: CHAP Challenge and Response

  For a *Challenge*, the *Code* field is 1, and the *Identifier* field is a unique number used to match the Response to the Challenge. The *Length* field defines the overall length of the packet and the *Value Length* field, the length of the *Value*. The *Value* field then contains a variable number of octets, and the Name field contains an implementation specific identification for the system transmitting the packet.

  In a *Response*, the *Code* field is set to 2. The *Identifier* field is used to match this response to the Challenge to which it relates, and the *Length*, *Name* and *Value Length* fields have the same meaning as they did for the Challenge. The *Value* field contains the one-way hash calculated over the Identifier concatenated with the secret, and the Challenge Value.

- **Success and Failure**

  If the Value in the Response is that expected by the Challenging peer, we now send a CHAP Success packet. If the Value is not that expected by the peer that issued the Challenge, a Failure is sent instead, and the link should be terminated with a Terminate Request LCP packet. The Success or Failure packet is therefore the third phase of the three way handshake. The format of the Success and Failure packets are similar and is shown in Figure 22-35.

  For a *Success*, the *Code* field has a value of 3, and for a *Failure*, a value of 4. In both cases the *Identifier* field is used to match the *Success/Failure* packet with the *Response* packet that caused it. The variable length *Message* field then contains implementation specific information whose length is determined from the overall *Length* field.

Figure 22-35: CHAP Success and Failure

22.5 PPP Link Quality Monitoring (LQM)

PPP is concerned with Wide Area Communications which, in general, are less reliable than LANs. Packets can be dropped due to insufficient buffer space being available, and packets can be corrupted due to line noise. Most importantly though, while the WAN link may be severely compromised by reliability, can we determine just how bad the problem really is? It is of course possible that an alternative route may be available (even at a lower speed). But how can we tell that the reliability of the primary link has dropped below acceptable thresholds?

Before the acceptance of PPP by vendors, there were of course many proprietary solutions. However, with inter-operability being the key to multi-vendor networks, we now need standards based solutions to networking problems. The Link Quality Monitoring protocol described in RFC 1333 achieves this by the peers exchanging a *Quality Report* that can then be used to calculate how many packets have been lost. Such a protocol, of course, relies on each peer maintaining a set of counters to track the number of packets and octets that have been transmitted and successfully received. These counters are then periodically transmitted in this *Link Quality Report* packet.

Since most devices today incorporate SNMP for management,[6] it makes sense to use the mandatory counters that SNMP defines. These counters associated with the *Interfaces* group, are therefore used to track the number of packets and octets that have been either transmitted or received. In addition, three further 32 bit counters are used as follows:

- **OutLQRs**
  Used to track the number of Link Quality Report packets sent.

- **InLQRs**
  Used to track the number of Link Quality Report packets received.

- **InGoodOctets**
  Used to track the number of octets that have been received in *good* Data Link layer packets. Unfortunately, the SNMP MIB II interface counter used to track inbound octets cannot be used since this counter also counts octets contained within packets that are either discarded or found to be in error.

22.5.1 LQM Configuration Option

In common with all PPP options, LQM is requested through a PPP configuration option, the general format of which is shown in Figure 22-36. In this instance, the *Type* field contains a value of 4, and the *Length* field 8. Following the *Length* field we then have a 16 bit *Quality Protocol* field that contains the quality protocol to be used – for LQR, this has the value $C025_{16}$, but of course any value could be contained here if we wish to use a proprietary extension. Finally a 32 bit field, the *Reporting Period*, is used to indicate the maximum length of time (in 1/100 second increments) between *Link Quality Reports* (LQRs). Where this field is zero the peer

6. SNMP is discussed in Chapter 20 and the Interfaces Group can be seen (in its entirety in Appendix C).

indicates that it will not maintain a timer, but that it will transmit its own LQR in response to a received LQR. Thus, a passive mode is achieved.

0	4	8	12	16	20	24	28	31
Type LQM-4		Length 8		Quality Protocol C025 for LQR				
Reporting Period								

Figure 22-36: LQM Configuration Option

22.5.2 Link Quality Report

At the reporting interval, or (if successfully negotiated) in response to a received LQR, the peer will transmit a Link Quality Report packet encapsulated in a PPP Data-Link frame. The format of the frame is shown in Figure 22-37.

The PPP Protocol Identifier is $C025_{16}$ – LQR. The Information field then contains a number of 32 bit fields that form the actual Link Quality Report.

The *Magic Number* field is the Magic Number negotiated with the Magic Number configuration option. Where no Magic Number has been negotiated, this field is always transmitted as zero. The *LastOutLQRs* field contains the value from the most recently received *PeerOutLQRs*. This field therefore indicates the number of LQRs that the peer should have received. The *LastOutPackets* field contains the value from the most recently received *PeerOutPackets*. Thus, this field indicates the number of packets that should have been received. *LastOutOctets* is copied from the most recently received *PeerOutOctets* and therefore indicates the number of octets that the peer believes it should have received. The *PeerIn...* and *PeerOut...* fields are then used to convey the number of LQRs received and sent by the peer.

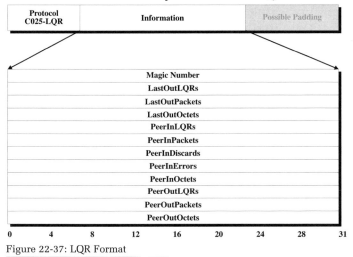

Figure 22-37: LQR Format

22.5.3 Gauging Link Quality

Where the quality of the link must be gauged, implementation specific methods are used. Generally, we can make the following assumptions:

- The LastOutLQRs can be directly compared to the PeerInLQRs to determine the number of *outbound* LQRs that have been lost.

- The LastOutLQRs can be compared with the OutLQRs to determine how many LQRs are still in the wide area link.

- The delta value (the change) in the PeerInPackets can, by comparison with the LastInPackets, be used to determine the number of outgoing packets lost over the link.

- The change in the PeerInOctets can be used to compare with the LastOutOctets to determine the number of octets lost over the outgoing link.

- The difference between the last LastInPackets and the PeerOutPckets can be used to determine the number of packets that have been lost over the incoming link.

- The difference between the LastInOctets and the change in PeerInOctets can be used to determine the number of lost octets over the incoming link.

- The change in the PeerInDiscards and the PeerInErrors can be used to determine whether the packet loss is due to congestion in the peer, or a physical failure in the link.

Of course, if the link is operating properly, then the whole idea of the LQR merely adds to what could already be an overloaded link. Where a problem exists however, the LQR can be invaluable in determining where the problem lies and therefore how to control it. For example where there is a loss of data over the link but the overall throughput is at least adequate, there would be no point in dropping it. However where the reporting interval is sufficiently short, we will be able to detect a failure and therefore take appropriate action.

Equally, where the link is good only in one direction, we can modify the reporting interval to accommodate this. Where the link is good incoming but bad outgoing for example, it would be inappropriate to shorten the reporting interval since our LQRs will probably be lost. On the other hand, incoming LQRs will inform us of exactly how bad the link is becoming. Of course were the situation to be reversed (that is *outgoing* is good but *incoming* is bad), we will lose a significant number of incoming LQRs but we should send our LQRs at a faster rate.

22.6 The Multi-Link Protocol

With the advent of emerging technologies such as *Integrated Services Digital Networking* (ISDN),[7] there opens a new opportunity to assign Bandwidth-on-Demand or *BonDing* as it is known. A single *Basic Rate* ISDN link comprises two

---

7. ISDN allows up to 30 x 64kb channels to be bound together to form *multiple-channel* pipes.

Bearer (or '*B*') Channels each with a bandwidth of 64kbs, and a *Primary Rate* service comprises up to 30 B Channels[8] (each of 64kbps). These channels can then be used to provide incoming calls from different remote sites, outgoing calls to different sites, multiple B Channel *pipes* to (or from) a single site, or any combination of these. Where multiple B Channels are bound together in this way, we use a Multi-Link protocol that ensures load balancing across all circuits. In use, Multi-Link can be described with Figure 22-38.

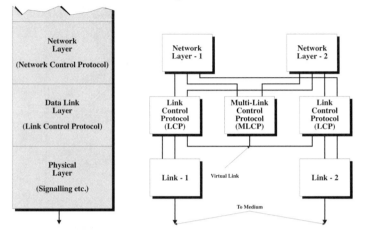

Figure 22-38: Multi-Link Model of Operation

22.6.1 Multi-Link Operation

Where we have multiple links, we obviously need to make best use of them by passing an equal amount of traffic over each. This then gives us a problem. For example, should we pass packets in equal number over each link, and if so, how can we ensure that this provides the best solution where the size of packets will differ? Equally, what will happen if the two links are of differing speeds? Although with technologies such as ISDN each link is the same, we must remember that Multi-Link is not restricted to only ISDN links. Thus, we must solve this dilemma if we are to make the best possible use of our links.

RFC 1717 defines a scheme for the transmission of packets over multiple links by fragmenting them at the transmitter and then reassembling them at the receiver. Small packets however, do not need to be fragmented and, to accommodate links of different speed, fragments neither need to be of equal size, nor do we need to send the same number of fragments over each link. Thus when Multi-Link is in operation, a further header (the Multi-Link Protocol Header) is required to control packet re-assembly. Figure 22-39 shows the format of a Multi-Link fragment.

Following the PPP *Link Layer* frame Header (described section 22.8), we find the PPP Multi-Link protocol itself identified with a *Protocol* field of $003D_{16}$, and

8. European Primary Rate services have 30xB Channels (known as E1) while in the US, there are only 24xB Channels (known as T1).

then a two or four octet header containing flags and a *Sequence Number*. The two flags (*B*, and *E*) are used to indicate the start (or *Beginning*) and *Ending* fragments in a PPP packet. The Sequence number is then 24 bits long (or 12 bits where it is negotiated through the LCP)[9] and contains a number that is incremented for each fragment transmitted. By using the Sequence number in this way, we are then able to re-order fragments and reconstitute the original PPP frame.

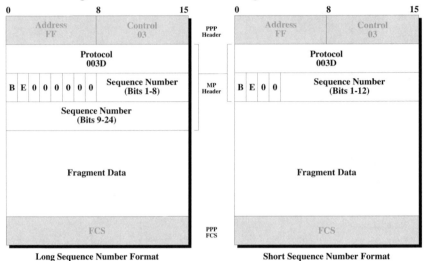

Figure 22-39: PPP Multi-Link Fragment Format

We saw in the LCP Configuration Options (section 22.3.4) that Multi-Link operation can be requested by either peer by sending a LCP Configuration Request containing a *Multi-Link Maximum Receive Reconstructed Unit* (MRRU) or a *Multi-Link Short Sequence Number* Header Format. In either case Multi-Link operation is being requested and, if the negotiation is successful, will be used. The *Endpoint Discriminator* option can then be used to determine whether the link should join an existing *bundle*, or whether a new *bundle* should be established. Since the Endpoint Discriminator alone does not indicate Multi-Link operation is being requested, it is also recommended that an authentication protocol (i.e. *PAP* or *CHAP*) is used to prevent malicious users from joining an existing link. This then provides the following four scenarios when deciding how our *bundled* links are handled:

- **No Discriminator and no Authentication**
  Here, all links must be joined to one bundle.

- **Discriminator but no Authentication**
  Where the Discriminator matches that used by the links of an existing bundle, the new link is joined to it. Where there is no Discriminator match, a new bundle is formed.

---

9. See Section 22.3.4 Multi-Link Short Sequence Number Header Format.

Communications Over Wide Area Links

- **No Discriminator but Authentication**
  Where the Authentication matches that of links in an existing bundle, the new link is joined to that bundle. Where the Authentication fails, a new bundle is formed.

- **Discriminator and Authentication**
  If the Discriminator and the Authentication both match with that of existing links, the new link will join that bundle. Where either the Authentication *OR* the Discriminator do not match, the new link will form the basis of a new bundle.

22.7 The Internet Protocol Control Protocol (IPCP)

PPP defines a number of Network Control Protocols (NCPs) designed to configure a link for operation with those specific Network Layer protocols. While other NCPs are beyond the scope of this book, the Internet Protocol Control Protocol (IPCP) – standardized by RFC 1332 – is described here since it is this that is responsible for the configuration of PPP links to carry IP datagrams.

IPCP uses the same exchange mechanisms as LCP, except that no NCPs are exchanged before the link has reached the *Network* phase. Once entered, IPCP packets are then encapsulated in PPP Data Link frames using a *Protocol* field containing the value 8021_{16}, and *Code* field values of 1 to 7 (*Configure Request, Configure Ack, Configure Nak, Configure Reject, Terminate Request, Terminate Ack*, and *Code Reject*). Once successfully negotiated, IP datagrams are then encapsulated in the *Information* field of PPP Data Link layer frames that have a *Protocol* field of 0021_{16} to represent IP.

22.7.1 IPCP Configuration Options

Three IPCP configuration options exist, of which one is now *deprecated* and is only used in older implementations to assure backward compatibility. The three options are:

- **IP-Addresses**
  Broadly, this option allows for the configuration of IP Addresses on dial up links. Now *deprecated*, this option has been superseded by the IP-Address option. As such, this option is only sent as a Configuration Request where a Configure Reject has been received in response to an *IP-Address Configuration* Request.

- **IP-Compression-Protocol**
  By default, although it may be desirable, IP over PPP does not use compression. Where compression is required, IPCP allows the negotiation of the compression protocol through an IPCP configuration option. The basic format of the option is shown over.
    The length of this NCP option is always at least 4 octets. The *Length* field therefore specifies a value of 4 or more. The *IP Compression Protocol* field is used to identify the compression protocol that is to be used. RFC 1332 defines only Van Jacobson Compression and states that the value in this field should be

$002D_{16}$. Obviously other, implementation specific, protocols can be used which will therefore require a different value to be used here. The *Data* field is used to contain additional information as required by the specific Compression Protocol to be used. For Van Jacobson Compression, the *Length* field is set to 6, and the *Data* field contains two single octet fields used to indicate the *Max Slot ID*, and the *Comp Slot ID*. These fields are discussed in section 22.7.2 below.

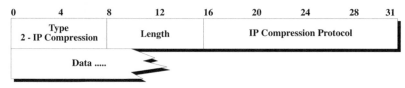

0	4	8	12	16	20	24	28	31
Type 2 - IP Compression		Length		IP Compression Protocol				
Data								

Figure 22-40: IP Compression Protocol Option

- **IP-Address**

  The IP-Address option allows a peer to either state the IP Address that it wishes to use, or to request that the remote peer provides the IP Address. In general then, this option allows the peer to negotiate the IP Address that should be used at the local end. The general format for this option is shown in Figure 22-41.

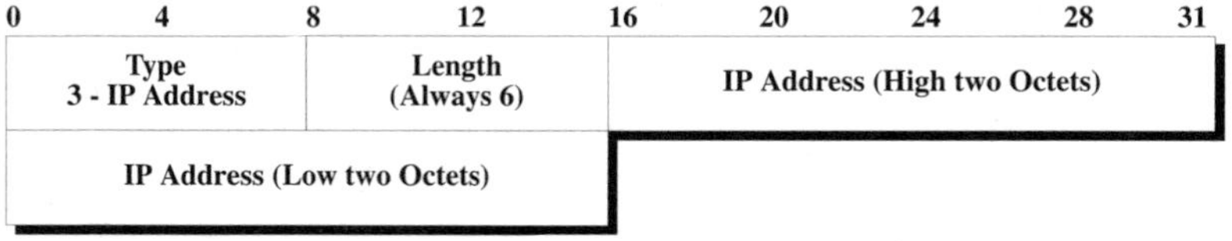

0	4	8	12	16	20	24	28	31
Type 3 - IP Address		Length (Always 6)		IP Address (High two Octets)				
IP Address (Low two Octets)								

Figure 22-41: IP Address Configuration Option

The *IP Address* field (the two, two octet values) contain either the IP Address that the peer wishes to use as it's local address, or zero. If all four octets are zero, it indicates that the peer wishes the IP Address to be assigned by the remote end of the link. Where the value is non-zero yet the value is unacceptable to the remote peer, the remote end will *NAK* the option and return a valid IP Address that will be used by the local end.

22.7.2   Van Jacobson Compression over PPP

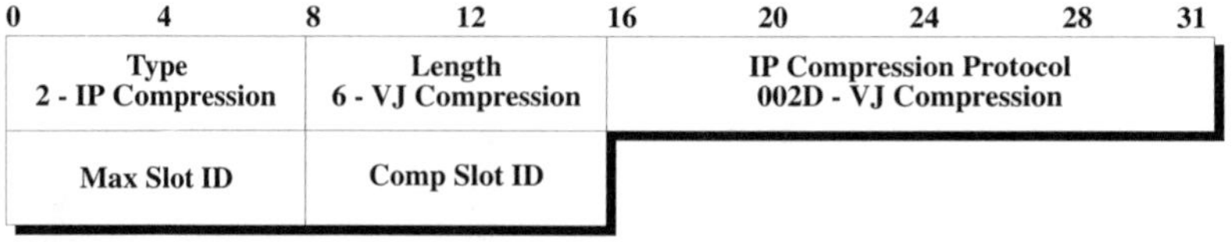

0	4	8	12	16	20	24	28	31
Type 2 - IP Compression		Length 6 - VJ Compression		IP Compression Protocol 002D - VJ Compression				
Max Slot ID		Comp Slot ID						

Figure 22-42: IP Compression Option for Van Jacobson Compression

As we saw in section 22.2.1, Van Jacobson Compression can be used to considerably reduce the size of TCP/IP headers. The IP Compression Protocol option, discussed in the previous section, is used to indicate that the peer is able to *receive* compressed packets and therefore operates unidirectionally. Where we wish to pass compressed traffic in both directions, each end must send an IP Compression Protocol option as shown in Figure 22-42.

The *Max Slot ID* field identifies the maximum number of *connection* slots (array entries) that the peer supports. This value however is actually one less than the maximum number since slots are counted from zero. The *Comp Slot ID* field determines whether or not the Slot number can be compressed. Where this field contains zero, the slot (connection) number field must be present and the *C* flag in the VJ header must be set. Where the field contains 1, the connection number may be omitted from the VJ Header where the connection has not changed (and correspondingly, the *C* flag will not be set).

Once successfully negotiated, PPP packets containing IP are then sent with the Protocol field set to one of the values from Table 22-5.

Table 22-5: VJ Compression Protocol Types

Value (Hex)	Description
0021	The IP protocol is not TCP, the packet is a fragment, or the packet cannot be compressed.
002D	The TCP/IP Headers are replaced by the Compressed Header.
002F	Uncompressed TCP – The IP Protocol field has been replaced by the Slot Identifier.

22.8 PPP Framing over Serial Links

PPP can be used over most Serial/WAN interfaces, with the only overriding requirement being that the link must be full duplex. For example, linking networks over Synchronous Point-to-Point connections (leased lines), or over Dial-Up Asynchronous links as would be the case for remote Internet access.

Table 22-6: PPP Framing and Associated RFCs

RFC	Description
1662	PPP in HDLC-Like Framing
1619	PPP over SONET/SD
1618	PPP over ISDN
1598	PPP in X.25

Most commonly, we find PPP used in environments requiring Higher Data Link Control (HDLC) like framing as described by RFC 1662. Other framing is possible, and these techniques are discussed in separate documents as indicated in Table 22-6. For our discussion, we shall consider only HDLC-like framing since this is the most common implementation over WAN links.

The Link Layer Frame now looks as shown in Figure 22-43.

The 8 bit *Flag* field is used to indicate the start (and end) of each frame. Only one *Flag* field is required between any two frames thus, as our diagram shows, the trailing *Flag* can be immediately followed by the *Address* field of the next frame. The *Flag* octet is a unique binary pattern (01111110_2, $7E_{16}$) that must be preserved at all cost. As such, a scheme known as zero-bit-insertion or bit stuffing, is used by the transmitter to insert an additional zero bit into the bit stream wherever five consecutive 1 bits exist. In the receiver, any zero bit that follows five consecutive 1's is then removed thus preserving the uniqueness of our Flag.

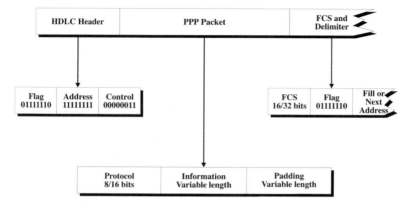

Figure 22-43: PPP in HDLC-Like Framing

The *Address* field is a single 8 bit value of all ones (FF). This address is equivalent to the All Stations address (Broadcast) but, although this may seem illogical, individual station addresses cannot be used at this time.

The *Control* field is always 8 bits in length and is always 00000011_2 (03_{16}). No other value can be used for this field. The *FCS* (Frame Check Sequence) field is either 16 bits (the default) or 32 bits (if negotiated through LCP Option Negotiation). The Frame Check Sequence is calculated over the entire frame including the *Address*, *Control*, *Protocol*, *Information*, and *Padding* fields. It does not include any *Start* or *Stop* bits (included for Asynchronous operation), any octets inserted for transparency,[10] the Flag field or FCS field itself.

22.8.1 Preserving Data Transparency

In order to transmit octets that otherwise have special significance, an *Escape* octet is defined as $7D_{16}$. Thus where a $7E_{16}$ legitimately exists in the data, this is replaced by an Escape sequence comprising two octets. For example, when transmitting a $7E_{16}$ within the data, we actually transmit $7D_{16}$ followed by the result of the Exclusive OR (XOR) of the octet to be transmitted, with the value 20_{16}. Our $7E_{16}$ is therefore transmitted as $7D5E_{16}$. Equally, should we wish to transmit the Escape octet ($7D_{16}$) itself, we actually transmit an Escape sequence of $7D5D_{16}$.

22.8.2 PPP Example using HDLC-Like Framing

In the final trace of this chapter, we see a complete exchange of LCP and NCP configuration packets between two routers as they negotiate to bring up a serial link. The routers are routing IP over an un-numbered PPP link and use OSPF as the routing protocol. All other protocols are bridged.

---

10. See section 22.8.1.

The trace itself is complete and is shown in a *raw* format to show as much detail as possible. For example, the frame header FF03$_{16}$ can be seen for each frame. Further decoding is then possible by referring to the previous sections in this chapter.

```
μSCOPE              PACKET TRACE DECODE REPORT          (c) T.Kenyon 1995

=======================μscope=====================================
Frame    : 1              Len    : 32           Error   : None
T Elapsed: 18:46:35:554   T Delta : 00:00:02:702
=========================[data:   32]=============================
0000  FF 03 C0 21 01 6C 00 1C 05 06 B2 A2 5A 70 15 12    ...!.l......Zp..
0010  58 59 50 4C 45 58 08 00 87 05 0D C6 00 02 00 00    XYPLEX.........
=======================μscope=====================================
Frame    : 2              Len    : 32           Error   : None
T Elapsed: 18:46:35:561   T Delta : 00:00:00:007
=========================[data:   32]=============================
0000  FF 03 C0 21 02 6C 00 1C 05 06 B2 A2 5A 70 15 12    ...!.l......Zp..
0010  58 59 50 4C 45 58 08 00 87 05 0D C6 00 02 00 00    XYPLEX.........
=======================μscope=====================================
Frame    : 3              Len    : 32           Error   : None
T Elapsed: 18:46:35:852   T Delta : 00:00:00:291
=========================[data:   32]=============================
0000  FF 03 C0 21 01 7F 00 1C 05 06 0A A2 77 14 15 12    ...!.......w...
0010  58 59 50 4C 45 58 08 00 87 02 3E 66 00 03 00 00    XYPLEX....>f....
=======================μscope=====================================
Frame    : 4              Len    : 32           Error   : None
T Elapsed: 18:46:35:859   T Delta : 00:00:00:007
=========================[data:   32]=============================
0000  FF 03 C0 21 02 7F 00 1C 05 06 0A A2 77 14 15 12    ...!.......w...
0010  58 59 50 4C 45 58 08 00 87 02 3E 66 00 03 00 00    XYPLEX....>f....
=======================μscope=====================================
Frame    : 5              Len    : 14           Error   : None
T Elapsed: 18:46:35:861   T Delta : 00:00:00:002
=========================[data:   14]=============================
0000  FF 03 80 21 01 0A 00 0A 03 06 C1 80 6B 10          ...!........k.
=======================μscope=====================================
Frame    : 6              Len    : 14           Error   : None
T Elapsed: 18:46:35:863   T Delta : 00:00:00:002
=========================[data:   14]=============================
0000  FF 03 80 21 01 0E 00 0A 03 06 C1 80 6C 1A          ...!........l.
=======================μscope=====================================
Frame    : 7              Len    : 11           Error   : None
T Elapsed: 18:46:35:863   T Delta : 00:00:00:000
=========================[data:   11]=============================
0000  FF 03 80 31 01 0A 00 07 03 03 01                   ...1.......
=======================μscope=====================================
Frame    : 8              Len    : 11           Error   : None
T Elapsed: 18:46:35:865   T Delta : 00:00:00:002
=========================[data:   11]=============================
0000  FF 03 80 31 01 0E 00 07 03 03 01                   ...1.......
=======================μscope=====================================
Frame    : 9              Len    : 40           Error   : None
T Elapsed: 18:46:35:869   T Delta : 00:00:00:004
=========================[data:   40]=============================
0000  FF 03 C0 21 0C 2E 00 24 94 AA 16 62 58 59 50 4C    ...!..$...bXYPL
0010  45 58 20 30 35 30 44 43 36 20 56 35 2E 30 2E 34    EX 050DC6 V5.0.4
0020  20 42 52 2F 34 36 30 00                            BR/460.
=======================μscope=====================================
Frame    : 10             Len    : 40           Error   : None
T Elapsed: 18:46:35:870   T Delta : 00:00:00:001
=========================[data:   40]=============================
0000  FF 03 C0 21 0C 31 00 24 0A A2 77 14 58 59 50 4C    ...!.1.$..w.XYPL
0010  45 58 20 30 32 33 45 36 36 20 56 35 2E 30 2E 34    EX 023E66 V5.0.4
0020  20 42 52 2F 34 36 30 00                            BR/460.
=======================μscope=====================================
Frame    : 11             Len    : 14           Error   : None
T Elapsed: 18:46:35:871   T Delta : 00:00:00:001
=========================[data:   14]=============================
0000  FF 03 80 21 02 0E 00 0A 03 06 C1 80 6C 1A          ...!........l.
=======================μscope=====================================
Frame    : 12             Len    : 14           Error   : None
T Elapsed: 18:46:35:873   T Delta : 00:00:00:002
=========================[data:   14]=============================
0000  FF 03 80 21 02 0A 00 0A 03 06 C1 80 6B 10          ...!........k.
=======================μscope=====================================
Frame    : 13             Len    : 11           Error   : None
T Elapsed: 18:46:35:873   T Delta : 00:00:00:000
=========================[data:   11]=============================
0000  FF 03 80 31 02 0E 00 07 03 03 01                   ...1.......
=======================μscope=====================================
Frame    : 14             Len    : 11           Error   : None
T Elapsed: 18:46:35:875   T Delta : 00:00:00:002
=========================[data:   11]=============================
0000  FF 03 80 31 02 0A 00 07 03 03 01                   ...1.......
```

DTE to DCE (ID=6C$_{16}$)
LCP Magic Number Configuration Request (B2A25A70$_{16}$).

DCE to DTE (ID=6C$_{16}$)
LCP Magic Number Configuration Ack (B2A25A70$_{16}$).

DCE to DTE (ID=7F$_{16}$)
LCP Magic Number Configuration Request (0AA27714$_{16}$).

DTE to DCE (ID=7F$_{16}$)
LCP Magic Number Configuration Ack (0AA27714$_{16}$).

DTE to DCE (ID=0A$_{16}$)
NCP (IPCP) Configuration Request (IP Address) 192.168.107.16.

DCE to DTE (ID=0E$_{16}$)
NCP (IPCP) Configuration Request (IP Address) 192.168.108.26.

DTE to DCE (ID=0A$_{16}$)
NCP (BCP) Configuration Request.

DCE to DTE (ID=0E$_{16}$)
NCP (BCP) Configuration Request.

DTE to DCE (ID=2E$_{16}$)
LCP Identification Packet. Data is implementation specific.

DCE to DTE (ID=31$_{16}$)
LCP Identification Packet. Data is implementation specific.

DTE to DCE (ID=0E$_{16}$)
NCP (IPCP) Configuration Ack (IP Address) 192.168.108.26.

DCE to DTE (ID=0A$_{16}$)
NCP (IPCP) Configuration Ack (IP Address) 192.168.107.16.

DTE to DCE (ID=0E$_{16}$)
NCP (BCP) Configuration Ack.

DCE to DTE (ID=0A$_{16}$)
NCP (BCP) Configuration Ack.

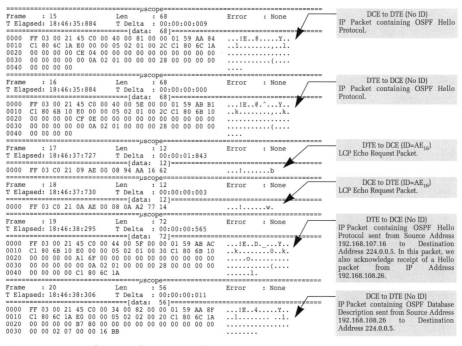

```
====================================μscope========================================
Frame    : 15              Len     : 68            Error    : None       DCE to DTE (No ID)
T Elapsed: 18:46:35:884    T Delta : 00:00:00:009                        IP Packet containing OSPF Hello
=================================[data:  68]===================================    Protocol.
0000  FF 03 00 21 45 C0 00 40 00 81 00 00 01 59 AA 84   ...!E..@.....Y..
0010  C1 80 6C 1A E0 00 00 05 02 01 00 2C C1 80 6C 1A   ..l........,..l.
0020  00 00 00 00 CE 04 00 00 00 00 00 00 00 00 00 00   ................
0030  00 00 00 00 00 00 0A 02 01 00 00 00 28 00 00 00 00  ..........(....
0040  00 00 00 00                                        ....
====================================μscope========================================
Frame    : 16              Len     : 68            Error    : None       DTE to DCE (No ID)
T Elapsed: 18:46:35:884    T Delta : 00:00:00:000                        IP Packet containing OSPF Hello
=================================[data:  68]===================================    Protocol.
0000  FF 03 00 21 45 C0 00 5E 00 00 01 59 AB B1   ...!E..@.^...Y..
0010  C1 80 6B 10 E0 00 00 05 02 01 00 2C C1 80 6B 10   ..k........,..k.
0020  00 00 00 00 CF 0E 00 00 00 00 00 00 00 00 00 00   ................
0030  00 00 00 00 00 00 0A 02 01 00 00 00 28 00 00 00 00  ..........(....
0040  00 00 00 00                                        ....
====================================μscope========================================
Frame    : 17              Len     : 12            Error    : None       DTE to DCE (ID=AE16)
T Elapsed: 18:46:37:727    T Delta : 00:00:01:843                        LCP Echo Request Packet.
=================================[data:  12]===================================
0000  FF 03 C0 21 09 AE 00 08 94 AA 16 62         ...!......b
====================================μscope========================================
Frame    : 18              Len     : 12            Error    : None       DCE to DTE (ID=AE16)
T Elapsed: 18:46:37:730    T Delta : 00:00:00:003                        LCP Echo Request Packet.
=================================[data:  12]===================================
0000  FF 03 C0 21 0A AE 00 08 0A A2 77 14         ...!......w.
====================================μscope========================================
Frame    : 19              Len     : 72            Error    : None       DTE to DCE (No ID)
T Elapsed: 18:46:38:295    T Delta : 00:00:00:565                        IP Packet containing OSPF Hello
=================================[data:  72]===================================    Protocol sent from Source Address
0000  FF 03 00 21 45 C0 00 44 00 5F 00 00 01 59 AB AC   ...!E..D._...Y..   192.168.107.16    to    Destination
0010  C1 80 6B 10 E0 00 00 05 02 01 00 30 C1 80 6B 10   ..k........0..k.   Address 224.0.0.5. In this packet, we
0020  00 00 00 00 A1 6F 00 00 00 00 00 00 00 00 00 00   .....o..........   also acknowledge receipt of a Hello
0030  00 00 00 00 00 00 0A 02 01 00 00 00 28 00 00 00 00  ..........(....   packet   from    IP    Address
0040  00 00 00 00 C1 80 6C 1A                            ......l.          192.168.108.26.
====================================μscope========================================
Frame    : 20              Len     : 56            Error    : None       DCE to DTE (No ID)
T Elapsed: 18:46:38:306    T Delta : 00:00:00:011                        IP Packet containing OSPF Database
=================================[data:  56]===================================    Description sent from Source Address
0000  FF 03 00 21 45 C0 00 34 00 82 00 00 01 59 AA 8F   ...!E..4.....Y..   192.168.108.26    to    Destination
0010  C1 80 6C 1A E0 00 00 05 02 02 00 20 C1 80 6C 1A   ..l......... ..l.  Address 224.0.0.5.
0020  00 00 00 00 B7 80 00 00 00 00 00 00 00 00 00 00   ................
0030  00 00 02 07 00 00 16 BB                            ........
```

Figure 22-44: Sample Trace Showing Complete Link Initialization

22.9 Summary

Wide Area links have an increasingly important role to play in joining our LANs together. Gone are the days of single vendor solutions where proprietary protocols could be used. Today, multi-protocol multi-vendor networks are the norm and inter-operability is the watch word for router manufacturers. PPP provides us with this standardized functionality, and allows multiple protocols to operate over a single link. Indeed, the rich functionality offered is probobaly more than most people would ever need however, by having all this available within a single protocol is certainly glamorous.

Serial dial-up links also take advantage of protocols such as SLIP and PPP. Certainly of the two, SLIP is now least popular since it does not provide features such as Compression, Authentication, or multiple protocol support. However, being simple means that it is easy to implement and has little or no overhead on slow speed links. PPP on the other hand, although being more complex, provides us with a whole suite of protocols that enhance its functionality with Network Control, Compression, and Authentication Protocols.

Creating a
Secure Internet
Environment

Many companies today are finding that the wealth of information available on the global Internet is invaluable. Companies are now exploiting the services that it offers such as Electronic Mail, On-line shopping, Advertising, and the abundance of information that is readily available – all just a mouse click away. Indeed, to many companies the Internet is its very life blood. So, given that companies need the resources of the Internet, it follows that their networks must be linked to it – therein lies our problem. How can we ensure that we can take full advantage of the Internet without unwanted intrusion from other Internet users?

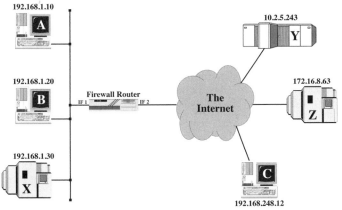

Figure 23-1: A Simple Network with Internet Connection

The answer lies in what has become known as *Firewall Security* where a router is configured through a series of filters, to provide a flexible yet secure gateway between networks. Almost all routers can be configured with filters limiting the data they pass. At the simplest level the router could be configured to forward packets only from certain networks however this can limit legitimate traffic. Another method is to limit protocols and/or to filter on parts of the packet themselves. There are many excellent books on this subject already and a complete discussion of every aspect of network security is certainly beyond the scope of this publication. However, in this chapter we shall discuss some of the areas that must be considered when implementing router security, based on protocols and specific packet elements.

When considering the configuration of routers to provide Firewalls of this type, we must first examine the protocols that will be used over the network(s) and the directions in which these protocols will be applied. For example, users on our network may need to send and receive electronic mail, download files by FTP, use Telnet to log into other hosts, and to look up information on the World Wide Web. It may be desirable though to prevent users from other networks from accessing any resources on our network. For this example, we shall consider the simplified, network of Figure 23-1 with access to Internet hosts and clients.

Here, our PC users on network 192.168.1.0 will need to legitimately access Internet resources on networks 10.0.0.0 and 172.16.0.0 along with hosts on our home network. Other users such as the one shown as a PC user at 192.168.248.12 may have no justification to access our machines however, and must be barred. So, let us take a look at the various protocols that might be utilized, their usefulness, and how they are actually used.

23.1 Internet Protocols

As we saw in Chapter 1, the Internet Protocol Suite is not limited to just TCP, and IP. Instead, we are dealing with a wide variety of protocols that work together to provide us with the rich functionality demanded by network users. Broadly, the protocols can be identified by the layer at which they operate with IP itself providing the centre of the communications environment. Thus, if we are to control their operation, we must understand not only how these protocols work, but also which protocols are used in conjunction with them.

In this chapter, we will not look at the protocols in detail since information on this is available elsewhere in other chapters. Instead, this chapter is designed to look at the operation of protocols only in terms of security.

23.1.1 Data-Link Layer Protocols

At the Data-Link layer, we really need only consider the Address Resolution Protocols ARP and RARP. These protocols, essential for the correct operation of IP, are broadcast at the Data-Link layer and as such will not be forwarded by routers. They are then of little overall concern in a secure environment.

- The Address Resolution Protocol (ARP)
  ARP frames are identified by the EtherType[1] 0806_{16} and are used to provide the dynamic mapping between IP and MAC addresses. The only real concern for this type of MAC frame is that routers can be configured to provide a proxy service (Proxy ARP) in a subnetted environment. This, due to its promiscuous nature, may be undesirable.

- The Reverse Address Resolution Protocol (RARP)
  RARP frames are used by hosts to determine their IP address when only in possession of their MAC address. This type of frame should not present any threat

---

1. EtherType refers to the contents of the Type field that directly follows the Source Address within an Ethernet frame.

Creating a Secure Internet Environment

to security unless the router is configured to provide a RARP service. In this case, intrusion is possible but it relies on the intruder being connected to the local network. RARP frames are identified by the EtherType 8035_{16}.

23.1.2 Transport Protocols

The most common IP transport protocols are TCP and UDP however, other protocols used in an IP environment must also be considered if we are to implement a useful security Firewall. These other protocols are direct users of IP that do not need a formalized Transport service and are typically management or routing protocols. As such they will be discussed separately.

- The Transmission Control Protocol (TCP)
  TCP is a user of IP and is identified by the IP protocol type[2] of 6. TCP provides a reliable transfer method that is usually used for user applications such as Telnet, FTP, HTTP (as used on the World Wide Web), and SMTP.
  In general, this is the safest and easiest protocol to control as far as routers are concerned although problems can arise in certain circumstances. These scenarios are discussed later.

- The User Datagram Protocol (UDP)
  UDP, again a direct user of IP, is identified by the IP Protocol type of 17_{10}. UDP is used to provide an unreliable transfer medium for application protocols such as the Domain Name System (DNS), the Simple Network Management Protocol (SNMP), and the Trivial File Transfer Protocol (TFTP).
  UDP can be very difficult to control since it can be easily forged, partly due to the fact that there are no handshaking procedures or acknowledgements built in. As such these packets can be extremely useful for probing destinations for valuable information. Typically, explicit filters must be used when this protocol is to be blocked by routers.

23.1.3 Management and Informational Protocols

These protocols are generally used to obtain or provide information to either applications, users/administrators, or network devices. Typically, it is more difficult to decide on whether to block these protocols than to actually implement the filters themselves, since some of these protocols are essential for the correct operation of IP.

- The Internet Control Message Protocol (ICMP)
  This protocol is a direct user of IP and is identified by the IP protocol ID 1. It is used for a variety of purposes. Reachability information is unquestionably key to the operation of IP as are many of the other features such as ICMP Redirect and Time Exceeded messages. Additionally, with the emergence of new Link State routing protocols, the newly introduced Router Discovery Protocol will play a much larger part in network management.

2. The Protocol Type field is part of the IP Datagram header and is discussed in Chapter 5.

- The Domain Name System (DNS)

  Unlike ICMP, DNS uses UDP (port 53_{10}) as a Transport protocol for most operations.[3] DNS is used to map Internet names to IP addresses primarily when attempting Telnet, FTP and WWW connections, and when delivering Mail. Obviously if our users need to use Internet resources, name queries must be forwarded from the local network to the Internet and responses must be returned. Equally, where the local network has a name server, requests may legitimately be received and of course responses will need to be sent.

  Care must be taken with this protocol since it can easily be abused. For example, using commonly available utilities,[4] a malicious user could establish the layout and structure of your network. True, the task would require much patience, but with only minimal information as a starting point a user could gain valuable insight into the hosts available on the local network.

- The Simple Network Management Protocol (SNMP)

  SNMP (UDP ports 161 and 162) is the de-facto standard for network management although associated with it are a number of problems. SNMP version 1 is inherently insecure and SNMP commands from unscrupulous users could be used to reconfigure the entire network.

  The main area of concern is that security is provided solely through the *Community String* that is transmitted un-encoded and is therefore visible to anyone with the appropriate equipment. As we have already said, UDP packets can easily be forged. Thus the Firewall router should block all incoming SNMP packets.

- The Bootstrap Protocol (BOOTP)

  The bootstrap protocol is generally used when boot loading network devices. Although the protocol relies upon UDP broadcasts using ports 67 and 68, it must be remembered that today's routers can be configured with UDP or BOOTP helpers[5] that allow these packets to pass. This makes the protocol routeable and therefore must be considered closely when discussing security.

  Because it is extremely unlikely that any Internet or remote device would legitimately require this protocol it should be blocked by the Firewall.

- The Kerberos Protocol (Kerberos)

  Kerberos is a security protocol using the services of TCP (port 88) and provides additional password level security to network devices and hosts. The actual passwords used are transmitted after encryption but, at least in theory, it is possible to decode them. If Kerberos is used on the local network, then these packets should not be forwarded unless it is absolutely necessary.

- The Network Time Protocol (NTP)

  The Network time protocol is extremely useful to network devices, distributing accurate time information and ensuring that all devices are synchronized. Using UDP port 123_{10}, an unwanted intruder could generate his own time packets causing both confusion, and in extreme cases, devices to revert to older pass-

3. UDP Zone Transfers use TCP however the same port number is used.
4. See Section 15.6 Looking Up DNS Information for further details.
5. Routers will not generally forward broadcast packets.

words. For example, Kerberos uses a dynamic password changing mechanism based upon time. Thus, by resetting the time, the intruder could force the server to re-use a previous password that had been *seen* on the network.

- The Finger Protocol (FINGER)
  Finger employs TCP (port 79) and is used to report on users that are either logged into or have accounts on network hosts. While the protocol does not provide sensitive information such as passwords etc., it can aid intruders in determining valid user names for host systems. If we are to create a secure environment, then we should block all incoming Finger packets.

- The Who Is or Nickname Protocol (WHOIS)
  This protocol uses UDP port 43 and allows users to look up information about Internet hosts and users. This protocol interrogates special databases at specific Internet hosts such as *rs.internic.net*, and supplies information such as:

  - The name (and address) of the organization that owns the Domain.

  - The actual name of the Domain.

  - The administrative and technical contacts for the Domain zone.

  - The names and addresses of sites that provide name service for the Domain.

  In general, since it is unlikely that we would have hosts running this service, it makes little difference if these packets are allowed through. Certainly our users may wish to interrogate Internet hosts for this information, so it would be wise to allow WHOIS traffic to pass.

23.1.4 Routing Protocols

These protocols are used to provide information relating to network connectivity and reachability.

Normally, connections to the Internet are made through a default route 0.0.0.0 rendering the need to block such protocols redundant. However, since it is possible to have these protocols enabled over Wide-Area links, a brief discussion is included here.

- The Routing Information Protocol (RIP)
  RIP was the first truly effective routing protocol and is still in widespread use today. It uses UDP broadcasts (port 520) which should be blocked by the router unless a UDP helper is in use. To make absolutely certain though, these packets should be filtered by the Firewall restricting them to the local network only.

- The Open Shortest Path First Protocol (OSPF)
  OSPF is a dynamic routing protocol that uses a Link State algorithm to determine true least cost paths. The protocol is a direct user of IP (identified by the IP protocol ID 89_{10}) and uses IP multicasts to relay routing information.
  As we saw in Chapter 14, since it is possible to forward such traffic, we should ensure that these packets are blocked at the Firewall. Generally how-

ever, this should not present a problem since OSPF multicasts are transmitted with a Time-to-Live of 1 restricting them from being forwarded through routers.

- The Exterior Gateway Protocol (EGP)
  EGP like OSPF travels in IP directly (IP protocol type 8) and was the original inter-Autonomous System routing protocol although, in truth, it offers very little over Static Routes. Your Internet provider may require that this protocol is used at the Firewall however where this is not the case, the router should block all incoming and outgoing EGP packets.

- The Border Gateway Protocol (BGP)
  This protocol is still very much under development at this time but it is designed to supersede EGP. BGP uses the reliable services of TCP (currently using port 179_{10}) and, like EGP, should be blocked unless your Internet provider specifically requests otherwise.

23.1.5 Application Protocols

It is for application protocols that all others exist. These protocols provide the user with access to the various hosts on the Internet and as such it is they that have to be controlled if our hosts are to be secure.

- Telnet
  This protocol provides users with a virtual terminal enabling them to connect to other, *remote*, systems. Telnet uses TCP (port 23_{10}) but has one major drawback in that no encryption is used. Thus, the password used by a user when logging on to a network host can be viewed on network analysis devices if they are available.

  Invariably most sites would wish to allow only explicitly defined users (by IP Address) or only allow outgoing calls to be made. Our Firewall then, should also be configured in a similar fashion.

- The File Transfer Protocol (FTP)
  As we know, FTP provides an effective system to enable the transfer of information and indeed, in practical terms, FTP could be said to offer a simple bulletin board. Typically local users will be allowed to FTP to Internet hosts. However in private networks, access from Internet users is normally either restricted to specific hosts or totally blocked.

  FTP operates by creating multiple concurrent connections. Here, the client initiates a static control session at TCP port 21_{10}, and the host responds to user requests by forming dynamic data transfer sessions using TCP port 20_{10} as its source. Alternatively, some administrators prefer that both control and data connections are initiated by the client. This, as we shall see later, is safer but relies on the FTP application on the host supporting the *Passive Open* command.

- The Trivial File Transfer Protocol (TFTP)
  TFTP provides a fast, *insecure*, method of transferring data. Many attempts have been made on hosts to make this more secure but this has the effect of limiting the scope of files that can be searched. The protocol is not reliable. It uses the User

Creating a Secure Internet Environment

Datagram Protocol port 69_{10} and another, dynamically assigned, port.

The use of UDP makes it easy to forge and thereby allows incoming calls to manipulate data on the host. As a result, the router being used as the Firewall should block any incoming and outgoing TFTP packets.

- The Simple Mail Transfer Protocol (SMTP)

  SMTP is arguably one of the major reasons for having an Internet connection in the first place. Mail is transferred using TCP port 25_{10}, normally to a mail server. From here it is then distributed to individual network users. True, there are other mail distribution systems in existence and the actual distribution of mail, and therefore the need to filter it will depend heavily on the particular system employed. One thing is clear though and that is SMTP must be passed in most cases.

  Setting filters for SMTP are very similar to those employed for Telnet and will be covered later.

- World Wide Web (WWW) access and the Hyper-Text Transfer Protocol (HTTP) is becoming extremely common at user sites. HTTP uses TCP port 80_{10} and can be treated in much the same way as Telnet. Typically for user sites, outgoing WWW access would be allowed but incoming packets should be barred.

- The Gopher Protocol (GOPHER)

  Gopher is essentially a specialist protocol designed specifically to search for information sources at known sites. In truth, it is unlikely that any normal user site would be bothered by such packets however the protocol is included here for completeness. Gopher uses TCP port 70_{10} and, as general rule, incoming packets should be blocked at the Firewall.

- The Network File System (NFS)

  The Network File System (NFS) and the Remote Procedure Call (RPC) protocols are designed for sharing file systems between hosts. They rely heavily on UDP calls using a variety of different ports. Thus, since it is unlikely that any user would actually wish to share a disk across the Internet, we should be able to safely block all such packets without affecting our users.

- NetBIOS Services

  This is typically used in LAN Manager, NT, and Windows for Workgroups environments. It can be transferred over various protocols including TCP/IP when adhering to RFCs 1001 and 1002 and it is therefore covered in this section. With NetBIOS, UDP broadcasts are used to announce the existence of a device using source ports $137\text{-}139_{10}$. However, due to the very nature of the protocol, it is recommended that the Firewall block all incoming NetBIOS packets.

23.2 Designing Secure Filters

In this section we shall consider the most common protocols and how they may be effectively filtered at the router. Each router vendor will implement filtering differently making it impossible to be specific. However, certain features are common to most vendors and it is these features that we shall consider.

Table 23-1: Protocol/Direction Configuration Guide

Protocol	Direction	
	Incoming	Outgoing
Telnet		
FTP		
SMTP		
etc........		

The first stage in creating filters is to decide exactly who will be using the Internet and through which protocols. Equally, we should decide if we will allow other Internet users access to our network. A simple table, similar to that shown on the left, can help us plan the filters and make our overall security system more effective. For example, filtering within routers is not without cost. Filter processing is performed at the expense of overall router performance. Our filters therefore must be as concise as possible, and where we have control over processing order, we should try to ensure that the filter responsible for eventually discarding or forwarding the packet is processed as soon as possible. This will guarantee that a packet to be discarded or forwarded, will be processed with the minimum of overhead.

Assuming that the majority of traffic should be filtered, we need to enable filtering and set the default filter such that ALL packets are discarded. Of course, if the majority of traffic should be forwarded, then we should perform the opposite function and enable filtering with a default that allows all packets to pass. This now ensures that our traffic is either discarded or forwarded at our option. For example, we may wish to discard all traffic by default, and then allow only certain protocols between the specific hosts that we identify.

Typically, there will be certain hosts on the network that are major service providers – DNS servers, SMTP mail gateways, FTP servers and Telnet hosts. User workstations are only likely to need to make calls to Telnet, FTP, and WWW destinations. Filters can therefore be created allowing specific service requests to appropriate destinations.

In the next sections we shall look at the operation of major protocols and discuss how specific filters should be built for each, based upon our network of Figure 23-1. Always remember that filters should be as generic as possible, so that they apply to multiple protocols and are therefore more flexible.

23.2.1 Telnet Filters

In the following figure, we see how a Telnet connection is formed and destroyed between the PC at address 192.168.1.20, and the host system at address 172.16.8.63.

Many sites will not have any restrictions placed on outgoing Telnet calls. Thus, to enable an outgoing Telnet session, we merely need to allow the TCP protocol to pass where the Destination ports is 23 and the packet arrives at interface 1 (IF 1) – the local interface of the router. If we wish to restrict this type of access to only certain stations, then we shall need to further qualify our filter by defining certain IP Addresses as well.

By defining a filter in this way (assuming that the deafault action is to discard) we have allowed *outgoing* Telnet sessions while *incoming* sessions remain barred.

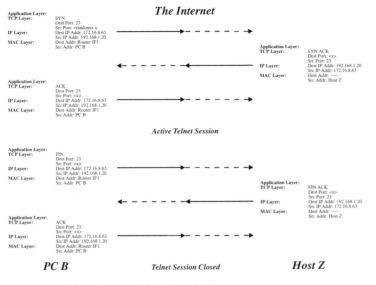

The Internet

Application Layer:
TCP Layer: SYN
Dest Port: 23
Src Port: <random> x
IP Layer: Dest IP Addr: 172.16.8.63
Src IP Addr: 192.168.1.20
MAC Layer: Dest Addr: Router IF1
Src Addr: PC B

Application Layer:
TCP Layer: SYN ACK
Dest Port: <x>
Src Port: 23
IP Layer: Dest IP Addr: 192.168.1.20
Src IP Addr: 172.16.8.63
MAC Layer: Dest Addr: -----
Src Addr: Host Z

Application Layer:
TCP Layer: ACK
Dest Port: 23
Src Port: <x>
IP Layer: Dest IP Addr: 172.16.8.63
Src IP Addr: 192.168.1.20
MAC Layer: Dest Addr: Router IF1
Src Addr: PC B

Active Telnet Session

Application Layer:
TCP Layer: FIN
Dest Port: 23
Src Port: <x>
IP Layer: Dest IP Addr: 172.16.8.63
Src IP Addr: 192.168.1.20
MAC Layer: Dest Addr: Router IF1
Src Addr: PC B

Application Layer:
TCP Layer: FIN ACK
Dest Port: <x>
Src Port: 23
IP Layer: Dest IP Addr: 192.168.1.20
Src IP Addr: 172.16.8.63
MAC Layer: Dest Addr: -----
Src Addr: Host Z

Application Layer:
TCP Layer: ACK
Dest Port: 23
Src Port: <x>
IP Layer: Dest IP Addr: 172.16.8.63
Src IP Addr: 192.168.1.20
MAC Layer: Dest Addr: Router IF1
Src Addr: PC B

PC B   *Telnet Session Closed*   **Host Z**

Figure 23-2: Telnet Session Establishment/Closure

To allow incoming Telnet sessions (which is generally not a good idea), we would then need to create a new filter such that TCP packets with a Destination Port of 23, arriving at the WAN interface (IF 2) of the router are also passed. Most commonly, such inbound access would be restricted, and we would allow access to only certain hosts from just a handful of trusted machines. Our filters would therefore have to be set accordingly.

One other *crucial* part of our network that must be considered in relation to Telnet is the Firewall Router itself. Most internetworking devices support a Telnet client that allows administrators to log in to them for management purposes. Thus, intruders must be stopped from gaining access to this key device or all our efforts will be in vain.

Typically, vendors use an *Access List* where the addresses of valid management stations are defined. Thus, the router itself will not accept incoming Telnet sessions from any device(s) not listed. In addition, it is normal for a degree of host level security to be implemented that requires users to identify themselves with either a name, a password, or both.

23.2.2   SMTP Filtering

When one Mail Server has information to send to another, it opens a TCP connection to it using Port 25. The actual call establishment and data transfer is almost identical to Telnet. Filtering is therefore treated in the same way, except in this case a filter should be employed that allows only the partner Mail Server to gain access.

23.2.3   FTP Filtering

FTP uses multiple calls making it difficult to control. Firstly, FTP uses a control session allowing the client user to send commands to, and receive responses from, the server. Data transfer sessions are then initiated to allow the movement of files between systems. Therein lies the problem. These Data Transfer sessions are normally initiated by the server leaving the client system with no control over which ports are used. The following figure shows a typical *incoming* FTP session where PC C makes a connection to Host X using TCP Destination port number 21_{10}.

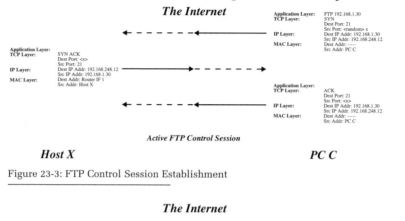

Figure 23-3: FTP Control Session Establishment

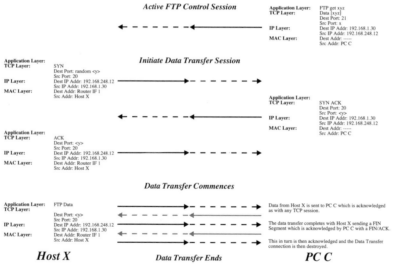

Figure 23-4: FTP Data Transfer Connection Establishment

Here we see the normal method of TCP session establishment resulting in the Control connection itself being set up. When the client then requests a file, the host (Host X) initiates a data transfer connection using a Source TCP port number of 20_{10} and a random Destination Port. This is shown in Figure 23-4 and assumes that the Control Session is already established. The problem is therefore evident. For the first part, we wish to allow *Control Session* access to our host, requiring the definition of several filters. One for IF 2 that permits packets

Creating a Secure Internet Environment

destined for our host with a destination TCP port of 21_{10} to pass, and a second for IF 1 that passes all traffic with a TCP Source Port of 21_{10}. The Data connection however will use a random destination port number making it impossible to track!

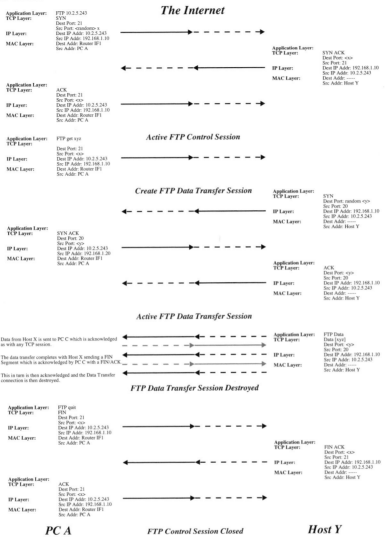

Figure 23-5: Example of an Outgoing FTP Session

To overcome this situation, we must now consider this data connection and we find that we have a similar situation to the Control Session. Firstly, a filter for IF 1 must be defined that allows packets with a source port of 20 and a source address of Host X to pass. Secondly, we must also define a filter for IF 2 that allows packets with a destination port of 20 to pass. If we are not careful though, we could open an unwanted portal from our network. To close this, we must define yet another filter for IF 1 that this time prevents TCP sessions using a destination port of 20 being established. Hence, one way connection establishment is assured.

Finally, although not shown in the figure, the user will eventually quit the FTP application and the Control Session will be destroyed using the same sequence of events as that shown in the Telnet example.

Next we shall consider an *outgoing* call made from our network. In this case, PC A makes a call to Host Y. The resultant connections and traffic are then shown in Figure 23-5. In this case, the filters are similar but reversed. Firstly, we must allow outgoing calls that use TCP Port 21 through IF 1 of the router. Since we will not know the addresses of the remote hosts, we must also allow any Destination IP Address to pass. Secondly, since we will need to establish Data Transfer sessions, we must also allow connections with a Destination Port of 20 to any device. If we do not wish to allow incoming sessions though, we must discard all packets that arrive at IF 2 with a Destination Port of 20.

Finally, it is worth considering the use of FTP *Passive Opens*. Although not supported by all hosts, this implementation of FTP does have the effect of allowing the client to make both the command and data connections. The local Network Administrator therefore has greater control over the filtering required.

For example, in Figure 23-6, our local PC (PC B) makes a connection to an Internet host (Host Z) with the following results:

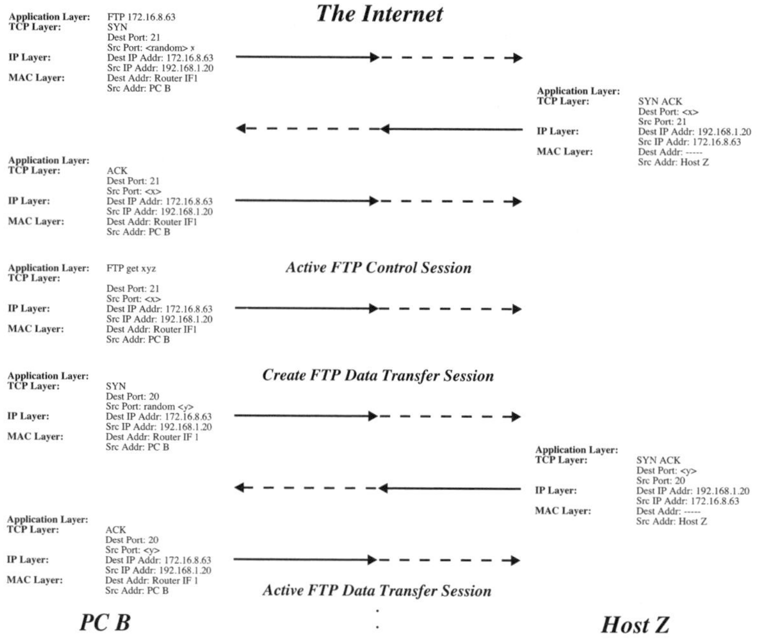

Figure 23-6: FTP Passive Open Example

In this example, although it does not show the connections being destroyed, it does show our local host is in control of both sessions. This method of FTP

Creating a Secure Internet Environment

then maintains the functionality of our network and Internet connections without sacrificing security.

23.2.4 DNS Filtering

You will recall that for DNS Zone Transfers (where *primary* and *backup* servers synchronize their tables), TCP is used with Source *and* Destination port number 53. For normal DNS queries we use UDP Destination Port 53 (and usually Source Port 53 also). Here, for simplicity, we shall assume that the primary and secondary DNS servers are not split across the Firewall since this would cause unnecessary complication at this stage. However, because DNS uses UDP (and UDP is easy to spoof) any filters implemented must be extremely explicit.

Figure 23-7 shows a simple DNS transaction where an outgoing DNS query is made from one DNS server within our local network, to another on the other side of the Firewall. This situation is common within the DNS and might be required for a recursive lookup.

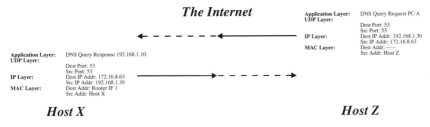

Figure 23-7: Example of an Outgoing DNS Query

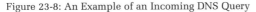

Here, the filter on IF 1 should allow the query to pass by specifying the Source and Destination port numbers (53), the protocol in use (UDP), and the address of the *internal* DNS server (the Source Address). Equally, the filter on IF 2 would be of a similar nature and again specify the address of the internal server. In this case though, the address would be specified as the Destination address.

For Incoming queries the situation is again similar with an external DNS server querying our internal server. Figure 23-8 shows a DNS server (Host Z), querying our local host (Host X) about the address of PC A.

Figure 23-8: An Example of an Incoming DNS Query

Within DNS, we should already be aware of the address of the external server. Thus, these filters would be similar to those described previously except that the filter on IF 1 would specify the *internal* server as a Destination address, and on IF 2, as a Source address. The major problem now is that anybody can query your internal server and therefore ascertain the addresses of all local devices.

This problem is recognized and much work is continuing in this area. One solution is to split the entire DNS name space such that an entire DNS is created internally, and a partial DNS is created externally. Internal devices then query their internal DNS, which may have to forward those queries as before. Internet queries however, are handled by the external DNS servers which, through their tables, are then restricted to only provide information on those devices which are allowed to be accessed by Internet hosts.

23.2.5 ICMP Filtering

ICMP is required to ensure the correct operation of IP. Carrying redirection and network reachability information as it does, this protocol is a required element of the Internet Protocol itself. Figure 23-9 shows our client station (PC B) attempting to connect to Host Y. In this example, the router receives a Destination Port Unreachable message indicating that the host is incapable of processing this protocol for whatever reason.

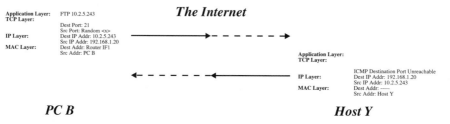

Figure 23-9: Destination Unreachable (Port) Example

Similarly the next example shows where a network has become unreachable. In this case it is our router that sends the ICMP Network Unreachable message.

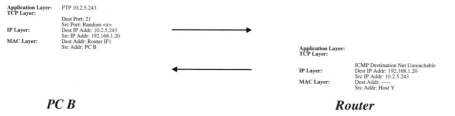

Figure 23-10: Destination Unreachable (Network) Example

One worry however, is that intruders might send ICMP Echo Requests (Pings) to our network in order to determine what IP addresses are in use and then map the network. Sadly, without extremely complex filters, this situation is difficult to avoid. We will almost certainly want to be able to originate Echo Requests targeted at Internet hosts, but we will probably want to discard any such requests from entering our network.

Creating a Secure Internet Environment

Figure 23-11 illustrates the effects of issuing ICMP Echo Requests by showing PC A sending an Echo Request to Host Z, and the corresponding response from the host.

In general, ICMP does not present a major security risk provided that all of the other filters are correctly implemented. True, a malicious user can determine which devices are on-line, but if we are blocking access by protocol and through correct host administration, security is still assured.

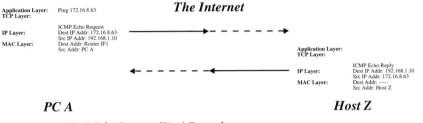

Figure 23-11: ICMP Echo Request (Ping) Example

23.2.6 SNMP Filtering and Management

SNMP can present a major risk to our network since most internetworking devices today can be totally re-configured using SNMP. Equally, most devices will accept an incoming Telnet session to a management port. We have already said that with this latter mode of management we may have no risk provided that the Telnet filter is correctly implemented. However, the manner in which devices handle an incoming Telnet session to themselves is implementation specific and we cannot rely on this.

As we have already said, most vendors implement some sort of Access List to limit who can Telnet to their devices. As such, it is worth checking with the vendor as to exactly what security measures exist. SNMP however, is another thing all together.

As we saw in Chapter 20, SNMP uses UDP – a protocol with no checks and therefore easy to forge. In addition, the current version of SNMP (version 1) provides no encryption and only a *loose* authentication technique. Thus, since it would be undesirable to have outsiders sending SNMP packets into our network, we will have to block them by UDP port number.

Although this will stop SNMP packets from entering our network, we must consider the possibility that we may have multiple sites connected through the Internet. Here if we wish to have a centralized department administering our network, blocking all SNMP packets may not be the solution. In this case we must now rely upon the SNMP *Community* strings that can be programmed into the device and the ability to configure a limited number of management stations from which SNMP requests will be serviced. Again, most devices today allow the configuration of management station addresses, thereby restricting who we will accept SNMP *Get* and *Set* commands from. Alternatively, returning to the Firewall, we could program a filter that only passes packets that carry SNMP from certain hosts.

23.3 Filters Types

Most routers allow filtering based upon the following criteria:

- The IP Protocol
  This is fundamental of course, since without the ability to filter on IP traffic, no security in an IP environment would be possible.

- TCP/UDP Destination Port Number
  The Destination Port for either TCP or UDP is used to identify the application or process to which the packet should be directed. For example, Telnet *listens* on Port 23 by default. Thus all Telnet traffic will generally be sent to this TCP Destination Port.

- TCP/UDP Source Port Number
  The Source Port Number identifies which TCP or UDP application or process sent the packet and therefore the return address. Source ports however, are normally allocated dynamically therefore making it difficult to filter based upon this information.

- The TCP SYN Flag
  When TCP connections are made, the two device involved will synchronize their sequence numbers through a process known as the *Three Way Handshake*. During this process, the station initiating the connection transmits its sequence number in a TCP Segment with the SYN Flag set. The response to this, is for the receiver to send an acknowledgement of the sender's sequence number indicated by the ACK Flag, and to send its own sequence number. Thus, the receiver sends a packet with both the SYN and ACK flags set.

  Many routers can detect these flags and filter accordingly. For example, if we wish to stop all incoming connections, we can discard all incoming packets that have *only* the SYN Flag set. This still allows outgoing connections, since the response to our SYN Segment would be a Segment that has both the SYN and ACK Flags set. Conversely, if we wish to block outgoing connections (but allow incoming connections), we could either block outgoing packets that have only the SYN Flag set, or block incoming packets that have any combinations of Flags that include SYN.

- IP Destination Address
  The IP Destination Address obviously identifies to which station(s) the packet is directed. Filtering incoming packets based upon this address therefore defines which stations on the local network can receive packets from the Internet. Equally, filtering outgoing packets by Destination restricts the Internet hosts to which our local hosts can connect.

- IP Source Address
  In just the same way that the Destination Address specifies the station(s) to which a packet is directed, the Source Address identifies the sending station. Incoming filters based upon Source Address can therefore identify specific Internet hosts that are allowed to access the local network. Similarly, outgoing filters based upon Source Address can be used to identify which of our local hosts may communicate with Internet hosts.

The actual order in which filters are processed and the precedence associated with each is obviously implementation specific. The documentation supplied by the router vendor should therefore be consulted before filters are implemented. One thing should be clear though and that is filtering does place a load (no matter how small) on the router itself. Thus, filters must be made as generic as possible in order to avoid duplicates.

23.3.1 IP Fragmentation and the SYN Flag

We saw above that some routers can be configured to discard packets that have the SYN Flag set and therefore prevent incoming connections. There is however, a subtle problem that must be addressed or at least highlighted since a potential loop hole in our secure environment exists.

Consider the case where a malicious user wishes to make a TCP connection to our local host system (Host X), but the router is discarding incoming TCP packets with the SYN Flag set. On the face of it our network appears to be secure. However, by generating special small packets that appear as IP Fragments, our router can be fooled.

Consider Figure 23-12. In this example the initial IP Datagram that contains the TCP SYN has been fragmented such that the first fragment contains the minimum amount of data (that is the first 8 octets of the TCP header). The TCP SYN Flag, which is contained in the second fragment will almost certainly be passed allowing the connection to be established. Unless the router is capable of detecting such events, Internet users can now access our local host.

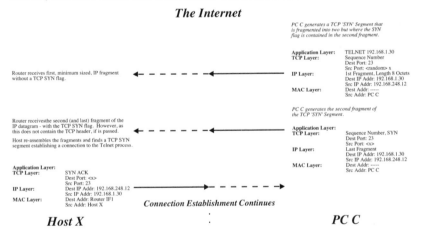

Figure 23-12: An Example of a Fragmented TCP SYN Segment

23.4 Other Considerations

So far we have considered the case of the Firewall router, however our concerns should not stop here. We all assume that our local networks are reasonably secure, but in truth there is nothing to stop our users from introducing unauthorized inter-networking devices and therefore obtain knowledge of our network. In short, we should never be complacent about the threat from within.

Equally, many companies today rely on a number of their employees either working from home, or spending a great deal of time out of the office. These people, along with other network users need to access network resources and to remain in contact with their colleagues, normally through dial-up lines. This then also represents a threat to network security.

23.4.1 Unauthorized Routers

In Chapters 9 to 13 we examined various routing protocols. For the Routing Information Protocol (RIP) Version 1, we saw that updates were passed through broadcasts and that no authentication was possible. A user introducing another router into our local network can therefore cause havoc with legitimate routers and potentially cause hours of network downtime. RIP II on the other hand, supports authentication and therefore overcomes this problem provided that it is implemented correctly, and that all routers participate.

OSPF has always supported authentication. Users therefore can cause little damage in an OSPF environment unless the router was configured without passwords. This is because routers configured with authentication passwords ignore those without. Over all then, RIP II or OSPF provide safer environments than say RIP.

23.4.2 Dial In Access

Many companies today employ staff that work either from home or spend a great deal of time on the road. These people typically dial in to the office network to update files, send and retrieve eMail and so on. Here there is another potential loophole in our security then since these, typically asynchronous, ports are open to the public telephone network.

In the case of the home worker or those people that always dial in from a specific number, the situation can be overcome by having the port dial the user back. This also allows for centralized billing since the cost of the call is also billed directly to the company. Where we have a user on the road, or one that may choose to dial in from anywhere in the world, this may not be possible. These users may choose to call from hotels and other establishments that have their own switchboards. Thus, dial-back is prohibited as an option. Clearly some other method of securing the ports must therefore be found.

In these cases, the Link Layer protocol must be used to provide the added security that we require. In Chapter 22 we saw how the Point-to-Point protocol (PPP) optionally provides authentication through the Password Authentication Protocol (PAP) and the Challenge Handshake Authentication Protocol (CHAP). So, by implementing a Password Authentication scheme, we can be assured that only bona-fide users have access through dial-in lines.

23.5 Summary

In this chapter, we have discussed various aspects of Internet security by pointing out some of the pitfalls and shortcomings with the Internet protocols. No network can be made *totally* secure since somebody will always try to break any system that you devise. In fact, many people consider the prospect of breaking security a challenge that cannnot be missed and although they may mean no harm can leave a security system in tatters.

We can make their task as difficult and frustrating as possible by implementing reasonably simple procedures and applying a degree of common sense to our network design. We have seen how, by using elements of the protocol suite itself, we can block traffic and therefore enhance ordinary host level security. Equally, it is hoped that this chapter has provided some *food for thought* about the types of protocols used in a normal network. The important point however, is that we should be able to control access without impairing functionality.

IP Version 6

If we have to look for limitations in the Internet Protocol Suite, one must surely be addressing. In today's networks the old 32 bit address is most woefully inadequate and urgently needs to be replaced by something that will cope with the explosive growth that is expected to continue. So what will it be?

The current thinking is that version 4 of IP (the current version, and that described in Chapters 4 and 5) should be replaced by version 6, or IP Next Generation (IPng) as it is sometimes called. But what are the implications of this and how will it operate in mixed V4/V6 environments? This chapter then details the IP Version 6 header, it's extensions and the changes required to ICMP.

24.1 IP Version 6 Enhancements

IP version 6 provides significant enhancements over the current, version 4, implementation. RFC 1883 defines these improvements in the following 5 areas:

- **Extended Addressing capability**
  Version 6 increases the IP address size from 32 to 128 bits. This address is then split into a greater number of hierarchical levels than merely Network ID, possible Subnet ID, and Host ID. In addition, Multicast routing is improved with a *scope* field and a new address type, the so-called *anycast* address. This new address is being defined so that a packet can be sent to any one of a group of nodes.

  Finally, there is no broadcast address for version 6. The concept of broadcasting with IP is now being superseded by multicasting.

- **Simplified Header Format**
  Some of the fields found in the IPv4 header have either been removed or made optional. This has the effect of reducing the number of CPU cycles associated with processing the majority of IP datagrams and also reduces the amount of bandwidth consumed.

- **Improved Extensions and Options**
  The way that IP options are encoded has been improved to allow for greater efficiency when forwarding, and provides a more flexible approach to new options in the future.

- **Flow Labelling**

  A concept of labelling packets as belonging to a particular *traffic flow* has been introduced. This enables the sender to request special handling such as a non default quality of service and/or real time service.

- **Authentication and Privacy**

  Additional extensions have been added that allow authentication, data integrity checking, and confidentiality although these are not discussed here.

24.2 IPv6 Addressing

As we have said, IP version 6 extends the addressing capability from 32 to 128 bits although, initially only approximately 15% of the address space has been allocated. In addition, version 6 has removed the concept of broadcasting but introduced the new concept of an *anycast* address. Address types are described below:

- **Unicast Address**

  Any packets sent to a unicast address are always delivered only to the interface identified by that address.

- **Anycast Address**

  An *Anycast* address is an identifier for a set of addresses typically belonging to different nodes. A packet sent to an anycast address is then delivered to one of the interfaces identified by that address. The interface chosen is normally the nearest as defined by the routing protocol in use.

- **Multicast Address**

  A Multicast address (as outlined in Chapter 14) is one that identifies a number of interfaces that will typically belong to different nodes. Packets sent to a multicast address are delivered to all interfaces identified by that address.

The actual ways in which addresses are assigned is similar to that used with Version 4 in that addresses are assigned to interfaces and not nodes. Equally, an interface may be assigned multiple addresses of any type (unicast, anycast, or multicast), and routers may use un-numbered interfaces for point-to-point links.

24.2.1 Representing Version 6 Addresses

You will recall from Chapter 4 that it is normal to represent the 32 version 4 address in what is known as dotted decimal notation. The main reason for this is that it would be impossible to attempt to remember long strings of binary numbers. Finding a method of representing 128 bit addresses is therefore both more difficult and most definitely required. RFC 1884 suggests three basic methods for representing addresses as follows:

- **Hexadecimal Representation**

  This is the preferred method of representing the address where the address is divided into 16 bit words and these are then represented by their hexadecimal equivalents with leading zeroes suppressed. The colon (:) is then used between each 16 bit value. Examples are:

19BD:3021:2538:B9D1:22C3:7719:8BD2:6836

A17B:1234:0:0:82FE:15BF:6697:7AC2

- **Suppressed Zeroes Representation**
  Some addresses may have long sequences of zeroes embedded, making them difficult to write efficiently. In this case, the zeroes may be removed and replaced simply by a double colon (::). For example:

1080:0:0:0:8:800:200C:417A	Becomes	1080::8:800:200C:417A
FF01:0:0:0:0:0:0:43	Becomes	FF01::43
0:0:0:0:0:0:0:1	Becomes	::1
0:0:0:0:0:0:0:0	Becomes	::

- **Mixed IPv4 and IPv6 Addressing**
  Where there are mixed IPv4/IPv6 nodes, addresses can be expressed as follows:

0:0:0:0:0:0:192.168.12.25   Or alternatively, where compressed;   ::192.168.12.25

Just as in version 4, the Class of address is defined by the leading bits. In version 6, the type of address is also defined in the same way. Table 24-1 shows the initial allocation of addresses as defined in RFC 1884.

Table 24-1: IPv6 Address Allocation

Allocation	Prefix (binary)
Reserved	0000 0000
Unassigned	0000 0001
Reserved for NSAP Allocation	0000 001
Reserved for IPX Allocation	0000 010
Unassigned	0000 011
Unassigned	0000 1
Unassigned	0001
Unassigned	001
Provider Based Unicast Address	010
Unassigned	011
Reserved for Geographic Based Unicast Addresses	100
Unassigned	101
Unassigned	110
Unassigned	1110
Unassigned	1111 0
Unassigned	1111 10
Unassigned	1111 110
Unassigned	1111 1110 0
Link Local Use Addresses	1111 1110 10
Site Local Use Addresses	1111 1110 11
Multicast Addresses	1111 1111

From the table, you will see that multicast addresses are distinguished from unicast addresses by the high order bits. A value of FF_{16} ($1111\ 1111_2$) identifies a multicast, while any other value indicates a unicast. Anycast addresses are in fact indistinguishable from unicast addresses and are taken from the unicast address space. Examples of these different types of addresses can be found in the following sections.

24.2.2 Unicast Addresses

Several different forms of unicast address exist such as the Provider Based Unicast Address, the NSAP Address, IPX Address etc. When looking at unicast addresses then, we must consider what the host is actually capable of doing. For example, the host itself may have no idea about the internal structure of a version 6 address. In this case, the address is merely a 128 bit address with no integral heirachy. Similarly, a host with some little sophistication may have knowledge of subnet prefixes. Here the address would have the high order bits used to define the subnet and the low order bits used to define the interface.

Most commonly though it is envisaged that the address will include a prefix that identifies the *Subscriber*, a *Subnet ID*, and an *Interface ID* as shown in Figure 24-1.

Subscriber Prefix	Subnet ID	Interface ID
n bits	80-n bits	48 bits

Figure 24-1: Unicast Address (Example 1)

The 48 bit *Interface ID* is the IEEE 802 MAC Address which allows us to realize certain benefits. Firstly, we are assured of a unique address globally. Secondly, we can achieve a level of self configuration since a host can now listen to say a router advertisement, and then configure itself to the same subnet by using its MAC Address as the *Interface ID*.

A second form of address (shown in Figure 24-2) is where the site might require a more hierarchical structure to its addressing. In this case, we can divide the *Subnet ID* into an *Area ID* and a *Subnet ID*.

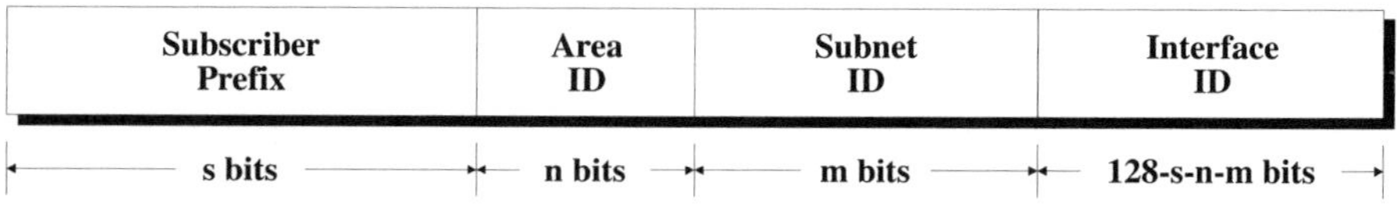

Subscriber Prefix	Area ID	Subnet ID	Interface ID
s bits	n bits	m bits	128-s-n-m bits

Figure 24-2: Unicast Address (Example 2)

Notice that in this latter example, the *Interface ID* need not be 48 bits in length. In this case, part of the space occupied by the *Interface ID* could be used to allow for additional layers of heirarchy within the organization. Here we would require some other administratively created scheme for Interface ID allocation.

It should be noted that two addresses are reserved.

- **0:0:0:0:0:0:0:0**

  This is known as the *Unspecified Address* and must never be assigned to any node. This address is used to indicate that an address is yet to be assigned, or could be used in the source address field of an IPv6 datagram sent by a host before it has learned its real address.

- **0:0:0:0:0:0:0:1**
  This is the *Loopback Address* and is used by a host to send datagrams to itself. As such, this address is never used outside the host.

24.2.3 Version 6 Addresses with Embedded Version 4 Addresses

Two types of address exist for version 4 hosts to co-exist in version 6 environments. The first type is used where we would want to *tunnel* IPv6 packets over an IPv4 infrastructure. In this case, the address has the high 96 bits set to zero, and the low 32 bits carry an *IPv4 address*. This is shown in Figure 24-3.

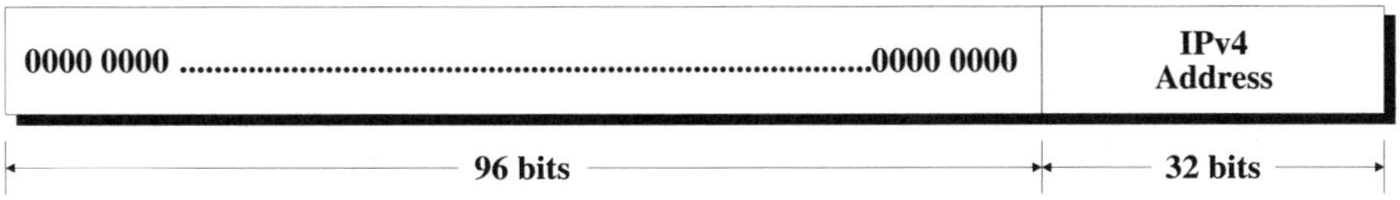

0000 0000 ....0000 0000	IPv4 Address
96 bits	32 bits

Figure 24-3: Address Type (Tunnelled IPv6)

In the second case, we are able to represent a host that does not support IPv6 (a so-called IPv4-only node). Here, we have the high order 80 bits set to zero, a 16 bit field of ones, and the *IPv4 Address* defined as the low 32 bits. Figure 24-4 shows this.

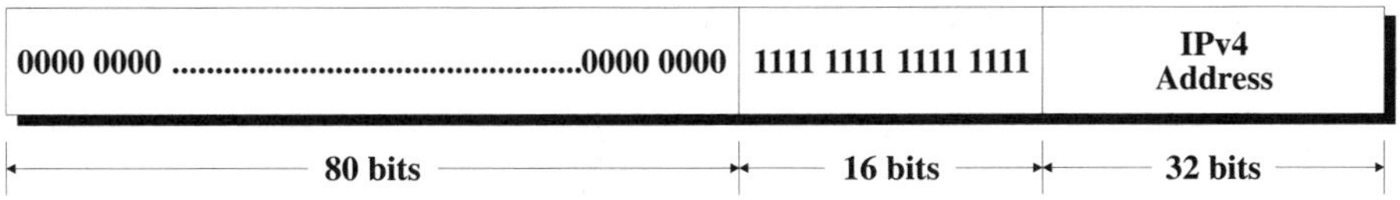

0000 0000 ....0000 0000	1111 1111 1111 1111	IPv4 Address
80 bits	16 bits	32 bits

Figure 24-4: Address Type (IPv4-Only Host)

24.2.4 Provider Based Global Unicast Addresses

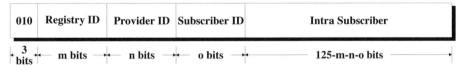

010	Registry ID	Provider ID	Subscriber ID	Intra Subscriber
3 bits	m bits	n bits	o bits	125-m-n-o bits

Figure 24-5: Provider Based Global Unicast Addresses

The format of the Provider Based Global Unicast Address is shown in Figure 24-5 and allows for a portion of the address to be assigned to registries who can then sub-divide this space and assign portions to providers. The *Registry ID* is used to identify the particular registry. The *Provider ID* identifies a specific provider, and the *Subscriber ID* is used to identify a specific subscriber attached to the Provider.

The *Intra Subscriber* portion of the address will probably be subdivided into a Subnet ID and an Interface ID. In any event, this portion of the address is defined by the individual subscriber.

24.2.5 Local Use IPv6 Unicast Addresses

Two types of Local Use Unicast Addresses exist. Firstly, there is the *Link-Local* address as shown in Figure 24-6, which is used by a single link only. This can then be used where there is no router, where auto-address configuration is used, or where neighbor discovery is used. The one golden rule is that routers must *never* forward packets that have a link-local source address.

1111111010
0000 0000.............................0000 0000
Interface ID
10 bits
n bits
118-n bits

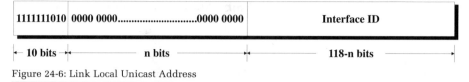

Figure 24-6: Link Local Unicast Address

The second type of local address is referred to as the *Site Local* address and is shown in Figure 24-7. These addresses are used by organizations that do not have a connection to the Internet. However, if the network should ever be connected to the Internet, then the *Site Local prefix* can be replaced by a *Subscriber Prefix.* This Subscriber Prefix then comprises all high order bits up to and including the Subscriber ID from the Provider Based Global Unicast Address described above.

In a similar vein to the Link Local address, routers must never forward packets that use *Site Local* source address outside of the site.

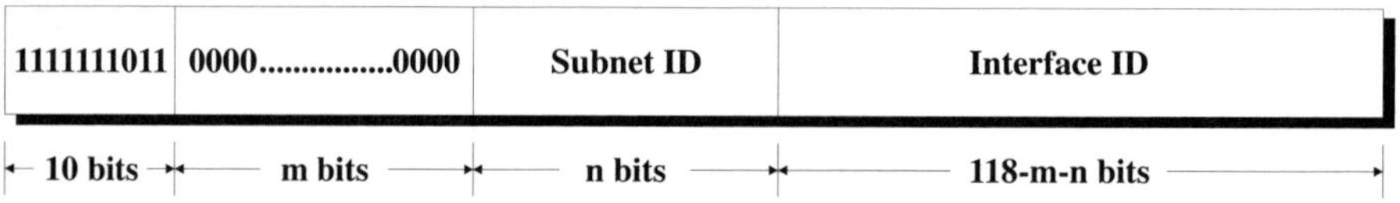

1111111011
0000...............0000
Subnet ID
Interface ID
10 bits
m bits
n bits
118-m-n bits

Figure 24-7: Site Local Unicast Address

24.2.6 The Anycast Address

The *Anycast* address is a new enhancement to Version 6. The anycast address can be assigned to more than one interface (typically belonging to different nodes) but a packet sent to an anycast address will always be delivered to the interface that is nearest, as defined by the specific routing protocol in use.

In use, the anycast address is actually the same as a unicast address. However, when such an address is assigned to multiple interfaces (making it an anycast), the interfaces *must* be configured in such a way that they know they are an anycast. In addition, two restrictions apply, namely, that an Anycast address should *not* be used as a source address, and that Anycast addresses should *only* be assigned to routers.

24.2.7 Multicast Addresses

As with version 4, IP version 6 *multicast* addresses are used to identify a group of nodes. Once again, like version 4, a single node may also be a member of any number of multicast groups. Figure 24-8 shows the format of version 6 multicast addresses.

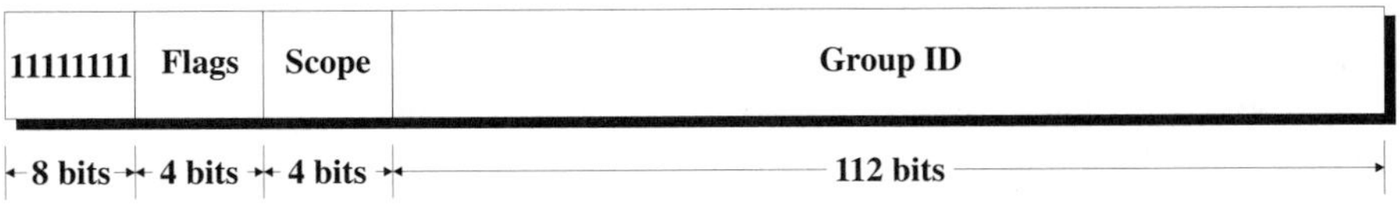

11111111	Flags	Scope	Group ID

⟵ 8 bits ⟶ ⟵ 4 bits ⟶ ⟵ 4 bits ⟶ | ⟵————————— 112 bits —————————⟶

Figure 24-8: Multicast Addresses

The 4 bit *Flags* field is organized with the highest order 3 bits reserved and the lowest order bit meaning *Transient*. This can therefore be described as 000T. Where the T bit is set on, this indicates that the group is a *transient* group (or non permanently assigned group). Where this bit is off, the group is *permanently* (globally) assigned.

Table 24-2: Assigned Scope Values

Scope	Description
0	Reserved
1	Node Local Scope
2	Link Local Scope
3	Unassigned
4	Unassigned
5	Site Local Scope
6	Unassigned
7	Unassigned
8	Organization Local Scope
9	Unassigned
A	Unassigned
B	Unassigned
C	Unassigned
D	Unassigned
E	Global Scope
F	Reserved

The *Scope* field (also 4 bits) is used to *limit* the scope of the multicast group. The 4 bits are then used as described by Table 24-2. For example, if we have the multicast address FF05:0:0:0:0:0:0:23, this would mean all members of group 23 are at the same site as the sender of the packet. Equally, if we had an address of FF0E:0:0:0:0:0:0:23. This would be taken to mean all members of group 23 in the Internet.

The use of the Transient flag is independent of the scope but, addresses that are identified as being transient have meaning only within the *Scope*. For example, FF15:0:0:0:0:0:0:23 at one site would bear no relationship to that address used at another site.

Multicast addresses which are permanently assigned (i.e. those beginning FF0x) but with a null Group ID are all reserved. In addition, several other groups are also reserved for specific usage, in particular FF01:0:0:0:0:0:0:1 and FF02:0:0:0:0:0:0:1 are reserved as the *All Nodes Multicast Addresses* and FF01:0:0:0:0:0:0:2 and FF02:0:0:0:0:0:0:2 are reserved as the *All Routers Multicast Addresses*.

24.3 IP Version 6 Header Format

As we have already said, the format of the version 6 header is much simpler than that of version 4. Figure 24-9 shows the general header format which is then described in the following text.

The 4 bit *Version* field has the same meaning as it did with version 4, in that it defines the version of IP being carried and therefore the format of the packet. This is now 6. The *Priority* field (4 bits) defines the priority of this packet relative to other packets from the same source. Values for this field in the range of 0 to 7 are used to indicate the priority of traffic for which the source host is providing congestion control (i.e. traffic that backs off in response to congestion). Table 24-3 then defines this traffic. Priority values of 8 to F are used to define non congestion controlled traffic. The lowest priority (8), is then used for those packets that the source is most willing to have discarded, and the highest (F), that which the sender is least willing to have discarded.

0	4	8	12	16	20	24	28	31

Version	Priority	Flow Label			
Payload Length			Next Header		Hop Limit
Source Address					
Destination Address					

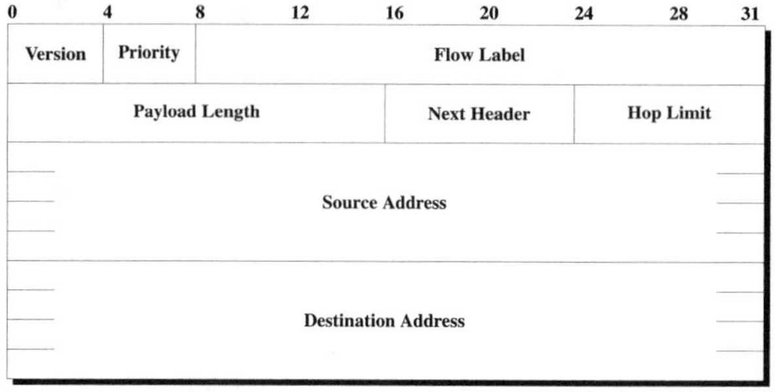

Figure 24-9: IP Version 6 Header Format

Table 24-3: Priority Values – Congestion Control

Priority	Description
0	Uncharacterized Traffic
1	Filler Traffic (e.g. news)
2	Unattended Data Transfer (e.g. Mail)
3	Reserved
4	Attended Bulk Transfer (e.g. FTP, NFS)
5	Reserved
6	Interactive Traffic (e.g. Telnet)
7	Interactive Control Traffic (e.g. Routing Protocols, SNMP)

The 24 bit *Flow Label* field is used by the source to identify packets for which special handling may be required. For example, the source may request that for a particular job, the packets are all handled with a special quality of service. In this case, all packets for that job will be labelled with the same *Flow Control Label*.

The 16 bit *Payload Length* field is used to specify the amount of data that follows the header. The *Next Header* field (8 bits) identifies the type of header that immediately follows the IP version 6 header. This field is the same as the version 4 *Protocol* field and indeed even uses the same protocol values for upper layer protocols. However, this field is also used to identify potential *Extension Headers* as described in the next section.

The *Hop Limit* is synonymous with the normal interpretation of the Time to Live field in the version 4 header in that it contains a value that is decremented by 1 for each node that forwards the packet. When this value reaches zero, the packet is then discarded as before. Finally, the 128 bit *Source* and *Destination* Addresses identify the source and destination hosts.

24.4 Extension Headers

As we have seen in the previous section, the version 6 header is much simpler than its version 4 counterpart. In truth though, much of this is because unlike version 4, version 6 packets can also carry a number of *header extensions* to indicate fragmentation information and routing information amongst other things. Figure 24-10 shows examples of how the IP version 6 headers might be arranged.

In general, extension headers are only examined by the destination node(s) and they are not examined by nodes en-route. The one exception to this is the Hop-by-Hop Options header that carries information that must be examined by all nodes en-route, and the destination itself. As such if the Hop-by-Hop extension header is present (indicated by a value of zero in the *Next Header* field of the version 6 header), it must immediately follow the IPv6 header.

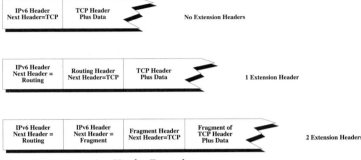

Figure 24-10: Extension Header Examples

The extension headers themselves determine whether or not the next header should be processed, thus extension headers must be processed in the order in which they appear. When processing extension headers, if the node finds a header that is unrecognizable, the packet is discarded and it sends an ICMP Parameter Problem packet. In general, the recommendation for the ordering of headers is as follows, and with the exception of the *Destination Options Header*, no header should appear more than once.

```
IPv6 Header
Hop-by-Hop Options Header
Destination Options Header
Routing Header
Fragment Header
Authentication Header
Encapsulation Security Payload Header
Destination Options Header      (where a second instance of this header is
                                present, this should only be processed by
                                the final destination of the packet).
Upper Layer Header
```

24.4.1 Options

Both the *Hop-by-Hop* and *Destination Options* Headers can carry a variable number of options encoded as a Type, Length, and Value. Figure 24-11 then shows this general form.

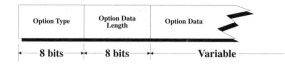

Figure 24-11: Option Format – General Form

The 8 bit Option Type field is encoded in such a way that the action to be taken if the option is not recognized, is determined from the highest order two bits. The third highest order bit is then used to specify whether the data associated with the option is allowed to change en-route. Table 24-4 shows the encoding of these bits.

Table 24-4: Option Type Encoding

Option Type Bits	Description
00xxxxxx	Skip over this option and continue processing the header
01xxxxxx	Discard the packet
10xxxxxx	Discard the packet and send an ICMP Parameter Problem message to the source
11xxxxxx	Discard the packet and send an ICMP Parameter Problem message to the source but only if the destination address was not a Multicast address
xx0xxxxx	Option Data does not change en-route
xx1xxxxx	Option Data may change en-route

8 octet alignment must be maintained thus, it is possible that options may require padding. There are two such types of padding options known simply as *Pad1*, and *PadN*. In the case of *Pad1* padding, a single octet of zero is placed in the options area of the header. No length or value fields are used.

Where more than one octet of padding is required, the *PadN* option is used. In this case, the *Option Type* is 1 (00000001) and the *Option Data Length* field is set to N-2 (where N is the number of padding octets). The *Option Data* then carries N-2 octets of zeroes.

24.4.2 Hop-by-Hop Options Header

The *Hop-by-Hop* options header is used to carry additional information that must be examined at every node en-route. The format of this options header is shown in Figure 24-12.

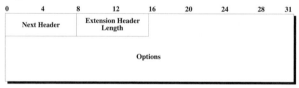

Figure 24-12: Hop-by-Hop Options Header

The *Next Header* field (8 bits) identifies the type of header that immediately follows this header. As we have already said, the value of this field will be the same as those used by IPv4. The 8 bit *Extension Header Length* field is the length of the header specified in 8 octet units but excluding the first 8 octets (i.e. n-1). The *Options* field is variable length and then defines the options that apply. Besides the *Pad1* and *PadN* options described earlier, the *Hop-by-Hop* extension header also supports one more option known as the *Jumbo Payload* option. This option, used to send packets with payloads greater than 65,535 octets (64k) is then shown in Figure 24-13.

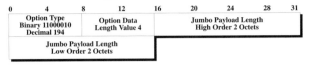

Figure 24-13: Jumbo Payload Option

The *Jumbo Payload Length* field (4 octets) is used to indicate the length of the packet in octets but excluding the IPv6 Header. Where this option is used, the *Payload Length* field in the IPv6 header must be set to 0 to indicate that it is not specifying the length.

24.4.3 Routing Header

The use of the *Routing Header* is similar in operation to the *Source Routing* options found in version 4. This header then defines a list of one or more intermediate nodes that must be visited en-route to the destination. The *Routing Header* is identified by a *Next Header* value of 43 in the preceding header and the format is shown in Figure 24-14.

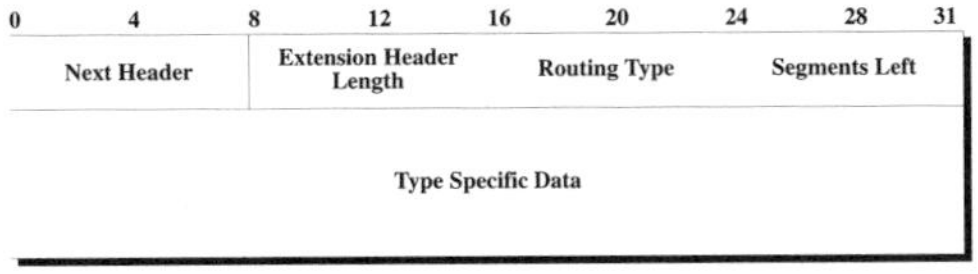

0 4	8 12	16 20	24 28 31
Next Header	Extension Header Length	Routing Type	Segments Left
Type Specific Data			

Figure 24-14: Routing Header General Format

The *Next Header* and *Extension Header Length* fields have the same meaning as before in that they identify the next header that is listed and the length of this header. The *Routing Type* field (8 bits) identifies the type of routing header that is present (for example *routing type 0* as defined below). The *Segments Left* field then defines the number of explicitly listed nodes that must still be visited before reaching the eventual destination of the packet. Finally, the *Type Specific Data* is a variable length field the format of which is determined solely by the *Routing Type* field.

The *Type 0 Routing Header* basically allows the source host to identify the hosts that must be visited along the route. The format of this extension header is shown in Figure 24-15 and can be described as follows.

The *Strict/Loose Bit Map* is a 24 bit map that indicates for each segment of the route whether or not the next destination must be a neighbor of the preceding address or not. If the bit is set on, then this indicates that *Strict Source Routing* is in use and that the next destination must be a neighbor. Where the bit is off, then

Loose Source Routing is assumed and the next destination need not be a neighbor. *Addresses 1 to n* then define the addresses of nodes that must be visited.

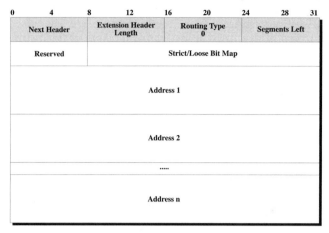

Figure 24-15: Route Type 0 Routing Header

24.4.4 Fragment Header

With version 4, fragmentation information is part of the IP header. In version 6, this functionality has been removed. Also, fragmentation in version 4 takes place at intermediate routing nodes. In version 6 however, any fragmentation required takes place at the source station only. No intermediate nodes may fragment packets en-route.

Where fragmentation is necessary to deliver a packet, the source station uses a *Fragment Header* extension that is identified by the value 44 in the immediately preceding header. The format of the Fragment Header is then as shown in Figure 24-16.

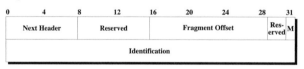

Figure 24-16: Fragment Header

Essentially, the Fragment Header provides the same functions as the *fragmentation* fields in the Version 4 header. The 13 bit *Fragment Offset* field is again used to identify the offset (in 8 octet units) of the data that follows this header relative to the start of the fragmentable part of the original packet. The *Identification* field is used to identify fragments that belong together, and the *M* flag is used to indicate the existence of more fragments. Notice though, that there is no "*Do Not Fragment*" flag. This is superfluous in version 6 since it is the source station that decides whether fragmentation is necessary and intermediate routing hosts are no longer allowed to fragment packets.

24.4.5 Destination Options Header

The *Destination Options Header* is only ever used to carry information that should be examined by a destination node. This option, identified by a value of 60 in the preceding header then has the *Next Header* field, the *Extension Header Length* field, and a variable length *Options* field. To date, only the *Pad1* and *PadN* options are allowed, however through this header any other option could be encoded.

24.4.6 No Next Header

Where there is no next header, then the *Next Header* field indicates a value of 59. This value is therefore valid in both an IPv6 header and any Extension Header.

24.5 IP Version 6 and ICMP

Because IPv6 introduces many changes to the way in which IP operates, it naturally follows that the *Internet Control Message Protocol (ICMP)* should also change. ICMP is an integral part of IP and is used to report errors that are found in IP packets and to carry out diagnostic functions.

Figure 24-17: ICMP General Format

ICMP messages are grouped into two classes, namely, *error* and *informational*. Error messages are easily identified since they have a zero in the high order bit of their Message Type fields. Since this field is 8 bits in length, error messages therefore have values between 0 and 127, while informational messages have values in the range 128 to 255. The general format of ICMP messages is shown in Figure 24-17.

The 8 bit ICMP Type field will be one of the 9 types as defined in Table 24-5. Each ICMP message is then preceded by a header (normally an IPv6 header) that has a *Next Header* value of 58 (as opposed to 1 in the Protocol field of IPv4). The *Type* field then defines the format for the remainder of the message and the *Code* field is dependent upon the Type of message being conveyed.

The *Checksum* field is calculated in the same fashion as Version 4 checksums. Again, it is the ones compliment of the sum of the ones compliment of each 16 bit word.

Table 24-5: ICMP Type Codes

Type	Description
1	Destination Unreachable
2	Packet Too Big
3	Time Exceeded
4	Parameter Problem
128	Echo Request
129	Echo Reply
130	Group Membership Query
131	Group Membership Report
132	Group Membership Reduction

24.5.1   Destination Unreachable

The Destination Unreachable message is generated by routers or receiving hosts when a packet is received that cannot be delivered. The format of the message is shown in Figure 24-18.

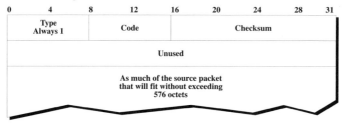

Figure 24-18: ICMP Destination Unreachable

The *Type* field is always 1. The 8 bit *Code* field further defines why the packet could not be delivered and is described by Table 24-6. In general, these Codes are fairly self explanatory however, some comment may need to be made about Code 2. This code is used where a router needs to forward the packet to a neighbor, but the next node listed is not a neighbor and the strict routing bit has been set.

Table 24-6: ICMP Code Field Values for Destination Unreachable Packets

Code Value	Description
0	No Route to Destination
1	Communication with Destination Administratively Prohibited
2	Not a Neighbor
3	Address Unreachable
4	Port Unreachable

24.5.2   Packet Too Big Message

The Packet Too Big message is always sent by a router when it receives a packet that cannot be forwarded because its size exceeds the *MTU* of the network over which the packet must be forwarded. The format is shown in Figure 24-19.

The *Type* field is always set to 2, and the *Code* field is unused (i.e. set to 0). The 32 bit *MTU* field is then set to the *Maximum Transmission Unit* of the next-hop link over which the packet should be forwarded.

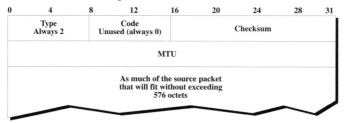

Figure 24-19: ICMP Packet Too Big Message

IP Version 6

24.5.3   Time Exceeded Message

As with version 4, the Time Exceeded message is used to inform the source host that either the *Hop Limit* (Time-to-Live), or the *fragment reassembly* time has been exceeded. The format of this message is identical to that of the *Destination Unreachable* message except that the *Type* field will be 3, and the *Code* field will be either 0 or 1. Where the *Code* field is 0, then the message is indicating that the *Hop Limit* has been exceeded, and where this is 1, that the *fragment reassembly* time has been exceeded.

24.5.4   Parameter Problem Message

This message is used where a problem with a field in the IPv6 header or an Extension Header has been detected. The format of this message is shown in Figure 24-20.

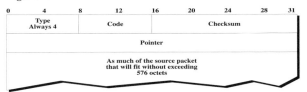

Figure 24-20: Parameter Problem Message

The 8 bit *Type* field is always set to 4. The *Code* field is set to 0 where an error is encountered in a Header field, 1 where we detect an unrecognized Next Header Type, and 2 where an unrecognized IPv6 Option is encountered. The 32 bit *Pointer* field then identifies the octet offset within the packet where the error was detected.

24.5.5   Echo Request/Reply Messages

As with version 4, ICMP has a built in reachability protocol by using ICMP Echo Request/Reply packets. The format is shown in Figure 24-21 and is similar for both the request and reply.

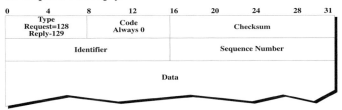

Figure 24-21: Echo Request/Reply Messages

For the *Request*, the *Type* field has a value of 128. In the *Reply*, this value is 129. In both cases the *Code* is set to 0. The *Identifier* and *Sequence Number* fields are then used to match Requests to Replies and any Data sent in a Request must be returned intact to the source station in the corresponding reply.

24.5.6 Group Membership Messages

These messages are used to convey *Multicast Group Membership* messages from nodes to neighboring routers. Three such messages exist, namely, the *Group Membership Query* (Type=130), the *Group Membership Report* (Type=131), and the *Group Membership Reduction* (Type=132). In all cases the *Code* field will have a value of zero. The general format of this message type is shown in Figure 24-22.

The *Maximum Response Delay* field, when used in a *Query* message, indicates the maximum time (in milliseconds) that *Report* messages may be delayed. Where the message type is a *Report* or *Reduction*, this field is ignored by receivers.

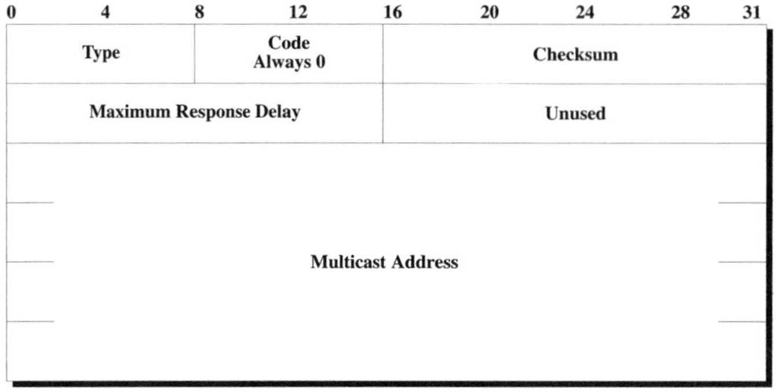

Figure 24-22: Group Membership Messages

24.6 Summary

Much work still remains to be completed concerning IP Version 6, and as such it is yet to be ratified as a standard protocol. Even when ratified change will not come overnight. Many millions of hosts currently implement version 4 and are unlikely to make the transition to version 6 immediately, if ever. For many years to come then, we will be using either version 4 as it stands today, or we will find ourselves using some type of interim where both version 4 and version 6 can co-exist happily.

One thing is certain and that is the current addressing scheme in place with version 4 can cope no longer and an alternative must be found. IP version 6 does provide us with a migration path, but change will come at a cost. Certainly, while we have to continue to support version 4, we will find that version 6 implementations are likely to support both V4 and V6. How routing will take place in this environment is still open to some debate and indeed how we can work in a mixed environment still needs much research. What overhead mixed environments will place on hosts and routers also remains to be seen. With increased speed and better technologies, it is likely that even if today's hardware cannot cope, tomorrow's certainly will.

A Glossary of Networking Terms

This appendix contains definitions of some of the most commonly used networking terms. There is no limit as to what could be included here, and indeed any attempt to cover every possible term would take a lifetime and even then it would never be complete. In addition, there is little that can be considered either unique or original. Much of this appendix was inspired by RFC 1392 and the reader should reference this document for further information about any term listed, or indeed any term that is not mentioned here.

Networking Terms

10Base2	Defined by IEEE 802.3b, this standard allows the Carrier Sense Multiple Access with Collision Detect (CSMA/CD) network access method to be used over 50Ω (RG58) co-axial cable. Sometimes referred to as "*Thin Ethernet*". See Chapter 3.
10Base5	The original specification for the CSMA/CD network access method (IEEE 802.3) defining 50Ω co-axial cable as the medium. Sometimes referred to as "*Thick Ethernet*". See Chapter 3.
10BaseF	Defined by IEEE 802.3j, this standard builds upon the original specification of CSMA/CD to include fibre optic medium. Three separate definitions exist, namely, 10BaseFB (synchronous inter-repeater links), 10BaseFP (a passive star topology), and 10BaseFL (a standardization of the Fibre Optic Inter-Repeater Link (FOIRL) specification). See Chapter 3.
10BaseT	A standard for the use of twisted pair medium in 802.3 environments. Defined in IEEE 802.3i, this is sometimes called "*UTP*" or "*Twisted Pair Ethernet*". See Chapter 3.
802.x	A set of standards developed by the IEEE. Several such standards now exist including 802.1, 802.2, 802.3, 802.4, 802.5 etc. See Chapter 2.
822 Header	*See RFC 822 Header.*
ABR	*See Area Border Router.*
Abstract Syntax Notation One	A formal language used in an OSI environment, and also to encode SNMP packets. See Chapter 20.
ACK	*See Acknowledgement.*
Acknowledgement	An indication that data has arrived at its intended recipient. Typically thought of as a Positive Acknowledgement where reliability is required, this indicates that the data has arrived without error. See also Negative Acknowledgement. See Chapter 7.
Address	A method of uniquely identifying a host (or person) within an internet. Several address types exist within an IP environment, namely, the Domain Name, IP Address, MAC Address, and when referring to a person, an eMail Address. See Chapters 4, 5, and 15.

Address Mask	*See Subnet Mask*
Address Resolution Protocol	A general purpose Layer 2 protocol designed to allow the mapping of Internet (or other protocol) Addresses to MAC Addresses. See Chapter 4.
Agent	A (typically) small piece of code (software) that is used to exchange information with some other device. For example, in an SNMP environment, the Network Management Station may request information from a managed device through its agent. See Chapter 20.
American National Standards Institution	A standards making body responsible for the approval of many standards in the USA. One such standard is X3T9.5, the standard describing FDDI.
American Standard Code for Information Interchange	A standard encoding scheme in common use within the computer industry. ASCII (as it is more commonly known) is based upon a 7 bit scheme but, although widely used, it is not the only scheme available. See also EBCDIC.
Anonymous FTP	Available on many FTP servers, anonymous FTP allows a user to gain access to public areas of the host without the need for a formal userid and password. See Chapter 17.
ANSI	*See American National Standards Institution.*
AppleTalk	Developed by Apple Computer Inc., this describes a protocol suite that allows Apple computers to exchange data. Several implementations exist including LocalTalk (a low speed proprietary system), EtherTalk (a 10Mbps system that runs over Ethernet), and TokenTalk (to run over Token Ring networks).
Application Layer	The uppermost layer (Layer 7) of the OSI Model, this layer provides access to the network environment. Application protocols such as FTAM reside at this layer. See Chapter 2.
ARCHIE	An Internet utility that gathers and indexes information on Internet resources.
Area Border Router	A router that spans two or more routing Areas and exchanges routing information between them. This router then assumes a special role and maintains multiple topological databases. See Chapter 11.
ARP	*See Address Resolution Protocol.*
AS	*See Autonomous System.*
ASBR	*See Autonomous System Boundary Router.*
ASCII	*See American Standard Code for Information Interchange.*
ASN.1	*See Abstract Syntax Notation One.*
Authentication	A method by which a person (or process) can identify itself. Several protocols within the Internet suite (such as PPP, RIP II, and OSPF) incorporate authentication methods. See Chapters 10, 11, and 22.
Autonomous System	A collection of networks under a single administration and employing a common routing policy. For example, an Autonomous System may run an Interior Gateway Protocol such as OSPF. See Chapters 11, 12, and 13.
Autonomous System Boundary Router	A router that joins different Autonomous Systems together. By its definition then, such a router will run multiple routing protocols. See Chapter 11.
Bandwidth	Generally, this is taken to mean the amount of data that can be passed over a particular communications channel.
Baseband Signalling	A communication method whereby only one signal may be present on the medium at any time. Ethernet is an example of such a system.

BGP	*See Border Gateway Protocol.*
Binary	A method of arithmetic using the base 2 therefore limiting the digits that can be used to 0 and 1. Normally, any binary number is written using the subscript 2 at the end to avoid confusion.
Bootstrap Protocol	A protocol that uses UDP and IP to allow network devices to determine (normally) start-up information. Typically, a diskless device may enquire its IP Address, the address of the server that has its image file, the address of the router that should be used, and the name of the file that should be used. See Chapter 19.
BootP	*See Bootstrap Protocol.*
Border Gateway Protocol	A protocol defined as being an Exterior Gateway Protocol, used to join Autonomous Systems together. See Chapter 13.
Bridge	A Store and Forward device, operating at Layer 2 of the OSI Model (the Data-Link Layer) used to segment traffic between LANs. See Chapter 3.
British Standards Institute	The standards making body responsible for approving standards applicable to the United Kingdom.
Broadband	A transmission method where multiple signals may co-exist on the network medium at the same time. Frequency Division Multiplexing is normally employed in this case.
Broadcast	A packet or frame destined for all devices on a network or internet a.k.a. a broadcast address. See Chapter 3.
Brouter	A combination device that is capable of routing specific frame types and bridging all others. See Chapter 3.
BSI	*See British Standards Institute.*
Byte	A basic unit of data transmission where each byte can be used to identify a single character. Normally bytes are 8 (binary) data bits in length however, since some systems use bytes that are longer than 8 bits, the term octet is generally used when referring to networking. *See also Octet.*
CCITT	*See Intn'l Telegraph & Telephone Consultative Committee.*
Checksum	A value that is calculated, based upon the contents of a packet, and then transmitted with it. A receiving station then performs the same calculation and compares its result with that received to ensure that the data has arrived intact.
Circuit Switching	A communication method that requires that a dedicated path be set up between two communicating hosts for the duration of the connection.
Client	A system that requests the services of another. For example, a device requesting a file using the File Transfer Protocol is a client of the host on which the file resides.
Congestion	A situation that arises in networking terms when data arrives at a rate faster than it can be processed.
Connectionless	A data communication method that does not require stations to agree to exchange data and therefore has no inherent acknowledgement capability. The Internet Protocol (IP) uses this method of communication however, where data is to be transmitted with positive acknowledgements, the Transmission Control Protocol (TCP) can be used create a connection oriented environment.
CRC	*See Cyclic Redundancy Check.*
CSMA/CD	Carrier Sense Multiple Access with Collision Detect. The transmission method used by Ethernet and IEEE 802.3. See Chapter 3.

Cyclic Redundancy Check	Used in Checksum calculations, the CRC provides the formula that is applied to the data as it is transmitted. Normally a polynomial function, the CRC is generated on transmission and checked on reception.
Datagram	The basic unit of transmission in an IP environment. IP packets are called datagrams and they each contain sufficient information to allow them to be routed between the source and destination host making them independent of each other. See Chapter 5.
DECnet	A proprietary networking protocol developed by the Digital Equipment Corporation (DEC) to link their machines together. Currently two implementations exist, namely, Phase IV which is totally proprietary, and Phase V which is based upon OSI protocols and is therefore open.
Default Route	A routing table entry that is used to route packets to networks that are not otherwise explicitly mentioned. The route (normally shown as 0.0.0.0) indicates to hosts and other devices that, in the absence of any other routing information, they should direct packets to the device advertising the default route for onward delivery. See Chapter 9.
Dialup	A method of communicating with a remote device over the Public Switched Telephone Network (PSTN). Such connections are therefore considered transitory rather than dedicated. See Chapter 22.
Dijkstra's Algorithm	An algorithm used to determine the best cost path between any two end stations. Dijkstra's algorithm is used in OSPF. See Chapter 11.
Disk Operating System	The operating system employed on many Internet hosts. The most commonly implemented Disk Operating System is Microsoft's MSDOS used on Personal Computers (PCs).
Distance Vector Algorithm	Otherwise known as the Bellman-Ford routing algorithm, this is a widely used method of gauging route quality. With this method, the quality of the route is based upon the number of networks that the packet must traverse. Protocols such as the Routing Information Protocol (RIP) use this method. See Chapter 10.
Distance Vector Multicast Routing Protocol	Although not widely implemented, this is a protocol that allows host group information derived from the Internet Group Message Protocol (IGMP) to be propagated throughout an internet. See Chapter 14.
DIX Ethernet	*See Ethernet.*
DNS	*See Domain Name System.*
Domain	There are many types of Domain such as a routing domain, named domain, and mail domain. In general, a domain can be considered as a group of entities sharing a common purpose. See Chapter 15.
Domain Name System	A host naming convention and protocol allowing the mapping of host names to IP Addresses. The Domain Name System also allows other information to be stored about hosts and networks such as the location of Mail Servers etc. See Chapter 15.
DOS	*See Disk Operating System.*
Dotted Decimal Notation	A method of representing a binary number in decimal. The most common implementation is the representation of IP Addresses where each octet of the 32 bit (4 octet) address is represented as its decimal equivalent separated from its neighbor by a dot. See Chapter 4.
DVMRP	*See Distance Vector Multicast Routing Protocol.*
E1	The term used to describe a digital line at 2.048Mbps.

EBCDIC	*See Extended Binary Coded Decimal Interchange Code.*
EGP	A generic name given to a group of routing protocols used between Autonomous Systems. See Chapter 12. *See also Exterior Gateway Protocol.*
EIA	*See Electrical Industries Association.*
Electrical Industries Association	A standards making body in the USA responsible for the introduction of many data communications standards. The most common EIA standard is possibly EIA RS-232.
Electronic Mail	The colloquial name for a system that allows network users to exchange messages. EMail is one of the most common network applications. See Chapter 18.
eMail	*See Electronic Mail.*
eMail Address	The address of an electronic mail user. Normally specified as a fully qualified Domain Name, this uniquely identifies a user anywhere within the internet. See Chapters 15 and 18.
Encapsulation	A method by which data from one logical layer (or protocol) can be carried within another. For example, TCP uses the services of IP and therefore is transported as IP data. As such, a TCP segment is said to be encapsulated within an IP datagram and the IP datagram is encapsulated within the physical frame i.e. Ethernet.
Encryption	This is a technique that allows the octets within a packet to be modified in such a way as to ensure that any device eavesdropping, will not be able to read the information. Data is encoded by the transmitter and then decoded by the receiver.
Ethernet	The original medium access system (developed by Digital, Intel, and Xerox) employing CSMA/CD. Ethernet defines a 10Mbps Baseband signalling system, originally developed for use with co-axial cable. This has since been enhanced by the IEEE and now uses multiple media types including Twisted Pair and Fibre Optic cables. *See also 10Base5, 10Base2, 10BaseT and 10BaseF.*
Extended Binary Coded Decimal interchange Code	A standard method of encoding characters to numeric codes, developed and used primarily by IBM.
Exterior Gateway Protocol	This term has dual meanings. Firstly, it describes a suite of routing protocols used to link Autonomous Systems together. Two such protocols exist, namely EGP and BGP. See Chapters 9, 12, and 13. Secondly, it is the name given to the original protocol for this purpose called the Exterior Gateway Protocol. *See Chapter 12.*
External Data Representation	A standard developed by Sun Microsystems for representation of data in a machine independent format.
FDDI	*See Fibre Distributed Data Interface.*
Fibre Distributed Data Interface	Developed by the American National Standards Institute (ANSI) as standard X3T9.5. This defines a 100Mbps ring topology that was originally developed for use over Fibre Optic cabling only. Today several variants exist that define other media, namely SMF-PMD (Single Mode fibre), MMF-PMD (Multi-Mode fibre), and TP-PMD (Twisted Pair).
File Transfer Protocol	A protocol that allows users on one machine to transfer files to/from another. *See Chapter 17.*
FINGER	A management protocol that allows one host machine to interrogate another network device to obtain information about valid or current users. *See Chapter 21.*

Fragment	A part of an IP datagram. When a router forwards a packet, it must know the maximum payload (data) allowed on the network over which the packet must pass. When the maximum amount of data allowed is less than the packet size, it must be broken into smaller pieces in an orderly fashion so that it may be re-built by the receiving host. Each smaller part is then called a fragment. See Chapter 5.
Fragmentation	The process by which packets are broken into smaller pieces in order to adhere to the constraints imposed by the network technology over which the data must pass. See Chapter 5.
Frame	The unit of data transfer at the Data-Link (Network Access) layer. The frame then contains header and addressing information as defined by the data-link layer protocol. See Chapters 2, 3, and 5.
FTP	*See File Transfer Protocol.*
Gateway	Within the context of the Internet Protocol Suite, a gateway is a router. In a more pure sense, a gateway normally translates application or other protocols. For example, TCP/IP to LAT allows a user running a Telnet session to attach to a LAT based host and vice-versa.
GOPHER	A simple protocol (and application by the same name) that allows a client host to access hierarchical information stored on a server.
HDLC	*See Higher Data Link Control.*
Header	This is the portion of a packet or frame that immediately precedes the data area. Typically, this will contain addressing and other control information.
Heterogeneous Network	A network that runs multiple network layer protocols such as IP, IPX, DECnet, etc. This is in direct contrast to a homogenous network where only a single protocol is employed.
Hierarchical Routing	An attempt to simplify the problems associated with routing in large networks by breaking the network into multiple levels. OSPF attempts to achieve this by introducing the concept of Areas. See Chapter 11.
High-Level Data Link Control	A general purpose Data-Link control protocol that is in wide use over WAN links.
Homogenous Network	A network that runs only a single network layer protocol (such as IP). This is in direct contrast to a Heterogeneous Network where multiple protocols are employed.
Hop	Within the context of routing, this term describes the quality of a route between a source and destination network. In this case, the path between stations is described as a series of hops (either router or network) that the data must take. See Chapters 9 and 10.
Host	A device (normally a user device) that resides on a network.
Host Address	The unique address assigned to a device on the network. Several addresses can be applied to a device, namely a MAC Address (at layer 2), an IP Address, or a name. See Chapters 3, 4, and 15.
Host Name	A name given to a device that uniquely identifies it. Names within an IP environment are generally referred to as Domain Names. See Chapter 15.
HTML	*See Hypertext Mark-up Language.*
HTTP	*See Hypertext Transfer Protocol.*
Hub	A device (typically a repeater) that allows multiple network devices to communicate.
Hypertext Mark-up Language	A language used to create pages of information used on the World Wide Web.

Hypertext Transfer Protocol	The protocol used to manipulate (upload and download) World Wide Web pages.
IAB	*See Internet Architecture Board.*
IANA	*See Internet Assigned Numbers Authority.*
ICMP	*See Internet Control Message Protocol.*
IEEE	*See Institute of Electrical and Electronic Engineers.*
IESG	*See Internet Engineering Steering Group.*
IETF	*See Internet Engineering Task Force.*
IGP	*See Interior Gateway Protocol.*
IGMP	*See Internet Group Management Protocol.*
In-Band	The term used to describe the transmission of information (normally management information) along with normal user data.
Institute of Electrical & Electronic Engineers	An American standards making body that has been responsible for the introduction and standardization of many, now commonly used, network access methods.
Integrated Services Digital Network	A Wide Area technology that allows the transmission of Voice, Data, Video and other information over a single cable. With the introduction of this service, ISDN is now emerging as the successor to many traditional leased circuits.
Interior Gateway Protocol	The collective term given to a suite of protocols that allow routers within an Autonomous System to exchange network reachability information. See Chapters 9, 10, and 11.
Intermediate System	An OSI term that is used to describe a device responsible for the forwarding of Network Layer data. This is analogous to a router.
Intermediate System-Intermediate System	The standard Interior Gateway protocol used in an OSI environment.
International Standards Organization	An international organization responsible for the introduction of many standards including those that are computer and communications related.
International Telecommunications Union	Formerly the CCITT, this standards making body works mainly in the telecommunications sector developing and introducing new standards. Many new and emerging technologies such as ISDN owe much to the work of this organization.
Intn'l Telegraph & Telephone Consultative Committee	Now part of the International Telecommunications Union (ITU), the CCITT (as it was referred to) is responsible for making recommendations regarding data communications.
Internet	The world wide network to which many businesses, educational establishments, and government departments now subscribe. The Internet (denoted by the capital I) is, in reality, a collection of networks interconnected for the common goal of global communications.
internet	An internet (denoted by a small i), is a collection of networks interconnected with routers and run primarily for private use.
Internet Address	*See Host Address.*
Internet Architecture Board	The technical body that oversees the development of the Internet. See Chapter 2.
Internet Assigned Numbers Authority	A central registry of all numbers associated with Internet protocols (Port Numbers, Protocol IDs etc.). Those numbers assigned are published at regular intervals through RFCs titled Internet Assigned Numbers documents, the most recent of which is RFC 1700.

Internet Control Message Protocol	A protocol that is considered as an integral part of IP used to report errors, and other information, and for rudimentary testing. See Chapter 6.
Internet Engineering Steering Group	A group that provides a first level technical review of all Internet standards and is responsible for the day-to-day management of the IETF. See also Internet Engineering Task Force. See Chapter 2.
Internet Engineering Task Force	A large group of individuals, vendors and researchers who are responsible for the evolution of the Internet protocols. See Chapter 2.
Internet Group Management Protocol	An integral extension to the Internet Protocol (IP) that allows host groups to be formed. This protocol then allows routers capable of multicast forwarding to determine where host group members reside and forward relevant multicasts to them. See Chapter 14.
Internet Protocol	The network layer protocol of the Internet Protocol Suite. The Internet Protocol is a connectionless, best efforts protocol that relies on upper layer protocols to provide reliability where required. See Chapter 5.
Internet Relay Chat	A protocol that allows Internet users to converse in real-time.
Internet Research Steering Group	The body that oversees the operations of the Internet Research Task Force. See also Internet Research Task Force. See Chapter 2.
Internet Research Task Force	The body that considers long-term Internet issues from a theoretical stand point. See Chapter 2.
Internet Society	A society that provides the forum for discussion of the operation and use of the Internet.
Internetwork Packet Exchange	A protocol loosely based upon Xerox's Internetwork Datagram Protocol (IDP) and developed by Novell. IPX is the Network Layer protocol used within Novell's NetWare architecture.
Inter-operability	The term used to describe the ability of software and/or hardware from multiple vendors to communicate seamlessly.
IP	*See Internet Protocol.*
IP Address	A form of Host Address applicable to the Internet Protocol Suite. In this address form, a 32 bit number (normally expressed in Dotted Decimal Notation) is used to uniquely identify each host within the internet. See Chapter 4 and also Host Address and Dotted Decimal Notation.
IPX	*See Internetwork Packet Exchange.*
IRC	*See Internet Relay Chat.*
IRSG	*See Internet Research Steering Group.*
IRTF	*See Internet Research Task Force.*
IS	*See Intermediate System.*
ISOC	*See Internet Society.*
IS-IS	*See Intermediate System- Intermediate System.*
ISDN	*See Integrated Services Digital Network.*
ISO	*See International Standards Organization.*
ITU	*See International Telecommunications Union.*
KERBEROS	A security system developed by the Massachusetts Institute of Technology (MIT) used to validate user access and using a system that encrypts data.
Kermit	A File Transfer Protocol (not FTP) that can be used to easily transfer files between hosts.
LAN	*See Local Area Network.*

LAT	*See Local Area Transport.*
Layer	Communications methods are described by functional models (architectures) to break the process into tasks that perform specific functions. These functions are then thought of as layers of the architecture which are, in turn, implemented as protocols. See Chapter 2.
Leased Line	A dedicated data circuit over which data may be passed. Leased lines are point-to-point Wide Area links (WANs).
Lineprinter Protocol	A general purpose protocol used to share printer resources over an internet. Used mainly in UNIX environments, the Line Printer Protocol allows client hosts to access other hosts known as Print Servers. See Chapter 21.
Link Quality Monitoring	A method of determining Link Quality by passing packets over a link. Mainly used in a WAN environment, one host sends diagnostic packets that contain the number of packets and octets sent. The receiving end then compares these figures with the number of packets and octets received, and from this determines how much data has been lost. See Chapter 22.
Link State Advertisement	Used in OSPF, this packet type is used to advertise information about reachable networks, the state of router interfaces, and the metrics associated with these interfaces. See Chapter 11.
Link State Algorithm	The algorithm used by protocols such as OSPF to determine the quality of a received route. This is in contrast to the Distance Vector Algorithm used by protocols such as RIP. See Chapter 11.
Link State Update	A packet type used by OSPF to advertise routing information. Link State Updates contain Link State Advertisements. See Chapter 11.
LLC	*See Logical Link Control.*
Local Area Network	A network that is designed to span no more than a few kilometers. Typically these networks would be Ethernet, Token Ring, or FDDI networks and have data transmission speeds of up to 100Mbps.
Local Area Transport	Developed by the Digital Equipment Corporation (DEC), this proprietary protocol is designed to allow users to connect to DEC hosts. It is extremely efficient in the way that it operates by allowing data from multiple sessions to be carried in a single packet. However, it operates at the MAC layer and it is therefore not routeable.
Logical Link Control	This is the upper part of the Data-Link layer and is defined by IEEE 802.2. Its purpose is simply to provide a uniform interface to the Network Layer regardless of the underlying network technology. See Chapter 2.
LP	*See Lineprinter Protocol.*
LQM	*See Link Quality Monitoring.*
LSA	*See Link State Algorithm and Link State Advertisement.*
LSU	*See Link State Update.*
MAC	*See Media Access Control.*
MAC Address	The hardware address of a device. Each device connected to a shared network technology such as Ethernet, Token Ring or FDDI will have such an address that uniquely identifies it. Do not confuse this with the IP Address which must also be uniquely applied to the device though, since IP Addresses are independent of the hardware.
Mail Exchange Record	A Domain Name System Resource Record that defines which device can handle mail for a particular domain. See Chapter 15.
Mail Exploder	Part of the mail delivery system that allows a single mail message to be delivered to multiple hosts.

Mail Gateway	A host that connects two or more electronic mail systems. These systems may be either similar or dissimilar.
Mail Server	A host that distributes electronic mail items in response to requests from the electronic mail system. See Chapter 18.
MAN	*See Metropolitan Area Network.*
Management Information Base	A set of parameters that can be manipulated to obtain information or configure network devices. See Chapter 20 and Appendix C.
Maximum Receive Unit	The maximum amount of data that can be received by a host. This figure particularly when applied to protocols such as the Point-to-Point Protocol (PPP) can be negotiated by each host connected to the link. See Chapter 22.
Maximum Transmission Unit	The maximum amount of data (payload) that can be carried by a particular network type. For example, Ethernet has a Maximum Transmission Unit of 1500 octets. See Chapter 3.
Media Access Control	The lower sub-layer of the Data-Link layer of the OSI Model. The term MAC Address is applied to the address at this layer, for example the Ethernet address of the host. See Chapter 2.
Metropolitan Area Network	The term applied to networks designed to span campuses or other medium sized areas. Obviously larger than LANs (yet smaller geographically than WANs), this describes an internet that covers a medium sized area.
MIB	*See Management Information Base.*
MIME	*See Multipurpose Internet Mail Extensions.*
MRU	*See Maximum Receive Unit.*
MTU	*See Maximum Transmission Unit.*
Multicast	The term used to describe a packet or frame destined for multiple (but not all) addresses on a network or internet.
Multi-Homed Host	A host that has more than one connection to a network.
Multi-Link Protocol	A protocol used to allow efficient load sharing over multiple Point-to-Point WAN links. See Chapter 22.
Multipurpose Internet Mail Extensions	An extension to the Internet Mail service that allows non-text items such as graphical, audio and fax data to be carried.
MX Record	*See Mail Exchange Record.*
NAK	*See Negative Acknowledgement.*
Namespace	A (typically) hierarchical naming system in which each name is unique. A typical example can be found in the Domain Name System (DNS). See Chapter 15.
NCP	See NetWare Core Protocols.
Negative Acknowledgement	An acknowledgement sent in response to a corrupted packet. Such negative acknowledgements normally require the transmitting station to re-transmit the data.
NetWare Core Protocol	A set of protocols used to support the Novell NetWare operating system. These protocols are at the very heart of NetWare operation and require the implementation of Novell's Internetwork Packet Exchange protocol (IPX). See Also Internetwork Packet Exchange (IPX).
Network	A data communications system used to interconnect computer systems either locally or remotely. See also Local Area Network (LAN), Metropolitan Area Network (MAN), and Wide Area Network (WAN).
Network Address	*See Host Address and IP Address.*

Network File System	Developed by Sun Microsystems to allow computers to access files over a network as if they were to reside on local disks. The Network File System is therefore independent of machine hardware or architecture.
Network Information Centre	A central administration that provides assistance and support to Internet users.
Network Link State Protocol	Developed by Novell, this protocol attempts to provide OSPF style functionality (Link State Algorithm support) to Novell NetWare.
Network Management Station	A station that implements a network management protocol such as SNMP and through In-Band management, manages devices in the network.
Network News Transfer Protocol	A protocol used for the posting and distribution of news articles.
Network Time Protocol	A protocol used to ensure accurate time services are available within an internet. See Chapter 21.
NFS	*See Network File System.*
NIC	*See Network Information Center.*
NLSP	*See Network Link State Protocol.*
NMS	*See Network Management Station.*
NNTP	*See Network News Transfer Protocol.*
Node	Another name for an addressable device connected to a network.
NTP	*See Network Time Protocol.*
Object Identifier	A means of identifying a particular Management Information Base (MIB) Variable. This is always specified as a variable length string of numbers separated by dots. See Chapter 20.
Octet	Eight bits of data are used to define an octet which can then be used to represent a single character. The term byte may sometimes be used however, since some machines define a byte as being longer than 8 bits, the term octet is generally used in networking. See also Byte.
OID	*See Object Identifier.*
Open Shortest Path First	One of the family of Interior Gateway Protocols (IGPs) that are designed to allow the exchange of routing information within an Autonomous System (AS). OSPF uses a Link State, rather than Distance Vector, Algorithm. See Chapter 11.
Open Systems Interconnection	A suite of protocols designed by the International Standards Organization (ISO). See Chapter 2.
OSI	*See Open Systems Interconnection.*
OSI Reference Model	A seven layer architecture used to describe the way in which computers can communicate. In addition, the model also defines the interfaces required between each layer so that multivendor networks can be created. See Chapter 2.
OSPF	*See Open Shortest Path First.*
Out-of-Band	A management technique where management data is sent outside of the normal data stream.
Packet	The basic unit of data transmitted across a network. The term packet can be used to describe the data at any level of the protocol stack. See also Frame and Protocol Data Unit.
Packet Internet Groper	A simple application that is used to test the reachability of network devices. Based upon the Internet Control Message Protocol (ICMP), this uses Echo Request and Reply codes. See Chapter 6.

Packet Switching	A communications method that requires packets to be individually routed between hosts.
PDU	*See Protocol Data Unit.*
PING	*See Packet Internet Groper.*
Point of Presence	A site that contains a collection of telecommunication equipment (normally modems) and allows users to gain access to other, larger, networks. This term is most commonly used by Internet service providers.
Point-to-Point Protocol	A protocol used over serial Point-to-Point links to allow the transmission of multiple protocols. See Chapter 22.
POP	*See Post Office Protocol.*
PoP	*See Point of Presence.*
Port	This has two meanings. Firstly, some may refer to the physical connectors of a device as ports. Within a TCP/IP environment however, the term is used to describe a de-multiplexing value so that data destined for a particular application can be uniquely identified. Both TCP and UDP use the concept of ports for this purpose. See Chapters 7 and 8.
Post Office Protocol	A Mail delivery protocol.
Postal Telegraph and Telephone	A telecommunications service provider. This is sometimes referred to as a PTT.
Postmaster	The person responsible for electronic mail at a particular site. See Chapter 18.
PPP	*See Point-to-Point Protocol.*
Protocol	A description of the rules and formats associated with the transfer of data.
Protocol Converter	A program that is used to convert between different protocols that serve the same purpose.
Protocol Data Unit	This is the more formal name for a packet. Each layer within an architecture will create Protocol Data Units (PDUs) which are then passed to the layer below for transmission. Equally, each layer accepts received PDUs from the layer below for processing.
Protocol Stack	A layered set of protocols that inter-operate to provide a network function. See Chapter 2.
Proxy ARP	Sometimes referred to as promiscuous ARP, this is a technique that allows one device (typically a router) to answer Address Resolution Protocol (ARP) requests generated by other devices. Most commonly used where a network has been subnetted, with more modern implementations, the reliance on this is now diminished. See Chapter 9.
PSTN	*See Public Switch Telephone Network.*
PTT	*See Postal Telegraph and Telephone.*
Public Switched Telephone Network	The normal telephone service provided by PTTs. A user accessing a network from a remote location may do so using a dial-up modem using the Public Switched Telephone Network.
Queue	A backup of packets that are awaiting transmission or processing.
RARP	*See Reverse Address Resolution Protocol.*
RCP	*See Remote Copy Protocol.*
RDP	*See Router Discovery Protocol.*
Reassembly	The process by which a previously fragmented packet can be re-assembled. Within TCP/IP, fragmentation takes place at the IP layer.

Thus, reassembly also takes place at this layer for received data that was fragmented. See Chapter 5.

Remote Copy Protocol	A protocol (and normally a program by the same name) that allows a file to be copied from one machine to another.
Remote Procedure Call	A protocol used for implementing a distributed client-server model of computing.
Repeater	A networking device that transparently propagates data from one segment to another. Repeaters are normally used to either increase network length or to increase the number of device connections. See Chapter 3.
Request for Comments	The vehicle by which Internet protocols are described and general information about proposed standards, experiments, and meeting notes are disseminated to the Internet community. See Chapter 2.
Reverse Address Resolution Protocol	A protocol, similar to ARP but allowing the resolution of IP Addresses where only the MAC Address is known. See Chapter 4.
RFC	*See Request for Comments.*
RFC 822 Header	The standard format for electronic mail messages. See Chapter 18.
RIP	*See Routing Information Protocol.*
RIP II	*See Routing Information Protocol.*
Rlogin	A virtual terminal application similar to Telnet except than in this variant we rely on trusted hosts. The user must therefore be known on the host to which access is desired. See Chapter 16.
Round Trip Delay Time	A measurement of the delays involved in sending data across a network.
Route	The path taken by data as it travels from one network to another. See Chapters 9, 10, 11, 12, and 13.
Routed	A program implemented on many UNIX hosts to propagate routing information.
Router	A Store-and-Forward device used to forward data from one network to another based upon network layer information. This term should not be confused with Source Routing which is a term used to describe a particular type of bridge. See Chapter 9.
Router Discovery Protocol	An extension to the Internet Control Message Protocol (ICMP) used to allow host systems to discover their local router(s). See Chapter 6.
Routing	The process of selecting the best path over which to send data destined for a distant network. See Chapters 9, 10, 11, 12, and 13.
Routing Domain	A group of routers that exchange routing information within an Autonomous System.
Routing Information Protocol	A Distance Vector based routing protocol. This protocol was the original routing protocol used with TCP/IP and has served the internet community well. Today two versions exist, namely RIP and RIP II. See Chapter 10.
RPC	*See Remote Procedure Call.*
Segment	The TCP unit of data transfer. TCP packets are therefore more correctly referred to as being segments. See Chapter 7.
Sequenced Packet Exchange	A reliable transport layer protocol used by Novell NetWare. This protocol (more commonly referred to as SPX) uses the services of IPX to transport it.
Serial Line IP	A simple protocol used to carry IP datagrams over serial lines. See Chapter 22.

Server	A machine used to provide resource to another host. These services may be File services, Print Services, or Naming services as found in the Domain Name System.
Simple Mail Transfer Protocol	A TCP based protocol used to transmit and receive electronic mail messages. See Chapter 18.
Simple Network Management Protocol	A protocol used to manage network devices. Originally developed for the management of IP hosts, SNMP can now also be used to manage IPX devices. See Chapter 20.
SLIP	*See Serial Line IP.*
Small Office/Home Office	A term introduced by Microsoft to describe the emerging market introduced by small businesses and home users.
SMDS	*See Switched Multi-megabit Data Service.*
SMI	*See Structure of Management Information.*
SMTP	*See Simple Mail Transfer Protocol.*
SNA	*See Systems Network Architecture.*
SNMP	*See Simple Network Management Protocol.*
SOHO	*See Small Office/Home Office.*
Source Routing	This term can have two meanings. Firstly, it can be used to describe a bridging protocol used primarily in Token Ring environments. Secondly, within IP, a host can predetermine the route that a datagram will take by loading a list of routers that it must visit. Two types of Source Routing exist when applied to an IP environment, namely Loose Source Routing and Strict Source Routing. See Chapter 5.
Spanning Tree Protocol	A simple protocol used in bridged networks to ensure a loop free topology. See Chapter 3.
Spoofing	The term used to fool a device into thinking that a response has been received.
SPX	*See Sequenced Packet Exchange.*
Std	A group of RFCs that define Internet standards. See Chapter 2.
Structure of Management Information	A set of rules governing the objects that can be accessed via network management. See also Management Information Base and Simple Network Management Protocol.
Stub Network	A Stub Network is one where there is only a single entry/exit point for traffic. See Chapter 11.
Subnet	A portion of a network that shares the same network address as other portions. These subnets are then distinguished through a Subnet Mask. See Chapter 4.
Subnet Address	The part of an IP Address that identifies the subnet on which the device resides. See Chapter 4.
Subnet Mask	A 32 bit mask which, when logically ANDed with an IP Address masks off the Host portion of the Address. See Chapter 4.
Switched Multi-megabit Data Service	A high speed public data network service.
Systems Network Architecture	An architecture developed by IBM to allow their machines to be networked. This architecture is proprietary.
T1	A U.S. standard communications facility used to carry data at 1.544Mbps.
T3	A U.S. standard communications facility used to carry data at 44.746Mbps.

Talk	A simple protocol that allows users at different machines to communicate in real time.
TCP	See Transport Control Protocol.
TCP/IP	The colloquial name given to the Internet Protocol Suite, derived from the two major protocols namely TCP and IP.
Telecommunications Industries Association	A U.S. standards making body.
Telnet	The Internet suite Network Virtual Terminal (NVT) Protocol allowing a workstation to access network hosts as if it were connected locally. See Chapter 16.
Terminal Server	A simple device used to take a raw RS-232 bit stream from a dumb terminal or other device, and packetise it for use on a LAN.
TFTP	*See Trivial File Transfer Protocol.*
TIA	*See Telecommunications Industries Association.*
Time-to-Live	A field within the IP datagram header that ensures the timely removal of packets that would otherwise endlessly circulate on networks. Such situations might occur due to router failure and the subsequent creation of routing loops. See Chapter 5.
TN3270	A variant of the Telnet protocol used to access IBM hosts.
Token Ring	A Local Area Networking system originally developed by IBM and standardized by the IEEE as IEEE 802.5. See Chapter 3.
Topology	This term is used to describe the geography of an internet. Through routing protocols, routers and hosts can then learn the topology of the internet.
TOS	*See Type of Service.*
Transceiver	A simple layer one Ethernet (IEEE 802.3) device that allows a device to be connected to a network. See Chapter 3.
Transit Network	A transit network is one that can pass data between networks. Thus, a transit network is one that has more than one attached router. See Chapter 11.
Translational Bridging	A bridge type that translates between one network type and another. See Chapter 3.
Transport Control Protocol	Used as a generic Layer 4 (OSI Model) protocol providing a reliable, connection oriented, communications environment. See Chapter 7.
Trap	Within an SNMP environment, a Trap PDU is sent from a managed device to a management station when it wishes to provide unsolicited information. See Chapter 20.
Trivial File Transfer Protocol	A UDP based protocol used to transfer files between devices. Although this is a general purpose file transfer protocol, it is typically employed where simplicity is required such as the loading of operating systems to diskless hosts. See Chapter 19.
TTL	*See Time to Live.*
Tunnelling	The process of encapsulating a foreign protocol within say an IP datagram so that it can be passed over an IP network.
Twisted Pair	A type of media referring to Twisted Pair cabling either (shielded or un-shielded). See also 10BaseT and Chapter 3.
Type of Service	A field within the IP datagram header used to define the way in which the datagram should be handled. Once set, this field can then be interrogated by routers and specific routes can be chosen based upon its contents. See Chapters 5 and 11.

UDP	*See User Datagram Protocol.*
Unicast	A packet or frame destined for just one device on a network or inter-net. For example, a Unicast Address is used to address a single host system. See Chapters 3 and 4.
UNIX	A host operating system originally developed by AT&T.
User Datagram Protocol	A connectionless transport protocol used within the Internet Protocol Suite. The protocol adds little to the basic services offered by IP with the exception of a de-multiplexing function. See Chapter 8.
Vines IP	The Network layer protocol used by the Vines network operating system from Banyan.
Virtual Circuit	A network service that provides a connection oriented service regardless of the underlying network technology.
WAIS	*See Wide Area Information Service.*
WAN	*See Wide Area Network.*
WHOIS	A program that allows a user to query database(s) of information regarding users, domain names, and networks. See Chapter 21.
Wide Area Information Service	A distributed information service.
Wide Area Network	A network created to span large geographic areas normally over serial lines. See Chapter 22.
World Wide Web	A hyper-text based distributed information system based on a client-server model. With the explosive growth of the Internet, there are now countless servers offering information on just about any subject imaginable.
WWW	*See World-Wide-Web.*
X	This is the generic name given to a TCP/IP windows system.
X.25	Developed by the CCITT, this specification describes how data can be passed over a public switched data network.
X.400	An ISO standard for Electronic Mail.
X.500	The ISO standard for electronic directory services.
X3T9.5	*See Fibre Distributed Data Interface (FDDI).*
XDR	*See External Data Representation.*
XNS	Xerox Network System. Originally developed by Xerox Corporation, XNS has now formed the basis for Novell's Internetwork Packet Exchange (IPX).
Yellow Pages	Originally this was the name for the Domain Name System imple-mented by Sun. Today, although many people still refer to this sys-tem as Yellow Pages, the more correct name should be the Network Information Service (NIS).
YP	*See Yellow Pages.*
Zone	A logical grouping of devices. This term is of particular importance to protocols such as AppleTalk where Apple machines are grouped into more user-friendly, named, zones.

Official Internet Protocol Standards (RFC 1800)

From time to time, RFCs are published that list the status of the various protocols and the RFCs that define them. Here, we list the status (Standard, Draft Standard etc.) of the individual protocols and the documents through which they are defined, based upon the information contained in RFC 1800.

B.1 Standard Protocols

Table B-1: Standard Protocols

STD	Protocol	Name	Status	RFC(s)
1		Internet Official Protocol Standards	Required	1800
2		Assigned Numbers	Required	1700
3		Host Requirements – Communications	Required	1122
3		Host Requirements – Applications	Required	1123
5	IP	Internet Protocol	Required	791
5	(amendment)	IP Subnet Extension	Required	950
5	(amendment)	IP Broadcast Datagrams	Required	919
5	(amendment)	IP Broadcast Datagrams with Subnets	Required	922
5	ICMP	Internet Control Message Protocol	Required	792
5	IGMP	Internet Group Multi-cast Protocol	Recommended	1112
6	UDP	User Datagram Protocol	Recommended	768
7	TCP	Transmission Control Protocol	Recommended	793
8	TELNET	Telnet Protocol	Recommended	854,855
9	FTP	File Transfer Protocol	Recommended	959
10	SMTP	Simple Mail Transfer Protocol	Recommended	821
11	MAIL	Format of Electronic Mail Messages	Recommended	822
11	CONTENT	Content Type Header Field	Recommended	1049
12	NTPV2	Network Time Protocol (Version 2)	Recommended	1119
13	DOMAIN	Domain Name System	Recommended	1034,1035
14	DNS-MX	Mail Routing and the Domain Name System	Recommended	974
15	SNMP	Simple Network Management Protocol	Recommended	1157
16	SMI	Structure of Management Information	Recommended	1155
16	Concise-MIB	Concise MIB Definitions	Recommended	1212
17	MIB-II	Management Information Base-II	Recommended	1213
19	NETBIOS	NetBIOS Service Protocols	Elective	1001,1002
20	ECHO	Echo Protocol	Recommended	862
21	DISCARD	Discard Protocol	Elective	863
22	CHARGEN	Character Generator Protocol	Elective	864
23	QUOTE	Quote of the Day Protocol	Elective	865

STD	Protocol	Name	Status	RFC(s)
24	USERS	Active Users Protocol	Elective	866
25	DAYTIME	Daytime Protocol	Elective	867
26	TIME	Time Server Protocol	Elective	868
33	TFTP	Trivial File Transfer Protocol	Elective	1350
34	RIP	Routing Information Protocol	Elective	1058
35	TP-TCP	ISO Transport Service on top of the TCP	Elective	1006
50	ETHER-MIB	Ethernet MIB	Elective	1643
51	PPP	Point-to-Point Protocol (PPP)	Elective	1661
51	PPP-HDLC	PPP in HDLC Framing	Elective	1662

B.2 Network Specific Standard Protocols

Currently, all Network Specific Standard Protocols have a status of Elective and are litsed below:

Table B-2: Network Specific Standard Protocols

STD	Protocol	Name	State	RFC(s)
	IP-ATM	Classical IP and ARP over ATM	Proposed	1577
	IP-FR	Multiprotocol over Frame Relay	Draft	1490
	ATM-ENCAP	Multiprotocol Encapsulation over ATM	Proposed	1483
	IP-TR-MC	IP Multi-cast over Token Ring LANs	Proposed	1469
36	IP-FDDI	Transmission of IP & ARP over FDDI Nets	Standard	1390
	IP-HIPPI	IP and ARP on HIPPI	Proposed	1374
	IP-X.25	X.25 and ISDN in the Packet Mode	Draft	1356
	IP-FDDI	Internet Protocol on FDDI Networks	Draft	1188
37	ARP	Address Resolution Protocol	Standard	826
38	RARP	A Reverse Address Resolution Protocol	Standard	903
39	IP-ARPA	Internet Protocol on the ARPANET	Standard	BBN1822
40	IP-WB	Internet Protocol on Wideband Networks	Standard	907
41	IP-E	Internet Protocol on Ethernet Networks	Standard	894
42	IP-EE	IP on Experimental Ethernet Networks	Standard	895
43	IP-IEEE	Internet Protocol on IEEE 802 Networks	Standard	1042
44	IP-DC	Internet Protocol on DC Networks	Standard	891
45	IP-HC	Internet Protocol on Hyperchannel Networks	Standard	1044
46	IP-ARC	Transmitting IP Traffic over ARCNET Nets	Standard	1201
47	IP-SLIP	Transmission of IP over Serial Lines	Standard	1055
48	IP-NETBIOS	Transmission of IP over NETBIOS	Standard	1088
49	IP-IPX	Transmission of 802.2 over IPX Networks	Standard	1132
52	IP-SMDS	IP Datagrams over the SMDS Service	Standard	1209

B.3 Draft Standard Protocols

Table B-3: Draft Standard Protocols

Protocol	Name	Status	RFC(s)
STR-REP	String Representation	Elective	1779
X.500syn	X.500 String Representation	Elective	1778
X.500lite	X.500 Lightweight	Elective	1777
BGP-4-APP	Application of BGP-4	Elective	1772
BGP-4	Border Gateway Protocol 4	Elective	1771

Protocol	Name	Status	RFC(s)
PPP-DNCP	PPP DECnet Phase IV Control Protocol	Elective	1762
RMON-MIB	Remote Network Monitoring MIB	Elective	1757
802.5-MIB	IEEE 802.5 Token Ring MIB	Elective	1748
BGP-4-MIB	BGP-4 MIB	Elective	1657
POP3	Post Office Protocol, Version 3	Elective	1725
RIP2-MIB	RIP Version 2 MIB Extension	Elective	1724
RIP2	RIP Version 2 Carrying Additional Information	Elective	1723
RIP2-APP	RIP Version 2 Protocol App. Statement	Elective	1722
SIP-MIB	SIP Interface Type MIB	Elective	1694
	Definition of Mngmnt Objects Parallel-printer-like	Elective	1660
	Definition of Mngmnt Objects RS-232-like	Elective	1659
	Definition of Mngmnt Objects Character Stream	Elective	1658
SMTP-SIZE	SMTP Service Ext for Message Size	Elective	1653
SMTP-8BIT	SMTP Service Ext for 8bit MIME Transport	Elective	1652
SMTP-EXT	SMTP Service Extensions	Elective	1651
OSI-NSAP	Guidlines for OSI NSAP Allocation	Elective	1629
OSPF2	Open Shortest Path First Routing Version 2	Elective	1583
ISO-TS-ECHO	Echo for ISO-8473	Elective	1575
DECNET-MIB	DECNET MIB	Elective	1559
	Message Header Ext. Of Non-ASCII Text	Elective	1522
MIME	Multipurpose Internet Mail Extensions	Elective	1521
802.3-MIB	IEEE 802.3 Repeater MIB	Elective	1516
BRIDGE-MIB	BRIDGE-MIB	Elective	1493
NTPV3	Network Time Protocol (Version 3)	Elective	1305
IP-MTU	Path MTU Discovery	Elective	1191
FINGER	Finger Protocol	Elective	1288
BOOTP	Bootstrap Protocol	Recommended	951,1497
NICNAME	WhoIs Protocol	Elective	954

B.4   Proposed Standard Protocols

All Proposed Standard Protocols have a Status of Elective.

Table B-4: Proposed Standard Protocols

Protocol	Name	RFC(s)
RREQ	Requirements for IP Version 4 Routers	1812
URL	Relative Uniform Resource Locators	1808
CLDAP	Connection-less LDAP	1798
OSPF-DC	Extension of OSPF to Support Demand Circuits	1793
TMUX	Transport Multiplexing Protocol	1692
TFTP-Opt	TFTP Options	1784
TFTP-Blk	TFTP Blocksize Options	1783
TFTP-Ext	TFTP Option Extension	1782
OSI-Dir	OSI User Friendly Naming	1781
MIME-EDI	MIME Encapsulation of EDI Objects	1767
Lang-Tag	Tags for Identification of Languages	1766
XNSCP	PPP XNS IDP Control Protocol	1764
BVCP	PPP Banyan Vines Control Protocol	1763
Print-MIB	Printer MIB	1759
ATM-SIG	ATM Signalling for IP over ATM	1755
IPNG	Recommendation for IP Next Generation	1752
802.5-SSR	802.5 SSR MIB using SMIv2	1749

Protocol	Name	RFC(s)
SDLCSMIv2	SNADLC SDLC MIB using SMIv2	1747
BGP4/IDRP	BGP4/IDRP for IP/OSPF Interaction	1745
AT-MIB	AppleTalk MIB	1742
MacMIME	MIME Encapsulation of Macintosh Files	1740
POP3-AUTH	POP3 Authentication Command	1734
IMAP4-AUTH	IMAP4 Authentication Mechanisms	1731
IMAP4	Internet Message Access Protocol V4	1730
PPP-MP	PPP Multilink Protocol	1717
RDBMS-MIB	RDBMS MIB – Using SMIv2	1697
MODEM-MIB	Modem MIB – Using SMIv2	1696
ATM-MIB	ATM Management Version 8.0 using SMIv2	1695
SNANAU-MIB	SNA NAUs MIB using SMIv2	1665
PPP-TRANS	PPP Reliable Transmission	1663
BGP-4-IMP	BGP-4 Roadmap and Implementation	1656
	Postmaster Convention X.400 Operations	1648
TN3270-En	TN3270 Enhancements	1647
PPP-BCP	PPP Bridging Control Protocol	1638
UPS-MIB	UPS Management Information Base	1628
AAL5-MTU	Default IP MTU for use over ATM AAL5	1626
PPP-SONET	PPP over SONET/SDH	1619
PPP-ISDN	PPP over ISDN	1618
DNS-R-MIB	DNS Resolver MIB Extensions	1612
DNS-S-MIB	DNS Server MIB Extensions	1611
FR-MIB	Frame Relay Service MIB	1604
PPP-X25	PPP in X.25	1598
OSPF-NSSA	The OSPF NSSA Option	1587
OSPF-Multi	Multicast Extensions to OSPF	1584
SONET-MIB	MIB SONET/SDH Interface Type	1595
RIP-DC	Extensions to RIP to Support Demand Circuits	1582
	Evolution of the Interfaces Group of MIB-II	1573
PPP-LCP	PPP LCP Extensions	1570
X500-MIB	X.500 Directory Monitoring MIB	1567
MAIL-MIB	Mail Monitoring MIB	1566
NSM-MIB	Network Services Monitoring MIB	1565
CIPX	Compressing IPX Headers Over WAN Media	1553
IPXCP	PPP Internetworking Packet Exchange Control	1552
CON-MD5	Content-MD5 Header Field	1544
DHCP-BOOTP	Interaction Between DHCP and BOOTP	1534
DHCP-BOOTP	DHCP Options and BOOTP Vendor Extensions	1533
BOOTP	Clarification and Extensions BOOTP	1532
DHCP	Dynamic Host Configuration Protocol	1541
SRB-MIB	Source Routing Bridge MIB	1525
CIDR-STRA	CIDR Address Assignment	1519
CIDR-ARCH	CIDR Architecture	1518
CIDR-APP	CIDR Applicability Statement	1517
	802.3 MAU MIB	1515
HOST-MIB	Host Resources MIB	1514
	Token Ring Extensions to RMON MIB	1513
FDDI-MIB	FDDI Management Information Base	1512
KERBEROS	Kerberos Network Authentication Server (V5)	1510
GSSAPI	Generic Security Service API: C-bindings	1509
GSSAPI	Generic Security Service Application	1508
DASS	Distributed Authentication Security	1507
	X.400 Use of Extended Character Sets	1502
HARPOON	Rules for Downgrading Messages	1496

Protocol	Name	RFC(s)
Mapping	MHS/RFC-822 Message Body Mapping	1495
Equiv	X.400/MIME Body Equivalencies	1494
IDRP	Inter-Domain Policy Routing Protocol	1479
IDRP-ARCH	Architecture for IDRP	1478
PPP/Bridge	MIB Bridge PPP MIB	1474
PPP/IP MIB	IP Network Control Protocol of PPP MIB	1473
PPP/SEC MIB	Security Protocols of PPP MIB	1472
PPP/LCP MIB	Link Control Protocol of PPP MIB	1471
X25-MIB	Multiprotocol Interconnect on X..25 MIB	1461
SNMPv2	Coexistence between SNMPv1 and SNMPv2	1452
SNMPv2	Manager-to-Manger MIB	1451
SNMPv2	Management Information Base for SNMPv2	1450
SNMPv2	Transport Mappings for SNMPv2	1449
SNMPv2	Protocol Operations for SNMPv2	1448
SNMPv2	Party MIB for SNMPv2	1447
SNMPv2	Security Protocols for SNMPv2	1446
SNMPv2	Administrative Model for SNMPv2	1445
SNMPv2	Conformance Statements for SNMPv2	1444
SNMPv2	Textual Conventions for SNMPv2	1443
SNMPv2	SMI for SNMPv2	1442
SNMPv2	Introduction to SNMPv2	1441
PEM-KEY	PEM – Key Certification	1424
PEM-ALG	PEM – Algorithms, Modes, and Identifiers	1423
PEM-CKM	PEM – Certificate-Based Key Management	1422
PEM-ENC	PEM – Message Encryption and Authentication	1421
SNMP-IPX	SNMP Over IPX	1420
SNMP-AT	SNMP Over AppleTalk	1419
SNMP-OSI	SNMP Over OSI	1418
FTP-FTAM	FTP-FTAM Gateway Specification	1415
IDENT-MIB	Identification MIB	1414
IDENT	Identification Protocol	1413
DS3/E3-MIB	DS3/E3 Interface Type	1407
DS1/E1-MIB	DS1/E1 Interface Type	1406
BGP-OSPF	BGP OSPF Interaction	1403
	Route Advertisement in BGP2 and BGP3	1397
SNMP-X.25	SNMP MIB Extension for X.25 Packet Layer	1382
SNMP-LAPB	SNMP MIB Extension for X.25 LAPB	1381
PPP-ATCP	PPP AppleTalk Control Protocol	1378
PPP-OSINLCP	PPP OSI Network Layer Control Protocol	1377
TABLE-MIB	IP Forwarding Table MIB	1354
SNMP-PARTY-MIB	Administration of SNMP	1353
SNMP-SEC	SNMP Security Protocols	1352
SNMP-ADMIN	SNMP Administrative Model	1351
TOS	Type of Service in the Internet	1349
PPP-AUTH	PPP Authentication	1334
PPP-LINK	PPP Link Quality Monitoring	1333
PPP-IPCP	PPP Control Protocol	1332
	X.400 1988 to 1984 Downgrading	1328
	Mapping Between X.400 (1988)	1327
TCP-EXT	TCP Extensions for High Performance	1323
FRAME-MIB	Management Information Base for Frame Relay	1315
NETFAX	File Format for the Exchange of Images	1314
IARP	Inverse Address Resolution Protocol	1293
FDDI-MIB	FDDI-MIB	1285
	Encoding Network Addresses	1277

Protocol	Name	RFC(s)
	Replication and Distributed Operations	1276
	COSINE and Internet X.500 Schema	1274
BGP-MIB	Border Gateway Protocol MIB (Version 3)	1269
ICMP-ROUT	ICMP Router Discovery Messages	1256
OSPF-MIB	OSPF Version 2 MIB	1253
IPSO	DoD Security Options for IP	1108
OSI-UDP	OSI TS on UDP	1240
STD-MIBs	Reassignment of Experimental MIBs to Standard MIBs	1239
IPX-IP	Tunnelling IPX Traffic Through IP Networks	1234
GINT-MIB	Extensions to the Generic Interface MIB	1229
IS-IS	OSI IS-IS for TCP/IP Dual Environments	1195
IP-CMPRS	Compressing TCP/IP Headers	1144
NNTP	Network News Transfer Protocol	977

B.5 Experimental Protocols

All Experimental Protocols have a status of Limited Use and are listed here:

Table B-5: Experimental Protocols

Protocol	Name	RFC(s)
	Content-Disposition Header	1806
	Schema Publishing in X.500 Directory	1804
	X.400-MHS use X.500 to support X.400-MHS Routing	1801
	Class A Subnet Experiment	1797
TCP/IPXMIB	TCP/IPX Connection Mib Specification	1792
	TCP and UDP Over IPX Networks with Fixed Path MTU	1791
ICMP-DM	ICMP Domain Name Messages	1788
CLNP-MULT	Host Group Extensions for CLNP Multicasting	1768
OSPF-OVFL	OSPF Database Overflow	1765
RWP	Remote Write Protocol – Version 1.0	1756
NARP	NBMA Address Resolution Protocol	1735
DNS-DEBUG	Tools for DNS Debugging	1713
DNS-ENCODE	DNS Encoding of Geographical Location	1712
TCP-POS	An Extension to TCP: Partial Order Service	1693
	DNS to Distribute RFC 1327 Mail Address Mapping Tables	1664
T/TCP	TCP Extensions for Transactions	1644
UTF-7	A Mail-Safe Transformation Format of Unicode	1642
MIME-UNI	Using Unicode with MIME	1641
FOOBAR	FTP Operation Over Big Address Records	1639
X500-CHART	Charting Networks in the X.500 Directory	1609
X500-DIR	Representing IP Infomation in the X.500 Directory	1608
SNMP-DPI	SNMP Distributed Protocol Interface	1592
CLNP-TUBA	Use of ISO CLNP in TUBA Environments	1561
REM-PRINT	TPC.INT Subdomain Remote Printing – Technical	1528
EHF-MAIL	Encoding Header Field for Internet Messages	1505
REM-PRT	An Experiment in Remote Printing	1486
RAP	Internet Route Access Protocol	1476
TP/IX	TP/IX: The Next Internet	1475
X400	Routing Co-ordination for X.400 Services	1465
DNS	Storing Arbitrary Attributes in DNS	1464
IRCP	Internet Relay Chat Protocol	1459
TOS-LS	Link Security TOS	1455

Protocol	Name	RFC(s)
SIFT/UFT	Sender-Initiated/Unsolicited File Transfer	1440
DIR-ARP	Directed ARP	1433
TEL-SPX	Telnet Authentication: SPX	1412
TEL-KER	Telnet Authentication: Kerberos V4	1411
MAP-MAIL	X.400 Mapping and Mail-11	1405
TRACE-IP	Traceroute Using and IP Option	1393
DNS-IP	Experiment in NS Based IP Routing	1383
RMCP	Remote Mail Checking Protocol	1339
TCP-HIPER	TCP Extensions for High Performance	1323
MSP2	Message Send Protocol 2	1312
DSLCP	Dynamically Switched Link Control	1307
	X.500 and Domains	1279
IN-ENCAP	Internet Encapsulation Protocol	1241
CLNS-MIB	CLNS-MIB	1238
CFDP	Coherent File Distribution Protocol	1235
SNMP-DPI	SNMP Distributed Program Interface	1228
IP-AX.25	IP Encapsulation of AX.25 Frames	1226
ALERTS	Managing Asynchronously Generated Alerts	1224
MPP	Message Posting Protocol	1204
ST-II	Stream Protocol	1190
SNMP-BULK	Bulk Table Retrieval with the SNMP	1187
DNS-RR	New DNS RR Definitions	1183
IMAP2	Interactive Mail Access Protocol	1176
NTP-OSI	NTP Over OSI Remote Operations	1165
DMF-MAIL	Digest Message Format for Mail	1153
RDP	Reliable Data Protocol	908,1151
TCP-ACO	TCP Alternate Checksum Option	1146
	Mapping Full 822 to Restricted 822	1137
IP-DVMRP	IP Distance Vector Multi-cast Routing	1075
VMTP	Versatile Message Transaction Protocol	1045
COOKIE-JAR	Authentication Scheme	1004
NETBLT	Bulk Data Transfer Protocol	998
IRTP	Internet Reliable Transaction Protocol	938
LDP	Loader Debugger Protocol	909
RLP	Resource Location Protocol	887
NVP-II	Network Voice Protocol	ISI-memo
PVP	Packet Video Protocol	ISI-memo

B.6   Informational Protocols

Informational Protocols have no status.

Table B-6: Informational Protocols

Protocol	Name	RFC(s)
NFSV3	NFS Version 3 Protocol Specification	1813
	A Format for Bibliographic Records	1807
SDMD	Ipv4 Option for Sender Directed MD Delivery	1770
SNTP	Simple Network Time Protocol	1769
SNOOP	Snoop Version 2 Packet Capture File Format	1761
BINHEX	MIME Content Type for BinHex Encoded Files	1741
RWHOIS	Referral Whois Protocol	1714
DNS-NSAP	DNS NSAP Resource Records	1706

Protocol	Name	RFC(s)
RADIO-PAGE	TPC.INT Subdomain: Radio Paging – Technical Procedures	1703
GRE-IPv4	Generic Routing Encapsulation over IPv4	1702
GRE	Generic Routing Encapsulation	1701
SNPP	Simple Network Paging Protocol – Version 2	1645
IPXWAN	Novell IPX Over Various WAN Media	1634
ADSNA-IP	Advanced SNA/IP: A Simple SNA Transport Protocol	1538
AUBR	AppleTalk Update Based Routing Protocol	1504
TACACS	Terminal Access Control Protocol	1492
SUN-NFS	Network File System Protocol	1094
SUN-RPC	Remote Procedure Call Protocol Version 2	1057
GOPHER	The Internet Gopher Protocol	1436
	Data Link Switching: Switch-to-Switch Protocol	1434
LISTSERV	Listserv Distribute Protocol	1429
	Replication Requirements	1275
PCMAIL	Pcmail Transport Protocol	1056
MTP	Multi-cast Transport Protocol	1301
BSD Login	BSD Login	1282
DIXIE	DIXIE Protocol Specification	1249
IP-X.121	IP to X.121 Address Mapping for DDN	1236
OSI-HYPER	OSI and LLC1 on HYPERchannel	1223
HAP2	Host Access Protocol	1221
SUBNETAGN	On the Assignment of Subnet Numbers	1219
SNMP-TRAPS	Defining Traps for use with SNMP	1215
DAS	Directory Assistance Service	1202
MD4	MD4 Message Digest Algorithm	1186
LPDP	Line Printer Daemon Protocol	1179

B.7 Historic Protocols

All Historic Protocols have a status of *Not Recommended*. They are however listed here for the sake of completion.

Table B-7: Historic Protocols

Protocol	Name	RFC(s)
BGP3	Border Gateway Protocol 3 (BGP-3)	1267/1268
	Gateway Requirements (was Std 4 – Required)	1009
EGP	Exterior Gateway Protocol (was Std 18 – Recommended)	904
SNMP-MUX	SNMP MUX Protocol and MIB	1227
OIM-MIB-II	OSI Internet Management: MIB-II	1214
IMAP3	Interactive Mail Access Protocol Version 3	1203
SUN-RPC	Remote Procedure Call Protocol Version 1	1050
802.4-MIB	IEEE 802.4 Token Bus MIB	1230
CMOT	Common Management Information Services	1189
	Mail Privacy: Procedures	1113
	Mail Privacy: Key Management	1114
	Mail Privacy: Algorithms	1115
NFILE	A File Access Protocol	1037
HOSTNAME	HOSTNAME Protocol	953
SFTP	Simple File Transfer Protocol	913
SUPDUP	SUPDUP Protocol	734
BGP	Border Gateway Protocol	1163,1164
MIB-I	MIB-I	1156

Protocol	Name	RFC(s)
SGMP	Simple Gateway Monitoring Protocol	1028
HEMS	High Level Entity Management Protocol	1021
STATSRV	Statistics Server	996
POP2	Post Office Protocol Version 2	937
RATP	Reliable Asynchronous Transfer Protocol	916
HFEP	Host – Front End Protocol	929
THINWIRE	Thinwire Protocol	914
HMP	Host Monitoring Protocol	869
GGP	Gateway Gateway Protocol	823
RTELNET	Remote Telnet Service	818
CLOCK	DCNET Time Server Protocol	778
MPM	Internet Message Protocol	759
NETRJS	Remote Job Service	740
NETED	Network Standard Text Editor	569
RJE	Remote Job Entry	407
XNET	Cross Net Debugger	IEN[1]-158
NAMESERVER	Host Name Server Protocol	IEN-116
MUX	Multiplexing Protocol	IEN-90
GRAPHICS	Graphics Protocol	NIC-24308

1. IEN stands for Internet Engineering Note, the predecessor of the RFC.

Management Information Base MIB II (RFC 1213)

The basic MIB II objects are defined by RFC 1213. This document defines 11 groups shown in the table below together with their OIDs. The following sections then briefly describe the 171 objects that make up this area of the management tree. It should be noted that many of the groups are considered *mandatory* thus, any SNMP compliant device should implement them allowing at least minimal management capability. Any compliant device will therefore be manageable, and will maintain these objects at the very least.

This list is not exhaustive but merely defines those objects specified by RFC 1213. As new protocols and network concepts are introduced, new groups are added and will continue to be so for many years to come.

Table C-1: SNMPMIB II Major Groups

Group	Name	OID	Description
1	system	1.3.6.1.2.1.1	Provides generic configuration information.
2	interfaces	1.3.6.1.2.1.2	Defines the number of physical interfaces and additional parameters associated with the definition of the interface type and status.
3	at	1.3.6.1.2.1.3	Marked as deprecated (since these objects are also found in the ip group) these objects contain the address translation table.
4	ip	1.3.6.1.2.1.4	These objects monitor the Internet Protocol (IP) used within the device.
5	icmp	1.3.6.1.2.1.5	Contains objects that return statistics on all aspects of ICMP.
6	tcp	1.36.1.2.1.6	Contains objects that monitor the Transmission Control Protocol (TCP).
7	udp	1.3.6.1.2.1.7	Provides statistical data on the User Datagram Protocol (UDP).
8	egp	1.3.6.1.2.1.8	These objects return statistics relating to the Exterior Gateway Protocol (EGP).
9	cmot	1.3.6.1.2.1.9	Originally designed so that this group could provide statistics and other information on CMOT as the transition to OSI protocols took place. This group however remains unused.
10	transmission	1.3.6.1.2.1.10	This group contains no directly defined objects. Instead it contains a subtree of groups relating to network access methods.
11	snmp	1.3.6.1.2.1.11	Provides statistical data on the SNMP. Although it was originally envisaged that the agent would be configured through this group, only statistical objects are currently defined.

C.1   System Group

This group is mandatory for all systems. Where a device is not configured to have a value for any of these objects a string length of zero is returned.

Table C-2: The System Group

Object	Name	Description
1	sysDescr	A text string of between 0 and 155 octets that contains the full name and version identification of the system's hardware type.
2	sysObjectID	The OID of the vendors authoritative identification of the network management subsystem (i.e. 1.3.6.1.4.1.33.1.2.3) so that the device type can be determined. In the example, this would be a device of type 1.2.3 from Xyplex.
3	sysUpTime	The integer time (in hundredths of a second) since the management part of the device was last reset.
4	sysContact	A text string (of between 0 and 255 octets) that can be used to identify the person responsible for this device.
5	sysName	A text string (of between 0 and 255 octets) that can be used to identify this device. By convention, this would be the fully qualified domain name of the device.
6	sysLocation	A text string (of between 0 and 255 octets) that can be used to identify the physical location of this device.
7	sysServices	An integer value between 0 and 127 that can be used to define the set of services offered by the device. The value starts at zero, but for each layer of the OSI model that the device offers services, 2 raised to the power (level-1) is added. A device that only performs routing would therefore have the value 4 (being $2^{(3-1)}$).

C.2   Interfaces Group

As with the System group, this group is mandatory. In contrast to the System group however, the interfaces group also includes sub-trees. Thus we see an absolute number of interfaces each of which has a number of associated objects.

Table C-3: The Interfaces Group

Object	Name	Description
1	ifNumber	An integer value that specifies the number of network interfaces on the device and regardless of their state.
2	ifTable	This is a sequence of IfEntry values. The number of actual entries within this table is determined by the value of ifNumber (with one table entry per interface. For example, a four port router would have 4 table entries with each entry made up of the values given in Table C-4 over.

C.2.1   The ifTable

For each interface we then have a number of objects within the ifTable as listed over:

Table C-4: The IfTable

Object	Name	Description
1	IfIndex	This object is an integer that contains the interface entry itself. Since each interface will have an entry and this defines the interface, it follows that this value will be between 1 and ifNumber.
2	ifDescr	A text string of between 0 and 255 octets that contains information about the interface.
3	ifType	An integer that defines the actual type of interface being described. As an example, if the interface was say 802.3, then this value would be 7. Equally, if the interface was FDDI it would be 15, and for PPP, 23.
4	ifMtu	An integer value that defines the largest datagram that can be either sent or received on the interface.
5	ifSpeed	An estimate of the interface's current bandwidth in bits per second.
6	ifPhysAddress	The physical address of the interface. If the interface does not have a physical address (for example a serial WAN link), then this object contains a zero length octet string.
7	ifAdminStatus	This is an integer value used to set the desired state of the interface. A value of 1 means up, 2 means down, and 3 means testing. In the testing state no operational packets can be passed.
8	ifOperStatus	This is an integer value used to indicate the current state of the interface. As before, a value of 1 means up, 2 means down, and 3 means testing. Again, in the testing state no operational packets can be passed.
9	ifLastChange	This is the value of sysUpTime at which the interface entered its current operational state. If the time has been reset since this value was set, the object contains a zero value.
10	ifInOctets	A counter used to indicate the total number of octets received at the interface.
11	ifInUcastPkts	A counter that indicates the total number of unicast packets received at the interface and passed to a higher layer protocol.
12	ifInNUcastPkts	A counter that indicates the total number of non-unicast packets received at the interface and passed to a higher layer protocol.
13	ifInDiscards	A count of the number of inbound packets that were discarded even though they had no errors. There are many reasons why a packet is discarded however, normally this would indicate resource errors within the device.
14	ifInErrors	The number of inbound packets that were discarded due to errors.
15	ifInUnknownProtos	The number of packets received at the interface that were discarded because the protocol was either unknown or not supported.
16	ifOutOctets	The total number of octets transmitted by the interface.
17	ifOutUcastPkts	The total number of unicast packets that higher level protocols requested be sent including those that were discarded.
18	ifOutNUcastPkts	The total number of non-unicast packets that higher level protocols requested be sent including those that were discarded.
19	ifOutDiscards	The number of outbound packets that were discarded even though there was no error detected. This could occur due to a lack of buffer space for example.
20	ifOutErrors	The number of packets that were not transmitted due to errors.
21	ifOutQLen	The length of the output queue (in packets).
22	ifSpecific	This is a reference to MIB definitions specific to a particular media type. E.g. If this interface is Ethernet, this object will refer to the document that defines Ethernet objects.

Interfaces Group

C.3 AT Group

The Address Translation (AT) group itself comprises just one table that has a number of entries providing protocol to physical address translation. This group is *deprecated* meaning that it has been superseded. The group is however considered mandatory since, previous implementations (MIB I) require it.

Table C-5: The AT Group

Object	Name	Description
1	atIfIndex	The interface on which this entry is used. This has the same value as ifIndex from the Interfaces group.
2	atPhysAddress	The physical address of the interface.
3	atNetAddress	The Network Address (protocol address) that corresponds to the atPhysAddresss at this atIfIndex.

C.4 IP Group

The IP Group is mandatory for all devices and provides information on the configuration and operation of the Internet Protocol running on the device. This group was modified significantly with the introduction of MIB II and now contains a table that supersedes the *deprecated* AT Group.

Table C-6: The IP Group

Object	Name	Description
1	ipForwarding	Whether or not this device is forwarding datagrams (i.e. whether it is acting as a router). This is an integer value of 1 where the device is a router, and 2 if it is not.
2	ipDefaultTTL	An integer value that is used for the Time-to-Live field in the IP Datagram header when no value was supplied by the Transport layer.
3	ipInReceives	A count of the number of datagrams received (including those with errors).
4	ipInHdrErrors	A count of the number of IP datagrams discarded because of an error in the header.
5	ipInAddrErrors	A count of the number of datagrams discarded because the Destination address in the IP header was invalid or incorrect for this type of device. For example if the device is not acting as a router and the destination address does not reflect the local network, then this would be considered an error.
6	ipForwDatagrams	The number of datagrams received by the device that require forwarding to another network.
7	ipInUnknownProtos	A count of the number of datagrams received, but discarded due to the protocol being either unknown or unsupported.
8	ipInDiscards	The number of datagrams that were discarded even though there was no physical problem that may have prevented them from being processed. One example may be a lack of buffers etc.
9	ipInDelivers	The number of datagrams received and delivered to IP user-protocols. In other words, delivered to another process on the device.

Object	Name	Description
10	ipOutRequests	The number of datagrams that were passed from another process on the device to the IP Layer for transmission.
11	ipOutDiscards	The number of output datagrams discarded even though there was no physical problem. Again buffer exhaustion may cause this to happen.
12	ipOutNoRoutes	The number of datagrams discarded because no route could be found to the destination.
13	ipReasmTimeout	An integer value that indicates the maximum time (in seconds) that received datagram fragments can be held while they are awaiting re-assembly.
14	ipReasmReqds	A count of the total number of IP fragments received that needed re-assembly.
15	ipReasmOKs	The total number of datagrams successfully re-assembled.
16	ipReasmFails	The number of datagrams that could not be re-assembled for whatever reason.
17	ipFragOKs	A count of the number of datagrams that have been successfully fragmented.
18	ipFragFails	The number of datagrams that needed fragmentation but could not be fragmented. For example, the Do Not Fragment flag may have been set.
19	ipFragCreates	The number of fragments that have been generated.
20	ipAddrTable	The table of addressing information relevant to this devices IP Address(es). See Table C.7 below.
21	ipRouteTable	The routing table for the device. See following Table C.8.
22	ipNetToMediaTable	The IP Address Translation Table replacing the AT Group. See Table C.9.
23	ipRoutingDiscards	A count of the number of routing entries discarded even though they had no errors. This could be due to buffer exhaustion.

C.4.1 IP Address Table

This table provides information about the IP Address(es) associated with each interface. Although simple in structure, it provides interface specific information relating to the MTU, Address, and Mask.

Table C-7: The IP Address Table

Object	Name	Description
1	ipAdEntAddr	The IP Address to which this entry pertains.
2	ipAdEntIfIndex	An integer value that is used to identify the interface. This has the same value as ifIndex.
3	ipAdEntNetMask	The subnet mask associated with the IP Address of this table entry.
4	ipAdEntBcastAddr	An integer that identifies the least significant bit of the broadcast address used. i.e. when an all zeroes broadcast is used, this will be 0. Equally, when an all ones broadcast is used this will be 1.
5	ipAdEntReasm-MaxSize	An integer value between 0 an 65535 which represents the largest datagram that the interface can handle.

C.4.2 IP Routing Table

The IP Routing Table provides us with information about the routes available to distant networks. This information includes the next hop router and various metrics that can be used.

Table C-8: The IP Routing Table

Object	Name	Description
1	ipRouteDest	The destination address for this route or the default route 0.0.0.0.
2	ipRouteIfIndex	An integer that identifies the interface through which the next hop to the destination is reached.
3	ipRouteMetric1	An integer value that defines the primary routing metric for the route as determined by the routing protocol.
4	ipRouteMetric2	An integer value defining an alternative routing metric.
5	ipRouteMetric3	An integer value defining an alternative routing metric.
6	ipRouteMetric4	An integer value defining an alternative routing metric.
7	ipRouteNextHop	The IP Address of the next hop for this route.
8	ipRouteType	An integer that defines the type of route. Valid values are: 1 Other, 2 Invalid, 3 Direct, and 4 Indirect with values 3 and 4 referring to direct and indirect routing respectively.
9	ipRouteProto	An integer value that identifies the mechanism through which this route was learnt. Sample values include 2 Local, 4 ICMP (i.e. Redirect), 5 EGP, 8 RIP, 13 OSPF, and 14 BGP.
10	ipRouteAge	An integer value that represents the time (in seconds) since the route was last updated.
11	ipRouteMask	The subnet mask that should be applied to the destination address.
12	ipRouteMetric5	An integer value defining an alternative routing metric.
13	ipRouteInfo	A value specific to the routing protocol responsible for this route.

C.4.3 IP Address Translation Table

This table replaces the deprecated AT group and, while the AT group is still included in the definition for backwards compatibility, it is unlikely that any future release will incorporate it.

Table C-9: The IP Address Translation Table

Object	Name	Description
1	ipNetToMediaIfIndex	An integer value that defines the interface on which this entry is effective.
2	ipNetToMediaPhys-Address	The Physical Address.
3	ipNetToMediaNet-Address	The IP Address that corresponds to the Physical Address above.
4	ipNetToMediaType	An integer value that defines the type of entry (mapping). Valid values are 1 Other, 2 Invalid, 3 Dynamic, and 4 Static.

C.5 ICMP Group

This group tracks statistical information about the Internet Control Message Protocol. Since ICMP is a required part of any IP implemenation, it follows that this group should also be considered mandatory.

Table C-10: The ICMP Group

Object	Name	Description
1	icmpInMsgs	A count of the number of ICMP messages that have been received (including those with errors).
2	icmpInErrors	A count of the number of ICMP messages received but with errors.
3	icmpInDestUnreachs	A count of the number of ICMP Destination Unreachable messages received.
4	icmpInTimeExcds	A count of the number of ICMP Time Exceeded messages received.
5	icmpInParmProbs	A count of the number of ICMP Paramter Problem messages received.
6	icmpInSrcQuenchs	A count of the number of ICMP Source Quench messages received.
7	icmpInRedirects	A count of the number of ICMP Redirect messages received.
8	icmpInEchos	A count of the number of ICMP Echo Request messages received.
9	icmpInEchoReps	A count of the number of ICMP Echo Reply messages received.
10	icmpInTimestamps	A count of the number of ICMP Timestamp Request messages received.
11	icmpInTimestamp-Reps	A count of the number of ICMP Timestamp Reply messages received.
12	icmpInAddrMasks	A count of the number of ICMP Address Mask Request messages received.
13	icmpInAddrMaskReps	A count of the number of ICMP Address Mask Reply messages received.
14	icmpOutMsgs	The number of ICMP messages that have been sent.
15	icmpOutErrors	The number of ICMP messages not sent dues to errors.
16	icmpOutDestUnreachs	The number of ICMP Destination Unreachable messages sent.
17	icmpOutTimeExcds	The number of ICMP Time Exceeded messages sent.
18	icmpOutParmProbs	The number of ICMP Parameter Problem messages sent.
19	icmpOutSrcQuenchs	The number of ICMP Source Quench messages sent.
20	icmpOutRedirects	The number of ICMP Redirect messages sent.
21	icmpOutEchos	The number of ICMP Echo Requests messages sent.
22	icmpOutEchoReps	The number of ICMP Echo Reply messages sent.
23	icmpOutTimestamps	The number of ICMP Timestamp Request messages sent.
24	icmpOutTimestamp-Reps	The number of ICMP Timestamp Reply messages sent.
25	icmpOutAddrMasks	The number of ICMP Address Mask Request messages sent.
26	icmpOutAddrMask-Reps	The number of ICMP Address Mask Reply messages sent.

C.6   TCP Group

This group is mandatory, but only for those devices that support TCP. Thus if a device (say a repeater) has the capability to receive Telnet connections for management purposes, it must support this group.

Table C-11: The TCP Group

Object	Name	Description
1	tcpRtoAlgorithm	An integer value used to indicate the timeout value used for re-transmitting any unacknowledged packets. A value of 1 indicates Other, 2 Constant, 3 rsre (MIL-STD-1778), and 4 Van Jacobson's algorithm.
2	tcpRtoMin	An integer value that represents the minimum value (in milliseconds) permitted by TCP for re-transmission.
3	tcpRtoMax	An integer value that represents the maximum value (in milliseconds) permitted by TCP for re-transmission.
4	tcpMaxConn	An integer value that defines the maximum number of TCP connections that the device can support.
5	tcpActiveOpens	A count of the number of times that TCP connections have made a direct transition from the CLOSED state to the SYN-SENT state.
6	tcpPassiveOpens	A count of the number of times that TCP connections have made a direct transition from the LISTEN state to the SYN-RCVD state.
7	tcpAttemptFails	A count of the number of times that TCP connections have made a direct transition to the CLOSED state from either the SYN-SENT or SYN-RCVD state plus the number of times that TCP connections have made a direct transition to the LISTEN state from the SYN-RCVD state.
8	tcpEstabResets	A count of the number of times that TCP connections have made a direct transition from either the ESTABLISHED or CLOSE-WAIT state to the CLOSED state.
9	tcpCurrEstab	The number of TCP connections currently established (i.e. those in either the ESTABLISHED or CLOSE-WAIT state).
10	tcpInSegs	A count of the number of TCP segments received (inc. errors).
11	tcpOutSegs	A count of the total number of segments sent.
12	tcpRetransSegs	A count of the total number of segments re-transmitted.
13	tcpConnTable	A table containing connection specific information. See Table C.12.
14	tcpInErrs	A count of the total number of TCP segments received in error.
15	tcpOutRsts	A count of the number of TCP segments containing the RST flag that have been sent.

C.6.1   TCP Connection Table

This table includes information about connections that are currently in progress. Tracking of connections can therefore be achieved.

Table C-12: The TCP Connection Table

Object	Name	Description
1	tcpConnState	An integer value that identifies the state of the connection. Sample values are: 1 Closed, 2 Listen, 3 SynSent, ... 5 Established, etc.

Object	Name	Description
2	tcpConnLocalAddress	The local IP Address for this TCP connection.
3	tcpConnLocalPort	An integer value between 0 and 65535 that identifies the local port number for this connection.
4	tcpConnRemAddress	The remote IP Address for this TCP connection.
5	tcpConnRemPort	An integer value between 0 and 65535 that identifies the remote port number for this connection.

C.7 UDP Group

The UDP group is deemed mandatory for all systems that support the UDP protocol. However, since these objects all refer to SNMP and SNMP relies upon UDP itself, this must be considered mandatory for any SNMP manageable device.

Table C-13: The UDP Group

Object	Name	Description
1	udpInDatagrams	A count of the total number of UDP datagrams delivered to processes on the device.
2	udpNoPorts	A count of the number of UDP datagrams received for which there was no application listening on the destination port.
3	udpInErrors	A count of the number of UDP datagrams received that could not be delivered due to errors. This does not include those that could not be delivered due to an incorrect port number though.
4	udpOutDatagrams	A count of the total number of UDP datagrams sent.
5	udpTable	A table that contains information about which ports the device is listening on. See Table C.14.

C.7.1 UDP Listener Table

The Listener Table provides a list of the well-known UDP ports that the device is using. For further information on UDP ports see Chapter 8.

Table C-14: The UDP Listener Table

Object	Name	Description
1	udpLocalAddress	The local IP Address for this UDP listener.
2	udpLocalPort	The local port number for this UDP listener.

C.8 EGP Group

The EGP group reports on information relating to the Exterior Gateway Protocol (EGP) and is considered mandatory for all devices that support it. Obviously Bridges and Repeaters would therefore be exempt.

Table C-15: The EGP Group

Object	Name	Description
1	egpInMsgs	A count of the number of EGP messages received without error.

Object	Name	Description
2	egpInErrors	A count of the number of EGP messages received with errors.
3	egpOutMsgs	A count of the number of EGP messages sent.
4	egpOutErrors	A count of the number of EGP messages not sent due to errors such as resource failures within the device.
5	egpNeighTable	A table of EGP Neighbors. See Table C.16.
6	egpAs	An integer used to define the Autonomous System Number (ASN) of this device.

C.8.1 EGP Neighbor Table

The EGP Neighbor Table provides information about the status of each neighbor (peer) with which the router has an association. This table is therefore significant if we wish to determine valuable routing information.

Table C-16: The EGP Neighbor Table

Object	Name	Description
1	egpNeighState	An integer value that defines the state of the local system with respect to its neighbor. Values are: 1 idle, 2 acquisition, 3 down, 4 up, and 5 cease.
2	egpNeighAddr	The IP Address of the neighbor to which this table entry applies.
3	egpNeighAS	An integer that identifies the Autonomous System Number (ASN) of the neighbor.
4	egpNeighInMsgs	A count of the number of EGP messages received without error from the neighbor.
5	egpNeighInErrs	A count of the number of EGP messages received from this neighbor that contained an error.
6	egpNeighOutMsgs	A count of the number of EGP messages sent to the neighbor.
7	egpNeighOutErrs	A count of the number of EGP messages that were not sent to this neighbor due to conditions such as resource errors etc.
8	egpNeighInErrMsgs	A count of the number of error messages (as defined by EGP) received from this neighbor.
9	egpNeighOutErrMsgs	A count of the number of error messages (as defined by EGP) sent to this neighbor.
10	egpNeighStateUps	The number of times that the device has transitioned to the UP state with this EGP neighbor.
11	egpNeighStateDowns	The number of times that the device has transitioned to the DOWN state with this EGP neighbor.
12	egpNeighInterval-Hello	An integer value that indicates the time (in hundredths of a second) between EGP Hello Command re-transmissions.
13	egpNeighIntervalPoll	An integer value that defines the time interval (in hundredths of a second) between EGP Poll Command re-transmissions.
14	egpNeighMode	An integer that defines the EGP polling mode of this device. When set to 1, the device is Active, and when set to 2, the device is Passive.
15	egpNeighEvent-Trigger	An integer that defines operator-initiated Start and Stop events. When set to 1 this object indicates Start, and 2 indicates Stop.

C.9   Transmission Group

RFC 1213 defines only the top level of this group and does not define any objects. In general, based upon the underlying technology of each interface on the device, the corresponding portion of the group will be mandatory. Definitions of the objects however, are contained in other documents. Chapter 20 contains tables of these documents to which reference should be made for further information.

C.10   SNMP Group

The SNMP group is again mandatory for all devices that implement SNMP. This group then defines objects that maintain statistical information about the protocol.

Table C-17: The SNMP Group

Object	Name	Description
1	snmpInPkts	A count of the number of SNMP messages delivered to the SNMP process.
2	snmpOutPkts	A count of the number of SNMP messages passed from the SNMP process to the Transport entity (UDP).
3	snmpInBadVersions	A count of the total number of SNMP messages that were received with an unsupported version number.
4	snmpInBad-Community-Names	A count of the total number of SNMP messages that were received but where the Community String was unknown.
5	snmpInBad-Community-Uses	A count of the number of SNMP messages received where the Community String used was not applicable to the operation requested.
6	snmpInASNParseErrs	A count of the number of ASN.1 or BER errors found in received SNMP messages.
7	Not Used	
8	snmpInTooBigs	A count of the total number of SNMP messages received with the 'tooBig' error indicated.
9	snmpInNoSuchNames	A count of the number of SNMP messages received where the Error Status field indicates 'noSuchName'.
10	snmpInBadValues	A count of the number of SNMP messages received with the Error Status field indicating 'badValue'.
11	snmpInReadOnlys	A count of the number of SNMP messages received with the Error Status field indicating 'readOnly'.
12	snmpInGenErrs	A count of the number of SNMP messages received with the Error Status field indicating 'genErr'.
13	snmpInTotalReqVars	A count of the total number of MIB objects that have been successfully retrieved as a result of GetRequest and GetNextRequest PDUs being received.
14	snmpInTotalSetVars	A count of the total number of MIB objects that have been successfully altered as a result of SetRequest PDUs being received.
15	snmpInGetRequests	A count of the total number of GetRequest PDUs that have been successfully processed.
16	snmpInGetNexts	A count of the total number of GetNextRequest PDUs that have been successfully processed.
17	snmpInSetRequests	A count of the total number of SetRequest PDUs that have been successfully processed.

Object	Name	Description
18	snmpInGetResponses	A count of the total number of GetResponse PDUs that have been successfully processed.
19	snmpInTraps	A count of the total number of Trap PDUs that have been successfully processed.
20	snmpOutTooBigs	A count of the number of SNMP messages generated with the value 'tooBig' in the Error Status field.
21	snmpOutNoSuch-Names	A count of the number of SNMP messages generated with the value 'noSuchName' in the Error Status field.
22	snmpOutBadValues	A count of the number of SNMP messages generated with the value 'badValue' in the Error Status field.
23	Not Used	
24	snmpOutGenErrs	A count of the number of SNMP messages generated with the value 'genErr' in the Error Status field.
25	snmpOutGetRequests	A count of the total number of SNMP GetRequest messages generated.
26	snmpOutGetNexts	A count of the total number of SNMP GetNextRequest messages generated.
27	snmpOutSetRequests	A count of the total number of SNMP SetRequest messages generated.
28	snmpOutGet-Responses	A count of the total number of SNMP GetResponse messages generated.
29	snmpOutTraps	A count of the total number of SNMP Trap messages generated.
30	snmpEnableAuthen-Traps	An integer value that is used to determine whether or not the device is allowed to generate traps when authentication failures are detected. A value of 1 indicates that this feature is enabled, while a value of 2 indicates that this feature is disabled.

Bibliography

Most of this book has been prepared directly from the relevant standards which, in the Internet world, is of course the *Request for Comments* document. In addition to other materials listed at the end of this section, many RFCs have been used in the preparation of the book and are listed below:

RFCs

114 A. Bhushan, "File Transfer Protocol", 04/10/1971.
768 J. Postel, "User Datagram Protocol", 08/28/1980.
791 J. Postel, "Internet Protocol", 09/01/1981.
792 J. Postel, "Internet Control Message Protocol", 09/01/1981.
793 J. Postel, "Transmission Control Protocol", 09/01/1981.
793 J. Postel, "Transmission Control Protocol", 09/01/1981.
821 J. Postel, "Simple Mail Transfer Protocol", 08/01/1982.
822 D. Crocker, "Standard for the format of ARPA Internet text messages", 08/13/1982.
826 D. Plummer, "Ethernet Address Resolution Protocol: Or converting network protocol addresses to 48bit Ethernet address for transmission on Ethernet hardware", 11/01/1982.
854 J. Postel, J. Reynolds, "Telnet Protocol specification", 05/01/1983.
856 J. Postel, J. Reynolds, "Telnet binary transmission", 05/01/1983.
857 J. Postel, J. Reynolds, "Telnet echo option", 05/01/1983.
858 J. Postel, J. Reynolds, "Telnet Suppress Go Ahead option", 05/01/1983.
859 J. Postel, J. Reynolds, "Telnet status option", 05/01/1983.
860 J. Postel, J. Reynolds, "Telnet timing mark option", 05/01/1983.
861 J. Postel, J. Reynolds, "Telnet extended options: List option", 05/01/1983.
862 J. Postel, "Echo Protocol", 05/01/1983.
863 J. Postel, "Discard Protocol", 05/01/1983.
864 J. Postel, "Character Generator Protocol", 05/01/1983.
865 J. Postel, "Quote of the Day Protocol", 05/01/1983.
866 J. Postel, "Active users", 05/01/1983.
867 J. Postel, "Daytime Protocol", 05/01/1983.
868 K. Harrenstien, J. Postel, "Time Protocol", 05/01/1983.
885 J. Postel, "Telnet end of record option", 12/01/1983.
903 R. Finlayson, T. Mann, J. Mogul, M. Theimer, "Reverse Address Resolution Protocol", 06/01/1984.
904 International Telegraph and Telephone Co, D. Mills, "Exterior Gateway Protocol formal specification", 04/01/1984.
917 J. Mogul, "Internet subnets", 10/01/1984.
919 J. Mogul, "Broadcasting Internet datagrams", 10/01/1984.
950 J. Mogul, J. Postel, "Internet standard subnetting procedure", 08/01/1985.
951 W. Croft, J. Gilmore, "Bootstrap Protocol", 09/01/1985.
954 E. Feinler, K. Harrenstien, M. Stahl, "NICNAME/WHOIS", 10/01/1985.
959 J. Postel, J. Reynolds, "File Transfer Protocol", 10/01/1985.

967   M. Padlipsky, "All victims together", 12/01/1985.

968   V. Cerf, "Twas the night before start-up", 12/01/1985.

1000 J. Postel, J. Reynolds, "Request For Comments reference guide", 08/01/1987.

1001 Defense Advanced Research Projects Agency, End-to-End Services Task Force, Internet Activities Board, NetBIOS Working Group, "Protocol standard for a NetBIOS service on a TCP/UDP transport: Concepts and methods", 03/01/1987.

1002 Defense Advanced Research Projects Agency, End-to-End Services Task Force, Internet Activities Board, NetBIOS Working Group, "Protocol standard for a NetBIOS service on a TCP/UDP transport: Detailed specifications", 03/01/1987.

1055 J. Romkey, "Nonstandard for transmission of IP datagrams over serial lines: SLIP", 06/01/1988.

1058 C. Hedrick, "Routing Information Protocol", 06/01/1988.

1075 S. Deering, C. Partridge, D. Waitzman, "Distance Vector Multicast Routing Protocol", 11/01/1988.

1084 J. Reynolds, "BOOTP vendor information extensions", 12/01/1988.

1091 J. VanBokkelen, "Telnet terminal-type option", 02/01/1989.

1096 G. Marcy, "Telnet X display location option", 03/01/1989.

1097 B. Miller, "Telnet subliminal-message option", 04/01/1989.

1112 S. Deering, "Host extensions for IP multicasting", 08/01/1989.

1119 D. Mills, "Network Time Protocol version 2 specification and implementation", 09/01/1989.

1122 R. Braden, "Requirements for Internet hosts – communication layers", 10/01/1989.

1144 V. Jacobson, "Compressing TCP/IP headers for low-speed serial links", 02/01/1990.

1149 D. Waitzman, "A Standard for the Transmission of IP Datagrams on Avian Carriers", 04/01/1990.

1155 K. McCloghrie, M. Rose, "Structure and Identification of Management Information for TCP/IP-based Internets", 05/10/1990.

1156 K. McCloghrie, M. Rose, "Management Information Base for Network Management of TCP/IP-based internets", 05/10/1990.

1157 M. Schoffstall, M. Fedor, J. Davin, J. Case, "A Simple Network Management Protocol (SNMP)", 05/10/1990.

1160 V. Cerf, "The Internet Activities Board", 05/25/1990.

1179 L. McLaughlin, III, "Line Printer Daemon Protocol", 09/04/1990.

1184 D. Borman, "Telnet Linemode Option", 10/15/1990.

1213 K. McCloghrie, M. Rose, "Management Information Base for Network Management of TCP/IP-based internets: MIB-II", 03/26/1991.

1231 E. Decker, R. Fox, K. McCloghrie, "IEEE 802.5 Token Ring MIB", 02/11/1993.

1243 S. Waldbusser, "AppleTalk Management Information Base", 07/08/1991.

1253 F. Baker, R. Coltun, "OSPF Version 2 Management Information Base", 08/30/1991.

1256 S. Deering, "ICMP Router Discovery Messages", 09/05/1991.

1269 J. Burruss, S. Willis, "Definitions of Managed Objects for the Border Gateway Protocol (Version 3)", 10/26/1991.

1271 S. Waldbusser, "Remote Network Monitoring Management Information Base", 11/12/1991.

1332 G. McGregor, "The PPP Internet Protocol Control Protocol (IPCP)", 05/26/1992.

1333 W. Simpson, "PPP Link Quality Monitoring", 05/26/1992.

1334 B. Lloyd, W. Simpson, "PPP Authentication Protocols", 10/20/1992.

1349 P. Almquist, "Type of Service in the Internet Protocol Suite", 07/06/1992.

1350 K. Sollins, "The TFTP Protocol (Revision 2)", 07/10/1992.

1353 K. McCloghrie, J. Davin, J. Galvin, "Definitions of Managed Objects for Administration of SNMP Parties", 07/06/1992.

1354 F. Baker, "IP Forwarding Table MIB", 07/06/1992.

1358 L. Chapin, "Charter of the Internet Architecture Board (IAB)", 08/07/1992.

1377 D. Katz, "The PPP OSI Network Layer Control Protocol (OSINLCP)", 11/05/1992.

1378 B. Parker, "The PPP AppleTalk Control Protocol (ATCP)", 11/05/1992.

1381 D. Throop, F. Baker, "SNMP MIB Extension for X.25 LAPB", 11/10/1992.

1382 D. Throop, "SNMP MIB Extension for the X.25 Packet Layer", 11/10/1992.

1389 G. Malkin, F. Baker, "RIP Version 2 MIB Extension", 01/06/1993.

1392 G. Malkin, T. Parker, "Internet Users' Glossary", 01/12/1993.

1406 F. Baker, J. Watt, "Definitions of Managed Objects for the DS1 and E1 Interface Types", 01/26/1993.

1407 T. Cox, K. Tesink, "Definitions of Managed Objects for the DS3/E3 Interface Type", 01/26/1993.

1414 M. St. Johns, M. Rose, "Ident MIB", 02/04/1993.

1461 D. Throop, "SNMP MIB extension for MultiProtocol Interconnect over X.25", 05/27/1993.

1471 F. Kastenholz, "The Definitions of Managed Objects for the Link Control Protocol of the Point-to-Point Protocol", 06/08/1993.

1472 F. Kastenholz, "The Definitions of Managed Objects for the Security Protocols of the Point-to-Point Protocol", 06/08/1993.

1473 F. Kastenholz, "The Definitions of Managed Objects for the IP Network Control Protocol of the Point-to-Point Protocol", 06/08/1993.

1474 F. Kastenholz, "The Definitions of Managed Objects for the Bridge Network Control Protocol of the Point-to-Point Protocol", 06/08/1993.

1493 E. Decker, P. Langille, A. Rijsinghani, K. McCloghrie, "Definitions of Managed Objects for Bridges", 07/28/1993.

1512 J. Case, A. Rijsinghani, "FDDI Management Information Base", 09/10/1993.

1513 S. Waldbusser, "Token Ring Extensions to the Remote Network Monitoring MIB", 09/23/1993.

1514 P. Grillo, S. Waldbusser, "Host Resources MIB", 09/23/1993.

1515 D. McMaster, K. McCloghrie, S. Roberts, "Definitions of Managed Objects for IEEE 802.3 Medium Attachment Units (MAUs)", 09/10/1993.

1516 D. McMaster, K. McCloghrie, "Definitions of Managed Objects for IEEE 802.3 Repeater Devices", 09/10/1993.

1525 E. Decker, K. McCloghrie, P. Langille, A. Rijsinghani, "Definitions of Managed Objects for Source Routing Bridges", 09/30/1993.

1552 W. Simpson, "The PPP Internetwork Packet Exchange Control Protocol (IPXCP)", 12/09/1993.

1559 J. Saperia, "DECnet Phase IV MIB Extensions", 12/27/1993.

1565 N. Freed, S. Kille, "Network Services Monitoring MIB", 01/11/1994.

1566 N. Freed, S. Kille, "Mail Monitoring MIB", 01/11/1994.

1567 G. Mansfield, S. Kille, "X.500 Directory Monitoring MIB", 01/11/1994.

1570 W. Simpson, "PPP LCP Extensions", 01/11/1994.

1583 J. Moy, "OSPF Version 2", 03/23/1994.

1584 J. Moy, "Multicast Extensions to OSPF", 03/24/1994.

1587 R. Coltun, V. Fuller, "The OSPF NSSA Option", 03/24/1994.

1595 T. Brown, K. Tesink, "Definitions of Managed Objects for the SONET/SDH Interface Type", 03/11/1994.

1597 Y. Rekhter, T. J. Watson, B. Moskowitz, D. Karrenberg, G. De Groot, "Address Allocation for Private Internets", 03/1994.

1598 W. Simpson, "PPP in X.25", 03/17/1994.

1604 T. Brown, "Definitions of Managed Objects for Frame Relay Service", 03/25/1994.

1611 R. Austein, J. Saperia, "DNS Server MIB Extensions", 05/17/1994.

1612 R. Austein, J. Saperia, "DNS Resolver MIB Extensions", 05/17/1994.

1618 W. Simpson, "PPP over ISDN", 05/13/1994.

1619 W. Simpson, "PPP over SONET/SDH", 05/13/1994.

1623 F. Kastenholz, "Definitions of Managed Objects for the Ethernet-like Interface Types", 05/24/1994.

1628 J. Case, "UPS Management Information Base", 05/19/1994.

1638 F. Baker, R. Bowen, "PPP Bridging Control Protocol (BCP)", 06/09/1994.

1661 W. Simpson, "The Point-to-Point Protocol (PPP)", 07/21/1994.

1662 W. Simpson, "PPP in HDLC-like Framing", 07/21/1994.

1700 J. Reynolds, J. Postel, "ASSIGNED NUMBERS", 10/20/1994.

1717 K. Sklower, B. Lloyd, G. McGregor, D. Carr, "The PPP Multilink Protocol (MP)", 11/21/1994.

1723 G. Malkin, "RIP Version 2 Carrying Additional Information", 11/15/1994.

1762 S. Senum, "The PPP DECnet Phase IV Control Protocol (DNCP)", 03/01/1995.

1763 S. Senum, "The PPP Banyan Vines Control Protocol (BVCP)", 03/01/1995.

1764   S. Senum, "The PPP XNS IDP Control Protocol (XNSCP)", 03/01/1995.J0

1771 Y. Rekhter, T. Li, "A Border Gateway Protocol 4 (BGP-4)", 03/21/1995.

1772 Y. Rekhter, P. Gross, "Application of the Border Gateway Protocol in the Internet", 03/21/1995.

1800 J. Postel, "INTERNET OFFICIAL PROTOCOL STANDARDS", 07/11/1995.

1883 S. Deering, R. Hinden, "Internet Protocol Version 6", 12/1995.

1884 S. Deering, R. Hinden, "IP Version 6 Addressing Architecture", 12/1995.

1885 A. Conta, S. Deering, "Internet Control Message Protocol (ICMPv6 for the Internet Protocol Version (IPv6) Specification", 12/1995.

Other References:

Comer D. E., Internetworking with TCP/IP Volume 1; Principles, Protocols, and Architecture, Second Edition (Prentice-Hall International Editions, 1991).

Comer D. E. and D. L. Stevens, Internetworking with TCP/IP Volume 2; Design, Implementation, and Internals, Second Edition (Prentice Hall International Editions, 1991).

Dickie M., Routing in Today's Internetworks: The Routing Protocols of IP, DECnet, NetWare, and AppleTalk, (Van Nostrand Reinhold, 1994).

Feit S., TCP/IP Architecture, Protocols, and Implementation, (McGraw-Hill, 1993).

Halsall F., Data Communications, Computer Networks and Open Systems, Third Edition, (Addison-Wesley, 1992).

Marsden B. W., Communication Network Protocols: OSI Explained, Third Edition (Chartwell-Bratt, 1991).

Smith P, Frame Relay; Principles and Applications, (Addison-Wesley, 1993).

Spragins J. D. with J. L. Hammond, and K. Pawlikowski, Telecommunications Protocols and Design (Addison Wesley, 1991).

Tanenbaum A. S., Computer Networks, Second Edition, (Prentice-Hall International Editions, 1989).

Tolhurst W. A., K. Blanton, and M. A. Pike, Using the Internet, Special Edition, (Que Corporation, 1994).

Bibliography

Index